Building Communication Theory

Dominic A. Infante
Kent State University

Andrew S. Rancer
Emerson College

Deanna F. Womack
Stonehill College

WAVELAND
PRESS, INC.
Prospect Heights, Illinois

Consulting Editors

Joseph A. DeVito
Robert E. Denton, Jr.

For information about this book, write or call:

Waveland Press, Inc.
P.O. Box 400
Prospect Heights, Illinois 60070
(708) 634-0081

Dedicated to Our Parents

Joseph and Maline Infante

Estelle and Jack Rancer

Ruth Fitzpatrick Fullerton and S. Grady Fullerton

Acknowledgements

We would like to thank our families for providing the love, support, and happiness which is necessary for a project such as this textbook. Our spouses — Sandy Infante, Kathi Dierks-Rancer, and Robert Womack — and our children — Laura Scott, Jeffrey Infante, and Aimee Rancer — offered encouragement and inspiration. Robert Womack also generously contributed his technical expertise and assistance. We are grateful to our colleagues who have influenced many of the ideas in this book and have helped us refine our ways of evaluating and teaching theory building. This text is the outgrowth of associations, collaborations, contributions, debates, and discussions too numerous to cite. We would like to mention William Gorden, Rebecca Rubin and Alan Rubin of Kent State University, the Communication Studies faculty of the University of Kansas and the Emerson College Division of Communication Studies. Joseph DeVito was extremely valuable in providing advice and motivation for this book. We also thank Neil Rowe of Waveland Press for his encouragement and Carol Rowe for her calm and patient guidance and for her ability to cut to the heart of a matter with her editorial pen.

D.A.I.
A.S.R.
D.F.W.

Contents

Theory Building in Major Approaches to Communication
Part II   89

6 Persuasion Approaches

7 Verbal Behavior Approaches

8 Nonverbal Behavior Approaches 231

Theory Building in Communication Contexts

Part III 267

9 Interpersonal Contexts 271

10 Organizational and Group Contexts 303

11 Mass Media Contexts 341

12 Intercultural Contexts   371

Preface

This book is designed to introduce college students to theories in the field of communication. A course with this purpose is offered at many levels in the curriculum. Sometimes the course in communication theory is the only communication course which a student takes. If that is the case, it is important that the material present a fairly detailed picture of the current thinking in the discipline. This should include the different approaches taken to understanding human communication, major theories within the structure of each approach, and representative research conducted to test the validity of theory building. It is important, in our views, that a book such as this reflect the current state of theory.

However, in addition to conveying current thinking, it is also important to reveal the traditions which gave rise to contemporary theory. The field of communication has a very rich intellectual history. Some of the great thinkers of ancient times, including Plato and Aristotle, devoted attention to human communication. In advancing a discipline, researchers frequently stand on the shoulders of those who preceded them. Early communication theorists have greatly influenced the development of the field. This book attempts to provide an appreciation for historical context.

For other students, the introductory course is the first of many which they will take in the field of communication. This book is designed to provide a solid foundation in basic communication theory which will serve the student well when pursuing advanced study. The possibility that students using this book might become more than casual students of communication was very much on our minds as we wrote this book. We attempted to reveal the importance of the field, the value of its teachings, and the richness of the discipline's thinking. We have tried to give "equal treatment" to the areas in which people specialize so that this book does not "persuade" the student to specialize in one area of the field instead of another. We intended this book to be used by communication majors or minors as a springboard to discover for themselves their strongest interests. It would be nice if equal treatment resulted in some students liking the major areas of the field equally. However, the current composition of the discipline suggests otherwise. Generalists are rather rare in the communication field; as in other disciplines, specialists are more the rule. A more realistic expectation might be that the first course in communication theory would provide a would-be specialist in organizational communication, for example, with an understanding and appreciation of the major models in other areas of the field.

This book has six distinctive features which set it apart from other introductory communication theory books. First, the book emphasizes the complementary relationship of theory building and research in the communication discipline. While the study of human communication is of interest to a number of academic fields, Gary Cronkhite explained persuasively in a recent article that the focus and scope of the communication discipline is defined by human symbolic activity. This book utilizes Cronkhite's conceptualization and rejects earlier models based on the "you cannot not communicate" notion. As a result, there is a strong emphasis on human symbolic activity. This turns our attention more to researchers in the field of communication and less to scholars in other disciplines who, although interested in communication, give it attention only insofar as communication enhances understanding of broad social processes such as risk taking, cooperation, apathy, violence, and prejudice.

A limited amount of work by scholars in fields such as social psychology will be discussed in this book. However, in comparison to earlier introductory communication theory textbooks, the attention will be less. In the 1960s, there was so little original theory building in the discipline that textbook writers in the communication field had little choice other than to "import" theories from related disciplines. However, that condition began shifting in the 1970s with Berger's Uncertainty Reduction Theory and McCroskey's Model of Communication Apprehension and then changed markedly in the 1980s. It will be evident to the reader that there is now no shortage of theory building in communication. The fact that this book is able to rely so heavily on the work of communication scholars may be viewed as a sign of the maturity of contemporary communication theory. This helps resolve the identity issue for the field which was raised often in the 1960s and 1970s.

A second feature of this book is that the coverage of theory is selective. In writing a book such as this, it is tempting to try to mention everything. The author trying to survey an entire field is limited to a brief mention of many theories because of the vast amount of theory and research in each area. At the other extreme, if too few theories are covered, a sense of the scope of theorizing is lost. We chose an intermediate position in order to emphasize how contemporary scholars build on past theory and research. This book presents overviews of areas of the field which include basic concepts and trends. Several theories are then discussed with a fair degree of depth. We hope this will be more intellectually satisfying for the student than reading "handbook-type" statements about theories. In selecting this middle course, we have included a sufficient number of theories to present an overview of the different theory building approaches in each. Our main concern has been to highlight the development of theory building in each area rather than a particular set of theories.

A third area of difference is that theories are positioned with respect to the laws, rules, and systems perspectives to studying communication. Since the mid-1970s, the communication discipline has recognized these three perspectives as acceptable ways to theorize about communication. The three approaches are distinctive; it is fairly easy to identify a given theory as falling within the assumptions of one approach or another. Although more advanced writings have made ample use of the laws-rules-systems idea, introductory works have ventured less into this framework. For the beginning student, we felt that this approach would best illustrate the different approaches to communication theory. As we will make clear, the nature of each perspective is easily understood and provides a meaningful framework for viewing theory building in communication.

A fourth feature of the book is that the trait approach to studying communication is presented. In terms of sheer quantity of research, this approach is probably the major one taken by researchers during the past fifteen years or so. A trait approach involves discovering what is characteristic of a person's communicative behavior—what regularities are consistent across situations. Researchers in the communication field tend to be either trait or situationist in terms of orientation. Situationists believe the factors in a given communication situation overwhelm characteristics of the individual so that the nature of the situation best explains communicative behavior. More and more contemporary theorists are emphasizing the interaction between traits and situational factors.

Interestingly, some introductory textbooks in communication include little or no discussion of the findings from trait research. This is puzzling since much of our current knowledge of communication involves traits. One of the most thoroughly researched topics in the history of the discipline is communication apprehension. Yet some books do not address this topic. What is the explanation? Although a large portion of recent research has been conducted by trait researchers, many of the textbooks have been written by situationists or rhetoricians who conduct a very different kind of research. We have tried to correct this fractional approach to communication theory. Both trait and situational research is included, and both are emphasized.

A fifth distinguishing characteristic of this book is that the student is taught how theories are tested. To complement the theories presented, we discuss how each has been studied by communication researchers. In addition, we have included material about communication research methods in the Appendix. In a recent issue of *Communication Education* (October, 1988), Lawrence Frey and Carl Botan emphasize the interdependence of theory and research and question "whether undergraduates are learning the research methods needed to fully appreciate and understand communication theory" (p. 250). We agree with Frey and Botan's concern. We would question how deeply a student understands a given communication theory if the student has no idea how to test the theory.

The sixth distinctive feature is the inclusion of a chapter on intercultural communication. The recent growth of theory building in this area has created sufficient material to justify such a chapter. In addition, the intercultural communication context provides an opportunity to trace differences and similarities in the communication process. Basic communication concepts have been examined in a variety of different contexts. For example, Berger's Uncertainty Reduction Theory is first presented in Chapter 9, the interpersonal chapter. Then, its extensions in the organizational and intercultural contexts are discussed in Chapters 10 and 12. This approach illustrates what we feel is one of the most important aspects of theory building: theorists often build on earlier work conducted by others in the field.

This book is divided into three parts. The first part provides an introduction and foundation. The three chapters conceptualize communication as symbol-using activity, discuss the nature of theories, and explain the laws, rules, and systems perspectives on communication. The second part of the book deals with theory building in several major approaches to understanding human communication. The first chapter reviews trends in the history of the field which led to current major lines of research. Each of the next four chapters focuses on a major approach: communication traits, persuasion, verbal behavior, and nonverbal behavior. The third part of the book deals with communication theory building contextually. A good deal of the literature in the field pertains to the set of circumstances where communication takes place, the context. Our approach is traditional in that four chapters cover theory building in interpersonal contexts, group and organizational contexts, mass media contexts, and intercultural contexts.

As we wrote this book, we were reminded of the excitement scientists feel as they create theories and conduct research to test them. Theory building is an exploratory process designed to extend the frontiers of knowledge. We are confident that the text will convince the reader of the importance of building theory. We also hope the book will lead the reader to share our enthusiasm for theory building in communication.

Part I

Theory Building
in
Communication

The purpose of this first section of the book is to orient you to theory building in the field of communication. In order to accomplish this, the three chapters are designed to provide understanding of the following topics: What is the nature of communication? How do theories function? and What approaches have been taken in building communication theories? After Chapter 3, you may want to read the material on communication research from the Appendix to help you better understand how communication theories are tested. The material in this Appendix is designed to follow logically from the discussion in Chapter 3.

The first chapter describes communication as a transactional process through which messages are exchanged and people relate to one another. Many different definitions of communication have been offered, each explaining communication from a different focus. Several central issues arise from these differences: Must a message be intentional to be considered communication? What does it mean to define communication as symbol-using behavior? Should we use the term *communication* to describe all verbal and nonverbal expression? The definition presented in this chapter corrects earlier definitions which claimed all behavior is communicative and thus obscured the significance of communication. Next, several reasons why communication is important to humans are discussed. The chapter concludes by examining some of the well-known descriptive models of communication which have been a part of the literature in the field for over twenty years.

The second chapter provides you with an understanding of the nature of theories. Theory is defined and explained. This chapter discusses major questions about theory such as the following: What is a theory? Are theories of communication different from other types of theories? Why do humans— both scientists and laypersons—invent theories? It becomes clear that theories are dynamic creations; they develop and change and are seldom stagnant. Testing theories allows us to see how they can be changed to make them better. This testing process involves providing a theory with the opportunity to fail or to prove itself wrong. The importance of testing suggests that evaluation of theories is an essential process. Without it, we would be unable to tell a good theory from a bad one. The criteria used in evaluating theories are examined along with the criteria for a good communication theory.

The third chapter presents a more macroscopic view of theory building in communication by examining the three major approaches or perspectives that have been taken in building theory. The laws perspective is the traditional approach which emphasizes the discovery of regularities or laws through empirical observation guided by a theoretical framework. There is a focus on modeling and testing causal relationships. Basically, this is the model of the physical sciences as applied to the social sciences. The rules perspective stresses that humans have free will, and this makes models of the physical sciences inapplicable. This approach emphasizes studying how people make choices, how they interpret and react to events, their intentions, their goals, the rules that they follow and the rules that they violate. The systems perspective is more general in that it stresses knowing how all of the parts of something function interdependently to adapt to an environment in seeking to attain certain goals. This approach emphasizes studying patterns of communication, inputs and outputs, and how the system moves toward a state of equilibrium.

Chapter 1

Introduction to Studying Communication

When you take your first course in a discipline, you sometimes are almost totally unfamiliar with what the discipline studies. In your first chemistry course you learn such things as the periodic table, covalent and ionic bonding of elements, and structural formulas which you probably were not aware of prior to taking the class. In other courses, you are very familar with the subject matter although you might not really understand it. For instance, if you took a course in meteorology, you would certainly be aware of the basic subject matter: weather, climate, storms, etc. You would take such a course to understand why familiar phenomena occur. You might learn that an unusually harsh winter was caused by a stationary high pressure system in the Pacific Ocean which directed the jet stream northward. Understanding such subject matter is useful and important not only for local forecasts but also for economic decisions such as the line of goods to stock in a store or the likely sales volume of weather-dependent businesses such as vacation resorts. Increased knowledge in one area allows us to build our understanding of other areas.

Your first course in communication is also one in which you are very familiar with the subject matter of the discipline. Because of your personal interactions and what you have experienced through the mass media, there are few, if any, communication behaviors which seem unfamiliar. As in our meteorology example, there is probably a great deal to learn about the "whys" of the phenomena. For instance, what can induce people to resist being persuaded? What predispositions influence how people communicate? How can you reduce your level of speech anxiety? What are the characteristics of a person

5

who is seen as a good conversationalist? How does the image people have of us influence how they react to our messages? How does your gender influence your verbal behavior? What nonverbal messages do we send to others?

Understanding these and many other concepts in this book will be achieved through the examination of *theory*. A theory is a set of related statements designed to describe, explain, and/or predict reality. As we shall observe in the next chapter, there are several types of theories of communication, and all are useful in providing explanations. It is important to realize that theories are useful not only on a very abstract level, but also as a basis for practical application. That is, theory guides practice. For instance, a theory of communication in organizations might imply that superiors should be trained to communicate in a certain style and that subordinates should be encouraged to communicate in other ways in order to make the organization more productive.

Defining Communication

There have been numerous attempts to define communication (Dance, 1970). In fact, nearly every book on communication offers its own definition! No author seems satisfied with other authors' definitions, and the proliferation goes on and on. Why is this? You would think if we know what communication is, we should be able to agree upon a definition. A reason for this predicament is there is no single approach taken to the study of communication; there are many (Fisher, 1978). Definitions differ on such matters as whether communication has occurred if a source did not intend to send a message, whether communication is a linear process (a source sending a message in a channel to a receiver who then reacts), or whether a transactional perspective is more accurate (emphasizing the relationships between people and how they constantly influence one another). Another factor in the lack of agreement on definitions is that the study of communication is not a precise science.

Measurement in communication research, as well as in other social sciences is inexact. In sciences such as chemistry there is very little error in measurement. In the measurement of weight, accuracy can be achieved to 1/10,000 of a gram, which is equivalent to about 1/4,500,000 of a pound. Such accuracy is not the case in the measurement of persuasion. We simply do not know enough to be able to predict, for instance, the precise impact a certain television commercial will have on buying behavior.

Some theorists believe that, since people have free choice and active minds, predicting human behavior is qualitatively different from predicting the weather. These theorists believe that we will never be able to make predictions about communication behavior that are as accurate as predictions about the physical world, no matter how sophisticated our theories become or how accurate our measuring instruments are. These theoretical differences will be discussed in more detail in Chapter 2.

What this discussion means in terms of defining communication is that people disagree on definitions of communication because they disagree on the nature of communication. This seems to be an unavoidable condition when a science is less precise. If something is clearly understood, it is possible to formulate a universally acceptable definition. For instance, a triangle is an enclosed straight, three-sided figure with three internal angles whose sum equals 180 degrees. Students of human behavior would assert that there is little hope of achieving an understanding of communication which equals the clarity of our understanding of the triangle. Communication has more properties than the triangle. Thus, an understanding of communication must be vastly more complex. The prospects for a universally accepted definition of communication are not good, at least not in the immediate future.

The fact that we have no universally accepted definition of communication is not a debilitating problem. Such a state of affairs is to be expected given our current level of understanding. What is important is that we continue studying communication and learning as much as we can about this very significant set of human behaviors. The more we learn, the more precisely we will be able to define communication. Studying a phenomenon allows us to define it. It is not true that to study something we must be able to define it. If at any time in our study of a phenomenon we stop and define it, the definition would simply represent our present thinking. As we learn more, we would surely change our definition. As you read this text, you might try defining communication at the end of each chapter. The chances are you will feel a need to re-define communication as you finish each chapter. The more you learn, the more you will see the inadequacies in your earlier definitions. As we said at the beginning of this section, a large number of definitions of communication have been formulated by writers. Table 1.1 presents some of those definitions. For the purposes of discussion, we have chosen to define communication as the stimulation of meaning through the exchange of shared symbols.

Characteristics of Communication

The Symbolic Nature of Communication

There are some issues about the nature of communication which emerge from these definitions. One important question is, "What makes human communication so powerful and distinctive?" If theorists can determine the answer, they can agree on what topics communication scholars should study. Cronkhite (1986) presented a cogent case for the communication discipline as one which focuses upon "human symbolic activity." A *sign* is something which stands

---

Table 1.1
Some Definitions of Communication

"Communication is the discriminatory response of an organism to a stimulus." (Stevens, 1950)

"the transmission of information, ideas, emotions, skills, etc., by the use of symbols—words, pictures, figures graphs, etc." (Berelson & Steiner, 1964)

"the eliciting of a response through verbal symbols." (Dance, 1967)

"communication has as its central interest those behavioral situations in which a source transmits a message to a receiver(s) *with conscious intent to affect the latter's behaviors*." (Miller, 1966)

"Human communication has occurred when a human being responds to a symbol." (Cronkhite, 1976)

---

for another thing. One type is a *symptom*; a cough, for example, is a symptom that one may be sick. Another type of sign is a *symbol*. Symbols are different from symptoms in that symbols are deliberately created to represent something. Once people realize what a symbol stands for, the symbol may be used by one person to cause another person to think of the thing represented by the symbol.

Cronkhite (1986) maintains human symbolic activity defines the very nature of communication. Other academic disciplines are interested in human symbols. However, the communication discipline is the only one which focuses primarily upon the *activity* of using symbols. He also includes a "gray" area, *ritual* activities, as long as a proportion of the activity is symbolic. A *ritual* is a third type of sign. It is one which is not entirely "natural," as in the case of a symptom, and not entirely created or arbitrary, as with a symbol. Instead, it is a bit of each. An example would be a growl to show that you are angry. Growling is natural in that it is a symptom of an emotional state which may have had its origin in our evolutionary past. However, it is somewhat symbolic because when we do growl, we do it, not in any haphazard way, but so that it does not sound too primitive. Such stylization represents symbolic activity.

The Intentional Nature of Communication

Another issue which arises from the list of definitions above is, "Has communication occurred if the source, the message sender, had no *intention* to *influence* the receiver of the message?" Let us say Jan overhears Joe telling someone to take a particular course because Professor Smith is interesting. Jan then registers for that course. Should we say communication occurred between Jan and Joe? Certainly, meaning was stimulated in Jan's mind by the verbal behavior of Joe. But does communication always occur whenever meaning is stimulated? If Jan told Professor Smith that Joe mentioned how interesting the class was, and Smith then approached Joe and said, "Thanks for talking so favorably with Jan about my course," Joe would probably be very puzzled and would think, "I don't remember talking with Jan about the course." Suppose you read research which suggests the amount of pupil dilation indicates how favorably a person feels about another. You then approach someone of the opposite sex. As you are talking, you notice the person's pupils are dilating. (Let us assume you do not know there is controversy among researchers as to the meaning of pupil dilation.) Should you assume the other person sent you a message communicating attraction? Once again, meaning was stimulated. But was it stimulated intentionally? Clearly no in this case because pupil dilation is an involuntary response. *Intentionality* seems necessary to identify behavior as communication behavior. If intentionality is not required to designate behavior as communicative, then mere existence is all that is needed. Thus, if you were to observe a patient lying in a hospital bed in a deep coma, we would have to say you were "communicating" with the person.

It has been argued by several authors that if a message is sent, then communication has occurred even though the person might not have intended to send the message specifically to you. However, the issue is whether there actually is a message. If you ask the person to repeat the "message," you would get only a puzzled look. When the other person is unaware he or she is influencing you, is this a case of what has been called "intrapersonal communication" (where you encode a message and then decode it)? If you read a message into another person's unintentional behavior, could it be that you are both the message creator and message consumer?

This issue illustrates a trend by some people to claim "everything is communication." Certainly communication is pervasive, but is it everywhere, all of the time? Somehow that view dilutes the significance of communication. There is an old saying that if something is everything, it is nothing. Such exuberance in staking out territory is not necessary. If we consider communication to occur *when humans manipulate symbols to stimulate meaning in other humans*, enough territory is claimed to justify a field of study. Humans unknowingly stimulating meaning in other humans is interesting, yet it is not the same as humans knowingly doing so. Why call the two the same thing? This view is not too narrow or restrictive. It allows for the complexity of human interaction but avoids the task of accounting for unintentional behavior. An important point is that we are not claiming it is always possible to determine intentionality. At times we cannot tell whether Sue sent a message to Anne or whether Anne both created and consumed a message about Sue. The issue is whether Sue sent a message. If Sue did so intentionally, communication occurred, regardless of Anne's reaction to the message.

Another reason for limiting communication to intentional behavior is to distinguish it from perception. Perception is an individual process by which individuals process and interpret sensory information. You might perceive that the walls of your classroom are painted "institutional green" or "institutional beige," but it would seem strange to say that you are communicating with the walls. Communication is a social rather than an individual process. Again, you might say that the painters communicated with you through the choice of color, but if you asked them to repeat their message, they might be puzzled. No message was intended. Instead, you observed and drew inferences from sensory data. On the other hand, communication would be the case if the painters said "We used those colors so you would know you were in school, and not at a party." While perception is an essential part of the communication process since it enables us to receive and interpret messages sent by others, not all perception involves communication. Human communication requires at least two people who intend to send and receive messages. The social nature of communication will be explored more fully in the next sections.

Communication As Planned Behavior

A conceptualization of communication plans provides a way of dealing with the issues raised in the previous section as to intentionality, what constitutes a message, and when symbols are actually manipulated. Viewing communication as planned behavior, in essence, makes it clear that intentions are a necessary element of the communication process. The notion of communication plans defines when human behavior represents communication and when it does not.

A *plan* is a set of behaviors which the person believes will accomplish a purpose (Cronkhite, 1976, Miller, Galanter, and Pribram, 1960). A general plan you might have is to graduate from college, to get a good job, to raise a family, and to retire comfortably. Some plans are more *specific*: take the car to the garage the first thing tomorrow, tell the mechanic to check the ignition system, etc. Plans are *hierarchically arranged* (Cronkhite, 1976). "If I don't graduate from college, I will work in my father's store." The plans we form are controlled by our beliefs, attitudes, and values (Cronkhite, 1976).

There are two types of communication plans: *verbal* plans and *nonverbal* plans. A verbal plan is what you plan to say in a *specific* or *general* communication situation. A plan for a specific situation might be: "When Joan congratulates me on my award, I will tell her she helped me greatly." A plan for a general situation could be: "Whenever people congratulate me, I will act humble and thank them for whatever assistance they provided." This assumes human communication behavior is *volitional*. People say what they plan to say. Some verbal plans are formed well in advance of the utterance while others are created and spoken immediately. For example, you may decide what to say when asked about your future profession years before you actually talk about it. However, you may form a plan about how you feel toward a particular presidential candidate only seconds before you speak. A verbal plan may be in the form of a *topical outline* where only the main ideas are specified. For instance, "Generally, I will say this proposal for property tax restructuring is unfair to low-income families and will lead to numerous problems at the state level." Or, a verbal plan may contain a complete specification of every desired word. For example, "The next time John loses his temper I will say, 'You're acting like a jerk again; I'm leaving.'"

Verbal plans also vary in terms of how *frequently* they are used. Some are used only once or a few times. Others are used habitually in recurring situations. For a large portion of our communication behavior, we use the same verbal plans, again and again. They work well, so we continue to use them. You can probably identify a large number of verbal plans which you use habitually. When someone asks you what you think about college you probably have a standard reply. This involves determining a verbal plan, executing it, deciding it accomplishes the desired purpose, and keeping it for use in future situations with slight modification as you see necessary. We revise verbal plans from time to time. What we say in a given situation usually represents a verbal plan that has evolved over a period of time. For instance, you may have a verbal plan for telling another person you do not want to date him or her again. After using it, you decide, "Well, I could have said that better." The next time you are in a similar situation you will revise your original plan and will "break the news" differently.

Nonverbal plans are another type of communication plan. Sometimes nonverbal plans precede or follow execution of verbal plans, but usually they are formed along with our verbal plans. An example of a nonverbal plan preceding verbal behavior might be, "I'll get that person to come over and meet me by looking engaging." Many nonverbal plans are formed along with verbal plans: "When she talks to me, I'll get a real pleasant expression on my face and look interested in her," or, "When I talk with my boss today, I'll look calm and confident." As with verbal plans, nonverbal plans can be general or specific, formed well in advance or formed at the moment, used once or habitually, revised or unrevised.

According to this concept, *human communication represents the execution of the individual's most recently adopted communication plan.* This means that to understand and predict communication behavior, it is necessary to understand and predict the person's communication plans. Research indicates that people learn to associate and/or anticipate consequences regarding their plans. How those consequences are perceived by the person permits a prediction of what the person will say.

The idea of communication plans provides a way to address the issue of whether communication has occurred if one person is unaware that his or her behavior is stimulating a response in another person. In terms of the communication plans framework, we would say communication has occurred if the individual's behavior may be traced to a plan. If it cannot be, communication did not occur even though meaning may have been stimulated in another person's mind. The individual does not have to be conscious at the moment that he or she is in the process of executing a communication plan. For instance, a woman might decide to change the color of her hair to platinum blond because she thinks that would communicate a glamorous image. Let us suppose that a male admirer sees her (she is unaware of him) and says to himself, "She is a glamorous looking woman." According to the communication plan perspective, that would be an example of communication. When it is not possible to attribute behavior to a communication plan, we would say no communication has occurred—meaning, perhaps—but no communication. Of course, it is not always easy to determine whether a communication plan stimulated behavior. Plans, like other forms of knowledge, are usually discoverable; the only limitations are the ingenuity and resourcefulness of the researcher.

According to this conception, messages are symbolic behaviors which are molded and energized by communication plans. This definition emphasizes the intentional and hence not accidental nature of human communication. Messages are expressed with verbal and nonverbal symbols. Plans, of course, are also composed of symbols. However, the symbols in a plan are not necessarily the same ones that will appear in a message. Human judgment and volition *transform* plans into action. Plans can be modified and adapted to the given situation. For instance, suppose you have a plan for refusing to drink beer when it is offered to you. What you say might vary according to the situation. You could say it is "sinful" when talking with religious people or "unhealthy" when talking with physical fitness enthusiasts. The transformation process allows for revisions of a communication plan. This complex human ability presents a formidable obstacle for attempts to simulate human communication through the use of computers.

According to a communication plans framework, communication does not always entail a great deal of thinking by the people involved. If we do not have a plan for a situation, then substantial thinking is involved. However, much of our communication behavior is *habitual* in the sense that we prefer to place ourselves in familiar situations where we have communication plans that are very dependable—they always seem to work for us. Life would be difficult if we had to examine each situation thoroughly to determine what to say. Instead, we form plans which are as robust as possible and cover as many circumstances as feasible. It is easier to talk if we have reliable plans.

This notion is similar to Langer's (1978) concept of "mindlessness." The idea is that people prefer to avoid cognitive activity because rest is desired more than expending effort. Thus, people like situations which they find familiar because they have plans which worked in similar past situations. Having a dependable plan means the person may go on "automatic pilot" and not have to think much in experiencing the situation. This analysis suggests that much human behavior is not unique or novel, but repetitive and hence predictable. If Langer is correct, this would call into question those theories of human behavior and awareness which depict people as always alert, forever thinking, and cognitively active as opposed to passive. Indeed, most of the theories may be subject to this criticism. Moreover, this conception challenges one of the most accepted ideas in the communication field, Berlo's (1960) notion of communication as *process.* Berlo's idea is that communication is a continual stream of unique behavior which is unrepeatable. The concepts of plans and mindlessness suggest that such a dynamic depiction of communication may be misleading. According to Berlo's model, predicting communication seems nearly impossible. However, in view of the framework in this section, much communication may be highly predictable because it is based on plans that people use and reuse, even if each situation itself is unique.

The Transactional Nature of Communication

The fact that communication is planned helps us recognize that communication is a *transactional process.* By that we mean communication involves people sending each other messages which reflect the motivations of the participants. People expect others to react to their messages and in turn expect to respond to the messages of others. When we communicate, we attempt to affect our environment; we understand that others also communicate to exert such influence. We anticipate a "give and take" in communication — an interaction of human motivations. One segment of an interpersonal relationship may be described as a *linear process.* "Please lend me a quarter for the candy machine" is an example of a simple one-thing-leads-to-another description, which is seldom adequate for communication. "I asked for a quarter and got only a frown" does not say much about the communication in that situation. Suppose the person you asked for money recently learned you had tried to date his girlfriend, but you did not know this. You thought you had been perfectly discreet. The frown would be understandable as a reaction in light of the additional information. We could present more details, but the point should be clear. Communication is a process of mutual influence in which participants' motivations interact. A simple linear process does not adequately explain the communication situation. Often, a linear description does not even identify the most important meaning in a communication situation. Not getting the quarter certainly was not the most important meaning present in that communication situation. To identify a single message source, a single message receiver, and a single effect of a message may be accurate, at best, for a very limited period of time. The thinking of the people involved in a communication situation, their characteristic traits, the factors in the physical and social environments, and how all these things interact are necessary for a more complete understanding of communication in the particular situation.

This transactional nature of communication means each communication situation is unique to a degree. A communication situation occurs with particular people, in particular physical and social circumstances, and during a particular period of time. Since what a person wants changes from one point in time to the next and since the physical and especially social environments are rarely if ever the same, we recognize that each of our communication experiences is at least fairly unique. We are able to distinguish among communication situations, even though the people and place may be the same.

Communication involves both *content* and *relationship* dimensions (Watzlawick, Beavin, & Jackson, 1967). When we communicate, we not only present information and points of view, we tell the other person about the relationship we perceive between us and him or her. We do not always use words to specify the relationship dimension. Often, we use our tone of voice, gestures, posture, or the physical situation to carry the relationship message. For instance, the relationship message in "please sweep the floor" is different depending upon whom you are addressing. If you were a supervisor talking to a subordinate, the relationship would be different than if a wife asked her husband to sweep the floor. With the subordinate the unspoken relationship part of the message would be "do this because I am your boss," while with the husband the message would be "do this because we are equals and it's your turn." Sometimes there is conflict between people not because of the content of a message but because of disagreement on the relationship dimension. For example, your subordinate may agree the floor needs sweeping but may not want to do it because he or she may believe you are going beyond your authority by issuing orders about floor sweeping.

The Contextual Nature of Communication

Another fundamental concept is that communication is *contextual*. A communication context is a type of situation in which communication occurs. Communication in one context will have different characteristics than communication in another context. For instance, there is much more feedback in family communication than in mass media communication. Of course there are basic components of communication which are present regardless of the context: message creator, message, and message receiver. The idea of communication and context is that the nature of the source, message, and receiver is different according to the situation. Thus, communication is distinctive to a degree because of where it occurs. This means, among other things, that the meaning derived from a message in one context can be substantially different from what is experienced in another context. For example, a story told in an interpersonal context such as a cocktail party may be viewed as very humorous. In another context such as a TV talk show, the very same story told by the same person with the same people from the cocktail party in the audience might be seen as not at all funny, in poor taste, and reflecting hostile, anti-social attitudes of the storyteller.

The idea that communication is contextual is a widely accepted idea in communication theory. There also is rather extensive agreement on the contexts. Generally, the contexts considered are:

1. Interpersonal (communication between two people)
2. Small Group (communication involving several people)
3. Organizational (communication within and between organizations)
4. Public (a speaker addressing a large audience)
5. Mass (communication which is mediated by electronic or print media)
6. Intercultural (communication between people of different cultures)

The acceptance of this typology is particularly evident in contemporary communication theory books. Nearly all have separate chapters on the nature of communication in the various contexts. You will find that to be the case in this book. The final four chapters examine communication theory building in the contexts where communication occurs.

The Functions of Communication

The last fundamental question concerns the uses or functions of communication. The great ancient Roman orator Cicero said the basic purposes of a speech are to entertain, to inform, and to persuade. In recent times the purpose to stimulate has been added. The distinction made between persuading and stimulating is that persuading involves changing a listener from pro to con or con to pro regarding the speaker's proposal, while stimulating means moving a person who is pro, for example, to become even more intensely pro. These purposes have been applied mainly to public speaking. Some contemporary theorists have developed further ideas on the functions which communication fulfills for humans.

Clark and Delia (1979) believe there are three basic objectives which operate in any communication situation. *Instrumental* objectives pertain to the communicator's goal. An example would be to have another person sign a petition. *Interpersonal* objectives are concerned with forming and maintaining relationships with other people. Thus, in a communication situation an interpersonal objective for a message source might be to motivate the message receiver to want only a professional and not a personal relationship with the source. *Identity* objectives involve the desired image which the person wants to communicate. For instance, a person might want to be seen as a very concerned citizen, always interested in helping poor people. Clark and Delia (1979) emphasize that the three objectives are not necessarily present equally in all situations. In a given situation, one objective might be more important than another objective.

Dance and Larson (1976) suggest that human communication has three functions which are realized without conscious effort. The functions are inherent, operating automatically for the individual. The first has been termed the *linking* function. This means communication is used to establish relationships between the individual and the environment. People use symbols to create a desired image to facilitate this linking to the environment. Thus, individuals might be very friendly in order to encourage others to include them in activities.

The *mentation* function means communication stimulates the development of higher mental processes. Mental growth is enhanced by communication. For example, using symbols encourages the development of *displacement*, the ability to move mentally from the present moment and circumstances to the future, to the past, or to solve problems in the immediate situation by going to a high level of abstraction. Displacement is a higher mental process which stimulates the child to move from egocentric (seeing self at the center of everything) to non-egocentric speech. Manipulating symbols may encourage the individual to see self with respect to other elements in the environment. Selecting symbols which are appropriate for a given receiver causes the source to consider the perspective of the other, an activity which is decidedly non-egocentric.

The *regulatory* function develops as the individual is influenced by persons and other things in the environment. During this period of dependency the child internalizes the ways of regulation, and this internalization constitutes learning. As a result the child learns how to regulate personal behavior. Later these methods are used to influence the behavior of other people. Thus, we have a need to influence our environment, and communication fulfills this need well. When we feel we are not able to influence events satisfactorily, a sense of helplessness can develop which can have very serious consequences in terms of mental health.

The Importance Of Communication

In Creating Cooperation

Because communication performs the functions discussed above, it plays a vital role in each of our lives. Humans are very interdependent. The arrangement of society is such that each of us depends upon the rest to provide what we need. Communication is very important in enabling people to coordinate their efforts and to produce a variety of goods and services which would be impossible if people were to work independently (Cronkhite, 1976). Beyond this macroscopic view, there are many examples in our individual lives when we use communication to enlist the cooperation of others. We ask people for directions when we are lost. We want our friends to support us when we take a stand on a controversial issue. We suggest a division of work for a task to our colleagues. It is probably fair to say that we do not live a day without asking for the cooperation of others and also cooperating with requests made by others.

Of course, some people get more cooperation than others. Communication skill is an obvious factor to explain this discrepancy. If people do not cooperate with us as much as we would like, it may be that our communication behavior is at fault. We have a need for *control* in our interpersonal relations (Schutz, 1958). If this need is not satisfied, we tend to feel powerless and view ourselves as relatively helpless, dependent upon the whims of others. It is possible to desire too much control. When this happens, others view us as burdensome and would rather not cooperate. We can ask too much of people. To be well adjusted interpersonally, we must learn what it is reasonable to ask of others and what we should reasonably give.

Erich Fromm's (1947) theory of character provides insights into certain kinds of cooperative communication behavior. There are four nonproductive character orientations. Each views cooperation differently and will communicate in distinctive patterns to enlist cooperation. The *receptive orientation* describes individuals who believe that good things are only received from others. Since this type of person depends on others to receive what is worthwhile and does not feel he or she has anything of value to give, relationships are rather one-sided. This person behaves pleasantly and acts favorably to maximize the chance that others will cooperate, but he or she is unable to reciprocate. If you were dealing with such a person, you would feel you were giving but not receiving. In a romantic relationship, you would feel you were not loved in return for the love you were giving. While the receptive orientation looks for gifts, the *exploitive orientation* thinks it is necessary to take things from others by force or cunning. Individuals with this orientation generally employ subtle or even overt threats when asking for cooperation. Deception is also a common tactic. The person may misrepresent a situation in order to get something from you. The *hoarding orientation* changes the focus for receiving what is good. This type of person believes he or she possesses what is good and wants to save, hoard, and protect it. Such individuals value orderliness and security above all. They will cooperate if they believe cooperation will help fortify their position and will not involve intrusion. They will ask for cooperation and give it on matters which involve restoring order or putting things back in their proper place. The *marketing orientation* also centers around the belief that the individual possesses what is good. Unlike the hoarding orientation, this person views himself or herself as a commodity with exchange value. An engaging personality and attractive physical appearance are prized because such characteristics make an effective package for the "product." This individual's communication behavior about cooperation reflects a desire to barter, or to get ahead by "delivering the goods."

When you ask such an individual to cooperate with you, you may get the feeling that you are going into debt and that the person will later expect something of you. As we said earlier, these four character types are seen as unproductive (Fromm, 1947). More desirable and satisfying cooperative communication behavior would indicate sincere respect and concern for the other person, a desire to realize one's potentialities, and a sense of how one's behavior will enhance his or her environment. Productive character orientation will be discussed in more detail in the section on entertainment below.

In Acquiring Information

The second key role of communication is to help us acquire information. Information or knowledge is probably our greatest possession. Humans have continuously accumulated information. Knowledge is power, and there may be no more striking example of this than at the international level where the nations which have the most information also have the most economically and militarily. Information is no less important on the more microscopic level. For various reasons we need a vast amount of information in our lives. Much of this information is useful. We want facts about candidates to reach a decision when we go to the polls. Information about the weather affects our plans for the day. The principles of gardening are necessary to produce vegetables in our backyard. If we want to be bankers, we need a knowledge of finance. However, other information simply satisfies our sense of curiosity with no apparent utility value. We read about the Bushmen of the Kalahari Desert because we are interested in extraordinary examples of survival. We listen to a lecture about black holes in space because we find the idea fascinating. We read a biography about a composer simply because we liked his or her music. The cliché states that people thirst for knowledge; that the thirst is unquenchable seems to be a permanent condition of being human.

Communication plays a very important role in acquiring information. Other than in cases of direct experience with our physical environment, information without communication is probably rare. Here's an example of purely physical information which you could acquire without communicating with other people. Let us say that you have just moved to another region of the United States and you wish to know where to catch a lot of fish. To do this independently you would have to roam the countryside and search for lakes and streams. Stay off highways because they contain signs, do not ask anyone about fishing waters, and do not consult a map, since all of these involve communication. Suppose you succeed in locating twelve lakes in a 15-mile radius from your new home without the benefit of communication. Would you have accomplished your goal which was to catch a lot of fish? No, and you would be very far from it. All bodies of water do not contain an ample fish population. In fact, few do.

Suppose you realize this and decide to communicate just once to find out which of the lakes contains the most fish so that you do not have to spend years finding this information for yourself. You ask a local expert; he names the best lake. Can you now proceed to accomplish your goal without further communication? Perhaps, but if the lake is large, you could spend the entire year there and not catch many fish. Even if you found the productive parts of the lake, there still is the matter of how to catch the fish. What bait, lures, and techniques work on this lake? You might catch a lot of fish without any human assistance. However, unless you are unusually lucky, it would take a very long time. Communication would not make the task easy, but it would make it simpler. Just find an experienced local fisherman and talk! Communication is vital in acquiring whatever information you need.

In this process of acquiring information, we have learned it is necessary to have a system of beliefs about the sources of information. According to Rokeach (1960), we have a set of beliefs about which sources are credible (believable) and which are not. Since we need information, we must know whether information is dependable. We have positive beliefs about highly credible sources and negative beliefs or disbeliefs about sources with low credibility. Consider the following piece of information: "Evidence indicates that Russia has been instrumental in manipulating the supply of oil in order to ruin the economies of free nations." Whether you believe that information will depend heavily upon its source. If it is announced by Dan Rather on the CBS evening news, and if Rather is a positive source for you, you probably would see this as a very plausible explanation for the energy problem. However, if the source is an extreme right-wing group you dislike greatly, you probably would dismiss the idea as highly implausible and as further proof of the "conspiracy mentality" of extremists.

In Self-Concept Formation

The third area in which communication is useful is in forming our self-concepts. A well-accepted principle of communication is that how we perceive ourselves greatly influences our communication behavior. You have heard the adage, "What you say is what you are." A more accurate rendition of this idea might be, "What you say is what you *think* you are." If you believe you are worthwhile and a success, you say this in many ways and on many occasions. Your verbal messages reflect optimism and an unpretentious confidence in yourself. Nonverbally, your posture, gestures, tone of voice, and facial expression say you have positive beliefs about yourself.

People sometimes exude too much self-confidence and seem overly poised. This communication behavior also reveals something about self-perception. This type of individual is probably uncertain about his or her self-worth and is attempting to convince others that he or she is productive and valuable. This attempt at social influence may be termed an *ego-defensive* set of communication behaviors. The person finds his or her unfavorable self-concept psychologically uncomfortable and seeks to remedy the condition by obtaining esteem from others. "My fears about myself must be wrong; how could I be a failure if people treat me like I am a success?" Of course, such self-deception is seldom sufficient to convince the individual of his or her worth, so the exaggerated communication behavior continues. This is not the only pattern of behavior which suggests an unfavorable self-concept. Other people say quite clearly in their verbal messages that they are pessimistic about their future, that they are helpless in their environments. Nonverbally, their facial expressions say they are depressed; this depression is also revealed by their tone of voice as well as in posture and gestures.

We say what we think we are. However, does communication play an additional role? Does communication influence what we think we are? That is, how does communication operate in the formation of our self-concepts? One theory claims our self-concept is a reflection of how we see ourselves in the responses of other people to us (Cooley, 1902). We communicate. Others observe our communication behavior and react to it. We observe these reactions, and they become the basis for deciding who we are. Hence, our communication behavior and the communication behavior of others control our self-concept. All of this is a very hopeful perspective about the idea of self-concept. It means we are partially responsible for the way we view ourselves because we stimulated the responses of others that resulted in our particular self-concept. There is hope because we can continue to communicate with people and obtain responses from them. People are discriminating. They respond differently according to the stimulus.

This is another way of saying you can change people's responses to you. You are partially responsible for and in control of your interpersonal world. This perspective says it is not valid for you to claim, "People do not show an interest in me, or in what I am doing, so I must not be an interesting person." Instead, this orientation to self-concept would want you to conclude, "People do not show an interest in me because I do not encourage them to; I do not show an interest in them." The explanation for this would lie in your communication behavior. You probably do not ask many questions about others' interests when you talk. You give little if any positive verbal and nonverbal reinforcement to others when they show an interest in you. What could you do, according to this perspective? You could ask sincere questions about the interests of others and show positive reactions to their responses to your questions. When people reciprocate by inquiring about your interests, you could show them that you are happy they asked. This should become an ongoing pattern in your interpersonal relations and not something you try only once.

The point we are trying to make is that communication has been important in the formation of your self-concept, and communication can be used to change your self-concept. We can change our communication behavior, and that will cause people to react differently to us. The new responses toward us will cause us to perceive ourselves differently. There is considerable reason for adopting this "communication orientation" to self-concept. We are happier in life if we have a favorable self-concept. We are not happy if we believe others have not treated us fairly or have not given us what we deserve. We are happier when we believe in the communication process, that communicating to the best of our ability will produce results. They may not always be exactly what we wanted, but they will be satisfying nevertheless because of our *sincere involvement in the process.*

In Entertaining

The previous discussion of the importance of communication gives the impression that humans are totally serious, goal-oriented, information-seekers who proceed through life in search of a kind of sober happiness. As we know, humans and other advanced animal species have a strong inclination towards entertainment. Once basic survival needs like safety and nourishment have been satisfied, it seems quite natural to occupy our time with less serious matters. Sometimes this sequence of survival-then-entertainment is not followed exactly. Some college students, for example, have even been known to place entertainment before survival in college. Some of our students have said if it were not for entertainment, they could not survive in college. The point is that entertainment is necessary.

Recall the discussion above of Fromm's (1947) unproductive and productive character orientations. Fromm said the productive character orientation involves a pattern of alternating between work and rest. We are more productive if we learn how to relax away from our work. Our diversions may be related to our work. For instance, if you are a comedian, you might enjoy going to night clubs when you are not working. The important issue is to find an enjoyable balance between work and play. Fromm emphasizes the idea of balance; if either work or play becomes disproportionate, the individual will not be as happy as when the two are in balance.

Communication is vital in this entertainment side of the productive character orientation. True, some of our diversions seem to involve no communication. We might paint in a private place and never discuss our paintings with anyone. However, most entertainment involves communication. Movies, plays, books, and magazines are some obvious examples. It has been said that entertainment is the main purpose of the mass media. While that claim may be debated, there seems little doubt that mass media provide us with much of our entertainment.

We sometimes find entertainment in the way a person communicates. We often watch a particular TV talk show not so much for the guests, but because we like listening to and watching the host. For instance, Johnny Carson's nonverbal behavior—the way he moves his eyes after a line and uses his voice to give additional meaning to words—adds to the entertainment value of the actual words he speaks. We like the way he says things and do not tire of his verbal and nonverbal mannerisms. It is not so much the jokes told by comedians but the way they are told that entertains us. Often leaders seem to be selected because of the way they express their ideas, even though the ideas may be rather commonplace.

Although communication behavior may be the main component in our working day, we often turn to communication for our entertainment. This is almost like a commercial fisherman going sports fishing on his days off. Social conversations represent one of the most common ways we are entertained by communication. For many of us, this is our chief form of entertainment. We enjoy talking with people. Such conversations may have no serious purpose. We may not want to accomplish anything other than to enjoy ourselves. The topics may be trivial and the talk may be shallow because the purpose is not rational dialogue but pleasant diversion.

Sometimes rational dialogue is entertaining. Some of us find arguing a source of entertainment. We perceive an argument over a controversial issue to be an exciting intellectual challenge, a verbal game of chess. The issue argued may not be important to us; what matters is the activity. If you are a surfer, a good wave is a good wave, whether it is in California, Hawaii, or even Ohio. (Although "surf's up" is not what you commonly hear on Lake Erie beaches!)

Returning to Fromm's conception of the productive character orientation for a moment, we should emphasize further the importance of balancing work and rest. If all of our communication behavior is task oriented, we are conveying a less than desirable impression of ourselves. Most people feel uncomfortable with someone who is totally production oriented. People also find it difficult to rely on someone who takes the opposite extreme, a preoccupation with entertainment. We may instinctively realize the validity of Fromm's notion that the healthy, productive person is one who alternates between work and rest. Our more favorable impressions are probably formed of people who have such an orientation.

In a Democracy

Our discussion has mainly emphasized that communication is important to the individual. We will now take a broader perspective and explore the significance of communication in a free society such as ours. What is unique about a free society? One distinguishing characteristic has been termed the "marketplace of ideas." People who have ideas are free to express them. If the ideas have merit, they will survive in competition with other ideas. This means freedom of speech is highly prized and protected from any possible erosion. It is assumed that people in the marketplace have the ability to select the best idea. Freedom of speech is crucial in order to assure that there will be a wide *variety* of ideas available. This increases the probability that a very good idea will be present in the group of available ideas. As in biological evolution, if there is no variety in a species, there is little chance of survival when the environment changes drastically (Cronkhite, 1976).

Communication is particularly prominent in *selecting* an idea from the marketplace of ideas. Aristotle believed that communication, especially persuasion, enabled people to discover what was good for society at a particular time and place. An example today might be whether or not nuclear power should be more strictly regulated. Public deliberation occurs with advocates and opponents for the various ideas or proposals attempting to persuade people. A major problem is that if all proposals are not represented by competent advocates, the best proposal may not survive. The superior proposal in a group of proposals is not always selected. The consequences of proposals must be clearly understood if the best decision is to be made. Advocates of an inferior proposal may deceive the audience by misrepresenting the superior proposal's advantages or potential disadvantages. If there were no competent spokesperson for the superior proposal, it would not be unusual for the audience to select the inferior proposal. People will do their best to make a good decision on an important matter. If their awareness of the issues has been reduced by deception or incompetence, even the best ideas will go unnoticed. This is why effective communication is so important in our society. People will select the best candidate, approve worthy issues by referendum, and support good changes in the status quo if the communication is of such a quality that the significant issues are understood. This idea of course is not new. It was central in the thinking of both Aristotle and the writers of our Constitution. A major goal of the field of communication has been to prepare students to be effective participants in a democracy. The study of communication is more extensive in the educational system of the United States than in any other country in the world. This is no accident. It is difficult to find a country which has more freedom of expression than the United States. Our very existence depends upon people making good decisions. As we have said, that is very unlikely without effective communication.

Despite the fact that our society is so advanced, we have not achieved complete equality of opportunity. Although there may be greater opportunity in the United States and discrimination is contrary to the law, your sex, race, religion, or national origin may affect your achievements. Even though this may be true, it does not mean that you as an individual must necessarily have less opportunity. Our society rewards people who are effective communicators; communicative ability is an "equalizer." For example, doors open for members of minority groups that would have remained closed if it were not for communication skills. Our society is not perfect, but that does not mean you cannot succeed in it. One reason the communication discipline is exciting is that we commonly observe people "getting ahead" because of improvements made in their communication skills. As you study the material in the rest of this book, it is important to keep in mind the vital role of communication in our private and public lives. Because communication is so important, building the best possible communication theories and models is perhaps the most important activity scholars in our discipline can undertake.

Descriptive Models Of Communication

In studying this book, it will become clear that there is no single comprehensive theory of the domain called communication. Not only is there no overall theory of communication, but there is no agreement as to what should and should not be included in such a theory. What we do have are numerous theories about the communication process. There are, for example, theories about: how people persuade one another; the initial stage of interaction in an interpersonal relationship; the communication apprehension that people experience; group communication and problem solving; violence and television. This book will introduce you to many of these theories which might be thought of as "partial theories" of communication since they deal with parts of a whole.

Although there are no comprehensive theories of communication to provide us with an overall view of the communication process, there are several *descriptive* models of communication which permit at least a "peek" at the overall process. The major difference between a descriptive model and a theory is that a theory provides not only a description of the area of interest but also an explanation for what occurs. This allows prediction about what will happen if certain conditions are created. Descriptive models do not provide an explanation or predictions. Instead, descriptive models identify relevant components of the process and attempt to describe how they operate. Often, the model only identifies the relevant parts. Despite the fact that they are extremely limited in what they tell us about communication, several models are worth examining because they help us begin thinking critically about communication, which is a necessary early step in theory building.

Some Basic Components and Concepts in Communication Models

In this section, we will discuss some of the components and concepts found in a large number of communication models. While these are by no means all the components found in communication models, their extensive recurrence makes their understanding a valuable guide to interpreting the communication models presented later in this chapter.

Source. A source in the context of communication models designates the originator of a message. Some communication scholars have differentiated between the concepts of "source" and "sender." A sender is one who transmits messages but does not necessarily originate them. An example of a sender could be a radio announcer reading an ad for the program sponsors. A source could be a single person, a group of people, or even an institution.

Message. A message is the stimulus which the source or sender transmits to the receiver. A message may be verbal, nonverbal or both. Tone of voice, gestures, and facial expressions are all examples of nonverbal messages. Usually, both verbal and nonverbal messages are conveyed in human communication transactions.

Channel. A channel is the means by which the message is conveyed from source to receiver. Channels may be air waves, light waves or even laser beams. Berlo's Source-Message-Channel-Receiver (SMCR) model of communication (discussed below) makes use of the five senses of human perception as channels in the communication process. The number of channels being used by an individual can affect the accuracy of a given message. For example, in which case could a job applicant present more information about himself or herself— on a telephone or in a face-to-face interview? Obviously the latter since the applicant would be using more sensory channels in conveying his or her message, and the interviewer would be doing the same in receiving that message. Using more than one channel in conveying a message increases the redundancy or repetition and, to a point, the accuracy of that message. When two messages partly overlap in meaning (B builds on A, reinforces A, or is a replication of A), *redundancy* is said to be present. Excessive redundancy or repetition, on the other hand, could be viewed by the receiver as an insult to his or her intelligence. When there is conflicting information presented over the verbal and nonverbal channels during a communication transaction, people may place a greater emphasis on the nonverbal cues. We will discuss this in greater detail in later chapters.

Receiver. The "receiver" is the destination of a given message. The receiver decodes and interprets the message which is sent (whereas the source/sender encodes a message and transmits it). In human communication transactions, it is important to note that all individuals function as source *and* receiver. Since humans perform both the functions of encoding and decoding, they have been labeled "transceivers."

Noise. Noise is any stimulus which inhibits the receiver's accurate reception of a given message. Noise is often classified as physical, psychological or semantic. Examples of *physical noise* would be the thunder of a jet airplane overhead, car horns blowing, or the blaring of a stereo system next door. *Psychological noise* occurs when an individual is preoccupied with thinking and therefore misses or misinterprets the external message. As you are sitting and listening to a lecture in class, you may be thinking of what you are going to eat for dinner or about the "lovers' quarrel" you had this morning with your boyfriend or girlfriend. If this activity prohibits the accurate reception of the professor's lecture, then psychological noise has occurred. *Semantic noise* occurs when individuals have different meanings for symbols and when those meanings are not mutually understood. For example, semantic noise occurs when you do not understand a particular word being used by another communicator or when the particular word or symbol used has many denotative or connotative meanings. When one of the authors moved to the midwest and ordered "soda," he was given an ice cream soda, rather than the plain carbonated beverage he thought he had ordered! Semantic noise occurred here. It is important to note that some element(s) of noise are always present in human communication transactions.

Feedback. Like all communication messages, feedback may be verbal or nonverbal, or both. Feedback is often called positive or negative. Positive feedback consists of those responses which are perceived as rewarding by the speaker, such as applause or verbal/nonverbal agreement. Negative feedback consists of those responses which are perceived as punishing or not rewarding. In public or interpersonal communication situations jeers, catcalls and frowns are examples of negative feedback. Even a complete lack of response on the part of the receiver could be perceived as negative feedback, since the source would have no cues by which to gauge the effects of the message produced. Thus, without feedback, a source would have no means of assessing how a message was being decoded, and subsequent inaccuracies might never be corrected. Since negative feedback implies that changes should be made, it is especially useful in helping us to send messages more effectively.

The Schramm Model of Communication

In 1954, Wilbur Schramm created his model of the communication process. It is a non-linear model, and it is diagrammed in Figure 1.1. Schramm's key point in this model of communication is the concept that we as communicators act as *both* source and receiver, encoder and decoder, in a given communication interaction. *Encoding* is defined as the process of taking an already conceived idea and getting it ready for transmission. *Decoding*, on the other hand, is the process of taking the stimuli that have been received and giving those stimuli meaning through your own individual interpretation and perception. In human communication transactions, the stimuli are signs and symbols.

Employing Schramm's model of communication, Person A encodes and transmits a message to Person B, who then decodes it, interprets its signs, symbols and meanings, and encodes another message as a result of Person A's initial transmission. Person A then acts as the receiver and decoder, and the entire system repeats itself. The message from Person B to Person A we call feedback. Feedback is included in the Schramm model of communication because we, as communicators, act simultaneously as both source and receiver. His model depicts the concept of communication as a process more accurately than some earlier models. The inclusion of feedback helps illustrate this process of communication.

While Schramm has contributed some new elements, his model is too simplified for us to fully understand human communication as a process. In addition, while he identified many key variables, he also neglected some. The

Figure 1.1
The Schramm Model of Communication

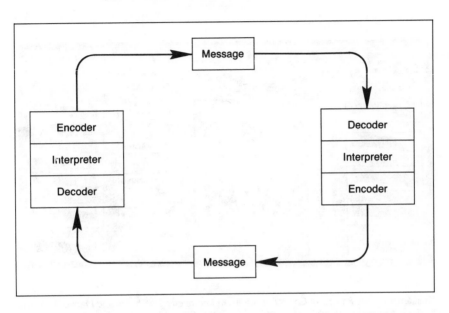

Reprinted with permission from W.L. Schramm (1954). *The Processes and Effects of Communication.* Urbana, IL: University of Illinois Press.

noise element, for example, is missing. Further, Schramm's model does not inform us about the channel of communication.

Berlo's SMCR Model of Communication

Berlo's (1960) Model of Communication goes into greater depth than previous models on certain key components. The concepts of source and receiver are expanded, and his treatment and representation of the channels of communication is different from that of other communication models. See Figure 1.2 for Berlo's Source-Message-Channel-Receiver (SMCR) model of communication.

The SMCR model examines four of the key variables which make up many of the models of communication: source, message, channel and receiver. The unique way Berlo defined channels of communication should be noted here. Berlo was the first researcher to treat the five senses as channels of communication. In addition, he expanded greatly on the concepts of source and receiver. Under source, Berlo listed such components as communication skills, attitudes, knowledge, social system and culture. These same components are part of the receiver's profile. They can either create noise in the system or increase accuracy and understanding in the communication encounter, depending on

Figure 1.2
Berlo's Model of Communication

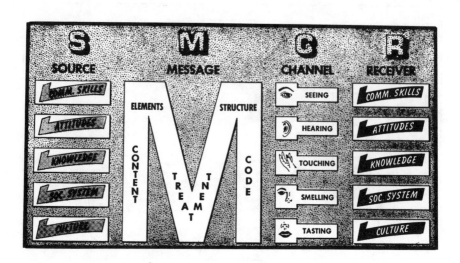

Diagram from *The Process of Communication: An Introduction to Theory and Practice* by David K. Berlo, Copyright ©1960 by Holt, Rinehart and Winston, Inc. Reprinted by permission of the publisher.

the individuals and the context at hand. However, noise is not explicitly labeled in this model, and feedback is also absent. Since Berlo's book stresses that communication should be viewed as a process, the omission of feedback is especially troubling. At a minimum, the model should have included a feedback loop (an arrow going from receiver back to source).

The McCroskey Model of Communication

The McCroskey model (1968) expands the concept of noise to include it in the encoding and decoding process, in the source and receiver, in the primary channel, and in the feedback channel. The McCroskey model also notes that noise may be evident prior to the communication act and after the communication act. This concept is often referred to as intrapersonal noise. The McCroskey Model of Communication is represented in Figure 1.3. The McCroskey model shows the intentional aspect of human communication and includes the terms feedback and "feedback-induced adaptation." Feedback-induced adaptation means that a source can adapt to a receiver's feedback by altering his or her subsequent messages and responses. In comparison to earlier models, the McCroskey model represents a more complete model of the communication process.

Figure 1.3
The McCroskey Model of Communication

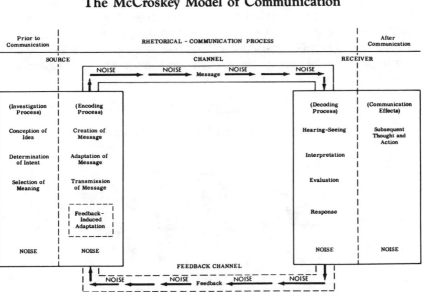

James C. McCroskey, *An Introduction to Rhetorical Communication, 5/E,* © 1986, p.6. Reprinted by permission of Prentice Hall, Inc. Englewood Cliffs, New Jersey.

The Ruesch and Bateson Model of Communication

The Ruesch and Bateson Model of Communication set forth in 1951 is concerned less with the traditional components of the communication process, (source, channel, message and receiver) than with four specific communication functions: evaluating, sending, channeling and receiving. The receiver can evaluate the source in two ways: verbally through the message content and nonverbally through vocal cues, facial expression, distance and body motion and movement. The source can evaluate the receiver in the same manner. In human communication, this evaluating as set forth in the Ruesch and Bateson model closely corresponds to the concept of feedback induced adaptation mentioned in the McCroskey model. In public speaking and mass communication contexts, a source can also evaluate a receiver or receivers. This is usually and preferably accomplished prior to the delivery of the message by the technique of *audience analysis.* Through audience analysis, the source attempts to find out the feelings, attitudes, beliefs and values of the group he or she will be addressing.

Sending is the act of transmitting a message to a receiver or group of receivers. Channeling is the selection of an appropriate channel or channels through which to transmit your message. Receiving is the act of obtaining and decoding messages.

   The process of communication for Ruesch and Bateson occurs at the same
time at four different levels of analysis. Level 1 represents the intrapersonal
level, or communication within the individual; Level 2 represents the interpersonal level, or communication between two people; Level 3 is the group
interaction level between many people; and Level 4 is the cultural level, which
joins large groups of people. The Reusch and Bateson Model of Communication is found in Figure 1.4.

Figure 1.4
The Ruesch and Bateson Model of Communication

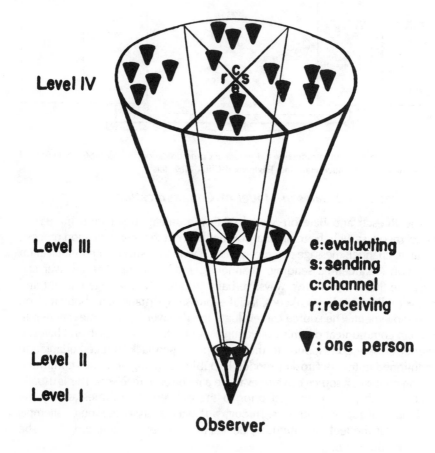

One of the most important functions of the Ruesch and Bateson model is that it shows overlapping fields of experience. Any one person can, and usually does, operate on more than one level of communication at any one time. Think of the classroom situation. You are sitting in class and you are thinking to yourself about some material just described by the instructor. This is an example of Level 1 in the model. Something about that material puzzles you, so you turn to your classmate on the left and ask her about it. Level 2 in the model is representative of this type of interpersonal communication. Finally, the entire class tries to discuss the concept, and there is great interaction between the class members. This is represented by Level 3 in the model, the group interaction level. Thus, in this example, the communication process was represented by three different levels of analysis.

The Westley-MacLean Model of Communication

The Westley-MacLean model of communication (1957) was designed specifically to deal with the process of communication in a mass communication context. However, the model of communication designed by Westley and MacLean can also be adapted to explain communication in other contexts as well. The model is diagrammed in Figure 1.5.

A key concept which the Westley-MacLean model includes is the intermediary in the communication process. Between the original source of the communication (A) and the ultimate receiver of the communication (B), there is often another person or persons (C) who might intervene or intrude on the communication process and encode the original source's communication for the receiver. The intervening person or persons in this process are referred to as *gatekeepers*. An example of a gatekeeper in mass communications is the editor of a newspaper or news show who intervenes between the reporter and the ultimate audience of the newspaper or news show. The editor may alter the story in some manner by intensifying certain parts or by deleting other parts. The editor thus fulfills the role of the gatekeeper or "filter" between the reporter covering the story and the ultimate receivers of the story. Examples of gatekeepers in interpersonal contexts include the neighborhood gossip who relays the news of the day to a friend or the person we ask to relay bad news to a third party.

The variable of feedback in the Westley-MacLean model is extremely important. There is a feedback channel not only between the ultimate receivers (B) and the gatekeeper (C), but also between the gatekeeper (C) and the source (A), as well as between the receivers (B) and the source (A).

An important concept becomes apparent in the model. Between the ultimate receiver of communication and the objects of orientation in one's sensory field, a constant process of filtering and abstraction occurs. Communication is always being shaped and altered due to individuals' own perceptions of reality, their attitudes, beliefs and values, and their past experiences and biases. We all see

Figure 1.5

The Westley-MacLean Model of Communication

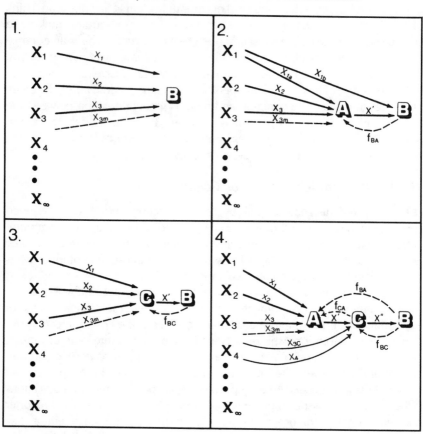

1. Objects of orientation (X_1 . . . X) in the sensory field of the receiver (B) are transmitted directly to him/her in abstracted form (X_1 . . . X_3) after a process of selection from among all Xs, such selection being based at least in part on the needs and problems of B. Some or all are transmitted in more than one sense (X_{3m}, for example).

2. The same Xs are selected and abstracted by communicator A and transmitted as a message (X') to B, who may or may not have part or all of the Xs in his/her own sensory field (X_{1b}). Whether purposively or non-purposively, B transmits feedback (f_{BA}) to A.

3. What Xs B receives may be due to selected abstractions transmitted by a non-purposive encoder C, acting for B and thus extending B's environment. C's selections are necessarily based in part on feedback (f_{BC}) from B.

4. The messages C transmits to B (X'') represent his/her selections from both messages to him/her from A (X') and C's selections and abstractions from Xs in his/her own sensory field (X_{3c}, X_4), which may or may not be in A's field. Feedback moves not only from B to A (f_{BA}) and from B to C (f_{BC}) but also from C to A (f_{CA}). Clearly, in the mass communication situation, a large number of Cs receive from a very large number of As and transmit to a vastly larger number of Bs, who simultaneously receive messages from other Cs.

Reprinted from Bruce H. Westley and Malcolm S. MacLean, Jr. "A Conceptual Model for Communications Research." (1957). *Journalism Quarterly, 34,* 31-38.

and interpret things differently. There could be a vast difference between the actual object of orientation and the ultimate receiver's interpretation, perception and decoding of a message about that object.

Summary

This chapter functioned as an introduction to the study of human communication by presenting several ideas which provide an orientation for the remainder of the book. Studying communication means acquiring an understanding of familiar phenomena. This is accomplished by examining theory building. Communication was explained as a transactional process which involves both content and relationship dimensions. Reasons for the lack of a precise definition of communication were reviewed. The symbolic nature of communication is a key feature which unites many communication theorists.

The issue of intentionality in defining communication was raised, and the position was taken that communication involves humans manipulating symbols to stimulate meaning in other humans. The issue of intentionality was addressed by considering communication as planned behavior. A conception of communication plans was explained to clarify this idea. Verbal and nonverbal plans were discussed along with the purposive and also habitual nature of communication.

The contextual nature of communication means that the nature of communication is influenced by the situation. The contexts usually considered are: interpersonal, small group, organizational, public, mass, and intercultural. The functions of communication have been viewed in several ways: as purposes of public speeches (inform, entertain, stimulate, persuade), as basic objectives of any communication (instrumental, interpersonal, identity), as inherent functions of speech communication (linking, mentation, regulatory). The importance of communication was covered with respect to: creating cooperation, acquiring information, self- concept formation, entertaining, and living in a free society.

Descriptive models of communication were reviewed because they provide an overall view of the communication process. Basic components of the models were: source, message, channel, receiver, noise, and feedback. Five descriptive models, which varied in how these components were depicted, were examined.

Questions To Consider

1. Why is it difficult to define communication in a way that is widely accepted?

2. According to the authors' definition, what is not recognized as communicative behavior? Why is it excluded?

3. Do you agree or disagree with the authors' definition? What is your personal definition of communication? Why have you chosen it?

4. What are the types of signs? How do they explain what is and is not communication?

5. What is the role of intentionality in communication? Do you agree with the authors' position? Why?

6. What does it mean to say that communication is a transactional process?

7. What are the important communication contexts? How does the context affect communication?

8. What functions does communication fulfill for human beings?

9. Why is communication important to humans?

10. What views of communication are provided by the descriptive models of communication? What are the strengths and weaknesses of each model?

11. Which model do you like best? Why? What does your personal model of communication look like?

References

Berelson, B., & Steiner, G. A. (1964). *Human behavior.* New York: Harcourt Brace and World.

Berlo, D.K. (1960). *The process of communication.* New York: Holt, Rinehart and Winston.

Clark, R.A., & Delia, J.G. (1979). *Topoi* and rhetorical competence. *Quarterly Journal of Speech, 65,* 187-206.

Cooley, C.H. (1902). *Human nature and the social order.* New York: Scribners.

Cronkhite, G. (1976). *Communication and awareness.* Menlo Park, CA: Cummings.

Cronkhite, G. (1986). On the focus, scope, and coherence of the study of human symbolic activity. *Quarterly Journal of Speech, 72,* 231-246.

Dance, F.E.X. (1967). Toward a theory of human communication. In F.E.X. Dance (Ed.), *Human communication theory: Original essays* (pp. 288-309). New York: Holt, Rinehart and Winston.

Dance, F.E.X.(1970). The concept of communication. *Journal of Communication, 20,* 201-210.

Dance, F.E.X. & Larson, C.H. (1976). *The functions of human communication: A theoretical approach.* New York: Holt, Rinehart and Winston.

Fisher, B.A. (1978). *Perspectives on human communication.* New York: Macmillan.

Fromm, E. (1947). *Man for himself.* New York: Rinehart and Winston.

Infante, D.A. (1980). Verbal plans: A conceptualization and investigation. *Communication Quarterly, 28,* 3-10.

Langer, H. (1978). Rethinking the role of thought in social interaction. In H. Harvey, W. Ickes, & R. Kidd (Eds.), *New directions in attribution research* (Vol. 2, pp. 35-58). Hillsdale, NJ: Lawrence Erlbaum.

McCroskey, J.C. (1968). *An introduction to rhetorical communication.* Englewood Cliffs, NJ: Prentice-Hall.

Miller, G.A., Galanter, E., & Pribram, K. (1960). *Plans and the structure of behavior.* New York: Holt, Rinehart and Winston.

Miller, G.R. (1966). On defining communication: Another stab. *Journal of Communication, 16,* 88-98.

Rokeach, M. (1960). *The open and closed mind.* New York: Basic Books.

Ruesch, J., & Bateson, G. (1951). *Communication: Matrix of psychiatry.* New York: W.W. Norton.

Schramm, W.L. (1954). *The processes and effects of communication.* Urbana, IL: University of Illinois Press.

Schutz, W.C. (1958). *The interpersonal underworld.* Palo Alto, CA: Science and Behavior Books.

Stevens, S.S. (1950). A definition of communication. *Journal of the Acoustical Society of America, 22,* 689-690.

Watzlawick, P., Beavin, J.H., & Jackson, D.D. (1967). *Pragmatics of human communication: A study of interaction patterns, pathologies, and paradoxes.* New York: Norton.

Westley, B., & MacLean, M. (1957). A conceptual model for communication research. *Journalism Quarterly, 34,* 31-38.

Chapter 2

Points of View About Theory

While the discussion of communication in Chapter 1 might have seemed quite familiar to you, questions about what theories are, why scientists create and modify them, and how theories may be compared and evaluated probably appear to be completely new topics for you to study. In fact, this is not the case. Each of us uses an unsophisticated type of theory building in our everyday lives. By comparing what you read about scientific theories to your own theory building processes, you will form a deeper awareness of the value of theory in understanding, predicting, and ultimately controlling communication in everyday life.

We shall define a theory as "A set of inter-related propositions that suggest why events occur in the manner that they do" (Hoover, 1984, p. 38). Propositions or hypotheses (relatively untested and tentative propositions) are statements about the relationships between concepts. In many ways, a hypothesis is a type of educated guess. If you have ever been puzzled about someone's behavior and tried to figure out the cause of it without directly asking the person, you probably formed a hypothesis to do so. Suppose you saw a friend walking across the street a short distance ahead of you. You called her name, but she did not respond. That event probably puzzled you. Normally we expect our friends to respond when we speak to them, especially if we address them by name. When your friend ignored you, you probably had several alternative hypotheses in mind: (a) Perhaps she deliberately ignored you because she was angry at you. (b) Perhaps she was worried and preoccupied and did not pay attention when you called. (c) Or maybe she did not hear you because a car screeched around the corner just as you spoke.

The hypothesis you chose to explain her behavior performed several functions for you. (1) It helped you to understand why an unexpected or unexplained event occurred as it did. (2) It helped you predict the future. If your friend is angry, she may continue to ignore you until the conflict between you has been worked out. If not, she may respond the next time you speak. (3) The hypothesis also allows you to control your communication behavior and to influence that of others. If you believe your friend to be angry, and you do not want to be publicly ignored, you will probably not speak to her again in public until you have settled the dispute in private. If she is preoccupied or could not hear you because of the noise of the car, maybe calling her name again will catch her attention.

Based on your hypothesis, you form a plan of action. You have not had an argument, so you decide that your friend probably did not ignore you deliberately. She does not look worried, so you discount the effects of internal interference with the communication process. The screeching car did come quite close to her and was quite loud, so you decide it must have prevented her from hearing you. Thus, you risk public rejection by calling her name again, louder than before. She turns and smiles, and your hypothesis-testing has been rewarded. You were able to understand puzzling behavior, to predict the likely effects of future actions, and to choose a future action based on those predictions. In this case, your action achieved the desired result, a friendly conversation rather than a public rejection. Although you still cannot be sure why your friend did not hear you the first time, you may now ask her questions to explore how she is feeling and whether or not the car frightened her.

By asking these questions, you may further narrow the range of possible hypotheses and decide whether the car or her own thoughts prevented her from hearing you. Or, by talking to her, you might discover some unexpected information which leads to a new hypothesis about the cause of her behavior. Perhaps she has just come from swimming and has water in her ears! Creating and testing hypotheses is an extremely valuable process, both for nonscientific behavior and for scientists. We count on our ability to explain, predict, and control communication behavior every day. When we try to perform successfully in a job interview, decide which classmate to ask to lend us notes, persuade parents to bend a rule or lend us money, or invite someone on a date, we are counting on the ability of the hypotheses we have formed through study and observation to allow us to predict and to control our environment. Theories, which consist of sets of related hypotheses, are used in a similar way by scientists. Four uses or functions of theories (Shaw & Costanzo, 1970, p. 7) are especially important.

Four Functions of Theories

(1) Theories Organize Experience

First, theories help scientists to organize a wide variety of experience into relatively few propositions. A theory of persuasion, for example, allows a scientist or persuasive speaker who knows the theory to summarize observations from many different persuasive situations. Instead of having to think about what persuaded the Rotary club to fund a scholarship last year, what persuaded you to vote for a political candidate in the last election, what persuaded a friend to help you research a term paper, and what was effective in countless other persuasive situations, a theory focuses attention on common features of these situations. The theory might suggest, for example, that for a well-educated audience, you should use comparatively more evidence than with a less-educated group. Quoting sources the audience members find to be highly credible or believable will be persuasive for both groups. The theory is a convenient way to focus our attention on some features of the environment—credibility of sources quoted in the speech, amount of evidence used, and the audience's educational level—while distracting attention from other features. In this case, our theory ignores such factors as the size of the audience, their age, race, gender, and the types of persuasive appeals used. The theory indicates which features of the environment we should pay attention to and, by their omission from the theory, which we can dismiss as irrelevant. Since no theory can include every possible environmental feature or variable, there is always a danger that potentially important variables may be overlooked. Nevertheless, in constructing the theory, we have considered certain features of the audience, the speaker, and the situation to be unimportant, either through testing them or by making assumptions, and have chosen to ignore these features in order to concentrate our attention on others.

Because theories focus our attention on some details and away from others, they may be compared to maps or fishing nets or sunglasses with different colored lenses. Like a map, a theory is a symbolic construction. No one map can show every possible feature of the territory it describes. If we want to drive to a new city, we use a different map from the one a geologist might use. Ours indicates highways; the geologist's probably omits highways, but indicates changing elevations of the land, bodies of water, and forests. Neither map can be described as "true" or "false." Each is more or less useful and accurate in portraying relevant features of the territory. A danger of using theories is that we forget they are maps and treat them as if they were the actual territory itself.

A friend of one of authors invented a story to illustrate this mistake. A small scouting team of soldiers during World War II had difficulty reporting back to their main unit. They had been given a map which indicated their rendezvous point on the other side of a large lake. Traveling at night, they were never able to locate the lake. Finally, more than eight hours past the rendezvous time, they came upon the rest of their unit. They angrily confronted the intelligence officer who had given them the map and berated him for indicating a lake that was not present. In the daylight, however, it soon became apparent that the blue area on their map was not the indication of a lake, but merely a spilled blob of ink. They had mistaken the map for the territory (Korzybski, 1958). They had such confidence in their map that they never questioned its accuracy or paid attention to its possible defects. Since no map can be identical to the territory—a map of Massachusetts, for example, would have to be the same size as the state itself to indicate every rock and ripple in the shoreline—every map reduces the richness of the actual territory to a few important details to serve the purposes of the user. The map is inherently incomplete and different from the territory.

The same is true of a theory. Because a theory consists of symbols—words or mathematical symbols, for example—it is never constructed of the same reality as the events it attempts to describe. Even though we communicate using words, a theory of communication uses different words than the persuasive speeches described above. In addition, the theory condenses the richness of many different persuasive episodes, each with a unique audience, context, purpose, speaker, and message, into a few highlights that are sufficient to explain why persuasion occurs and to predict the conditions under which it will occur in the future. In this sense, then, theory is inherently *reductionistic*. It reduces all the verbal and nonverbal cues of a real communication encounter to a few propositions that are general enough to apply to a variety of situations. If we forget that every theory has advantages and disadvantages, highlights certain variables and ignores others, we are in danger of mistaking the map for the territory. We are likely to confuse the usefulness of the theory with the reality of the communication episodes it purports to explain or predict. Since scientists constantly test and refine their theories, treating the theory as though it were the communication event being studied would imply that the event changed every time a theory was modified.

This, of course, is not the case. Take, for example, the Babylonian theory of the universe, which taught that the earth rode through the sky on the back of a turtle. This view was rejected in favor of Ptolemaic astronomy, which stated that the sun revolved around the earth. Now we accept the Copernican theory that the earth revolves around the sun. When those theories changed, the earth did not suddenly jump off the back of the turtle or switch from being orbited by the sun to being the sun's satellite. What changed were human explanations of empirical events observed by astronomers. Perhaps one day the Copernican theory that the earth orbits the sun will seem as ridiculous as the turtle theory seems to us. After all, only forty years ago students were taught in school that the atom was the smallest particle of matter and that it could not be split. Yet today scientists routinely investigate sub-atomic particles! What changed was not the atom, but our understanding of it and our theories about it. Later in this chapter we will explore the ways in which theories are tested, modified, and replaced. The point for now is that the theory is just a symbolic representation of the reality it attempts to describe and explain.

A similar point is made by Stephen Toulmin when he compares a theory to a fishing net (1961). Suppose you are fishing for commercial tuna with nets that have webbing five inches apart. It follows that you will catch no fish smaller than five inches in diameter. Yet it would be foolish to conclude that no small fish existed in the ocean you were trawling. Your net can only catch the fish for which it was designed. Of course, you could use a net with very small mesh, but that would result in much wasted effort. If you are fishing for tuna, you use a tuna net, not a net that will catch thousands of minnows. Otherwise, you would spend all your time emptying the net so that it would not break when the heavy tuna swam into it. Catching every possible fish of any size would be almost as frustrating as catching no tuna after a hard day's work. The danger lies in forgetting the size of your net. If your persuasion theory does not say anything about gender differences, it would be a mistake to conclude that there are no male-female differences in persuasion, unless you had found no such differences through previous investigation. Because a theory is a symbolic construction which focuses our attention on some variables and away from others, every theory has weak points. It is important to remember what the theory's weaknesses are and to be aware that they are features of the map, not the territory; that they are characteristics of the fishing net you are using, not necessarily characteristics of all the fish that swim in your theoretical ocean.

Toulmin also refers to theories as "intellectual spectacles" (1961, p. 104). Like a pair of sunglasses with blue lenses, the theory used by a layperson or scientist tints the world that is observed. Someone who has sunglasses with brown lenses will see a slightly different world. The world itself appears to change color when you change pairs of glasses, but in reality the color change is caused by the change in your observational tools. Using a different theory, like using a different map or net, will focus the scientist's attention differently and perhaps cause him or her to see different phenomena or to catch different fish.

Students in our classes frequently provide excellent models for discussion. One student, Lee, believed that being assertive was the most effective way to communicate in job interviews. However, Lee was not completely confident about the theory because of contradictory advice. Some authors of books on the subject suggested taking control of the interview to make sure important points were covered. Other authors advised letting the interviewer lead, so as not to appear too aggressive. Lee became quite excited about conducting a research project to discover the best presentation style for job interviews; what was the appropriate level of assertiveness for being invited for a second interview or being offered the job?

You may find this example naive (or risky given the importance of employment interviews!), yet it is a case in which a real individual tried to explain, predict, and control a job search using a real theory. Perhaps your theory of how to impress interviewers is different; your theory may focus on being a good conversationalist, appearing poised and relaxed, having a strong resume, or being a persuasive speaker. In any case, the categories highlighted by your theory are those that you have *chosen* to highlight, not categories that are "dictated" by the real world. The fact that your theory of interviewing involves behavior that is more commonly perceived as beneficial than the theory of taking control of the interview does not in itself make your theory better than Lee's. The categories serve as the color of your sunglass lenses or the size of the webbing in your net. Different categories will cause the theorist to be interested in different facets of behavior and to behave in different ways to get a job. We will use this interviewing example later to illustrate how theories may be compared, evaluated, changed, and even rejected.

(2) Theories Extend Knowledge

The examples above bring us to the second function of a theory (Shaw & Costanzo, 1970): it enables us to go beyond the data observed and extend our knowledge to events which we have not yet encountered. While a theory is based on what we observe, it allows us to go beyond observation and to gain new insights into specific behavior. Astronomers, for example, imagined that there were black holes before data consistent with the presence of a black hole had been observed. Their theories led them to expect to observe something which no one had yet experienced. Predicting the future is a by-product of the fact that a theory allows us to extend our knowledge beyond what we have actually observed.

Another aspect is that the relationships between propositions that make up the theory may tell us something about the event that we could have observed but never looked for before. Since prediction refers to foretelling or making statements about the future, this function of theory is not really a predictive one. Instead it has to do with relationships between variables. The persuasion theory developed above, for example, predicts a relationship between the level of education of the audience and the amount of evidence used. We might directly observe this relationship by presenting a speech with a great deal of evidence to separate audiences, one of educated and one of relatively uneducated people, and observing the difference in how many of the audience members were persuaded to agree with us. Or we might observe the effect of *other* variables on educated and uneducated audiences, observe the effects of evidence on only educated audiences, and hypothesize a different relationship for uneducated groups given other effects we have experienced. Suppose we have observed that uneducated audiences are more likely to be persuaded by emotional appeals and that educated audiences are unlikely to be persuaded by emotional appeals but very likely to be persuaded by the use of evidence. We may infer the relationship between the use of evidence and uneducated audiences, then predict the outcome of some future experiment, and test that prediction to see if the relationship we have inferred from propositions already tested is correct. If an interviewer tells you that the only person with whom she ate lunch today just received a speeding ticket, and a friend tells you he has just had lunch with the interviewer, you can infer that your friend received a speeding ticket, even though that information was not contained in either of the spoken statements.

(3) Theories Stimulate and Guide Further Research

The second function of theory, that it allows us to see implications that are not evident from individual observations (Shaw & Costanzo, 1970), leads to the third function—theories stimulate and guide the direction of further research. For example, the fact that educated and uneducated audiences are persuaded by different amounts of evidence might suggest that there are other differences in what is persuasive to these two types of audiences. If evidence makes a difference, organization might also be an important variable in persuasion. Predictions indicated by the theory may be tested by further research. The findings of this research may support the theory, or may indicate that the theory should be rejected or modified.

This function of stimulating future research is often called the *heuristic* function of a theory. The English word "heuristic" comes from the Greek verb *eureka*, literally translated into English as, "I have found it!" When California miners exclaimed, "Eureka!" they meant they had found gold. A theory leads to "gold" for researchers because it points the way to look for further knowledge and explanations. A theory that is particularly fruitful in leading to additional research is known as a heuristic theory. We shall discuss this characteristic of theories later in the section about how theories are compared and evaluated.

(4) Theories Perform an Anticipatory Function
(Mandler & Kessen, 1959)

Because theories indicate relationships and lead to predictions and, thus, to further research, they allow us to anticipate events we may never have encountered (Shaw and Costanzo, 1970). For example, theories of physics and of gravity allow scientists to calculate the gravity of planets never explored by humans. An intercultural communication theory might predict, for instance, how you should greet a visitor from outer space, even though no scientist has yet entertained such a visitor. In the words of Shaw and Costanzo (1970), "In a sense, we may say that theory provides a bridge to something 'out there' and thus makes our world seem more logical, reasonable, and organized (p. 9)."

How Do Theories Develop and Change?

The discussion above about the heuristic function of theories clearly indicates that theories are not static; theories are constantly growing and changing. Scholars have identified three types of changes. During "normal" times (Kuhn, 1970), theories grow by extension and intension (Kaplan,1964). When a theory grows by extension, it adds knowledge and expands to include more concepts. For example, the persuasion theory in which we compared the factors that lead to persuasion in educated and uneducated audiences grew by adding the concept of organization to the original variables of amount of evidence and source credibility. The theory relating assertiveness to successful interviewing might grow in the same way. Suppose Lee finds that both being assertive and following the interviewer's lead are equally effective in getting him second interviews if he is relaxed and wears a "lucky" tie. The theory has grown by extension through the addition of two variables: being relaxed and type of tie.

A theory that grows by intension grows by developing a deeper understanding of the original concepts and variables. Thus, if we found through investigation that our category of educated vs. uneducated audiences was rather imprecise, we might improve the ability of our theory to predict persuasion by further dividing our concept of audience education. Originally our variable of audience education consisted of two categories: educated and uneducated. Suppose we refined our variable to include six levels of audience education: (1) those who have not completed grade-school, (2) grade-school graduates, (3) technical school graduates, (4) high school graduates, (5) college graduates, and (6) those with some graduate school education. Perhaps further research would lead to a finding that audiences of high school graduates (level 4) were more likely to be persuaded by large amounts of evidence than audiences with less than a high school education (levels 1 and 2), but that persuasion of audiences with some graduate education (level 6) depended more on the type than on the amount of evidence. Our theory would have grown by intension, exploring more fully variables already contained in the theory.

The third way in which theories grow is suggested by Thomas Kuhn (1970) in a famous book entitled *The Structure of Scientific Revolutions*. In studying the history of science, Kuhn found that sometimes a theory that everyone accepted as useful is rejected for a theory containing a new metaphor. In other words, people stop fishing with one kind of theoretical net and exchange it for another. They change from deciding which style of blue-lensed sunglasses is most attractive and opt for a completely new color of lens. Kuhn terms this type of theoretical growth a scientific revolution. Scientific revolutions constitute a type of major change in which long-accepted theories are rejected in favor of theories that indicate new metaphors, new concepts, or other new ways of knowing.

A scientific revolution often comes about when some problem in a field cannot be solved by current theories or paradigms. Just before a scientific revolution occurs, some scientists become dissatisfied with the current theories. They believe that there are important questions the accepted theories fail to answer. They pose questions that may not previously have been considered important, or introduce new concepts to explain puzzling phenomena. Often the new theories or paradigms are developed to help scientists account for anomalies, unexplained events or findings resulting from research under the old paradigm. As advocates of the new theory persuade other scientists to accept their questions and explanations as important, a group of supporters of the new theoretical paradigm begins to grow. The supporters of the new paradigm engage in argument with defenders of the old explanation systems. The defenders may believe the new theories are inaccurate and the questions they answer rather unimportant. They believe the old questions are the most important ones, and the old paradigm is superior because it best answers the old questions. The new paradigm may even make predictions which contradict predictions made by theories of the old paradigm. Supporters of the new paradigm and defenders of the old one conduct debates (often heated debates!) in the scientific literature and at conventions. It may take several years, even several generations, for scientists to abandon the old paradigm. During this time, increasing support is found for the new theory. Finally, the new paradigm gains enough support to become the majority view.

This is the type of change that occurred when the Babylonian theory that the earth rode on the back of a turtle was rejected for the Ptolemaic theory that the sun revolved around the earth. Another revolution occurred when astronomers accepted Copernicus's theory that the earth revolved around the sun. As we pointed out above, obviously the earth did not jump from the turtle's back, then change its orbit. What changed was the picture of reality proposed by the theory. You can imagine that scientific revolutions, like political revolutions, result in sweeping changes since all science in the field to that point has been conducted with the assumption that the basic theory was a very accurate representation of reality. When astronomers came to accept the Copernican theory, they had to re-evaluate not only their hypotheses about the sun and earth, but also all their propositions about the relationships of the other planets and the moon. A whole way of thinking, or family of theories, was rejected in favor of a new one. In Chapter 3, we will discuss three families or perspectives on theory that communication scientists have used to build communication theories.

How Are Theories Tested?

The fact that theories perform certain key functions and that they change in the three ways indicated above should lead you to ask how theories are evaluated. How may theories be compared and judged? What is the basis for accepting one theory and rejecting another? You will recall that we began the chapter with the argument that the goal of theory is to explain, predict, and ultimately control behavior. These are the properties of theory that are tested and judged. Competing theories may be compared to see which explains better or which predicts more accurately. Some scientists will prefer a theory that has clear implications for controlling behavior, like our earlier persuasion theory that provides information about how to approach educated and uneducated audiences. The three goals of explaining, predicting, and controlling are the primary standards against which theories are tested and evaluated.

In the social sciences, theories are tested by using empirical research, that is, research that depends on observation or experiments. The scientist tests the phenomena and hypothesized relationships by observing them or by conducting an experiment which is expected to give the hypothesized result.

1. The first step in empirical research is to form a hypothesis. Recall our earlier example about Lee who wanted to discover how assertive to be in job interviews. For example, suppose Lee hypothesizes that one needs to be more assertive if the job is more competitive in order to obtain a second interview or a job offer.

2. The second step is to decide how the concepts and relationships in the hypothesis may be observed. Suppose Lee divides possible job interviews into two groups, high and low levels of competitiveness. In order to confirm the categories assigned to the jobs, Lee checks with friends. After finding a high rate of agreement about a particular job's desirability, Lee must decide what will count as relatively more or less assertive behavior. Asking questions will be the general behavior category. Alternating asking questions with the interviewer will count as more assertive behavior; waiting to ask questions until the end of the interview will count as less assertive. Again Lee checks with friends and professors to make sure that they agree with the judgments about the different levels of assertiveness. A scientist would want to use a large sample of interviewers and also different interviewees to test the force of the relationship. However, since this experiment was designed to measure interviewers' reactions to one student, Lee will be the only interviewee. Flipping a coin will determine whether to schedule interviews with more or less competitive jobs first so that personal preference does not influence the experiment. The coin toss indicates the first interview should be for a less competitive job. Lee places in a hat the names of five companies which offer jobs in this category, then randomly selects a name.

3. The third step is to carry out the experimental procedure. Lee signs up for an interview at the campus placement center, prepares answers to likely questions, then dresses appropriately and arrives on time for the interview. The same procedure is repeated—alternately interviewing more assertively for more competitive jobs and less assertively for less competitive jobs—

until all ten companies on the list have been covered. The number of rejections and acceptances from each group (more and less competitive positions) are then tallied.

4. The fourth step is to interpret the meaning of the observations to decide whether to accept or reject the hypothesis. After the hypothesis has been tested, the theorist must explain what the results mean in terms of the theory. Those results may lead to theoretical revisions, extensions, or to new hypotheses.

An important point to note here is that a theory or hypothesis can never be "absolutely proven." We accept as "fact" the statement, "All cats have four legs," yet at the same time we realize that it is not absolutely true. We are probably aware of cats that, because of a birth defect or accident, have three or even five legs. Yet we consider them exceptions to the rule, not disproof of it. Why? Because the number of cats that have four legs is so overwhelmingly large, we consider "four legs" to be a typical property of "catness"; anything else is an anomaly. What would we have to do to prove the statement true beyond a shadow of a doubt? Conduct an empirical investigation, an attempt to observe events directly. One way to test our theory would be to try to confirm our hypothesis by "proving it to be true." To do this, we would have to examine **all cats** in the world. Yet even that, if we could manage it, would not be enough, because our proposition does not specify a particular time. Therefore, to prove absolutely, beyond a shadow of a doubt, that all cats past, present and future have four legs, we would have to examine **all cats** that have ever lived or ever will live, in addition to those presently alive. Obviously this task is impossible. A similar logic may be extended to the "proof" of any scientific hypothesis or theory. (Since we have just established that it is absolutely impossible to prove any theory beyond a shadow of a doubt, the word "proof" is placed in quotation marks. The more accurate scientific term is "confirm" or "support.")

If it is futile to try to confirm a theory absolutely, what can we do? We can seek to *disconfirm* it. Instead of looking for four-legged cats, we look for cats that have some other number of legs; any other number will do to disconfirm our hypothesis. As stated above, doubtless we would find some cats without four legs, but we would find such a small number that we would consider them anomalies. Scientists differ on the number of "exceptions" necessary to disconfirm or disprove a theory. Since everyone agrees with our hypothesis, "All cats have four legs," it would be easy to persuade people that three-legged or five-legged cats are exceptions, not indications that the theory is wrong. In the case of scientific research, if a theory is new and relatively untested, sometimes one example that counteracts the theory's prediction is enough to falsify the theory. There is no certain number of "negative" or counter-examples required in order for scientists to reject the theory. The number depends on the consensus of scientists in that particular field of science. This consensus is likely to be influenced by how new the theory is, by who has developed the theory and who is conducting the research, and by how nicely the theory fits with currently accepted theories. The key point to remember is that the logic of science dictates that scientists should always try to disconfirm their theories, since it is impossible to confirm them absolutely.

Because of this logic of disconfirmation, we do not speak of a theory as "true" or "false," any more than we declare a pair of blue-lensed sunglasses to be "true" and brown-lensed ones "false." Rather, theories are stronger or weaker (and sometimes rejected), more or less valuable for our particular purposes, just like the different pairs of sunglasses or nets of different sizes. Every theory has advantages and disadvantages. No theory can be proved beyond a shadow of a doubt. Therefore, it is very difficult to judge the merit of a particular theory.

Let us return to our experiment involving assertiveness and job interviews. Recall our hypothesis, "The more competitive the job, the more assertive the student must be to obtain it." Suppose Lee finds that none of the companies offer a job. What does that result indicate about the hypothesis? Should it be rejected? Perhaps, but it is also possible that Lee was not assertive enough. Perhaps the experiment should be repeated with a change to initiating the greeting and handshake before the interviewer does. Perhaps waiting until the end of the interview to ask questions was too passive. A better test of the hypothesis might be to greet the interviewer first and to ask questions halfway through the time period. What about the opposite result—all the companies offer jobs. Does that mean the hypothesis should be rejected? That result certainly might indicate that assertiveness is irrelevant in obtaining jobs, but it might also indicate that some degree of assertiveness is essential. Perhaps Lee picked just the right degree of assertiveness, so that both parts of the hypothesis are true. What conclusion does Lee draw if, as most often happens, the results are mixed: some companies in both groups offer jobs? Is the hypothesis correct or incorrect? Was assertiveness essential or irrelevant? Were the types of behavior inappropriate, were there "inside" candidates, or were there other reasons unrelated to the experimental hypothesis why the job was not offered? Lee has not really designed the experiment clearly enough to test the hypothesis.

Either the hypothesis must be revised, or, if the problem lies in the experiment, it must be redesigned to test the hypothesis more effectively. Lee should identify an additional group of relatively less and more competitive jobs, then behave less assertively in all the interviews, asking questions about halfway through the scheduled time. Again, there are several possible results.

1. If only the less competitive employers offer jobs, the data will support the hypothesis. However, one experiment is usually not sufficient to confirm a hypothesis that is this complicated. To convince scientists that interviewing assertively is the most important variable in obtaining jobs, the results of

this experiment must be replicated. It would be highly desirable for someone not associated with the theory, someone relatively more objective, to conduct a similar study and to repeat the results. Perhaps then the theory might be seen as a real alternative to currently accepted theories of interviewing.

2. If all the employers offer jobs, Lee should revise his hypothesis to focus on some variable other than assertiveness or be even less assertive than before.

3. If none of the companies offer jobs yet assertiveness still seems to be a factor, Lee should find some way of communicating that is mild enough to influence the less competitive companies but not so assertive as to induce the more competitive employers to offer jobs. Or perhaps Lee should accept the evidence as disconfirming the hypothesis. Variables other than assertiveness may be more important. Interviews with employers who have both accepted and rejected Lee in the past would reveal what factors influenced their decisions. This information about what communication behaviors are effective in interviews could lead to the development of a new theory which includes variables other than asssertiveness.

Two concepts discussed above lead us to a discussion about how theories are comparatively evaluated. In situation 1 above, when the data appear to confirm the hypothesis, we suggested that having additional independent researchers repeat the experiment would lend strong support to the theory. The experimental results would then be judged reliable. Experimental findings are reliable if they can be repeated so that anyone who follows the same procedure will achieve the same results. Reliability, or repeatability, is an important criterion, for example, in medicine. A vaccine should work against the disease no matter who administers it so long as that person is trained. If the vaccine works only when administered by its developer, it is of relatively little use because the number of people who may be helped would be severely limited. Such a situation would also cause scientists to wonder whether the cure was the result of the vaccine or of some psychological effect the particular scientist had on patients.

Situation 3 above suggests that scientists are also concerned about the validity of a theory or experiment, the ability to measure what the theory purports to measure. For example, both the validity and reliability of polygraph machines used as lie detectors have been questioned. The machines actually measure nervous arousal through skin temperature, pulse, and the like. Critics of lie detectors point out that the machine does not measure directly whether or not someone is lying. In fact it measures how nervous someone is. The theory behind the machine indicates it will detect the increase in nervous arousal experienced when someone who has been telling the truth tells a lie. By comparing readings when the person being investigated tells a known lie and known truth with readings obtained when the person is questioned about the suspected behavior, the polygraph operator can detect whether or not the person is lying. In fact, some pathological liars do not become more aroused when they lie than when they tell the truth, and some very nervous suspects may become even more nervous as the questioning proceeds, causing them to appear to be lying when they are not. While the polygraph may provide a valid measure of nervous arousal, it does not give a valid measure of truth-telling. The reliability of polygraph readings is also doubtful. A great deal of training is necessary to read a polygraph accurately, and operators may interpret the readings differently. Two different operators often reach opposite conclusions about the truthfulness of witnesses, especially if they have different levels of training and experience. Critics charge that the instrument's readings are so difficult to interpret that the polygraph is unreliable in determining truthfulness in criminal investigations. Because of validity and reliability problems, the results of polygraph examinations are often not admissible as legal evidence.

The above analysis indicates the interactive relationship between theory and research. Research is used to test and revise theories, and theories are needed to indicate what variables and relationships should be examined. The chapter in the appendix discusses research methods in more detail. A summary of the concepts above is sufficient for our purposes here. Theories are tested by a four-step process:

1. Hypotheses are formed.
2. Scientists design appropriate methods of observing the variables and relationships posited by the theory.
3. The observations or experiments are conducted and results obtained.
4. The results are interpreted as offering support or disconfirmation of the theory. Often the results are ambiguous, and the research methods must be redesigned or the theory revised in light of the new data.

This section has presented two important criteria for good research: validity and reliability. In the section which follows, we shall examine how the relative merits of theories may be compared.

How Are Theories Evaluated and Compared?

As you might expect, different scientists have different criteria for what makes a "good" theory. We have chosen to discuss nine criteria which are typical (Shaw & Costanzo, 1970). Different scientists view some of these as essential and others as desirable but not absolutely essential; there is general agreement that these criteria are the important ones to discuss. Since there is disagreement, we shall try to indicate theories which fail to meet the criteria but are generally accepted. After you finish reading this section, you should become aware of how often scientists disagree about theories, and how personal the choice of a good theory is. Remember, too, that these criteria reflect the three goals of theory presented at the beginning of the chapter: to explain, predict, and control reality. In a sense the criteria below are scientists' answers to the question, "How can you decide which theory does the best job of predicting, explaining and enabling scientists and laypersons to control reality?"

Necessary Criteria

Shaw and Costanzo (1970) believe only three qualities are necessary for a good theory; the other six are desirable but not essential. In fact, as we shall see, these three are debatable, but your authors believe the list to be a good one.

1. *Logically consistent.* First, a good theory must be logically consistent. It may not contain contradictory propositions. One must not be able to make opposite predictions from the same theory. For example, a theory that allowed us to predict that well educated audiences are most likely to be persuaded by large amounts of evidence and indicated, in another part of the theory, that well educated audiences are most likely to be persuaded by small amounts of evidence would be contradictory. Obviously the audience cannot be *most* likely to be persuaded by both large and small amounts of evidence. A theory with internal contradictions would be rejected by scientists.

In fact, the last statement is not absolutely true. Currently, in physics, for example, two incompatible theories are used to explain the behavior of light. For some purposes light is conceptualized as traveling in waves. For other purposes, physicists describe light as composed of particles. These two theories require different assumptions and posit different properties about light. Until one unifying theory can be found to explain the apparently contradictory properties of light, physicists accept two incompatible theories; they have no other alternative.

2. *Consistent with accepted facts.* Second, during "normal science," i.e. not during a scientific revolution (Kuhn, 1970), a theory ought to be consistent with known data. We shall define data or facts as statements generally accepted as true by the scientific community. For example, if someone invented a theory of water that predicted water would freeze at 50 degrees Fahrenheit (F), that theory would be rejected as inconsistent with the fact that water freezes at 32 degrees F. and remains liquid at 50 degrees F. The currently accepted facts are assumed to be true until proven otherwise.

The "normal science" limitation on this criterion is an important one. During scientific revolutions, the new theory or paradigm will likely be inconsistent with facts that support the current theory. For example, the "fact" that the earth revolves around the sun (contained in the Copernican theory) is inconsistent with the "facts" of the Ptolemaic theory of the universe, which had long been accepted as "true" before Copernicus advanced his competing theory. Thus, during normal science, Copernicus's theory would have been rejected as inconsistent. It required a scientific revolution to overturn established ways of viewing the world and to allow a new set of "facts" to be accepted. A theory that would be rejected during a period of normal science might prevail and come to be universally accepted as the result of a scientific revolution.

3. *Testable*. A third essential criterion suggested by Shaw and Costanzo (1970) is the criterion of testability. A good theory must be testable, that is, able to be disproved or falsified. Notice that the preceding sentence does not imply that the theory has been disproven, only that scientists could conceive of a situation which would constitute disproof and possibly lead to rejection of the theory. Shaw and Costanzo present psychoanalytic repression as a theory which is unable to be tested or disproved (1970, p. 13). The theory of repression predicts that people may deal with traumatic events by forgetting, or repressing, their memories. For example, victims of violence or sexual abuse may not be able to remember the incident. They are repressing the memory of the trauma in order to protect themselves from recalling painful events. However, the theory does not specify that traumatic events will always be repressed, nor even when they are most likely to be repressed. Thus, if a victim cannot remember the incident, that fact counts as an example of the theory of repression. If a victim does remember, that fact does not disprove the theory because the theory does not say memory will always be repressed. *Both remembering and its opposite, not remembering, count as "proof" for the theory.*

An example of such a theory in the field of communication is cognitive dissonance. Cognitive Dissonance Theory states that holding two contradictory or inconsistent beliefs leads to psychological discomfort. Someone who (a) believes that he is handsome but also (b) believes that others find him physically repulsive will experience dissonance, or psychological tension. According to Festinger (1957), people have a psychological drive to reduce dissonance. Thus, the man described will attempt to resolve the tension in some way.

Festinger's research suggests many methods for reducing dissonance. We shall mention just four. (1) First, the man might change one of the cognitive elements, a or b above. He might decide that he is not handsome after all, or might believe that others also believe him to be handsome. (2) Second, he might devalue the elements, deciding that his attractive personality is much more important than his appearance. (3) Third, he might distort or misinterpret information about the beliefs, perhaps believing that others are only teasing when they tell him he is ugly. (4) Fourth, he might seek information which agrees with his own position, perhaps asking his parents for confirmation that he is handsome. *Notice that virtually any cognitive readjustment the man performs counts as evidence in favor of dissonance theory.* If he changes his mind, he confirms the theory. If he maintains his current beliefs, he also confirms it. If he lies to himself by distorting incoming information, interpreting insults as jokes or believing that people mean the opposite of what they tell him, his behavior still serves as evidence confirming the theory.

The theory is used to persuade others by showing them that they simultaneously hold two inconsistent beliefs, or by persuading them to believe something inconsistent with their present beliefs. For example, a speaker might try to persuade an audience that believes strongly in the Ten Commandments and also in capital punishment that capital punishment violates the commandment, "Thou shalt not kill." The speaker would indicate to the audience that they should change their minds and oppose capital punishment, thus resolving the psychological tension. If the audience members change their minds after hearing the speech, their action confirms the theory because changing one's mind is one way that dissonance can be reduced. However, notice that *not changing their minds* also counts in favor of the theory. If the audience members seek consonant information, information consistent with their current beliefs, by talking afterwards with friends about their reasons for favoring capital punishment, this behavior also confirms the theory. *Any action taken by the audience is predicted by the theory. Nothing they could do would count against the theory.* Thus, this theory, which has been widely used for thirty years by scholars in psychology, communication studies, political science and other fields, is not testable.

Cognitive dissonance fails to meet Shaw and Costanzo's essential criterion of testability, yet many scientists find it a very useful explanation of some psychological forces underlying the persuasion process. It is an example of a circular, or untestable, theory that has had a long life and is still used by scientists, despite its disadvantages, because of its supposed explanatory power. We shall examine dissonance theory further in Chapter 6.

As we have seen, all three criteria that Shaw and Costanzo (1970) claim are mandatory have been or are currently being violated by one branch of science or another. When no theory that meets all three criteria is available, scientists must make do with the theoretical choices they have. This situation has led to the simultaneous acceptance of the particle and wave theories of light. The purposes of a theory—to explain, predict, and control behavior—are so important that a theory may make up for a weakness in one of the areas by its strength in another. This is the case with Cognitive Dissonance Theory and many others. The six criteria which follow are desirable, but Shaw and Costanzo (1970) do not view them as mandatory; many theorists would agree that these six are less essential that the first three criteria.

Desirable Criteria

1. *Simple.* Hoover (1984) argues that, "Social knowledge, if it is to be useful, must be communicable, valid, and compelling. In order to be communicable, knowledge must be in clear form" (p. 7). Shaw and Costanzo (1970) argue that a good theory is one that is as simple as possible. The principles of the theory should be stated clearly so that they can be communicated to other scientists. Predictions from the theory should be straightforward.

2. Parsimonious. Similar to simplicity, the concept of parsimony implies simplicity of deductive structure. In other words, a parsimonious theory contains as few propositions as possible. A theory that relies on ten variables and their relationships to explain attitude change is to be preferred to one that takes twenty steps. In order to save time and energy, and because some scientists find an elegance in simplicity, when theories have equal explanatory and predictive power, parsimonious theories are to be preferred to complex ones.

3. Consistent with related theories. This criterion for a good theory is similar to requirement 2 above, that a good theory must be consistent with known data. The difference is that criterion 6 is concerned with theoretical, not empirical, consistency. Again, this criterion is likely to be violated during times of scientific revolution. Even during normal science, theories may be inconsistent with one another. As you read above, this is the case with the wave and particle theories of light in physics. Physicists are seeking one theory that would explain the wave and particle discrepancy. It is possible that such a theory might rely on a new metaphor, indicating that light travels in neither particles nor waves. If so, this new theory might be inconsistent with current theories yet be accepted because it helps to solve a problem that puzzles scientists.

Suppose that someone were to invent a theory of interpersonal communication which implies that trust is unimportant. The theory discusses the development of relationships with no mention of trust and no need for the concept. Since trust is considered to be a keystone of interpersonal relationships and self-disclosure (the degree to which you reveal information about your self-concept to others), the new theory would be viewed with much skepticism. Scientists would expect it to have a low probability of being confirmed because it contradicts a widely accepted component of many current theories.

4. Interpretable. As we have emphasized throughout this chapter, the purpose of a theory is to help us to explain, predict and control behavior. The process of theory building often begins with a description of the nature of reality, for example, the stages through which interpersonal friendships normally progress or what happens when someone is persuaded by a speaker. If a theory is difficult for scientists to relate to the real world, the theory has little value, since the purpose of communication theory is understanding, predicting, and controlling everyday communication events. As Kurt Lewin wrote, "There is nothing so practical as a good theory" (Cited in Thayer, 1982, p. 21). The idea that a theory should be practical may surprise you; many people view theory as mysterious and of little use to ordinary people. Nothing could be further from the truth. Recall the earlier discussion of the functions of theory. Theories are necessary to direct scientific research. A theory indicates which features of the phenomenon under investigation should be paid attention to and which ignored. For example, Lee's theory of interviewing and assertive communication stresses being assertive rather than preparing better answers or maintaining eye contact in order to be hired. If a theory cannot easily be connected by scientists to the real world, it will have lost a major part of its usefulness and will be difficult to test or disprove.

5. *Useful*. Theories should be useful, not only in explaining and guiding behavior as noted above, but also for the advancement of science. This is the heuristic function of theory discussed earlier: its ability to stimulate further research and hypotheses. Even though cognitive dissonance was criticized earlier as a theory that cannot be tested and disproved, many scientists praise cognitive dissonance for its heuristic power; it has stimulated research in many different fields of social science for the past thirty years.

6. *Pleasing to the Mind*. Stephen Toulmin (1961), in *Foresight and Understanding*, his important book on the philosophy of science, concludes that, ". . . we can never make less than a three-fold demand of science: its explanatory techniques must be not only (in Copernicus' words) 'consistent with the numerical records'; they must also be acceptable—for the time being, at any rate—as 'absolute' and 'pleasing to the mind'"(p. 115). As we mentioned earlier, scientists disagree on what criteria are essential for a good theory, and Toulmin's last criterion is certainly an interesting one. Some scientists argue that theories that are parsimonious, that explain a large number of events with relatively few principles, are inherently beautiful and elegant. This inner beauty and simplicity somehow strikes a chord for theorists. Many physicists evaluate Einstein's theory of relativity as especially elegant in this way. Regardless of the form of the theory, there is something mysterious and personally compelling about the impact of theory on the mind of a scientist. Scientists try not to be so caught up in their personal biases that they lose objectivity, or at least intersubjectivity, the ability to find "truths" that other scientists will also recognize as "true." Nevertheless, a scientist or theorist has a very personal involvement with theory building.

Polanyi (1958) has discussed a concept that addresses the mystical "resonance" that scientists sometimes feel from a theory. This feeling that the theory is somehow "right" or "true," Polanyi terms "personal knowledge." As the term implies, personal knowledge is a subjective experience on the part of the scientist, yet Polanyi argues that it is not the result of bias nor blindness to disconfirming evidence. Rather, personal knowledge is a feeling that the scientist has that one theoretical path rather than another is the right road to take. Once the theory has been developed, the scientist uses traditional research to demonstrate its strength to other scientists. Personal knowledge is a type of "evidence" found within the scientist's intellectual and emotional response to the theory that causes him or her to pursue a particular direction with confidence that the path will lead to important discoveries.

While personal knowledge is an individual phenomenon, scientists as a group may also have a special feeling about a particular theory. The judgment of a group of scientists that a theory is unusually elegant or "right" seems to be what Toulmin means when he says that a theory must be "pleasing to the mind." Because of their training in the scientific method and in research, scientists share a common culture and values. As a result of those shared values, the truly inexplicable impact of a theory upon the community of science may result in the common judgment that the theory is exceptionally pleasing or intellectually satisfying. Conversely, if a theory does not "feel right," chances are that it will not be accepted for very long; a better theory will be found to take its place, in part because of scientific dissatisfaction with the original theory.

What Should Be the Criteria for a Good Communication Theory?

Disagreement over what a good theory would look like also extends to the field of communication. Two important points of controversy will be presented below. As you read them, try to form your own criteria for a good communication theory. Imagine what an ideal theory of communication would look like. Decide on your answer to the two questions posed below. Then review the "necessary" and "desirable" criteria for theories presented above. Which do you believe are truly necessary? This exercise will be useful, in part, because you will then be able to compare your ideal theory with important communication theories currently discussed by scientists and presented in later chapters of this book.

What should be the scope of a good communication theory?

In Chapter 1 you read a discussion about the characteristics of human communication and learned about some disagreements over the definition of communication and its characteristics. Some theorists are searching for a communication theory which will apply to many different communication contexts; for example, a theory that would describe interpersonal, group, and public communication. Such a theory must be fairly general because of the obvious differences between, say, television news and going on a date. The Sender-Message-Receiver model we presented in Figure 1.1 in Chapter 1 is typical of such theories. A major theoretical family or paradigm that focuses on common features across contexts is systems theory, which will be discussed in Chapter 3.

Other scientists believe that a theory that covers many communication contexts will overlook key features of the different types of communication. For example, a communication theory that accurately portrays the key features of both the mass communication and interpersonal communication contexts would have to combine such important concepts as technology and mediated communication with key interpersonal variables such as trust and relationship formation. Many, perhaps most, scientists believe the contexts in which communication occurs are so varied and so individually important that it is best to focus theory building on only one particular context.

This scientific disagreement is a disagreement about what is the most desirable scope of a communication theory. The scope of a theory refers "to the number of different kinds of behaviors that the theory attempts to explain" (Shaw & Costanzo, 1970, p. 11). As Shaw and Costanzo emphasize, there is no reason to assume that a theory with broader scope is better than a narrower theory, one that focuses on only one communication context. Each theory must be judged on its own merits. The preference for a theory of broad or narrow scope is one on which scientists differ. Which would you prefer: a general theory of communication that explains all types of communication or several specific theories that explore the particular features of different communication contexts separately? If you prefer the latter, realize that the result might be a situation like that in physics with the wave and particle theories of light; communication scholars might find themselves with theories that are contradictory or at least incompatible. On the other hand, perhaps communication contexts are so varied that a unified theory is an impossible dream. At present, this is a matter of speculation and debate.

Is it more important for a communication theory to explain or to predict behavior?

By now you should be familiar with the goals of theory: to explain, predict, and control. In fact, there is an even more basic goal. Since the social scientific study of communication is comparatively new, many theories of communication at present are merely descriptive. They identify what variables or concepts are important in a particular communication event. Some are best referred to not as theories, but as models, like the ones you read about in Chapter 1. Models are generally mathematical or pictorial representations of events. Theories may or may not contain models, but they are usually distinguished from models in that theories attempt not only to identify key concepts and the relationships between them, but also to indicate why the particular relationships occur. So, for example, a theory of interpersonal communication might not only indicate that there is a reciprocal relationship between trust and self-disclosure, but also explain why trust increases self-disclosure and self-disclosure increases trust. There is general agreement that a minimum requirement for a good communication theory is that it describe phenomena.

The explanation and prediction functions of theory, while often compatible, are not always so. The Babylonian theory of astronomy accurately predicted lunar eclipses and new moons because the Babylonians had carefully observed nature and performed mathematical calculations that led to these predictions (Toulmin, 1961). Yet the Babylonians had no understanding of why the events occurred. "To discover that events of a certain kind are predictable—even to develop effective techniques for forecasting them—is evidently quite different from having an adequate theory about them, through which they can be understood," writes Toulmin (1961, p. 30). Toulmin contrasts Babylonian astronomy, which predicted well but did not explain, with Newton's theories of physics. Toulmin believes, "No scientific theory has ever provided a more striking advance in our understanding of Nature than Newton's" (1961, p. 31). Yet Newton's theory, which explained why eclipses, but not earthquakes, can be precisely forecast was incorrect in many of its annual forecasts of eclipses. It did not accurately predict.

Scientists are in agreement that the best communication theories should *both* explain and predict, but rarely do communication theories do both. As the example above from physics illustrates, many theories do a better job of one function than the other. If you could not have both, which would you prefer? A theory that predicts without adequate explanation? Such a theory, by making accurate predictions, might lead to further insight and discoveries about the causes of the regular patterns the theory has identified. On the other hand, a theory that adequately explains gives a scientist understanding that the scientist might be able to refine to make future predictions. In fact, there is debate over what constitutes an adequate explanation. Some scientists believe that identifying regular patterns of cause and effect in nature constitutes an explanation. So, for example, identifying the mutually reinforcing relationship between trust and self-disclosure counts as a sufficient explanation according to some theorists. Others, however, want to know why the relationship exists in terms of why individuals choose to self-disclose more to those whom they trust and vice-versa. What the first scientist might consider an adequate explanation, the second would reject as superficial. The difference in the level of preferred explanation reflects a difference in the assumptions that theorists make.

As we shall discuss in more detail in Chapter 3, theories in communication and other fields tend to cluster in paradigms, or families. These theories are grouped together because they reflect the same perspective on communication; that is, they adopt the same assumptions about what is important and how it can best be discovered. In some sense, these theories are like fishing nets made of different material but with the same size mesh, or sunglasses with different style frames but the same color of lenses. As Chapter 3 explains, some families of theories are better at explaining and others at predicting. Some scientists would argue that we have relatively few theories that both predict and explain because our field is relatively new. Others claim that predicting human choice can never be as precise as predictions in physics, for example, and that explanation should be our primary goal. This debate goes to the heart of what the fundamental nature of human communication is all about, and we will explore the controversy in detail in the next chapter.

Summary

Like any other theory, a communication theory is a symbolic creation designed to explain why phenomena occur in the patterns we observe. The three basic goals of theory are to explain, predict and control. Theories have four major functions: they organize experience, extend knowledge, stimulate and guide further research, and allow scientists to anticipate events they may not yet be able to observe. During normal scientific times, theories develop by extension, growing to encompass more variables, and by intension, further refining their explanations of the variables included. Scientific revolutions may also occur. During such times theories that have long been confirmed are rejected in favor of theories which use new metaphors and perhaps contradict accepted "facts." Theories cannot be proven; they can only be disconfirmed when scientists discover that evidence does not support hypotheses generated by the theory. The scientific method allows scientists to test theories so that conclusions are reliable and valid.

Scientists disagree on the criteria which distinguish good from inadequate theories. We have suggested three essential criteria for a good theory: logical consistency, consistency with accepted facts, and testability. Desirable criteria include: simplicity, parsimony, consistency with accepted theories, interpretability, usefulness, and the indescribable quality that a theory be pleasing to the mind. After reading the chapter, you should have formed your own opinion about what an ideal theory of communication would be like. How broad should be its scope? If it does not both explain and predict, which criterion is more important to you? If you can answer these questions, you will be able to compare your ideal theory with the actual theories discussed in Parts II and III. Before reading about specific communication theories in detail, you should understand more about the theoretical perspectives currently used by communication researchers and the research methods scientists use to test their theories. These topics will be presented in Chapter 3. More detail about research methods is available in the Appendix.

Questions to Consider

1. What is a theory?
2. In what ways do theories organize experience?
3. How do theories extend knowledge?
4. Explain the heuristic function of a theory.
5. How do theories allow us to anticipate something we have never encountered?
6. In what three ways do theories develop and change?
7. How are theories tested?
8. Why is testing theories by the process of disconfirmation necessary and valuable?
9. List and explain the nine criteria for evaluating theories. Which do you feel are necessary for a good theory? Desirable? Give reasons for your choices.
10. What should be the criteria for a good communication theory?

References

Arnoult, M. D. (1972). *Fundamentals of scientific method in psychology.* Dubuque, IA: Wm. C. Brown.

Festinger, L. (1957). *A theory of cognitive dissonance.* Stanford, CA: Stanford University Press.

Hoover, K. R. (1984). *The elements of social scientific thinking* (3rd. ed.). New York: St. Martin's Press.

Kaplan, A. (1964). *The conduct of inquiry.* San Francisco: Chandler.

Korzybski, A. (1958). *Science and sanity: An introduction to non-Aristotelian systems and general semantics* (4th ed.). Lakeville, CT: International Non-Aristotelian Library Publishing Company.

Kuhn, T. S. (1970). *The structure of scientific revolutions.* Chicago: University of Chicago Press.

Littlejohn, S. W. (1983). *Theories of human communication.* Belmont, CA: Wadsworth.

Mandler, G., & Kesson, W. (1959). *The language of psychology.* New York: Wiley.

Polanyi, M. (1958). *Personal knowledge.* Chicago: University of Chicago Press.

Shaw, M. E., & Costanzo, P. R. (1970). *Theories of social psychology.* New York: McGraw-Hill.

Thayer, L. (1982). What would a theory of communication be for? *Journal of Applied Communication Research, 10,* 21-28.

Toulmin, S. (1961). *Foresight and understanding: An enquiry into the aims of science.* New York: Harper Torchbooks.

Chapter 3

Covering Laws, Rules and Systems Perspectives

Paradigms and Communication Theory

In Chapter 2 we introduced the concept of paradigms. Paradigms are "grand models" or sets of theoretical assumptions shared by many theories. Individuals use paradigms as guides to develop and to test questions about the phenomena they are studying. Usually scientists, including communication scientists, tend to favor one paradigm over another. Because paradigms are "world views" which are generally accepted by the scientific community at large, a given scientist is somewhat limited in his or her choice of paradigms from which to operate. When a communication scholar adopts a particular paradigm or theoretical perspective, that paradigm will help define not only the questions to be asked but, to a large extent, the methods of discovering answers to those questions. To a lesser, although significant degree, the theoretical perspective chosen may also help define what are acceptable answers to the questions posed.

At times in the history of science, scholars and scientists have been limited in their choice of paradigms. A particular theoretical perspective would be so well developed and enjoy such widespread support that the vast majority of researchers would employ that paradigm. When a sufficient amount of evidence accumulated to question the core assumptions of that paradigm, new paradigms were introduced to try to account for discrepancies. If enough evidence was found for the superiority of one model over another, a *paradigm shift* took place. One paradigm eclipsed another in adoption and support. Soon, the "new" paradigm became the dominant one.

Contemporary communication scientists, researchers and theorists are working in a period of time when several paradigms are operating simultaneously. Each model has an inherent set of assumptions which provides questions to ask about communication behavior, methods to try to discover answers to those questions, and even some "established" answers. Although each of the theory building perspectives we will explore has a different set of assumptions which guide research activity, none of the paradigms has achieved total dominance in our field. Because human communication is such a complex and multifaceted phenomenon, contemporary communication scientists seek the theoretical perspective which they believe will *best* help them answer a specific research question. While communication scholars may have a preference for one paradigm over another when they conduct their research, the critical review process of our field encourages researchers to be open to several perspectives when conducting scientific inquiry.

Three theory building perspectives currently enjoy widespread popularity and acceptance in communication research. Each of these perspectives will be described and examples of communication research illustrating the three models for inquiry will be presented. As you examine each perspective, you may find that one particularly appeals to you. Remember that each paradigm outlined has been used by communication scholars to generate much outstanding research; each has strengths and weaknesses, friends and enemies. Each model has helped provide answers to very complex questions about human communication behavior. The three paradigms are: the covering laws perspective, the human action perspective (including the rules approach) , and the systems perspective.

The Covering Laws Perspective

This perspective, sometimes referred to as the *classical model* or the *logical positivist model*, is the oldest and most frequently employed in contemporary communication theory and research. The covering laws approach became the dominant method of inquiry in the communication arts and sciences when our discipline incorporated a behavioral science orientation during the early 1960s. This pattern of discovery has also been widely used in other social science disciplines such as psychology. The laws perspective did not originate in the social sciences. Theorists and researchers from the physical sciences (e.g., biology, chemistry, physics) employed the covering laws model (logical positivist thought) well before psychologists and communication scholars embraced it.

To understand fully the covering laws perspective, we should examine its underpinnings in logical positivism. Logical positivism represents one particular "way of knowing." It asserts that we can only "know" something in two ways: (1) we can see, taste, touch, smell, or hear it; or (2) we can discover it through some type of logical derivation. Thus, according to the logical positivists we come to "know" something if we can gather information about it through our senses or if we can discover it through logical examination or mathematical modeling. For example, physicists and astrophysicists used high level mathematical modeling to discover the forces that create weightlessness long before we had the capacity to experience the effects during space travel. The concept of "weightlessness" was uncovered through this logical discovery and modeling process before anyone actually felt the effect.

A third crucial premise of logical positivism suggests that there are certain regularities in nature which can be observed and/or discovered. These regularities are called "laws." Laws are universal. Once established, that law transcends time and space. The physical sciences have provided us with many law-governed regularities such as, "At 100 degrees Celsius, water will boil," or, "With the proper velocity, mass, acceleration and wind, an airplane will fly." The laws of thermodynamics derived from physics have helped us discover how to make aircraft fly. Of course, these law-governed regularities do not eliminate the possibility that human error might create havoc with our plans! We will address this point again later in the chapter.

As with the examples above, the underlying structure of a law generally follows this form:

If X, then Y

If X (some antecedent condition) exists, then Y (some consequent effect) will occur. The existing law predicts that X will *cause* Y.

We have now articulated a concept that is crucial to our understanding of the covering laws model: causation or causality. An inherent assumption of the laws approach to communication suggests that we can understand human communication behavior if we uncover those antecedent conditions which cause consequent effects. The laws approach emphasizes cause and effect relationships. People communicate the way they do because some prior condition caused them to respond to a message in certain ways. Advocates of the covering laws model of communication are continually seeking to discover what preceding conditions will cause people to respond in various ways. If we discover those conditions, then we can re-create them and have people respond the way the law governed generalization indicates they will. In this way, we can better *explain* our environment, *predict* outcomes, and ultimately *control* our environment.

Prediction is another important characteristic of the law-governed perspective in human communication. Advocates of this approach try to use their knowledge about antecedent conditions to predict how people will respond or behave in communication situations. Researchers in the fields of advertising and marketing are particularly interested in discovering the conditions which *cause* people to react to packaging and advertising. If research had found that the color red is more eyecatching than other colors and that red creates more psychological arousal, then we could predict with accuracy that people would generally be more responsive to a product packaged in red.

We have just made a law-like proposition involving human behavior. Stating it another way, if X (packaging is red), then Y (the product may be more easily seen and more psychologically arousing). In addition, we have alluded to another important aspect of the covering laws perspective, the generalizability of law-like statements. Proponents of the laws approach probe for law-like generalizations which hold true across many situations and many different time periods. This is what we meant when we stated that laws transcend time and space. If an antecedent condition is found to be the cause of a consequent effect today, the law predicts the same effect will occur a month from today, a year from today, perhaps even several decades from now! In addition, if the law-like generalization holds true for one group of people, then it should also hold true for many different groups of people as well.

Earlier in this chapter we mentioned one of the law governed generalizations regarding an airplane's ability to fly. The laws of physics predict that given a certain velocity, mass, acceleration, wind and wing span, an airplane will take off and fly. This law governed statement has been found to be true—barring the possibility that human error may alter the situation. Notice that this introduces a qualifier into the prediction. There are certain conditions which would falsify our other example, as well. Water will boil at 100 degrees Celsius—if we have the water at sea level. If we are at the top of a very high mountain, the water might have to be heated several degrees above 100 degrees Celsius before it would boil. What we are suggesting is that laws exist under certain conditional constraints.

The Positivistic versus The Probabilistic Conception of Laws

According to the framework of the logical positivist tradition, laws cannot be broken. That is, if certain antecedent conditions cause a certain consequent effect, once those conditions have been introduced, the consequent effect will *always* result. *Every* time X occurs, Y will *always* follow. In fact, the logical positivist approach believes that the consequent effect will occur 100 times out of 100 if the antecedent conditions are in effect. Under the appropriate environmental conditions, every time a sodium (Na) atom is introduced to a chlorine (Cl) atom, they will joint to form NaCl or salt. This result will be observed 100 times in 100 trials. The "laws" of chemistry prevent any other consequent effect from occurring. The sodium and/or chlorine atoms are not free to choose whether they want to be joined (bonded) in any given situation. The strict logical positivist or mechanistic approach to laws works quite well in the fields of chemistry and physics.

While we trust our lives to the laws of physics that an airplane will *always* take off and fly, many communication theorists and scholars would agree that human beings do not act in the same fashion as atoms or molecules. Most contemporary communication theorists would admit that the human being differs from those particles because we have some choice in how we respond to stimuli in our environment. Human beings have volition and can, to some degree, exercise their choices even in the presence of certain *antecedent conditions* which have a strong causal relationship to some consequent outcomes.

Communication theorists who advocate this particular view of laws and causality are called probabilists. Miller and Berger (1978) have suggested that most communication theorists advocating the covering laws approach to building communication theory today have rejected the strict mechanistic view of laws and have opted for a probabilistic orientation. The probabilistic view of laws asserts that given a certain antecedent condition (X), outcome or consequent effect (Y) will occur with (P) degree of probability, under certain conditions. Let us consider an example of a communication "law" regarding the use of evidence in persuasive communication. Stated in its most basic law-governed fashion, "Using evidence in a persuasive message will cause listeners to accept that message more than they would a persuasive message without evidence." The probabilistic view of laws might suggest that using evidence in a message will produce more persuasion "70 percent of the time."

Further, probabilistic law-governed communication theorist would establish certain conditions that must exist in order for that law to hold true even 70 percent of the time. In the example above, they might state that the evidence must be timely and current because extremely old evidence might be more harmful than no evidence at all. Second, they might suggest that the evidence must be new to the listeners. Third, they might suggest that the evidence should come from sources that are believable to the audience because of expertise and trustworthiness. Probabilistic law-governed communication theorists recognize that human beings do have choice or volition even when confronted by extremely strong causal relationships. These scholars also recognize that some laws or regularities in nature regarding communication behavior exist only under certain specific conditions.

Discovering Certain "Laws" of Communication

For the last thirty years, communication theorists and scholars have attempted to uncover some "laws" or regularities involving human communication behavior. Much of this research activity has centered around the area of persuasion or attitude change. One of the earliest attempts was conducted at Yale University by Hovland, Janis and Kelley (1953). Some of the major research findings of the Yale Studies in Communication will be detailed in Chapters 4 and 6 of this text.

The Yale communication research team was essentially interested in discovering certain conditions which would make individuals more susceptible to the persuasive influence of others. The use of propaganda in World War II and the Korean War, the introduction and rapid diffusion of commercial television and the world-wide increase in advertising focused attention on persuasion and social influence. Through a series of systematic research studies, Hovland and his associates sought to discover the many source, message, channel and receiver characteristics which would enhance such influence. They found that certain characteristics of a message source increased that source's persuasive impact on an audience. The higher the source's perceived credibility (believability, expertise, trustworthiness), the more likely an audience member would be persuaded. They also observed that physical appearance affected persuasion. In general, the more physically attractive the message source, the more the source persuaded the audience.

Regarding characteristics of the message itself, the Yale communication researchers discovered that well-organized messages were more persuasive than disorganized messages. Messages with more evidence or testimony had more impact than other types of messages. Messages containing modest amounts of information designed to frighten a receiver into believing or doing what the persuader wanted (fear appeals) had more impact than messages which did not contain any fear-arousing information.

Characteristics of an audience were also investigated. Educational level, sexual composition, and level of self-esteem were a few of the audience/receiver characteristics that received research attention in the Yale Studies on Communication. One interesting finding that emerged was that two-sided messages (messages that contain both your position and a few arguments from the opposing side which you refute) worked best with more educated audiences.

More recently, certain law-like generalizations have been discovered in the area of interpersonal attraction. The question of what makes people like each other has received considerable attention from theorists in communication and social psychology (see Chapter 9). Certain factors have been discovered which contribute to attraction or liking between people: attitudes in common, similar backgrounds, and physical resemblance. Examples of law-like generalizations in the area of interpersonal attraction might include: "People are more likely to be attracted to others with similar rather than different attitudes" and "Physically attractive people are more likely to develop relationships with others who are also physically attractive." Several studies (Berger, 1977; Berscheid & Walster, 1978; Huston, 1974) have indeed found that relationships between two people, one of whom is highly attractive and the other is highly unattractive, are unusual. There are many more law-like generalizations that have been discovered in the area of interpersonal attraction and relationship development during the last several years. These findings will be presented in Chapter 9.

The "Tools" of the Law-Governed Communication Researcher

As we have stressed, the concept of causality is central to the law-governed approach to communication. In an effort to demonstrate causal relationships between communication variables, researchers use a very important method or set of tools, the experimental model. The experimental model is used by researchers to create controlled situations in order to test the effect of antecedent conditions on subsequent outcomes. The experimental model is the only method researchers can use to establish *causal* relationships between communication variables. The research methods chapter in the Appendix details concepts central to the experimental model such as variables, experimental design, and control.

To illustrate the use of the experimental paradigm, let us consider a person's general tendency to argue or to defend his or her beliefs—trait argumentativeness. Two of the authors decided to explore this topic. They wanted to investigate whether individuals who like to argue would behave differently when arguing with people who hesitate to voice their opinions than with people who quickly express their opinions. Similarly, would individuals who avoid argument behave differently when talking to people who like to defend their beliefs versus people who try to avoid disputes?

Four experimental situations were created. In one, individuals high in argumentativeness were led to believe that they would have to argue informally with another person who was also very argumentative. In the second, high argumentatives thought they were going to argue with an opponent dissimilar to themselves, a low argumentative individual. The third experimental condition participants were low argumentatives who thought they were going to argue with someone similar to themselves. In the fourth condition, low argumentatives thought they would argue with someone dissimilar, a highly argumentative adversary. The results of this experiment revealed that high argumentatives were more motivated to argue than low argumentatives. In addition, it was discovered that highly argumentative individuals were most motivated when they expected to argue with another high argumentative. This experiment demonstrated that motivation to argue is influenced not only by a person's own underlying tendency, but also by expectations about the adversary. Highly argumentative individuals were especially likely to be influenced by expectations about their partner.

Strengths and Weaknesses of the Laws Perspective

While the covering laws approach to building theory has enjoyed widespread support and adoption in the communication arts and sciences, it has also recently received criticism. Some of the major strengths and weaknesses of the laws approach to communication follow.

Strengths of the Laws Perspective

1. The laws approach to communication seems especially useful in helping us make *predictions* about human communication behavior. The laws approach to communication has uncovered many causal relationships between communication variables. For example, many of the findings of the Yale Studies on communication continue to receive support. The use of evidence to help persuade an audience under certain conditions (see Chapter 7) is one such relationship.

2. Advocates of the laws approach suggest that theory building in communication is strengthened by utilizing findings from studies conducted using this perspective. Our understanding of communication apprehension (fear or anxiety associated with communication), for example, has been greatly enhanced by nearly two decades of effort by McCroskey and his associates (e.g., Daly and McCroskey, 1984). They have continuously tested the many factors associated with this trait and have painstakingly constructed new predictions based on previous results. Our knowledge about this subject increases with each additional effort.

Weaknesses of the Laws Perspective

1. Critics suggest that the laws approach, especially the positivist tradition, does not place enough emphasis on human choice, free will and interpretation of stimuli. They suggest that the primary tool used in laws research, the experimental model, is best left to researchers and theorists in the physical sciences who do not have to be concerned with issues of human choice and interpretation.

2. The laws approach can help us make predictions about how people will behave *in general*. Critics state that the laws approach cannot, with any degree of certainty, help us predict how any single individual will behave. For example, using research that suggests that including messages designed to frighten an audience slightly (moderate fear appeals) in a persuasive speech is effective, you might conclude that some percentage of one hundred audience members will change their minds and vote for your proposal. However, the laws approach will not help you know who the particular people are who will change their minds. The focus is on the group, not the individual.

3. Other critics of the laws approach maintain that breaking down communication events into separate parts does not contribute to theoretical advancement. They claim that this method, often referred to as *variable analysis*, oversimplifies human communication. Jesse Delia says variable analysis "fails to reflect the interwoven texture of the processes participating in human communication" (1975, p. 2). These critics

suggest that communication is so complicated that studying only one variable at a time misleadingly reduces a very complex event to a very simple one.

Human Action Perspectives

The human action perspective encompasses the rules approach and was developed in reaction to some of the more extreme followers of the covering laws perspective. Philosophers of science such as Winch (1958) argued that human beings cannot be studied using models developed for the physical sciences because humans are *qualitatively* different from natural events. Predicting whether water will or will not freeze at a given temperature is very different from predicting whether or not a marriage between two people will succeed. Throughout this book, we shall refer to the rules perspective as typical of the philosophical assumptions held by scientists who adopt the human action perspective about theory building.

For the covering laws perspective, the true nature of reality is contained in regular patterns that occur in nature. Followers of the rules and other human action perspectives believe that the true nature of reality is *subjective experience*. In order to understand a communication event, you must understand the individual's perception of that event, not just the event itself. Scientists adopting the rules perspective try to predict behavior by grouping together people who understand or interpret events similarly, or who make choices for similar reasons.

For example, suppose you want to persuade your classmates to stop smoking. You realize that the American Cancer Society often tries to frighten television viewers through its commercials, and you wonder whether a fear appeal will be persuasive in a classroom situation. If you turn to previous research using fear appeals, you will find many studies concerning the level of fear appeal used in the persuasive message: high, moderate or low. In an experiment using dental hygiene as the topic of the persuasive message, a low fear appeal might consist of a mild speech mentioning the dangers of getting a cavity. A moderate fear appeal might mention tooth decay and show pictures of decayed teeth. A strong fear appeal would mention tooth decay and gum disease and include very graphic pictures of badly diseased gums—such as those you probably avoid looking at in your dentist's office.

A rules or interpretive theorist would caution that in order to understand the persuasive effects of low, moderate, and high fear appeals, the scientist must ask the audience how they interpreted the message. It is not enough to know that test audiences rated the three messages as mild, moderately and strongly threatening. One must know how members of the target audience for the experiment viewed the message in order to interpret the results. The rules or human action perspective's "way of knowing" is to understand the subjective experience of people acting in the situation. The rules theorist would attempt to understand the communication behavior as experienced by the audience members, who are assumed to be intentional, purposeful beings rather than merely reactors to stimuli or events. The rules theorist would then make predictions for people who interpret the message in a certain way.

The laws theorist might divide the audience into three groups. Members of each group would hear the same type of message, one with either mild, moderate, or strong fear appeals. The rules theorist would be more likely to divide the audience based on how they perceived the message—those who were mildly frightened, moderately frightened, or strongly frightened— regardless of what speech they heard. Then both scientists would proceed to study the effect of fear on attitude change. The rules theorist is not so much concerned with the stimulus or antecedent conditions—the speech—as with how the audience interpreted and responded to it. For example, someone with dental problems might have been very frightened by the speech which contained a mild fear appeal.

A distinction made by sociologist Schutz (1967) is helpful at this point. Schutz said that human behavior can be explained by two types of motives which he called in-order-to-motives and because-motives. We may apply these terms to the covering laws and rules perspectives. Because-motives are related to past events, while in-order-to-motives are related to goals you hope to accomplish in the future. According to Schutz, a because-motive is a reason for some action based on an event that happened in the past. For example, a child may run from dogs after having been bitten by a dog in the past. The motive for the behavior rests in some past event that influences present behavior. This type of motive is very much like a covering laws explanation; the child runs from the dog (subsequent behavior) because of some previous event (antecedent condition).

The rules perspective emphasizes the second of Schutz's explanations for behavior, the in-order-to-motive. Schutz says that human beings are goal-oriented. They behave in ways that will best enable them to reach the goals that they strive for. An *in-order-to-motive* is the mental picture of a goal that someone wants to attain. Schutz says that we think of such goals in the future. Thus, if your goal is to graduate from college, you think of the goals as *already having been completed.* That is, you might picture yourself in cap and gown at graduation, or applying for your first job with degree in hand. So you are taking college or university classes *in order to* graduate from college. You consciously choose your actions in order to reach a particular goal.

It is interesting to notice that *the same event can be explained by both types of goals,* a reason why we claim that the rules and laws perspectives may sometimes indicate different approaches to the same question. For example, think about why you decided to attend college in the first place. Was it because your parents had instilled in you a respect for education? That would be a because-motive; you went to college because of a past influence by your parents. Or you might have chosen a particular college because your friends were going there and you wanted to be with them. That's an in-order-to-motive. As you sent in your forms, you probably pictured yourself enjoying future activities with your friends. Even though a behavior may be explained by both past influences (because-motives) and future goals (in-order-to-motives), the covering laws and rules perspectives tend to have different emphases. The covering laws perspective emphasizes the effect of previous experiences, while the rules perspective emphasizes the importance of goals for the future. Thus, under covering laws, the individual is seen as reacting to a prior stimulus. Under the rules or human action perspective, the individual is seen as proactive, choosing actions in order to accomplish goals.

No communication scientist operating under the covering laws perspective would deny that individuals are goal-oriented. Rather, a covering laws researcher believes that the majority of human behavior is heavily influenced by past events or previous stimuli, and that understanding those events and stimuli is the best way to predict behavior. A rules researcher does not deny that past experiences influence behavior but feels that the influence of goals is even stronger. A rules researcher would point out that two people with the same negative experience may react to the experience very differently. The rules researcher deliberately chooses to de-emphasize the past event itself in order to focus attention on the individual's *interpretation* of that event and the way it fits into the individual's goals for the future.

Scientists adopting human action perspectives believe that *subjective experience* describes the true nature of reality. What is important, then, is not what actually happens, but what individuals perceive happened, because we behave as though our perceptions were reality. After all, if you feel people have deliberately told lies about you, you will treat them as though they had spread false rumors, whether or not they actually did. Your behavior is based on what you believe happened. So your behavior is not based on "absolute reality" but on your perceptions of what is real.

Theorists taking human action perspectives believe that human behavior can be predicted because people make purposeful choices about their actions. In order to understand behavior, we must examine the goals which led the person to choose to behave a certain way. People are persuaded because they deliberately choose to change their minds, not because the speaker happened to use the "right" tactic. The speaker's persuasive tactics influenced the audience, but the *audience* controlled that influence, not the speaker. If behavior is chosen by individuals to help them reach their goals, you must ask them what goals led them to act as they did. A rules study of persuasion might conclude that a persuasive speech was effective because people felt that to stop smoking now would help them live longer. The fear appeals made them afraid of getting lung cancer. However, suppose the researcher's interviews with the audience indicated it was the new information—stopping smoking reduces the probability of getting lung cancer even for former smokers—that led the audience to decide to quit. The fear appeals played little part in their decision.

The hypothetical study above provides clues about the research tools that rules theorists use. They use methods which will allow them to investigate individual experience and interpretation of events. Some examples of these tools are questionnaires, interviews, and descriptions of what someone would say in response to a certain situation. Participants in a study might be asked to write a persuasive speech or to write what they would say if a romantic partner made a certain type of statement. A rules researcher would then try to understand what goals the participant tried to accomplish or why he or she used certain persuasive tactics. The key point is that the rules or interpretive researcher tries to understand the subjective reality of people in order to explain and predict their behavior.

According to the rules perspective, these choices are made by following individual or social rules for decisions. Following these rules is assumed to be a freely-chosen act that allows people to accomplish their goals. For example, there is an unwritten rule in most college classes regarding attendance. Some professors even write their attendance requirements on the syllabus. If the requirement is not written and is not made clear orally in class, you may have to figure out what the professor's attendance rule is. You would probably do so by asking students who have had the class before, talking to a teaching assistant if there is one, reading the course description in a department or university handbook, or by asking other students in the class what they have heard. After you have learned the rule, either by hearing or reading it or by figuring out for yourself what the professor considers a reasonable number of absences, you then decide whether or not to obey it.

This type of choice or decision is precisely what rules researchers find interesting and valuable in understanding human behavior. Realize that you really do have a choice. There may be negative consequences if you fail to follow the rule, but you may decide to accept them. This is not to imply that you have a great mental debate each day to decide whether or not to attend class. Some choices are made so frequently that we are rarely conscious of making them. The point is that we have control over our actions and can choose to follow or to break rules. Rules theorists are interested in the reasons why we make a particular choice. They are also interested in how people create rules and why they create particular rules rather than others.

We now turn to two examples of theories which follow the assumptions of the human action perspective. One example is an interpretive theory and the other a rules theory. While these theories share common assumptions about human beings, they are quite different in the types of communication behavior which they study. The first to be discussed is Kelly's (1955) Personal Construct Theory, which has come to be known in the field of communication as Constructivism.

Personal Construct Theory, or Constructivism

Kelly believed that all humans act like naive scientists, trying to understand, predict and thereby control their environments. By this phrase, Kelly meant that we are always trying to understand things which happen to us so that we can cause good events to occur and avoid bad ones. Let us examine how an ordinary street beggar acts as a naive scientist. If you have observed the behavior of panhandlers, you may have noticed that they do not approach everyone who passes by. Since it is painful to be rejected over and over, they try to approach people who are most likely to give them money. How can they tell who will give and who will not? Kelly says they use perceptual categories called *constructs* to help them make this prediction.

Imagine that a panhandler classifies passersby as "generous-not generous." Based on individual experience, he has discovered that people dressed in business suits are not generous, while people with children usually give him money. Similarly he has learned that people in military or police uniforms do not give, while people wearing habits, clerical collars, or other clothing with religious connotations usually do give. Just possibly he has discovered that people with dark hair are more likely to respond to his appeals than are blondes and redheads. The panhandler then has a *personal construct*, a pair of opposite mental categories expressed by the labels "generous" and "not generous," that is described below:

Panhandler One's Construct

Generous	Not Generous
religious clothing	police or military uniforms
dark hair	lighter hair
with children	without children
casual clothes	business suits

The panhandler will use his "generous-not generous" construct to predict and control his environment. He will "size up" approaching passersby and decide whether or not to ask for money based on his personal construct system. (Realize that your authors are unaware of any scientific evidence predicting generosity on the basis of hair color.) The connections made by the panhandler are not scientific facts so much as patterns repeated in his experience and influenced by what others might have told him. In fact, another panhandler may have had just the opposite experience!

We can imagine a female panhandler who has the construct described below:

Panhandler Two's Construct

Generous	Not Generous
women	men
gray hair	not gray hair
without children	with children
in uniform	not in uniform

Both panhandlers try to control their environments—maximize money received and minimize insults and rejections—by using their constructs to predict which passersby are most likely to give and by approaching only those people. Notice that there may be inconsistencies in their constructs. How would the second panhandler respond to a man in uniform without children? Would she ask for a handout because two of the three relevant characteristics—walking alone and being in uniform—indicated generosity? What would the male panhandler do in the case of a red-haired priest?

In part, this difficulty may be resolved by understanding that constructs are hierarchically organized; that is, some are more important than others. Perhaps both panhandlers have discovered that the most important distinction in assessing the generosity of givers is hair color. Thus, the male panhandler would **not** approach the red-haired priest because, in a case when two predictions conflict, hair color has been his most reliable predictor in the past. We all have many, many constructs, and our construct systems cannot be completely consistent even when we organize our constructs at different levels of importance. According to the rules perspective, human behavior can never be absolutely predictable because of the element of individual choice involved. People may behave differently depending on their moods and on the situation. At times beggars may be so hungry that they approach everyone who passes by. Even though our constructs are imperfect and human behavior is complicated and puzzling, we still use personal constructs to guide our actions toward the accomplishment of our personal goals.

The above discussion of panhandlers has probably left you feeling slightly uncomfortable because of the way we used the terms generous and not generous. (We deliberately avoided making the opposite of generous to be stingy). Perhaps your personal constructs of "generous" and "not generous" are completely unrelated to giving handouts to street beggars. You might label such giving as saintly/futile, or even foolish/harmful (if you believe it supports alcoholism, for example). Your individual idea of generosity may be related to behaviors such as helping out needy friends with a loan, giving to charitable causes, or always picking up the check when dining with friends. The example is designed to show that each of us creates our own constructs and construct systems. We are influenced by our families, by society and culture, and by past experiences, but each of us has a unique set of constructs because our experiences and interpretations of them are different from anyone else's. It is easy to see the importance of cultural influences on constructs. If you are from a country such as Japan where almost everyone has dark hair, you probably do not connect hair color with either generosity or stinginess since you have seen people with the same hair color behave in both ways.

A final interesting characteristic of constructs is that they change. Some of the changes come naturally as we grow from childhood to maturity. Our constructs become more abstract, dealing with personality not just with physical appearance, for example. They become more differentiated as we learn that not all males or females behave the same way; some individuals are generous and some are not. Constructs may change not only with increasing maturity but also in response to our experiences. Suppose you had decided that everyone who is intelligent is also shy because all the very intelligent people you had known were bashful. Then you met another very intelligent person who was an extrovert! You might have taken *shy* off your list of connections with the construct *intelligent-unintelligent* because of one startling exception or because you frequently found exceptions to this mental rule. In part, the fact that constructs change explains how we can overcome stereotypes: through personal experience with members of the stereotyped group.

Researchers have extended Kelly's psychological theory to the field of communication. In one study of persuasion, Clark and Delia (1976) demonstrated that children with more fully developed construct systems were able to construct more advanced persuasive messages than children with simple, relatively unconnected constructs. Clark and Delia believed that people who had many constructs related in many different ways would be better persuaders than people who possessed simple constructs with few connections between them. They believed that "cognitively complex" children would be better able to imagine how the person they wanted to persuade understood the world and, therefore better able to present a persuasive message that would appeal to their target audience.

During the experiment, Clark and Delia asked their participants to imagine that they had found a puppy which they could not keep. They were told to tell the female experimenter what they would say to a female stranger to convince her to take care of the puppy for them. The researchers developed categories for coding the children's tape-recorded messages. As their theory predicted, Clark and Delia found that the older children—those with more mature and complex construct systems—used the most advanced persuasive strategies. The least sophisticated messages indicated only the request: "Would you please keep the puppy?" The next level of sophistication revealed only the child's perspective: "Please keep the puppy. I want you to keep it." The next highest level of messages showed the child's awareness of possible objections the stranger might have: "Please keep the puppy. It won't cost much to feed." The most sophisticated—and theoretically most effective level—of messages offered some benefit to the stranger: "Please keep this puppy. It will be a good watchdog for you."

Even though Clark and Delia do not explicitly state that their theory is based on the rules perspective, we have included it here because it is typical of human action or interpretive approaches which form the broad philosophical perspective into which rules theories also fit (Delia, O'Keefe, & O'Keefe, 1982). (You will read a slightly different interpretation of personal constructs in Chapter 5). Kelly's basic assumptions, outlined above, emphasize individual understanding and choice-making. The research methods used by the constructivists also focus on individuals' choices of strategies to reach a goal. The researchers assume that even children have persuasive goals and ask the children to give an example of how they would persuade a stranger. Overall, the focus of the research is on the child's understanding of the task (persuading the stranger) and how that understanding contributes to communication effectiveness.

The Coordinated Management of Meaning

The Coordinated Management of Meaning (CMM) is one of the most fully developed and researched communication rules theories. Cronen, Pearce and Harris (1982) explicitly describe their theory as an example of the rules perspective. When you compare the Coordinated Management of Meaning (CMM) with constructivism, you will see that all human action and interpretive theories have in common the philosophical assumptions that humans are choice-makers and that individual meanings and interpretations are the key to understanding human communication behavior. Whereas research based on constructivism tends to focus on the person sending a message, CMM, as a rules theory, emphasizes the social nature of communication. According to CMM, what happens in a conversation is the result of the rules followed by each party and what happens when the two sets of rules meet. CMM theorists believe that while individuals may choose their rules for conversing, the conversation that results is controlled jointly by the people involved. The focus of CMM is on the speech acts that people perform while communicating.

There are three basic parts to the CMM Theory: the context of a conversation, rules for interpreting the words and actions used (we will call them *definition rules*), and rules for deciding how to behave when someone says something or behaves in a particular way (i.e. performs a particular speech act. We will call these *behavior rules*). Let us examine these rules in a hypothetical negotiation between business executives from two different countries, the United States and Japan. To make the example clearer, we will assume that neither is familiar with the other's culture or with basic principles of doing business in an intercultural environment.

From the United States negotiator's perspective, the conversation occurs in a *context* called *business negotiations.* The American views the negotiation as a business transaction. During this type of conversational episode, it would be appropriate to state one's business, make offers and counter offers, use negotiating tactics to gain as much as possible, then return home. Topics of conversation such as family, hobbies, religion and politics would be out of place in this context, although brief inquiries about family or sports might be used as small talk to "break the ice." The American is especially eager to return home soon to save the high hotel bills and other costs of doing business in Japan.

The Japanese executive also views the negotiation as a business transaction. However, for the Japanese, business transactions are an extension of one's social and family life. One would not do business with strangers, so much time should be spent developing personal relationships before one discusses contracts. You can probably guess the ways in which the two different contexts will influence the conversation! Here is the discussion:

> **AMERICAN:** Well, it's nice to meet you. Let's get down to business.
>
> **JAPANESE:** Fine. I thought we might go out to dinner tonight, then to the Kabuki tomorrow. I want to show you my country since this is your first visit.

After several days composed primarily of social activities during which the American executive is growing increasingly impatient and the Japanese executive is feeling increasingly rushed by the American's insistence on discussing the contract, they begin the contract talks. The conversation below takes place after four hours of intensive discussion:

> **AMERICAN:** This is my last price. Take it or leave it. I have to be back at my desk by Monday, and this is the best I can do. How about it?
>
> **JAPANESE:** I know you are trying very hard to give us a good price for our products.
>
> **AMERICAN:** It's a deal, then.
>
> **JAPANESE:** (Long silence...)
>
> **AMERICAN:** Fine, I'll have my people draw up the papers for your approval. We'll meet here again tomorrow morning.
>
> **JAPANESE:** Yes, I'll see you tomorrow.
>
> *American's thoughts upon leaving:*
>
> Great! I can be on the plane tomorrow night! That would put me back in the office by the end of the week. The Japanese are easier to deal with than I thought. They agreed to all of our terms.

Japanese's thoughts upon leaving:

How abrupt these Americans are! I can see that we have our work cut out for us if we are ever to agree on a contract! And how rude they were to use threats: "Take it or leave it"! How uncivilized to refuse our hospitality. They acted as though someone was forcing them to go to the evening entertainments we had planned for their enjoyment! Tomorrow will be a long day.

One of the strengths of the Coordinated Management of Meaning Theory (CMM) is its ability to explain puzzling conversations such as the one above. Both negotiators misunderstood each other to such an extent that they had very different expectations about what would happen on the next day. It almost seems that they participated in different conversations. CMM helps researchers understand such outcomes by understanding how the two negotiators' rule systems interact.

The *context* for each negotiator's set of rules was presented above. Now let us examine their conversational rules. Remember that definition rules help people interpret what the other person's words or actions mean, while behavior rules tell us what to do in response to a particular speech act. (You will read more about Speech Act Theory in Chapter 7). First, notice that both negotiators understood the American's statement, "Take it or leave it," as a threat. Both used the same *definition rule* for interpreting that speech act. Their *definition rule* was something like this: "Take it or leave it" counts as a threat. But they apparently had different behavior rules. The American's rule seems to have been, "When threatened during negotiations, return the threat or make a counter-offer." The Japanese rule might have been, "When threatened during negotiations, ignore such impolite behavior so as not to embarrass the other person by calling attention to his or her bad manners. Do not respond in an impolite way." (Note that overt disagreement would be considered impolite by the Japanese but accepted, even expected, by the American.) The first two sentences reveal that the negotiators had similar *definition rules*, but different *behavior rules*. Both understood the American was making a threat, but they disagreed about the proper response to the speech act "threat."

The second and third pair of statements reveal two conflicting definition rules. The Japanese executive's silence was interpreted differently by the two negotiators. In America, silence means agreement. In Japan, it means just the opposite. Notice that the definition rules are based on cultural values which support overt expressions of conflict in the United States but which support public harmony, and thus suppression of overt conflict, in Japan. The culture provides part of the context for understanding the negotiators' rules. Thus, the different definition and behavior rules caused the American to misinterpret the silence and the Japanese businessman not to understand that the American really expects to sign a contract the next morning.

The Coordinated Management of Meaning has been applied most often to therapeutic situations, such as marriage counseling, in which a therapist attempts to diagnose a couple's communication problems and to suggest ways of overcoming them. Our presentation of CMM has been greatly oversimplified but sufficient for you to understand how the theory might be used to analyze the conversational rules used by a husband and wife. It explains how the rules of different people combined to produce a conversation in which they misunderstand each other, yet were still able to communicate.

There are several popular theories based on the human action perspective. We chose to present Constructivism and Coordinated Management of Meaning because they have generated and continue to generate the majority of rules and other human action studies conducted using quantitative research. They provide a good comparison and contrast of theories developed from the rules and other human action perspectives.

Strengths of the Rules and Other Human Action Perspectives

After reading about two examples of human action theories, you may have been able to identify strengths and weaknesses of this perspective.

1. Proponents of human action perspectives such as rules believe that the major strength of this perspective lies in its implicit assumptions about human beings. They argue that a theory that views humans as active choice-makers is most appropriate for the study of human communication. Many theorists, researchers, and students of communication are attracted to this perspective because of the importance it places on human choice and interpretation. Rules researchers believe that rules provide the best description of human nature and how to observe it and that the rules perspective values what is distinctly human, while the covering laws perspective does not.

2. Perhaps because of this set of assumptions, theories developed from the rules and other interpretive perspectives are especially useful in helping us to understand why communication takes place as it does. Rules researchers probe beneath surface relationships to explore people's meanings and interpretations of events. By doing so, they provide what many consider more satisfactory explanations of human behavior than those discovered using the covering laws perspective.

Weaknesses of the Rules and Other Human Action Perspectives

1. The major disadvantage of the rules and other human action perspectives lies in their inability to *predict* the future. Human action theories such as constructivism and the Coordinated Management of Meaning tend to provide better understanding of behavior that has already occurred than predictions of future events. Theories based on

the human action perspective require more extensive knowledge of individuals' interpretations and rules than we have in all but the most intimate communication settings.

For example, constructivism explains why some people are able to develop more sophisticated (and presumably more effective) persuasive messages than are others. Constructivists do predict that a more effective strategy will be used by a more cognitively complex person. However, it is difficult to predict what particular strategy a cognitively complex persuader will use. We can predict that it will be more advanced than one used by a cognitively simple persuader, but we cannot predict exactly what form or topic it will take, other than to say that it will reflect the perspective of the target audience.

The Coordinated Management of Meaning is most useful for analyzing conversations which have already occurred. It is impossible to predict an exact conversation. Our American and Japanese negotiators would not find the Coordinated Management of Meaning very useful except in analyzing after the fact why the negotiations had broken down.

2. A second criticism of human action and rules research related to the first disadvantage is that fewer empirical studies have been conducted from the rules perspective than from the covering laws approach. Rules theorists defend themselves against this charge by reminding us that since rules is a newer perspective, it has had a shorter time than covering laws to influence research. Thus, it is reasonable to expect fewer rules studies than covering laws studies because covering laws is an older perspective. Covering laws researchers maintain that the utility of the rules perspective can be assessed only after sufficient data has been accumulated to test it. The field of communication awaits the outcome of these studies.

The Systems Perspective

The systems perspective is the newest of the three paradigms used in communication theory. It was first introduced by von Bertalanffy (1968), a biologist, in an attempt to find principles common to all types of systems. von Bertalanffy believed that science is unified so that all types of systems—biological, physical, and chemical ones, for example—have common properties. Systems theory as a communication perspective is not an attempt to find properties common to all systems. However, communication scholars have found some of the principles von Bertalanffy developed to be useful in studying communication.

Systems theory is somewhat different from the laws and rules perspectives in that systems theorists do not advocate a particular "way of knowing." A system could be held together with laws, or with rules, or connected with both laws and rules. The contribution of systems theory is a set of concepts which help us to understand communication not as an isolated event, but as a system.

A system is a set of interdependent units which work together to adapt to a changing environment. An organization is one type of system and a good one to use as an example in discussing communication systems. Communication systems are *open systems*, that is, they interact with their environments. An organization communicates with customers, suppliers, the government, and other groups of individuals or institutions that form its environment. If it were a *closed system* which did not communicate with its environment, it would die, because closed systems tend toward entropy, chaos or total disorganization. Organizations receive inputs such as raw materials from their environment, transform those inputs in some way (such as using research information to create an advertising campaign), then send outputs back to the environment. During the transformation process, different departments of the organization may send outputs to each other for further processing.

A system is hierarchical. That is, the system can be broken up into smaller units, subsystems, which are part of larger suprasystems. The personnel department of an organization is a subsystem of the larger organization, which may be a subsystem of a multinational corporation, the suprasystem. The fact that the suprasystems and subsystems are interdependent leads to the systems property called *nonsummativity*. The whole system is more than the sum of the contributions of each individual part. A cake is a good example of a system. To make a cake, you add butter, sugar, flour, eggs, baking soda and other ingredients, perhaps chocolate flavoring. When you bake the cake, it changes into something that is more than the individual characteristics of the ingredients. You cannot take the cake apart and retrieve the eggs or the chocolate flavoring. Even though you added just a bit of chocolate, the flavor changed the entire cake. The baking soda permeated the entire mixture and caused the cake to rise. The chemical interaction that created the cake changed the ingredients and created something new. A cake is more than just the individual parts added together, as you might add layers to a sandwich.

Every system is like a cake in the sense that if you take away or change one individual part, the entire system is affected. If the sales department of an organization has problems, the entire organization may lose profits. Perhaps the production department will have to make fewer cars, or even lay off workers on the assembly line, because of a problem in a completely different department.

Cybernetic systems try to maintain a balance with their environments through a process called *homeostasis*, or self-regulation. After a change in the environment, the system adapts to maintain an equilibrium. It may not be the same equilibrium point as before the change, but the system comes to some balance point. For example, many United States manufacturing companies laid off workers during the last recession. When times got better, many, but not all, workers were rehired. The system maintained a balance, but the balance resulted in fewer jobs than the equilibrium point before the recession. A thermostat is also an excellent example of a cybernetic system.

One of the most interesting system properties is called *equifinality*. Equifinality means that there are many different ways by which a system may reach the same end state. Systems are *teleological*; they are designed to reach specific end states or goals. If an organization has a goal of increasing profits, it may reach the goal by increasing sales, by decreasing labor or materials costs, by increasing prices, or by adapting in other ways. Because of equifinality, researchers looking at an organizational outcome cannot know immediately what has caused the outcome. If profits increased, researchers would have to study the system closely to discover which of the many factors just listed contributed to raising profits. Communication researchers concerned with a decrease in morale must examine many possible causes in order to recommend an appropriate solution.

The systems perspective on communication is complex, reflecting the complicated nature of communication. It encourages communication students to be concerned about the environment or audience. Many of the terms applied to other types of systems are useful in shedding light on communication in our complex society, especially communication in organizations. Due to its "holistic" orientation, the attraction of using the systems approach to the study of human communication is strong. Our definition of a system, a set of interdependent units working together to adapt to a changing environment, conjures up thoughts of at least two communication systems that are well-suited for scholarly investigation from this perspective—organizations and families. Indeed, these two types of systems have received the most attention from communication theorists operating from a systems perspective. Due to the nonsummative nature of a system, one of the most important concerns for a systems researcher or theorist is the investigation of relationships and interactions of each individual part of the system with the others, and with the environment. Since most interactions in human systems (such as families and organizations) involve communication, communication theorists and researchers are well prepared to study these interactions. As a result, several studies employing the systems approach in communication have focused on the exchange of information and the development and maintenance of relationships among the members of a system.

To best illustrate how the systems perspective has been employed in communication, let us examine one type of system that is common to all of us—the family. Communication behavior is an integral part of a family system (Bavelas & Segal, 1982). The relationships and interactions between the various members of a family are the materials that actually constitute "the family." Four discrete, non-interacting, non-communicating individuals, although they may live under the same roof, do not necessarily constitute a family. In employing the systems perspective to study a family, you will not be able to identify the essence of the family—their relationships and interactions—if you simply study each member in isolation. The systems perspective requires that you focus attention on the whole family and that you see each individual member only in the context of the whole family. The essence of the concept of family rests with the communication and interaction of its members. Even when the various members of a family are spread far and wide over several geographic locations, communication and interaction form bonds which hold the system together.

As previously stated, open systems are characterized by a great deal of exchange and interaction with their environment. Because families could not exist in isolation from others and their environment, families are considered open systems. The boundaries of the family are open to interactions with many others, such as neighbors, friends, and colleagues to name but a few. And, a single family may exist in the context of a much larger extended family. Bavelas and Segal (1982) suggest that the extended family may actually be considered an environment. This type of environment would consist of several nuclear families. Each nuclear family would contain sub-systems consisting of spouses, children, grandparents, cousins and the like. It is also possible to identify the environment in a much broader fashion when discussing family interaction from a systems perspective. The environment could be taken to mean a given culture and/or climate in which the family exists. You may recall that one characteristic of a system is the attempt to maintain a balance with its environment through homeostasis or self-regulation.

How does a family system attempt to adjust communicatively to changing environmental conditions? How is family communication affected by a change in the environment? These questions call forth several areas worthy of attention by communication theorists and scholars interested in family communication. Two communication students (Bellefontaine & Florea, 1983) attempted to study how a change in the environment caused a change in the communication interactions of the members of several families. The students were interested in examining how a change in the environment, poor economic conditions leading to the unemployment of the family provider, caused a change in family interaction and communication patterns. The students were specifically interested in examining how the unemployment of the family provider affected how frequently family members communicated, shared personal feelings, and argued, and how the self-esteem of the family members changed. Four families agreed to participate in this study. In each family, the husband/father was unemployed for a period of between one to six months. Using several methods to gather data (i.e., surveys, interviews with family members, observations), the researchers discovered that several changes in family communication patterns did indeed occur.

With the provider more accessible and available during the period of unemployment, communication between the family members increased.

Husbands and wives reported a slight increase in overall disclosure of feelings to each other. Understandably, the husbands' feelings of self-esteem decreased. However, in several of the families studied, the wives reported increases in feelings of self-worth and self-esteem. Finally, all families noted increases in the frequency of social conflict and family dispute. As one father stated, "As a consequence of being laid off, I was home more often and saw things I normally didn't have to deal with. Consequently, there were more areas of conflict."

This study of family interaction helps illustrate several key concepts of the systems perspective as applied to communication. It demonstrates the concept that a system is a set of interdependent units all working together. When the main provider was laid off, the other members of the system tried to find jobs in order to keep money flowing into the system. The study also demonstrated the systems maxim that a change in one part of a system, of necessity, creates changes in other parts of the system. In this case, when the husband/father became unemployed, the other family members were affected financially and communicatively. However, each system tried to maintain a balance through self-regulation. If possible, the wife went to work, and the husband assumed more of the domestic responsibilities. Increased communication resulted from the need for all members of the system to get used to the new family arrangement. The other adjustments noted by the researchers, such as changes in social conflict and levels of self-esteem, reflect the complex and interactive nature of the family system.

As with the other theory building approaches to human communication, the systems perspective has a set of strengths and weaknesses associated with it.

Strengths of the Systems Perspective

1. The systems approach is a flexible and open perspective from which to study human communication. Advocates of this approach state that it does not impose a series of perceptual constraints or biases on researchers to force them to focus only on certain elements in a communication situation. Laws theorists focus on trying to identify causal relationships among communication phenomena, while rules theorists focus primarily on trying to identify social norms or individual interpretive patterns which guide communication behaviors in various contexts. Systems theorists however, valuing breadth and generality in their theories, attempt to focus on all patterns of interaction and relationship within a communication event.

2. Human communication is such a complex phenomenon that it requires a broad-based, multi-leveled investigatory schema. For example, many factors contribute to the breakup of a marriage and family. If one were to interview just the husband, or the wife, or the children alone, a partial and incomplete picture of the trouble would result. The systems

approach opts for studying the effects of all the factors involved, alone *and* in interaction. Advocates of the systems perspective feel that the laws and rules approaches are too narrow to investigate fully the complex interaction of the large number of factors that make up a communication event.

3. Advocates of the systems perspective state that this perspective utilizes *situation-specific* generalizations and thus is a more appropriate perspective to employ than the laws approach which uses universal generalizations. Many communication theorists feel that communication is culture specific. If communication is culture bound, then the universal generalizations identified by laws approach are not truly universal, but only true for the culture of the scientists or research participants. Systems theorists do not attempt to make universal generalizations.

Weaknesses of the Systems Perspective

1. Critics suggest that the systems perspective is too broad and too general to be useful in building theory in applied contexts. As we argued about communication in Chapter 1, if everything can be described as a system, then looking at phenomena as systems is not useful because this way of theorizing does not add insight. Instead, systems theory just makes explicit concepts which we intuitively understand from observation of the world around us. If it is equally valid to draw the boundaries of an organizational system around a work group, a department, a manufacturing plant, and an entire company, what benefit is gained by examining a department as a subsystem rather than a suprasystem? If both are equally valid, it should make no difference which approach we take. It would be impossible to test which level of observation was best.

2. While uncovering many important interactions and relationships involving communication in human systems, the systems perspective does not yield a great deal of explanatory power. Cahn (1981) suggests that its application fails to explain events previously unexplained. Critics suggest that the systems perspective does not help shed light on *why* things happen the way they do. Recall that explanation is one of the most important goals of a theory. An advocate of the systems approach, Monge (1973) notes that scientists developed theories which predicted the motion of planets before they had one that explained it. Perhaps future researchers may be able to develop systems theories with greater explanatory power.

3. Critics state that while the systems approach has many advocates, it has yet to generate much empirical or theoretical research. This is a very complex weakness of the systems approach which, at its core, may

reflect our discipline's desire to conduct research and publish findings rapidly. The effort to investigate the interrelationships and interactions of the many parts of a system is not only costly, but very time consuming. Examining all possible interactions between units of the system requires a relatively long term research focus. Many communication scholars are not prepared to spend the vast amount of time and money required to engage in an all-encompassing research study of changes in a system over time.

Summary

In this chapter we have examined three major perspectives on communication theory: covering laws, human action approaches exemplified by the rules approach, and the systems perspective. As you have learned, scientists from different perspectives make different assumptions, ask different questions, study the questions in different ways, and are interested in different types of answers. Researchers operating from the covering laws perspective emphasize cause and effect relationships, while rules researchers emphasize choice in the creation of individual and social rules. Systems theorists emphasize the interactions between the parts of an interdependent system and de-emphasize the role of individuals.

Your own experience has probably led you to feel more comfortable with one of these perspectives, or perhaps you will be tempted to adopt the perspective favored by your instructor. As you read Part II, Theory Building in Major Approaches to Communication, keep in mind the three "grand models" presented in this chapter. Try to imagine why your authors believe a particular theory is an example of a given perspective. For example, ask yourself, "Why is this theory an example of the laws approach? What cause-effect relationships does it propose? Might rules or systems provide a better explanation of the communication behavior being studied? How would theorists from the other two perspectives approach this research question?" Ask the same types of questions for rules and systems theories. You will see that more research has been conducted using the laws perspective than any other. If you have not taken a course in research methods, reading the chapter on research methods in the Appendix before you proceed to Part II will give you a better understanding of how theories are tested in communication experiments.

Questions to Consider

1. What is a paradigm?
2. What are the main assumptions of the covering laws approach to communication theory?
3. How appropriate to the study of communication is a probabilistic conception of laws?
4. What are the strengths and weaknesses of the laws perspective?
5. What are the major assumptions of the rules approach to communication theory?
6. How does the emphasis on intentions and goals distinguish the rules approach?
7. What are the assumptions of constructivism as a human action perspective?
8. How does the Coordinated Management of Meaning Theory explain communication?
9. What are the strengths and weaknesses of rules and other human action perspectives?
10. What are the main assumptions of the systems approach to communication theory?
11. What are the strengths and weaknesses of the systems approach?
12. Explain the nonsummativity property of systems.
13. Which perspective might be the most useful for you to adopt in studying communication? Why do you prefer this one? What are its disadvantages?
14. What questions about communication will you attempt to answer using this perspective?

References

Bavelas, J.B., & Segal, L. (1982). Family systems theory: Background and implications. *Journal of Communication, 32,* 99-107.

Bellefontaine, A., & Florea, J. (1983, March). *The effect of unemployment on family communication: A systems examination.* Paper presented to the DePauw University Communication Honors Conference, Greencastle, Indiana.

Berger, C.R. (1977). The covering laws perspective as a theoretical basis for the study of human communication. *Communication Quarterly, 25,* 7-18.

Berscheid, E., & Walster, E.H. (1978). *Interpersonal attraction* (2nd ed.). Reading, MA: Addison-Wesley Publishing Co.

Bertalanffy, L. von (1968). *General systems theory.* New York: Braziller.

Cahn, D.D. (1981, May). *A critique of Bertalanffy's general systems theory as a "new paradigm" for the study of human communication.* Paper presented to the International Communication Association, Minneapolis, Minnesota.

Clark, R.A., & Delia, J.G. (1976). The development of functional persuasive skills in childhood and early adolescence. *Child Development, 47,* 1008-1014.

Cronen, V.E., Pearce, W.B., & Harris, L.M. (1982). The Coordinated Management of Meaning: A theory of communication. In F.E.X. Dance (Ed.), *Human communication theory* (pp. 61-89). New York: Harper & Row.

Daly, J.A., & McCroskey, J.C. (1984). *Avoiding communication.* Beverly Hills, CA: Sage Publications.

Delia, J.G. (1975, November). *Communication research and the variable analytic tradition: A critique of three papers.* Paper presented to the Speech Communication Association meeting, Houston, Texas.

Delia, J.G., & Grossberg, L. (1977). Interpretation and evidence. *Western Journal of Speech Communication, 41,* 32-42.

Delia, J.G., O'Keefe, B.J., & O'Keefe, D.J. (1982). The constructivist approach to communication. In F.E.X. Dance (ed.), *Human communication theory* (pp. 147-191). New York: Harper & Row.

Hovland, C.I., Janis, I.L., & Kelley, H.H. (1953). *Communication and persuasion.* New Haven, CT: Yale University Press.

Huston, T.L. (1974). *Foundations of interpersonal attraction.* New York: Academic Press.

Kelly, G.A. (1955). *A theory of personality: The psychology of personal constructs.* New York: Norton Library.

Miller, G.R., & Berger, C.R. (1978). On keeping the faith in matters scientific. *Western Journal of Speech Communication, 42,* 44-57.

Monge, P.R. (1973). Theory construction in the study of communication: The systems paradigm. *Journal of Communication, 23,* 5-16.

Rancer, A.S., & Infante, D.A. (1985). Relations between argumentativeness and the argumentativeness of adversaries. *Communication Quarterly, 33,* 209-218.

Schutz, A. (1967). *The phenomenology of the social world.* Chicago, IL: Northwestern University Press.

Winch, P. (1958). *The idea of a social science and its relation to philosophy.* Atlantic Highlands, NJ: Humanities Press.

Part II

Theory Building in Major Approaches to Communication

Part Two is designed to provide you with background from the extensive and rich history of the field of communication. After exploring the origins of modern theory, four major areas of communication theory are introduced: communication traits, persuasion, verbal behavior, and nonverbal behavior. These represent four major lines of communication research which have been investigated without being tied to a specific situation in which communication takes place (context). Ideas concerning persuasion, for instance, are assumed applicable in some form regardless of the context in which they occur. In contrast to this section of the book, Part III will discuss theory building in particular communication contexts.

The history outlined in Chapter 4 will give you a sense of how communication was conceived in earlier times. Communication theory had its roots in ancient Greece, especially in the works of the great philosophers Plato and Aristotle. The ancient Romans were also very interested in communication and made substantial contributions. The additions to theory were fewer during the Middle Ages and the Renaissance. However, in more recent times there has been a rebirth of interest in human communication. Rhetorical theorists such as Kenneth Burke are discussed along with other influences such as information theory, the Yale Studies, Berlo's process model, and contextual approaches.

Chapter 5 examines what has probably been the most extensively researched approach to communication for the past ten years or so. This is the concept of communication traits, which had its beginning in the study of personality by psychologists. Early research on personality and communication is reviewed first; four types of communication traits are then discussed. Apprehension traits cover feelings of fear and anxiety about communication. Presentation traits comprise ways or styles of presenting verbal and nonverbal messages. Adaptation traits concern the different ways individuals adjust or adapt to the people with whom they communicate. Aggression traits involve tendencies to use force; these can be constructive or destructive to communication. The theories presented in Chapter 5 provide excellent illustrations of the covering laws approach.

Chapter 6 discusses persuasion. Prior to the current line of research on communication traits, persuasion was probably the most popular research area. Persuasion is conceptualized in this chapter as changing one's attitude about a proposal. Persuasion research on several variables is considered. The source credibility approach to persuasion is discussed in some detail. Several covering laws theories of persuasion are examined: cognitive dissonance, ego-involvement, affective-cognitive consistency, and learning theory. Methods to prevent persuasion are also reviewed. Finally, a rules theory of persuasion is presented.

Chapter 7 focuses on verbal behavior theory and research. This has been a consistently popular area of study for the past several decades. Basic concepts such as symbols, meaning, codes, and perception are discussed. Research on how language communicates power, status, and a number of factors including fear, intensity, and opinion is examined. Three areas of verbal behavior research are reviewed in some detail: verbal plans, speech accommodation, and conversational and discourse analysis. Searle's Speech Act Theory, which forms the basis for the Coordinated Management of Meaning rules theory, is also presented.

Chapter 8 covers nonverbal behavior approaches. Nonverbal communication has emerged not only as one of the most popular areas of research in the communication field but also as an area of interest to the general public. The effectiveness of verbal and nonverbal codes in communicating about different topics is discussed, along with ideas concerning intentionality, the influence of context, emotional leakage, and the functions of nonverbal communication. Nonverbal message codes examined are kinesics, eye and facial behavior, vocalics, physical appearance, proxemics, touch, and time. The chapter emphasizes that not all nonverbal behavior is communicative; previous concepts sometimes confused noncommunicative behavior with nonverbal messages.

Chapter 4

The Development of Approaches to Communication

Although the modern discipline of communication as taught in American universities today is fairly new, its roots are very old. The kinds of questions that current communication scholars find interesting and that you are exploring in your classes were first discussed by some of the most famous people in Western civilization. In this chapter, we shall explore the history of rhetoric and communication theory from its early roots in the ancient world to contemporary trends in communication. Narrowly defined, rhetoric includes the principles of how to make a good speech, especially persuasion (Randall, 1960). More broadly, rhetoric may be considered the use of symbols to achieve a particular response from other human beings (Thonssen, Baird, & Braden, 1970). Using the latter definition, modern rhetoricians study both verbal and nonverbal influence strategies including the strategies used in mass media, which you will study more fully in Chapter 11.

The first part of this chapter will briefly summarize some of the questions addressed by the ancients. As the study of persuasive speaking, rhetoric played an integral role in the lives of famous Greeks and Romans. Later, Christian writers such as St. Augustine were interested in rhetorical training for preachers. Rhetoric comprised a major portion of the curriculum of the first universities. Finally, we will consider the changes in the conceptualization and study of rhetoric through the Age of Enlightenment into the Victorian era. The second part of the chapter will discuss in more detail current theoretical trends in the discipline. In the section on social scientific approaches, you will learn of the contributions of psychologists and sociologists and the beginnings of scientific experimentation in communication. The role of literary critics such as Kenneth Burke in the development of the discipline will be covered in the section on rhetorical approaches. The chapter will close with contemporary trends in contextual approaches. This final section covers contributions of contemporary theorists, some of whom are teaching in communication departments today.

The Classical Period

The Rhetoric of the Iliad and Odyssey

Although we often think of Plato and Aristotle as the first rhetorical or communication theorists, their writing was influenced by early Greek poets such as Homer. Several characteristics of what the Greeks considered to be effective public address can be seen through the speeches of heroes in the *Iliad* and the *Odyssey*. The ninth book of the *Iliad* is especially fruitful for the study of heroic speeches; it contains speeches by Odysseus, Phoenix, and Ajax, who try to persuade Achilles to rejoin the Greek troops in battle. All three speeches display a concern for style of language, are adapted to the hearer Achilles, and reflect a concern of the speakers for their roles as persuaders (Kennedy, 1980).

The Pre-Socratic Philosophers

A second important influence on the thought and rhetorical theory of Plato and Aristotle was the work of earlier theorists, the pre-Socratic philosophers, who lived from the beginning of the sixth to the middle of the fifth century B.C. The pre-Socratic philosophers used knowledge gained from Egypt and the Orient about astronomy and natural events to help them answer questions such as, "How did the universe come into being?" They were the first to question and investigate the myths of creation by using logic and empirical observation (Kirk & Raven, 1957). Their efforts formed the beginnings of Western scientific thought (Jaeger, 1976).

The study of the ideas of the pre-Socratic philosophers is very much a detective story pieced together by inference from scant evidence, since very few of their writings have survived for us to read (Womack, 1985). Much of what we know about the pre-Socratic philosophers exists in the form of quotations by writers such as Plato and Aristotle. Nevertheless, we can summarize two basic trends in pre-Socratic philosophy. One tradition is presented by Parmenides, who was born about 515-510 B.C., approximately forty-five years before Socrates (Kirk & Raven, 1957).

Parmenides. One of the most interesting questions for all the pre-Socratics involved the changes of the seasons, birth, and death. In nature, plants, animals, and humans are constantly being born (coming into Being, or Existing) and dying (becoming Notbeing, or Nonexistent). Our physical senses indicate that plants and animals come from Notbeing into Being, then pass into Notbeing again. Parmenides rejected this idea. He believed instead that the physical senses were not to be trusted; they deceive us by making things appear to pass in and out of Being. Reason was the only way that humans could know truth. Using logic, Parmenides concluded that reality consists of one unified whole. The way of reason, not observation with the senses or popular opinion, was the road to truth. Plato is generally considered to have followed in the tradition of Parmenides.

Heraclitus. The second tradition is represented by Heraclitus, who was born about 544-541 B.C. Heraclitus believed that life is made up of conflicting opposites (such as Being and Notbeing), which constantly supplant each other. The nature of reality is one of change, and it is this change which provides stability. The world "rests by changing" (Jaeger, 1976, p. 183). What is permanent is change. Unlike Parmenides, Heraclitus trusted human nature and the senses. Heraclitus believed that since humans are part of the universe and subject to natural laws they hold within them the laws of the universe. Thus, humans share a community because of their common nature. They can trust their senses to help them know the true nature of reality. Aristotle followed in the philosophical tradition of Heraclitus (Kirk & Raven, 1957).

The Sophists

Protagoras, the earliest *sophist*, was born in 481 B.C. (Zeller, 1980). The sophists travelled throughout the Greek city-states teaching rhetoric. The term *sophist* comes from *sophos*, the Greek word for wisdom. Except for Protagoras, the sophists were not philosophers so much as teachers of practical knowledge. A sophist was someone knowledgeable or especially clever about effective speaking or arguing. Perhaps the best English equivalent is *professor* (Guthrie, 1971). Similar to the Greek poets, sophists performed an educational role— teaching young men how to give effective speeches before the political assembly and lawcourts. Most sophists were not native Greeks but traveled to Athens because of the demand for their services. Trials in Athens were held before juries of at least 201 members and consisted of a speech by the plaintiff followed by an address from the defendant. There were no lawyers; citizens spoke for themselves in court (Kennedy, 1980).

Although there were differences between individual sophists, some of which will be indicated below, they generally had several characteristics in common. They were itinerant, travelling from city-state to city-state, teaching the young men, then moving on. They charged fees for their services, so most of their clients belonged to influential, wealthy families and were potential statesmen. The sophists taught rhetoric, or persuasion. They were most concerned with effectiveness. For instance, what tactics would persuade a jury or other audience? Any argument that would persuade the jury to agree with the speaker was acceptable. Therefore, they taught their students to analyze both sides of a question, not just the arguments for their own positions. They claimed to teach virtue—to make the young men wiser and better citizens through their instruction—rather than merely training young men in specific skills. In general, the sophists were disliked by Plato and other Athenians because they were not Athenian citizens and because they displayed their skill in public lectures in addition to teaching the young. They competed with each other in speech-making for prizes at festivals such as the Olympics (Guthrie, 1971). The sophists were both rhetoricians (those who studied the principles of rhetoric) and orators (those who practiced speech-making). Communication scholars today use the Greek word *rhetor* to refer to someone who is both a rhetorician and an orator.

Some of the most famous sophists were Protagoras, Gorgias, and Isocrates. Protagoras believed that taking either side of an argument in debate was ethical because what might seem false to one man might seem true to another. What one person liked, another disliked. Similarly, the same person might like and dislike the same thing at different times, just as someone might refuse a certain food when sick but enjoy it after recovering from the illness. Therefore, "a man was the sole judge of his own sensations and beliefs, which were true for him so long as they appeared to be so. Since there was no absolute or universal truth, no one needed to consider, before attempting to make an individual, a jury or a state change its mind, whether or not he would be persuading them of a truer state of affairs" (Guthrie, 1971, p. 267). Protagoras was a humanist and was clearly influenced by the relativistic philosophy of Heraclitus, as Plato indicates (Zeller, 1980). Because he taught pupils to argue both sides of a question, Protagoras has been called the father of debate (Thonssen, Baird, & Braden, 1970). Protagoras also founded the science of Greek grammar and taught grammar to his students (Zeller, 1980). Although Plato criticizes the sophists harshly, he describes Protagoras fairly and notes that Protagoras was famous long after his death (Zeller, 1980). None of Protagoras' writings have survived.

Gorgias. Another important sophist, Gorgias lived at the same time as Protagoras. He came from Leontini, a city in Sicily. Ancient authorities agree that he lived to a remarkable age, at least 105 (Durant, 1939; Guthrie, 1971). Like Protagoras, he charged very high fees, ten thousand drachmas (about $10,000) per pupil (Durant, 1939). Unlike Protagoras, Gorgias did not claim to teach virtue or to make his students better citizens (Zeller, 1980). He did teach rhetoric, the power of persuasion. Some of Gorgias' writings still survive. In the available summary of *On the Non-Existent,* or *On Nature,* Gorgias develops a logical argument to prove: "(1) that nothing exists (2) if anything existed it could not be known and (3) if it could be known it could not be communicated to others" (Zeller, 1980, pp. 86-87). In *On the Non-Existent,* Gorgias uses Parmenidean arguments to ridicule Parmenides' logic by using it to prove a conclusion opposite that of Parmenides. Two of his model speeches, "Encomium of Helen" (in praise of Helen of Troy) and "Defense of Palamedes," reveal another characteristic for which Gorgias was famous, his beautiful use of style and the Greek language. His speeches are filled with poetic devices, and his oratorical style became a fad in Athens when he came there at about the age of sixty as an ambassador from Leontini.

Isocrates. The sophist and logographer Isocrates was one of Gorgias' pupils (Guthrie, 1971). A *logographer* was a rhetorician who wrote speeches for delivery by others, but was not a public speaker himself. Unlike other sophists, Isocrates did not travel; pupils came to him and stayed for a required period of time in the school he opened in about 392 or 393 B.C. Several of Isocrates' speeches have survived. His students were encouraged to imitate his style, which was extremely smooth and composed of long, balanced sentences. He avoided unusual or poetic words. Both Gorgias and Isocrates used "stylistic features that were permanently influential on Greek prose" (Kennedy, 1980, p. 34). Unlike Gorgias, Isocrates emphasized moral character in his students; he believed that the study of rhetoric and politics could make students better citizens. This emphasis on virtue in the orator influenced the educational principles of the later Roman rhetoricians Cicero and Quintilian. The history of structured public speaking training and its special importance for citizens in a free society can be traced back approximately twenty-three hundred years to the school of Isocrates the sophist (Kennedy, 1980).

Aspasia. Some scholars believe that during the 4th and 5th centuries B.C. Greek women were cloistered and confined to their homes. However, courtesans had more freedom than wives or slaves and did play a role in the rise of Greek rhetoric. They lived in their own homes and were free to attend lectures, which afforded the opportunity to improve their conversation with wealthy and well-educated patrons. Aspasia, the concubine of Pericles, founded a school of philosophy and rhetoric in about 450 B.C. She taught wives and daughters of good families as well as men (Durant, 1939). In Plato's dialogue *Menexenus*, the character Socrates indicates that he studied in her school and credits her as the author of the speech, "The Funeral Oration of Pericles," which has survived to our time.

Philosophical Rhetoric

At the same time that the sophists flourished, another tradition represented by Socrates and his pupil Plato began to take root. Socrates, a contemporary of Protagoras, lived from 469-399 B.C. Socrates "resembled the sophists superficially" (Kennedy, 1980, p. 41) in that he was a teacher and was interested in the power of words. However, Plato pictures him as the chief opponent of the sophists. Socrates did not charge fees for his instruction, nor did he claim to have special knowledge or to teach virtue to young men. He preferred a question-and-answer method (dialectic) rather than lecturing his pupils or giving model speeches. This method is illustrated in many of Plato's dialogues. Unlike Gorgias and the other sophists, he was skeptical of the role of rhetoric. Socrates left no writings (Kennedy, 1980); we are familiar with him primarily through the dialogues of his pupil, Plato.

Plato. Foremost among the followers of Socrates was Plato, who wrote many dialogues which have survived today. Plato was born about 429 B.C., and was a contemporary of Isocrates, Gorgias, and Protagoras. A follower of the philosophical tradition of Parmenides and a student of Pythagorean philosophy, he founded a school called the Academy (Durant, 1939). His wealthy students, both men and women, were not charged fees, but their parents often made large donations. The principal subjects he taught were mathematics and philosophy. Among his many famous pupils were Aristotle and Demosthenes (Durant, 1939). Plato's dialogues are important contributions to Greek literature as well as to philosophy.

The Gorgias. Written about 387 B.C. when the sophist Gorgias was probably still alive, this dialogue says that rhetoric is not a true art but a "knack." True arts are based on knowledge, but rhetoric is based on experience gained from trial and error. This contrast of knowledge with experience shows the influence that the pre-Socratic tradition (represented by Parmenides) had on Plato. Absolute Truth exists, but it is not revealed through experience with the senses. Instead, dialectic triggers a process by which the participants recall knowledge which they have possessed since before they were born. Kennedy describes Plato's theory of dialectic:

> Dialectic is a faculty of discovering available arguments to answer proposed questions, and in Plato it is the only acceptable form of philosophical reasoning. It follows a method of division of the question and definition of the factors involved, testing hypotheses as they are advanced. In theory the leader of the discussion does not know . . . what the conclusion will be . . . but . . . his [the Platonic Socrates'] hypotheses often work out with a feeling of inevitability. Plato would say that this is because new truth is not discovered, but rather old truth is recollected: we all existed before birth and we know much more than we can immediately remember. In contrast to dialectic, rhetoric involves a preselected arbitrary conclusion: that a defendant is guilty or that the assembly should follow a particular policy or that a certain proposition is feasible. The orator chooses those arguments which prove or seem to prove the conclusion to which he is committed, whether or not it is true. (Kennedy, 1980, p. 46).

As Kennedy indicates, Plato favors dialectic and disdains rhetoric because rhetoric produces only opinion, not absolute Truth. The *Gorgias* indicates that the only valid rhetoric is one used to serve Truth and justice.

The Phaedrus. Written later than the *Gorgias*, this work by Plato describes the characteristics of a "true art" of rhetoric. Some scholars trace Aristotle's handbook *The Rhetoric* to the ideas of the *Phaedrus*. It provides an especially beautiful example of Plato's literary style. In the dialogue, Socrates explains that rhetoric is "a kind of leading the soul by means of words, not only in lawcourts and public assemblies" (Kennedy, 1980, p. 56) but also in private (Brownstein, 1965). Socrates believes that the "true art" of rhetoric has five characteristics. (1) It must be based upon Truth arrived at by dialectic; the subject must have been defined and logically analyzed until its proper nature is understood. (2) The rhetor must analyze the audience. (3) The organization of the speech should be adapted to the type of audience; one should provide complex speeches for complex souls and simple speeches for simple souls. (4) The speaker should only attempt to instruct the hearer about justice, honor, and goodness, which are Truths "written in the soul of the listener" before birth; the speaker helps listeners to recall what they already know. (5) The speech should be the speaker's own "legitimate child"; it should not try to persuade an audience to believe something the speaker thinks is false (Phaedrus 277 b5-c6) nor should speakers debate both sides of a question as did Protagoras' pupils. According to Socrates, the person who knows Truth, who can defend his position, and who can refute others' opinions, is a philosopher, literally "a lover of wisdom." Socrates criticizes written speech as inferior to oral rhetoric because writing encourages forgetfulness and because it is apt to be misinterpreted. If it falls into the hands of those who do not understand it, it cannot correct or refute their misunderstandings, as someone engaged in the dialectical process of question-and-answer could.

The *Gorgias* and *Phaedrus* indicate that Plato shared some philosophical assumptions with the followers of the contemporary covering laws perspective discussed in Chapter 3. Like covering laws philosophers, Plato believed that there was a Truth independent of human beings. There were fixed laws governing nature which humans had merely to discover (even though Plato believed they could not be discovered through observing nature but must be remembered through dialectic with other philosophers). These laws or Platonic forms did not vary with societies or individuals but were constant and independent of human influence. Knowledge of Truth was the foundation of Plato's philosophical system.

Aristotle. Aristotle was born in 384 B.C., studied with Plato beginning in 367 B.C. and remained a member of Plato's Academy for twenty years (Kennedy, 1980). He left the Academy shortly before Plato's death and became the tutor of Alexander the Great. A year before Alexander became king, Aristotle opened his own academy, the Peripatetic School, in Athens. The *Rhetoric* of Aristotle is the earliest existing public speaking handbook, and much of what is taught today in departments of communication studies has roots in Aristotle's theory of rhetoric. Unlike Plato's dialogues, the *Rhetoric* is a set of lecture notes, not a polished literary work.

While the *Rhetoric* is the only handbook which exists from that time period, there had been earlier examples which undoubtedly influenced Aristotle. When democracy was suddenly introduced at Syracuse in Sicily in 467 B.C., citizens who previously had little need to speak persuasively in public were forced to testify on their own behalf about the ownership of property. "A crisis in education" arose surrounding the subject of rhetoric (Kennedy, 1980, p. 18). Corax and Tisias were two Sicilians who, like the sophists, charged a fee to teach others the techniques of how to argue and make speeches in the lawcourts. The principles of Corax and Tisias were written down in notes, copied, and sold. By the end of the fifth century B. C., many handbooks on effective public speaking were available. The handbooks concentrated on judicial rhetoric and focused on the organization of speeches in lawcourts. Such speeches were divided into five parts: introduction, narration, proof, refutation and conclusion. Some handbooks discussed style, especially the choice of diction and use of ornamental language (Kennedy, 1980).

Like these handbooks, Aristotle's *Rhetoric* was meant to be a practical guide for public speaking. In Book I, Aristotle defines rhetoric and places it within his philosophical system (Kennedy, 1980). Rhetoric is the "counterpart of dialectic" (Rhetoric I.1.1354a 1). Unlike Plato, Aristotle limits dialectic to "the form of reasoning built on premises which are generally accepted." For example, rhetoric could be used today to persuade an audience of citizens that a nuclear power plant was safe or unsafe. While technical knowledge about nuclear physics might be necessary to persuade an audience of physicists, rhetoric allows a speaker to discover what arguments will persuade a lay audience. Rhetoric will not discover new technical knowledge or truth about nuclear physics. Instead, dialectic and rhetoric help guide a speaker's reasoning in order to convince the audience.

Instead of focusing on the emotions, Aristotle believes rhetoricians should center their attention on the modes of persuasion. The form of *deductive demonstration* used in rhetoric is the enthymeme, a syllogism with one premise frequently suppressed, so that the audience helps to complete the persuasive form by "filling in the blanks" (Bitzer, 1959). For example, today's speaker might persuade an audience to avoid saccharine because saccharine has been shown to cause cancer in laboratory rats. The missing logical connection is that substances which cause cancer in rats are also likely to cause cancer in humans. The form of *inductive proof* used in rhetoric is the example. By using several examples of substances that cause cancer in both rats and human beings, the rhetor can lead the audience to draw the general conclusion that all substances which are dangerous to rats are also dangerous to humans.

Aristotle suggests four reasons for using rhetoric: (1) Since truth has a natural tendency to prevail over falsehood in a "fair fight," if truth fails to win a case, the speaker must be at fault. Speakers must be trained in rhetoric to make sure that truth has a "fighting chance" to show its natural superiority. (2) Since not everyone is capable of following complicated arguments or understanding technical matters, rhetoric is useful for persuading a popular audience. (3) Rhetoric trains speakers to argue both sides of a question, not in order to deceive the audience, but to better prepare the speaker to refute arguments of the opponent. Aristotle notes that, of all the arts, only dialectic and rhetoric prepare one equally well to draw opposite conclusions, even though the supporting evidence on both sides will not be equivalent. Rhetoric and dialectic are morally neutral but should be used by the speaker only for moral ends (Rowland & Womack, 1985). (4) Finally, rhetoric should be studied as a form of verbal self-defense (*Rhetoric*, I, 1-1355a 21-1355b 7).

After justifying the study of rhetoric, Aristotle discusses the three types of *rhetorical proof* central to the art (Book 1, Chapter 2). By using three classes of persuasive appeals or proofs, the rhetor accomplishes his or her goal to lead the audience to make some judgment or come to some conclusion. Some types of proof or evidence are concrete rather than rhetorical and are outside the boundaries of the art. These are known as *inartistic proofs* and need only to be *used* by the rhetor. The three types of *artistic proofs* or appeals must be *invented* through the words of the speech itself. In Greek they are *ethos*, *pathos*, and *logos*. Roberts' translation in the outline of the *Rhetoric* provides a more thorough understanding than is commonly found in public speaking textbooks. He translates *ethos*, *pathos*, and *logos*, respectively, as "(1) the speaker's power of evincing a personal character which will make his speech credible; (2) his power of stirring the emotions of his hearers; (3) his power of proving a truth, or an apparent truth, by means of persuasive arguments" (1941, p. 1318). Kennedy notes that emotional appeals are important because they influence the judgment of the audience: "they will come to a different conclusion, for example, when they are angry than when they are pleased" (Kennedy, 1980, p. 68).

Since the three types of proofs are used by the rhetor to lead the audience to reach some type of judgment, Aristotle divides rhetoric "on the basis of three kinds of audience which a speaker can address in a speech: judges of past action, judges of future action, and spectators" (Kennedy, 1980, p. 72). Audiences who judge past action are juries in the law courts; they must decide whether or not someone committed a particular act and so are concerned with justice. Legislators, who make judgments about what action is desirable in the future, deliberate about whether a proposed policy is expedient for the city-state. The hearer-as-spectator refers to ceremonial or display oratory, sometimes called by its Greek name, *epideictic*. Funeral orations and classroom exercises in praise or blame of historical figures comprise this category. In the case of display oratory, the audience is asked to make a judgment about whether the person mentioned should be praised or blamed: Should Helen of Troy be blamed for causing the Trojan War? Perhaps the closest counterparts we have today are the eulogies spoken in praise of the dead at funerals and the types of orations traditionally given by politicians at Fourth of July ceremonies praising the character of all Americans or of local heroes.

In Book II of the *Rhetoric*, Aristotle discusses the other forms of proof, those provided by the character of the speaker and the frame of mind of the audience. The effective *rhetor* should choose material for the speech that will create in the audience a particular impression of the speaker. The rhetor must demonstrate evidence: (1) of the virtues of character prized by the audience, (2) of practical wisdom, a kind of elevated common sense related to practical ways of governing society to reach good ends, and (3) of goodwill. The audience must feel that the speaker intends good for them and is not trying to deceive or manipulate them for his own purposes. Chapters 1-20 of Book II, which discuss the emotions, have been compared to a work on psychology. Aristotle tells his readers under what circumstances a particular emotion may be aroused, toward whom the emotion is directed, and the reasons for feeling it. For example, in Chapter 10 he defines envy as pain someone feels when his equals have good things that he himself does not have.

In the remainder of Book II, Aristotle again discusses logical argument and enthymemes. Aristotle here provides a list of *topoi*, common topics that a rhetor could use as an aid to analyzing the materials of any case, no matter what the subject. Chapter 23 introduces 28 lines of reasoning that could be used on a variety of different subjects. For example, cause-to-effect reasoning is discussed. If the effect is present, then the cause must also be present. If money is missing from a bank and no bookkeeping mistake has been made, someone must have committed a crime. Using the same line of reasoning, you might argue in court that if a gun was fired, someone must have pulled the trigger, whether accidentally or on purpose. Kennedy suggests that Chapter 23 would make an excellent index to enthymemes (1980). At the end of Book II, Aristotle provides some material on refuting an opponent's arguments.

Book III contains Aristotle's discussion of style, arrangement, and delivery. This part of the *Rhetoric* is similar to the material contained in the handbooks and emphasized by the sophists, although Aristotle provides a more philosophical treatment of style and arrangement than did other authors (Kennedy, 1980). Even though Aristotle apologizes for having to deal with such a lowly subject as delivery, he does outline topics such as volume, pitch, and rhythm of the voice that would comprise an art of delivery. Aristotle defines four qualities which contribute to effective style: clarity, appropriateness, proper use of metaphor to give the style distinction, and correct grammar. These qualities were modified to become a standard list of stylistic virtues found in the works of later Greek rhetoricians (Kennedy, 1980). Unlike other writers, Aristotle claims that there are only two basic parts to an oration: (1) the statement of purpose, or thesis, and (2) the proof. Although he criticizes the longer list of divisions presented in the handbooks, he does discuss introduction, statement, proof, refutation, cross examination, and conclusion in terms of how they are actually used by speakers in court and in the legislative assembly.

Because many of his writings were lost for centuries, Aristotle has been primarily influential on rhetoric in the 20th century (Kennedy, 1980). Prior to that time, his ideas were transmitted primarily through the work of his student Theophrastus, who wrote works on delivery and style, and other Greek authors. Nevertheless, of all the theories discussed in this chapter, Aristotle's rhetoric represents the most important because it is "the first orderly, systematic attempt to set down the principles of the art of public speaking" (Thonssen, Baird, & Braden, 1970, p. 75).

Hellenistic and Roman Rhetoric

After the defeat of the Greeks by Macedon in 338 B.C., the influence of Greek schools and rhetoric spread around the eastern Mediterranean, and Greek prose style underwent major changes. A simplified form of the Attic dialect of Greek, called *koine*, was spoken as a universal language throughout Alexander the Great's empire. Two competing groups developed among rhetoricians, (1) those who preferred the style of the 4th and 5th century Attic writers and such orators as Thucydides and Demosthenes, and (2) those who preferred an artificial and flowery style somewhat similar to that of Gorgias, mainly orators from Asia minor. The two groups, known as the Attics and the Asianists, disagreed as to whether the simple or flowery style was the appropriate standard for effective oratory. The works of Theophrastus, who succeeded Aristotle as head of the Peripatetic School, were written during this time (3rd century B.C.).

Cicero

"The greatest Roman orator and the most important Latin writer on rhetoric" (Kennedy, 1980, p. 90) lived from 106-43 B.C. Cicero's works combine ideas from the philosophical rhetoricians as well as the sophists and writers of the handbooks (Kennedy, 1980). Cicero wrote most about invention, creating material for the speech. *De Inventione* was influential on rhetoricians "for the next fifteen hundred years" (Kennedy, 1980, p. 90). Cicero believed rhetoric was a part of politics. He cited Aristotle's division of rhetoric into three types, judicial, legislative, and display oratory, and mentioned the five canons of rhetoric: invention, arrangement or organization, style, memory and delivery. He also discussed *stasis*, a concept invented by Hermagoras, a Greek writer of the second century B.C. *Stasis*, which Cicero called *constitutio*, is "the first conflict of the two sides of a case, resulting from the rejection of an accusation" (Kennedy, 1980, p. 92). For example, in judicial rhetoric, a defendant accused of committing a crime may deny guilt. The issue of the defendant's guilt or innocence is a point of *stasis*. Cicero discussed four types of *stasis* conflicts, mentioned the differences between simple and complex cases, and extended invention to deliberative or legislative oratory. He also discussed six parts of an oration. Cicero's treatment of invention emphasized the speech itself, rather than the speaker or audience, and was intended for orators (Kennedy, 1980).

Material from the time of Cicero on arrangement, delivery, memory, and style may be found in *The Rhetorica ad Herrenium*, a work which is similar to *De Inventione* and falsely attributed to Cicero. *The Rhetorica ad Herrenium* contains the earliest extant discussion of delivery, covering aspects of voice and movement. Voice quality, consisting of volume, stability, and flexibility, is discussed. "Physical movement or gesture is coordinated with the three tones, and advice is given on use of the face, arms, hands, body, and feet. In moments of pathetic [emotional] amplification it is even appropriate to slap the thigh and beat the head" (Kennedy, 1980, p. 98). "The discussion of memory in *The Rhetorica ad Herrenium* . . . is the best account of the subject in any ancient treatise" (Kennedy, 1980, p. 98). Mnemonic systems, such as relating a list of items to be remembered to a physical setting, were presented. For example, the speaker might imagine a banquet table with pictures which symbolize the main points at the places of the diners. By remembering the imaginary scene, the speaker can remember main points by mentally picturing each successive place at the table. The discussion of style in *The Rhetorica ad Herrenium* is not original, but is a good summary of the general consensus of first century rhetoricians (Kennedy, 1980). There were three kinds of style: grand, middle, and plain; these are also mentioned in Cicero's work *The Orator* (not to be confused with *De Oratore*). These are primarily differentiated by the use of ornamental language such as figures of speech. Grand style was very ornamental, similar to that of the Asiatic school, while plain style was clear and moderate, similar to that of the Attic orators mentioned above (Thonssen, Baird, & Braden, 1970). The qualities of good style are discussed, but the author does not specify when to use different styles (Kennedy, 1980).

According to Kennedy, Cicero's "greatest legacy is his own oratory, which is closely associated with his vision of the orator . . . in *De Oratore*" (1980, p. 100). Cicero's major contribution to the technical theory of rhetoric is the duties of an orator: proving the case to be true, winning the hearts of the audience, and arousing in the audience the proper emotion for the case. These also appear in *The Orator* and are translated as "to prove, to delight, and to stir" (Kennedy, 1980, p. 100). In *De Oratore*, three duties of the speaker are associated with the grand, middle and plain styles, and Cicero adds advice about when each is appropriate: "plain for proof, middle for pleasure, and grand for emotion" (Kennedy, 1980, p. 100).

Quintilian

Quintilian (actually Marcus Fabius Quintilianus) lived a century after Cicero, from about A.D. 40-95. "From about A.D. 71 to 91 he held an official chair of rhetoric paid for by government funds, giving lectures to large groups of students and criticizing their rhetorical exercises . . ." (Kennedy, 1980, p. 100). Quintilian presents a rhetorical theory similar to Cicero's, but his most important contribution is that he integrates rhetorical theories to form a complete system for the education of a rhetor. His treatise the *Education of the Orator* is the longest existing Latin work on rhetoric. An important feature of this work is that Quintilian presents historical surveys of rhetorical theory on the topic at hand, including disagreements, which he attempts to resolve. Quintilian's educational theory, the goal of which is to produce a great orator, takes the student from birth to adulthood; rhetoric is "the centerpiece in the training of the citizen" (Kennedy, 1980, p. 101). Like Isocrates, Quintilian emphasizes the moral quality of the orator.

The Second Sophistic

In the first century B.C., during Quintilian's lifetime, Greek and Roman rhetoric became more and more like the rhetoric of the sophists because *rhetors* emphasized style and the magic of language rather than inventing proofs and discussing the relationship of rhetoric and philosophy. An influential work about style entitled *On the Sublime* was written just before the beginning of this period. With the decline of democracy at Greece and Rome, teachers gave their pupils classroom exercises that were unrelated to actual events in their lives. Exercises concerned questions of value, historical or legislative themes, or "fictitious cases in imitation of the lawcourts" (Kennedy, 1980, p. 37). For example, pupils might try to compose a speech in response to one of Demosthenes. In one of these exercises presented by Quintilian and entitled "The Poor Man's Bees," the speaker represents a poor man whose bees were killed by poison sprinkled by the rich man who owned the flower garden next door. The poor man sues the rich man for damages. The speech ends with a section praising bees, who are considered virtuous because they work without being trained by man and live in hives which are models of civic organization (Clarke, 1953, pp. 248-250). This period is called the Second Sophistic because of the similarities to sophistic rhetoric, especially in the emphasis on style and the use of model speeches.

Augustine

Augustine (A.D. 354-430), the most important Christian rhetorical theorist, began his career as a teacher of rhetoric in Thagaste, moved to Carthage and Rome, then held the chair of Rhetoric at Milan from 384-386. After becoming a Christian through the influence of the sermons of Ambrose, bishop of Milan, Augustine resigned his position as a teacher of rhetoric. In 391 he became a priest, and in 395 he was installed as a bishop in Hippo. Many of Augustine's writings, which include sermons, letters, commentaries, and longer works, are available for us to read. Augustine's most explicit statement of rhetorical theory is contained in his work *On Christian Doctrine*, especially Book IV, which was completed in 426-427 (Kennedy, 1980). Augustine made three major contributions to rhetoric. (1) He revived the rhetorical teachings of Cicero, (2) he avoided the excessive emphasis on style typical of the Second Sophistic, and (3) he "[set] . . . a high ideal of Truth before the Christian preacher" (Thonssen, Baird, & Braden, 1970, p. 120).

In Book IV of *On Christian Doctrine*, "Augustine reestablished the pursuit of Truth as the guiding principle of public speaking" (Thonssen, Baird, & Braden, 1970, p. 120). In this regard, Augustine may be considered a follower of Plato and Parmenides because he believed in an absolute standard of truth. Unlike Heraclitus and Protagoras, he rejected opinion as a source of knowledge. As a Christian preacher and bishop, Augustine located the source of truth not in natural laws nor in Platonic forms, but in God's law which could be found in Scripture. Augustine emphasized the practical focus of rhetoric for "persuading Christians to lead a holy life" (Corbett, 1965, p. 545); there was no role for rhetoric in conversion since conversion was accomplished by the Holy Spirit. Augustine suggested that preachers use rhetoric to teach Truth because evil rhetors were using it to defend error and sin. Augustine adapted Cicero's three functions of rhetoric to the purposes of the Christian teacher, who should "conciliate those who are opposed, arouse those who are remiss, and teach those ignorant of his subject" (*On Christian Doctrine*, IV.6-26, cited in Kennedy, 1980, p. 156). Unlike Quintilian, Augustine did not believe that one had to be morally good to be an effective rhetorician or even an effective preacher. "[H]e realized that even a vicious preacher could induce his audience to follow Christ if he were skillful enough in the manipulation of his suasive resources" (Corbett, 1965, p. 545).

In *On Christian Doctrine*, Augustine set forth rhetorical principles for those who teach the Scriptures. First, they must discover the Truth; then they must teach what they have learned, both to present the Truth and to correct false ideas. Teachers should thoroughly understand the Scriptures to be able to explain the parts which were metaphorical or which contained other types of signs that point to subtle meanings. The teacher could use the writings which were clear to help explain those which were not. Augustine did admit the possibility that some parts of the Scriptures might be interpreted in more than one way. When such ambiguity arose, the teacher should prefer the interpretation which was consistent with more explicit Scriptures and with Church doctrine. The context must also be considered (Kennedy, 1980).

The role of dialectic for the preacher was to interpret the intent of God as revealed in the Scriptures, much as for Plato the role of dialectic was to help philosophers remember the truths they had seen before birth. Augustine admitted that sometimes the rules of logic and reason must be used in interpreting Scripture, but considered this a dangerous practice. Augustine believed that dialectic, mentioned in *On Christian Doctrine* in the form of definition, division, and partition, had a role for the teacher because "valid inference was instituted by God, and then observed by men" (Kennedy, 1980, p. 154). Thus, ideas from the Greek and Roman rhetoricians might be adapted by the Christian as long as they were True ideas created by God.

Augustine believed that the teacher must be familiar with stylistic forms not only to use them in speaking, but also to interpret Scriptures which contain metaphorical and other stylistic devices; clarity was the most important virtue of style for the Christian teacher. He discussed appropriateness of style in Scriptural passages, but believed ornamentation and correctness to be of little importance for the teacher. Like Cicero in the *Orator*, Augustine advocated using the plain style for teaching, middle style for delighting, and grand style for persuading (Kennedy, 1980). Augustine believed that the height of eloquence had only been achieved if one succeeded in persuading the audience. The influence of Augustine permitted rhetoric to retain its role in education at a time when Church writers mounted attacks on virtually all elements of Greco-Roman culture. For example, Tertullian rejected Greek literature including the poems of Homer because of references to "false gods" (Murphy, 1974). Augustine's justification allowed rhetoric to remain a part of the Christian educational system.

Rhetoric in the Middle Ages

Roman Educational Influence

The period from A.D. 400 to 1050 has been called an age of transition (Murphy, 1974). The two major influences on rhetoric throughout the Middle Ages were the tradition of Augustine on the one hand, and the narrower, more formulary tradition of Martianus. Martianus Capella, in *The Marriage of Philology and Mercury*, written about A.D. 410-427, introduced the Roman curriculum which in the Middle Ages became the seven liberal arts (Kennedy, 1980). The four-year elementary curriculum included grammar, logic (what Aristotle called dialectic), and rhetoric, all subjects which deal with words. Students practiced declamation exercises like those suggested by Quintilian and other Latin rhetoricians. In the three-year advanced curriculum, students studied four subjects governed by mathematical concepts: music, arithmetic, geometry, and astronomy (Murphy, 1974). However, rhetoric had become so focused on style "that the product of such training was a glib, clever 'entertainer' rather than a resourceful orator in command of all the available means of persuasion. Accordingly, the art of rhetoric stood still, if it actually did not retrogress, despite the prominent position that rhetoric held in the curriculum" (Corbett, 1965, pp. 544-545). This role for rhetoric is quite different from its position in classical schools, in which rhetoric and grammar were the principal subjects taught (Kennedy, 1980).

Arts of Preaching and Letter-Writing

Apart from such classroom exercises, in the middle ages rhetoric consisted primarily of the study of the arts of preaching, reflecting the tradition of Augustine, and letter-writing, reflecting an emphasis on style and figures of speech. Both of these traditions relied heavily on the rhetorical theory of Cicero.

Homilies, informal sermons based on interpretation of a scriptural text, were the most important type of sermon (Kennedy, 1980). The homilies of the Venerable Bede (A.D. 673-735) are examples of the practice of Christian rhetoric in England in the 7th century. Books on the art of letter-writing had titles such as *Flowers of Rhetoric*, written by Alberic around A.D. 1050, *Art of Versification* by Matthew of Vendome, and the *New Poetry* by Geoffrey of Vinsauf, the latter two written in the late twelfth and thirteenth centuries (Kennedy, 1980). These handbooks were primarily designed to train students to write formal diplomatic and legal correspondence of the kind required in civil and religious courts.

Rhetoric in the Universities

From the eleventh to thirteenth centuries, the seven liberal arts, including rhetoric, continued to influence education. They formed the basis for the French cathedral schools, especially the one at Chartres which became prominent in the eleventh century. The cathedral school of Chartres was the predecessor of our modern universities. If you have taken a required freshman university course in public speaking, you have participated in an educational tradition that has its roots in the educational system of Athens at the time of Aristotle and Plato. In fact, it was during the "renaissance of the twelfth century" that the study of rhetoric returned to its Greek roots. The works of Aristotle, which had largely been lost in Greek and Latin throughout the Middle Ages, became available through translations by Arab writers. A Latin translation in 1240 of an Arabic commentary on the *Rhetoric* attributed to Al-Farabi and a Latin translation of the *Rhetoric* itself by William of Moerbeke in 1270 were widely available, but at that time the *Rhetoric* was studied primarily for its moral and political philosophy in Books I and II, rather than for Aristotle's rhetorical theory.

Rhetoric During the Renaissance

Classical Revival

With the Italian Renaissance, classical rhetoric again became a strong educational and cultural influence during the fourteenth, fifteenth, and sixteenth centuries. George Trebizond (1395-1472) introduced the Greek tradition of Aristotle to the West through his *Five Books of Rhetoric*. Erasmus wrote works on letter writing and preaching which were influenced by Quintilian and Cicero. His most influential work on the varieties and formulas of expression included "one hundred and fifty ways to say (in Latin) 'Your letter pleased me very much' and two hundred ways to say 'I shall remember you as long as I live' " (Kennedy, 1980, p. 206).

The Province of Rhetoric Narrowed

Work by the fifteenth century Italian writers was continued by the Dutch scholar known as Rudolph Agricola (1444-1485). Agricola and Philipp Melanchthon (1497-1560), a Protestant leader who was a friend of Martin Luther, viewed rhetoric as a subordinate part of dialectic. In an effort to study and classify the arts, Peter Ramus (1515-1572) followed Agricola by including in dialectic such traditional rhetorical subjects as invention, judgment, arrangement, and memory. Omer Talon (1510-1562), a close associate who wrote several versions of a *Rhetoric*, limited rhetoric to style and delivery. Like the authors of the arts of letter-writing, Ramus reduced rhetoric to a focus on the speech itself and completely stripped it of the concern with speaker and audience reflected in the great Greek and Roman writers (Kennedy, 1980).

The Flourishing of the Philosophy of Logic

The seventeenth and eighteenth centuries were the beginning of the age of science. During this time, French, British, and American schools were strongly influenced by the development of logical theory. The British philosopher John Locke, who had once been a lecturer on rhetoric at Oxford, criticized rhetoric as deceptive and too much concerned with superficial concepts like figures of speech, but Locke's essay on human understanding did reveal a role for rhetoric similar to that of Plato, as a tool used to teach others about truth.

Fenelon's French Rhetoric

Heavily influenced by questions about the relationship of truth to preaching was Fenelon's dialogue, which has been called "the greatest work on classical rhetoric written in French and the finest statement of the philosophical strand of the tradition since antiquity" (Kennedy, 1980, p. 222). Fenelon's dialogue, written in the late 1670s, combined the rhetorical theory of Plato with the Christian rhetoric of Augustine. Fenelon emphasized rhetorical invention without neglecting style and delivery. His criteria for rhetorical excellence were that the orator remain loyal to Truth and nature while attempting to persuade the audience (Kennedy, 1980).

Rhetoric in the Eighteenth Century

George Kennedy identifies four themes in the eighteenth century study of rhetoric (1980). The emphasis on technical rhetoric after the manner of Cicero and the broader neoclassical rhetoric influenced by Fenelon formed the first two of these trends. Technical rhetoric was found especially in elementary education and consisted primarily of the teaching of figures of speech and the Roman system of common topics. The third trend, the Elocutionary

Movement, which had some basis in sophistic rhetoric, was begun by Thomas Sheridan, who founded a school to teach correct English speech to pupils from various British dialect areas. The fourth trend consisted of an effort to develop a new rhetoric based on "the theory of human nature and human knowledge" (Kennedy, 1980, p. 233) being developed by British Empiricist philosophers such as David Hume.

George Campbell's Philosophy of Rhetoric (1776)

Rather than relying on the classical structure of arts of rhetoric, George Campbell, a professor of divinity at the University of Aberdeen, developed a theory based on the new science of human nature. According to Campbell, the new knowledge of human nature should be used to draw general principles explaining different types of rhetorical effectiveness. In America more than thirty editions of Campbell's work were printed, and it was frequently adopted as a textbook in college rhetoric courses (Kennedy, 1980).

Hugh Blair's Lectures on Rhetoric and Belles Lettres (1783)

Hugh Blair, a minister and Regius Professor of Rhetoric at the University of Edinburgh, was important not so much for his original theoretical contribution as for his role in preserving a rhetorical tradition. Blair's lectures conserved traditional concepts of rhetoric and integrated them into the new belles lettres movement. In the lectures Blair discussed oral rhetoric, drawing on the work of Isocrates, Gorgias, Cicero and especially Quintilian. However, Blair believed that the circumstances of his time were so different from those of the classical period that oratory as an art form was not possible. Thus, his primary emphasis was on rhetorical eloquence through the written word (Kennedy, 1980).

Rhetoric in the Modern Period

It is especially interesting to note the changing role of rhetoric (and now communication) in the curriculum of American universities during the last two hundred years. In 1806 at Harvard, nineteen years before he became President, John Quincy Adams was the first person to hold the Boylston Professorship in Rhetoric and Oratory. This chaired professorship survives today, but it was changed from a chair of rhetoric to a chair of belles lettres, and then to a professorship of poetry (Kennedy, 1980). Today there is no department of spoken rhetoric or communication at Harvard. As of this writing, the holder of the Boylston chair is Seamus Heaney, an Irish poet.

Perhaps one reason for the decline of the importance of rhetorical instruction was the manner in which it was taught in American colleges and universities in the nineteenth century. Lectures by John Quincy Adams indicated he believed that everything important on the subject of rhetoric had been written by Aristotle, Cicero, and Quintilian. Modern rhetoricians needed merely to learn the ancients; there was no role for them to play in the development of rhetorical theory. By ignoring the philosophical concerns of a broader theory of rhetoric, followers of the Elocution Movement also left spoken rhetoric without the strong theoretical foundation necessary to claim its rightful place in the university. The Elocution Movement had a substantial influence on the teaching of rhetoric in American universities in the 19th and early 20th centuries. Followers of the Elocution Movement emphasized standards for developing "correct" speech, including inflection and body movement. The elocution period endorsed "scripted speech," in which every phrase had a "correct" pronunciation and accompanying delivery style. The elocution period began to wane during the early 1900s, but interest in the oral performance of literature continued to grow. The study of oral interpretation blossomed. Entire departments of speech dedicated themselves to the theory and practice of literature in performance.

Communication as a modern academic discipline began in the 1910s when separate departments of speech began to emerge in American universities (Kneupper, 1985). Just before World War I, speech teachers separated from the National Council of Teachers of English to form an independent professional association, the National Association of Academic Teachers of Public Speaking. The National Association of Academic Teachers of Public Speaking later changed its name to the Speech Association of America. As that title implies, the organization reflected an "orality alliance" of faculty concerned with "speech production and performance," including professors of communication education, theatre, oral interpretation, speech and hearing science, and, in the 1930s, broadcasting (Delia, 1987, p. 78). The Speech Association of America became the Speech Communication Association. That name reflects the development and growth of the study of communication in the 1900s, which is the subject to be examined in the next part of this chapter.

Increased Interest in Communication Study

During the first part of the 1900s, academic interest in speech, rhetoric, argumentation, journalism and writing flourished. The invention and diffusion of radio in the 1920s and television in the late 1940s significantly expanded interest in communication studies. Scholars and practitioners added another dimension, the mediated dimension, to their study of communication. The emergence of mass communication stimulated scholarly and practical interest in the influence of these new media (see Chapter 11).

During this period, scholars from other disciplines such as psychology, sociology, anthropology, and political science also began systematic investigations into aspects of communication. Since communication and the exchange of symbols are central to these fields, a great deal of research activity took place. This research activity examined critical components involving the communication process.

Psychologists and social psychologists such as Herbert Kelman, William J. McGuire, Leon Festinger, Elihu Katz, Charles E. Osgood, Carl I. Hovland, Irving L. Janis and Harold H. Kelley studied the influence of attitudes, beliefs and values (see Chapter 6). These scholars developed research programs which probed such relevant communication issues as, "What source, message, channel and receiver variables most influence outcomes of persuasive messages?" Scholars such as Theodore Newcomb and Donn Byrne began research campaigns to investigate the development of interpersonal relationships, liking and attraction (see Chapter 9). Other scholars such as Kurt Lewin investigated factors such as altruism or helping behavior, group leadership patterns and small-group decision-making (see Chapter 10).

Sociologists such as Paul Lazarsfeld investigated the influence of the mass media on society. The concept of the "mass society" emerged (see Chapter 11). Contemporary sociologists helped chronicle and explain the changing nature of modern society. Erving Goffman, another sociologist, examined the role of ritualized exchange on relationship development and social communication. Anthropologists, cultural anthropologists in particular, investigated concepts relevant to nonverbal communication. Ray Birdwhistell developed the science of *kinesics*, the study of body motion and movement. Edward T. Hall advanced the study of *proxemics*, the use of personal space (see Chapter 8). These and other critical components of nonverbal communication were first systematized and categorized by cultural anthropologists who had direct interest in human communication.

Political scientists such as Harold Lasswell began to explore the influence of communication in shaping world opinion. The study of propaganda and mass persuasion emerged from these efforts. The examination of interpersonal and informal communication on voting behavior was stimulated by these interdisciplinary scholars (see Chapter 11).

During the late 1940s and 1950s the study of rhetoric and speech expanded considerably. In addition to the increased interest in mass communication came increased interest and awareness of *psycholinguistics*, or the psychology of language. The production and enhancement of speech sounds was advanced by speech scholars trained in voice, diction and articulation. Renewed interest in the forms, methods and materials of argument and debate emerged.

The science of speech and language production developed. Scholars, practitioners and therapists interested in understanding and improving people's ability to speak and hear led to the development of research and theory building in speech pathology and audiology, now often referred to in department titles as Communication Disorders.

Interest in drama and theatre continued to grow throughout the decades. Departments of Speech and Theatre often became large enough to justify and demand their separation into two distinct areas of study. Newly created Departments of Speech and Departments of Theatre grew in academic stature and size.

It is clear that the period shortly after the second world war evidenced rapid growth and increased interest in the communication arts and sciences. To chronicle every major development from 1940 to the present is well beyond the scope and purpose of this chapter, and indeed this book. To mention every major contributor to the scholarly, theoretical, instructional, practical, and therapeutic growth of this discipline is a task also well beyond this chapter. In the next several sections we will trace the development of several contemporary approaches to communication. We will include examples of *social scientific approaches* which contributed to the development of communication theory and which have had an enduring effect on contemporary thought. We will sample some contemporary *rhetorical approaches* which have contributed to the development of our discipline. We will also explore the development of several contemporary *contextual approaches* to communication study. These contextual approaches appear to reflect one current direction that the communication discipline is taking. Several of these approaches will receive extensive treatment in Part III of this text, "Theory Building in Communication Contexts."

Major Approaches in the Development of Contemporary Communication Theory

The Yale Studies on Communication

Shortly after World War II, Carl I. Hovland, Irving L. Janis and Harold H. Kelley developed a research program to investigate systematically factors associated with attitude change and persuasion. This program continued for well over a decade. The major findings of this effort are summarized in their seminal text, *Communication and Persuasion* (1953). Because the bulk of the experimental work was conducted at Yale University, this research program became known as the Yale communication research program. Chapters 6 and 7 of this text provide a more extensive treatment of the major findings that emerged from this program. The Yale approach to persuasion and communication was largely based on *cognitive learning theory*: "opinions, like other habits, will tend to persist unless the individual undergoes some new learning experiences" (p. 10). Hovland and his colleagues believed that individuals who are exposed to persuasive messages may change their attitudes through a type of learning process.

The bulk of the Yale Studies are classified into four major headings, each examining one major component in the communication process. The researchers believed that the source of communication was of primary importance in determining the potential success of a persuasive effort. Factors associated with the credibility of a communicator were assessed to determine their influence on persuasion. Not unlike Aristotle's conception of *ethos*, the Yale Studies examined a communicator's perceived expertise and trustworthiness as factors which influence the acceptance of a persuasive message. Findings from the Yale Studies suggest that if we view a communicator to be highly expert and trustworthy, there is a greater likelihood we will accept that source's positions. The Yale Studies identified several factors that influence the relationship between source credibility and persuasion. Some of those factors are mentioned in Chapters 6 and 7.

The second major heading, the content of the message, describes efforts to identify the primary message variables which influence attitude change and persuasion. The researchers sought to identify certain types of motivating appeals which stimulate a receiver's emotions. Their research supported the contention that emotional appeals could assist in the change of attitudes. In particular, the influence of fear-arousing messages was studied.

The Yale studies also examined the organization of persuasive messages. Hovland and his colleagues felt that the order of persuasive appeals could influence attitude change and persuasion. Other factors such as implicitly or explicitly stating a conclusion, the presentation of one side versus two sides of an issue, and the primacy-recency ordering of arguments (placing the strongest argument first or last) could influence persuasion.

The nature of the receiver and audience predispositions/characteristics were examined to determine their influence on persuasion. The Yale Studies focused on the influence of group membership or group affiliation as factors in the resistance to a persuasive message. Certain individual personality factors associated with receivers' susceptibility to persuasion were also examined. Level of ego-involvement and initial attitudes toward a message were investigated. The relationships between intelligence, self-esteem, aggressiveness and social withdrawal were examined for their influence on persuasion.

Changes in a person's overt verbal behavior in response to persuasive messages were also studied. Will an individual willingly and voluntarily express or verbalize a newly acquired opinion or attitude? How long will a person retain the newly acquired attitude? These questions were also addressed by the Yale Studies on communication.

Contributions. The Yale Studies had a major impact on the development and advancement of communication theory. As Delia (1987) states, "Hovland's emphasis on attitude change through communication. . . served to bring these topics to center stage for communication researchers" (p. 64). The Yale Studies stimulated almost two decades of research on attitude change and persuasion, much of it conducted by contemporary communication researchers such as Gerald R. Miller, James C. McCroskey, John W. Bowers, and their colleagues.

Many scholars now credit the Yale Studies with moving the communication discipline into the social scientific approach (Sypher, Davenport-Sypher & Haas,

1988). Importing social psychological research methods into the communication discipline helped bring other constructs such as interpersonal attraction, leadership, and group decision-making to the attention of communication theorists and researchers. Delia states, "By 1970, American communication research was utterly dominated by social psychological approaches" (1987, p. 65).

Hovland and his colleagues acknowledged that the topics of their concern closely paralleled Harold D. Lasswell's formula of: who (the source) says what (the message) to whom (the receiver) with what effect (the consequence) (Smith, Lasswell, & Casey, 1946). This focus led to the development of Berlo's frequently cited model of the communication process (Berlo, 1960; see Chapter 1). The Yale communication research program has been said to have *heuristic value* since it stimulated numerous research studies on the influence of communication in persuasion.

Limitations. While the Yale approach to communication contributed greatly to the development of communication theory, critics argue that the program suffered from several limitations. Some contemporary communication scholars have argued that the Yale researchers were incorrect in their assumption that learning and attitude change are related (Smith, 1982). The approach has also been classified as *atheoretical,* or lacking a theoretical framework to draw upon. Critics challenge the Yale Studies' reliance on cognitive learning theory to provide explanations of *why* changes in attitudes lead to changes in behavior (Smith, 1982).

Communication rules theorists also challenge the findings of the Yale studies with the very paradigm on which they were based. One characteristic of the Yale approach was its reliance on the law-governed, causal model of inquiry. The majority of Yale results were obtained from experimental research conducted under controlled conditions (see the chapter on research methods in the Appendix). Communication rules theorists such as Smith argue that the findings are limited in that they "focus on what messages 'do to' people, rather than what people 'do with' messages" (1982, p. 236). Despite these possible limitations, the Yale approach to communication had a tremendous influence on the development of contemporary communication research.

An Information Approach to Communication

The Shannon and Weaver Model of Communication did much to advance the information theory approach to communication. Claude Shannon, scientist at the Bell Telephone Laboratory, and Warren Weaver, a professor of mathematics, advanced their theory with the publication of two papers jointly referred to as *The Mathematical Theory of Communication* (1949). This theory is frequently referred to as the information theory of communication. Through information theory, concepts such as channel (the communication medium) and noise (interference) were brought to the attention of the communication discipline (see Chapter 1) and have surfaced with increasing frequency and regularity in both popular magazines and scholarly journals.

In an effort to discover the systematic and mathematical foundation for communication, Shannon and Weaver sought to identify the quickest and most efficient way to get a message from one point to another. Their goal was to discover how communication messages could be converted into electronic signals most efficiently, and how those signals could be transmitted with a minimum of error. In order to do this, Shannon and Weaver had to quantify the information contained in messages. They also had to determine the amount of distortion or *noise* in the channel used to transmit the messages (Hawes, 1975). According to the theory, transmission of the message involved sending information through electronic signals. "Information," in the information theory sense of the word, should not be confused with "information" as it is usually understood. Conventionally, information is thought of as what we know; we think of information in terms of meaning. However, information theorists view information quite differently. According to Shannon and Weaver, information is defined as "a measure of one's freedom of choice when one selects a message" (p. 9). Hawes suggests that information "refers not to the content contained in a message but to all possible messages that could be transmitted" (1975, p. 87).

In order to understand this concept of information, we must consider another concept, *uncertainty*. Uncertainty occurs when you are unsure about something, or when you do not know exactly what will happen in a given situation. In information theory, information and uncertainty are closely related. *Information* refers to the degree of uncertainty present in a situation. Uncertainty also relates to the concept of predictability. When something is completely predictable, it is completely certain, so it contains very little, if any, information. For example, the letter U almost always follows the letter Q in the English language. Thus, the letter U is almost completely predictable in words that start with Q. If you were playing the television game "Wheel of Fortune," you could easily guess that the second letter of a word beginning with Q must be U. You would not need to spend money to buy a vowel. If another player revealed that the second letter in the word was U, you would know nothing more than you had previously known. You would have gained no information. One way to understand information in terms of this theory is to think of it as potential information, or as *all possible knowledge that you do not yet have* with regard to a subject.

A related term, *entropy*, is also important in information theory. Entropy refers to the degree of randomness, lack of organization, or disorder in a situation. A situation which is highly random, or unpredictable, is characterized as highly entropic. Thus, the more entropy in a system, the less predictability. The less predictability, the greater the potential information. Since you need more messages to predict the outcome of a complex situation than a simple one, the complex situation is said to contain more information.

Information theory introduced a concept to our vocabulary which is being heard with greater frequency today—*bit*. A bit is a measure of the actual amount of information in a message. Bit comes from the condensation of the term "binary digit." In the binary digit system, there are only two digits, 0 and 1. Computers make use of the binary code of 0's and 1's. Every piece of "information" that a computer receives or transmits is reduced to a pattern of electrical impulses like those controlled by a light switch, such as "on," represented by a 1, and "off," represented by a 0. The American Standard Code for Information Interchange, commonly referred to as ASCII, has converted all the letters of the alphabet, both upper and lower case, and all the numerals from 0 through 9 into combinations of 0's and 1's.

Redundancy is another concept which has emerged from the information theory approach to communication. Redundancy is the opposite of information. Something that is redundant adds little, if any, information to a message. Redundancy is important because it helps combat *noise* in a communication system. If a professor is asked to repeat something in class because a student was daydreaming, the statement which is repeated does not add any information to those students who heard it the first time. The repeated message was totally redundant. However, the message may serve as a reinforcement to those who heard it the first time. The repetition provides confirmation that the message was recorded accurately. Redundancy adds little to the amount of information, but a great deal to reinforcing messages sent. Some research indicates that reinforcement is related to attitude change and persuasion (see Chapter 6). This may help explain why we hear commercials repeated with such frequency on television and radio.

Contributions. The language of information theory is symbolic, and its symbols are those of mathematics (Hawes, 1975). Information theory concepts do much to challenge our conventional understanding of the concept of information. Information theory has, however, contributed to the clarification of certain concepts such as noise, redundancy and entropy. These concepts are inherently part of the communication process.

Critics of the information theory approach to communication argue that the theory has limited utility when applied to human communication. One major criticism of the theory is that it does not deal with meaning, and meaning is most important in the context of *human* communication. According to information theory, a message may contain a great deal of information and still contain little meaning. The definition of communication as the stimulation of meaning in another is clearly not addressed by the information theory approach. Information theory concentrates on the transfer of electronic signals, not on the meaning generated when receivers interpret those signals. The information theory approach to communication has provided us with a rich set of concepts and propositions to draw upon when needed. These concepts are especially useful for theorizing about message transmission using computers and the electronic media. Indeed, the information theory approach still emerges as useful when our discipline examines human-machine interaction.

Berlo's "Process" Approach to Communication

At about the time that information theory developed, a group of "new" scholars in communication emerged. David Berlo and his contemporaries were firmly rooted in speech and rhetorical studies. At the same, time they were strong advocates of adopting a behavioral science approach to studying human communication. This new generation of communication scholars developed research programs designed to explore the traditional problems of speech performance and speech training. They also studied other issues such as the process of persuasion, small-group communication and small-group decision-making, and language and communication.

David Berlo (1960) published a book which did much to advance the concept of communication as a *process*. Berlo's book dramatically influenced the emerging social scientific orientation to the study of communication, and his approach has persisted throughout the last three decades. Communication definitions which describe communication as the process of exchanging symbols or a process in which many interrelated variables influence each other reflect Berlo's influence. His process approach to communication theory argues that events and relationships are dynamic, continuous and constantly changing. All the factors involved in a process are in continuous interaction with each other simultaneously; all of the variables affect and influence each other. An example from biology illustrates the concept. The *digestive process* is a complex procedure involving many variables which work together to break down food into chemicals, nutrients and wastes. Berlo (1960) argues that communication is most accurately thought of as a process. Communication as a process involves the interaction of factors or variables. These variables all act upon each other simultaneously to influence the direction, flow and outcome of an interaction. Communication cannot be isolated or separated from other events, either internal or external.

Berlo (1977) suggests that the concept of process has been used by communication theorists in several ways. When asked to define communication, many scholars claim that it is not definable because it is a *process*. That is, attempts to define communication would render it static when communication is dynamic. In this context, communication is referred to as a process without a distinct beginning, an end, or a set of boundaries. This view assumes that everything is related to everything else, and reminds us of the systems approach to communication. Process has also been viewed as "complex organization of an individual or group of individuals" (Berlo, 1977, p. 13). This approach suggests that relationships should be the unit of analysis in communication. Process, therefore, is seen as the "organization of relationships." Others view process as a change over time. Process is also seen as an activity, as in information *processing*. Berlo argues, "Communication processes are subsets of information processes in that they consist of symbolic informational activity" (1977, p. 23).

Imagine sitting in your 11:00 AM class. The instructor is lecturing and asking a series of questions of the class members. What are some of the variables that are influencing the flow, direction and outcome of this interaction? We can use the Source-Message-Channel-Receiver (SMCR) Model developed by Berlo (1960) and described in Chapter 1 to examine some of them. How dynamic and interesting is the professor when she delivers the lecture? What is her mood that morning? What is the topic of the lecture? How interested are you and the other class members in the topic? How technical or abstract is the material? How much jargon is used in conveying the information? How prepared is the class to respond to the questions posed by the instructor? Does one class member dominate the interaction? What about the time of day? Are you hungry and thinking about lunch? Are you tired because you stayed up late the previous night? Are you thinking about the upcoming semester break? Are you assessing and processing the dispute you had with your roommate the night before? What is the temperature of the classroom? Is the instructor's handwriting legible to you? Is this a course which was required, or is it an elective?

These are a few of the factors that affect the process of communication in the classroom. If we spent eight hours a day during the next month, we probably could not list all the variables that comprise the communication process in that context. Each of these factors is important in its own right, and each influences the others. If you are tired and hungry, then you may miss some of the concepts presented. It suffices to say that the process of communication is quite complex. We can list the "ingredients," but we must not forget that it is the simultaneous *interaction* of these variables that makes up the process of communication.

Style Specific or Special Communication Theories

Ernest Bormann has provided a valuable taxonomy to identify the two classes of communication theory which we will consider next. Bormann (1980) argues that scholars have confused theories which deal with specific communication practices of particular groups with more general propositions accounting for broad classes of events covering many groups. Bormann calls the former *style-specific* or *special* communication theories, and the latter *general* theories of communication. These two kinds of theories represent different kinds of knowledge and serve different functions (Bormann, 1980, p. 59).

Special theories concern communication styles or practices of given rhetorical communities. A rhetorical community is a "group of people who participate in a rhetorical style and share common rhetorical visions from within the perspective of that style" (Bormann, 1980, p. 61). Rhetorical communities are groups of people engaged in interaction in which the participants understand the rules, customs and conventions of "appropriate" or "correct" communication.

These special theories guide the actual practice of communication within the group according to a predetermined, normative style. Style-specific or special communication theories are bound by time and space. That is, the theory is primarily useful to particular groups of people in a particular time frame. Several style-specific communication theories will be noted here. Earlier in this text, we mentioned the elocution movement. During the elocution period, public communication or public speaking was extremely stylized, rigid and formal by today's standards. Most phrases and words had a "correct" pronunciation and a precise delivery style. If a speaker were to utter the phrase "the brilliant sun shone upon the city," the speaker would be taught the "correct" pronunciation of each of those words and the "correct" body posture and gestures used to accompany those words. Elocution can be considered one example of a style-specific or special communication theory.

Try to imagine how strange it would seem to us today if our politicians or public speakers communicated under the rubric of elocution theory. Every phrase and manner of delivery would be "scripted out" for the speaker. Today, this style of public address would appear exceedingly rigid and unnatural at best! Observing a public speaker delivering a message under the stylized practices of elocution theory would conjure up images of the robot-like figures one observes in amusement parks like Disneyland. The usefulness of any style-specific theory diminishes considerably if you observe it in a different time frame or if it is used by a different group of people.

Another special communication theory relates to the authentic relationship style of interpersonal communication popular in the 1960s. This theory advocates that communicators create social awareness and growth and establish authentic and meaningful relationships with each other. Communicators are urged to create a warm, trusting communication climate. In order to do so, they must engage in such behaviors as risk-taking, self-disclosure, and openness. People are encouraged to respond to another's messages with emotionality. Sensitivity groups and encounter sessions were created in order to teach people how to communicate in this human relations style, just as elocution classes were created to teach people how to communicate appropriately in that style.

Style-specific theories are also culture-bound. This means that the style is appropriate primarily for the given culture or group which practices it. To extend the theory beyond that culture might be inappropriate and even counterproductive. For example, our western theories of argumentation are style-specific and primarily relevant to our western culture. Western theories of argumentation suggest that opinions of others on controversial issues should be verbally attacked with data, warrants and claims if we disagree with them (see Infante, 1988; Infante & Rancer, 1982; Toulmin, 1959). These theories explain how to construct arguments and counterarguments during conflict situations. Courses dealing with these theories are offered at many colleges, often under the title "Argumentation" or "Argument and Advocacy: Theory and Practice."

The argumentative approach to social conflict is highly culture-bound and western in cultural orientation. That is, the norms and rules of other cultures, specifically eastern cultures, do not endorse or advocate an attack-and-defend orientation for managing conflict. In eastern cultures, a verbal attack on another person's position on an issue, delivered publicly, would be a severe violation of social etiquette! Thus, special communication theories such as theories of argument apply only within a particular culture.

General Theories of Communication

According to Bormann (1980), general theories are universal explanations which account for broad classes of events. General theories are similar to the theories developed in the natural and physical sciences. General theories attempt to provide accounts of human communication behavior based upon generalizable regularities. Thus, general theories may be applicable and relevant to many different groups and cultures, across many times. When scholars provide explanations of communication behavior that cut across given styles, then general communication theories are developed. General theories describe features or aspects of communication common to many different rhetorical communities.

Because general theories are not culture-bound, the propositions which undergird these theories may be applied to many different people and cultures. That is, a general theory has as much usefulness in predicting and/or explaining the communication behavior of an American as it does an Australian. As general theories are not time-bound, the propositions which undergird the theory might be as true today, or fifty years from now, as they were fifty or one hundred years ago.

Cognitive Dissonance

Festinger's (1957) Theory of Cognitive Dissonance has been identified as a general theory which developed out of the cognitive consistency approach to persuasion. Cognitive Dissonance Theory suggests that individuals who hold two contradictory ideas, or ideas contradicted by their behaviors (e.g., saying "I don't like horror movies," then watching them on television) will experience psychological discomfort called dissonance. This discomfort motivates people to change their attitudes, their behaviors, or both. Cognitive dissonance reflects an attempt by scientists to construct a general theory. It suggests that, like gravity, feelings of cognitive dissonance may be experienced by many people at many different times across human history. Bormann states, "The assumption is that the cognitive dissonance phenomenon is an unvarying human drive that can account for Julius Caesar's crossing the Rubicon as well as predict the behavior of a cigarette smoker in the future who reads of new evidence of the danger of smoking" (1980, p. 171). Cognitive dissonance theory will be explained in greater detail in Chapter 6.

Symbolic Convergence

Another general theory which has been useful in applied communication research is called *symbolic convergence*. It deals with the general human tendency to interpret, and give meaning to signs and symbols. Convergence refers to the way people try to unite their own private symbolic "worlds" to achieve what has been described as a "meeting of the minds." When individuals communicate in such a way that their own private symbolic "worlds" begin to come together, they begin to share symbol systems. During this convergence process, people share their individual fantasies, dreams and meanings and begin to interpret signs and symbols in similar ways.

It is argued that the process of symbolic convergence occurs when individuals share group fantasies (Bormann, 1980). This process can occur in small-group encounter sessions, in focus groups, or in an audience during the delivery of a public speech or the viewing of a television show or movie. The films *Rocky* and *Rambo* include images, symbols, dramatizations and narratives that tend to draw audience members together into a common "symbolic world." The group fantasies which emerge create common dreams, goals and values for the audience. Typically, this type of film depicts "underdogs" overcoming humble or difficult beginnings, fighting against the establishment and winning, thereby triumphing over the injustices of the world. As Bormann (1972) suggests, when group members share a number of fantasies over a period of time, they begin to share the same heroes and villains, and they applaud the same actions. These group fantasies make it easier for individuals to communicate with each other.

Symbolic Convergence Theory also suggests that people often share a particular *fantasy-type*. This involves sharing the same story, but with different characters and slightly different events. Bormann (1980) compares a fantasy-type to a recurring script in the group's culture. Political parties are held together by common fantasy types. Bormann suggests that members of the Republican Party often emerge with the same fantasy type, one which depicts the Democrats as too liberal, fiscally irresponsible, and the creators of inflation, imbalanced budgets and economic chaos. Democrats on the other hand often emerge with a fantasy type which depicts the Republicans as too conservative, swayed by big business and corporate interests, and unsympathetic to the working person and the poor. Bormann argues that Symbolic Convergence Theory represents a general theory of communication because it transcends rhetorical communities and various communication contexts. The sharing of group fantasies is "assumed to include all human collectives in the past, now, and in the future, regardless of cultural differences and rhetorical style" (Bormann, 1980, p. 254).

Burke's Dramatism

The final general theory to be discussed is Burke's rhetorical theory called *dramatism*. Kenneth Burke has been a major influence in the development of contemporary communication theory. His works span the literature of the humanities and social sciences, and his contributions to contemporary rhetorical theory are numerous. Burke has been cited by scholars in the fields of philosophy, sociology, theology, psychology, and literature.

Burke (1966) recognizes that human beings are symbol-making, symbol-using and symbol-misusing animals. The ability to create and manipulate symbols is what distinguishes human beings from other animals. Humans alone, Burke argues, use symbols and are reflexive creatures. That is, human beings can communicate, and they can communicate about their communication. For example, we can deliver a presentation in our speech class and can then talk about this presentation with others. Dogs, on the other hand, can bark, but they cannot bark about the nature of barking. Burke argues that symbols influence behavior because motives are an inherent part of human communication. Motive "refers to action by way of communication behavior" (Stewart, Smith, & Denton, 1984, p. 87) and is often viewed as a *completed action* (Golden, Berquist, & Coleman, 1978). In other words, persuading, a communicative action, fits Burke's definition of a motive. Behavior can be explained or justified by appealing to a motive. Burke is interested in how motives influence communication behavior. He believes that if we understand the motives of individuals, we are better able to understand their perceptions of reality.

Burke's notion of dramatism is at the core of his theory, a theory grounded in the symbolic nature of communication. As much of human action is symbolic, the theory provides a means of analyzing human action. Dramatistic theory has been called a "communication theory of human behavior" (Stewart, Smith, & Denton, 1984, p. 90). A key concept in dramatistic theory is *identification*. Burke believes that an important goal of communication is identification. When we communicate, we try to develop a "common bond" with our audience. When we attempt to persuade an individual or group, we try to establish a sense of rapport or similarity with them. Burke (1950) argued, "You persuade a man only insofar as you can talk his language by speech, gesture, tonality, order, image, attitude, idea, identifying your ways with his" (p. 55). In order to create identification with an audience, several options are available to a communicator. You can participate in or observe the actions and behaviors of the group. For example, if you wanted to persuade the members of your college class to elect you Class President, you could participate in social functions sponsored by the class. You could try to dress like the class members. This might mean refraining from spiking your hair or wearing leather pants. Adopting and understanding the language of the group helps foster identification. Using group expressions, if done honestly and adroitly, will increase identification. Using examples that are easily understood by the audience and emphasizing shared experiences between you and the audience also create identification. For example, in your quest for the class presidency, you may suggest that as a dormitory resident, you, too, are troubled by the lack of space, privacy and decent meals.

Among Burke's lasting contributions to communication theory is the development of a model of rhetorical criticism called the *dramatistic pentad*. The pentad is "a method for analyzing symbolic acts so that we can recognize the important relationships between symbolic acts and the environment in which they occur" (Stewart, Smith, & Denton, 1984, p. 85). Burke's pentad includes five parts: the *act* (what is occurring, the rhetorical event); the *agent* (the leading players in the rhetorical event); the *agency* (the means to accomplish the rhetorical purpose); the *scene* (the physical, temporal, cultural, and environmental setting of the rhetorical event) and the *purpose* (the desired outcome of the rhetorical event). By identifying the individual elements of the pentad and examining their interrelationships, scholars can understand why a rhetorical event such as a speech has had a particular effect on an audience. Using the pentad, scholars can suggest why a persuasive speech succeeded or why it failed.

Burke's dramatistic theory and his method of pentadic analysis have been extremely useful to scholars attempting to explain and predict human communication behavior. The dramatistic approach to rhetorical criticism has been used in a wide variety of communication events ranging from analyzing the inherent characteristics of formal organizations (Tompkins, Fisher, Infante, & Tompkins, 1975) to assessing the rhetorical dimensions of a multiple murder and suicide (Fisher, 1974).

Contextual Approaches to Communication

During the early development of the discipline, the focus of communication theorists was much narrower than it is today. Primary emphasis was placed on studying message effects. As Berger and Chaffee (1987) note, the study of communication was dominated by the study of public and mass persuasion. As the communication discipline grew in size, it also grew in scope. One-way, linear models were abandoned in favor of process models of communication. Interest in the role of communication in developing social and personal relationships grew. Alternative methodologies and paradigms for building communication theory were adopted. Research emphasis broadened to include both applied studies and attempts to build general theories. Communication scholars no longer depended on other disciplines such as social psychology to create theories. With increasing frequency, communication theories were being advanced by scholars trained primarily in the communication arts and sciences. This trend continues today.

Concomitant with this growth has been the development of contextual approaches to the study of human communication. Attempts to develop an all-encompassing, general theory which explains a wide range of communication behavior across contexts have been met with frustration. During the last decade, communication theorists have been attempting to build theories which have greater utility when applied to specific communication contexts. Part III of this text will detail several theory building efforts in the major contexts of human communication. It is our belief that this contextual approach marks the current state of theory building in our discipline. Two communication associations, the Speech Communication Association and the International Communication Association, have created interest groups and divisions for scholars interested in research and theory building in communication contexts. Examples of theory building efforts are presented in Chapters 9 through 12 of this text. In this chapter, we will introduce a few of the many contexts which are receiving attention from communication theorists.

The Interpersonal Communication Context

Dyadic or two-person communication was one of the first contexts to receive attention from communication theorists. As the field began to grow, greater emphasis was placed on understanding the impact of communication on social relationships. Theorists began research programs designed to explain communication in interpersonal or one-on-one contexts. Understanding the role communication plays in (1) developing relationships, (2) our attraction to others, (3) disengaging from relationships, and (4) general interpersonal influence has been the focus of much research and theory development. Research efforts in interpersonal communication have included a re-examination of persuasion in the one-on-one context. Referred to as studies on "compliance-gaining," this body of research emphasizes persuasive efforts which account for the emotions and needs of the target, the person being persuaded, as well as for the nature of the interpersonal relationship (Miller, Boster, Roloff, & Seibold, 1977). Chapter 9 will present several contemporary lines of inquiry in interpersonal communication.

The Organizational Communication Context

During the late 1940s and early 1950s scholars became interested in the academic study of organizational or business communication. Since that time it has emerged as a large and clearly identifiable context of communication. W. Charles Redding, one of the pioneers in the study of organizational communication, indicates that the term "organizational communication" did not emerge until the late 1960s or early 1970s (Redding, 1985). The "roots" of the study of organizational communication can be found in rhetorical theory, industrial psychology, traditional management theory, business English, and the human relations school of organizational thought. Putnam and Cheney (1985) propose that organizational communication developed from contexts such as public address, persuasion, interpersonal, small-group and mass communication.

Four major lines of inquiry seem to have dominated the study of organizational communication (Putnam & Cheney, 1985). Communication channels in the organization, communication climate, network analysis and superior-subordinate communication appear to have occupied much of the theory building efforts in organizational communication. Chapter 10 will present several contemporary lines of inquiry in organizational and group communication.

The Political Communication Context

Interest in political communication marks another contextual approach in the discipline. Scholars interested in how messages and/or campaigns influence voting behavior have produced several large research programs and theory building efforts. Communication theorists have also studied how the mass media and advertising influence attitudes toward political candidates. Some of the earliest studies on the influence of the mass media examined issues such as voting for a United States President (Lazarsfeld, Berelson, & Gaudet, 1944). Communication scholars today study the influence of communication on the political process as well as the influence of politics on communication.

The Health Communication Context

Communication in the health care context has received attention from communication theorists (Kreps & Thornton, 1984; Thompson, 1986). Communication is extremely important in doctor-patient, nurse-patient, and doctor-nurse interaction. In the health care context, providing adequate and accurate information may be the key to effective treatment and recovery. In 1988 in an effort to communicate accurate information to all its citizens, the United States Department of Health and Human Services sent every American household a seven page brochure on "Understanding AIDS." This was a large scale effort designed to provide accurate information to the American public about a very serious health problem and is an excellent example of the importance of communication in health care.

The development of a trusting and open relationship between health care providers and their patients impacts on treatment and cure. If you have ever visited a doctor or dentist who lacked interpersonal communication skills or a "good bedside manner," then you are aware of just how important communication is in the health care context. As Pettegrew and Logan (1987) state, "If progress is to be made in health communication research at the interpersonal level, communication theories must be embraced more fully" (p. 679).

The Mass Communication Context

Since the advent of radio and television, communication theorists have spent considerable time investigating the influence of the mass media on people's behavior and the influence of people's behavior on the media. Mass communication scholars study the roles culture, society and the individual play in the production of mass communication content (McQuail, 1987). Mass communication theorists have also investigated the effects of exposure to the media on an individual's behavior. A number of theories have been developed to explain how such exposure shapes our perceptions of the world. Chapter 11 of this text will explore several theory building developments in mass media contexts.

The Intercultural Communication Context

As the world grows smaller, it is more and more likely that we will interact with individuals from different cultures. Each culture has its own set of norms, rules, values and customs. Individuals involved in cross-cultural interaction often find communication to be quite difficult, if not frustrating. Failing to observe cultural norms and rules during communication may result in misunderstandings, some with rather severe consequences, like the unintended insult in the American-Japanese business negotiation described in Chapter 3. If you have ever travelled abroad, you may remember a time when something you said, or the way you said it, created an awkward moment. One of our favorite examples of such an interpersonal difficulty concerns an American just learning to speak Mandarin Chinese. In Mandarin the words "teacher" and "old rat" are distinguished only by the pitch and emphasis with which they are pronounced. They would be Romanized almost identically: "teacher" is *laoshur* and "old rat, " *laoshu*. The American, who had trouble pronouncing the tones that differentiate Chinese words, called his teacher an "old rat"!

Communication theorists are creating theories of intercultural communication to help individuals interact with those of other cultures. These theories explain why some cross-cultural communication interactions are successful, while others are not. Several of these theories will be presented in Chapter 12 of this text.

Assessing Contextual Theory Building Efforts

Some scholars argue that the contextual approach to communication may encourage fragmented research and theory-building. They suggest that since communication occurs in thousands of different contexts, "there is the possibility for confusion and overlap in theory and research efforts" (Chaffee & Berger, 1987, p. 538). These cautions, however, are balanced by the many powerful and useful theories developed by communication scholars employing a contextual approach. The explanatory power and practical value of contextual theories indicate that the trend toward developing our knowledge of communication processes in specific contexts will continue well into the 1990s.

Summary

This chapter has attempted to trace the history of the study of communication with two goals in mind: (1) to trace the development of the questions and problems that concern communication theorists today, and (2) to indicate the rich educational heritage in which students participate through the study of rhetoric and communication. From the earliest development of western philosophy to contemporary research on media and advertising, rhetoric and persuasion have been a central focus of communication studies. Around 400-300 B.C. sophists such as Gorgias and Protagoras travelled from city to city to prepare students to argue cases in the lawcourts and political assemblies. Plato and Aristotle developed theories of rhetoric firmly grounded in the philosophical tradition of their time, yet designed to aid those who wished to study the practical art of rhetoric. In the first century A.D., Roman rhetoricians such as Cicero and Quintilian classified rhetorical topics and styles and set forth a system for educating orators which was influential even on American universities. In the fourth century A.D. Augustine developed a theory of rhetoric for training Christian preachers and teachers.

Various parts of the classical traditions were emphasized from the time of Augustine until the 1700s, when a philosophy of logic led some scholars to develop modern rhetorical theories and others to limit rhetoric to the study of delivery alone. Since the beginning of the twentieth century, a renewed interest in the classics has strengthened the traditional strain of rhetoric, which has intertwined in Departments of Speech Communication and Communication Studies with the study of communication, including mass communication, by social scientists. As this chapter has shown, the field called communication has a long and rich tradition as well as an adaptive and energetic modern focus. Although rhetoric and communication theories have been developed by scholars from different traditions using different methods, their complementary focus provides both breadth and depth to help scholars better understand an important phenomenon in the lives of all human beings. As a student of communication, you are participating in an ancient and honorable, yet exciting and very modern enterprise.

Questions To Consider

1. What was the nature of communication training in ancient Greece?
2. Who were the sophists?
3. What were Plato and Aristotle's major contributions to communication theory?
4. What basic ideas about communication were predominant during the period of ancient Rome?
5. What was communication theory like during the Middle Ages?
6. What form did communication theory take during the Renaissance?
7. How is your communication training similar to that taught in the first universities?
8. What were the communication theory trends during the eighteenth, nineteenth, and early twentieth centuries?
9. How did the Yale Studies revolutionize communication research? What were the main topics of investigation?
10. What is the focus of information theory? Define *information* as it is used in this theory.
11. What is communication like according to Berlo's Process Model?
12. Explain the difference between specific and general communication theories.
13. What are the main concepts in Burke's dramatism?
14. Explain the contextual approach to communication. List several communication contexts in which theories are currently being developed.

References

Aristotle. (1941). *The basic works of Aristotle.* (R. McKeon, Ed. & introd.). NY: Random House.

Berger, C. R., & Chaffee, S. H. (1987). The study of communication as a science. In C. R. Berger & S. H. Chaffee (Eds.), *Handbook of communication science* (pp. 15-19). Newbury Park, CA: Sage.

Berlo, D. K. (1960). *The process of communication.* New York: Holt, Rinehart and Winston.

Berlo, D. K. (1977). Communication as process: Review and commentary. In B. D. Ruben (Ed.), *Communication Yearbook, I* (pp. 11-27). New Brunswick, NJ: Transaction.

Bitzer, L. F. (1959). Aristotle's enthymeme revisited. *Quarterly Journal of Speech, 45,* 399-408.

Bormann, Ernest G. (1980). *Communication theory.* Reissued 1989. Salem, WI: Sheffield.

Bormann, E. G. (1972). Fantasy and rhetorical vision: The rhetorical criticism of social reality. *Quarterly Journal of Speech, 58,* 396-407.

Brownstein, O. L. (1965). Plato's Phaedrus: Dialectic as the genuine art of speaking. *Quarterly Journal of Speech, 51,* 392-398.

Burke, K. (1966). *Language as symbolic action.* Berkeley: University of California Press.

Burke, K. (1950). *A rhetoric of motives.* New York: Prentice-Hall.

Chaffee, S. H., & Berger, C. R. (1987). Contexts of communication: An introduction. In C. R. Berger & S. H. Chaffee (Eds.), *Handbook of communication science* (pp. 537-539). Newbury Park, CA: Sage.

Clarke, M. L. (1953). *Rhetoric at Rome: A historical survey.* London: Cohen and West.

Corbett, E. P. J. (1965). *Classical rhetoric for the modern student.* New York: Oxford University Press.

Delia, J. G. (1987). Communication research: A history. In C. R. Berger & S. H. Chaffee (Eds.), *Handbook of communication science* (pp. 20-98). Newbury Park, CA: Sage.

Durant, W. (1939). *The life of Greece.* New York: Simon and Schuster.

Festinger, L. (1957). *A theory of cognitive dissonance.* Stanford, CA: Stanford University Press.

Fisher, J. Y. (1974). A Burkean analysis of the rhetorical dimensions of a multiple murder and suicide. *Quarterly Journal of Speech, 60,* 175-189.

Golden, J. L., Berquist, G. F., & Coleman, W. E. (1978). *The rhetoric of Western thought.* (2nd ed.). Dubuque, IA: Kendall/Hunt.

Guthrie, W. K. C. (1971). *The sophists.* New York: Cambridge University Press.

Hawes, L. C. (1975). *Pragmatics of analoguing: Theory and model construction in communication.* Reading, MA: Addison-Wesley.

Hovland, C. I., Janis, I. L., & Kelley, H. H. (1953). *Communication and persuasion.* New Haven, CT: Yale University Press.

Infante, D. A. (1988). *Arguing constructively.* Prospect Heights, IL: Waveland Press.

Infante, D. A., & Rancer, A. S. (1982). A conceptualization and measure of argumentativeness. *Journal of Personality Assessment, 46,* 72-80.

Jaeger, W. (1976). *Paideia: the ideas of Greek culture, I* (2nd ed.). Trans. Gilbert Highet. New York: Oxford University Press.

Kennedy, G. A. (1980). *Classical rhetoric and its Christian and secular tradition from ancient to modern times.* Chapel Hill: University of North Carolina Press.

Kreps, G. L., & Thornton, B. C. (1984). *Health communication: Theory and practice.* Reissued 1989. Prospect Heights, IL: Waveland.

Kirk, G. S., & Raven, J. E. (1957). *The presocratic philosophers: A critical history with a selection of texts.* Cambridge: Cambridge University Press.

Kneupper, C. W. (1985). Developing rhetoric as a modern discipline: Lessons from the classical tradition. In C. W. Kneupper (Ed)., *Oldspeak/Newspeak: Rhetorical transformations* (pp. 108-118). Arlington, TX: Rhetoric Society of America.

Lazarsfeld, P. F., Berelson, B., & Gaudet, H. (1944). *The people's choice: How the voter makes up his mind in a presidential campaign.* New York: Columbia University Press.

McQuail, D. (1987). *Mass communication theory: An introduction.* Beverly Hills, CA: Sage.

Miller, G. R., Boster, F., Roloff, M., & Seibold, D. (1977). Compliance-gaining message strategies: A typology and some findings concerning effects of situational differences. *Communication Monographs, 44,* 37-51.

Murphy, J. J. (1974). *Rhetoric in the Middle Ages: A history of rhetorical theory from Saint Augustine to the Renaissance.* Berkeley and Los Angeles: University of California Press.

Pettegrew, L. S., & Logan, R. (1987). The health care context. In C. R. Berger & S. H. Chaffee (Eds.), *Handbook of communication science* (pp. 675-710). Newbury Park, CA: Sage.

Pierce, J. R. (1961). *Symbols, signals, and noise.* New York: Harper & Row.

Plato. (1971). *The collected dialogues of Plato including the letters.* E. Hamilton & H. Cairns, Eds. Princeton, NJ: Princeton University Press.

Pomeroy, S. B. (1975). *Goddesses, whores, wives, and slaves: Women in classical antiquity.* New York: Schocken.

Putnam, L. L., & Cheney, G. (1985). Organizational communication: Historical development and future directions. In T. W. Benson (Ed.), *Speech communication in the 20th century* (pp. 130-156). Carbondale, IL: Southern Illinois University Press.

Randall, J. H., Jr. (1960). *The making of the modern mind: A survey of the intellectual background of the present age.* New York: Columbia University Press.

Redding, W. C. (1985). Stumbling toward identity: The emergence of organizational communication as a field of study. In R. D. McPhee & P. K. Tompkins (Eds.), *Organizational communication: Traditional themes and new directions* (pp. 15-54). Beverly Hills, CA: Sage.

Rowland, R. C., & Womack, D. F. (1985). Aristotle's view of ethical rhetoric. *Rhetoric Society Quarterly, 15,* 13-32.

Ruben, B. D. (1988). *Communication and human behavior* (2nd ed.). New York: Macmillan.

Shannon, C. E., & Weaver, W. (1949). *The mathematical theory of communication.* Urbana, IL: University of Illinois Press.

Smith, B. L., Lasswell, H. D., & Casey, R. D. (1946). *Propaganda, communication, and public opinion.* Princeton, NJ: Princeton University Press.

Smith, M. J. (1982). *Persuasion and human action.* Belmont, CA: Wadsworth.

Stewart, C. J., Smith, C. A., & Denton, R. E. (1984). *Persuasion and social movements.* Prospect Heights, IL: Waveland Press, Inc.

Sypher, H. E., Davenport-Sypher, B., & Haas, J. W. (1988). Getting emotional: The role of affect in interpersonal communication. *American Behavioral Scientist, 31,* 372-383.

Thompson, T. L. (1986). *Communication for health professionals.* New York: Harper & Row.

Thonssen, L., Baird, A. C., & Braden, W. W. (1970). *Speech criticism* (2nd ed.). New York: Ronald Press.

Tompkins, P. K., Fisher, J. Y., Infante, D. A., & Tompkins, E. L. (1975). Kenneth Burke and the inherent characteristics of formal organizations: A field study. *Communication Monographs, 42,* 135-142.

Toulmin, S. (1959). *The uses of argument.* Cambridge: Cambridge University Press.

Womack, D. F. (1985). Why Plato ignored Democritus. In C. W. Kneupper (Ed)., *Oldspeak/Newspeak: Rhetorical transformations* (pp. 127-141). Arlington, TX: Rhetoric Society of America.

Zeller, E. (1980). *Outlines of the history of Greek philosophy* (13th ed.). (W. Nestle, Rev.; L. R. Palmer, Trans.) New York: Dover. (Original work published 1931).

Chapter 5

Trait Approaches

If a scholar from another academic discipline were to go to communication research journals to determine how communication is studied, a trait approach would be immediately apparent. Skim through several recent volumes of journals such as *Human Communication Research, Communication Monographs*, and *Communication Quarterly*, and you will find a consistently high percentage of articles based on the idea of communication traits.

What is a communication trait? The concept originates in personality theory from the field of psychology. Our definition of a communication trait will thus not be unlike that of a personality trait. The major difference is that the idea of communication traits is only concerned with communicative behavior. A brief review of several definitions of personality provides a basis for defining communication traits.

> Personality is the dynamic organization within the individual of those psychological systems that determine unique adjustments to his environment. (Allport, 1937, p. 48)
>
> Personality is that which permits a prediction of what a person will do in a given situation. (Cattell, 1950, p. 2)
>
> Personality is an abstraction or hypothetical construction from or about behavior . . . . a trait is a construction or abstraction to account for enduring behavioral consistencies and differences . . . .(Mischel, 1968, pp. 4-5)
>
> Personality is a stable set of characteristics and tendencies that determine those commonalities and differences in psychological behavior (thoughts, feelings, and actions) of people that have continuity in time and that may

or máy not be easily understood in terms of the social and biological
pressures of the immediate situation alone. (Maddi, 1972, p. 9)

Personality is the governing organ of the body . . . . (Murray, 1951, p. 436)

This sampling of definitions reveals that the study of personality aims at
understanding human behavior. As stated earlier, the study of communication
traits is more focused because the interest is on communicative behavior—
when individuals manipulate what are generally recognized as verbal and
nonverbal symbols in order to stimulate meaning in others. The study of
personality encompasses this and much more. Traits such as compulsiveness,
masochism, tolerance for ambiguity, richness of fantasy, and rigidity are studied.
Although such traits certainly might affect *how* we communicate, they do not
constitute communicative behavior *per se*.

In view of these definitions, we may define a *communication trait* as a
hypothetical construct which accounts for certain kinds of communicative
behaviors. A *hypothetical construct* is a concept which is thought to represent
reality, to structure reality and to give it meaning. Researchers invent
hypothetical constructs for a purpose—to explain communicative events. If
another hypothetical construct is invented to explain the same domain, the
old and the new constructs can be compared to determine which provides
the more satisfying explanation. For instance, the construct "gullibility" might
be invented to explain why some people are so easily influenced. Someone
else might come along later and say that the construct "low self-esteem" better
explains the lack of resistance to persuasion. It might be claimed that the notion
of gullibility cannot explain the fact that easily influenced people are not *always*
persuaded. Further, self-esteem might be a better explanation because it can
be shown that raising the esteem of low self-esteem persons reduces their
persuasibility. Self-esteem would predict variations in response to persuasion,
but gullibility would not. Gullibility permits only an unsatisfying explanation
for variability: "people are not as gullible in some situations as in others."

It is important to note that while a hypothetical construct in the social
sciences is invented to represent and characterize something, scientists cannot
absolutely prove the construct by observing it empirically with the five senses.
For instance, the most prominent hypothetical construct in the history of the
social sciences is probably *attitude*. An attitude is usually defined as a
predisposition to respond favorably or unfavorably toward an object (topic,
event or person). This seems clear, for example, when we think of how favorable
our feelings are toward a particular food. To say we have a favorable attitude
toward that food makes sense. Remember, however, that "attitude" is a
hypothetical construct, an invention to explain behavior. No one has actually
ever seen an attitude. Radical behaviorists have even denied the concept of
attitude and have explained behavior by reinforcements in the environment.
In their opinion, you eat a certain food not because of your attitude toward

it but because your family expects you to eat it, and you have been positively reinforced when you did.

Communication traits are also hypothetical constructs. Those that we will examine in this chapter have an appeal because they appear to give meaning to certain communication behaviors and provide explanations which would not otherwise exist. Remember, however, that we do not know that a given trait is "real." Researchers assume that if it is real, the data from a study will take a certain form. If it does, the researcher essentially says, "I'm right so far; the data don't contradict my assumptions. Now let's gather some different data to see if there is further proof." This process never really ends because somewhere along the line it will be possible to invent a different construct which explains the data better.

A major criticism of trait approaches is that they "beg the question." For instance, it is not very helpful to say some people argue a lot because they are high in trait argumentativeness. Using a label for a trait as an explanation for behavior does not say much. However, the criticism is a "straw man" argument (describing and then refuting a position which no one actually holds) because trait researchers do not simply use the trait label to explain the behavior. Instead, a theoretical framework is used. The label "high in argumentativeness" applies to people who argue frequently. That label does not explain *why* they argue. The last section of this chapter will present a theoretical explanation which assumes competing motives and how people's perceptions interact with those motives to cause them to argue in a particular situation.

One of the reasons for the popularity and appeal of such traits as asser-tiveness, openness, friendliness, attentiveness, and aggressiveness is that it is easy to think of people whose personality is defined mainly by one or another of these traits. Communication traits provide a basis for what to expect from others in various situations. We usually want to be able to predict how others will respond to us. We would prefer to reduce uncertainty in dealing with others (Berger & Calabrese, 1975). Becoming aware of communication traits may provide an acceptable basis for reducing uncertainty, for knowing what to expect.

Traits, Contexts, and States

Distinctions are sometimes made between trait, contextual, and state behaviors. Trait behavior is assumed to be consistent across situations. That is, one's behavior regarding a trait is expected not to vary greatly from one situation to the next, nor from one point in time to the next. This does not mean that there should be *no* variability in trait behavior. Rather, types of behavior are usually predictable and reasonably consistent. Thus, a person who is assertive in one situation tends to be assertive in another. A person who is unassertive at age 13 tends to be unassertive at 23, 33, 43, and so forth. This does not mean that a given situation exerts no influence on behavior. A situation might, for instance, stimulate an unassertive person to speak up for his/her rights. In general, trait approaches maintain that there is a fairly high degree of consistency in trait behaviors across time and situations. This idea has sparked a good deal of controversy which we will review in the next section.

A *contextual* view of communication behavior contends that behavior is characteristic within contexts but varies across contexts. Some examples of contexts would be family, school, or work. In this view, how one communicates on the job is not a good predictor of how one communicates at home. Communication competence is sometimes claimed to be contextual. For instance, being a competent communicator in public speaking situations does not mean one will be a competent interviewer or cocktail party conversationalist. Similarly, a good interpersonal communicator may be a poor public speaker. This position contradicts that of a trait theorist who would expect someone who is very competent in one communication situation to be highly competent in all situations. The popularity of examining communication contextually is indicated by textbooks (such as this one) which have separate chapters on communication in interpersonal, organizational, and mass media contexts. This approach indicates a belief that communication may be very different in each context, different enough to require separate theories to explain how it occurs.

A *state* differs from a trait because state behavior varies from one situation to another. Trait communication apprehension predicts a uniform level of fear will be associated with real or anticipated communication situations (McCroskey, 1970). State communication apprehension fluctuates with different circumstances. At times your fear might vary from your general trait behavior. You might normally be relatively free from fear about communicating (low in trait apprehension) but might experience a good deal of state apprehension in a specific situation. For example, a student who had usually been confident in public speaking situations, trembled and was almost speechless when she had to pray in front of three thousand people at her graduation. She reported that if she had not written out the prayer beforehand, she would have been too afraid to think of a single word!

Trait behavior, as we noted earlier, can be expected to vary somewhat across situations. In fact, to exhibit precisely the same communication behavior regardless of the situation might indicate that a person is neurotic with obsessive-compulsive symptoms (Infante, 1987a). Trait theorists do not deny that the situation influences behavior. The dispute between trait, situationist, and state theorists concerns degree: how *much* does the behavior vary? Are situations basically different from one another and do their varying characteristics force us to behave in ways that are unique to the given situation? Or, do we tend to place ourselves in situations which we view as functionally equivalent, thus enabling us to repeat favorite behaviors? These questions pertain to the issue of how consistent a person's behavior is across different situations, an issue which has stirred an interesting controversy in personality research.

The Cross-Situational Consistency Issue

The issue concerns whether traits exist and has involved extensive controversy by personality theorists (for reviews see Epstein, 1979; Mischel, 1973). The issue of the stability of behavior across situations has been debated several times in the field of psychology. The most recent controversy began with personality theorist Walter Mischel's (1968) analysis that a correlation of about .30 seems to be the limit of the relationship of behavior in one situation to behavior in another situation. Thus, if we were to observe how *sociable* a group of people appeared to be in one situation by noting the number of greeting smiles and then observed the same people in a different situation, the correlation would be rather low. A 1.00 correlation represents a perfect relationship; behavior in one situation could be predicted with perfect accuracy from behavior in another situation. In our example, if the rank order of the individuals in terms of the number of smiles were exactly the same in the first situation and the second, the correlation would be 1.00. Joe Smith smiled the most in both situations, Sally Jones was second in both, etc. A .30 correlation is low; it indicates considerable variability in smiling behavior from the first to the second situation. Joe Smith ranked first in smiling in situation one but ranked tenth in situation two. While a 1.00 correlation means perfect consistency, .30 means there is some but not much consistency between two sets of observations.

Those who support this idea have been termed *situationsists*. In the social sciences, a situationist believes situations primarily determine behavior because situations are unique and present different demands on the individual. People experience these demands and try to adapt their behavior to the environment. Behavior therefore is shaped by the situations. Since situations are seldom the same, behavior is not consistent across situations. Basically, this position maintains that personality is overwhelmed by the situation. For instance, a person may not be as sociable in one situation as compared to another because one situation is more task oriented and the participants simply do not have as much time or opportunity to act sociably.

Situationists also argue that stability in behavior across situations may be more in the mind of an observer of a person than in the person's actual behavior. That is, we may have a need to see others as consistent because this reduces uncertainty in our lives. We want others to be predictable and dependable because it is easier to deal with reliable than with unreliable behavior. Perhaps due to wishful thinking, we see people as cross-situationally consistent even if they are not; we distort the .30 relationship and make it closer to 1.00.

Traits, according to this view, are more in the minds of perceivers than in the behavior of social actors.

The *trait* position maintains that broad predispositions which explain behavior do exist. Trait theorists argue that a major reason why some research has failed to find consistent behavior across situations is that the studies were conducted in laboratory environments which placed people in unrealistic positions. Forcing people to behave one way or another in artificial situations does not demonstrate that the individuals are also inconsistent in real life. According to the trait view, our personality traits predispose us to seek certain situations which allow us to "be ourselves," to behave characteristically, or to act in ways which reflect our uniqueness. If studies are not designed to permit people to select the situations in which they communicate, then the theory of traits is not being fairly tested by researchers.

A trait approach to personality assumes that there are "ways of behaving" that we associate with the people in our lives. You have probably heard someone say, "That is so much like her to do that," or "I just knew he would do that." We tend to think of people in terms of a cluster of *central traits*. One person might be known best for being friendly, assertive, dominant, competitive, and cheerful, while another person might be shy, neat, polite, anxious, and creative. All traits are not equally important to everyone's personality. For a given trait, some people will show stronger patterns than others across situations, depending upon how important the trait is in the makeup of that individual's personality. For example, the person described as friendly, assertive, dominant, competitive and cheerful might be consistently assertive but might not show strong patterns regarding non-central traits such as neatness.

Another major reason why low cross-situational consistency has been noted, according to trait theorists, is that too few behaviors have been observed in studies. A behavior such as smiling in one situation may not be related to smiling in another because situations can influence behavior to some extent. The idea of a trait is not that behavior in *two* situations should be consistent, but that there should be a pattern across *many* situations. A person who is very sociable (high in the sociability trait) might be friendly in one situation but not in another. However, in looking at the person's sociability behavior across a large number of situations, a distinct pattern should emerge. For example, behavior might be characterized as sociable in 35 out of 40 situations. A person who is not very sociable (low in the trait) might be sociable in Situation 1 and Situation 2, yet he or she should not be very sociable over time. Sociable behavior might occur in only 8 out of 40 situations. A good deal of research indicates that such trait patterns do exist (for example see Block, 1971; Costa & McCrae, 1980; Epstein, 1979; Stagner, 1977).

The *interactionist* position emerged from the conflict between trait and situationist theorists. Interactionists maintain that behavior in a particular situation is a *joint* product of a person's traits and of variables in the situation.

To ignore either of these influences on behavior results in less understanding of a person's actions. The interactionist position represents an attempt to integrate trait and situationist positions—to show they are compatible and not inherently antagonistic. According to an interactionist approach, trait and situational variables interact with one another to produce behavior. This means they influence one another and thereby create something which is unique, behavior which cannot be explained by the person's traits alone or by the situation alone. For instance, to predict whether a person will ask someone to turn down loud music, we must know not only whether the person has an assertive personality trait but also important characteristics of the situation. Is the loud music interfering with study for final exams? If the music is not blocking an important goal such as passing a difficult course, even an assertive person may say nothing. The interactionist position emphasizes the need to consider both trait and situational factors in predicting behavior.

Communication theories tend to be either trait or situationist in nature. It has been recommended that communication research should take an interactionist approach instead of the more fragmented approach of examining only traits or only situations (Andersen, 1987; Infante, 1987b). Ignoring one factor leads to less than complete knowledge of communication. In the final section of this chapter we will examine a theory of argumentativeness which represents a recent communication theory that takes an interactionist approach.

The cross-situational consistency debate in psychology has been important for the field of communication because it caused scholars to realize that there are trait and situationist approaches to communication also. Unlike the field of psychology, trait and situationist researchers in communication have largely ignored one another. The situationist models of communication are inadequate because they cannot explain the many results found in trait research. Trait models are lacking because they cannot account for differences in behavior due to the situation. It seems obvious that combining the trait and situationist approaches would be desirable, and taking an interactionist approach is a promising way for researchers to do so.

This debate in psychology has also been valuable because it has largely answered the question of how consistent behavior is across situations. Research indicates that behavior is consistent when enough relevant situations are considered. Personality traits are meaningful, and to view communication behavior in terms of communication traits is a valid way to study humans. In addition to demonstrating cross-situational consistency, the research has suggested other areas in need of study. The focus on consistency has revealed not only that inconsistency occurs, but that scientists do not yet adequately understand why it occurs. Models need to be developed to account for differences in behavior. Is a given difference due entirely to occurrences within the situation? Is someone very sociable at parties but very quiet when working as a librarian? Or is there a trait such as a need for novelty or variety that would predict that very sociable individuals choose jobs in which sociable behavior is appropriate? While it is important for researchers to investigate regularities in communication, unexpected, novel, and creative communicative behavior may be even more challenging to study.

Personality Traits and Communication

Personality theory and research by psychologists has been of interest to communication researchers for the past several decades. Many communication studies have explored how personality influences communication, especially in persuasion situations. We will briefly survey some of the major traits which have been examined (for a review of this literature see Steinfatt, 1987).

Persuasibility

Research reported in the book *Personality and Persuasibility* (Hovland & Janis, 1959) suggests that there is a personality trait which predicts how much a person is influenced by persuasion attempts, regardless of the topic, source, or situation. This idea appears to be valid. Some people seem easy to persuade. They rarely resist pressure to move in one direction or another. This willingness to change can be viewed as persuasibility. Also, other individuals seem consistently difficult to persuade. They rarely budge on any issue. In essence, they seem resistant to persuasion.

The idea of a persuasibility trait appears to be an uncomplicated way to explain susceptibility to social influence. However, conceptually the matter is not so clear. Is there such a trait, or are there other personality traits sometimes related to persuasion which create the illusion of a general persuasibility trait? In that regard, the traits which follow have been found to be related to persuasion. The amount of persuasibility indicated by each trait, when viewed as a whole, could create the impression that there is a more global persuasibility trait.

Self-Esteem

Self-esteem refers to how favorably the individual evaluates self and is a trait which is related to persuasion (Infante, 1976). When individuals have low self-esteem, they lack self-confidence in general, and they have little faith that their positions on controversial issues are valid. When told by a speaker that their positions should be changed, they tend to believe the speaker, "The speaker must know what is right on this, for I certainly do not know." Low self-esteem is a psychologically uncomfortable state which people would like to change. One way to get more favorable feelings about self is to obtain favorable feedback from valued others. A persuasion situation with an esteemed source presents that opportunity. To agree with a source can result in a favorable reaction, being liked by the source. Also, adopting an esteemed source's ideas provides a means for identifying with the source, and this perceived similarity can increase self-esteem; e.g., "I must not be so bad because I am similar to ..., who is very well regarded."

High self-esteem, on the other hand, is thought to be related to low persuasibility. When people feel very good about themselves, they are also confident about their positions on controversial issues since opinions are a part of one's identity. Satisfaction with oneself usually discourages change. Therefore, individuals with high self-esteem tend to resist persuasion.

Dogmatism

Rokeach (1960) conceptualized dogmatism in terms of individuals' willingness to consider belief systems other than the ones which they hold. A belief system is represented by what one associates with an object or issue. Open-minded individuals are willing to consider other sets of beliefs, even if they feel very strongly about an issue. Dogmatic or closed-minded persons are unwilling to do so. They have a set of beliefs for an issue, and they do not want to be bothered by other belief systems.

Dogmatic people find it very difficult to separate a source from the source's message. Thus, if a dogmatic person likes a source, he or she tends to accept the source's message; if they dislike a speaker, rarely will the speaker's message persuade them. The open-minded person, however, has no trouble reacting differently to source and message; e.g., "I can't stand the speaker, but he makes a good point." When the source is viewed as credible, dogmatism is associated with persuasion. This is especially true when the persuasion topic is not very important to the individual. Dogmatic people tend to be rather easy to persuade when given a credible source and a less important topic. This also suggests that open-minded persons are not necessarily easy to persuade. When the source is credible and the topic rather unimportant, open-minded people are more difficult to persuade than dogmatic individuals.

Machiavellianism

The trait of Machiavellianism refers to an orientation in which people believe that manipulating others is a basic strategy of social influence (Christie & Geis, 1970). Individuals who are high in Machiavellianism think it is ethical to tell people only what they want to hear, to use the receivers' doubts, fears, and insecurities to motivate action, and even to distort facts so they become more acceptable. Generally these people are willing to use whatever strategy works in persuasion; they are very pragmatic. High Machiavellians tend to be less emotional than other people and act rather detached. In a debate on the issue "Does the end justify the means?", high Machiavellians would tend to argue "yes." Persons with a high level of this trait have a strong need to influence others, they like leadership positions, and they are usually dominant rather than submissive in their relations with other people.

Low Machiavellians, on the other hand, are very nonmanipulative in dealing with people. They want to avoid pressuring others, to allow others maximum freedom to decide for themselves. Low Machiavellians tend to have little need to dominate and influence others. They tend to be more emotional than high Machiavellians in discussing a controversial issue.

Cognitive Complexity

Cognitive complexity may be thought of as a trait that pertains to our system of personal constructs. Remember that a construct is a bi-polar pair of terms such as honest-dishonest or exciting-dull, which we apply to our environment to obtain meaning. People in a society share a common core of constructs because of their shared culture, resulting in some fairly "standard" meanings. However, people also develop pairs of idiosyncratic constructs, opposites that are rather unique to the individual. The pair humorous-deadly would be an example of an unusual pairing. Individuals experience meaning in a situation depending upon which constructs they apply and which pole of each construct is associated with the situation (for example, either *exciting* or *dull*). The basic idea is that people use their construct systems to "construct" reality (Delia, 1977). Reality is not "out there somewhere." It is in your head; you create your reality with your construct system.

Cognitive complexity, then, may be thought of as a characteristic or trait of one's construct system. You will remember from Chapter 3 that someone who is cognitively complex has a greater number of constructs which are both more abstract and more interconnected than someone who is cognitively simple. Cognitive complexity is important because it is related to important communication processes. The greater one's cognitive complexity, the better able one is to imagine how *other* people view a situation. Social perspective-taking ability is a key determinant of successful communication. With this ability one is able to understand another person's concerns by seeing things from his or her perspective. This means the more complex person is better able to adapt a message to a particular receiver. If a message is not adapted to the audience, it seems impersonal, generic, and often less than relevant. Since the probability of success in persuasion is usually lower if the message is not tailored to the likes and dislikes of the receiver, cognitively complex sources should be better persuaders.

Need for Social Approval

People vary in their need for social approval and the extent to which they fear social disapproval (Crowne & Marlowe, 1960). According to this idea, a source who offers social approval, or threatens social disapproval when the receiver has a strong need for approval, ought to be very persuasive. Various forms of opinionated language specified by Rokeach (1960) provide a way to test this relationship. *Opinionated acceptance* language expresses a favorable attitude toward those people who agree with the speaker; e.g., "Intelligent and responsible people will agree that my proposal is needed." *Opinionated rejection* language states a negative attitude toward those who disagree with the speaker's position; e.g., "Only a bigoted fool would oppose this plan." Opinionated acceptance language represents social approval, while opinionated rejection constitutes social disapproval. Baseheart (1971) found support for the idea that opinionated language leads to more persuasion when people have a strong need for social approval. In such a circumstance, opinionated rejection was as successful as opinionated acceptance in stimulating persuasion. Having a strong need for social approval probably heightens a person's sensitivity to language which suggests the speaker is evaluating the receiver in some way.

Communication Traits

Communication traits may be viewed as personality traits which are concerned particularly with human symbolic behavior. Therefore, communication traits represent a subset of the larger set of personality traits, and definitions of personality traits given at the beginning of this chapter are relevant to communication traits. An adaptation of Mischel's (1968) definition to make it more communication oriented could be: *A communication trait is an abstraction which is constructed to account for enduring consistencies and differences in individuals' message sending and message receiving behaviors.* We will examine four classes of communication traits in this chapter: apprehension, presentation, adaptation, aggression.

Apprehension Traits

Communication Apprehension

Due to a most ambitious research program by James C. McCroskey and his associates, communication apprehension is probably the most thoroughly researched topic in the history of the communication discipline (for a good overview of the research see Richmond & McCroskey, 1985). Hundreds of studies have been conducted during this and the past decade. As a result, an impressive body of knowledge exists. In 1970 McCroskey defined communication apprehension as "a broadly based anxiety related to oral communication" (p. 270). This definition was expanded in later work to "an individual's level of fear or anxiety associated with either real or anticipated communication with another person or persons" (McCroskey, 1977, p. 78).

There are four types of communication apprehension (CA). *Traitlike CA* is the relatively stable degree of anxiety a person experiences across communication contexts (public speaking, meetings, interpersonal and group communication) and over time. Traitlike CA reflects a personality orientation and has been the major focus of study. Although people tend to be consistent across contexts and time, in some people communication apprehension varies across contexts. This is termed *Context-Based CA*. For instance, some people are more fearful of speaking before a large crowd than of taking part in a group discussion. Or, some people have little fear of giving speeches but are uncomfortable talking with people on a one-to-one basis. Thus, it is meaningful to consider the context when studying CA.

Audience-Based CA is fear experienced when communicating with certain types of people regardless of the time or context. The particular audience members trigger the fear reaction. A person who is apprehensive about communicating with parents, for instance, will experience CA when giving a speech if the parents are in the audience even though the person has little fear of public speaking. The person experiences fear similar to that felt when talking with the parents interpersonally.

Situational CA is the degree of fear experienced in talking with a given person or persons in a given situation. This is the apprehension created by variables unique to a particular situation. People who are high in CA are not always fearful, and low CAs sometimes do experience fear. What accounts for this inconsistency with one's trait? Variables in the given situation probably best explain such discrepancies. For instance, a person who is low in CA might become apprehensive if the person is told a great deal depends upon a superior performance. Pressure can result in even very confident people "choking" in terms of performance.

There is basically only one internal effect of CA; the person feels psychologically uncomfortable. Manifestations of this feeling are "butterflies" in the stomach, shaking hands and knees, dry mouth, excessive perspiration, elevated heart rate, increased respiration rate, and increased blood pressure. What does it mean for someone to experience this internal effect on a regular, traitlike, basis? The research is striking in terms of how debilitating it is to be apprehensive about communication. For instance, people with high CA are perceived by others as less competent, have less academic success, take jobs with lower communication requirements, are less satisfied with work, are not viewed as leaders, and are seen as less friendly and less attractive than people with low CA. Richmond and McCroskey (1985) conclude that the more talkative, low CA person "is perceived to be more competent in general, more communicatively competent, less anxious about communication, more composed and extroverted, more assertive and responsive, generally a leader and an opinion leader, more friendly and sociable, and more attractive" (p. 60).

There are several speculations about what causes CA. A *low self-esteem* explanation posits that people fear communication when they have an unfavorable concept of self and therefore anticipate that they will do poorly. A *parental reinforcement* model predicts that when children are positively reinforced for communicating, they communicate more and develop less CA. On the other hand, when children are negatively reinforced by being told not to disagree with adults or are reinforced inconsistently by being allowed to talk at the dinner table one day but not another, they learn to withdraw from communication and therefore become apprehensive about it because they have learned to expect punishment afterwards. An *inherited trait* explanation suggests that traits such as sociability are inherited. Persons who inherit a low sociability trait are especially susceptible to developing CA if their communicative behavior is not positively reinforced.

Three additional causes are linked to methods for reducing CA. *Excessive activation* as a theory of cause says that fear of communication is a result of a physiological overreaction to an event—trembling, difficulty in swallowing, or temporary loss of memory. If the person is taught to control the overreactions, CA for all practical purposes is reduced. A method of therapy, *systematic desensitization*, is based on this assumption and appears to work very well. This involves learning to relax while thinking about various kinds of anxiety-producing communication events. *Inappropriate cognitive processing* posits that what high CA and low CA people experience physically is very similar, but, what they "think" they experience is very different. The physical sensation of "butterflies in the stomach" may be perceived by some people as a mild, normal reaction to public speaking, whereas other people interpret it as a major loss of control. Thus, to change CA, one needs only to change one's mind about communication. *Cognitive restructuring* is a therapy method employed for this. It involves identifying and changing irrational beliefs about self and also formulating new positive beliefs. The *inadequate communication skills* model of CA maintains people are apprehensive about communication because they know they are not very good at the activity. Fear is a quite normal and predictable response to a situation that one does not know how to deal with competently. The treatment approach for this is *communication skills training*. This is a very popular approach exemplified by speech and communication courses in educational institutions.

Receiver Apprehension

Wheeless (1975) maintained that CA is a multi-faceted construct which includes dimensions pertaining to sending and receiving information in formal and informal contexts. The Personal Report of Communication Apprehension (PRCA) questionnaire developed by McCroskey (1970) focuses on fear of sending messages. A typical item on the scale is, "I look forward to expressing my opinion at meetings." If people are apprehensive about sending messages, it seems reasonable to speculate that they may also be anxious about receiving messages from others. According to Wheeless (1975), receiver apprehension "is probably related more to fear of misinterpreting, inadequately processing, and/or not being able to adjust psychologically to messages sent by others" (p. 263). The Receiver Apprehension Test (RAT) was developed by Wheeless (1975) to measure this trait. His research suggests receiver and source apprehension appear to be two separate dimensions of CA. When dimensions are separate or independent, they are not related to one another. Thus, if you are high in source apprehension, you are not necessarily high in receiver apprehension.

For receiver apprehension, formal and informal communication contexts are not separate. This means the degree of receiver apprehension one feels in one context such as a public speech is similar to the degree experienced in other contexts such as talking with a friend. Someone's level of receiver apprehension in one situation can be predicted from knowing about his or her receiver apprehension in another context. Wheeless' research suggests this is also true for source apprehension.

Writing Apprehension

Daly and Miller (1975) developed the Writing Apprehension Test (WAT) to study fears about writing. Their conception of writing apprehension is that some people fear evaluation of their writing behavior, expect to fail in activities requiring writing, and avoid situations where writing is a requirement. The WAT is used in the field of English to study and help people who suffer from these fears. The correlation between oral communication apprehension (as measured by the PRCA) and written communication (as measured by the WAT) is about .30. This suggests there is a weak relationship between oral and written apprehension. You cannot predict very accurately whether a person who is apprehensive about oral communication will also be apprehensive about written communication.

Unwillingness to Communicate

The three types of apprehension which we discussed may be viewed as facets of a broader, more global, trait—unwillingness to communicate. Burgoon (1976) conceived of this as "a chronic tendency to avoid and/or devalue oral communication" (p. 60). Source, receiver, and writing apprehension can be reasons why a person is unwilling to communicate. However, there are several other reasons, each contributing to the broad nature of this trait.

Social alienation results when people do not adopt societal values and norms but instead develop feelings of insecurity, isolation, and powerlessness. Socially alienated people are unwilling to communicate because they are distrustful. *Introversion* is responsible for some unwillingness to communicate because the introvert places less value on communication and therefore has less need for it than the extrovert. *Self-esteem* is a part of the unwillingness to communicate syndrome because individuals who have low self-esteem expect others to react negatively. As a result, they are less motivated to communicate because they expect to fail. A related reason for an unwillingness to communicate is *skills deficiency*; people communicate less when they realize they do not possess a level of skill adequate for successful communication (Richmond & McCroskey, 1985). Finally, people might be unwilling to communicate when they are *ethnically/culturally divergent* (Richmond & McCroskey, 1985). When people are members of an ethnic minority, for example, they may be hesitant to communicate with people who represent the majority because the majority may criticize the use of language by the minority. Their unwillingness to communicate results from wanting to avoid the stress of dealing with critical people. The next section discusses the second type of communication traits, traits which influence the ways in which we orally convey our personalities to others.

Presentation Traits

Predispositions toward Verbal Behavior

Mortensen, Arntson, and Lustig (1977) created a questionnaire to measure Predispositions toward Verbal Behavior (PVB), the first type of presentation trait to be discussed. Their definition of this predisposition is similar to that of a personality trait: "an internalized cognitive map of the structure of interactions, a metacode of formal relations governing the interplay of verbal activity between self and others" (p. 147). This definition follows that of Shontz (1965), who said the study of personality "is defined by its concern for inferred mediational processes that account for organization in the behavior of the individual" (p. 7). The basic idea here is that the global features of our verbal behavior are rather consistent from one situation to the next. Sometimes we make our speech sound like that of the person with whom we are speaking; if the person sounds excited, we put some excitement in our voices. There do seem to be unique, characteristic ways that each of us uses his or her voice. These patterns may be controlled by a trait, our predispositions toward verbal behavior. What are the features of our voice that tend to be consistent, traitlike? Mortensen and Arntson (1974) identified five: (1) hesitating, pausing; (2) vocal forcefulness; (3) length of utterances; (4) verbosity; (5) dominance.

If people have a "cognitive map" that they follow in behaving verbally, the extent to which the cognitive map which people say they follow actually corresponds to their verbal *behavior* is an important issue. Mortensen and Arntson (1974) discovered such a correspondence. They interviewed 72 persons who scored either high, moderate, or low on the PVB scale and found that those who scored highest had the most verbal activity and that their own perceptions of their verbal characteristics were more favorable than those of persons who were low on the trait. Moderates fell between these two extremes. There is thus some evidence that the PVB trait works like a cognitive map that people are aware of and use to guide their verbal behavior.

Communicator Style

The next presentation trait, communicator style, concerns a more specific type of self-presentation and was developed from a model by Robert Norton (1978, 1983). Communicator style is concerned with the *ways* messages are communicated, not with the content of messages. According to Norton (1978) communicator style is "the way one verbally and paraverbally interacts to signal how literal meaning should be taken, interpreted, filtered, or understood" (p. 99). Style gives form to content and accumulates over time so that we develop an overall, more global impression of a person's communicator style (Norton, 1983, p. 283). A person is eventually perceived as having a particular style as a communicator.

Communicator style may be viewed as an overall impression, a *communicator image*, which is composed of at least ten traits: impression leaving, contentious, open, dramatic, dominant, precise, relaxed, friendly, attentive, and animated. The degree to which an individual possesses each of these traits contributes to the person's image. With ten traits a large number of possible combinations exist; for example, high on two of them, moderate on three, low on five. Each configuration of the set of traits creates a different overall impression. For instance, a person who is dominant, animated, and friendly is perceived as very different from another person who is also dominant and animated, but is unfriendly. The unfriendly trait might be so prominent that impressions of this person's other prominent traits might be perceived more negatively when compared with the same traits in someone else. The unfriendly trait might lead to the dominant and animated traits being viewed as manipulative and not-to-be-trusted. How a person's traits combine, therefore, is crucial to the overall image that is created.

We will review briefly the meaning of each of the traits which comprise communicator style. *Impression leaving* is the tendency to try to create a lasting image in the minds of receivers. This is a goal which the person is aware of when talking with people. *Contentious* is a disposition to challenge others when disagreements occur, to argue with others. While arguing constructively is a very positive trait (to be discussed later), contentiousness appears to be a somewhat negative trait because it involves arguing too much, getting "carried away" by the emotion in a situation, being unwilling to end an argument gracefully and instead pursuing it to "the bitter end." *Open* is a trait which means liking to reveal feelings, thoughts, and personal information. The person takes pride in being honest and in not hiding things from others. *Dramatic* style involves telling jokes and stories to illustrate points, exaggerating for emphasis, and generally creating the impression of "acting" when talking with people. *Dominant* denotes coming on strong, speaking frequently, taking leadership roles, and wanting to control social situations. *Precise* includes insisting that people document what they are saying and that they give definitions. Generally, a person with this trait tries very hard to be accurate and thorough. *Relaxed* means not having nervous mannerisms in speech or bodily communication; pride is taken in appearing relaxed in stressful situations. *Friendly* involves praising, encouraging, and expressing liking for others. *Attentive* is the tendency to listen carefully to people, to be able to repeat back what others say, and to act so that people know you are listening. *Animated* is a trait which signifies extensive use of eyes, face, and gestures to express meaning.

Infante and Gorden (1981) used the communicator style model to investigate communication between superiors and subordinates in organizations. They explored how similarities and differences in the communicator styles of an employee and a boss related to the employee's satisfaction. Are there certain traits on which subordinates like to be similar to their bosses, and are there other traits on which subordinates like to differ? The study found employees were most satisfied when dramatic and animated traits were similar but relaxed, open, and attentive traits were different. Subordinates might like to be similar to superiors on dramatic and animated traits because if a boss is different (much more dramatic and animated than the subordinate), the subordinate may be uneasy and perhaps feel somewhat inferior because the boss exerts so much more energy than the subordinate.

In another study Gorden, Infante, and Braun (1986) investigated the communicator style traits of fashion innovators and fashion laggards. A fashion innovator was conceived as one who adopts recent fashion changes, while a fashion laggard was one who adopts a fashion change after a long time, or one who never adopts it. The study found that fashion innovators, when compared to fashion laggards, were higher on impression-leaving, dramatic, friendly, and animated traits. These traits comprise what has been called the "energy expenditure" dimension of communicator style. This finding supported the hypothesis that people who communicate at a high energy level would also "dress for the part." That is, they would wear more dramatic, attention-getting, and current fashions.

Disclosiveness

Self-disclosure, revealing intimate information about oneself, is a presentational trait which plays an important part in the development of close relationships. The general model is that trust is developed and strengthened when both persons self-disclose and show support for the partner's disclosures. Thus, one person reveals something—a like, a fear, a secret goal—and, if the other person is supportive, this revelation encourages more, and more intimate, disclosures. The other person may feel a need to reciprocate the disclosure, so the individuals might take turns sharing. It is probably impossible to develop a close personal relationship without self-disclosure. In fact, not to self-disclose is probably a way of telling another person that you do not want the relationship to progress to a more personal or intimate level. Wheeless (1978) developed a scale to measure the tendency to self-disclose as a trait. According to Wheeless, disclosiveness represents "a person's predilection to disclose to other people in general—his or her generalized openness in encoding" (1978, p. 144). Wheeless' model specifies that, for persons to be high in disclosiveness, they must also trust others a great deal. Thus, people who are not very trusting will be especially cautious about revealing feelings to others.

The Disclosiveness Scale measures the trait of self-disclosure in terms of five dimensions. The *intent* dimension involves the degree of awareness that one is revealing information about self. Having intent to self-disclose may mean that the individual views disclosure as a strategy in relating to other people. *Amount* pertains to the frequency of disclosure relative to other types of messages in interpersonal communication. *Positiveness* is a subscale which measures the extent to which the information revealed about self is positive or negative. *Depth* refers to how superficial or intimate the information is. The *honesty* dimension involves the sincerity of disclosure.

Clothing Predispositions

Another form of self-presentation is the clothing that we wear. Certainly clothing is used to protect the body from the elements of nature, but humans also use clothing symbolically: clothing communicates. The language of dress expresses how we feel about ourselves and can provide information about a person's values, profession, and attitudes toward sex. Research suggests clothing is important in interactions with others. For instance, studies have found the well-dressed individual is picked up more often when hitchhiking, receives help more readily, obtains directions more easily, has his/her space invaded less, receives more tips, and is followed more when crossing a street against the light. Moreover, well-dressed people tend to create first impressions of success, power, positive habits, and the ability to earn money.

A questionnaire to measure clothing predispositions was developed by Rosenfeld and Plax (1977). The scale has four dimensions. *Clothing consciousness* involves liking to "dress up," spending much time dressing, having people notice what one is wearing, being in style, spending a good deal of money on clothes, and keeping up with the latest fashion news. *Exhibitionism* as a dimension of one's clothing predispositions means liking clothes which are sexy, close-fitting, revealing, and have bold designs. *Practicality* implies less concern for fashion and beauty than function and a strong inclination toward comfort; e.g., "all that I care is that it keeps me warm." The *designer* dimension pertains to the individuals' desire to be a model or a clothes designer.

This scale was used in a study by Gorden, Tengler, and Infante (1982), who speculated that individuals' clothing predispositions should have important consequences in the workplace. They reasoned that individuals would be more satisfied with their jobs and successful when their clothing predispositions matched usual expectations for proper attire on the job. The results of a study of 300 employees from more than 200 companies revealed that employees who were high in clothing consciousness dressed more conservatively on the job (dressed as expected), were more satisfied with their jobs, and received more promotions. People who were high in exhibitionism dressed more casually on the job, and they received fewer promotions. How one dresses on the job may communicate to superiors whether the individual accepts company values. Individuals whose clothing indicates they do not support company values may be ignored when promotions and other important job decisions are made.

Adaptation Traits

In contrast to the presentation traits just discussed, adaptation traits influence how we adapt to conversational partners. Three major categories of adaptation traits, rhetorical sensitivity, communication competence, and interaction involvement will be discussed in this section.

Rhetorical Sensitivity, Noble Self, Rhetorical Reflector

Hart, Carlson, and Eadie (1980) positioned a trait called *rhetorical sensitivity* with respect to two other traits, *noble self* and *rhetorical reflector*. Persons who are *noble selves* believe in expressing exactly what they think or feel. To do otherwise, they believe, betrays their "real self." Thus, a noble self who dislikes something feels compelled to express that dislike even though other people might not want to hear such a negative assessment, or even though the negative comments might create difficulties for the speaker. Noble selves do not value flexibility in adapting to different audiences. Noble selves view the idea of presenting a message one way to some people and another way to other people as misrepresenting their true beliefs. They believe a message should be created to suit self, not others. Thus, the noble self tends to have a script (a sequence of events which a person expects in a situation) for a given topic and uses that script, with little change, in all situations in which the topic is discussed. For instance, if a noble self has a script of critical views on the President's domestic policy, she says about the same thing when talking to the President's supporters as when talking with critics. No attempt is made to appease the listener, to put the message in more "acceptable" terms.

The *rhetorical reflector* is at the other end of this spectrum. Rhetorical reflectors conceive of their "selves" not as fixed entities but as social "characters" who take on whatever role is necessary for the particular situation. "Self" is a servant of the person and of necessity is highly changeable and adaptable. Rhetorical reflectors take pride in seeing the type of person needed in a situation and then becoming that person. They see flexibility as a most important trait. They emphasize "telling people what they want to hear," expressing a position on an issue in terms of the attitudes, values, hopes, fears, and desires of the receiver. The rhetorical reflector believes in being the kind of person others want him or her to be. This does not mean being dishonest. For rhetorical reflectors honesty is not the issue. Their concern is with the *requirements* of the situation. What type of person are people looking for and what do they want to hear? As you would expect, the scripts of the rhetorical reflector are not as fixed as those of the noble self. Rhetorical reflectors probably have very general scripts for controversial issues and situations which they adapt to the given situation.

Rhetorical sensitivity is intermediate with respect to the noble self and rhetorical reflection extremes. According to Hart, Carlson, and Eadie (1980), the rhetorically sensitive person believes there is no single self but a complex network of selves, such as father, husband, accountant, church member, golfer. Rhetorically sensitive persons do not adopt the constantly changing character of the rhetorical reflector, but neither do they agree with noble selves that individuals have only one immutable self. Rhetorical sensitives are flexible, but they neither sacrifice their values to please others nor ignore the needs of other people when communicating with them. Rhetorical sensitivity avoids the rigidity of the noble self and the chameleon character of the rhetorical reflector. While the rhetorical reflector sees messages as a means to please others, the rhetorical sensitive is more concerned with the function of messages in creating understanding. Thus, messages on a topic vary from audience to audience in terms of what it takes to make an idea clear and meaningful to people. The rhetorical sensitivity trait involves an appreciation for the idea that communicating ideas and feelings to people need not be either rigid nor overly accommodating.

A study of more than 3000 college students (Hart, Carlson, & Eadie, 1980) found noble selves tended to be single, Democratic, liberal, live in cities in the eastern U.S., come from larger, lower income families, and be more likely to take pride in their ethnic origins. Rhetorical reflectors tended to be conservative, women, 21 years or older, married, academically noncompetitive, conservative Protestants, regular churchgoers, and to come from low to middle socioeconomic classes. Rhetorical sensitives were more likely to be male, competitive, from higher income, upper middle socioeconomic classes, low in ethnic identification, and Republican or politically Independent. In other research Gorden and Infante (1980) found that freedom of speech was valued most by noble selves and least by rhetorical reflectors. Rhetorical sensitives were slightly less likely to value freedom of speech than noble selves. These results were consistent with the socio-political orientations of noble selves (liberal) and rhetorical reflectors (conservative) found by Hart, Carlson, and Eadie (1980). People with more liberal ideologies tend to be more supportive of the exercise of the First Amendment.

Communication Competence

Communication competence is an adaptation trait which has received a good deal of attention by communication researchers (for instance see Rubin, 1982, 1985; Spitzberg & Cupach, 1984; Wiemann, 1977). Communication competence involves *appropriateness* and *effectiveness* and may eventually be found to involve other traits. Appropriateness means verbal and nonverbal communication which results in no loss of face for the parties involved. Effectiveness refers to the speaker's achieving communicative goals. There is some controversy as to whether communication competence is a trait or whether it is contextual or situational. If communication competence is a trait, then it is context free and is an attribute of the individual. Thus, if a person communicates competently in one context (at work), the person would tend also to communicate in a competent manner in other contexts (at school or at a party). Basically, a trait approach maintains there is considerable consistency in communication competency across a variety of situations.

A contextual approach maintains that our communicative behavior is influenced greatly by elements of context: the time, place, activity, and people involved. The nature of communication on the job, for instance, is greatly different from communication in the family. Therefore, contextual theorists maintain, having the skills to be good at one does not insure that one will be good at the other. In other words, according to a contextual approach, you may be effective in getting subordinates to be more productive but might fail in motivating your children to work harder. Some research supports this contextual view of communication competence (e.g., Onyekwere, Rubin, & Infante, 1987).

Unfortunately, there has been little research to resolve the trait versus contextual controversy. There is some intuitive appeal of a trait approach since we can usually think of some people who are such good communicators that they never appear to communicate inappropriately or ineffectively. On the other hand, there are some persons who never do seem to measure up to the standards of competent communication. Thus, cross-situational consistency for some people seems high. However, such individuals may represent the extremes (high and low) of the distribution of people in terms of communication competence. People who are more moderate in communication competence may be much less consistent across contexts. That is, communication competence may be contextual for people who are neither extremely good nor poor communicators. Thus, a person who is moderate in terms of trait communication competence might be very competent in some contexts such as work groups, low in others such as intimate relationships, and moderately competent in the remainder such as social functions.

There is a further possibility that communication competence contains a trait component but is also influenced by the context or situation. The real explanatory power of a trait aspect of competence may be the way the trait interacts with factors in the particular situation. The trait examined in the next section represents such a possibility.

Interaction Involvement

Interaction involvement has been defined as "the extent to which an individual participates with another in conversation" (Cegala, Savage, Brunner, & Conrad, 1982, p. 229). Individuals who are highly involved tend to focus their attention on self, the other person, the situation, and the topic of communication. They are able to integrate their thoughts, feelings, and experiences with the interaction as it develops. People who are higher in interaction involvement generally are viewed as more competent communicators. Persons who are low in interaction involvement tend to be "removed" from the situation. They seem to be preoccupied with other things, to be distracted, and to have a difficult time remembering the content of conversations. Typically these individuals are judged as low in communication competence.

People can vary at times in how much involvement they experience. For instance, persons who are usually highly involved in conversations may occasionally find themselves experiencing low involvement. Despite such fluctuation there appears to be a characteristic level of interaction involvement which people prefer. Therefore, interaction involvement appears to be very trait-like. Cegala (1984) does emphasize an interactionist position—that factors in the given situation such as the degree of competitiveness can affect the amount of interaction involvement experienced.

Research suggests there are three aspects or dimensions of interaction involvement. *Responsiveness* according to Cegala et al. (1982) "is a tendency to react mentally to one's social circumstance and adapt by knowing what to say and when to say it" (1982, p. 233). This reaction pertains to appropriateness and involves such aspects as alertness, judgment, and creativity. *Perceptiveness* "is an individual's general sensitivity to: (1) what meanings ought to be applied to others' behavior; and (2) what meanings others have applied to one's own behavior" (Cegala, 1984, p. 321). Perceptiveness is concerned with social intelligence in the sense of assessing meanings important to the competent communicator. *Attentiveness* "is the extent to which one tends to heed cues in the immediate environment, especially one's interlocutor" (Cegala, 1984, p. 321). Attentiveness reflects the individual's awareness of what comprises the environment.

Taken together, responsiveness, perceptiveness, and attentiveness are three tendencies which determine the individual's level of interaction involvement. Being high on all three or low on all three is an easy pattern to imagine. However, other combinations are possible. For instance, a person might be high on perceptiveness and attentiveness but lower on responsiveness. Such a person is competent in terms of the cognitive aspects of communication competence, but is not able to be responsive putting the knowledge into action.

Research has focused on how interaction involvement relates to other interaction traits such as communication apprehension, nonverbal communication, and leadership style. Cegala (1984) found that highly involved individuals could better process information and recall details of conversations. Also, they had stronger egos, felt more positive and friendly, prouder, and stronger than persons low in interaction involvement. According to Cegala (1984), for low involvement persons, conversations with strangers may create uncertainty, which results in greater fear or anxiety. Similarly, to low involvement people a competitive situation also represents a threat, which results in fear.

Aggression Traits

Although not typical of the majority of our communicative behaviors, the final type of traits to be discussed, aggressive communication, tends to be very important because of its consequences. A communicative behavior "may be considered aggressive if it applies force physically and/or symbolically in order, minimally, to dominate and perhaps damage or, maximally, to defeat and perhaps destroy the locus of attack. The locus of attack in interpersonal communication can be a person's body, material possessions, self-concept, positions on topics of communication, or behavior" (Infante, 1987a, p. 158). Thus, communication is aggressive when a person tries to "force" another person to believe something or to behave in a particular way. To force someone means to put such pressure on them that they do not really have a choice. According to a recent model of aggressive communication (Infante, 1987a), this force can be constructive or destructive in interpersonal relations. Aggression is constructive if it facilitates interpersonal communication satisfaction and enhances a relationship. Examples of physical aggression which can do this are sports, games, and playfulness such as mock assaults. Examples employing symbolic aggression might be defending one's rights without infringing upon the rights of other people, as in persuading someone to cooperate on a new venture. On the other hand, aggressive communication is destructive when it produces dissatisfaction and reduces the quality of a relationship. Destructive types of physical aggression include violence against persons (e.g., spouse-beating) and violence directed at objects (e.g., crushing someone's favorite hat). Examples of destructive symbolic aggression include insulting a person, swearing at someone, and expressing bitter resentment.

Infante's (1987a) model of aggressive communication maintains that symbolic aggression is energized by a set of four personality traits. The idea is that the aggressive dimension of our personalities is not composed of a single trait but rather is a complex combination of competing predispositions. Two of these traits are constructive, and two are destructive. The generally constructive traits are assertiveness and argumentativeness, while the usually destructive traits are hostility and verbal aggressiveness.

Assertiveness

Assertiveness may be defined as "a person's general tendency to be interpersonally dominant, ascendant, and forceful" (Infante, 1987a, p. 165). Alberti and Emmons (1974), who were influential in popularizing assertiveness training, said assertiveness involves people acting in their own best interests, defending their rights without undue anxiety, expressing honest feelings comfortably, and exercising their rights without denying others' rights.

Lorr and More (1980) developed a questionnaire for measuring assertiveness and discovered four major dimensions. *Directiveness* involves leadership, taking charge in group situations, and seeking positions where one can influence others. *Social assertiveness* occurs when the individual is able to start conversations with strangers, feels comfortable around a wide variety of people, and generally is able to initiate desired relationships. *Defense of rights and interests* is a dimension of assertiveness which pertains, for example, to a person's willingness to return a purchase which is defective, to tell others when they are creating a disturbance, or to confront people who are taking advantage of the person. *Independence* involves maintaining personal convictions even when in the minority and receiving pressure from the majority to conform.

Lorr and More's (1980) research suggests there are low to moderate relationships among the four dimensions. Thus, if you are very directive, for instance, you are not necessarily likely to be very socially assertive. With four dimensions a variety of combinations are possible, so that many people tend to be assertive in some ways but not in other ways. At the extremes, some people are assertive in all four ways, while others are not assertive at all.

Assertiveness training has been popular for a number of years. Its purpose is to teach people who are low in assertiveness how to behave assertively. The focus of this training has been primarily on the defense of rights and interests dimension, with some degree of attention paid to social assertiveness. A variety of assertiveness training programs have emerged. Some are designed for a particular group of people such as assertiveness training for women. Others constitute a form of psychotherapy. The programs vary greatly in length. An assertiveness "workshop" for nurses, for instance, might last an evening or weekend, while an assertiveness program in psychotherapy can be quite lengthy.

Assertiveness is conceived as a generally constructive aggressive trait. It is aggressive because it involves using verbal and nonverbal symbols to create a force which dominates in such ways as taking control of a group activity, getting what one deserves, or stopping violations of one's rights. Of course, dominance could be destructive if such actions are used to hurt other people as in making a person seem foolish when you insist on your rights. If that happens, the trait of hostility, rather than assertiveness, is involved. Hostility will be discussed later in this chapter.

Argumentativeness

Argumentativeness is a subset of assertiveness since all arguing is assertive, but not all assertive behavior involves arguing. Argumentativeness is defined as a person's tendency to present and defend positions on controversial issues while attempting to refute the positions which others take (Infante & Rancer, 1982). Argumentativeness includes two competing motives: the tendency to approach arguments and the tendency to avoid arguments. The person's argumentativeness trait is the difference between the approach and avoidance tendencies. The more the desire to approach exceeds the desire to avoid arguments, the more argumentative the individual tends to be.

The Argumentativeness Scale is a questionnaire which measures these tendencies (Infante & Rancer, 1982). A person who is highly argumentative has strong approach and weak avoidance tendencies, while a person low in argumentativeness is low on approach and high on avoidance. There are at least two types of moderate argumentatives. A moderately argumentative person with "conflicting feelings" is high on both approach and avoidance. This person would like to argue often, but strong feelings of anxiety about arguing hold him or her back. This type of moderately argumentative person tends to argue only when the probability of success is high, such as arguing with someone who has little knowledge of the controversial issue. A moderately argumentative person termed "apathetic" is low on both approach and avoidance. This individual does not like arguing controversial issues, but does not really dislike the activity either. This type of moderately argumentative person argues mainly when the incentive for success is high—when there is something of importance to be gained by arguing.

Infante and Rancer's (1982) model of argumentativeness is an *interactional model* of personality because it suggests that a person's motivation to argue in a given situation is a function both of the person's argumentativeness trait and of the influence of situational variables. The situation is represented in their model by the individual's perceptions of the probability and importance of success and of failure in arguing. These perceptions of the situation interact with one's trait to produce one's motivation to argue in a given situation. This model can explain why a person who is high in trait argumentativeness does not always argue, or why a person who is low in the trait does argue at times. The model predicts that, in a given situation, high argumentatives will not argue if they perceive that failure is likely and important and that success is unlikely and unimportant. Further, there are situations in which persons low in argumentativeness do argue. This does not happen often, but, when it does, it is because these individuals perceive that arguing in the situation is likely to produce an important outcome and there is low likelihood that bad consequences will occur.

A good deal of research suggests that arguing produces valuable outcomes. (Infante, 1987a; Johnson & Johnson, 1979). For instance, arguing has been shown to produce more learning by stimulating curiosity about the topics argued. Arguing is also related to greater social perspective-taking ability because arguing with others requires understanding their vantage points and engaging in less egocentric thinking and more mature reasoning. Arguing has been associated with enhanced credibility; when people argued more, they were viewed as more believable. Other research has found highly argumentative individuals to be more skilled and competent communicators, less easily provoked to use verbal aggression, and more likely to succeed as supervisors in work situations. A recent book (Infante, 1988) suggests that, since arguing is associated with so many positive outcomes, it might be considered a basic skill that should be taught to all children fairly early in their schooling. Being unable to argue effectively may represent an unneccessary handicap since it is not difficult to learn how to argue well.

Hostility

Unlike argumentativeness, hostility can be thought of as a broad tendency to be angry. Hostile people are often angry. Hostility, in terms of communication, has been defined as symbolic expression of irritability, negativism, resentment, and suspicion (Infante, 1987a). *Irritability* is communicated by having a very quick temper in response to the slightest provocation, being generally moody and grouchy, showing little patience, being exasperated when there is a delay or something goes wrong, and being rude and inconsiderate of others' feelings. *Negativism* is expressed by refusing to cooperate, expressing unwarranted pessimism about the outcome of something when other people are very hopeful, and voicing antagonism concerning authority, rules, and social conventions. *Resentment* is a dimension of hostility which involves expressing jealousy and hatred, brooding about real or imagined mistreatment so that feelings of anger develop, and indicating that others do not really deserve success. *Suspicion* is communicated by expressing an unjustified distrust of people, expecting that others do not have goodwill, believing that others are planning to harm you, and treating people as if their characters are flawed.

Hostile persons might vary along these four dimensions. For instance, one hostile person might be high on resentment but low on the other three components. Another person might be high on suspicion and negativism and moderate on the other two dimensions. A person high on all four aspects would be particularly hostile.

As explained in the previous section for argumentativeness, an individual's perceptions of a situation can modify the behavior normally predicted by the person's trait. For example, a person who is very high on the negativism dimension of hostility might express no antagonism toward an authority figure in a particular situation and might cooperate readily. In the same situation, another person who is low in negativism might curse the authority figure and refuse to cooperate. In the first case the hostile urges toward the authority might be suppressed because the person has a stronger need such as impressing a member of the opposite sex. In the second case, the usually mild individual might behave in a hostile manner because of a belief that he/she was betrayed by the person in the position of authority.

Analysis of the hostile personality by Berkowitz (1962) is particularly illuminating. He explained that the hostile person is not one who is chronically angry. Rather, the person has learned to behave aggressively, a trait which remains latent until aroused by frustration. Frustration stimulates anger. In time, merely thinking about a frustrating event can produce the anger. The frustration is sometimes generalized in the person's mind, so that even very ambiguous situations or events are seen as frustrating. For instance, a person who sees his father as frustrating might come to view all men that way.

Berkowitz points out that hostile responses are learned. They can be influenced, for example, by the disciplinary method one experiences as a child. Punitive methods including spankings are associated with children's becoming aggressive, while nonpunitive methods such as rewards for desired behavior can help children restrain hostile words and actions. To a degree, a child learns from parents whether or not to behave aggressively. If a child is physically punished for not behaving in a particular way, and if the child then behaves as the parent desires, the lesson learned is, "Hitting someone must be a good way to influence people; it certainly worked on me!"

Berkowitz also explained that encouraging people to talk about frustrations or to vent anger is not an effective way of avoiding aggression. In fact, just the opposite happens. Talking about the hostile urge rekindles the anger, and thus aggression becomes more likely, not less likely, since anger is necessary for aggressive behavior. Encouraging someone to talk about a frustration only facilitates the learning of the hostile response. Berkowitz's idea challenges a core concept of expressive forms of psychotherapy in which the patient is led to "talk through" hostile urges. It also calls into question the practice, sometimes popular in interpersonal communication courses, of encouraging students to "open up," to express their true feelings concerning their relations with others. Instead, Berkowitz's framework suggests that individuals should be taught non-hostile, rational methods for dealing with frustrating situations and should avoid mentally rehearsing hostile responses. Thus, if a husband and wife have bitter verbal fights over money, they could be taught methods of argumentation so that they can debate rather than fight about finances.

Verbal Aggressiveness

As in the case of argumentativeness, which is a subset of assertiveness, verbal aggressiveness is a subset of hostility. That is, hostility is the more global trait of which verbal aggressiveness is a facet. Thus, as a subset of hostility, all verbal aggression is hostile. Verbal aggressiveness is defined as the trait of attacking the self-concepts of people instead of, or in addition to, their positions on topics of communication (Infante & Wigley, 1986). While a physically aggressive person tries to inflict bodily pain, a verbally aggressive person attempts to create mental pain. A verbally aggressive person tries to hurt others by making them feel bad about themselves. In a sense, a "verbal punch" is thrown at a person's concept of self.

There are many types of verbally aggressive messages. All are forms of insults: character attacks, competence attacks, personal background attacks, physical appearance attacks, curses, teasing, ridicule, profanity, threats, and nonverbal emblems. You probably recognize most of these and may have been the victim of some. The last on the list, nonverbal emblems, may seem to contradict the idea of "verbal" aggression. However, a nonverbal emblem is functionally equivalent to a word. Thus, to roll your eyes when someone says something can be a rather severe attack on the person's competence. An exaggerated look of disbelief would also be an insulting nonverbal emblem.

Verbal aggression produces a number of effects in interpersonal communication. The most fundamental effect is self-concept damage. A person can recover from many types of physical aggression such as being punched in the nose. However, recovery from some forms of verbal aggression does not occur, and the effects can last for a lifetime; for instance, telling a child he has a "pig's nose." Of these two examples, the punch was probably the "kinder" of the aggressive acts.

Verbal aggression also leads to some temporary effects in interpersonal communication: hurt feelings, anger, irritation, embarrassment. Verbal aggression sometimes results in deterioration or even termination of the relationship. A very serious effect of verbal aggression, from a personal and a social perspective, is that verbal aggression sometimes leads to physical violence. A good deal of research suggests murder, for example, is commonly preceded by verbal aggression in the form of threats, character attacks, or ridicule.

There are at least four causes of verbal aggression (Infante, Trebing, Shepherd, & Seeds, 1984). *Transference* is a psychopathological basis for verbal aggression. People attack with verbally aggressive messages persons who remind them of an unresolved conflict. For instance, if as a child a person was humiliated by someone older, the person might create a target for retaliation later in life by projecting the undesirable characteristics of that particular older individual onto all persons in the class "older." Because of this transference, the person would feel justified and derive pleasure when saying something verbally aggressive to any older man. *Disdain* as a cause means that dislike for a person motivates attacking that individual with verbally aggressive messages as a means for communicating that dislike. *Social learning* means people use verbal aggression because they are rewarded for using it; e.g., people laugh when one person "puts down" another person. Also, people learn things vicariously by observing someone "modeling" the behavior—seeing a "hero" on TV use verbal aggression. The fourth cause is that verbal aggression sometimes results from an *argumentative skill deficiency*. If people do not know how to argue skillfully, they resort to attacking self-concepts because they are unable to attack positions on topics. This "misdirected" attack is less likely when one is skilled at arguing positions.

It is difficult to say how much of the verbal aggression in society is due to each of the four causes. However, the first two causes are probably responsible for a rather small portion. That is, psychopathologies are not pervasive in the population, and we structure our lives so that we talk as little as possible with others we dislike. Probably social learning and argumentative skill deficiencies are responsible for much of the verbal aggression in society. If this is the case, there is hope that the destructiveness of verbal aggression can be reduced substantially. Education can be a solution. People, especially children, can be taught how to argue constructively and thus reduce the inclination to use verbal aggression. Children can be taught methods for dealing with verbal aggression when it does occur.

Summary

This chapter explored trait approaches that have been taken in order to understand human communication. The approach has its origin in the study of personality in the field of psychology. The trait approach was contrasted with situationist and interactionist positions. Distinctions were made between trait, contextual, and state behaviors. The cross-situational consistency of behavior issue was reviewed because of its relevance to understanding traits. Personality traits which have been of interest to communication researchers were reviewed: persuasibility, self-esteem, dogmatism, Machiavellianism, cognitive complexity, and need for social approval. Four classes of communication traits were discussed: apprehension, presentation, adaptation, aggression. In the apprehension traits category, we examined communication apprehension, receiver apprehension, writing apprehension, and unwillingness to communicate. The presentation traits presented were predispositions toward verbal behavior, communicator style, disclosiveness, and clothing predispositions. The category of adaptation traits included rhetorical sensitivity, noble self, rhetorical reflector, communication competence, and interaction involvement. The last class of communication traits explored consisted of aggression traits: assertiveness, argumentativeness, hostility, and verbal aggressiveness.

The next three chapters will investigate other types of communication and the theories that have been developed. Chapter 6 shifts from a consideration of individual traits to what was once the most extensively studied communication phenomenon, persuasion.

Questions To Consider

1. How is a communication trait similar to a personality trait? How are the two concepts different?
2. What is a hypothetical construct? How do constructs affect theory building?
3. Explain the difference between trait, contextual, and state behaviors. Why is it useful to make these distinctions? Which approach do you think best explains communication?
4. What implication does the cross-situational consistency of behavior have for understanding communication?
5. What are the major personality variables studied in communication research?
6. What communication traits involve apprehension about communication?
7. What communication traits are concerned with the presentation of verbal and nonverbal messages?
8. What communication traits deal with the ways in which we adapt our communication to audiences and situations?
9. What communication traits are aggressive in nature?
10. How does the argumentativeness model reflect an interactional explanation of arguing?

References

Alberti, R.E., & Emmons, M.L. (1974). *Your perfect right: A guide to assertive behavior* (2nd ed.). San Luis Obispo, CA: Impact.

Allport, G.W. (1937). *Personality: A psychological interpretation*. New York: Holt.

Andersen, P.A. (1987). The trait debate: A critical examination of the individual differences paradigm in interpersonal communication. In E. Dervin & M.J. Voigt (Eds.), *Progress in communication sciences* (Vol. 7, pp. 47-52). Norwood, NJ: Ablex.

Baseheart, J.R. (1971). Message opinionation and approval-dependence as determinants of receiver attitude change and recall. *Speech Monographs, 38,* 302-310.

Berger, C.R., & Calabrese, R.J. (1975). Some explorations in initial interaction and beyond: Toward a developmental theory of interpersonal communication. *Human Communication Research, 1,* 99-112.

Berkowitz, L. (1962). *Aggression: A social psychological analysis*. New York: McGraw-Hill.

Block, J. (1971). *Lives through time*. Berkeley, CA: Bancroft.

Burgoon, J.K. (1976). The unwillingness-to-communicate scale: Development and validation. *Communication Monographs, 43,* 60-69.

Cattell, R.E. (1950). *Personality: A systematic, theoretical, and factual study.* New York: McGraw-Hill.

Cegala, D.J. (1984). Affective and cognitive manifestations of interaction involvement during unstructured and competitive interactions. *Communication Monographs, 51,* 320-335.

Cegala, D.J., Savage, G.T., Brunner, C.C., & Conrad, A.B. (1982). An elaboration of the meaning of interaction involvement: Towards the development of a theoretical concept. *Communication Monographs, 49,* 229-245.

Christie, R., & Geis, F. (1970). *Studies in Machiavellianism.* New York: Academic Press.

Costa, P.T., & McCrae, R.R. (1950). Still stable after all these years: Personality as a key to some issues in adulthood and old age. In P.B. Baltes & O.G. Brim (Eds.), *Life-span development and behavior* (Vol. 3, pp. 65-102). New York: Academic Press.

Crowne, D.P., & Marlowe, D. (1960). A new scale of social desirability independent of psychopathology. *Journal of Consulting Psychology, 24,* 349-354.

Daly, J.A., & Miller, M.D. (1975). The empirical development of an instrument to measure writing apprehension. *Research in the Teaching of English, 9,* 242-249.

Delia, J. (1977). Constructivism and the study of human communication. *Quarterly Journal of Speech, 53,* 66-53.

Epstein, S. (1979). The stability of behavior: I. On predicting most of the people much of the time. *Journal of Personality and Social-Psychology, 37,* 1097-1126.

Gorden, W.I., & Infante, D.A. (1980). Attitudes toward free speech: Trends, measurement and individual difference considerations. In P.E. Kane (Ed.), *Free speech yearbook 1980* (pp. 115-125). Annandale, VA: Speech Communication Association.

Gorden, W.I., Infante, D.A., & Braun, A.A. (1986). Communicator style: Is the metaphor appropriate? *Communication Research Reports, 3,* 13-19.

Gorden, W.I., Tengler, C.D., & Infante, D.A. (1982). Women's clothing predispositions as predictors of dress at work, job satisfaction, and career advancement. *Southern Speech Communication Journal, 47,* 422-434.

Hart, R.P., Carlson, R.E., Eadie, W.F. (1980). Attitudes toward communication and the assessment of rhetorical sensitivity. *Communication Monographs, 47,* 1-22.

Hovland, C.I., & Janis, I.L. (Eds.) (1959). *Personality and persuasibility.* New Haven: Yale University Press.

Infante, D.A. (1976). Persuasion as a function of the receiver's prior success or failure as a message source. *Communication Quarterly, 24,* 21-26.

Infante, D.A. (1987a). Aggressiveness. In J.C. McCroskey & J.A. Daly (Eds.), *Personality and interpersonal communication,* (pp. 157-192). Newbury Park, CA: Sage Publications.

Infante, D.A. (1987b). Enhancing the prediction of response to a communication situation from communication traits. *Communication Quarterly, 35,* 305-316.

Infante, D.A. (1988). *Arguing constructively.* Prospect Heights, IL: Waveland Press.

Infante, D.A., & Gorden, W.I. (1981). Similarities and differences in the communicator styles of superiors and subordinates: Relations to subordinate satisfaction. *Communication Quarterly, 30,* 67-71.

Infante, D.A., & Rancer, A.S. (1982). A conceptualization and measure of argumentativeness. *Journal of Personality Assessment, 46,* 72-80.

Infante, D.A., Trebing, J.D., Shepherd, P.E., & Seeds, D.E. (1984). The relationship of argumentativeness to verbal aggression. *Southern Speech Communication Journal, 50,* 67-77.

Infante, D.A., & Wigley, C.J. (1986). Verbal aggressiveness: An Interpersonal model and measure. *Communication Monographs, 53,* 61-69.

Johnson, D.W., & Johnson, R.T. (1979). Conflict in the classroom: Controversy and learning. *Review of Educational Research, 49,* 51-70.

Lorr, M., & More, W.W. (1980). Four dimensions of assertiveness. *Multivariate Behavioral Research, 2,* 127-135.

Maddi, S.R. (1972). *Personality theories: A comparative analysis.* Homewood, IL: Dorsey Press.

McCroskey, J.C. (1970). Measures of communication-bound anxiety. *Speech Monographs, 37,* 269-277.

McCroskey, J.C. (1977). Oral communication apprehension: A summary of recent theory and research. *Human Communication Research, 4,* 75-96.

Mischel, W. (1968). *Personality and assessment.* New York: John Wiley and Sons.

Mischel, W. (1973). Towards a cognitive social learning reconceptualization of personality. *Psychological Review, 80,* 252-253.

Mortensen, C.D., Arnston, P.H., & Lustig, M. (1977). The measurement of verbal predispositions: Scale development and application. *Human Communication Research, 3,* 146-155.

Mortensen, C.D., & Arnston, P.H. (1974). The effect of predispositions toward verbal behavior on interaction patterns in dyads. *Quarterly Journal of Speech, 60,* 421-430.

Murray H.A. (1938). *Explorations in personality.* New York: Oxford University Press.

Murray, H.A. (1951). Toward a classification of interaction. In T. Parsons & E.A. Shils (Eds.), *Toward a general theory of action* (pp. 434-464). Cambridge, MA: Harvard University Press.

Norton, R.W. (1978). Foundations of a communicator style construct. *Human Communication Research, 4,* 99-112.

Norton, R.W. (1983). *Communicator style: Theory, applications, and measures.* Beverly Hills, CA: Sage Publications.

Onyekwere, E.O., Rubin, R.B., & Infante, D.A. (1987, November). *Communication competence in arguments as a function of argumentativeness and ego-involvement.* Paper presented at the meeting of the Speech Communication Association, Boston.

Richmond, V.P., & McCroskey, J.C. (1985). *Communication: Apprehension, avoidance, and effectiveness.* Scottsdale, AZ: Gorsuch Scarisbrick, Publishers.

Rokeach, M. (1960). *The open and closed mind.* New York: Basic Books.

Rosenfeld, L.B., & Plax, T.G. (1977). Clothing as consciousness. *Journal of Communication, 27,* 24-31.

Rubin, R.B. (1982). Assessing speaking and listening competence at the college level: The Communication Competency Assessment Instrument. *Communication Education, 31,* 19-32.

Rubin, R.B. (1985). The validity of the Communication Competency Assessment Instrument. *Communication Monographs, 52,* 173-185.

Shontz, E.C. (1965). *Research methods in personality.* New York: Appleton.

Spitzburg, B.H., & Cupach, W.R. (1984). *Interpersonal communication competence.* Beverly Hills, CA: Sage Publications.

Stagner, R. (1977). On the reality and relevance of traits. *Journal of General Psychology*, *96*, 155-207.

Steinfatt, T.M. (1987). Personality and communication: Classical approaches. In J.C. McCroskey & J.A. Daly (Eds.), *Personality and interpersonal communication* (pp. 42-126). Newbury Park, CA: Sage Publications.

Wheeless, L.R. (1975). An investigation of receiver apprehension and social context dimensions of communication apprehension. *The Speech Teacher, 24*, 261-265.

Wheeless, L.R. (1975). A follow-up study of the relationships among trust, disclosure, and interpersonal solidarity. *Human Communication Research, 4*, 143-157.

Wiemann, J.M. (1977). Explication and test of a model of communication competence. *Human Communication Research, 3*, 195-213.

Chapter 6

Persuasion
Approaches

Persuasion was once the most frequently researched topic in the communication field. Scholars were enthusiastic about the prospect of unraveling the mysteries of social influence. Such a goal was indeed exciting because of the importance of persuasion. People influencing one another is a basic process in society. To gain control over this process would be a monumental achievement. The scientific knowledge would allow people to predict and to control persuasion. The power inherent in this idea is staggering. In fact, you might be thinking it probably was best the feat was not accomplished! We are not implying that persuasion researchers were intent on discovering how to control masses of people. Prediction and control are, however, outcomes of successful scientific research. In some fields such as astronomy, researchers do not achieve control since they are unable to manipulate the objects of study. Research programs in persuasion were initiated to build knowledge so that a relatively complete understanding of the subject could be achieved. Inherent in such knowledge is prediction and control.

You may be relieved to learn that the persuasion process did not yield much to the onslaught of thousands of experiments. Many relationships were explored in this research. However, laws were not discovered which would permit precise, scientific-like predictions. Perhaps it was this resilience that contributed to the decline of persuasion research. If you were to thumb through the volumes of communication journals in your college library, you would find the number of persuasion studies began to decline in the early 1970s. By the end of the decade, the earlier torrent of studies had subsided to barely a trickle.

In reviewing the history of persuasion research, it is clear that although communication researchers conducted numerous studies in the 1950s and 1960s, they did not develop new theories about the subject (see McGuire, 1969, for an excellent synthesis through the late 1960s). Persuasion theories were devised by social psychologists. Communication researchers typically based their research on these psychological models. If you were to examine, for example, the 1969 volume of *Speech Monographs* you would find many more references to sources in social psychology than to communication sources.

The lack of original theorizing, the heavy borrowing from other disciplines, and the abandonment of an area of research after a relatively short period of time may suggest that the communication field never really had a serious interest in the scientific study of persuasion. Actually, the focus has changed. "Traditional" persuasion research has been replaced by a broader model of *social influence*. Earlier research focused on how a relatively formal speech or essay influences a person. More recent research examines how people try to influence one another in many ways: how do we convince people to agree with us, how do we induce others to like us, how do we end an interpersonal relationship, what techniques should be used to control classroom behavior, what tactics are effective for resisting another's attempt to persuade us, what is the role of argument or verbal aggression in interpersonal relations? An examination of contemporary research suggests that the communication field's fascination with persuasion has matured into a more global interest in social influence. Moreover, if earlier research implied at least a tacit quest for laws which would enable prediction and control, the more contemporary research seems to have settled for prediction. The vast majority of recent social influence research in the communication discipline examines correlations between variables that affect social influence. Variables seldom are manipulated by scientists in controlled, laboratory situations in order to study what *causes* persuasion. Instead, variables are measured and related to one another to determine the strength of the association.

Conceptualizing Persuasion

At its most basic level, persuasion may be thought of as attitude change toward a source's proposal which has resulted from a message designed to alter beliefs about the proposal. A proposal is a recommended course of action. For instance, "We should give a piece of land in our state back to Native Americans," or, on a more personal level, "Let's go to the movies tonight." Attitude is defined as how favorably we evaluate something. This is represented by feelings such as good versus bad, right versus wrong, nice versus awful, valuable versus worthless. An example of an attitude toward a proposal might be, "I feel giving that piece of land to the Native Americans is extremely good and right, moderately nice, and slightly valuable." A belief is a perception of how two or more things are related. In terms of persuasion, beliefs are perceptions of the consequences of a proposal. For instance, "If we return the land to the Native Americans, a number of farmers will have to be relocated."

If a persuader wants to influence a specific behavior, the first concern is usually attitude. If we want to influence someone to sign a petition, we need to address the individual's attitude toward the object of the petition. If the petition proposes returning a tract of land to Native Americans, persuasion involves presenting a message which will help the person form favorable beliefs about giving land to a Native American tribe; e.g., "A previous wrong would be corrected." If beliefs about the proposal are positive, the attitude toward the proposal will be favorable. Of course, if beliefs are negative, the attitude will be unfavorable. A mixture of positive and negative beliefs results in a moderately favorable or unfavorable attitude, depending upon the proportion of positive to negative beliefs.

By persuading a person to favor a proposal, a persuader provides justification for the receiver to *choose* to behave in a particular manner. In order to have persuasion and not some other social influence process such as coercion or compliance, the receiver must feel free, not constrained, to choose. Thus, *perceived choice* is a distinguishing characteristic of persuasion. If coercion is used, no choice is perceived; e.g., "The person is holding a gun to my head, so I had better sign the petition." An individual's attitude toward the proposal is also unchanged under compliance; however, beliefs pertaining to the receiver's relationship with the source are activated; e.g., "You should sign this petition because you owe me a favor."

Thus, when one person influences the behavior of another person, social influence has occurred but not necessarily persuasion. Persuasion uses symbols to modify an attitude to achieve a particular behavior. Attitude represents a predisposition to behave. In persuasion the source is willing to let success depend upon attitudinal influence. In other types of social influence the source is unwilling to allow the person's behavior to be controlled by the person's attitudes. Instead the source applies force or pressure as a substitute for the motivation provided by attitudes. Coercion involves the use of physical aggression and verbal aggression as substitutes for attitudinal influence. Verbal aggression uses symbols to apply pressure to a person's self-concept (Infante & Wigley, 1986). Examples include threats, insults, ridicule, and profanity.

Compliance involves more subtle forms of psychological pressure: "I (and/or others) will like you if you comply"; or "I (and/or others) will dislike you if you do not comply." There are many compliance-gaining strategies for each of these two forms. An example of the first is, "I will do something for you if you do this for me." "Our friends will be disappointed if you do not do this," illustrates the second. Instead of allowing the receiver's attitude toward the proposal to control the receiver's behavior, the source in a compliance situation implies that the desired behavior will make the receiver more socially accepted.

Placing persuasion within the framework Belief Change→Attitude Change→ Behavior Change helps to clarify whether persuasion took place. Persons can be influenced to *behave* in a certain way which can lead them to change their attitudes and beliefs about the object of behavior. This would be the reverse of the model above. We might encourage a friend who dislikes fishing to go on a fishing trip by saying, "This trip is a chance to renew our friendship." If the person enjoys the experience (forms positive beliefs about fishing), the attitude toward fishing becomes more favorable. This situation would not constitute persuasion because it was not a message by one person that caused the other person to change an attitude toward fishing. Instead, engaging in the behavior produced the attitude change. No message was presented before the behavior. However, a message is necessary for persuasion. The fishing trip was not a message because it was not an intentional exchange of symbols. For example, catching a large fish was not symbolic activity because the fish did not manipulate symbols in stimulating a feeling of exhilaration in the person. Thus, through coercion or compliance a person can be induced to behave in a certain manner which can lead to attitude change. However, the steps involved in coercion or compliance are different from the belief-to-attitude-to-behavior model.

Six Dimensions of Persuasion Situations

It is apparent that the many persuasion situations which we experience are not the same. But how do they differ? We can say that people differ physically in terms of height, weight, and body type. Can we be nearly as precise with persuasion situations? Because of research by Cody and McLaughlin (1980), we are able to measure persuasion situations. They identified six ways that one situation can differ from another. We will examine each briefly. Keep in mind that there are many other ways in which situations may differ. In terms of persuasion, however, these six dimensions are especially important.

The first dimension is *intimacy*. A very intimate situation would be one in which the source has a highly personal, meaningful, and perhaps intimate relationship with the receiver. The second is *dominance*. This involves one person in the persuasion situation usually being dominant and the other person usually being submissive; one person essentially controls the behavior of the other. The third is *resistance*. Situations vary in terms of how agreeable the receiver is to the object of persuasion. The fourth, *rights* involves the justification that the source has for asking the receiver to do something, whether or not the source has reasonable grounds for the request. The fifth is *personal benefits.* This dimension includes what the source would gain by succeeding in the persuasion attempt and may also reflect advantages for the receiver in fulfilling the source's wishes. The sixth is *long-term consequences.* Situations vary in terms of whether the persuasion will have short-term or long-term consequences for the relationship between the source and receiver. When the relationship is an intimate one, the persuasion attempt could have very long-term consequences. However, persuasion between strangers usually will have only short-term relationship consequences.

It is important that a persuader consider these six dimensions. For instance, threats do not work well in intimate relationships or where there are long-term consequences. If the source stands to gain substantially from the persuasion, the receiver needs to be convinced of the source's trustworthiness. If the source does not appear to have the right to advocate something, attention must be given to establishing why one has the right to speak. If the receiver is very resistant to the source's proposal, a good deal of time may have to be spent explaining why the proposal is needed.

Self-Awareness and Persuasion

In studying persuasion, one can form the impression that the persuader is constantly thinking: analyzing the receiver, situation and topic; composing the message a split-second before delivering it; continually monitoring feedback from the receiver; and adjusting the message, along with delivery, to the feedback. The idea of the source being so aware of everything and so active in encoding and delivering a message suggests almost a "frantic" model of persuasion, portraying a persuader not only as completely alert but also as actively controlling the shape, content, and sound of the message.

Recent conceptions suggest that this may not be the case (for a review see Roloff, 1980). Individuals seem to follow a cognitive course of "least resistance" in communication which leads them to rely upon previously prepared scripts. A script is a meaningful sequence of events which a person expects in a situation as either an observer or a participant (Abelson, 1976). Thus, in a given type of situation a person may find that a certain message was effective. In a situation which appears similar to previous ones, the person simply recalls the message and repeats it, modifying perhaps a word or two. Thus, the persuader essentially reads from a previously prepared script. This requires very little effort and allows the source to communicate on "automatic pilot."

The idea that receivers are not very attentive, that their minds wander away from the message, is an ancient one. Add to it the recent notion of a source similarly preoccupied, and we have a model of persuasion where the source and receiver are physically present in the situation but mentally "in-and-out." According to script theory, this probably is more the rule than the exception. Perhaps a reason why this may be the case is that our personalities predispose us to prefer certain situations. Given a choice, we approach some situations and avoid others. Thus, we usually find ourselves in familiar situations. Because we are seldom in an unusual situation, we are seldom without a script. That is, having been in certain types of situations virtually guarantees that we possess a script that has enjoyed at least some previous success. Among other things, this suggests that we do not do much composing of original messages. We usually can recall a script that is appropriate. If not, we revise one that is close to what is needed.

Approaches to Understanding Persuasion

We will not attempt a comprehensive review of persuasion theory in this chapter (for more thorough treatments see Bostrom, 1983; Miller, Burgoon, & Burgoon, 1984). Instead, we will focus on five approaches and theories which have stimulated the most persuasion research in the field of communication. Then we will turn to theories explaining how to resist persuasion. We will end the chapter with a rules approach to persuasion.

(1) The Variable-Analytic Approach

A good deal of persuasion research, especially early research in the 1940s, 50s, and 60s, explored specific variables in the persuasion process because they seemed to be important, not because they were part of a particular persuasion theory. Thus, numerous variables relating to the source, message, channel, and receiver in persuasion were examined through experiments. A good deal of the early research on the source in persuasion tried to determine how sources who are more and less believable (source credibility) influence attitude change and what factors influence source credibility (Andersen & Clevenger, 1963). We will examine source credibility in the next section. You might also want to reread the section in Chapter 5 on rhetorical sensitivity, an approach to studying how likely sources are to adapt their messages to the demands of the situation.

A large body of research on the message in persuasion exists (for summaries, see Bostrom, 1983; Burgoon & Bettinghaus, 1980; Cronkhite, 1969). At least three categories seem relevant: message structure, message appeals, and language. The message structure research investigated such variables as: whether the strongest argument in a message should be placed first (anti-climactic arrangement), last (climactic), or in the middle of the message (pyramidal) (Gulley & Berlo, 1956); whether two-sided messages are more persuasive than one-sided messages (Hovland, 1957); whether the opposition's argument should be refuted before or after presenting one's own case (Thistlethwaite, Kamenetsky, & Schmidt, 1956); and whether the speaker or receiver should draw conclusions from arguments in the speech (Tubbs, 1968). Message appeals explored were the use of: fear or anxiety appeals (Janis &

Feshbach, 1953); evidence (McCroskey, 1969); reward appeals (McCroskey & Wright, 1971); humor (Gruner, 1965, 1970); logic (Scott & Hurt, 1978); emotion (Ruechelle, 1958); and self-esteem (Spillman, 1979). Language variables included language intensity (Bradac, Bowers, & Courtright, 1979); use of qualifiers for arguments (Feezel, 1974); rhetorical questions (Zillman, 1972); opinionated language (Infante, 1975a); and obscenity (Bostrom, Baseheart, & Rossiter, 1973).

The channel in persuasion has received a limited amount of research. A major focus has been on comparing live, tape-recorded, and written messages for differences in persuasiveness (Knower, 1935; Wilkie, 1934).

The receiver in persuasion has been studied in a variety of ways (for a good summary, see Bostrom, 1983, pp. 180-201): sex (Scheidel, 1963); ego-involvement (Sereno & Bodaken, 1972); and attitude intensity (Mehrley & McCroskey, 1970). Probably the major way the receiver has been studied is in terms of personality. Some of the traits investigated have been persuasibility (Hovland & Janis, 1959); authoritarianism (Adorno, Frenkel-Brunswik, Levinson, & Sanford, 1950); dogmatism (Rokeach, 1960); self-esteem (Infante, 1976); richness of fantasy (Infante, 1975b); and tolerance of ambiguity (Infante, 1975c). Several of these were discussed in Chapter 5.

These are just a sample of the persuasion variables that have been investigated. You might expect that numerous persuasion principles were discovered. However, that is not the case. Despite the vast amount of research, the conclusions are very tentative, subject to numerous qualifications. For instance, a message which tries to frighten the receiver will vary in its persuasiveness depending upon how important the topic is, how believable the source is, and how specific the solutions presented are. Thus, a high fear message can be more persuasive than a low fear message when the source is highly believable and the solution for the problem is very specific, but only if the topic is important to the receiver. The inability of this research to offer law-like statements, such as "Intense fear is more persuasive than mild or no fear," has been viewed as a major criticism. Another criticism has been that since variable-analytic research investigates a variable without first developing a theory of persuasion, it does not advance theory-building in persuasion. That is, critics claim that persuasion research should test persuasion theories.

Despite the rather serious criticisms, it is possible to find value in this research. Much of the research was done in an earlier era when there was little theory. The research served to "identify the territory," to suggest what the important variables might be. The research stimulated thinking about persuasion (it had *heuristic* value). What began as relatively simple variable-analytic research sometimes resulted in a rather sophisticated theory of persuasion. For example, Burgoon, Jones, and Stewart's (1975) message-centered model of persuasion had its beginning in the language intensity research. An additional value of variable-analytic research is that its painstaking search for law-like principles of persuasion revealed the complexity of persuasion. Time after time, the results of experiments had to be stated in the tentative, highly qualified manner of the fear appeal example presented above. If scientific research is supposed to reveal the nature of what is studied, variable-analytic research may have accomplished that rather well. We think of persuasion as a dynamic process, involving numerous factors which can control differences in social influence. Little is static, and success is often equated with being able to adapt to the fluidity of the persuasion situation. It took many variable-analytic studies to bring this picture into semi-clear focus. Now we at least have a better idea about what persuasion involves.

(2) The Source Credibility Approach

A great deal of research has been based on the second major persuasive approach, the idea that source credibility is important in explaining persuasion (for summaries and analyses see Andersen & Clevenger, 1963; Bostrom, 1983; Cronkhite & Liska, 1976; Delia, 1976). Generally, the research has failed to establish that source credibility is a necessary condition for persuasion. That is, some studies find that credible sources persuade more people, while other studies find no relationship between attitude change and source credibility. Such inconsistency seems strange, especially since the idea that credibility affects persuasion seems self-evident, hardly worth investigating.

The Factor Model (A Covering Laws Approach). There are three major models of source credibility in the communication field: factor, functional, and constructivist. The factor model of credibility has been dominant for the past 2500 years, since the time of Aristotle. The other approaches are recent (Cronkhite & Liska, 1976; Delia, 1976). As you read in Chapter 4, Aristotle said *ethos,* the Greek term for source credibility, is one of the three major ways speakers persuade audiences. The others are *logos,* the words, ideas and arguments in the speech, and *pathos,* arousing the audience's emotions and feelings. Aristotle said there are three aspects of credibility: a source's competence or expertise, character, and good will toward the audience. Over the years these came to be viewed as dimensions or *factors* of credibility. A factor is a cluster of perceptions that seem to pertain to the same thing: perceptions of a source's intelligence, authoritativeness, and informativeness all contribute to the source's perceived expertise.

According to the factor model, source credibility is represented by how favorably the receiver judges the source on each of the factors of credibility. Thus, credibility exists in the mind of the receiver; it is not an actual characteristic of the source like eye color or hair color. If a source has an I.Q. of 160, is a published author on the subject of her speech, and presents an enormous amount of information on that topic, that does not mean that the audience will necessarily view her as an expert. One person may consider the source an expert on the topic, while another person may not. Credibility is strictly in the eye of the beholder.

In the past 30 years, research which has taken a factor approach has found that the expertise dimension appears distinct from the character dimension. Thus, sources viewed as experts are not necessarily also thought to have good character. Some may be seen that way while others may not; one factor does not depend upon the other. In the case of character and good will, however, the factors are not distinct. They seem to be dependent. If we believe sources have our best interests in mind, we also perceive them as having good character. If we think they are trying to deceive us, we also rate them as immoral. Thus, character and good will are dependent; they "go together."

The research has discovered a number of other variables which may affect credibility: energy (dynamism), sociability, power, impact, mental balance, cultivation, and charisma. Critics wonder, if credibility is a list of factors, how long is the list? Does a longer list imply a better understanding of credibility (Cronkhite & Liska, 1976)? This raises the issue of whether a "laundry list" of factors really tells us anything. Does understanding or does confusion increase with each new factor discovered? Another criticism of the factor approach is that the model does not specify whether a receiver uses all of the factors in assessing a source's credibility. A plausible expectation is that in some persuasion situations some factors matter more than other factors. Some factors matter more for some receivers than for others. Thus, the characteristics used to judge the source's credibility can change with different sources, situations, and audiences. These and other criticisms of the factor model have led to the development of two additional models of credibility.

The Functional Model (A Covering Laws Approach). The functional model of source credibility views credibility as the degree to which a source satisfies the receiver's needs. Three simultaneous processes occur in a persuasive situation. First, the receiver becomes aware of the source's characteristics. Some, like height and voice quality, are observable; others, like education and social status, must be inferred. Second, the receiver determines criteria for judging the source in the situation. That is, the receiver becomes aware of the functions that the source could serve for the receiver, e.g., to provide recent information, to entertain. Third, the receiver compares the characteristics with the functional criteria. An audience at a banquet might judge the extent to which a speaker has both informed and entertained them. The more needs that are fulfilled by the source, the more credible the source is. For example, the more the audience enjoyed the speech, the more credible they consider the speaker (Cronkhite & Liska, 1980).

Another group of researchers developed a method for measuring credibility according to the functional approach and then compared the functional model to the factor model to determine which explains persuasion best. The two models performed equally well in explaining differences, so the test was inconclusive. However, since the factors did not explain persuasion better than a general measure of credibility, the functional model was judged to be promising (Infante, Parker, Clarke, Wilson, & Nathu, 1983).

The Constructivist Model (A Human Action Approach). Although most of the research on source credibility has been conducted from a covering laws perspective, another recent approach, the constructivist model, has been developed using the interpretive or human action paradigm. Constructivism, as an approach to communication, maintains that people construct their reality. Individuals are active participants in their social universe, creating meaning by using their personal construct systems to explain and control their experiences. You will remember from the discussion in Chapter 3 that a construct can be viewed as a bi-polar pair of judgments which create a continuum. Right-wrong and honest-dishonest are examples of constructs. Some are determined by culture, such as honest-dishonest. Others may be defined by the individual. A fun-loving party-goer might have dull-drunk as a construct which might be meaningless to someone else. People have highly individualized construct systems which they actively use to create meaning in communication situations. If we are to understand source credibility, we need to learn how people use their systems of personal constructs to form, reinforce, and change images of people in persuasion situations (Delia, 1976).

Source credibility, according to the constructivist model, involves learning what it is about the source that leads the receiver to accept or to reject the source's proposal. It is not necessary to understand the receiver's entire construct system, but it is essential to learn what constructs the receiver used to judge the source in a particular situation. Constructivists do this by asking the receiver questions in order to learn what constructs the receiver applied. Two major concerns are, "What questions should be asked?" and "What should be done with the answers?" (See, for example, the debate about which method should be used to study persuasive strategies: Boster, 1988; Burleson & Wilson 1988; Burleson, et al. 1988; Hunter, 1988; and Seibold, 1988).

The constructivist researchers feel their method is more accurate for discovering the constructs people really use. Researchers using other models sometimes distribute checklists to determine receiver attitudes. If handed a checklist, the receiver might recognize the pairs of adjectives provided as possibilities for audience members to use to judge a speaker and might check those off, whether or not the receiver had actually used them to evaluate the source. Receivers might also check off adjectives that they know their friends use or that they think their public speaking teachers would approve of, rather than indicate their own constructs. The receivers might overlook or not be aware of their own constructs when consulting a checklist. The constructivists prefer to have receivers write down their impressions of the source. Next, researchers pick out the adjectives recorded by each receiver and compare them to see if there are systematic differences (Delia, O'Keefe, & O'Keefe, 1982). Most of the constructivist studies have concerned the cognitive structures of message sources (see for example Crockett, 1965; Delia & Clark, 1977; O'Keefe, 1984; O'Keefe & Delia, 1982; O'Keefe & Sypher, 1981; Samter, Burleson, & Basden-Murphy, 1989).

Since the constructivists have concentrated their research on sources rather than receivers and on how people form impressions of others in general rather than on how audiences form impressions of speakers, very little research specifically investigates the constructivist model of credibility. One typical impression-formation study is presented here because it tests the axiom that people are evaluated differently in different contexts. It seems natural to generalize from this finding that people evaluate speakers according to criteria which vary from situation to situation. The constructivist researchers gave students information to read about a college student named Walt. Half of the information described Walt in social situations, the other half in work situations. The students read positive information about Walt's work behavior and negative information about Walt's social behavior, or vice versa. The participants then wrote a description of Walt as though they were describing him to a friend who had not met him. Half the students were told that their friend would soon be working with Walt on an academic project; the other half were told their friend would be meeting Walt in an informal social setting. Not surprisingly, the researchers found that people judged Walt primarily in terms of the information relevant to the situation in which they expected their friend to meet him. If they had read a positive description of Walt's social behavior but a negative description of his work behavior and they expected their friend to meet Walt at a party, the overall impression of Walt was favorable. If they had read a negative description of social behavior and a positive description of work behavior, the overall impression was unfavorable. The same pattern held true for the work setting (Delia, Crockett, Press, & O'Keefe, 1975).

This experiment indicates that people view different characteristics of others as more or less important, depending on the situation. In terms of this theory, receivers evaluate sources using different constructs for different situations. Thus, the constructivists believe there is no overall list of factors or functions that can be applied to study source credibility. Instead, one must study common elements in constructs that receivers typically use to evaluate sources. The outcome of this research would be lists of typical constructs related to credibility of entertainers, public speakers, teachers, or politicians, for example. These lists would be expected to vary slightly with different receivers and to be quite different for individuals from different cultures. Further development of a way to differentiate source credibility from other types of impressions and to measure credibility might provide ways to compare the constructivist model with the factor and functional approaches. Then it might be possible to conduct a "grand test," pitting the three models against one another to see which best predicts persuasion. Since the constructivists believe that source credibility is best studied as another instance in which people form impressions (Delia, 1976), they have not been interested in creating more specific methods or conducting such a test.

(3) Cognitive Dissonance Theory

A third approach to persuasion is Leon Festinger's Cognitive Dissonance Theory (1957). It is the most thoroughly researched of a family of cognitive consistency theories and therefore the one we shall discuss in this chapter (for a review of other consistency theories see Kiesler, Collins, & Miller, 1969). Consistency theories of persuasion are based on the idea that inconsistency is psychologically uncomfortable. Inconsistency results when we believe A should have a certain relationship to B, but does not, or when A has an unexpected undesirable relationship with something. For instance, inconsistency would be felt if we see that a program to reduce poverty in our city is not reducing hunger among children as we had expected. Instead, the program is reducing hope and aspirations among poor people.

Cognitive Dissonance Theory assumes that two beliefs are related either in a state of consonance or dissonance. A state of consonance is characterized by consistency: "I like my sorority, and my good friend likes my sorority." Dissonance is marked by inconsistency: "I like my sorority, but my good friend does not like it." The idea is that it would "bother" us (we would feel dissonance) if our friend did not also value what we value, and we would be motivated to get rid of the uncomfortable feeling. A central tenet of the theory is: the more the mental discomfort (dissonance), the more we are motivated to change something to make things comfortable.

The theory identifies a number of factors that influence the amount of dissonance experienced. Perhaps the most important one is whether the person's self-concept is involved in the dissonant relationship. If one belief is, "I just said that I liked a task that I really hate" ("I lied"), and a second belief is, "I am an honest person," the dissonance involves self-concept, our mental picture of the kind of person we are. What will be done to reduce dissonance? Research suggests individuals tend to change so that their attitude toward the task is more favorable, "I just said I liked a task that I actually do like." This change in attitude permits consistency with the belief, "I am an honest person." We try to protect our self-concepts by rationalizing our actions and decisions so we do not "look bad" to ourselves. Changing the second belief to "I am dishonest" would also have restored consistency: "I lied" and "I am dishonest." However, we seldom reduce dissonance by changing a favorable belief about ourselves.

This principle can be used to explain the results of a classic study by Aronson and Mills (1959). In order to join a very dull discussion group, individuals were required either to recite a list of sexual terms (mild initiation) or to recite a list of "obscene" words (severe initiation). The research participants were then asked how much they liked the group. Did the severe or the mild initiation lead to greater liking for the group? In line with the theory's prediction, persons given the severe initiation liked the group more. Why? Because they experienced more dissonance. Their beliefs could be characterized as: "I am not stupid," so "I just put forth a great effort, and I got something worthwhile." To conclude that the group was worthless would force the belief about self to be: "I am stupid" since "I just put forth a great effort for little reward." Individuals who experienced the mild initiation did not distort their feelings about the group. "I am not stupid," and "I got little benefit from the discussion, but I did not put much into it, so I have not lost."

Dissonance can be reduced in many ways besides changing beliefs as in the example above. Attitude change toward a speaker's proposal and attitude change toward the speaker are two basic methods of resolving dissonance. Attitude change toward the speaker might involve criticizing the source of the information: "I won't listen to the American Cancer Society public service announcement warning about the health risks of smoking because the American Cancer Society is biased against cigarette smoking." Other methods of reducing dissonance are not as obvious. Selective exposure involves seeking information which supports your opinion but avoiding information which is unfavorable toward your opinion. The listener can also misinterpret the speaker's position so that the speaker seems to agree with the listener. One could also consider the dissonant elements unimportant so that the dissonance does not really matter. "The new car I just bought has little pick-up, but I really don't need power and speed in a car anyway." Another alternative is to add consonant elements to "drown out" the dissonance. "Besides, my new car has great lines, a beautiful interior, an excellent stereo, and perfect handling."

A basic idea about persuasion from dissonance theory is that to persuade people you must cause them to experience dissonance, then offer your proposal as a way to get rid of the dissonance. A persuader might try to make receivers feel dissonance about United States energy policies then present a proposal for developing alternative energy sources such as extracting energy from shale rock or coal, to free the United States from dependence on foreign oil. When a speaker arouses dissonance, the receiver will try to reduce it, using one of the methods listed above. However, dissonance can also be reduced by adopting or agreeing with the speaker's proposal. Although there is no guarantee that the audience will reduce dissonance by changing their minds, the speaker does have a chance to achieve persuasion.

According to the theory, if no dissonance is aroused, there will be no persuasion. People do not change an attitude unless they feel they need to change it. Feeling dissonance provides the motivation to change. The theory predicts that to persuade someone, you must first "upset" the person (make them feel dissonance) concerning your proposal. If you fail to persuade the audience, perhaps the dissonance they felt was not great enough to motivate action.

(4) Ego-Involvement, or Social Judgment Theory

This fourth approach to persuasion is distinctly different from cognitive consistency theories of persuasion. Ego-involvement or social judgment theory

(Sherif, Sherif, & Nebergall, 1965) predicts successful persuasion by a message depending upon how the message is related to the person's current beliefs. Research in physiological psychology indicates if a person is given an "anchor" in making judgments, objects which are close to the anchor are seen as more similar to the anchor than they really are (they are *assimilated*). Objects which are far from the anchor are perceived as even more dissimilar than they really are (they are *contrasted*). If you were handed a bar and told it weighs 10 pounds, you would probably judge too low when asked to guess what a 12 pound bar weighs. You probably would judge the 12 pound bar as just about the same as the 10 pound anchor; you would assimilate it. Next, if asked to guess the weight of a 40 pound bar, you probably would judge it heavier than it really is. It would seem more distant from the anchor; the contrast effect would occur.

What does this have to do with persuasion? Ego-involvement or social judgment theory indicates that assimilation and contrast effects also occur in persuasion. *Assimilation* constitutes persuasion; a *contrast effect* represents a failure to persuade. In the case of persuasion, the receiver's position on the topic of the persuasive message serves as the *anchor*. If a speaker slightly opposes gun control and you moderately oppose it, you tend to interpret the speaker's position as basically the same as yours. On the other hand, the more you favor gun control and the more the speaker opposes it, the greater the likelihood that you will view the speaker's position as more extreme than it really is. Basically, we accept assimilated messages but reject contrasted messages.

Although interesting, the assimilation-contrast notion leaves several questions unanswered. Under what conditions are messages assimilated or contrasted? Why do two individuals with the same position on an issue react differently to the same message about the issue, one person assimilating the message while the other person contrasts it? The concepts of latitude of acceptance, rejection, and noncommitment are needed to answer these questions. The *latitude of acceptance* represents all statements which the person finds acceptable, including the favorite position, the anchor. In Figure 1, the latitudes of acceptance for two individuals are illustrated. In our example, the hypothetical issue has a span of 11 positions. Notice that Chris and Pat have the same most acceptable position (A) or anchor belief: "final exams should be optional in elective courses." Chris rejects statements 6 and 7 while Pat basically agrees that final exams should be optional for students with either an A or B or an A, B or C average. The *latitude of rejection* represents all of the positions on the issue which the person rejects (finds objectionable). In Figure 1 the two persons have latitudes of rejection which vary in width. Pat rejects only statement 1, the position that final exams should be required of all students, while Chris rejects statements 1-7. Rejected statements are indicated by *r* in Figure 1.

Figure 6.1: Ego-Involvement or Social Judgment Theory

	Chris										
Topic Positions:	1	2	3	4	5	6	7	8	9	10	11
	r	r	r	r	r	r	r	nc	a	A	a

	Pat										
Topic Positions:	1	2	3	4	5	6	7	8	9	10	11
	r	nc	nc	nc	nc	a	a	a	a	A	a

A = most acceptable position
a = other acceptable positions
r = positions which are rejected
nc = positions on which the person is neutral

Position Statements

11. Final exams should be optional for all students.
10. Final exams should be optional for graduating seniors.
9. Final exams should be optional in elective courses.
8. Final exams should be optional for students with an A average.
7. Final exams should be optional for students with an A or B average.
6. Final exams should be optional for students with an A, B or C average.
5. Final exams should be optional for students with a passing average.
4. Final exams should be optional at the professor's discretion.
3. Final exams should be required only of freshmen.
2. Final exams should be required only of freshmen and sophomores.
1. Final exams should be required of all students.

The *latitude of noncommitment* consists of all positions which the person neither accepts nor rejects. The person is noncommittal or neutral on these issues. In Figure 1, this is represented by *nc*, statement 8 for Chris and statements 2-5 for Pat. The latitudes of acceptance, rejection, and noncommitment determine whether a given person will assimilate or contrast a message. Messages falling in the latitudes of acceptance or noncommitment will be judged closer to the favorite position (anchor belief) than they really are (assimilated). Messages falling in the latitude of rejection will be judged farther away (contrasted). According to ego-involvement theory, a basic principle of persuasion is that to change a person's most acceptable position on a topic, the message must fall within the person's latitude of acceptance. A persuader can also attempt to widen the latitude of acceptance by advocating a position in the person's latitude of noncommitment. If successful, the persuader will widen the receiver's latitude of acceptance, thus creating a larger "target" for a second persuasion attempt.

The latitudes also indicate whether the person is *ego-involved*. Examine the examples in Figure 1. One of the individuals is highly ego-involved in the topic while the other is low in ego-involvement. According to the theory, high ego-involvement is characterized by a narrow latitude of acceptance (the person's own favorite position is about the only position accepted), a wide latitude of rejection (almost everything other than one's own position is rejected), and a narrow latitude of noncommitment (nearly all positions are either accepted or rejected; the person is neutral about very few positions). Low ego-involvement is opposite. The latitude of acceptance is wide (people are able to accept several other positions on the issue besides their anchor position), the latitude of noncommitment is wide (there are many positions on the topic that the person is neutral about), and the latitude of rejection is narrow (there is not much left to reject if one accepts most positions and does not care about most of the remaining ones).

In Figure 1, it is apparent then that Chris is highly ego-involved and Pat is not ego-involved with final exam regulations. According to the theory, even though they both hold the same most acceptable position (statement 10), they would react differently to a message which advocated position 6. Chris would contrast the message because it falls in the latitude of rejection; it would be "heard" as a more extreme message than it actually is. On the other hand, Pat would assimilate the message, perceive it closer to the anchor (position 10) than it really is because it is one of the positions the person finds acceptable. Thus, Pat would be persuaded by the message; Chris would not.

This theory permits us to conceptualize how persuasion can be achieved with a highly ego-involved individual. In our example, to persuade Chris to change from position 10 to position 2 would take many messages. One message would not be enough—it would be contrasted. Persuasion would require many messages over a long period of time, each gradually expanding the latitude of acceptance and slowly moving the favorite position (anchor belief). This probably is a realistic view of persuasion. It is very difficult to persuade someone who is very ego-involved in a topic. The theory represents this idea clearly. When a person is highly ego-involved, a "one-shot" attempt to persuade the individual is surely doomed to failure. A "persuasive campaign" composed of many messages over a period of time is a more realistic way to try to change someone who is ego-involved.

(5) Value-Expectancy Theory

The fifth major approach to persuasion is based on the idea that the value we expect from something controls our attitude (e.g. Fishbein & Ajzen, 1975; Rosenberg, 1956). Persuading a person involves changing the value that they expect to receive from the object of persuasion. For instance, if you expect many good things to result from a proposal and someone convinces you that not only will the good things not happen but bad will actually result, you will change your attitude toward the proposal. If someone convinces you that making final exams optional would result in lower grades and more pressure during midterm exams, you might oppose a change in final exam policy. You would shift from pro to con on the proposal. This represents persuasion in its most basic form. Why would you change your mind? There are two major explanations.

Affective-Cognitive Consistency. One explanation is based on affective-cognitive consistency (Rosenberg, 1956). This theory states that we have *affect* and *cognitions* regarding a topic and that we try to make the two consistent. Affect involves our attitude—how favorably we evaluate an object. Cognitions are beliefs about what is related to the object. In persuasion the most common beliefs deal with the consequences of adopting a proposal. The theory says if we believe that good consequences will result from a proposal, we will favor it. This happens because of our natural tendency toward affective-cognitive consistency, similar to the concept of consistency discussed earlier under Cognitive Dissonance Theory. Affective-cognitive consistency proposes a law of cognitive behavior: if you change a person's beliefs about a proposal the attitude will "automatically" change in the same direction and to the same degree as the belief changes. For instance, if we believe that making finals optional will result in higher grades and less end of semester pressure, we are likely to support the new final exam policy. Likewise, if we are certain that optional exams will mean lower grades and more pressure, we will oppose the change.

If there really is a law that humans seek out cognitive consistency, then it should not only cause a change in beliefs to produce a change in attitudes, but it should also cause a change of attitudes to lead to a change in beliefs. Rosenberg (1960) designed a study to test this idea. He hypnotized people and changed their attitudes toward a program by post-hypnotic suggestion. He found that once attitudes changed from favorable to unfavorable the individuals then proceeded to change their beliefs about the program from good ones to bad. They did this completely by themselves. No persuader told them, "This program will produce bad effects." This study represents some convincing evidence that we try to make our feelings and beliefs about a topic consistent.

It does not require hypnotism for people to change beliefs about a proposal by themselves, without a persuader saying a word about the beliefs. Another researcher found that when a person favors a proposal and a speaker argues convincingly that several bad consequences will result from the proposal, the individual then begins to believe that the *good* consequences are less likely, even though the speaker discussed only *bad* consequences. If a speaker causes you to dislike a proposal that you had liked by saying it would produce bad results, you would then tend to doubt that it would produce all of the good effects you had previously associated with it. Research also shows that arguing that good consequences are unlikely is not as effective as arguing that bad consequences are likely. In fact, listeners liked a speaker less who said good consequences were unlikely. A basic strategy in persuasion might be to try to convince people that things they have not thought were related to a proposal are in fact closely associated with it. For example, people might never have thought about increased stress during midterm exams when they evaluated the new final exam policy. People seldom like to be told they are wrong. Instead, they prefer to change beliefs themselves after they have been convinced bad things are likely to result from a proposal. A flat statement that higher grades will not be the result of the new system would be less effective than introducing the idea that midterms will be more stressful.

The same ideas would apply to a persuader who is trying to convince a receiver to favor a proposal. The receiver believes bad consequences are likely and good consequences are unlikely. The speaker would argue that good grades (good consequences) are likely. Should the speaker try to refute the receiver's beliefs that certain bad consequences are likely? Although it may be tempting, research suggests this could be counterproductive. It may be best to provide receivers with facts about good consequences and allow the receivers to decide for themselves that they have placed too much emphasis on the bad possibilities. Rather than trying to convince the receiver that high stress will not result from the change in final exams, the speaker should emphasize that good grades will result. Of course, if you are asked directly about possible bad consequences, you should not dodge the issue. What we are saying is it may not be a good strategy to volunteer arguments which contradict receivers' current beliefs. By allowing receivers themselves to reconcile privately held beliefs about likely consequences with a message which maintains very different consequences, the speaker, in essence, is inviting the receiver to participate in the message. The receiver is free to complete parts that are unspoken or implied (Infante, 1975c).

Learning. Learning theory provides a second explanation for persuasion from a value-expectancy framework. The idea here is that we *learn* to associate consequences with proposals, characteristics with people, and attributes with objects (Cronkhite, 1969). The affect (feelings) elicited by a consequence becomes connected (conditioned) to the proposal. The proposal is then identified with those emotions. Thereafter, mentioning the proposal arouses the associated emotions. If four negative consequences—lower grades, more pressure, more term papers, and fewer opportunities to raise the final average—have been conditioned to our proposal for changing the final exam policy, the receiver's attitude will represent the total of the negative feelings from the four consequences. This idea comes from classical conditioning in psychology. In Pavlov's famous conditioning experiments, a dog came to respond to a bell in the same way that it responded to having meat powder placed in its mouth—it salivated. Response to the meat powder was conditioned (connected) to the bell by placing the powder in the dog's mouth immediately after ringing a bell. After a while, the dog salivated in response to the bell alone. It could be argued that this conditioning process is like persuasion. In a series of advertisements for example, consequences are paired with a proposal in hopes that people's reactions to the consequences will become attached (conditioned) to the proposal. If the conditioning is successful, the proposal itself will produce a reaction in the audience which would be equal to their reaction to the associated elements. Mentioning a change in policy regarding final exams would have the same effect as actually stating the probability of lower grades, more pressure, more term papers and less chance of changing the final average. Conditioning will be responsible for arousing the audience's dislike without the necessity of repeating the consequences.

Persuasion, then, involves conditioning new affect (feelings) to the proposal and allowing previous (unwanted) associations to weaken. The goal is to extinguish the relationship between the proposal and previous associations. For instance, a persuader might try to have someone who opposes the new final exam policy believe that three good consequences would result from the proposal: less end of semester pressure, more time to devote to other activities, and fewer "all-nighters." These would be "new" consequences in that the receiver had not considered them before. The idea is that a person's attitude is controlled by the beliefs that are the strongest or most important (Fishbein & Ajzen, 1975). If the persuader convinces the audience about three good consequences, the new beliefs will be the ones receivers are most aware of, and they will "push" earlier beliefs to a lower level of awareness. If the receiver is less aware of a belief, that belief has less effect on the receiver's attitude.

Besides adding new beliefs to the receiver's thinking about a proposal, a persuader can increase the salience (awareness) of old beliefs. A receiver who opposes the new final exam policy may have beliefs about good consequences such as more free time to search for a summer job. But those beliefs might not be as salient as beliefs about bad consequences such as lower grades in the fall term. The strategy would be to make the audience more aware of the good beliefs, thus decreasing awareness of the negative beliefs. What would make the good beliefs more salient? First, a speaker could present facts and reasons to demonstrate why the good consequences are likely to happen if the proposal is adopted. Second, the speaker could show how important the good consequence will be to the receivers and their friends. The audience would become less aware of the negative beliefs because the mind can be aware of only so many things at a time. As with affective-cognitive consistency theory, the speaker should avoid mentioning the negative beliefs since they will become more salient if the audience thinks about them. According to learning theory, what is uppermost in awareness (salience), determines one's attitudes.

Preventing Persuasion

We turn now to theories that explain how to prevent persuasion. In emphasizing how to persuade people, it is easy to forget that the reverse is often our goal. It is not unusual for us to want another person to resist being influenced by a third party. We might want a wavering Democrat to resist appeals to vote Republican. In a sense, we try to "persuade" a person not to be persuaded. There have been five approaches taken in persuasion research to the problem of how to prevent persuasion.

The *behavioral commitment* approach advises public statements about positions. If you know that someone supports your proposal, you would want him or her to express that opinion publicly. When other people learn someone holds a given position, it is more difficult for that person to change the position. Since the position has been associated with the individual, "losing face" might result from changing what was previously declared.

The *anchoring* approach is based on the idea that someone will be less likely to change a position if the position is anchored or "tied" to things that are significant for that person. With this approach you would try to convince an individual that valued others (friends, family, etc.) agree with the position and/or that reference groups (religious, political groups, etc.) also agree. Additionally, you might try to have the person see that important values (freedom, for instance) are upheld by the position. Changing an opinion would involve disagreeing with family and friends and would violate group norms and undermine values.

A third approach is creating *resistant cognitive states*. People are more difficult to persuade when they are in certain frames of mind. The major research finding in this area is that when persons experience an increase in self-esteem, they are particularly resistant to persuasion because people who feel high self-esteem believe they are valuable; they are confident and therefore less likely to say they were wrong in holding a position that a persuader tries to change. It is relatively easy to raise or lower self-esteem in a research laboratory. The main technique for raising self-esteem is to lead individuals to believe they have succeeded at an important task. Conversely, believing they have failed lowers self-esteem. Since a person with low self-esteem is particularly easy to persuade, an ethical issue arises. Is it acceptable to try to persuade someone who has just experienced failure? The person may be especially vulnerable at that time and to try to attempt persuasion may be taking advantage of him or her (Infante, 1976).

Training in critical methods is an approach which has met with mixed results. The idea appears sound. Train people to think critically when listening to a speech, to recognize fallacies in reasoning, to detect propaganda techniques, and they will not be so easily persuaded. In one study, students were trained in methods for critically evaluating speeches. Later they listened to a tape recorded speech. Women in the study were persuaded less than untrained women. However, male participants were persuaded more than untrained men, perhaps because the critical methods learned had taught them to pay more attention to the message. American culture may also have taught men to be more firm in their positions than women; therefore, men may pay less attention than women to opposing positions. The training might have neutralized this cultural effect and made men more sensitive to the message (Infante & Grimmett, 1971).

Inoculation theory is the fifth approach (McGuire, 1964). This theory assumes that preventing persuasion is like preventing a disease. To keep a dangerous virus from causing a disease, the body can be inoculated with a weakened form of the disease-producing virus. The body's immune system will then create antibodies to destroy that type of virus. If the actual virus does invade the body at a later date, the defense will be in place and will prevent the disease. In order to prevent persuasion, according to this biological analogy, the person's cognitive system needs to be inoculated so a defense is in place when a strong persuasive message "invades the mind." How does cognitive inoculation work? The counterpart of the weakened virus would be weak arguments in support of an opponent's position. In theory, when an audience hears the weak arguments, they think of refutations for them. These refutations, like antibodies against a disease, form the foundation for attacking stronger arguments which the audience hears later. Thus, preventing persuasion from this approach involves "strengthening" the mind's defense systems so they will be able to destroy strong attacking arguments.

A Rules Theory of Persuasion

With very few exceptions, persuasion theories have been developed from the covering laws perspective. So far, all the theories in this chapter except for the constructivist approach to source credibility have been covering laws theories. As you remember from Chapter 3, covering laws theories are usually concerned with the conditions which *cause* persuasion. A causal relationship can be stated in law-like form. For example, the more dissonance a message produces, the more attitude change there will be in favor of the proposal. In essence scientists following the laws approach search for regular patterns in the way people respond to persuasion, patterns that allow the researcher to predict whether or not the audience will change their minds. Laws theories have relied heavily upon the construct "attitude." Persuasion, therefore, has been conceptualized in terms of attitude change toward the object of a proposal.

The rules approach to persuasion rejects the ideas (1) that there are causal conditions in the environment which control persuasion and (2) that attitudes are necessary to understand persuasion. Instead, the rules approach emphasizes that people make choices because they have free will (See Chapter 3).

Choice-making behavior and factors (such as rules) that influence choice are sufficient to explain persuasion. The rules perspective stresses that people are active information processors who form intentions to behave. These intentions are influenced by the outcomes a person expects from behaving a particular way. Through experience with the consequences of certain behaviors, the person forms rules which guide future behavior. Rules may be individual, but people are likely to adopt rules taught by society. For example, offering your hand for a handshake is behavior related to a rule for "being polite." You may choose to violate this rule, but doing so may lead people to think you are rude.

Smith's (1982a, 1982b, 1984) Contingency Rules Theory is an example of a rules approach to persuasion. Instead of considering attitudes the central construct in persuasion, Smith utilizes the idea of *cognitive schemas*, expectations about (1) the attributes that a given object will have or (2) expectancies about the consequences of behaving in a particular manner. These schemata function as *contingency rules* that both shape the way something is viewed and structure behavior. Let's consider a proposal to finance education by requiring mandatory public service to qualify for a student loan. A contingency rule about an attribute of this proposal might be, "Proposals are worthless if they create more federal bureaucracy." An example of a contingency rule for a consequence of opposing the proposal could be, "My family will not like my opposing the educational loan bill because my tuition might then cost them more, and they value saving money." Smith suggests that rules such as these explain persuasion better than the traditional concept of attitude. Thus, whether we sign a petition supporting a particular student loan bill will depend not so much on our attitude toward the bill, but on how we apply rules for judging government programs. Smith's research has supported her theory that rules can be used to understand persuasion.

According to Smith's Contingency Rules Theory, rules are used to create responses to persuasive messages. *Self-evaluative rules* associate persuasive behavior with the way we think we are and the way we want to be perceived by others. If we believe we are helpful, we would want to be known as helpful individuals. *Adaptive rules* associate persuasive behavior with consequences such as health, safety, good relationships with valued others, economic gains, and status; e.g., "If others consider me helpful, they will like me." Smith stresses that behavioral contingency rules are contextual. This means that the consequences we perceive vary according to such situational differences as whether the individuals are equal in power, whether we are ego-involved in the topic, whether we are calm or anxious, whether the receivers are friendly or hostile, and whether or not we have an intimate relationship with the receivers. In some situations certain consequences are considered (certain rules are activated) which guide behavior. In other situations, other rules are activated. For example, someone in a social situation might apply rules relating arguing to being liked—"go along to get along." Thus, the person would avoid arguments. In a class discussion, the same person might follow rules that tell him or her to agree only if classmates accurately summarize course material. "Don't agree unless the speaker is correct, or the teacher and classmates will think you haven't done your homework."

Rules guide what we say when we want to persuade people and also guide how we respond to others' messages. We use both types of contingency rules, those that concern our evaluation of self and those that concern evaluation of consequences. Smith's approach implies that to understand persuasion we should focus on the choices that people make with regard to the rules they activate in a persuasive situation. A limited number of studies have tested some of the ideas of the theory (Smith 1982a, 1982b, 1984). Although the results are promising, there is too little research at this time to decide whether the theory's claim that rules explain persuasion better than laws is valid.

Summary

In this chapter, we defined persuasion as attitude change toward a source's proposal. Persuasion differs from coercion because audience members can choose to agree or disagree. In this framework, belief change leads to attitude change, which can then produce behavior change. Adapting to the audience and the situation make persuasion more effective. Six dimensions of persuasion situations were identified: intimacy, dominance, resistance, rights, personal benefits, and long-term consequences. The implications for persuasion concerning recent research on self-awareness was discussed. Several major lines of persuasion research were covered: the variable-analytic approach, the source credibility approach, cognitive dissonance theory, ego-involvement or social judgment theory, affective-cognitive consistency theory, learning theory. Next, we discussed five approaches to resisting persuasion: behavioral commitment, anchoring, inducing resistant cognitive states, training in critical methods, and inoculation theory. Finally, the contingency rules theory of persuasion was presented.

As we said at the beginning of this chapter, persuasion research has changed greatly in recent years. Current researchers are especially interested in how people influence one another in interpersonal relationships. We think it is important for persuasion research to continue with the enthusiasm it has enjoyed in the past. Persuasion is an important topic for communication study since success depends upon how well the persuader manipulates verbal and nonverbal symbols. The growth of the advertising and public relations professions provides another persuasive context to which communication theory can be applied.

Of course, there are other ways of influencing another person's behavior. Two particularly distasteful methods are physical aggression and coercion.

Persuasion is infinitely more desirable than these alternatives because the process of persuasion, more than the other methods, respects the dignity and best features of humans. Persuasion offers hope for people to resolve differences in a satisfying and constructive manner. Therefore, research which enhances our understanding of this process is inherently valuable.

Questions To Consider

1. Discuss how the construct "attitude" is used to conceptualize persuasion.
2. What are the major dimensions of persuasive situations?
3. How do the ideas of self-awareness and communication scripts contribute to our understanding of persuasion?
4. What is the variable analytic approach to understanding persuasion?
5. How is persuasion studied according to the source credibility approach?
6. What are the differences between the factor, functional, and constructivist models of source credibility?
7. What is Cognitive Dissonance Theory? How does the theory explain persuasion? List several ways of reducing dissonance.
8. How is persuasion explained according to ego-involvement or social judgment theory?
9. What are the main ideas of affective-cognitive consistency theory?
10. List 5 ways of preventing persuasion.
11. What are the assumptions of Smith's Contingency Rules Theory? How does it explain persuasion?
12. Explain the role of self-evaluative rules and adaptive rules in Smith's Contingency Rules Theory. Compare these rules to behavior and content rules of the Coordinated Management of Meaning Theory discussed in Chapter 3.

References

Abelson, R. (1976). Script processing in attitude formation and decision making. In J. Carroll and T. Payne (Eds.), *Cognition and social behavior* (pp. 33-45). Hillsdale, NJ: Lawrence Erlbaum.

Adorno, T. W., Frenkel-Brunswik, E., Levinson, D. J., & Sanford, R. N. (1950). *The authoritarian personality*. New York: Harper & Row.

Andersen, K., & Clevenger, T., Jr. (1963). A summary of experimental research in ethos. *Speech Monographs, 30*, 59-78.

Aronson, E., & Mills, J. (1959). The effect of severity of initiation on liking for a group. *Journal of Abnormal and Social Psychology, 59,* 177-181.

Boster, F. J. (1988). Comments on the utility of compliance-gaining message selection tasks. *Human Communication Research, 15,* 169-177.

Bostrom, R. N. (1983). *Persuasion.* Englewood Cliffs, NJ: Prentice-Hall.

Bostrom, R. N, Baseheart, J., & Rossiter, C. (1973). The effects of three types of profane language in persuasive messages. *Journal of Communication, 23,* 461-475.

Bradac, J. J., Bowers, J. W., & Courtright, J. A. (1979). Three language variables in communication research: Intensity, immediacy, and diversity. *Human Communication Research, 5,* 257-269.

Burgoon, M., & Bettinghaus, E. P. (1980). Persuasive message strategies. In M. E. Roloff & G. R. Miller (Eds.), *Persuasion: New directions in theory and research* (pp. 141-169). Beverly Hills, CA: Sage.

Burgoon, M., Jones, S. B., & Stewart, D. (1975). Toward a message centered theory of persuasion: Three empirical investigations of language intensity. *Human Communication Research, 1,* 240-256.

Burleson, B. R., & Wilson, S. R. (1988). On the continuing undesirability of item desirability: A reply to Boster, Hunter and Seibold. *Human Communication Research, 15,* 178-191.

Burleson, B. R., Wilson, S. R., Waltman, M. S., Goering, E. M., Ely, T. K., & Whaley, B. B. (1988). Item desirability effects in compliance-gaining research: Seven studies documenting artifacts in the strategy selection procedure. *Human Communication Research, 14,* 429-486.

Cody, M. J., & McLaughlin, M. L. (1980). Perceptions of compliance-gaining situations: A dimensional analysis. *Communication Monographs, 47,* 132-148.

Crockett, W. H. (1965). Cognitive complexity and impression formation," In B. A. Maher (Ed.), *Progress in experimental personality research,* (Vol. 1, pp. 47-90). New York: Academic Press.

Cronkhite, G. (1969). *Persuasion: Speech and behavioral change.* Indianapolis: Bobbs-Merrill.

Cronkhite, G., & Liska, J. R. (1976). A critique of factor analytic approaches to the study of credibility. *Communication Monographs, 43,* 91-107.

Cronkhite, G., & Liska, J. R. (1980). The judgment of communicant acceptability. In M. E. Roloff & G. R. Miller (Eds.), *Persuasion: New directions in theory and research* (pp. 101-139). Beverly Hills, CA: Sage.

Delia, J. G. (1976). A constructivistic analysis of the concept of credibility. *Quarterly Journal of Speech, 62,* 361-375.

Delia, J. G., & Clark, R. A. (1977). Cognitive complexity, social perception, and the development of listener-adapted communication in six-, eight-, ten-, and twelve-year old boys. *Communication Monographs, 44,* 326-345.

Delia, J. G., Crockett, W. H., Press, A. N., & O'Keefe, D. J. (1975). The dependency of interpersonal evaluations on context relevant beliefs about the other. *Communication Monographs, 42,* 10-19.

Delia, J.G., O'Keefe, B.J., & O'Keefe, D.J. (1982). The constructivist approach to communication. In F.E.X. Dance (Ed.), *Human communication theory* (pp. 147-191). New York: Harper & Row.

Feezel, J. D. (1974). A qualified certainty: Verbal probability in argument. *Speech Monographs, 41,* 348-356.

Festinger, L. (1957). *A theory of cognitive dissonance.* Stanford: Stanford University Press.

Fishbein, M., & Ajzen, I. (1975). *Belief, attitude, intention and behavior: An introduction to theory and research.* Reading, MA: Addison-Wesley.

Gruner, C. R. (1965). An experimental study of satire as persuasion. *Speech Monographs, 32,* 149-154.

Gruner, C. R. (1970). The effect of humor in dull and interesting informative speeches. *Central States Speech Journal, 21,* 160-166.

Gulley, H., & Berlo, D. (1956). Effects of intercellular and intracellular speech structure on attitude change and learning. *Speech Monographs, 23,* 288-297.

Hart, R. P., Carlson, R. E., & Eadie, W. F. (1980). Attitudes toward communication and the assessment of rhetorical sensitivity. *Communication Monographs, 47,* 1-22.

Hovland, C. I. (Ed.) (1957). *The order of presentation in persuasion.* New Haven: Yale University Press.

Hovland, C. I., & Janis, I. L. (Eds.) (1959). *Personality and persuasibility.* New Haven: Yale University Press.

Hunter, J. E. (1988). Failure of the social desirability response set hypothesis. *Human Communication Research, 15,* 162-168.

Infante, D. A. (1973). The perceived importance of cognitive structure components: An adaptation of Fishbein's theory. *Speech Monographs, 40,* 8-16.

Infante, D. A. (1975a). The effects of opinionated language on communicator image and in conferring resistance to persuasion. *Western Journal of Speech Communication, 39,* 112-119.

Infante, D. A. (1975b). Richness of fantasy and beliefs about attempts to refute a proposal as determinants of attitude. *Speech Monographs, 42,* 75-79.

Infante, D. A. (1975c). Differential functions of desirable and undesirable consequences in predicting attitude and attitude change toward proposals. *Speech Monographs, 42,* 115-134.

Infante, D. A. (1975d). The Socratic effect in response to speeches opposing a proposal. *Central States Speech Journal, 26,* 201-206.

Infante, D. A. (1976). Persuasion as a function of the receiver's prior success or failure as a message source. *Communication Quarterly, 24,* 21-26.

Infante, D. A. (1980). The construct validity of semantic differential scales for the measurement of source credibility. *Communication Quarterly, 28,* 19-26.

Infante, D. A., & Grimmett, R. A. (1971). Attitudinal effects of utilizing a critical method of analysis. *Central States Speech Journal, 22,* 213-217.

Infante, D. A., Parker, K. R., Clarke, C. H., Wilson, L., & Nathu, I. A. (1983). A comparison of factor and functional approaches to source credibility. *Communication Quarterly, 31,* 43-48.

Infante, D. A., & Wigley, C. J. (1986). Verbal aggressiveness: An interpersonal model and measure. *Communication Monographs, 53,* 61-69.

Janis, I. L., & Feshbach, S. (1953). Effects of fear-arousing communications. *Journal of Abnormal and Social Psychology, 48,* 78-92.

Kiesler, C., Collins, B., & Miller, N. (1969). *Attitude change: A critical analysis of theoretical approaches.* New York: John Wiley.

Knower, F. R. (1935). Experimental studies of attitude change I: A study of effect of oral argument on changes of attitude. *Journal of Abnormal and Social Psychology, 6*, 315-347.

McCroskey, J. C. (1969). A summary of experimental research on the effects of evidence in persuasive communication. *Quarterly Journal of Speech, 55*, 169-176.

McCroskey, J. C., & Wright, D. W. (1971). A comparison of the effects of punishment-oriented and reward-oriented messages in persuasive communication. *Journal of Communication, 21*, 83-93.

McGuire, W. J. (1964). Inducing resistance to persuasion: Some contemporary approaches. In L. Berkowitz (Ed.), *Advances in experimental social psychology* (Vol. 1, pp. 191-229). New York: Academic Press.

McGuire, W. J. (1969). The nature of attitudes and attitude change. In G. Lindzey & E. Aronson (Eds.), *Handbook of social psychology* (Vol. 3, pp. 136-314). Reading, MA: Addison-Wesley.

Mehrley, R. S., & McCroskey, J. C. (1970). Opinionated statements and attitude intensity as predictors of attitude change and source credibility. *Speech Monographs, 37*, 47-52.

Miller, G. R., Burgoon, M., & Burgoon, J. K. (1984). The function of human communication in changing attitudes and gaining compliance. In C. C. Arnold & J. W. Bowers (Eds.), *Handbook of rhetorical and communication theory* (pp. 400-474). Boston: Allyn & Bacon.

O'Keefe, B. J. (1984). The evolution of impressions in small working groups: Effects of construct differentiation. In H. E. Sypher & J. L. Applegate (Eds.), *Communication by children and adults* (pp. 262-291). Beverly Hills, CA: Sage.

O'Keefe, B. J., & Delia, J. G. (1982). Impression formation and message production. In M. E. Roloff & C. R. Berger (Eds.), *Social cognition and communication* (pp. 33-72). Beverly Hills, CA: Sage.

O'Keefe, D. J., & Sypher, H. E. (1981). Cognitive complexity measures and the relationship of cognitive complexity to communication: A critical review. *Human Communication Research, 8*, 72-92.

Rokeach, M. (1960). *The open and closed mind.* New York: Basic Books.

Roloff, M. E. (1980). Self-awareness and the persuasion process: Do we really *know* what we're doing? In M. E. Roloff & G. R. Miller (Eds.), *Persuasion: New directions in theory and research* (pp. 29-66). Beverly Hills, CA: Sage.

Rosenberg, M. J. (1956). Cognitive structure and attitudinal effects. *Journal of Abnormal and Social Psychology, 53*, 367-372.

Rosenberg, M. J. (1960). Cognitive reorganization in response to the hypnotic reversal of attitude affect. *Journal of Personality, 28*, 39-63.

Ruechelle, R. C. (1958). An experimental study of audience recognition of emotional and intellectual appeals in persuasion. *Speech Monographs, 25*, 49-58.

Samter, W., Burleson, B. R., & Basden-Murphy, L. (1989). Behavioral complexity is in the eye of the beholder: Effects of cognitive complexity and message complexity on impressions of the source of comforting messages. *Human Communication Research, 15*, 612-629.

Scheidel, T. M. (1963). Sex and persuasibility. *Speech Monographs, 30*, 353-358.

Scott, M., & Hurt, T. (1978). Social influence as a function of communication and message type. *Southern Speech Communication Journal, 43*, 146-161.

Seibold, D. R. (1988). A response to "Item desirability in compliance-gaining research." *Human Communication Research, 15,* 152-161.

Sereno, K., & Bodaken, E. (1972). Ego-involvement and attitude change: Toward a reconceptualization of persuasive effect. *Speech Monographs, 39,* 151-158.

Sherif, C. W., Sherif, M., & Nebergall, R. W. (1965). *Attitude and attitude change: The social judgment-involvement approach.* Philadelphia: Saunders.

Smith, M. J. (1982a). Cognitive schemata and persuasive communication: Toward a contingency rules theory. In M. Burgoon (Ed.), *Communication Yearbook 6* (pp. 330-362). Beverly Hills, CA: Sage.

Smith, M. J. (1982b). Contingency rules theory of persuasion: An empirical test. *Communication Quarterly, 30,* 359-367.

Smith, M. J. (1984). Contingency rules theory, context, and compliance behaviors. *Human Communication Research, 10,* 489-512.

Spillman, B. (1979). The impact of value and self-esteem messages in persuasion. *Central States Speech Journal, 30,* 67-74.

Thistlethwaite, D. L., Kamenetsky, J., & Schmidt, H. (1956). Refutation and attitude change. *Speech Monographs, 23,* 14-25.

Tubbs, S. (1968). Explicit versus implicit audience conclusions and audience commitment. *Speech Monographs, 35,* 14-19.

Wilkie, W. H. (1934). An experimental comparison of the speech, the radio, and the printed page as propaganda devices. *Archives of Psychology, 25,* No. 169.

Zillman, D. (1972). Rhetorical elicitation of agreement in persuasion. *Journal of Abnormal and Social Psychology, 21,* 159-165.

Chapter 7

Verbal Behavior Approaches

"Human beings are the only creatures on earth that can talk themselves into trouble." This statement suggests that communication and language are responsible for many of the difficulties that people experience every day. If you think carefully about your encounters over the last few weeks, you may be able to recall several instances in which you "talked yourself into trouble." Perhaps you told someone that they were "interesting," only to discover that rumors had spread across campus about your new intimate relationship! You might have made what you thought was a small joke in class and suddenly found yourself in disfavor with the professor because of your "wisecrack." If you promised your mother that you would vacuum the house "real soon," she might have been upset because you did not do it that *morning*.

If these examples sound familiar, you are aware of the difficulties that exist when people communicate. Some students assume that the formal study of human communication will be an "easy" subject to master. Newcomers to the field have remarked, "communication must be a real easy subject. After all, I have been communicating since I was born and talking since I was three years old."

Signs, Symbols, and Signals

Some of the difficulty in understanding and practicing effective communication can be traced to the core of verbal communication, *language*. Language can be thought of as a collection of signs, symbols, codes and rules which are used to construct and convey messages. These elements form the medium through which we communicate our ideas, desires and feelings. Language is "a productive system capable of displacement and composed of rapidly fading, arbitrary, culturally transmitted symbols" (DeVito, 1988, p. 81). This definition highlights several important characteristics of spoken and written words.

Displacement means that language permits us to discuss topics that cut across time and space, reality and fantasy. Messages delivered today can influence events and people in other times and in other cultures. The speeches and letters of Dr. Martin Luther King, Jr., written in the early 1960s in the United States, are now influencing a new generation of individuals in the U.S. and South Africa.

Rapid fading means that verbal messages must be received immediately after they are sent, or they will be lost. Although books, audiotape, videotape, laser disks and other devices allow us to store our signs, symbols and signals temporarily, information stored on even the best of video- or audiotape, the sturdiest disk drive, or the finest quality paper will eventually decay and lose information in the information theory sense (See Chapter 4).

The concepts *sign*, *symbol*, and *signal* are related and often confused with each other. *Signs* stand for or represent something else. The object or concept the sign represents is called a referent. There are two types of signs: natural signs are called *signals*; artificial or conventional signs are called *symbols*. Signals stand in a direct one-to-one relationship with what they represent. They are not ambiguous or arbitrary but are linked with specific responses. Cronkhite (1986) defines a signal as, "That type of sign that stands for its significate by virtue of a natural relationship, usually by some relationship of causality, contingency, or resemblance" (p. 232). Signals technically cannot be arranged because they occur naturally; they are discovered, not created. This definition of signal differs significantly from common usage of the term "traffic signal." In order to avoid confusion, Cronkhite has substituted the word *symptom* for *signal*. A "symptom is a sign that bears a natural relationship to that for which it stands" (Cronkhite, 1986, p. 232). For example, thunder, lightning and dark clouds are symptoms of an approaching rainstorm. Calloused hands are a symptom of physical labor. High temperature, sneezing, and congestion are symptoms of a head cold or flu.

Signs also exist as conventional, human-made, artificial phenomena called *symbols*. Artificially created or conventional symbols provide meaning when a particular society has agreed on what they will look like and what they will represent. Increase in foreign travel has necessitated the creation of international traffic signs. These signs are now found on major freeways and highways across the U.S. and Western Europe. For example, a sign with a hand facing you, palm exposed, means **stop**. The meaning of that sign is becoming universally accepted.

One important characteristic of symbols is that they are *arbitrary* and *ambiguous*; they do *not* have a direct relationship with their referents. The word *elephant*, for example, does not possess any of the physical characteristics of a large animal. Unlike a physical sign or signal, a symbol can have many referents. A picture of an elephant in a children's book is another possible referent for the word-symbol *elephant*. The picture of the elephant is also a nonverbal symbol of the animal. Just like the word, the picture stands for, or represents, something other than itself.

A third category of sign behaviors which are neither totally arbitrary nor symptomatic has been called *rituals*. The clenching of a fist or the fidgeting and foot-shuffling which occurs just before the end of a class are examples of rituals (Cronkhite, 1986, p. 234).

The communication discipline has focused largely on the study of human *symbolic activity*. Although research has been conducted into forms of non-symbolic behavior and some communication scholars still argue that "all behavior is communication" (see Chapter 1), other scholars including Cronkhite (1986) have suggested that the focus of our field needs to be more narrowly and realistically defined. They argue that primary attention should be focused on the effects of symbol systems and those who use them. The study of language and verbal behavior is inherently connected to the study of human symbolic activity.

Language and Meaning

The symbols used to create language are arbitrary and ambiguous. Yet communication is a process of exchanging mutually understood symbols to stimulate meaning in another (Steinfatt, 1977). Indeed, human language exists in order to allow us to share meanings. If symbols themselves do not contain meaning, how then is meaning created out of symbols? Meaning is accomplished when human beings *interpret* symbols. Meaning is a human creation; "Words don't mean; people mean." That is, the meaning of symbols is supplied by people and their culture. Symbols themselves carry no innate meaning; they may mean one thing to one person and something different to someone else. For example, the word-symbol *rock* can mean a hard substance found in quarries, a type of contemporary music, or a valuable stone set in a ring.

An eleven-year-old boy noticed that his mother was unusually quiet and did not appear to be "herself." When he asked his mother what was wrong, she replied that she was feeling depressed and did not know why. The son suggested that his mother see a psychiatrist to find out what was wrong. Before he could finish his sentence, he noticed that both of his parents became quite angry. They admonished him for being rude and impolite to his mother and "punished" him by sending him to his room! The boy honestly did not understand why he was being punished, or why his parents had reacted so strongly. The parents soon forgot the incident, but it continued to haunt the boy. Several years later, while studying language and communication at college, he finally understood what had happened. To the mother and father, the word psychiatrist meant "doctor who treats crazy people." To the son, *psychiatrist* meant "counselor, advisor, and mental health professional who helps people understand their problems." The two generations had very different meanings for the symbol *psychiatrist*.

We learn meanings from our past experiences, from the mass media, and from interactions with friends, family, and authority figures. Even though the meaning of a given symbol can appear quite similar, no two people have the *exact* same meaning for the symbol. If people do not share the same meaning for symbols, how is communication possible? In order to answer this, we must distinguish between two types of meaning, *denotative* and *connotative*.

Denotative refers to the "actual" or "agreed upon" meaning or meanings of a word. Denotative meaning is frequently referred to as the literal or "dictionary" meaning of a word. Connotative meaning refers to subjective associations—the personal and emotional attachments that people associate with a word or symbol. Connotative meaning contains all of the judgments and evaluations that individuals have for a word or symbol. The word *college*, for example, has both denotative and connotative meaning. Its denotative meaning is, "An institution of higher learning furnishing courses of instruction usually leading to a bachelor's degree." Its connotative meaning can differ considerably. One connotative meaning might be, "A place to party for four or more years." Another connotative meaning for college is, "An institution which will prepare me to get a job." Yet another connotative meaning could be, "The place where I became an adult and learned responsibility." Communication could not occur if people did not operate with some denotative meanings. Dictionaries are created to provide us with the "correct" or "accepted" definitions of words. We still run into difficulty, however, when the dictionary provides us with multiple definitions of symbols! For example, twelve different definitions of "college" may be found in a large dictionary.

Language and Perception

Culture strongly influences the way a linguistic system develops and is transmitted. Language, as a set of signs, symbols and signals, has a grammar associated with it. All languages have their own unique organization patterns. Communication becomes possible when individuals share a system of order or grammar. Linguists and semanticists Benjamin Lee Whorf and Edward Sapir suggested that the language system we learn from our culture has a profound influence on how we interpret the world: "Language shapes perceptions of reality."

Theory of Linguistic Relativity

This hypothesis, (labelled Whorfian, Sapir-Whorf, or the Theory of Linguistic Relativity) contains two fundamental principles: (1) All higher levels of thought depend on language; and (2) The structure of the language we use influences the way we understand our environment (Chase, 1956, vi). The Theory of Linguistic Relativity has never been tested through scientific experiments. Little if any research has explored the relationship between linguistic structure and actual behavior. Cronkhite (1976) states that the theory "would be impossible to 'prove' even if it were true" (p. 271). We have no way of interpreting reality without thinking thoughts expressed in some language. Suppose we met a being from outer space who could perceive but had no means to communicate. Without language we could not share this creature's understanding of the world.

One study did lend support to the Theory of Linguistic Relativity. It indicated that people with differences in words for colors perceive colors differently. The researchers discovered that differences in the ability to recognize and recall colors is associated with the availability of names for those colors (Brown & Lenneberg, 1954). For example, people from cultures with a word for a particular shade of blue such as *azure, sapphire,* or *royal* would be more likely to perceive differences in shades of blue than those who had only one word for blue. People with the limited vocabulary could recognize shade differences once they had been pointed out but would be unlikely to perceive the shade on their own since their language did not stimulate them to distinguish hues of the same color. Since languages develop in part in response to environmental conditions, a language is likely to have many words for classifying phenomena important to its physical and cultural environment. For example, the Eskimo language has many different words for snow. Eskimos are more likely to notice and think about differences in snowfalls than are native speakers of English who have only a single term for snow. English leads us to "lump" all types of snow together and to ignore differences that the Eskimo highlights (Cronkhite, 1976).

Much of the data that Whorf reports compares standard American English vocabulary to the language structure of the Native American Indian language Hopi. The Hopi and Standard American English linguistic systems have very different rules for the discussion of "time." Time in the Hopi system is a psychological time, rather than a quantitative measure. For the Hopi, the concept of time varies with each person and cannot be given a number larger than one. The Hopi do not say, "I stayed five days," but, "I left on the fifth day" (Whorf, 1956, p. 216).

The Sapir-Whorf hypothesis is important because it suggests that there is a connection between one's language and one's behavior. If language shapes perception and perception shapes behavior, then language can strongly influence one's actual behavior. American Standard English contains a great many polarized words—pairs of opposites. Think of the bi-polar adjectives thick and thin, smart and stupid, tall and short, ugly and beautiful. Now try to think of a word that will fit exactly in the middle between those bi-polar adjectives. The English language provides us with a ready store of opposites but does not provide us with many "moderate" words. We have difficulty finding them and using them (DeVito, 1986).

How does this linguistic situation influence our behavior? Let us suppose that your friend shows you a new outfit he or she has just purchased and asks your opinion of it. Suppose your attitude is somewhere right in the middle between love and hate. You don't want to say, "It's okay," as that answer sounds somewhat vague. What other alternatives quickly come to mind? "Nice" and "fair" do not accurately reflect your feelings. Thus, you are almost "forced" to say that you "love" or "hate" it. The constraints imposed on you by the linguistic system influence what you say. Indeed, you may then come to like the outfit more or less (another pair of opposites!) based on the word you chose.

Question Phrasing

A further illustration that language influences verbal responses is the recent finding that how questions are phrased affects perception and the responses given to the questions. Loftus' (1979, 1980) research has demonstrated that the way eye witnesses are questioned in court alters the witnesses' memories and biases their testimony. In one experiment Loftus showed participants a film of an automobile accident, then asked one of two questions: (1) "Did you see *the* broken headlight?" or (2) "Did you see *a* broken headlight?" In reality there was no broken headlight on the film, but participants asked about "*the* headlight" were more likely to report that they saw one. "The" biased perception because it implied a broken headlight existed. Participants then interpreted the question to mean, "Did you see it?" rather than, "Was a headlight broken?" In a second study participants were asked what speed the vehicles in a film of a traffic accident had been traveling. Half the participants were asked, "About how fast were the cars going when they *smashed* into each other?" The others were asked, "About how fast were the cars going when they *hit* each other?" The group who heard the *smashed* description estimated the speed as much faster than the *hit* group. Even though both groups saw the same film of the accident, the word *smashed* created an expectation that the accident was more serious and thus the cars must have been travelling very fast. In addition, the effects of the questions appear long-lasting and influence other perceptions. One week after seeing the film, participants in both groups were asked, "Did you see broken glass?" Although no broken glass appeared in the film, the *smashed* group were much more likely to say they had seen it. Thus, the original question biased what was perceived and remembered; at a later date, people answered a new question in terms of their altered memories of the accident.

Research has also demonstrated that limiting the range of responses to a question affects a person's memory. The researcher questioned people about headache remedies then asked one of two questions: (1) "In terms of a number, how many other products have you tried: 1, 2, 3?" or (2) "In terms of a number, how many other products have you tried: 1, 5, 10?" The group who heard the first question reported an average of 3.3 additional products tried, while the second group remembered trying an average of 5.2 products. The restrictive wording of the first question discouraged thorough memory searching (Loftus, 1979, 1980). Loftus' research indicates that it is very easy to structure a question to manipulate a particular answer, a fact well known to trial attorneys who cross-examine witnesses! Although the differences in how questions are phrased may be subtle and might not be noticed except by language experts, questions strongly affect the answers people give. Even though we use language almost every waking minute to communicate or think, we are still not aware of its power. Researchers are continuing to probe the subtle nuances of language to understand how it affects communication.

Language and Power

Power, control, and status are at the core of many social relationships (Giles & Wiemann, 1987). More powerful speakers can exercise greater control over a communication interaction and even the entire relationship (Wiemann, 1985). Can you recall a situation where language made you feel powerless or low in status? Perhaps you remember a time when you felt inadequate because of your conversational partner's vocabulary level. Some individuals, for example, report feeling "left out," "ignorant," and "passive" when they communicate with their physicians. Doctors who lack effective communication skills often appear to "talk down" to their patients. They do this by using professional jargon and "buzz words" and by interrupting when patients ask questions.

Communicating Power, Status and Control

Several forms of verbal behavior are commonly used by people in powerful or powerless positions. As you encounter each example, review whether you have used any of these forms in your own speech or writing. What conclusions might others draw from your communication?

Verbal Intensifiers. Verbal intensifiers are adverbs such as *so, such,* and *quite,* and expressions such as "It was *really* nice." By increasing the intensity of the emotion being conveyed, intensifiers also serve to reduce the strength of an utterance. Instead of saying, "I'm upset with my roommate," the inclusion of a verbal intensifier would modify the utterance to "I'm *so* upset with my roommate." The language implies that usual expressions are inadequate to convey the speaker's extreme emotion.

Verbal Qualifiers. Verbal qualifiers also reduce the strength and impact of an utterance. Examples frequently cited are "you know," "possibly," "perhaps," "I guess," and "in my opinion." Instead of saying, "A communication degree will prepare me well for many careers," a lower status or less powerful speaker might add a verbal qualifier to the statement: "In my opinion, a communication degree will prepare me well for many careers." The new statement sounds as if the speaker doubts that hearers will agree.

Tag Questions. In this form of verbal behavior, the speaker adds or "tags on" a question to the end of a statement. Tag questions often weaken the assertions of the speaker. Note, for example, the difference in the strength of the following statements: "Billy Joel is a great singer and songwriter," and "Billy Joel is a great singer and songwriter, isn't he?" The second speaker appears to be insecure and seeking reassurance. Some scholars argue that tag questions are used to draw a response from reluctant communicators (Pearson, 1985). However, tag questions appear to weaken the verbal behavior of the speaker by making assertions appear less certain.

Lengthening of Requests. The power and status of a speaker is often related to lengthening of requests. For example, if you want someone to open the window, you may say, "Open the window." If you want to appear more polite you might add, "Please open the window." People who add additional words to their requests are making "compound requests." Lengthening a request also serves to soften the request and suggests that the speaker is less powerful, less assertive, and of lower status. For example, some speakers may add the additional phrase, "If it is not too much trouble" to the sentence above. While lengthening a request appears to signal politeness, it also seems to make the speaker appear to be more tentative, hesitant and weak.

Sex, Gender and Power: Differences in Verbal Behavior

Over the last two decades scholars have studied sex differences in verbal behavior. Several recent books have examined this rapidly increasing body of communication research in great detail (Bate, 1988; Pearson, 1985; Stewart, Cooper & Friedley, 1986). Much of the early research indicated that females tend to use more verbal intensifiers, qualifiers, tag questions and lengthening of requests than males (Lakoff, 1975; Pearson, 1985). Because of this, "female speech" was often characterized as less powerful and assertive than "male" speech.

During the last fifteen years, society has become more sensitive to verbal displays of power. The feminist, senior citizen, gay and lesbian, black, disabled and Hispanic movements have also had a significant impact on the language choices we make (Bate, 1988). During the last twenty years, the description preferred by members of the Negro race has changed from *colored* to *Negro* to *Black*. Recently, Jesse Jackson has advocated the use of *African American*, a term that appears to be gaining popularity. The women's movement, in particular, has done much to alter the verbal behavior of males and females. It has sensitized us to expressions of power and status in speech. As a consequence of this heightened sensitivity, changes have occurred in people's language. We now avoid using the masculine pronoun *he* to stand for both males and females, and we avoid sex-stereotyped job titles such as *policeman* in favor of the gender-neutral *police officer*. Like *Mr.*, the title *Ms.* does not require a speaker or writer to know someone's marital status to address her politely. Bradac (1988) notes that additional research must be conducted on the interaction of context and linguistic indicators of power. He poses several questions that communication theorists need to investigate. For example, Is it sometimes possible to increase power by hedging or being indefinite in language? Will high power persons such as corporate presidents be able to enhance their power if they use low-power forms of verbal behavior? How will people respond to a woman C.E.O. who uses "feminine speech"?

Verbal Codes

A code is "a set of rules for converting one sign system into another" (Ellis, 1982, p. 53). The written alphabet is a code whereby language sounds are translated into written symbols. Other codes include the Morse code (the alphabet converted into a series of dots and dashes), scientific notation (symbols denoting chemicals and compounds, such as NaCl for sodium chloride), and a computer coding system called ASCII (American Standard Code for Information Interchange assigns a binary digit to all the characters of the alphabet and punctuation symbols). Codes have existed for quite some time. The military uses codes to disguise information and messages which might be intercepted by an enemy. During World War II, British military officials successfully broke the German code; the information gained shortened the war and led to an Allied victory. We employ codes whenever we formulate a message and prepare it for transmission or receive a message and interpret its meaning. In Chapter 1 we identified those processes as *encoding* and *decoding*. Codes act as strategies or plans of language use (Ellis, 1982).

Codes are often determined by the relationship between individuals and the larger social structure. Researchers identify a linguistic code by observing a given culture over time. They observe and record specific and frequently occurring features of the linguistic system to determine the linguistic rules communicators use. DeVito (1986) and Ellis (1982) suggest that certain co-languages have developed with their own distinctive verbal codes. They cite Black English as one example of a co-language which has its own unique verbal code.

Verbal codes as strategies or plans of linguistic use are influenced by situational factors. The choice of language used is an interaction of the language system, the situation, and the choices available to the speaker. Ellis (1982) suggests "There is a systematic relationship between language and the environment, and codes function to organize this relationship" (p. 55). For example, speakers may consciously switch back and forth between linguistic codes. After several years in college, your language style will probably differ from your pre-college days. You will have a greater repertoire of linguistic choices. The sophistication and expansion of your vocabulary and additional training in grammar affects your conversation. On the other hand, you probably have not forgotten the grammar, vocabulary and linguistic coding system used in your pre-college days. You can move from one code to another with greater proficiency, engaging in *code-switching*. If you doubt your code-switching ability, go to a local club you may have frequented before college and interact with the patrons there. You will probably find yourself switching verbal codes in order to seem more like your friends. On several occasions, friends have teased one of your authors for using the linguistic code of "The Professor" in informal social conversations!

The Enthymeme

Much communication takes the form of informal or "everyday" argument. In argument, people attempt to "manage" conversations by using rules. Conversational arguments, however, are not as complete as more conventional or "formal" arguments. Conversational arguments do not always link premises with conclusions as in formal argument. These "incomplete" arguments are attempts to reach agreement between the communicators (Jackson & Jacobs, 1980).

One rhetorical device particularly relevant to the discussion of both formal and informal argument is the *enthymeme*. The enthymeme, an incomplete chain of deductive reasoning, has been studied since antiquity and holds a central place in Aristotle's rhetorical system (See Chapter 4). An enthymeme is an argument created by the joint efforts of communicators or by a speaker and the audience. When speakers use enthymemes, they sometimes allow their receivers to draw the conclusion the speaker wants them to draw. For example, opponents of nuclear power suggest that nuclear power plants cannot be considered one hundred percent safe and that they pose a significant danger to surrounding residents. They point to the problems which occurred at the Three Mile Island and Chernobyl nuclear power plants. The unsupplied conclusion they hope the audience will draw is, "If we build nuclear power plants, they will explode, and people will be killed." This second level of argument is often implicit in the message and is rarely directly stated. When anti-nuclear power speakers deliver messages on this topic, they often use enthymemes to allow the receivers to draw their own conclusions and thus participate in persuading themselves (Bitzer, 1959).

In conversation, enthymemes are constructed from questions asked or objections raised by a receiver. Unlike more conventional interpretations of how the enthymeme works, Jackson and Jacobs (1980) argue that the use of enthymemes helps achieve agreement because the receiver does not object to the speaker's claim. The enthymeme's minimalist form makes it seem less like an argument than a conversation. Thus, the conversational partner uses the rules of conversational turn-taking—give and take, requests for clarifications and elaboration—rather than the rules for arguing or debating. The enthymeme provides an appropriate amount of support for a conversational argument without supplying too much support. Too much support may make conversational partners more aware of points of disagreement.

Reaction to Verbal Messages

Throughout the last four decades, communication theorists have identified several variables which appear to influence our reaction to verbal messages (Sussman, 1973). The majority of research has focused on four verbal message variables and their influence on message acceptance: *fear appeals, evidence, language intensity,* and *opinionated language.*

Fear Appeals

The study of fear-arousing message content has its roots in antiquity. Aristotle discussed the use of fear and other emotions in the *Rhetoric.* Aristotle suggested that speakers must understand the emotional predispositions of their audience and then use that knowledge as one of the "available means of persuasion" (See Chapter 4). Modern research considers a fear appeal to be an argument which takes the following form:

1. You (the listener) are vulnerable to a threat.

2. If you are vulnerable, then you should take action to reduce your vulnerability.

3. If you are to reduce your vulnerability, then you must accept the recommendations contained in this message.

4. Therefore, you should accept the recommendations contained in this message. (Boster & Mongeau, 1984, p. 371).

A typical fear appeal might be a variation on the following:

1. Smoking has been found to increase the chances for disease and death.
2. Since you do not want disease or death, you must do something to prevent them.
3. An effective way to prevent these outcomes is to stop smoking.
4. Therefore, you must stop smoking.

During an average evening, we may witness several fear-arousing messages contained in television commercials. From smoke detectors to life insurance, advertisers make frequent use of the fear appeal to influence consumers.

The contemporary study of fear in persuasion can be traced to the work of Janis and Feshbach (1953). In their seminal study, high school students were randomly assigned to one of two experimental groups who heard messages on dental hygiene. For one group, a *moderate* fear appeal was used; for the other, a *high* fear appeal was created. A third group of students was also tested. They served as a *control group* and were exposed to an entirely different message on the structure and operation of the human eye. The high fear appeal urged dental care and recommended vigorous and proper brushing of the teeth; pictures of rotting gums and decaying teeth accompanied the message. In the moderate fear appeal, these pictures were omitted. Janis and Feshbach discovered that the moderate fear appeal was more effective than the high fear appeal in changing students' attitudes toward proper brushing and dental care.

These findings led to several decades of experimental research testing the reflationship between level of fear in a message and attitude change. Some studies discovered the opposite outcome: attitude change was more likely when a high fear appeal was used (Beck & Davis, 1978). (See Miller, 1963, for a summary and analysis of the early research). Because experimenters sometimes arrived at different results when they studied fear appeals, scientists tried to reconcile these contradictions.

Six Explanations of Fear Appeal Findings

Boster and Mongeau (1984) reviewed six explanations of fear appeal effects. The *drive explanation* suggests that the fear aroused by a persuasive message creates a state of drive which receivers find unpleasant. Individuals experiencing this state of drive are motivated to reduce it by changing their attitudes and/or behaviors. According to the drive explanation, the greater the amount of fear in a message, the greater the attitude change in the direction recommended by the message.

The *resistance explanation* suggests that as perceived fear in a message *decreases*, individuals' attitudes and/or behaviors will move closer to those recommended in the message. The rationale is that receivers will pay attention to messages low in threatening content; they will resist messages which are more threatening. Low fear appeals are less threatening than high fear appeals. Thus, messages containing low fear appeals are more likely to be heard than messages containing high fear appeals.

According to the *curvilinear hypothesis,* when receivers are either very fearful or very unafraid, little attitude or behavior change results. High or low levels of fear are either too strong so that individuals block them out or are too weak to produce the desired effect. Messages containing *moderate* amounts of fear-arousing content are most effective in producing attitudinal and/or behavior change.

The *parallel response explanation* suggests that fear-arousing messages activate fear control and danger control processes in listeners. *Fear control* is a coping process by which receivers strive to reduce the fear created by the message. *Danger control* refers to a problem-solving process in which listeners search for information on how to deal with the threat presented. These two processes interact to influence message acceptance. According to the parallel response explanation, when a fear-arousing message primarily activates the *danger control* process, a *high* fear appeal will most influence attitudes and/or behaviors. When a fear-arousing message primarily activates the *fear control* process, a *low* fear appeal is most influential.

The *protection motivation explanation* states that a receiver's attitude toward the topic is a result of the amount of "protection motivation" produced by the message. Protection motivation refers to receivers' drives to avoid or protect themselves from a threat. As protection motivation increases, conformity to attitudes and/or behaviors recommended in the message also increases. Thus, the greater the fear in a message: (1) the more likely a threat will occur; and (2) the greater the ability to deal with the threat by following the recommendations provided in the message; thus (3) the greater the attitude and/or behavioral change in the direction of the message.

The sixth explanation is labelled the *threat control explanation.* This explanation suggests that reactions to fear appeals are dependent upon logical, not emotional, factors. A fear-arousing message stimulates *response efficacy* and *personal efficacy* processes in listeners. Response efficacy refers to the receiver's perception of how effective the recommended attitudes or actions will be in reducing or eliminating the threat. Personal efficacy refers to whether or not the receiver is capable of taking the actions recommended by the message. These two responses combine to produce *threat control.* Threat control is a person's perceived probability of success in controlling the threat. This explanation suggests that, as threat control increases, listeners will adopt attitudes more closely corresponding to the recommendations of the message. As fear increases in a message, so too should the amount of attitude and/or behavioral change in the listener.

Boster and Mongeau (1984) concluded that all six explanations were less than adequate in explaining the results of experiments studying fear-arousing messages and persuasion. None of the six explanations was completely consistent with the evidence. Several problems were highlighted. First, researchers were not creating strong enough fear appeals. If manipulations of fear in messages were not strong enough to produce fear in listeners, then it was impossible for any relationship between fear and attitude or behavior change to emerge. Second, other demographic variables and personality traits interacted with fear appeals to affect attitudes and behavior. In particular, *age*, *trait anxiety* (See Chapter 5), and whether the participant *volunteers* for the study were offered as potential moderators of the fear-attitude relationship. Contrary to conventional wisdom, low-anxiety, older volunteers seemed to be more susceptible to fear appeals than high anxiety, younger nonvolunteers.

Sussman (1973) also provided a similar suggestion regarding the influence of mediating variables on the fear-attitude relationship. He argued that Aristotle warned, "Such variables as coping style, self-esteem, perceived vulnerability to danger, and chronic anxiety may mediate the response to a fear appeal" (p. 209). Despite the attention paid by researchers to understanding the fear-attitude relationship, additional theory and research is needed to uncover more satisfactory explanations. Because the use of fear appeals in messages is very common, the results of such research should be of interest both to applied communicators such as advertisers and to scholars.

Evidence in Messages

When we hear the term *evidence*, images of attorneys arguing cases come to mind, as depicted in the television show "L.A. Law," for example. Clearly evidence is a critical component in any trial. Evidence is also an important verbal behavior variable in less formal communication contexts. Speakers seeking to persuade an audience to accept their claims have been told to use evidence. When we become the target of a persuasive effort, we usually challenge our adversary to *prove* the case to us. When a new drug claims to prevent baldness, all but the most desperate or trusting of souls require some type of evidence before they spend huge sums of money on it.

Since ancient times, communication theorists have suggested "the importance of evidence in the establishment of individual belief systems" (Florence, 1975, p. 145). Evidence consists of "factual statements originating from a source other than the speaker, objects not created by the speaker, and opinions of persons other than the speaker that are offered in support of the speaker's claims" (McCroskey, 1969, p. 170). A slightly different definition is "any statement of fact, statement of value, or definition offered by a speaker or writer which is intended to support a proposition" (Florence, 1975, p. 151). Contemporary communication courses, especially argumentation and public speaking, also stress the relationship between evidence and persuasion. Yet despite these theories, the findings of almost two decades of communication research do not appear to support a direct, positive association between evidence and persuasion. It has not been conclusively shown, for instance, that an audience will be more easily persuaded if more evidence is presented (Florence, 1975). Reviewing over twenty studies on the influence of evidence in persuasion, McCroskey (1969) concluded that several variables interact with evidence to produce changes in attitudes or increases in perceived speaker credibility. He offered the following generalizations regarding evidence and other variables.

Evidence and Source Credibility. There is a relationship between the use of evidence and the credibility or believability of the speaker. If a speaker is already perceived to be very credible, including "good" evidence will do little to change attitudes or enhance speaker credibility. However, speakers who are perceived as low-to-moderate in credibility may increase their credibility by employing evidence. This increase in perceived credibility may in turn increase attitude change.

Evidence and Delivery Effectiveness. In several studies on evidence and message topic, McCroskey (1969) believed that other factors were influencing the evidence-attitude change relationship. By interviewing participants after the experiments, he discovered that the quality of the delivery seemed to make a difference. To investigate the relationship further, he conducted several studies using a well-delivered and a poorly delivered version of live, audiotaped and videotaped presentations. The amount and type of evidence were the same for each version in each medium. From these studies, he found that: (1) including good evidence will influence attitude change very little if the message is delivered poorly; (2) including good evidence can influence attitude change and speaker credibility immediately after the speech or tape if the message is well-delivered, the speaker initially has only low-to-moderate credibility, and the audience has little prior knowledge of the evidence. Since these results were consistent for studies using audiotape, videotape, and live messages, he concluded that the medium of presentation has little effect on the use of evidence in persuasion.

Prior Familiarity of Evidence. McCroskey also believed that prior familiarity with evidence should be considered when assessing the evidence-persuasion relationship. Post-experimental interviews led him to conclude that "old" evidence does little to influence listeners. "Old" evidence has already been heard and processed cognitively. If any dissonance had been created by the message, it would either already have been resolved, or defense mechanisms would have been created to prevent a recurrence of dissonance. These assumptions are consistent with explanations derived from information theories (see Chapter 4) and Cognitive Dissonance Theory (see Chapter 6). When McCroskey conducted a study to test these assumptions, he found that, in order for evidence to affect listeners' attitude change or perceptions of the source immediately, the evidence must be "new" to the listener. Including evidence has little, if any, impact on receivers if they are already familiar with it before they hear it again in a persuasive message. McCroskey (1969) concluded that while considerable information has been uncovered about the influence of evidence in persuasion, communication theorists must continue their research efforts.

McCroskey's call was heeded by Florence, who examined the theoretical foundations of previous research and reformulated the existing theories concerning evidence and persuasion. Florence (1975) argued that evidence influences persuasion only if the proposal, idea or policy it supports is *desirable* to the audience. He also suggested that both the credibility of a source of evidence and the evidence itself influence the desirability of a proposal. More recently, Hample (1977, 1979, 1981) developed a theory of argument in which evidence plays a major role. In this theory, the relative power of evidence was measured. Hample argued that the power of evidence is one of the best predictors of attitude change. Since evidence is a key verbal message variable in the communication process, researchers will no doubt continue to examine its influence in persuasion.

Language Intensity

One of the verbal behavior variables most frequently studied during the last twenty-five years is the intensity of a speaker's language in a persuasive message. *Language intensity* is "the quality of language which indicates the degree to which the speaker's attitude toward a concept deviates from neutrality" (Bowers, 1964, p. 345). Speakers who use intense language exhibit more emotion and utilize stronger expressions, opinionated language, vivid adjectives, and more metaphors than speakers using less intense language. For example, during a period of strained relations, President Ronald Reagan made a public speech calling the Soviet Union an "evil empire." This term is clearly stronger and more intense than if the President had referred to the Russian government as a "difficult power."

Language intensity is related to a communicator's use of metaphors, modifiers and obscure words. Bowers and Osborn (1966) tested whether sex and death metaphors used in the conclusions of speeches would have greater persuasive impact than less intense, more literal conclusions. For a literal conclusion, Bowers and Osborn used the statement, "Too long, we ourselves have stood by and permitted the ruination of our western economies by those who have proclaimed the doctrine of protective tariff." In the metaphorical conclusion, they made use of the sex metaphor by substituting the word "rape" for "ruination." They found that speeches with metaphorical conclusions were more persuasive than speeches with literal conclusions. This finding contrasts with a previous study (Bowers, 1963) in which highly intense language produced less attitude change than low intensity language. However, metaphors were not used in the earlier study.

Carmichael and Cronkhite (1965) reasoned that the frustration level of a receiver interacts with language intensity of the speaker to affect persuasion. They speculated that a very intense persuasive message would be less effective when listeners are frustrated. Since frustrated people are already aroused, they should reject an intense message because it would push their level of arousal too high into an "uncomfortable zone." Carmichael and Cronkhite tested this relationship and found that frustrated listeners reacted less favorably to a highly intense message. Language intensity, however, made no difference to listeners who were not frustrated.

Bradac, Bowers, and Courtright (1979) conducted an extensive review of over twenty studies which examined the language intensity variable. They developed thirteen generalizations about the relationship between intense language and persuasion. They agreed with Carmichael and Cronkhite (1965) that less intense messages are more persuasive when the arousal (stress) level of listeners is high. They also found that language intensity interacted with several other variables to influence attitude change. Receivers hearing intense language will be more likely to change their attitudes when: (1) they view the speaker as highly credible; (2) the speaker is male; (3) the speaker advocates a proposal which the receivers already support; and (4) the receivers are low in arousal and stress. These findings are useful to political and organizational communicators. For example, a male sales manager wishing to increase quotas for the coming quarter and speaking to a staff which has just experienced record sales should use highly intense language to motivate them. Similarly, a political advisor confidently urged President Bush to use intense metaphors when speaking to the Veterans of Foreign Wars about a constitutional amendment to outlaw burning the American flag.

Opinionated Language

Opinionated language, a form of highly intense language, has received much attention from communication theorists and researchers (Rokeach,1960). When speakers use opinionated language, they indicate both their attitudes toward the topic and their attitudes toward those who agree or disagree with them (Miller & Lobe, 1967). For example, a speaker might proclaim, "Only a fool would oppose the construction of nuclear power plants across the country," or, "Any intelligent person recognizes the danger in building nuclear power plants." The first statement is considered an "opinionated-rejection" statement. This type of statement reflects an unfavorable attitude toward people who disagree with the speaker. The second statement is considered an "opinionated-acceptance" statement. This type of statement expresses a favorable attitude toward people who agree with the speaker about the topic.

Researchers have conducted several studies on the effect of opinionated language. Miller and Lobe (1967) examined the effect of opinionated language in persuading open- and closed-minded listeners. They created a proposal advocating outlawing the sale of cigarettes, a proposal with which they knew the audience disagreed. For one audience, two opinionated-acceptance and two opinionated-rejection statements were inserted in the message. For the other group, no opinionated statements were inserted. The messages were otherwise identical and were attributed to the same highly credible source. They found that opinionated language is more persuasive (if the source is highly credible) than non-opinionated language. They reasoned that using opinionated language strengthens the intensity of the bond between the message *source* and the message *proposal*. When a highly credible source uses opinionated language, receivers think the speaker feels very strongly about an issue. Receivers are likely to change their attitudes to agree with the speaker. Using opinionated language also helps speakers emphasize the rewards listeners can expect if they accept the speaker's recommendations. Another study found that a highly trustworthy male speaker was more persuasive when he used opinionated language, but an untrustworthy speaker was more persuasive when he used non-opinionated language (Miller & Baseheart, 1969).

Other researchers have investigated the relationship between opinionated language and intensity of initial attitude toward a topic (Mehrley & McCroskey, 1970). A message containing opinionated language may be more or less persuasive depending on listeners' *initial* attitudes toward the topic. When listeners initially hold strongly negative or positive attitudes toward a topic, messages containing non-opinionated language enhance persuasion. However, when listeners hold relatively neutral attitudes, opinionated language results in greater persuasion. These findings can be explained by dissonance theory (see Chapter 6). The more a speaker pressures receivers to change their attitudes, the less their attitudes will change. When listeners are initially neutral, non-opinionated language statements are not strong enough to change attitudes. Speakers would be wise to use opinionated language with neutral audiences. When listeners hold intense attitudes toward proposals, the opposite is true. Opinionated language statements are considered too strong, so that speakers who use opinionated language with intense listeners may find less attitude change and lower credibility ratings. The complicated effects discovered by researchers led Mehrley and McCroskey (1970) to conclude that no simple generalizations can be made about the effects of opinionated language. They suggest that the use of opinionated language "may be dependent upon the interaction of a variety of source, message, and receiver variables" (p. 48).

Several years later, other researchers examined opinionated language used in forewarning messages. *Forewarnings* are messages which warn the audience by mentioning the type of arguments an opposing speaker will present. For example, parents often warn their children not to accept candy or rides from strangers. Politicians often warn voters about upcoming attacks by their opponents. In studies of forewarnings and opinionated language, participants read an excerpt from a "symposium TV program," then indicated their reactions to the program. On the first page of the booklet containing the synopsis, participants read a message from either an authoritative (professor) or less authoritative (freshman student) "warner." This "warner" used either opinionated or non-opinionated language to warn the reader about another authoritative (a second professor) or less authoritative (a second student) speaker. Examples of opinionated statements included: "Any intelligent person will come to this same conclusion after considering the matter," and, "Only the most uneducated individual will accept the arguments that he is going to present. . . ." For less authoritative speakers, using a non-opinionated warning yielded greater persuasion. However, the use of opinionated language by an authoritative warner was effective in reducing the impact of a persuasive message. Thus, opinionated language appears to be one way to motivate listeners to resist persuasion (Infante, 1973).

A follow-up study tested whether opinionated language strengthened the attitudes of those later exposed to a message with which they disagreed. Each participant received both a "pro" and a "con" speech. Two groups received the "pro" speech before the "con" speech, and two groups received the "pro" speech after the "con" speech. One group received six opinionated rejection statements in the "pro" speech, and one group received six non-opinionated statements in the "pro" speech. Participants read the speeches then evaluated the proposal and the character and authoritativeness of the two speakers. The "pro" speaker was viewed as less authoritative and less moral when he used opinionated language. With a favorable audience, using non-opinionated language seems to make the audience resistant to prior or subsequent persuasive efforts (Infante, 1975).

Studying opinionated language has helped theorists develop "guidelines" for persuaders. Salespeople, advertisers, politicians and public relations practitioners can use these findings to make their messages more successful. For example, speakers at a Democratic political convention should avoid using opinionated language when warning the party faithful about what the Republicans will say. Instead, the audience will find the speakers more persuasive if they avoid using opinionated language to "put down" supporters of the other party.

Theoretical Approaches to Verbal Behavior

The Verbal Plan Perspective

Having explored the effects of four experimental variables on persuasion, we now consider four broader theoretical approaches to language. The Verbal Plan Perspective maintains that to understand someone's communication it is necessary to understand the individual. How an individual organizes thoughts and feelings (cognitive structure) combined with underlying traits and predispositions will determine verbal behavior (see Chapter 6). Recall from Chapter 1 that a *verbal plan* is what someone plans to say in a specific or general communication situation. (You might wish to review the discussion of verbal plans in Chapter 1 and affective-cognitive consistency in Chapter 6.) Whether or not you use a verbal plan probably depends upon affective-cognitive consistency. When we form a verbal plan, we are offering a *proposal* to ourselves. We consider our own proposal much like we consider a proposal presented to us by another person. That is, we weigh the consequences of the proposal in terms of *desirability, likelihood,* and *importance* (Infante, 1980). If the good consequences outweigh the bad, we have a favorable attitude toward the plan and probably will use it. If we believe the bad consequences outweigh the good, we will not use it.

Imagine you are a candidate for student representative to the board of trustees and you are in a discussion when someone says: "The university administration does not really care about us as individuals; we are just numbers to them." This statement causes you to become aware of an attitude object, your university's administration, and the various beliefs you have about it. Let us say you have a very positive set of beliefs. Your dean helped you when you had a personal problem. One of the vice-presidents congratulated you on an academic achievement. The president sent you a personal letter of thanks for your service on a committee. Faculty and students you trust have told you the administrators at your school are very competent. In a matter of seconds you form a verbal plan: "Wait a minute. I have had some really good experiences with this administration, and I think they really are interested in us as individuals." Next, you consider consequences of using your plan. Suppose you believe 4 consequences will occur and judge those results as follows: (1) Others will perceive you as a forceful advocate (desirable, likely, and important); (2) You will correct misconceptions that are unfair to current administrators (desirable and important, but unlikely); (3) Others will consider you a "lackey" of the administration (very undesirable, important, and very likely); and (4) Others will not support your candidacy for student representative to the Board of Trustees (very undesirable, important, and likely). The two negative consequences outweigh the two desirable ones, since one desirable consequence is likely and the other unlikely. Thus, the theory predicts you would not use this verbal plan. Instead, you might say to yourself, "I'd better not say that. I might be better off saying: Sure this administration could be more sensitive to student needs, but we can change that. I intend to try by running for student representative to the Board of Trustees." Guided by the faults you found in the previous plan, you form a new one and decide whether to use it. This is another way of saying affective-cognitive consistency was a factor in your cognitive structure which motivated you to change your communication.

The actual time we spend considering a verbal plan varies greatly. We might spend days pondering a plan to ask our boss for a raise but only seconds to ask a friend for a ride into the city. Or, we might not think at all about whether to voice a particular verbal plan because it is part of a larger plan that we have previously decided should be executed. For example, if you are a wife, a plan for communicating with your husband might be: "Whenever something is bothering me, I will talk about it immediately because honest communication is best for our relationship." Thus, you would not weigh consequences every time you mentioned something that was bothering you. Life would be rather difficult if we had to check each situation to determine whether it was affectively and cognitively consistent. Instead, we formulate plans which are as sound as possible to cover as many circumstances as we can.

A final point concerns how favorable our verbal plan is toward the object. At times, we say what we feel. At other times, we speak more or less favorably than we actually feel. This happens because in some situations we perceive that people we value expect us to agree or disagree on an issue. In the example above, the student spoke less positively about the administration in order to agree with others. Why do we form such verbal plans and then execute them if they do not represent how we truly feel about an object? The main reason is we decide the bad consequences of expressing exactly how we feel outweigh the good consequences. If we were to tell our host that his or her cooking was terrible, the host would be embarrassed and the nature of the friendship might change. We like our plans to produce more good than bad consequences, so we would select another plan, one which would not express our true feelings about the food but which would produce consistency in the social situation. "Thanks for a wonderful evening; I really enjoyed everything." Research suggests that how much we deviate in our verbal behavior from our true feelings is a function of our attitude, the degree we believe valued others wish us to speak favorably or unfavorably, and the degree to which we are motivated to please others (Infante, 1980). In addition, when expectations of valued others do not influence a communication situation, people tend to say what they feel (Infante, 1979). Thus, verbal behavior and attitude correspond when we perceive that what others want us to say is different from our own attitudes but we have little or no motivation to comply with those expectations. For example, we know a restaurant server wants us to say the food is good, but we feel little pressure to say it is good if we dislike it, so we might say: "The chef may have had a bad day."

Speech Accommodation Theory

A second theory of verbal behavior is Speech Accommodation Theory (SAT), which examines underlying motivations and consequences of shifts in verbal

behavior (Giles & Wiemann, 1987; Street & Giles, 1982). Speech Accommodation Theory was derived from a number of social psychological principles
including similarity-attraction (see Chapter 9), social exchange (see Chapter
9) and causal attribution (see Chapter 6). Two premises are central to Speech
Accommodation Theory: (1) During communication, people try to accommodate or adjust their style of speech to others. (2) They do this in order to gain
approval, to increase communication efficiency, and to maintain positive social
identity with the person to whom they are talking. A core assumption of SAT
is that our *perceptions* of another's speech determine how we will evaluate
and behave toward that person. Two speech strategies, convergence and
divergence, are central to this theory. In both speech convergence and
divergence, the movement toward or away from the speech style of the other
is motivated by an assumption about the other's speech style (Giles, Mulac,
Bradac, & Johnson, 1987). Using *convergence*, individuals adapt to each other
by slowing down or speeding up speech rate, lengthening or shortening pauses
and utterances, and using certain forms of politeness, tag questions and verbal
intensifiers in their speech. For example, interviewees often shift their rate and
duration of speech when they want to sound likable to an interviewer.
Salespeople often converge their speech styles with those of customers (Giles,
Mulac, Bradac, & Johnson, 1987). *Divergence* refers to the way speakers accentuate vocal and linguistic differences in order to underscore social differences
between speakers. In some situations, communicators often deliberately wish
to maintain a social distance between themselves and others. Speech divergence is likely to occur when individuals believe that others are members of
undesirable groups, hold distasteful attitudes, or display unsavory appearances
(Street & Giles, 1982).

Use of Convergent Strategies. Researchers have explored situations in which
people use convergent and divergent forms of speech. In the area of gender
and communication, Wheeless (1984) found that individuals classified
according to gender orientation (masculine, feminine, androgynous, undifferentiated) rather than biological sex differed in their language use. Feminine
and undifferentiated individuals were more accommodating than masculine
and androgynous individuals. This finding is consistent with research which
shows that "feminine language" is viewed as more considerate, cooperative,
helpful, submissive, and accommodating (Stewart, Cooper & Friedley, 1986).

Stereotypes or expectations of others' abilities often influence the speech
convergence process. For example, some nurses use "baby talk" to the
institutionalized elderly, regardless of the individual's actual capabilities. Blind
persons report that people who communicate with them often shout, slow
down, or avoid addressing them at all (Giles, Mulac, Bradac, & Johnson, 1987).
Such "overconvergence" gives the person a sense of being talked down to
and detracts from effective and satisfying communication.

Speech convergence suggests that people find approval from others satisfying.
The greater the need for social approval, the greater the tendency for speech

convergence. Power also plays a part in the degree to which convergence will be exhibited. Powerless individuals tend to adopt the verbal and vocal styles of those with power. This finding helps to explain some of the sex differences in verbal behavior. Females may use speech convergence in organizational communication contexts in order to "say the right thing" and to "fit in" among organizational superiors, usually males. Communication theorists interested in gender and communication have identified the "double-bind" women are faced with in the organization when they are asked to "speak like a man, but act like a lady."

Giles reports that in several instances speech accommodation may be a scripted behavior. Individuals may "automatically" use a convergence script to make their speech appear more similar to another's (Giles, Mulac, Bradac & Johnson, 1987). To borrow a concept from a previous theory, we may have a speech convergence *verbal plan* ready to use when we need it.

Use of Divergent Strategies. On the other hand, groups with strong ethnic pride often use speech *divergence* or speech *maintenance* to underscore that identity and distinctiveness (Giles, Mulac, Bradac, & Johnson, 1987). In Chapter 5 we reviewed the research on the communication trait *rhetorical sensitivity*. We identified three types of individuals (noble selves, rhetorical sensitives, rhetorical reflectors) regarding their tendency to display "real" attitudes and values. Of those three groups, the *noble selves* would be more likely to use speech divergence as a way of maintaining their identity.

Speech divergence is also purposefully used to accentuate differences between communicators. We may adopt a more formal, jargon-laden speech style when we wish to highlight educational differences. Occasionally, speech divergence is used as a power marker or to control the behavior of others. One professor uses speech divergence as a way to gently and humorously remind students that she has the power to determine when class will end. When students shuffle their feet and rearrange their books toward the end of a class period, the professor has been heard to say, "I see that you are engaging in significant leave-taking behaviors!" Giles and his colleagues report that we sometimes slow down our speech rate when we are talking with people who speak rapidly in order to slow them down. Parent-child interaction is another context in which speech divergence is frequently exhibited. As a child, you may have known you were "in trouble" when your parent called for you by using your first, middle, and surnames. This divergence was an attempt to increase the perceived (or real) status differences between parent and child.

While Speech Accommodation Theory has generated considerable research, Giles and his colleagues suggest that more questions need to be answered. For example, how do one's speech accommodation behaviors change during the course of a lifetime? What is the relationship between speech accommodation and empathy? What nonverbal features make up convergent and divergent accommodation strategies? Giles, Mulac, Bradac, and Johnson (1987) have suggested that when the theory and research have been developed to include nonverbal behavior, the theory should be relabelled Communication Accommodation Theory. Meanwhile, communication scholars will explore these issues and continue to refine the theory.

Speech Act Theory

Although the perspective of Speech Act Theory is quite different from the representational theory of language (sign, symbol, signal) presented earlier in the chapter, Speech Act Theory is included here because it forms the basis for the Coordinated Management of Meaning rules theory presented in Chapter 3. It is a perspective adopted by many scholars of communication, including some of the conversational analysts described below. Speech Act Theory is most commonly associated with the language philosopher John Searle (1969). According to Searle, to understand language one must understand the speaker's intention. Since language is intentional behavior, it should be treated like a form of action. Thus Searle refers to statements as speech acts. It is important to note that the action is performed by the speaker uttering the words, not by the words themselves. According to Searle, understanding the speaker's intention is essential to capture the meaning. Again, words do not "mean," people "mean." Without the speaker's intention, it is impossible to understand the words as a speech act.

Four Types of Speech Acts. In elementary school you were probably taught types of sentences that mirror the speech act perspective. For example, you were taught that you could make a statement, ask a question, make a request, and give a command. Searle emphasizes that the same words may perform all four of these speech acts; to understand the meaning, one must infer the speaker's intention. For example, you might say to someone, "I wonder what time it is." A friend hearing that remark may understand that you are just wondering, making a statement. If you approach someone you do not know at a shopping mall and say the same words, the person normally understands them as a question. The words now mean "What time is it?" Furthermore, the stranger may realize that you are really requesting him or her to tell you the time, changing the meaning to, "Would you please tell me what time it is?" The phrase, "Do you have the time?" is most often answered with the time of day, not by "yes" or "no." In other words, we understand the phrase to be a request to provide the time, not a question about whether or not we know the time. If you are waiting on the corner for a stoplight to change and a police officer says, "I wonder what time it is," you might interpret the words to be a command, "Tell me the time." The very same words can constitute many different kinds of speech acts. Searle believes these acts are the basic unit of meaning in communication. He does not emphasize symbols or signs or words or phrases, but units of language which combine to form a speech act. A speech act may be a word such as "Why?", a phrase, "How long?"

or a sentence. Searle classifies speech acts as one of four types. These four types are presented below in hierarchical order from most basic to most complex.

Utterance acts involve merely uttering strings of words like singers vocalizing, "Mi, mi, mi, mi." The singers do not intend to make any sort of statement; they are merely "warming up," tuning their "instruments" like an orchestra.

Propositional acts are those which make a reference, as in the representational theory of language presented at the beginning of the chapter. The sentence—"This is an elephant."—spoken by a child reading a picture book merely connects the picture in the book with the word *elephant*. The child is not communicating with anyone, but saying out loud what she has learned. Note that, according to Searle, the words themselves do *not* refer; instead, *the speaker refers*. Referring is a type of propositional act.

Illocutionary acts consist of the types of acts you learned in elementary school like promises, questions, and commands. They are speech acts uttered to communicate the speaker's intention to the listener. For example, if you say, "I'm hungry" as an illocutionary act, you intend to have someone else understand your physical state. You are not merely uttering words or making a connection between yourself and the state of hunger; you are trying to communicate with someone else. It is true, however, that you are also performing an utterance act and a propositional act whenever you perform an illocutionary act because your illocutionary act consists simultaneously of uttered words and of references. What is different is that by performing an illocutionary act a speaker is said to "mean something." You mean that you are hungry, whereas the child performing a propositional act above was just "talking to herself."

Whenever a person performs an illocutionary or perlocutionary act, the next type to be discussed, he or she also performs utterance and propositional acts. Searle (1969) explains the relationship:

> [I]n performing an illocutionary act one characteristically performs propositional acts and utterance acts. Nor should it be thought from this that utterance acts and propositional acts stand to illocutionary acts in the way buying a ticket and getting on a train stand to taking a railroad trip. They are not means to ends; rather, utterance acts stand to propositional and illocutionary acts in the way which, e.g., making an 'X' on a ballot paper stands to voting. (p. 24)

Utterance and propositional acts are not ways one can perform an illocutionary act but part of the act itself. The same illocutionary act (stating that you are hungry) can be performed by different utterance and propositional acts: "I'm hungry," "I'm ready to eat," or "I'm starved." Because the intent is the same, the illocutionary act is the same. This idea is the counterpart of that discussed above. The same sentence can constitute different kinds of acts, and speakers can use different sentences to perform the same type of speech act. The common element is not the words themselves nor the events to which the speaker refers, but the speaker's intention to utter a particular kind of act.

The fourth type of speech act, a *perlocutionary act*, is performed knowing the effect the act may have on the listener. In other words, the speaker uses the act to elicit some behavioral response from the listener. For example, if you are at a friend's house when you say, "I'm hungry," you are probably performing a perlocutionary act requesting food. Of course, the perlocutionary act must include an illocutionary act (your friend understands the words are intentionally expressed and directed toward him or her), a propositional act (the connection between you and the state of hunger), and an utterance act (whatever string of words you chose to perform the perlocutionary act, in this case, "I'm hungry").

Definition and Behavior Rules. Searle believes that speakers perform acts by observing two types of rules. Constitutive or definition rules (as we called them in discussing the Coordinated Management of Meaning Theory in Chapter 3) "create or define new forms of behavior" (Searle, 1969, p. 33). Like a rule in football specifying what counts as a touchdown, definition rules define or create speech acts by specifying what counts as a command or request. Without the rule defining a touchdown, we could not explain how to score one. Definition "rules often have the form: X counts as Y in context C" (Searle, 1969, p. 35) so that, "A touchdown is scored when a player has possession of the ball in the opponents' end zone while a play is in progress" (p. 34). Regulative or behavior rules (as we called them in Chapter 3) govern types of behavior that already exist. For example, behavior rules in the game of football tell how play of the game proceeds, such as who kicks off first. Behavior rules usually take the form "'Do X' or 'If Y do X'" (Searle, 1969, p. 34). Since "speaking a language is performing acts according to rules" (Searle, 1969, p. 34), definition and behavior rules tell one how to speak a language correctly, that is, how to perform speech acts.

Language, then, is rule-governed behavior. Native speakers apply rules in new situations and recognize deviations from the patterns specified by the rules as "wrong." Robin misunderstood a foreign server in a restaurant who asked, "Do you want rice or potatoes?" and responded, "Yes." The server did not follow the behavior rules of English intonation, which specify a pause between *rice* and *or*, a rising inflection on *rice* and a lower, level tone on *potatoes* to indicate two responses from which the speaker is to choose. Instead, the server spoke (quite rapidly) with no pause and a rising inflection on *potatoes*. Robin understood the question as, "Do you want rice pilaf?" Breaking the rules caused Robin to misunderstand the server's meaning. If the server had spoken more slowly, Robin might have realized the server was breaking a behavior rule of English intonation which governs forced-choice questions. Then Robin could have reevaluated the interpretation and realized what the server meant. If Robin had been teaching English to someone who was not a native speaker, Robin would have corrected the intonation pattern because it did not "follow the rule." Even though native speakers may not be able to articulate the rules of their language, they habitually use them in conversation and recognize deviations as incorrect. Performing speech acts requires a speaker both to intend the act and to follow definition and behavior rules. As Searle (1969) expresses it, "Meaning is more than a matter of intention; it is also at least sometimes a matter of convention" (p. 45).

Speech Act Theory has contributed to the rules perspective in communication because it provides a basis for examining what happens when speakers use different definition and behavior rules. By analyzing the rules used by each speaker, researchers can better understand why conversational misunderstandings have occurred. Recently, Brenders (1987) has criticized the Coordinated Management of Meaning theorists for incorrectly adapting Searle's theory for their own purposes. The strengths and weaknesses of using Speech Act Theory to study communication are still being debated. Nevertheless, Searle's contribution is an important one which has had a broad influence on communication and other disciplines. Some of the same assumptions about language as a type of symbolic action are reflected in the conversational analysis approach presented below.

The Conversation and Discourse Analytic Perspectives

A fourth major verbal theory approach is concerned with patterns and forms of language activity. The analysis of conversational form and content has evolved into a body of knowledge referred to as discourse or conversational analysis. Scholars from several branches of social science including sociology, psychology, linguistics, anthropology, and communication are responsible for research and theory building efforts in this area. Discourse analysis has been called one of the most promising new methods for the study of interpersonal communication (Jacobs, 1988).

Although the terms are often used interchangeably, there are subtle differences between the *discourse* and *conversational* analysis perspectives. One of the major differences lies in the coding of natural conversation. Researchers investigating the properties, patterns, and forms of discourse use natural conversation as the primary form of data. When analyzing conversational data, the *discourse* analyst favors a narrower coding procedure and greater statistical treatment of the data. *Conversational* analysts favor a broader descriptive method, choosing to include the subtleties of communication which would be lost with a more narrow coding procedure (Hopper, Koch, & Mandelbaum, 1986).

Conversational analysis conceives language as communicative action. That is, those who study language structure and flow believe that conversation is governed by rules which are implicitly known by speakers (Jacobs, 1980). Conversational analysts attempt to understand the rules of conversational action and how people use those rules to engage in natural discourse. For example, some of the research questions considered are:

1. How do people in conversation signal the exchange of speaking turns?
2. How do speakers coordinate talk with eye gaze, body movement, and other action?
3. How do partners identify and "repair" problems which occur in conversations following "failures"?
4. How does conversation function in settings such as interviews, court hearings, or card games?
5. How do we label sections of talk?
6. What role do stories play in conversation?
7. How are disclaimers used to set the stage or offset potentially offensive or sensitive remarks?
8. How do people directly and indirectly respond to questions? (Knapp, 1984)

Conversational analysts are concerned with the ability to use language appropriately in several communication contexts. Scholars suggest that this ability is one dimension of *communication competence* (see Chapter 5). Individuals are judged communicatively competent not simply because they follow the rules but by how they use the rules. A competent rule user can skillfully manipulate the rules of conversation and can violate certain conversational rules to achieve a given purpose (Jacobs, 1980).

One of the most important aspects of conversational effectiveness is managing conversations. The ability of people to know when to start and when to stop talking is a fundamental concern of discourse analysts. A competent linguistic rule user is someone who can monitor the discourse of another and recognize the "points of possible completion." These points are moments during a conversation where the speaking turn can change. We are sure you can remember a conversation you were engaged in which seemed to be "out of sync." You may have spoken while the other person was talking. At times, both of you may have talked "on top" of each other's utterances. More likely than not, this type of conversation did not seem satisfying to you. Discourse analysts refer to this as simultaneous talk or overlap in talk. Overlaps are distinguished from interruptions. Overlaps are talk that begins during a change of speaker turn but does not interfere with the current speaker's completion of her turn (McLaughlin, 1984).

Those places in a conversation where a change of speaking turn is possible have been formally defined as *transition relevance places* (TRPs) (Hopper, Koch, & Mandelbaum, 1986). At each transitionally relevant place, a speaker may continue talking or may relinquish the turn and allow the other person to talk.

The competent communicator recognizes TRPs by such conversational characteristics as falling intonation at the end of an utterance, drawing out the final syllable of a word, or by nonverbal cues such as changes in eye gaze.

Methods of Conversational Analysis

One characteristic of conversational analysis research is the use of actual dialogue as primary data. When you read a study conducted from the conversation analytic perspective, you often see a transcription of naturally occurring dialogue. The analyst examines the details of the conversation and arrives at a characterization of the discourse. On the basis of this characterization, claims are made about the linguistic properties of the conversation (Jacobs, 1988). Hopper, Koch, and Mandelbaum (1986) describe four types of activities used by researchers to conduct discourse analysis: *recording, transcribing, analyzing* and *reporting*. They explain how these activities are carried out and offer a set of recommendations for the researcher.

Recording. Record conversations that would have occurred whether or not you recorded them. Before recording a conversation, obtain permission of all parties involved. If recording is not possible in natural situations, "role-playing" of conversations may be used. Although audiotape is often used, videotape provides a richer source of data. Try to record two-party conversations rather than multi-party conversations, which are more difficult to code and decipher. Reduce background noise as much as possible during the recording process.

Transcribing. Transcribing involves repeated listening to the recording. Start transcribing at the beginning of the tape. Use conventional symbols to indicate the verbal and vocal characteristics of the conversation. For example, underlining in transcripts indicates stress of the underlined sounds. Capital letters indicate loudness, and colons denote "stretched" sounds. The use of variable speed playback devices are helpful in deciphering exact beginnings, endings and overlaps in speech. Transcribe recordings until elements come into focus and until you see patterns recur.

Analysis. Listen to the recordings repeatedly and use the transcripts as you follow the recordings. Focus your attention on brief segments of dialogue. Listen to each segment at least twenty times while taking frequent notes. Number each line of the transcript for easy reference. Listen in groups to the transcribed recordings. Any claims you make about the characteristics of the conversation must be supported by details found in the recordings. Examine and describe the details of the conversation in order to sharpen your initial observations. Other analysts should be able to listen to the recordings, study the transcripts, read your written report, and reach the same conclusions you do.

Reporting. State your conclusions clearly and provide evidence for them. Account for any exceptions you may observe or reservations you may have. The format of the report may vary. You can examine an entire single conversation or a conversational "fragment." You may choose to focus your report on a particular conversational characteristic, such as responses to compliments. Interaction sequences such as turn-taking or conversational openings and closings may be the focus of your report. Try to describe the events in detail rather than report only the numbers related to your observations. For example, do not limit the report to how many turn changes occurred with different speakers (Hopper, Koch, & Mandelbaum, 1986, pp. 174-182).

Characteristics of Conversation Management

Conversational analysts have investigated a broad range of factors associated with the development, maintenance and management of natural discourse. McLaughlin and her colleagues have investigated the production of *self-serving utterances* or "bragging" (McLaughlin, Louden, Cashion, Altendorf, Baaske, & Smith, 1985), *awkward silences* (McLaughlin & Cody, 1982), *compliance-gaining attempts* (McLaughlin, Cody, & Robey, 1980) and *failure events in conversations* (McLaughlin, Cody, & O'Hair, 1983). Much of this research is summarized by McLaughlin (1984). Nofsinger (1976) has also examined conversational rules used in answering questions indirectly.

The research on discourse analysis has identified several characteristics commonly found in natural conversation. *Turn-taking* is a fundamental conversational characteristic uncovered by discourse analysts. During turn-taking there is an exchange of speaker and listener roles. Turns are viewed as "opportunities at talk" into which utterances are slotted (McLaughlin, 1984). Turn-taking is managed through competent conversational interaction.

Speech acts such as requests and compliments have also been studied. *Requests* have been found to vary in politeness and directness. *Compliments* are utterances in which the speaker bestows upon the listener some positively valued attribute or property. *Preventatives*, devices used by speakers to gain permission to violate conversational rules, have been noted. One frequent type of preventative is the disclaimer. For example, prior to telling an offensive ethnic joke, a person might say, "I'm Chicano, so I can tell this one" (McLaughlin, 1984, p. 204). Several types of preventatives such as *credentialling*, "Some of my best friends are, but . . .," and *sin license*, "This really shouldn't be said here, but . . ." have been identified. *Repairs* are conversational devices used to smooth or reduce "troubles" after a conversational rule has been violated. One of the most frequently heard forms of repair is the utterance, "I was only kidding," used after a conversational remark has hurt or upset a listener.

The analysis of conversation provides the communication discipline with sound methodological techniques to examine verbal communication. One advantage of this method of analysis is that conversations are found everywhere in both formal and informal contexts. The conversational analyst needs only a good recording device to begin the data-gathering process. One disadvantage which you have probably recognized is that this type of research requires much time and attention to detail. Secretarial and time costs associated with transcripts can be extremely high compared to the costs of other research methods. Discourse and conversational analysts believe that the rich data and detailed findings which emerge are worth the investment.

Summary

Many theories of communication account for the verbal behavior of individuals. Language is at the core of verbal behavior, and human beings are distinct in their ability to use language, including signs, symbols and signals. Language helps shape our perceptions and influences our behavior. Four variables which influence our reaction to verbal messages were identified: fear appeals, evidence, language intensity, and opinionated language. Research findings related to the influence of these variables on conformity to message recommendations was reviewed. In addition, four theoretical approaches to verbal behavior were presented. The Verbal Plan Perspective helps us understand and predict a person's verbal behavior. A verbal plan is what you plan to say in a specific or general communication situation. People create and use verbal plans in conversations. Speech Accommodation Theory suggests that people accommodate or adjust their style of speech in order to gain approval, maintain social identity, and make communication more effective. Speakers use convergence to adapt to another's speech style and divergence to maintain social distance between themselves and others. Searle's version of Speech Act Theory forms the basis of definition and behavior rules used in the Coordinated Management of Meaning communication theory discussed in Chapter 3. According to Searle, in order to understand what a speaker means, we must understand not only the speaker's words but the speaker's intention. Finally, the Conversational Analysis Perspective was discussed. Conversational analysts attempt to understand the rules of conversational action. They identify conversational rules and ways people use those rules to manage conversation. Four steps (recording, transcribing, analyzing and reporting) in conducting discourse analysis were discussed. Turn-taking, requests, compliments, preventatives and repairs have been identified as important characteristics of conversational management.

Questions to Consider

1. What are signs, symbols, and signals?
2. How does language result in meaning?
3. How do denotative and connotative meaning differ?
4. According to the Sapir-Whorf hypothesis, what is the relationship between language and our perceptions of reality?
5. In what ways does language communicate power and power-lessness?
6. What is code-switching?
7. How may everyday arguments be thought of in terms of the enthymeme?
8. What are the major verbal behavior variables which have been investigated by communication researchers?
9. How is communication conceived and explained according to the Verbal Plan Perspective?
10. What does Speech Accommodation Theory predict about our speech style?
11. Explain Searle's idea of a speech act. Name some definition and behavior rules you follow in using language.
12. How is communication studied by conversational and discourse analysts?

References

Bate, B. (1988). *Communication and the sexes*. New York: Harper & Row.

Beck, K.H., & Davis, C.M. (1978). Effects of fear-arousing communications and topic importance on attitude change. *Journal of Social Psychology, 104*, 81-95.

Bitzer, L.F. (1959). Aristotle's enthymeme revisited. *Quarterly Journal of Speech, 45*, 399-408.

Boster, F.J., & Mongeau, P. (1984). Fear-arousing persuasive messages. In R.N. Bostrum (Ed.), *Communication Yearbook 8*, (pp. 330-375). Beverly Hills, CA: Sage.

Bowers, J.W. (1963). Language intensity, social introversion, and attitude change. *Speech Monographs, 30*, 345-352.

Bowers, J.W. (1964). Some correlates of language intensity. *Quarterly Journal of Speech, 50*, 415-420.

Bowers, J.W., & Osborn, M. (1966). Attitudinal effects of selected types of concluding metaphors in persuasive speeches. *Speech Monographs, 33*, 147-155.

Bradac, J.J. (1988). Language variables: Conceptual and methodological problems of instantiation. In C.R. Tardy (Ed.), *A handbook for the study of human communication: Methods and instruments for observing, measuring, and assessing communication processes* (pp. 301-322). Norwood, NJ: Ablex.

Bradac, J.J., Bowers, J.W., & Courtright, J.A. (1979). Three language variables in communication research: Intensity, immediacy, and diversity. *Human Communication Research, 5,* 257-269.

Brenders, D. A. (1987). Fallacies in the Coordinated Management of Meaning: A philosophy of language critique of the hierarchical organization of coherent conversation and related theory. *Quarterly Journal of Speech, 73,* 329-348.

Brown, R.W., & Lenneberg, E.H. (1954). A study in language and cognition. *Journal of Abnormal and Social Psychology, 49,* 454-462.

Carmichael, C., & Cronkhite, G. (1965). Frustration and language intensity. *Speech Monographs, 32,* 107-111.

Chase, S. (1956). Forward. In J.B. Carroll (Ed.), *Benjamin Lee Whorf: Language, thought and reality.* (pp. v-x). Cambridge, MA: The M.I.T. Press.

Cronkhite, G. (1976). *Communication and awareness.* Menlo Park, CA: Cummings.

Cronkhite, G. (1986). On the focus, scope, and coherence of the study of human symbolic activity. *Quarterly Journal of Speech, 72,* 231-246.

DeVito, J.A. (1986). *The interpersonal communication book* (4th ed.). New York: Harper & Row.

DeVito, J.A. (1988). *Human communication: The basic course* (4th ed.). New York: Harper & Row.

Ellis, D.G. (1982). Language and speech communication. In M. Burgoon (Ed.), *Communication Yearbook 6* (pp. 34-62). Beverly Hills, CA: Sage.

Florence, B.T. (1975). An empirical test of the relationship of evidence to belief systems and attitude change. *Human Communication Research, 1,* 145-158.

Giles, H., Mulac, A., Bradac, J.J., & Johnson, P. (1987). Speech accommodation theory: The first decade and beyond. In M. McLaughlin (Ed.), *Communication Yearbook 10* (pp. 13-48). Newbury Park, CA: Sage.

Giles, H., & Wiemann, J.M. (1987). Language, social comparison, and power. In C.R. Berger & S.H. Chaffee (Eds.), *The handbook of communication science* (pp. 350-384). Newbury Park, CA: Sage.

Hample, D. (1977). Testing a model of value argument and evidence. *Communication Monographs, 44,* 106-120.

Hample, D. (1979). Predicting belief and belief change using a cognitive theory of argument and evidence. *Communication Monographs, 46,* 142-146.

Hample, D. (1981, May). *Models of arguments using multiple bits of evidence.* Paper presented at the annual meeting of the International Communication Association, Minneapolis, MN.

Hopper, R., Koch, S., & Mandelbaum, J. (1986). Conversation analysis methods. In D.G. Ellis & W.A. Donohue (Eds.), *Contemporary issues in language and discourse processes* (pp. 169-186). Hillsdale, NJ: Lawrence Erlbaum.

Infante, D.A. (1973). Forewarnings in persuasion: Effects of opinionated language and forewarner and speaker authoritativeness. *Western Journal of Speech Communication, 37,* 185-195.

Infante, D.A. (1975). Effects of opinionated language on communicator image and in conferring resistance to persuasion. *Western Journal of Speech Communication, 39,* 112-119.

Infante, D.A. (1979). Predicting response to semantic-differential scales from verbal behavior. *Southern Speech Communication Journal, 44,* 355-363.

Infante, D.A. (1980). Verbal plans: A conceptualization and investigation. *Communication Quarterly, 28,* 3-10.

Jackson, S., & Jacobs, S. (1980). Structure of conversational argument: Pragmatic bases for the enthymeme. *Quarterly Journal of Speech, 66,* 251-265.

Jacobs, S. (1980). Recent advances in discourse analysis. *Quarterly Journal of Speech, 66,* 450-472.

Jacobs, S. (1988). Evidence and inference in conversation analysis. In J.A. Anderson (Ed.), *Communication Yearbook 11,* (pp. 433-443). Newbury Park, CA: Sage.

Janis, I.L., & Feshbach, S. (1953). Effects of fear-arousing communications. *Journal of Abnormal and Social Psychology, 48,* 78-92.

Knapp, M.L. (1984). Forward. In M.L. McLaughlin, *Conversation: How talk is organized.* Beverly Hills, CA: Sage.

Lakoff, R. (1975). *Language and woman's place.* New York: Harper & Row.

Loftus, E.F. (1979). *Eyewitness testimony.* Cambridge, MA: Harvard University Press.

Loftus, E.F. (1980). *Memory.* Reading, MA: Addison-Wesley.

McCroskey, J.C. (1969). A summary of experimental research on the effects of evidence in persuasive communication. *Quarterly Journal of Speech, 55,* 169-176.

McLaughlin, M.L. (1984). *Conversation: How talk is organized.* Beverly Hills, CA: Sage.

McLaughlin, M.L., & Cody, M.J. (1982). Awkward silences: Behavioral antecedents and consequences of conversational lapse. *Human Communication Research, 8,* 299-316.

McLaughlin, M.L., Cody, M.J., & O'Hair, H.D. (1983). The management of failure events: Some contextual determinants of accounting behavior. *Human Communication Research, 9,* 208-224.

McLaughlin, M.L., Cody, M.J., & Robey, C.S. (1980). Situational influences on the selection of strategies to resist compliance-gaining attempts. *Human Communication Research, 7,* 14-36.

McLaughlin, M.L., Louden, A.D., Cashion, J.L., Altendorf, D.M.,Baaske, K.T., & Smith, S.W. (1985). Conversational planning and self-serving utterances: The manipulation of topical and functional structures in dyadic interaction. *Journal of Language and Social Psychology, 4,* 233-251.

Mehrley, R.S., & McCroskey, J.C. (1970). Opinionated statements and attitude intensity as predictors of attitude change and source credibility. *Speech Monographs, 37,* 47-52.

Miller, G.R. (1963). Studies on the use of fear appeals: A summary and analysis. *Central States Speech Journal, 14,* 117-125.

Miller, G.R., & Baseheart, J. (1969). Source trustworthiness, opinionated statements, and response to persuasive communication. *Speech Monographs, 36,* 1-7.

Miller, G.R., & Lobe, J. (1967). Opinionated language, open- and closed-mindedness and responses to persuasive communications. *Journal of Communication, 17,* 333-341.

Nofsinger, R.E. (1976). Answering questions indirectly. *Human Communication Research, 2,* 171-181.

Pearson, J.C. (1985). *Gender and communication.* Dubuque, IA: Wm. C. Brown.

Rokeach, M. (1960). *The open and closed mind.* New York: Basic Books.

Searle, J. R. (1969).*Speech acts: An essay in the philosophy of language*. Cambridge: Cambridge University Press.

Steinfatt, T.M. (1977). *Human communication. An interpersonal introduction.* Indianapolis, IN: Bobbs-Merrill.

Stewart, L.P., Cooper, P.J., & Friedley, S.A. (1986). *Communication between the sexes: Sex differences and sex-role stereotypes.* Scottsdale, AZ: Gorsuch Scarisbrick.

Street, R.L., Jr., and Giles, H. (1982). Speech accommodation theory: A social cognitive approach to language and speech behavior. In M. Roloff & C.R. Berger (Eds.), *Social cognition and communication* (pp. 193-226). Beverly Hills, CA: Sage.

Sussman, L. (1973). Ancients and moderns on fear and fear appeals: A comparative analysis. *Central States Speech Journal, 24,* 206-211.

Trenholm, S. (1986). *Human communication theory.* Englewood Cliffs, NJ.: Prentice-Hall.

Wheeless Eman, V. (1984). A test of the theory of speech accommodation using language and gender orientation. *Women's Studies in Communication, 7,* 13-22.

Whorf, B. (1956). *Language, thought, and reality.* New York: John Wiley.

Wiemann, J.M. (1985). Interpersonal control and regulation in conversation. In R.L. Street, Jr. & J.N. Cappella (Eds.), *Sequence and pattern in communicative behavior* (pp. 85-102). London: Edward Arnold.

Chapter 8

Nonverbal Behavior Approaches

Communication often involves more than a verbal message. We typically send and receive several messages simultaneously. Messages sent without using words are called "nonverbal" messages. For instance, a person's verbal message concerning a new shirt you are wearing might be, "I really like your new shirt." If the person accompanied the verbal message with nonverbal behavior such as erratic eye contact, a downward twist of the lower lip, words spoken in a slightly higher than average pitch, shoulders turning away from you, eyes blinking, and feet shuffling, you might decide that the verbal message was inconsistent with the nonverbal cues. Which would you tend to believe? Probably you would conclude the person really does not like your new shirt and is simply trying not to offend you.

Our example suggests that nonverbal communication is important because it is highly believable. We realize that understanding what people mean is central to how effective we are socially. Determining what people mean is not always easy because deception is a common strategy. For example, individuals believe one thing but say they believe something else, claim to pay attention but are actually thinking of something else, and say they will behave one way while intending to behave just the opposite. Because of the disagreement over definitions of communication presented in Chapter 1, we will include behaviors that do not actually constitute "messages" according to our definition. These nonverbal cues, while not examples of intentional communication, often accompany verbal messages and help us to interpret them.

The better we can "read" people, the more we know what to expect and can plan accordingly. Understanding nonverbal communication is a very valuable social tool.

There is widespread interest in nonverbal communication by both the general public and those in the communication field. Books such as Fast's (1970) *Body Language* have enjoyed extensive popularity. In the communication discipline, nonverbal behavior is one of the major lines of research (for an overview of research see Burgoon, 1985), and there are numerous books on the subject (for instance see Knapp, 1980; Leathers, 1986; Richmond, McCroskey, & Payne, 1987). Nonverbal behavior is thought to be at least as important as verbal behavior in understanding communication. The nonverbal code may be viewed as a language, one that we begin learning early in life just as we do the verbal code.

The popularity of nonverbal communication makes it necessary to emphasize that it is not a "cure-all" for social problems; studying nonverbal communication does not guarantee social effectiveness. The textbooks mentioned above make this clear; they do not exaggerate the importance of this area. Popular books, on the other hand, have not always been so cautious. They sometimes characterize nonverbal codes as "secret weapons" which when learned will help you conquer any task. However, nonverbal communication is only one dimension of communication competence. Other aspects including competence with the verbal code, constructing effective arguments, and good delivery are also very important.

Affective-Cognitive Dimensions of Communication

The potency of verbal and nonverbal communication varies according to what is being communicated. Understanding the *affective* and *cognitive* dimensions of communication will clarify the variation. The affective dimension includes the communication of emotion (such as anger, love, fear or happiness), attitude (how much something is liked or disliked, for example), and predispositions (such as anxiousness, confidence, or depression). These feelings can be communicated by the verbal code, but the task is difficult. For instance, when you try to tell a friend how much you love another person, you may feel that you have not really been understood. Some ideas are difficult to put into words but can be expressed very clearly nonverbally. Simply observing how a person looks at another communicates a good deal about the degree of love, for instance. Nonverbal behavior is particularly effective in communicating affect.

The verbal code, on the other hand, is more effective when the goal is to communicate thoughts or cognitions. The cognitive component of communication refers to *beliefs* about what is and/or is not related to the object of communication. You can have beliefs about attributes, characteristics, and consequences of an object. For instance you might believe that a candidate for the Presidency is honest, sincere, friendly, and an expert in domestic issues, but a novice in foreign affairs. Beliefs have to do with how things are related. This might also be thought of as "an idea" or "thinking." Typically, abstract processes such as spatial reasoning are necessary to comprehend a belief. These processes are very difficult to express nonverbally. The verbal code seems to have been designed especially for communicating the cognitive aspects of our internal processes. In our example, expressing beliefs about a candidate's relationship to domestic issues and foreign affairs could be done verbally without much difficulty. However, to do this nonverbally would be a nearly hopeless task. Expressing affect for the candidate through the nonverbal code could be accomplished very easily. A negative opinion about the candidate could be expressed with a look of disapproval; positive feelings could be expressed with smiles, head nodding, or clapping.

Contextual Nature of Nonverbal Communication

The idea that the meaning of a message is dependent upon its context is important in understanding nonverbal communication. A context involves a situation and variables in the situation which make it different from other contexts. These differences occur along the lines of who, what, how, why, where, and when. The characteristics of the context influence the meaning of a message. Take a symbol such as a handshake. In a situation where you are introduced to someone, the handshake might indicate, "I'm very glad to meet you," while the very same behavior in greeting an old friend could mean, "I'm so glad to see you again." A handshake with rivals before a contest can mean, "May the better person win"; after closing a business deal, "It was a pleasure to do business with you"; after a bitter quarrel, "Let's put this fight behind us." The behavior is essentially the same in all of these examples. However, the meaning is considerably different. The reason is quite simple; we have learned that a given symbol (or set of symbols) means one thing in one situation but something different in another. Thus, the meaning of a message is influenced by context. We should note the context in which a message is presented when we decide on its meaning.

Despite the fact that the contextual nature of communication is discernible, some of the popular books on nonverbal communication overlook this concept. Instead, they suggest that certain nonverbal behaviors mean only one thing and ignore the other possible meanings that could be created by changes in the situation. For instance, a possible interpretation of a woman talking to a man with her arms folded in front of her is that she is signaling unavailability; he is "closed out." What if this behavior occurs in a chilly room or even in a warm room by a woman who has just come in from the cold? In such cases, the nonverbal arm behavior might say nothing about the woman's desire for a relationship. It is misleading to treat a set of nonverbal behaviors as a formula for social knowledge. In certain circumstances it might be true that "a woman is interested in you if she moves her shoulders back, is slightly flushed, and tilts her head to one side a bit." These behaviors might indicate interest in an intimate setting. If you are walking across campus to your next class, they might signal that she had a good workout at the gym, is stretching her deltoids, and is reacting to the muscle stimulation.

Nonverbal Behavior and Intentionality

In Chapter 1 we clarified that all human behavior is not communicative behavior. Communication occurs when people use symbols to stimulate meaning in other people. Symbols are only one of several things that can stimulate meaning. Nonsymbolic behavior can involuntarily stimulate a response. A woman may fold her arms for many reasons. If sending a message about unavailability is not one of her reasons, then communication about approachability does not occur when she folds her arms. Of course, an interested male might "read meaning into" her behavior. She cannot stop people from thinking. Meaning can be stimulated by both symbolic and nonsymbolic elements. If a man's arm folding is nonsymbolic regarding accessibility, imagine his confusion if a woman said, "Why did you just send me a message which said you are unavailable?" His response, in the terminology of this book might be, "I only tell you something when I send a message to you. I cannot stop you from seeing meaning in non-message behavior. If you do, do not act as though I am saying something to you. Realize that you are creating meaning for yourself which may have no relation to my ideas and feelings."

Perhaps one of the reasons the area of nonverbal communication has become so popular is that nonverbal behavior provides clues to detecting attitudes, traits, and deception. There are many examples. A drooping posture reveals depression. Pupil dilation shows interest. Frequent head nodding indicates a feeling of lower status. Deception is signified by less forward body lean. Nervousness is evidenced by fewer gestures. Such behaviors seem to reveal information that people themselves usually would not volunteer. As such, these nonverbal behaviors appear to be a valuable means for understanding people. Despite this appeal, the behaviors in question usually do not constitute communication since action with symbols is not apparent. Instead, they seem more like symptoms (See Chapter 7) as defined by Cronkhite (1986), e.g., A symptom of depression is a drooping posture. Judee Burgoon (1985), probably the leading nonverbal communication researcher in the communication discipline, supports this interpretation.

Similarly, *emotional leakage* probably is a consequence of the perception of symptoms. Emotional leakage is the term used to describe when a person's true feelings "leak out" through one or more nonverbal channels. Unknowingly, or at a very low level of awareness, individuals reveal their true emotions because of their nonverbal behavior. If you are bored with a conversation but pretend you are interested, emotional leakage might occur if your laughter were less relaxed and you used fewer vocal expressions and head nods. The idea that a person's boredom would leak out and foil the person's attempt to create a particular impression is intriguing. However, the "leaky" behaviors probably are not symbolic. Instead, they are most likely symptoms. As such they have the potential to stimulate meaning. As our conception of communication makes clear, all meaning does not result from communication. Although highly provocative, "emotional leakage" is not a communication concept because nothing is communicated. Instead, one-way meaning is formed which occurs only in the mind of the observer. Communication is a "two-way" process involving social behavior and a deliberate message on the part of the sender. A person may create meaning because of naturally occurring symptoms or behaviors which cannot easily be controlled. Of course, even behaviors such as blinking in response to a threatening movement can be controlled. However, symptomatic behavior usually has nothing to do with symbols.

Nonverbal Communication Abilities

People vary widely in how well they encode and decode written and spoken messages. Since individuals range from very high to very low in verbal language abilities, we would expect to find differences in nonverbal communication as well. Research suggests that the ability to encode and decode nonverbal behavior may be an attribute of certain personality traits. People who are extroverted are more skilled at portraying emotions through vocal and facial codes. Introverts are less able to communicate emotions nonverbally, if for no other reason than they have not had as much practice due to their tendency to withdraw from people.

Self-monitoring of expressive behavior is another trait which appears related to nonverbal encoding ability (Snyder, 1974). High self-monitors are very aware of the impression they make on others. They are able to assess their behavior and reactions to it and make adjustments in their performance accordingly; high self-monitors are very adaptive. High self-monitors are also skilled at communicating emotions nonverbally when compared to low self-monitors. Having the motivation to monitor one's behavior with respect to the reactions of others appears necessary for the development of the ability to encode nonverbal messages skillfully.

Greater encoding skill by high self-monitors has been investigated in terms of deceptive communication (Miller, de Turk, & Kalbfleisch, 1983). Research participants were asked to tell the truth or to lie about the feelings that they had while viewing pleasant or unpleasant slides. Both high and low self-monitors took part in the experiment. Participants either spoke immediately or were given 20 minutes to rehearse what they would say. Observers viewed videotapes of the participants' messages and judged whether the individual was telling the truth or not. When rehearsal was permitted, high self-monitors were more effective in deceiving observers. The more time highs had to practice their behavior, the more successful they were. Low self-monitors who had not rehearsed displayed more pauses and had a higher rate of nonfluencies such as "um". This experiment confirmed the hypothesis that high self-monitors would be more effective in deceiving others.

There may be a sex difference in the ability to communicate emotions facially and vocally (Zaidel & Mehrabian, 1969). Females seem to be more skilled than males. One explanation for this is that culture has taught females to be more expressive and to reveal emotions. Males, on the other hand, have been conditioned to be more stoic and to inhibit expression of feelings. Because males engage less in emotionally expressive behavior, they are less skilled at encoding it. Nonverbal decoding ability is also related to sex. Rosenthal and his associates (1979) developed the PONS (Profile of Nonverbal Sensitivity) test to measure ability to decode nonverbal messages. One of the most consistent results in research which has used this test is that females tend to score higher in comparison to males. The finding that females are higher in both nonverbal encoding and decoding abilities further illustrates the point that the two abilities are related. That is, if you are high on one, you tend to be high on the other; if you are unskilled regarding one, you tend to be unskilled regarding the other.

A cultural sex-role explanation would be that women are better at decoding nonverbal messages because they have to be skilled "people-readers." Females need this ability because they do not have as much of the power in society. If you are vulnerable, you need to be sensitive to the moods and emotions of those who have the power because your success in influencing powerful others depends upon timing. Thus, nonverbal decoding ability may be a "survival" behavior which women have developed to cope with being in a position of low power in society. The sociologist Rosabeth Moss Kanter (1977) has hypothesized a similar explanation for the behavior of Jewish males in turn-of-the-century America. Since they were discriminated against and not promoted to high positions in business, they worked to become valued assistants to those in power. They were able to advance because they had learned to "read" behavior and thus to gain favor with those more powerful than themselves. Thus, the sex difference in the ability to read nonverbal behavior may have nothing to do with biology but much to do with social structures that empower some and disadvantage others. Those with little power learn to decode nonverbal behavior to curry favor with the powerful; they learn to obtain indirectly the power which society prevents their gaining through more direct means.

Although females generally score higher on the PONS test, there are some males who score as well or better than most females. These tend to be males who are in professions which are very communication oriented and which require sensitivity to the needs of others. Teachers, clinical psychologists, and actors are examples. This finding further supports the social-influence explanation given above for male-female differences in nonverbal behavior.

High scorers on the PONS test differ from low scorers in several ways in addition to gender. Low scorers tend to be younger. Just as with verbal language, nonverbal ability seems to improve with age. High scorers tend to function better socially, have closer same-sex relationships, and predict future events with greater accuracy.

In developing the PONS, Rosenthal experimented with the amount of time a scene was shown to people. He found when exposure was reduced from five seconds to 1/24 of a second, some people were still able to identify the emotion portrayed. These individuals who appeared to be especially sensitive to the nonverbal code reported that they had less satisfactory relationships with other people. Perhaps it is possible to see "too much" in the behavior of others, and this creates dissatisfaction with people. That is, extreme accuracy in decoding may make one more aware of the "common deceptions" which are a regular component of social interaction. Common deceptions refer to "white lies," behaving one way but preferring something else, or concealing the truth because of a desire to protect someone's feelings.

Functions of Nonverbal Communication

Functional approaches have been used extensively to examine a number of areas in communication such as credibility, persuasion, and mass media. Viewing nonverbal communication in terms of the functions that it fulfills for the individual is similarly valuable. We will briefly examine six important functions.

Sending Uncomfortable Messages

Some messages are difficult to send verbally but much easier to present nonverbally. Overt delivery of the message verbally would have a high potential for resulting in embarrassment, hurt feelings, discomfort, anxiety, and anger. One example of such a message involves initiating or preventing interaction. For instance, at a party Jamie might realize that Sean across the room wants to approach and talk. If Jamie does not want to meet Sean, a possible verbal message would be, "Don't bother coming here to talk with me; I don't want to get to know you." Of course, that is a difficult message to present in a social situation. An "easy way" to deliver the idea would be advantageous. Nonverbal codes such as eye and facial behavior and the directness of body orientation accomplish this very well. In fact, even in a crowded room, probably only Sean would be aware of Jamie's message of discouragement.

Once interaction has been initiated, another difficult message is to inform someone that you wish to terminate the interaction. Imagine that Sean in our previous example ignored the nonverbal message and approached Jamie anyway. A possible verbal message which would serve the purpose would be: "Why did you come across the room to talk with me? Couldn't you see I'm not interested? Please leave." As in the earlier example, this would be a most difficult message to deliver verbally. Nonverbally, the task would be easier. Jamie could avoid eye contact, turn so as not to face Sean directly, and talk in short phrases with little expression (sound bored).

These examples illustrate that messages which are essentially negative in nature are communicated with efficiency by the nonverbal code. However, some types of positive messages also are easier to say nonverbally. One example is communicating love. Some people find it difficult to say "I love you" and instead rely upon eye behavior, touch, and close proximity. Another example is communicating favorable internal states such as feeling very good about oneself. Nonverbally, this can be done by sounding confident (vocally), reflecting this feeling in facial behavior, and walking with a confident gait.

Forming Impressions Which Guide Communication

Nonverbal communication is especially useful in the process of forming first impressions. Initial interaction and the early stages of a relationship are influenced a good deal by the first impressions which people form of each other. Gerald Miller's (1978) developmental approach to interpersonal communication provides a way to conceptualize this. Communication between people is viewed as ranging from impersonal to interpersonal. At the *impersonal* end of the continuum, people use sociological variables such as age, sex, and race to form an impression which guides what to say and how to say it. When communication is impersonal, you rely on stereotypes and other assumptions about what people are like to guide your communicative behavior. We typically place a good deal of importance on first impressions because we do not want to say something that the other will view as foolish. We are strongly motivated to reduce uncertainty about the other so that we can predict with confidence how to and how not to communicate. (You will read more about this process in the discussion of Uncertainty Reduction Theory in Chapter 9.)

When communication is *interpersonal*, the impression of the other which guides interaction is based mainly upon *psychological* data. In comparison to sociological data, psychological is more personal. The major types of psychological data are values (broad, very strong beliefs which guide behavior), attitudes (like or dislike for things), and personality (traits which define the person). Thus, when communication is interpersonal, it is less stereotypic and is individualized according to the psychological characteristics of the people involved.

The nonverbal messages which we send contribute substantially to the first impression others form of us. This impression then guides how people talk with us in the early stage of interaction. Many of these messages pertain to physical appearance—fashion, grooming, body type, and attractiveness. For instance, the first impression that you make might be: a black male, late teens, highly fashion conscious, very neat and clean looking, a "physical fitness" type who values being attractive. These cues would provide a basis for others to guess how to communicate with you. For instance, clothes or physical fitness would be "excellent bets" for successful topics of communication.

Nonverbal cues provide data relevant to your psychological characteristics. If the cues are clear, communication moves from the impersonal to interpersonal levels more readily. The cues just discussed, fashion consciousness and physical fitness, are examples. Other cues derive from nonverbal codes such as the way we use our voices. For instance, a person might sound very self-confident or move very confidently. Another individual's movements might suggest nervousness or apprehension about something. If the nonverbal cues are not clear, then there is the tendency for communication to remain at the impersonal level. For instance, if the messages from your eyes, face, and body movements make it unclear whether you are a very cautious or a carefree person, a person talking with you will exercise discretion, selecting only "safe" topics such as the weather, one's major, or home town.

Making Relationships Clear

In addition to *content*, communication has a *relationship* dimension (Watzlawick, Beavin, & Jackson, 1967). Content refers to the topic of the message. For instance, a parent might say to you, "Did you have a nice time at the party last night?" The content is clear. It has to do with how favorable your experience was with the party. The relationship dimension refers to the interpersonal relationship between the individuals, and this influences how the message will be handled. For instance, you might respond, "Oh, I had a marvelous time!" If a particular friend had asked the question, you might have said: "I had a marvelous time . . . until I reached the point where I had too much to drink." The relationships we have with people exert a powerful force on our communicative behavior.

Nonverbal communication functions to establish and clarify the relationship dimension of communication. It does this very well because at times the relationship message would be offensive if spoken verbally. For example, "I am your boss even though you do not like it." Communicating such a message without words serves to "soften" the message, making a destructive outcome of the situation less likely. If the relationship is not clarified, the danger of a misunderstanding increases. For instance, in the early stages of a new job you might be uncertain as to whether you must comply with what a certain person tells you to do. This uncertainty could result in your responding to the person with indifference when the other person's expectation was for you to be compliant. This would be a costly mistake if the person was your superior and not a peer.

There are many types of relationships which are important in communication. Some of these are parent-child, superior-subordinate, husband-wife, friendship, sibling, and dominant-submissive power roles. Others are based on competition, cooperation, liking, love, or disdain. Nonverbally, we tell one another what we believe the nature of our relationship to be. If there is correspondence between the parties, the relationship dimension of communication can recede to the background. For instance, if you want to be dominant in a relationship, you might communicate that by steady eye contact, holding the floor most of the time, interrupting and touching the other person more. If the other person accepts this relationship definition, there is no problem. Nonverbally, this acceptance might be communicated by eyes cast downward while looking "up" to you, frequent head nods, and passive smiles. On the other hand, if the nonverbal messages which people send to one another about the nature of their relationship are not congruent, then the definition of the relationship becomes an issue and usually predominates until resolved. When a relationship issue emerges, it becomes more likely that the attempt to define the relationship will shift from the nonverbal to the verbal code. That is, it is easier, less disruptive, and less offensive if we tell one another nonverbally of the nature of our relationship. If this fails to produce an agreeable outcome, then more overt communication is necessary; there is a need to talk about the relationship.

Regarding our earlier example, suppose you are new on a job and respond with indifference to someone who says you should stop what you are doing for a while and work at a different task. Suppose further that this person's eye contact was not steady and the tone of voice was unsure—two behaviors which do not indicate a superior relationship. Because the command is incongruent with the nonverbal cues, it probably would be necessary to clarify the relationship verbally. This could be done by having your supervisor explain to you whom else in the organization you must obey.

Regulating Interaction

Regulating our interaction with others is a fourth major function of nonverbal communication. Imagine the following: two people recognize one another in a college library. They begin to talk in a pleasant tone with occasional laughter. They take turns talking with little silence between utterances. After about 15 minutes the conversation ends, and they return to separate places in the library. Imagine further that both individuals derived considerable satisfaction from the interaction. That is, our example is one of successful communication. The episode described, although commonplace according to our experience, could be viewed with amazement as an example of complex human activity made to look easy. A major reason why communication events such as this go smoothly is they are carefully and skillfully regulated. The central regulating mechanism appears to be nonverbal communication. As a regulator, nonverbal behavior operates in terms of *initiating interaction, clarifying relationships, directing turn-taking, guiding emotional expression* and *leave-taking.*

Greeting behaviors which suggest a desire to interact are largely nonverbal. In our example, each person could send such messages by raising eyebrows while widening the eyes, raising the chin with a smile, and perhaps waving the hand in greeting. When the individuals approached one another and positioned themselves about three feet apart, the conversation could begin.

During the conversation, several nonverbal behaviors regulate the interaction. We discussed the function of clarifying relationships in the previous section. Directing turn-taking involves communicating when you want the floor and when you are or are not willing to relinquish the floor. When we want the floor (our turn to speak), a number of nonverbal messages may be used: throat clearing, vocal sounds such as "uh, uh," opening the mouth as if beginning to speak, raising eyebrows and opening eyes wide. Willingness to give up the floor is indicated by pausing, looking to the other as if searching for a response, nodding approval to begin, or gesturing toward the person to begin. Wanting to hold the floor when someone desires to talk is expressed by increasing volume somewhat, employing an aggressive tone in the voice, breaking eye contact and adopting a determined facial expression.

Guiding emotional expression involves the tone of the conversation. Nonverbally we say whether the tone should be happy, sad, angry, hurried, or serious. As we explained earlier, nonverbal communication is especially effective at expressing the affective or emotional dimension of communication.

Regulating leave-taking is accomplished nonverbally in many ways (Knapp, Hart, Friedrich, & Shulman, 1973). Messages which indicate a desire to end the conversation include breaking eye contact and glancing around the area, looking at a watch, shuffling feet, and leaning in the direction of the exit. The actual leave-taking will either be positive or negative, depending upon desire for future communication. Some positive nonverbal messages are a handshake, a smile, and a wave. Negative messages include an abrupt ending, turning and leaving with no goodbye, an angry goodbye, and a gesture of disgust upon exiting.

Influencing People

Nonverbal communication appears to be very important in the process of persuasion. Certainly the verbal message matters. However, there is increased awareness that people are influenced by nonverbal messages as well. Whether the verbal message is accepted seems to depend upon how well the persuader communicates nonverbally. Since the adage, "It's not what you say but how you say it," surely is an overstatement, a restatement may be appropriate: "What you say cannot escape how you say it."

There are several types of nonverbal messages which can enhance a source's persuasiveness. Some pertain to physical appearance, such as dress and grooming that appeal to the receiver. Others have to do with body movement or eye and facial behavior such as creating a dynamic image, a sincere look, or appearing sociable. Also of importance is vocal behavior, meaning the way the voice is used. This entails sounding dynamic and interesting. These nonverbal messages all contribute to the individual's *image* or total impression. In political communication especially, there is increased use of terms such as image building, image management, and image rebuilding or repairing. The use of these terms acknowledges the principle that one's nonverbal messages are not independent of the verbal message. Perhaps this causes you to think that the influence process, whether it occurs in the political, business, or personal arena, is extremely superficial because appearances matter so much. However, there is a very good reason for this. People pay close attention to persuaders' nonverbal behavior as a basis for deciding whether to *trust* the person. Trust is a necessary condition for persuasion in almost all cases.

A person's nonverbal behavior provides a major source of data to decide on a person's character. Dress, grooming, and facial behavior give us clues as to what kind of person the source is. Eye behavior is usually emphasized as a criterion for deciding whether to trust someone. Voice is also a focus. What kind of person do we look for in deciding trust? The answer is rather well established in terms of research. We are more attracted to people and trust them when they are similar to us (Infante, 1978). Similarity tends to breed attraction, and the more our nonverbal behavior says to a person, "As you can see, I am a lot like you," the more the person probably will trust you. This is true mainly because they know what to expect from a similar other. They think the person is guided by similar values.

This analysis has identified an approach to nonverbal communication in persuasion which has been termed *nonverbal response matching* (Infante, 1988). The idea is for the persuader to match the receiver's nonverbal behavior so that a bond of trust develops because the receiver perceives similarity between self and the persuader. For instance if the receiver talks fast with short, quick gestures, the persuader would adopt this style in order to identify with the receiver. This is not mimicry, which is a form of insult. Instead, it is a message that says, "I understand how you are, and I like being that way myself." This behavior confirms the saying, "Imitation is the sincerest form of flattery." Studies which compared successful salespersons to mediocre ones revealed that the successful sellers used response matching while the unsuccessful ones did not (Moine, 1982). Clearly, our nonverbal behavior provides important input in our decision about whether to trust others.

Reinforcing and Modifying Verbal Messages

Finally, one of the most basic functions of nonverbal communication is to affect the verbal message. The verbal and nonverbal messages are often produced together. As such, there is not one message but several, comprising a *set* of messages. The idea of a set emphasizes that things go together, influence one another, and the whole is more than simply a sum of the parts (See the discussion of Systems Theory in Chapter 3). Thus, a given configuration of nonverbal messages along with certain words will communicate one thing, while the very same words with a different set of nonverbal messages will communicate something else. Nonverbal communication may reinforce or modify the verbal message.

Nonverbal communication serves to reinforce verbal messages in a variety of ways. Gestures are used to illustrate size ("the fish was this big. . ."), position ("I was here; the fish jumped there. . ."), effort ("I struggled to keep the rod tip high while he pulled real hard . . ."), movement ("I reached into the water quickly and picked up the fish by the lower jaw."). Facial, eye, and vocal behavior are especially effective in emphasizing the emotional content of a message. For instance, if you are talking about a social problem such as hunger in America, nonverbal messages can be sent to reinforce the message of seriousness which you hope to convey verbally. While you were discussing the problem, your face, eyes, and voice could express sympathy and gravity. While discussing a proposed solution such as a guaranteed job program, your face, eyes, and voice could communicate hope, enthusiasm, and confidence.

At times, nonverbal messages are used to modify verbal messages. This is especially likely when we do not want our words to be taken literally. There are at least four ways this happens. One is when it is socially desirable to say one thing, but we want to express our displeasure with the contents of the verbal message. For example, imagine working for a company that invested much of its resources in a new but very unsuccessful product. In talking with co-workers your verbal message might be, "Oh, yes, our . . . is a wonderful innovation." Nonverbally, with eyes, face, and tone of voice, you might say that the product is not so wonderful and actually not much of an innovation either. Another circumstance is in using mock verbal aggression. You will recall (Chapter 6) that verbal aggression attacks a person's self-concept in order to deliver psychological pain. Mock verbal aggression includes verbal playfulness commonly termed "kidding" or "teasing." However, just as with mock physical assaults such as playful wrestling, one must be careful because a miscalculation can result in injury. Receiving a birthday present wrapped in paper which reads, "Happy birthday to a sweet old buzzard," may or may not be taken as a joke! Third, nonverbal messages are used to modify the verbal message in requests. Terry asks Dale for something, and Dale responds "yes" even though Dale would rather have said "no." Common nonverbal messages which are used to say, "OK, I will if you *really* want me to," include expressing the verbal message with little enthusiasm, looking away before saying yes, and breathing out while drooping the shoulders (as if burdened by a great load). In the fourth situation the individual's verbal messages create a certain image, but the person wants to modify that to say, "I am not exactly what you think" or "There is more to me than you realize." For instance, a person's verbal messages might leave no doubt that she is a lawyer, but her nonverbal messages might add, "I am opposed to this culture and seek to change it." These messages might come from very unconventional grooming (brightly colored spiked hair) and dress (wearing beads and buckskin clothes) and from negative nonverbal messages when talking about the status quo in America.

Nonverbal Message Codes

There are several types of nonverbal messages which we send and receive in the process of communication. We have learned to symbolize in many ways other than words. We will examine those message codes in this section.

Kinesics

Kinesics entails the study of bodily movement. The skeletal and muscular systems of the human body make possible a great variety of motions. The study of these motions and the muscles involved is very important to fields concerned with physical rehabilitation. For instance, understanding the motions involved in pitching a baseball can be used to prescribe an exercise program for a pitcher recovering from shoulder surgery. In terms of communication, we are not interested in the full spectrum of human movement. Rather, our concern is with those movements which have acquired symbolic meaning. These movements are sometimes termed "body language." In this section we will focus on movements below the neck. In the next section we will consider facial and eye behavior.

Ekman and Friesen (1969) developed a typology of five kinds of body movements that function communicatively. *Emblems* are movements which are functionally equivalent to words. That is, an emblem acquires meaning in a way that is very similar to how a word acquires meaning, so emblems may be used in place of words. Think of the emblems which have these verbal equivalents: "Come here"; "Hi"; "Goodbye"; "That's A-OK"; "I surrender"; "I would like a ride in your vehicle"; "Stop"; "I want three of those"; "Oh, how stupid of me." The number of emblems in American culture is said be only a hundred or so. Since emblems are movements which are clearly symbolic, intentionality is obvious. This clearly communicative nature is not always present in some of the other types of movements. In some of the types discussed below, a movement might simply be a symptom of an emotional state rather than a deliberate attempt to send a message.

Illustrators represent another example of movements that are usually intentional. While emblems can be independent of verbal messages, illustrators are used in conjunction with words to assist the receiver in understanding the intended meaning. As with emblems, illustrators also are learned and performed at a high level of awareness. Some types of illustrators are gestures which emphasize certain words. A rather classic gesture in this regard is a downward stroke of the hand and forearm to emphasize a particular word. Other movements seem to follow a rhythm, not unlike a musical rhythm. In fact, it has been suggested that any interpersonal communication situation is characterized by a tempo and people in the situation move and talk according to the tempo; for instance, you enter on the down beat. Further, we are disturbed when the people we talk with do not stay in tempo and thus are out of beat. Another type of illustrator involves description, as in "It was this high." Finally, gestures can attempt to draw a picture of something.

Affect displays are body movements which express emotion. The face probably communicates affect better than any other body movement. Whether it expresses emotion better than the voice, however, is debatable. Affect displays are not always intentional and do not always represent symbolic activity. Symbolic activity which is clear with emblems and illustrators is not always so with affect displays. However, there are many cases in which affect displays do clearly communicate and are obviously message behaviors. These cases occur mainly when the speaker wants to display certain emotions instrumental to accomplishing a goal. For instance, a teacher "puts on a happy face" because students respond better when the teacher is happy. Or, a speaker shows great enthusiasm because it is believed to be "catchy." These examples of messages indicate that an affect display can be an influence strategy. Other affect displays are simply signs of an emotion and are not symbols. For instance, if Lyn presents some startling facts to Marty, the look of surprise on Marty's face would not represent communication unless Marty wanted Lyn to believe surprise had occurred. There are numerous instances in which people use affect displays as message behavior. Thus, there is no need to claim all displays of affect as communicative symbols.

Regulators are movements used to regulate the interaction between people. This idea was discussed earlier as one of the functions of nonverbal communication. Besides examining the nonverbal behaviors which people use to regulate interaction, we may consider whether people vary in their use of regulators. Perhaps some individuals attempt to exercise more control in initiating interactions, governing the flow of communication in the situation, and deciding when to terminate an interaction. Several speculations can be derived from our discussion of traits in Chapter 6. Assertiveness, the tendency to be interpersonally ascendant, dominant, and forceful, is perhaps the most obvious choice for a trait related to the use of regulators. More assertive individuals probably will influence the start, course, and finish of an interaction. Fear of communication (communication apprehension) may be negatively related to regulating activity; the more communication apprehension, the less often the person initiates interaction. Interaction involvement, on the other hand, may be positively related. If one is more involved, he or she may try to have the interaction flow a particular way.

Adaptors are behaviors which once served a purely physical need but have been "adapted" to serve other needs. Scratching the head originally relieved an itch but has been adapted to express confusion. People typically have a number of adaptors which serve as expressions of their personalities. For example, Johnny Carson touches his tie and face and shrugs his shoulders in certain ways that are distinctly "Johnny" and thus become a means for conveying his image. Two types of adaptors discussed by Ekman and Friesen (1969) are self adaptors and object adaptors. *Self adaptors* involve touching or doing something to one's body: biting nails, pulling the ear lobe, smoothing hair, or rubbing the nose. *Object adaptors* involve such acts as clicking a pen, chewing gum, rubbing a piece of jewelry, handling a piece of paper, or tugging on a piece of clothing. Determining the meaning of these behaviors is difficult because they may be performed at a low level of awareness. If they are only signs of an internal state such as anxiety, they do not represent communication, even though they may stimulate meaning. However, there are adaptors which we knowingly use, perhaps because we feel the behavior says something about us. These, of course, constitute communication because the behavior is made to symbolize something, in this case our image. The behavior does not necessarily have to say something good about us to be communicative. For instance, Lee might deliberately smoke much of the time yet dislike the idea that others might consider that behavior self-abusive. For Lee, smoking constitutes communication because Lee uses cigarettes knowing they can symbolize something. At one time some people smoked because they thought smoking cigarettes symbolized "being cool." That behavior too represented using an object adaptor to communicate a message.

Posture involves body position more than body movement. We will examine it briefly since posture can function as a message, especially in terms of the source's attitude toward self and toward the receiver. However, as explained earlier, posture functions as a symptom rather than a symbol much of the time and therefore often does not represent communication. James' (1932) research identified four types of posture. *Approach* is a positive, attentive, accepting posture characterized by a forward lean of the body. *Withdrawal* is a negative, rejecting, refusing posture expressed by drawing back and/or turning away. *Expansion* conveys a proud, arrogant, or conceited attitude and involves an expanded chest, erect shoulders and head, and at times a backward leaning trunk. *Contraction* suggests a depressed, dejected mood and entails a forward leaning trunk with drooping shoulders, a bowed head, and a sunken chest. *Body orientation* refers to the degree a speaker's shoulders and hips are turned in the direction of the receiver. More direct body orientation indicates a more favorable attitude toward the receiver. Thus, a more negative attitude toward the receiver may be the case when the speaker's shoulders are facing the receiver at an angle.

Eye and Facial Behavior

Eye behavior has received considerable attention as an important source of information about people. There are stories of people in business who refuse to talk with someone who is wearing sunglasses because the person's eyes are hidden by the glasses. An adage claims, "Never trust someone who is unwilling to look you right in the eye." Interestingly, research has discovered some support for the idea that deceivers maintain less eye contact than truthtellers (Greene et al, 1985; Miller et al, 1983). However, a model of deception by Hocking and Leathers (1980) suggests that when people want to avoid detection, they attempt to control behavior which is stereotypic of liars. Less eye contact is one of these stereotypic behaviors, and it can be controlled if the person has time to prepare for the deception. Other behaviors such as vocal disfluencies ("uh, um") are much more difficult to control and increase when someone lies, even when there is time to rehearse. When a person uses eye contact to communicate truthfulness, whether or not the person succeeds, the behavior represents communication because it was intended to symbolize something.

In addition to deception, eye behavior has been examined in terms of communicating *attitude*, *interest*, and *dominance-submission*. Attitude is perhaps illustrated best by the look of two lovers. This is a favorable attitude at its most extreme and is characterized by a look that is at once extremely peaceful, warm, intense, and focused, not willing to be distracted. The opposite, an extremely negative attitude, is typified by great tension on the eye lids (which partially closes them) and a hard, cold stare with little blinking.

Attention has been given to pupil dilation as an indication of attitude. Given controlled light (since the pupils are very sensitive to any change), the pupils dilate when a person feels favorable. Thus, the pupils provide an involuntary measure of attitude. This idea has proved to be controversial. It is more likely that pupil dilation indicates *interest* in the object of attention rather than attitude. Another possibility is that pupil dilation is a measure of cognitive effort; the more cognitive effort, the more the pupils dilate. Although interesting, the idea of pupil dilation has little to do with communication since it is clearly a symptom of something, whether that be attitude, interest, or effort. Since pupil dilation is an involuntary response, it is easy to see that symbolic activity is not involved. If pupil size could be manipulated to symbolize something, that would be a different matter. For instance, some research suggests a woman is perceived as more beautiful if her pupils are dilated (Hess, 1975). If a woman takes a drug to dilate her pupils because she thinks it will enhance her beauty, then pupil dilation would represent a message and thus be an example of nonverbal communication.

Interest and disinterest can also be communicated by eye behavior. The eye behaviors which show interest are eye lids opened rather wide and sustained eye contact with a relaxed look (if tensed instead of relaxed, those behaviors suggest fear). Disinterest entails drooping eye lids, little eye contact, eyes glancing around as if looking for something. The idea of showing interest in someone pertains to the notion of attentiveness. Research suggests that attentiveness is an important part of the communication style of subordinates in the work situation (Infante & Gorden, 1989). Subordinates who were more attentive tended to be those with satisfactory job performance.

Dominance and submission can be communicated nonverbally with eye behavior. If one person wants to be dominant in a relationship with another, this message can be sent with the eyes by a rather firm stare at the other person with little blinking and by appearing to be looking down at the person, even if both people are standing on the same level. Submissiveness is suggested by avoiding eye contact from time to time with eyes cast downward and by appearing to look up to the other person even if the two are on the same level.

Research on eye contact (Argyle, 1967) indicates that it follows an expected pattern depending upon whether the individual is the source or the receiver. The source is expected to look at the receiver for several seconds and then to look away briefly, to break eye contact occasionally. By comparison, the receiver should sustain more eye contact; however, eye contact should not be held long enough to be considered a stare. A failure to maintain the expected pattern of eye contact, especially if one makes contact too little, may cause others to think we have low self-esteem. The person may appear not to have enough confidence to face others and to be afraid of normal activity. Making too little eye contact may also create the impression that we have a negative attitude toward our conversational partner. This impression results from the facts that we look more at people we like and that averting our eyes is normally a conscious activity. When we look away, we are motivated to do so and know what we are doing. Eye contact is thus considered symbolic. Usually, we are communicating something by looking or not looking at someone. Of course, not all eye aversions indicate a negative attitude. Breaking eye contact is sometimes used to say the interaction should end (Knapp et al., 1973).

Facial behavior is also extremely expressive. Our face naturally expresses emotions we are experiencing internally, and we all realize this occurs. Moreover, we know that there are many times when we do not want to reveal what we feel because that information could be used by others against us. For example, if we are playing poker and draw a good hand, a look of glee could cause others to fold. Thus, we sometimes want our facial expressions to be neutral rather than to convey what we are feeling (Richmond, McCroskey, & Payne, 1987).

In other circumstances, we want the emotion we feel to show. However, we try to project a stronger or weaker emotion than we actually feel; we attempt to amplify or depreciate the intensity of the emotion. For instance, if you receive a gift you are only mildly favorable toward, you might, by your facial (and eye) behavior, convey that you "absolutely love" the gift. Depreciation is necessary in situations where you want something desperately but to show that intensity is counterproductive. Thus, your choice would be to express a more moderate degree of desire. Purchasing a car is an example where displaying less emotion would be beneficial.

Finally, there is another class of situations in which our interests would best be served if our facial behavior presented a different emotion from the one we actually feel. A salesperson who is feeling depressed because of family problems knows a look of depression will not put customers in the proper frame of mind for a sale. Thus, the person will smile and try to look happy. In this instance, facial behavior is used to create certain impressions in others regarding an emotional state. Facial behavior can be used to symbolize something. Some nonverbal codes are more intentional than others; some often represent symbolic activity while others seldom symbolize anything. Facial behavior is particularly intentional, perhaps because it is so visible during communication and we are so aware of it.

Leathers' (1986) analysis of the research on facial behavior suggests at least five things are communicated by the face. Two are communication outcomes which we discussed regarding eye behavior: attitude (like–dislike) and interest–disinterest. A third outcome was also covered earlier when we explained that facial behavior can be manipulated in terms of amplification and depreciation of emotions. Facially we can express emotional intensity and our degree of involvement in the situation.

Two additional outcomes are fairly unique to the face, although the voice also shares these functions. First, the face reveals the amount of control people have over their emotional expression. A person who is not skilled at using a neutral expression ("poker face"), at amplifying and depreciating expressions, or at expressing an unfelt emotion cannot disguise this lack of ability. Do these weak attempts constitute communication? Yes; message behavior does not have to be successful to be considered communication. If a person attempts to use a message code, no matter how ineptly, that activity along with the receiver's reaction to it represents communication. A probable response to much of our communication behavior is that people assess our competence at least some of the time. We are aware that other people evaluate our social behavior. Because of our need to maintain a favorable self-concept, a common goal in communication situations is to be perceived as a competent communicator.

Finally, Leathers (1986) points out that facial behavior expresses our understanding or confusion over the content in a message. The face and the voice are particularly good at revealing confidence and understanding or a lack of confidence and confusion. These are fairly difficult expressions to conceal, and it is difficult to feel one but express the other. Think about times you have been confused; was it easy to act as if you were confident and to pretend that you understood the message?

Vocalics

Along with facial behavior, the way we use our voice contributes greatly to the emotional meaning in face-to-face communication. Psychologist Albert Mehrabian (1981, p. 77) proposed the total feeling communicated by a message is comprised of 7% verbal, 38% vocal, and 55% facial codes. Perhaps the most surprising percentage is the small proportion of emotion expressed by words. In fact, these findings were due more to the research methods Mehrabian used than to the actual percentage of emotional content communicated by verbal or nonverbal channels. However, as explained earlier, the verbal code functions best in the cognitive dimension of communication, and the verbal and nonverbal codes combine to form a set of behaviors which are best interpreted together. It makes little sense to discuss which channel, verbal or nonverbal, communicates what meaning since we most often receive communication along both channels simultaneously.

Vocalics involves the meaning stimulated by the sound of the voice. A good deal of the sound of the human voice is under the control of the speaker. There is considerable awareness of the vocalic dimension of communication because speakers hear themselves speak. We may reasonably conclude that vocal intonation is intentional because speakers know that they control their voices and can change how they sound. Thus, if we hear a person speak with a very excited voice, we assume he or she has chosen to sound excited. However, not all aspects of the human voice can be controlled by the speaker. Vocal quality is partially due to the physical configurations of one's larynx and vocal chords. When vocal quality cannot be controlled, it is not message behavior even though it stimulates meaning. The meaning is merely a "one-way" interpretation on the part of the receiver.

Speakers have little or no control over several aspects of the sound of their voices. Modal pitch and resonance are two factors which influence greatly whether the person sounds like a male or female. The female voice is pitched about an octave above the male voice, and the resonance chambers (throat, oral cavity, nasal cavity) are smaller for women. These physical differences affect the tones produced by the larynx and explain why male and female voices are distinct. If you have had singing lessons, you know it is possible to enhance the tonal quality of your voice, especially in terms of producing a strong, even vibrato (the vibrating quality of the voice). Other aspects of the tone are fairly impervious to change. One is the "lyric" quality of the voice. This pertains to the freshness or youthfulness of the voice. As the voice gets older, it becomes "darker" and sounds more aged. Even the vocal techniques of great singers such as Enrico Caruso could not prevent this change in lyric quality.

Some vocal qualities can be controlled and therefore are means of communication. Rate, volume, pitch, articulation, and pronunciation are important examples. Rate regulates the amount of time it takes to say words. Skilled speakers vary their rate considerably by slowing for emphasis or speeding through other parts of a message. Volume affects loudness and can vary from a whisper to a shout. Speaking with little variation creates what is called a "monotone" voice. Monotone does not mean literally talking on the same pitch (the stereotype of a talking computer sounds that way). Pitch refers to the number of vibrations per second of the vocal tone. Making the voice go higher and lower to emphasize words and to display emotions (for instance, a higher voice is more excited) is relatively easy to do. Articulation involves shaping the basic sound in the larynx in order to produce the various sounds of the vowels and consonants used to form words. If a person's articulation is clear, receivers easily hear each sound in a word. Pronunciation is the articulation of a word according to the accepted or standard usage. Common mistakes are accents on the wrong syllable, adding an incorrect sound for the correct sound (such as ath-uh-lete for ath-lete), and omitting sounds (a-lum-num for a-lu-mi-num).

These five vocal qualities represent vocal behaviors: how we use our voice when expressing words. The voice also is used to make sounds such as laughing, yawning, sighing, grunting, and "fillers" inserted in the void between thoughts ("uh"), sometimes called "vocalized pauses." A stereotypic behavior of unskilled speakers is the frequent use of vocalized pauses. Some vocal sounds might qualify as what Cronkhite (1986) termed *rituals*. Such signs are somewhat natural and might have origins in evolution. They have since become stylized, performed in a certain way, and are now symbolic. A person might grunt while making a great effort. The sound is now restrained so that people will not think the person is crude. The person thus communicates both the physical effort and the effects of civilization!

Vocalics, sometimes called paralanguage, is another important aspect of communication. As with facial behavior, vocalics is particularly effective in communicating emotion. Since we have commented on this earlier, we will examine other messages produced by the way we use our voices. The voice is put to use in managing interactions. In requesting a turn, we use vocal sounds such as "uh, uh." When we have the floor and do not want to yield to someone who uses "uh, uh" or actually begins to speak, we increase the volume of our voices and adopt a more determined tone to "ward off" the intruder. We commonly indicate that we are yielding the floor by hesitating a bit and allowing our voices to "trail off" (decrease in volume, pitch, and rate). Another way interaction is managed is by encouraging and discouraging others using vocal sounds. For instance, sounds such as "Hmm" or "Uh-huh" can either encourage or discourage, depending upon whether they are vocalized with a friendly or hostile tone.

Education and social status are communicated by the way we use our voices. One of the things we learn in college, for instance, is how a professional in any given field should sound. You recognize how people sound in college and probably soon are able to shift vocalics depending upon whether you are at college, at your part-time factory job, or on the streets of a big city. For example, you might express less variety in pitch with your "professional" voice.

Attitude toward the receiver is revealed by vocalics. If speakers do not want to reveal their true feelings toward the receiver, then they manipulate vocal behavior to express the desired attitude. As with other vocalic messages, this one is often utilized in conjunction with other nonverbal messages such as facial behavior.

The way the voice is used appears to send a message about how much expertise we have on a topic. The voice can reflect great confidence and security about the information in a message, creating the impression that a speaker really knows the topic. On the other hand, if speakers are hesitant, use vocalized pauses, and sound uncertain, receivers doubt the speaker's expertise. Of course, such a speaker might actually be an expert, while a confident sounding person might be a complete fraud. Vocalics represents such a potent communication code that other, conflicting messages sometimes are ignored, and we believe the message sent through vocalics.

In relationships we use our voices to say how we feel about ourselves, especially in task situations. The degree of confidence that we have in our abilities is expressed typically by the way we talk about what needs to be done and how it should be done. Another context in which self-esteem is expressed readily is in intimate interpersonal relationships. There probably is some truth to the adage, "You cannot love someone else if you do not love yourself." It is very difficult not to tell someone with whom you are attempting to build an intimate relationship just how you feel about yourself.

Messages about one's sex role are communicated by the way the voice is used. For instance, a male who values a "traditional male" role and a male whose psychological gender is "traditional female" will use their voices in very different ways. The stereotypic voices of the "macho" male and the "effeminate" male provide examples.

Sexual arousal and desire are expressed vocally with clarity. In fact, it generally is considered "crude" to verbalize sexual desire. Instead, the expectation seems to be that the message should be sent by vocal, facial, and touching behavior. Although very difficult to do, great writers such as Tolstoy have penned memorable scenes of lovers communicating in this manner.

Physical Appearance

Our physical appearance is a message code because a good deal of how we appear is under our control. We exercise choice to appear one way or another by selecting clothes and artifacts (such as ties or scarves), by grooming, and by attempting to enhance attractiveness and body shape. There are aspects of physical appearance which are not alterable but nevertheless can function as nonverbal messages if they have symbolic value. These aspects include sex, race, beauty, height, and body characteristics. For instance, race would be a nonverbal message if a white person running for President spoke in an all black church and said, "From the early days in America there have been a line of white people who have been true champions of the rights of black people. I am the only person running for President who is from that mold." Through advances in medical technology we may now change some parts of our physical appearance which previously had been immutable. A few examples are the shape of the nose, the alignment of teeth, and the color of our eyes. There are some gray areas. For instance, is the shape of your body genetically determined? Were you born with a certain number of fat cells or is your eating and exercise behavior responsible for body weight and shape?

Several physical appearance message codes have received considerable attention by researchers. We will first examine dress. Beyond protection from the elements, humans cover their bodies for a variety of reasons. Clothing is used to enhance beauty; people select clothing they think makes them "look good." How we dress perpetuates tradition (the Native American headdress or Indian *sari*) and reinforces such aspects of culture as sexual identity (women wear dresses). Clothing sometimes indicates authority and roles. For example, law enforcement officers often wear uniforms with insignia of rank, and supervisors in a factory may wear dress suits and ties while subordinates wear work clothes.

The language of dress provides considerable information about how we feel about ourselves. For instance, someone who wears exercise clothes in public expresses the identity of one who values physical fitness. Attire is assigned meaning, and several experiments have explored the nature of that meaning. The well-dressed person is picked up more often when hitchhiking, receives help and directions more readily, receives more tips, and is followed more often than someone who is not well dressed when crossing the street against the light. Other research suggests well-dressed people create first impressions of success, power, good habits, and the ability to earn money. A study by Gorden, Tengler, and Infante (1982) studied attire on the job and the attitudes of 300 women from more than 200 organizations. They found that women who were more clothing-conscious dressed more conservatively on the job (colored blazer, matching skirt), and were more satisfied with their jobs than less clothing-conscious women. Women who liked dressing in sexy clothes on the job were more exhibitionistic in terms of their clothing attitudes and received fewer promotions. Thus, not dressing conservatively on the job may violate organizational norms and result in being "passed over" when opportunities arise for promotion. This finding supports advice given by Molloy (1977) in his popular book on dress.

Other researchers (Gorden, Infante, & Braun, 1985) investigated how fashion innovativeness is related to other aspects of a person's communicative behavior. Fashion innovativeness is the extent to which an individual is "current" in his or her dress or how willing the person is to adopt the most recent fashion trends. The fashion innovator is probably saying nonverbally, "I am with it.

I know what is in *Elle* or *Gentleman's Quarterly*, and I like it. I am at the forefront when it comes to dress." The results (all research participants were women) revealed that high as compared to low fashion innovators were more animated and dramatic in their communicator styles (high energy), more friendly, and had more desire to leave an impression on people. People who have high energy and dramatic, impression-leaving identities may use dress as one of the means for expressing themselves.

Physical attractiveness has been investigated extensively by researchers in the field of psychology. A limited amount of research on this variable has also been conducted in the communication discipline. This research points to a strong advantage that physically attractive people have in communication situations (see Berscheid & Walster, 1974). Attractive people are judged more favorably in terms of desirable personality traits, are expected to succeed more, are assumed to be happier, are perceived higher in credibility, and receive less punishment for a wrongdoing in comparison to their less attractive counterparts. This is only a partial list of findings. Moreover, the effects of beauty appear resistant to change. A study by Infante, Pierce, Rancer, and Osborne (1980) found less attractive people were perceived more favorably in terms of success and ability when their pictures were accompanied by very likeable first names. Thus, an approved name cancelled some of the disadvantage of being less attractive. However, when pictures of very attractive people with very undesirable first names were presented, the individuals were rated just as favorably in terms of success and ability as the same pictures given with very likeable names. This suggests the effects of being attractive are so strong that they are not diminished easily. Research findings such as these may be used in courtroom settings to explain judgments by the jury about witnesses and defendants. Television teaches us that attorneys have defendants in criminal cases dress their very best to look as attractive as possible. Perhaps it is difficult for a jury to believe that a "nice-looking" defendant could commit a horrible crime.

Berscheid and Walster (1974) said a possible explanation for the advantages of physical attractiveness is the stereotype, "What is beautiful is good." Unless we have been mistreated by an attractive individual, we assume the stereotype to be true and treat people accordingly. This results in prestige value being associated with physical attractiveness. That is, we think it is prestigious to have relationships with attractive people.

Earlier research suggests that women who are physically attractive send a message to that effect; when they are no longer able to use such a message code, they are less happy (Wilson & Nias, 1976). Social values have not emphasized as strongly the importance for men to be physically attractive. Their happiness may depend more upon success in business and power. Speculation is that because women in our society have little power, they must rely upon advantages such as physical attractiveness to gain power over others. When beauty fades, they probably experience a loss of influence. Although beauty is primarily determined by nature, the communicator can exercise a degree of control over it through grooming, cosmetics, physical fitness, or even cosmetic surgery.

Research by Sheldon (1940, 1954) and others suggests that the basic shape of our bodies has message value because we have learned to associate certain traits with people who are shaped one way or another. The *mesomorph* has an athletic build with wide, muscular shoulders and a low body fat level. We associate dominance, enthusiasm, assertiveness, and competitiveness with these characteristics. The *ectomorph* is thin with shoulders and hips about equal in width and an appearance which seems to lack physical strength. Ectomorphs are believed to be tense, anxious, cautious, and withdrawn. The *endomorph* has a heavy look with hips wider than shoulders, stomach protruding, and a high body fat level. We generally assume such persons are contented, easy going, jolly, and kind. If the shape of our bodies symbolizes certain traits, we might be more motivated to improve our physical fitness. More favorable attributions seem to be assigned to the more athletic body shape. Like physical attractiveness, body shape may be determined basically by nature. However, with extensive effort, it is possible to change from an ectomorph or an endomorph to a mesomorph.

Proxemics

Proxemics describes how people use space to communicate. *Territoriality* and *personal space* are concepts which have received considerable attention from scholars in nonverbal communication because of the importance we attach to the space around us and how using space "says" things to people. From the time of the pioneering research by Hall (1959, 1966), it has been clear that proxemics represents a message system that is often used with more than a minimal level of awareness.

Territoriality refers to claiming rights to an area. The concept was borrowed from studies which determined territoriality can explain a good deal of animal behavior. Why does an animal roam in a geographic area, but only so far? It urinates on the perimeter of the area and responds very aggressively to boundary violations. The answer is the animal has claimed rights to an area and is determined not to relinquish what the animal believes is its own. Territorial behavior has survival value because it spreads a species rather evenly throughout an area, regulating density and thus creating less drain on resources. Since some territory is more desirable than others, it is taken by the fittest of the males in male-dominant species. Females gravitate toward males who occupy the best territory, increasing the chance that superior genes will survive. Human territorial behavior is thought to be a remnant of biological evolution. Perhaps the clearest evidence of human territorial behavior is that nations have established borders and have responded to encroachments with war. Individuals do not often respond to a violation of territory with extreme aggression.

However, shooting a stranger who invades your home, for instance, generally does not result in criminal charges being filed.

We encounter examples of territoriality in private and public contexts every day. At home, we can use fences or shrubbery to mark boundaries. Inside the home, certain areas are designated by function and are seen to belong to the person fulfilling the function. For instance, in a family with traditional sex roles, the kitchen "belongs" to the wife and the garage to the husband. Territory is also claimed within areas not "owned" by an individual. Thus, within the family room a husband might have his chair and the wife hers. Violations of territory typically are acknowledged, but treated lightly; "If you don't get out of my kitchen, I am going to put you to work." Territorial behavior is not unusual in public places. Markers such as coats, books, and purses are placed in an area to convey the message that temporary rights to the place have been claimed. An assumption is that even if a place is public, people can reserve rights for themselves. Although territory can be marked informally by leaving your coat on a seat, society also is structured so that you can formally reserve a seat. At a football game, security forces are available to enforce the rights of possession you acquired when you purchased a ticket.

Personal space refers to the zones of space which surround us, regardless of where we are. Hall's (1959, 1966) work suggests that there are at least four distances which have meaning in communication. The distance for a given zone can expand or contract according to factors in the situation. However, culture has taught us that certain distances have certain meanings. Further, there are differences across cultures in the meanings attached to personal space. Picture a South American and a British diplomat talking. The South American tries to get very close to the British individual, who backs away trying to keep distance between them. Hall points out the serious breakdown in communication in this situation. One thinks the other is too pushy and insensitive to intimate space, while the other feels personally rejected by a cold and aloof counterpart. However, the problem is not one of attitudes but the fact that the two people are speaking different languages in terms of proxemics. Individuals from different cultures have different expectations about the distance one should keep during a conversation.

The distance for the *intimate zone* according to Hall ranges from physical contact to about 18 inches. Recall all messages have content and relationship dimensions. The distance 0-18 inches pertains to the relationship dimension. Violations of space expectations are noticed and are assumed to be symbolic, to function as a message. Thus, if a woman expects a man to be from 0-18 inches from her and he stands 30 inches away, she may think something is wrong in terms of their relationship. The *casual personal* distance extends from 18 inches to 4 feet. This is a common zone for engaging in interpersonal communication since many interpersonal interactions are with friends or people with whom we have at least a casual relationship. The *socioconsultative* zone spans from about 4 feet to 10 feet. This distance is normally used in the work situation or in talking with someone in a professional capacity such as lawyer-client. The *public* zone begins at 10 feet and ranges to where we can be seen and heard. Communication at such distances tends to be formal.

Judee Burgoon's (1978; Burgoon & Jones, 1976) theory of nonverbal violations of expectations has enhanced understanding of proxemics in communication. Through social norms we form expectations about how others should behave nonverbally. For example, strangers do not engage in touching. Also, we form expectations about how certain individuals will behave. "The first thing my roommate always does is put his arm around my shoulder." Another assumption is that we have attitudes toward these behaviors. Some we like; others we dislike. Finally, it is assumed these behaviors are meaningful. Often the meaning depends upon the situation and the relationship between the individuals. Thus, for example, "a caress may convey sympathy, comfort, dominance, affection, attraction, or lust" (Burgoon, Coker, & Coker, 1986, p. 497).

Based on these assumptions, a proxemic violation is viewed as positive or negative depending upon whether the communicator is liked or disliked. Thus, outcomes in a communication situation will be more favorable if a *liked* communicator sits *closer* to us than expected (positive violation of the distance norm) rather than conforming to the distance norm. Disliked communicators have more favorable outcomes if they conform to the distance norm. According to the model, a source's violation of nonverbal expectations causes emotional arousal in the receiver; anything out of the ordinary makes us take notice. The nature of our relationship with the source controls how we feel about the violation of expectations. If we like the source, we seem to appreciate being treated uniquely in the sense that the source does not follow the norms. However, if we dislike the source, we seem to prefer the ordinary (conforming to norms) and view violations negatively. Thus, Burgoon's model posits that it is not just a matter of identifying nonverbal behavior violations and the outcomes. Instead, who does the violating (the source) matters greatly, and this must be accounted for in order to tell whether the violation was positive or negative.

Touch

The use of touch to communicate, *tactilics*, could be considered a special case of the nonverbal message code which we just discussed, proxemics. That is, touch involves the minimum distance between people—zero—and thus means physical contact. Because the skin is a sensory organ, we are distinctly aware when we are being touched by another person. We are able to differentiate being touched by something inanimate (clothing or a chair, for example) from being touched by a person. Likewise, we are clearly aware of the difference in touching another person as compared to touching an animal or an inanimate object.

Touch is a potent nonverbal message code, one that stimulates meaning in some interesting and significant ways. It may be our most basic or primitive code (Knapp, 1980); a fetus' physical contact with its mother provides meaning — warmth, comfort, security. Once a baby is born, it is very important that touch continues. If it does not, physical development is retarded, and death becomes more likely. This has been documented in studies of institutionalized infants. Hospitals discovered that infant mortality rates dropped when procedures were changed to include holding and cuddling a baby several times a day.

This suggests that we have a need for touch. Because the skin is an organ, a lack of stimulation can be debilitating. This is rather obvious for our other sensory organs. For instance, how do you react to an environment where there is no sound? Total quiet is nice for a while but can become unnerving. To cope with sound deprivation, you may begin to hum, whistle, or sing, or to change the sound environment by turning on a radio or TV.

Touch deprivation appears to function similarly. If we lack touch stimulation, we often solicit it. We could put our arm around a loved one so he or she will do the same. When such an activity is not possible, we touch ourselves in order to fulfill touching needs. For instance, if we are upset about something we might rub our hands together, run a hand across our mouth and cheeks, rub our heads, wrap our arms around our torso and massage our sides with our hands.

Leathers (1986) suggests that touch is particularly effective as a message code in communicating *specialized emotional meanings, power,* and *status.* Two emotional meanings which touch communicates clearly are warmth and sympathy. If we wish to comfort and reassure someone who has had an unfortunate experience, nonverbal messages such as a compassionate look and a comforting tone of voice are helpful. However, holding the person or putting an arm around his or her shoulders, is particularly effective. Another emotional meaning which can also be communicated clearly by touch is hostility.

Physical aggression in the form of shoving, hitting, slapping, grabbing, or shaking creates a vivid feeling of hostility. When touch attempts to produce pain, the communication climate is clearly destructive. However, this type of touching, as with all message codes, is dependent upon context for meaning. Thus, shoving, pushing, and grabbing behavior between spouses in their kitchen may mean spouse abuse, while very similar behaviors on a basketball court in a one-on-one game may mean the spouses are having a very good time at play. Although physical aggression often is a destructive form of touch, it can be constructive, especially in athletics, games, mock assaults, rescue operations, and theatre.

Power and status are also communicated effectively by touch (Leathers, 1986). Frequent touching is associated with greater power and status. Thus, it is more likely for supervisors to touch their subordinates than it is for subordinates to touch their boss. Touching may be a way of communicating power, of telling people they have less power or status than you. Not to touch may be a way of acknowledging that we are power-vulnerable.

According to Mehrabian (1981), touching is especially effective in communicating liking. By touching someone we are saying we choose to approach rather than to avoid them; we are attracted to rather than repelled by them. We learn to expect touching in certain situations, and we develop a rather complex set of expectancies about touching in a wide range of situations. If our expectations for touching are violated in a given situation, the violation has meaning. The nature of that meaning will depend upon such factors as whether more or less touch was received than expected and our attraction to the violator (for a theory of proxemic violations see Burgoon, 1978). For instance, if you receive more touch than you had expected from someone you consider attractive, you will find that more rewarding than receiving that same amount of touching from someone you find less attractive. Further, it is punishing to receive less touching than expected from an attractive other. This reinforces Mehrabian's (1981) point that withholding touching when it is expected in a communication situation can stimulate a variety of negative feelings. Such manipulation of the touch code can tell other people quite clearly that you are unhappy with them.

Although we all seem to have a need to be touched, Hall (1959, 1966) suggests there may be individual differences in this need. Some of the differences are due to culture. For instance, there is less touch in British and American cultures than in Latin American and Mediterranean cultures. This can result in breakdowns in intercultural communication. For instance, imagine a male Italian tourist talking with an American man in Washington, D.C. The Italian pats the American on the upper arm to emphasize a point, then squeezes the American's forearm to suggest importance. The American is uneasy with the physical contact and is unable to hide his discomfort completely. The Italian perceives the uneasiness and takes it to be a sign that the person does not want to talk. The conversation ends prematurely. The American is perplexed, the Italian is very disappointed. The failure to communicate effectively was due to the men speaking different languages in terms of the nonverbal touching code. Unless each participant is aware of the other's underlying nonverbal codes, misunderstandings are fairly inevitable.

An analysis by Heslin and Alper (1983) suggests we may conceptualize touch as serving five functions in nonverbal communication. *Functional-professional* touch is impersonal. The purpose is business-like, and the person being touched is seen more as a task-object than a thinking-feeling-caring individual. There are many professional-client relationships in which this applies. Doctor-patient, nurse-patient, hair stylist-client, and tailor-customer are a few examples. *Social-polite* touch is part of the greeting behavior in a culture. This involves acknowledging people, expressing goodwill, and starting interaction in a positive manner. Common touching behaviors in this regard are handshaking, hugging, and kissing. Of course, culture has specified who kisses whom, the kind of kiss, etc. *Friendship-warmth* touch involves reinforcing the bond of friendship which has developed between people. There is considerable cross-cultural variability here. For instance, in some Mideastern countries it is acceptable for two male friends to walk on a street holding hands. *Love-intimacy* touch also is reinforcing; however, the relationship in this case is an intimate one. Stroking a person's hand or face are examples. However, some behaviors are idiosyncratic to the particular relationship. A wife might rub her husband's temples when he sits down after returning from work or vice versa. *Sexual-arousal* touch is energized by the individual's sex drive and functions to satisfy sexual needs.

Time

Chronemics is the study of how time is used to communicate. It is also a study of the way time functions in communication. There is a difference between these two objectives. The first implies that time is used to symbolize something—that time is manipulated by the individual to create meaning in another person. For instance, a university administrator who keeps a student waiting might want to impress upon the student that the administrator is a very busy person and that the student should be "grateful" for the time he/she is given by the administrator. This use of time is clearly communicative according to our definition of communication. Remember from Chapter 1 that communication is when humans manipulate symbols to stimulate meaning in other humans.

How time functions in communication is different. Time is not manipulated; it is not a message to be studied. Instead, different conceptions of time are viewed in terms of the associated messages. For instance, writers in the area of nonverbal communication often discuss *biological time*. This refers to the various cycles or rhythms that our bodies follow. *Ultradian* cycles occur about every hour and a half. Our attention, for example, seems to follow a ninety minute cycle where it progresses from its lowest point and then peaks. How attentive one is in a conversation could be viewed in terms of this cycle. The "biological time" pattern could be used to explain, for instance, how inattentiveness produced a bad decision. Another example is *circadian* time. This involves daily cycles. The idea that some people are "larks" and others are "owls" is often discussed with reference to circadian cycles. Larks are "morning persons." They are most alert, highest in energy, and vigorous during the morning hours. Their most creative and best work is accomplished during these hours. Owls, on the other hand, are the opposite. While the larks are beginning to "run down" during the early evening hours, the owls are beginning to peak in terms of performance. Many owls do their best work late at night. Thus, communication could be studied in terms of circadian time and how it affects creative performance.

Most of the writing by scholars in the nonverbal area has been on the second objective: how time functions in communication. In addition to biological time, cultures are discussed in terms of whether they have past, present, or future time orientations. For instance, in a past oriented society such as Great Britain there is great emphasis on tradition; the present is placed in the context of what has already happened. Attention also has been given to Hall's (1959) conception of the different kinds of time. For instance, *formal* time involves creating weeks from days, months from weeks, years from months, etc. Also, time is valued by some cultures and appears as a tangible resource. The question "Could I have five minutes of your time?" illustrates this attitude. *Informal* time refers to how culture treats time. Punctuality is an example. In some cultures, being punctual means being no more than a few minutes late; in other cultures, 45 minutes late is considered "on time."

The study of time orientations and personality by Mann, Siegler, and Osmond (1972) is an interesting way to view how time functions in the individual's communicative behavior. These researchers studied the use of time by different personality types identified by Carl Jung, one of the originators of psycho-analysis. There are four basic types of personality; each experiences time in unique ways which affects their communicative behavior. The *thinking type* perceives time as flowing from the past to the future with the present as a time for assessing where an idea, for instance, has been and where it is probably headed. The past is seen in a detached manner, more as history than as drama. Thinking types enjoy being logical, plotting issues out through time, discovering principles and processes for a problem. There is a particular love of planning. Often personal gratification is sacrificed to actualize a plan. This type sees time as linear; there is no particular emphasis on past, present, or future. The other types of personality each emphasize one of these time periods.

The *feeling* type associates the emotional part of past experiences with what is occurring in the present. According to Mann, Siegler, and Osmond (1972) feeling types "need to continue to see things in ways that were popular and appropriate in their younger days. They are trapped in the remembrance of things past" (p.79). This extreme loyalty to the past makes change difficult for a feeling type. For example, if an opinion is associated with a strong emotion, to change the opinion is tantamount to renouncing the past. This type has trouble being punctual. For instance, if a feeling type were engaged in a conversation which stimulated memories of a valued past experience, it would be difficult to end the discussion even if the person were late for an appointment. The feeling type personality might recognize that the lack of punctuality could create future problems, but fails to act because the past outweighs the future.

The *sensation* type perceives time mainly in terms of the present. The existence of things is most important; where they have been or where they are going are relatively unimportant. Sensation types are realists. As a result, their time orientation makes them particularly competent in dealing with crises and making split second decisions. Thinking types are not so able in this regard. It takes time to weigh alternatives and to think something through thoroughly. Sensation types are not burdened by a belief about thoroughness; they act immediately. In a crisis, immediate action is often what is needed rather than a carefully weighed action. Because of their emphasis on the present, sensation types do not tolerate delays. In order to delay gratification, for instance, one needs to see time as flowing. However, sensation types see time as fixed in the present. As with the other personality types, communication reflects one's time orientation. The sensation type is more likely not to venture from the present verb tense.

The *intuitive* type views time primarily in terms of the future. What will be seems more real to the intuitive type than what currently exists. This type is preoccupied with what is possible. Life is spent looking ahead, trying to see around the next bend in the road—a road which never is straight since one bend always leads to another. To the other personality types, the intuitive seems unrealistic and flighty. The intuitive gets frustrated with other people because they do not share his or her vision of the future. Thus, others seem to be "dragging their feet." Intuitives feel they must change the world in order to realize their visions of the future. This sense of mission, when it is combined with the trait of extroversion, creates charisma. This ability to inspire others with a vision of what could be is perhaps the intuitive's greatest talent. (Mann, Siegler, & Osmond, 1972).

These examples of how the perception of time distinguishes different personality types illustrates that time functions in communication and influences the messages formed and the way the messages are received. Time is viewed as a part of the context created by the people involved. To study time in this manner represents communication research. However, such research does not illuminate *how* time communicates. In a sense, much of the writing on nonverbal communication is misleading because writers do not differentiate the use of time symbolically from time as a psychological and social factor which influences message production and message reception. To blend the two creates confusion over what is and is not communication, a problem we addressed in Chapter 1.

To demonstrate the problem further, imagine a study is conducted and finds that very rigid, dogmatic people are extremely punctual in terms of appointments. What does this say about communication? Does this mean the dogmatic person's punctuality "communicates" his or her rigidity to another person? No. According to the framework of this book, punctuality probably is a symptom (Cronkhite, 1986) of a particular psychological state. Punctuality, for instance, is communicative behavior only when the individual uses it as a symbol to create meaning. This could be represented by a person looking at a watch and thinking "I better hurry; I do not want to be late and seem like I'm not dependable."

A review of the nonverbal literature indicates that more attention needs to be given to the symbolic use of time. This does not mean that we should abandon models such as the personality and time perception one just discussed. However, more needs to be learned about time as symbolic behavior. There are many uses which need to be systematized. For example, in what ways do companies manipulate time in order to increase productivity? At least two uses come to mind. Management tells subordinates that "time is money." Thus, to waste time is to throw away money while saving time means gaining money. Also, some companies have utilized the symbol "flex-time." This involves giving the worker a choice in structuring starting times and working hours. Trying to get a worker to respond to the symbols "time equals money" and "flex-time" are examples of treating time symbolically. With further study, it should be possible to discover many more examples of the communicative uses of time. This would confirm Edward T. Hall's (1959) original pioneering speculation that time communicates in many clear and forceful ways.

Summary

Nonverbal communication is one of the most popular areas of study in the communication field because nonverbal communication is highly believable and at least as important as the verbal code. While nonverbal behavior functions best in communicating affect, verbal language more efficiently expresses cognitions. The meaning of nonverbal behaviors is highly dependent upon the communication context. Your authors believe intentionality is a necessary condition for nonverbal behavior to be considered communicative. Otherwise, the behavior is usually a symptom. Research indicates that females are more skilled in nonverbal encoding and decoding, perhaps because females generally have less power in our society. Several functions of nonverbal communication were discussed: to express messages which are uncomfortable to present verbally, to form impressions which are used to guide communication, to clarify and establish the nature of the relationship between the people who are communicating, to regulate the interaction between people from beginning to end, to persuade people by conveying a basis for trust, and to reinforce and modify verbal messages. Various nonverbal message codes were examined: kinesics, eye and facial behavior, vocalics, physical appearance, proxemics, touch and time. The discussion emphasized how symbolic activity is utilized for each code and determined when nonverbal behavior does not involve communication.

Questions to Consider

1. Do verbal or nonverbal codes communicate cognitive messages more effectively? Affective messages?
2. Explain what it means to say that the meaning of nonverbal messages is highly contextual.
3. Explain how your authors use intentionality to determine whether nonverbal behavior is or is not communicative.
4. Is emotional leakage properly considered a communication concept?
5. List and explain the 6 functions of nonverbal communication.
6. What factors influence one's ability to encode and decode nonverbal messages?
7. What types of nonverbal messages have been studied extensively?
8. How do nonverbal and verbal messages relate to each other, especially when someone tries to deceive us?
9. Why does nonverbal response-matching stimulate trust?
10. How can Cronkhite's concept of ritual be used to distinguish between nonverbal behavior which is communicative and that which is not?

References

Argyle, M. (1967). *The psychology of interpersonal behavior*. Baltimore: Penguin.

Berscheid, E., & Walster, E. (1974). Physical attractiveness. In L. Berkowitz (Ed.), *Advances in experimental social psychology* (Vol. 7, pp. 157-215). New York: Academic Press.

Buller, D. B., & Burgoon, J. K. (1986). The effects of vocalics and nonverbal sensitivity on compliance: A replication and extension. *Human Communication Research, 13*, 126-144.

Burgoon, J.K. (1978). A communication model of personal space violations: Explication and an initial test. *Human Communication Research, 4*, 129-142.

Burgoon, J.K. (1985). Nonverbal signals. In M.L. Knapp & G.R. Miller (Eds.), *Handbook of interpersonal communication* (pp. 344-390). Beverly Hills, CA: Sage.

Burgoon, J.K., Buller, D.B., Hale, J.L., & de Turk, M.A. (1984). Relational messages associated with nonverbal behaviors. *Human Communication Research, 10*, 351-378.

Burgoon, J.K., Coker, D.A., & Coker, R.A. (1986). Communicative effects of gaze behavior: A test of two contrasting explanations. *Human Communication Research, 12*, 495-524.

Burgoon, J.K., & Jones, S.B. (1976). Toward a theory of personal space expectations and their violations. *Human Communication Research, 2*, 131-146.

Burgoon, J.K., & Koper, R.J. (1984). Nonverbal and relational communication associated with reticence. *Human Communication Research, 10*, 601-626.

Cody, M.J., & O'Hair, H.D. (1983). Nonverbal communication and deception: Differences in deception cues due to gender and communicator dominance. *Communication Monographs, 50*, 175-192.

Coker, D.A., & Burgoon, J.K. (1987). The nature of conversational involvement and nonverbal encoding patterns. *Human Communication Research, 13,* 463-494.

Cronkhite, G. (1986). On the focus, scope, and coherence of the study of human symbolic activity. *Quarterly Journal of Speech, 72,* 231-246.

Ekman, P., & Friesen, W. (1969). The repertoire of nonverbal behavior: Categories, origins, usage, and coding. *Semiotica, 1,* 49-98.

Fast, J. (1970). *Body language.* New York: Pocket Books.

Gorden, W.I., Infante, D.A., & Braun, A.A. (1985). Communicator style and fashion innovativeness. In M.R. Solomon (Ed.), *The psychology of fashion* (pp. 161-175). Lexington, MA: D.C. Heath.

Gorden, W.I., Tengler, C.D., & Infante, D.A. (1982). Women's clothing predispositions as predictors of dress at work, job satisfaction, and career advancement. *Southern Speech Communication Journal, 47,* 422-434.

Greene, J.O., O'Hair, H.D., Cody, M.J., & Yen, C. (1985). Planning and control of behavior during deception. *Human Communication Research, 11,* 335-364.

Hall, E.T. (1959). *The silent language.* Greenwich, CT: Fawcett.

Hall, E.T. (1966). *The hidden dimension.* Garden City, NJ: Doubleday.

Heslin, R., & Alper, T. (1983). Touch: A bonding gesture. In J.M. Wiemann & R.P. Harrison (Eds.), *Nonverbal interaction* (pp. 47-75). Beverly Hills, CA: Sage.

Hess, E.H. (1975). *The tell-tale eye.* New York: Van Nostrand Reinhold.

Hocking, J.E., & Leathers, D.G. (1980). Nonverbal indicators of deception: A new theoretical perspective. *Communication Monographs, 47,* 119-131.

Infante, D.A. (1978). Similarity between advocate and receiver: The role of instrumentality. *Central States Speech Journal, 24,* 187-193.

Infante, D.A. (1988). *Arguing constructively.* Prospect Heights, IL: Waveland Press, Inc.

Infante, D.A., & Gorden, W.I. (1989). Argumentative and affirming communicator styles as predictors of satisfaction/dissatisfaction with subordinates. *Communication Quarterly, 37,* 81-90.

Infante, D.A., Pierce, L.L., Rancer, A.S., & Osborne, W.J. (1980). Effects of physical attractiveness and likeableness of first name on impressions formed of journalists. *Journal of Applied Communication Research, 8,* 1-9.

James, W.T. (1932). A study of the expression of bodily posture. *Journal of General Psychology, 7,* 405-437.

Kanter, R.M. (1977). *Men and women of the corporation.* New York: Basic Books.

Knapp, M.L. (1980). *Essentials of nonverbal communication.* New York: Holt, Rinehart and Winston.

Knapp, M.L., & Comadena, M.E. (1979). Telling it like it isn't: A review of theory and research on deceptive communications. *Human Communication Research, 5,* 270-381.

Knapp, M.L., Hart, R.P., Friedrich, G.W., & Shulman, G.M. (1973). The rhetoric of goodbye: Verbal and nonverbal correlates of human leave-taking. *Speech Monographs, 40,* 182-198.

Knapp, M.L., Wiemann, J.M., & Daly, J.A. (1978). Nonverbal communication: Issues and appraisal. *Human Communication Research, 4,* 271-280.

Leathers, D.G. (1986). *Successful nonverbal communication: Principles and applications.* New York: Macmillan.

Mann, H., Siegler, M., & Osmond, H. (1972, December). Four types of time and four ways of perceiving time. *Psychology Today*, pp. 76-77, 79-80, 82, 84.

Mehrabian, A. (1969). Significance of posture and position in the communication of attitude and status relationships. *Psychological Bulletin, 71*, 359-372.

Mehrabian, A. (1981). *Silent messages: Implicit communication of emotions and attitudes* (2nd ed.). Belmont, CA: Wadsworth.

Miller, G.R. (1978). The current status of theory and research in interpersonal communication. *Human Communication Research, 4*, 164-178.

Miller, G.R., de Turk, M.A., & Kalbfleisch, P.J. (1983). Self-monitoring, rehearsal, and deceptive communication. *Human Communication Research, 10*, 97-117.

Moine, D.J. (1982). To trust perchance to buy. *Psychology Today, 16*, 50-54.

Molloy, J.T. (1977). *The women's dress for success book*. Chicago: Follett.

Richmond, V.P., McCroskey, J.C., & Payne, S.K. (1987). *Nonverbal behavior in interpersonal relations*. Englewood Cliffs, NJ: Prentice-Hall.

Rosenthal, R., Hall, J.A., DiMatteo, M.R., Rogers, P.L., & Archer, D. (1979). *Sensitivity to nonverbal communication*. Baltimore, MD: Johns Hopkins University Press.

Sheldon, W.H. (1940). *The varieties of human physique*. New York: Harper & Row.

Sheldon W.H. (1954) *Atlas of men: A guide for somatotyping the adult male at all ages*. New York: Harper & Row.

Snyder, M. (1974). Self-monitoring of expressive behavior. *Journal of Personality and Social Psychology, 30*, 526-537.

Watzlawick, P., Beavin, J.H., & Jackson, D.D. (1967). *Pragmatics of human communication: A study of interaction patterns, pathologies, and paradoxes*. New York: Norton.

Wilson, G., & Nias, D. (1976). Beauty can't be beat. *Psychology Today, 10*, 96-103.

Zaidel, S.F., & Mehrabian, A. (1969). The ability to communicate and infer positive and negative attitudes facially and vocally. *Journal of Experimental Research in Personality, 3*, 233-241.

Part III

Theory Building in Communication Contexts

Part III of this book examines theory building in particular contexts. The idea that communication is highly contextual is widely accepted. A message which has one meaning in one context can take on a much different meaning in another context. Thus, a good deal of theory building in communication has dealt with a particular class of situations. While there are many ways of specifying contexts or classifying situations, the one used in this book is probably the most accepted. Theories are examined in terms of interpersonal, small group, organizational, mass media, and intercultural contexts.

Chapter 9 discusses theory building in interpersonal communication contexts. This is one of the most active research areas in the field. Some of the early influences of the 1960s are mentioned. Differences in the laws, rules, and systems perspectives are stated. Several interpersonal communication theories are then examined in some detail. The laws perspective is represented by Uncertainty Reduction Theory, which has had perhaps the most significant impact on interpersonal communication recently. Predicted Outcome Theory and its relationship to Uncertainty Reduction Theory is discussed. Exchange theories are discussed in general, and Equity Theory is explained in some detail. Interpersonal attraction is examined from the viewpoint of Reinforcement Theory. The rules approach is represented by the Rule-Based Model of Relationship Development and by the Theory of Perceived Understanding. The systems perspective is represented by studies of dominance in marital relationships.

Chapter 10 explains theory building in small group and organizational contexts. Some of the classical sources of organizational communication theory are identified. A laws theory, the Independent-Mindedness Theory of organizational communication is discussed in detail. Uncertainty Reduction Theory as applied to organizational communication is also examined. A rules theory, the Coordinated Management of Meaning, is discussed as it has been applied to organizational communication. Two systems theories of organizational communication are covered. Weick's Theory of Organizational Information represents a model combining systems and rules. Structural-Functional Systems Theory exemplifies theories of systems governed by laws. Group communication is discussed by utilizing the Interaction System Model, an Input-Output Model representing the laws perspective, and Symbolic Convergence Theory, a human action approach.

Chapter 11 teaches about theory building in mass media contexts. Basic questions explored by mass media researchers are identified. The Reflective-Projective Theory of mass media effects is reviewed. The functions of mass media in society are discussed next. Major theories of mass communication are also surveyed. These include the Two-Step Flow Theory, Diffusion Theory, Five Functions of Mass Media in Society, Agenda-Setting Theory, the Theory of Mediated Interpersonal Communication, the Theory of Uses and Gratifications, and Cultivation Theory. Also, Lull's Rules Theory of Mass Media and Audience Behavior is examined.

Chapter 12 deals with theory building in intercultural contexts, currently a fast-growing area of the communication field. Factors which have led to an interest in intercultural communication are discussed. The Whorfian hypothesis is applied to intercultural communication, and intercultural differences in nonverbal behavior are identified. The influences of value differences, stereotypes, prejudice, high- and low-context cultures, and cultural training on communication are examined. The laws approach of Uncertainty Reduction Theory is examined in the intercultural context. The Coordinated Management of Meaning, a rules theory, is applied to intercultural communication. Finally, Kim's Systems Theory of Intercultural Communication is presented.

Chapter 9

Interpersonal Contexts

The Development of Interpersonal Communication Study

During the late 1950s and early 1960s, few communication scholars were engaged in research and theory building about interpersonal relationships. The focus instead was on how attitudes, beliefs, and values could be altered via public and mass communication messages. During this period, research and theory building in interpersonal interaction were conducted primarily by sociologists, social psychologists and anthropologists. The study of dyadic, or one-on-one, communication did not begin in earnest until the mid-1960s. Researchers then investigated how communication could be used to develop and improve interpersonal relationships with friends, lovers, and spouses. The aura of the 1960s with messages about peace, understanding, and cooperation prompted many institutions of higher education to offer courses dealing with the development and improvement of human relations.

The first synthesis of early empirical research efforts included studies of social psychologists. In the early 1970s scholars published the first textbooks in interpersonal communication (Giffin & Patton, 1971; Keltner, 1970; McCroskey, Larson & Knapp, 1971). By the mid to late 1970s, the communication discipline was heavily involved in researching and theorizing about interpersonal communication and relationship development. Most of this research in interpersonal communication was borrowed from works in social psychology. By the mid to late 1970s and 1980s, several theories of interpersonal communication and relational interaction had been formulated.

A Multi-Perspective Orientation to Interpersonal Communication

Throughout this text, we have attempted to illustrate the variety of theory building options available by showing the differences between laws, human action (rules), and systems approaches to communication (see Chapter 3). This chapter will introduce you to examples of interpersonal or relational communication theories from each of these perspectives. Recall that advocates of the *law-governed* approach to communication theory emphasize the causes of interpersonal communication. *Rule-governed* researchers and theorists stress the influence of individual choice and free will. *Systems* scholars stress the interaction, interdependence and coordination of behavior between individuals. They examine the entire "interpersonal system," which can range in size from the friend-lover, friend-friend, or husband-wife dyad to a larger extended family system or social network. Systems scholars believe that "to understand the process of mutual adaptation in interpersonal communication, it is necessary to focus on moment-to-moment changes during interactive events" (Knapp & Miller, 1985, p. 15). As each theory is described, you will see how the underlying perspective shaped the development of the theory.

Uncertainty Reduction Theory

One example of a theory developed from the *law-governed* approach is *Uncertainty Reduction Theory* (URT) (Berger, 1979; Berger & Calabrese, 1975). URT was initially presented as a series of axioms and theorems which describe the relationships between uncertainty and several communication factors. The theory seeks to explain and predict interpersonal communication during the *beginning* of an interaction. One core assumption of this theory is that when strangers meet, they seek to *reduce uncertainty* about each other. Simultaneously, people seek to increase their ability to predict their partner's and their own behavior in the situation. Interviews, first dates, and interactions with foreigners are situations in which we are highly uncertain. One of the major problems we face when we first meet people is the uncertainty of predicting their behavior. If we could predict others' behavior, we could choose more appropriate behaviors ourselves. (Recall that one goal of theories is to help us control our environment). According to URT, different types of communication occur during three stages of first meetings.

Three Stages of Initial Interactions

Some information about others is easily revealed. Physical appearance cues can indicate another's sex, age, and economic or social status. This information is then supplemented with additional biographic and demographic information obtained during the *entry phase* of relationship development. Much of the interaction in this entry phase is controlled by communication rules and norms. For example, it is considered improper to ask strangers for intimate details about their personal behavior. When communicators begin to share attitudes, beliefs, values, and more personal data, the *personal phase* begins (Berger & Calabrese, 1975). During this phase, the communicators feel less constrained by rules and norms and tend to communicate more freely with each other. The third phase of initial interaction is the *exit phase*. During this phase, the communicators decide on future interaction plans. They may discuss or negotiate ways to allow the relationship to grow and continue. However, any particular conversation may be terminated at the end of the entry phase.

Uncertainty Reduction Axioms

Uncertainty Reduction Theory was developed to describe the interrelationships between uncertainty, the amount of verbal communication, information seeking, similarity and attraction, the intimacy level of the communication content, nonverbal expressions of affiliation, and the rate at which individuals engage in equal amounts of information exchange. The seven axioms offered in Uncertainty Reduction Theory take the form of "If . . ., then . . ." statements typical of the law-governed approach. The first axiom of the theory suggests that, if uncertainty levels are high, the amount of verbal communication between strangers will decrease. The more we learn about someone, the less uncertain we are, and the amount of verbal communication increases.

Two other factors which reduce uncertainty between communicators are information seeking behavior (Axiom 3) and the degree of similarity individuals perceive in each other (Axiom 6). When strangers first meet and interact, the amount of information they seek from each other is quite high. As a relationship progresses, the amount of overt information-seeking behavior decreases. The degree of perceived similarity (in background, attitudes, appearance) between communicators also reduces uncertainty. (Perceived similarity is one of the components of interpersonal attraction theory and will be discussed in more detail below.) Similarity between strangers helps reduce uncertainty because the number of alternative explanations for the person's behavior decreases. Individuals use cues about similarity and dissimilarity (especially background and attitude cues) to help them understand why other people communicate as they do. For example, if I am talking with Dana, who comes from a large city similar to mine, then I would have some basis to explain why Dana uses an assertive or aggressive communication style. Similarity in background, real or imagined, may help us explain and predict attitudes and beliefs. Indeed, Berger (1979) found that perceived background similarity led to predictions of attitude similarity.

If communicators are very uncertain, URT suggests they will exchange information and will self-disclose at about the same rate. Axiom 5 states that high levels of uncertainty will produce high and about equal rates of information exchange between communicators. Under conditions of high uncertainty such as when strangers meet, an imbalance in the exchange of information may create tension. One person may be accused of dominating the conversation, and the relationship may be terminated.

Nonverbal expressions of interest and attention also increase as uncertainty decreases (Axiom 2). Communicators may exhibit more direct eye gaze, touch more, and sit closer to each other. As uncertainty is further reduced, more intimate communication messages may be exchanged (Axiom 4). As uncertainty is further reduced, self-disclosing statements reveal more intimate information and may rapidly move the relationship from the entry phase. The final result of less uncertainty is that communicators like each other more overall (Axiom 7) because they feel they know and understand each other better.

Figure 9.1
Uncertainty Reduction Axioms

1. A high level of uncertainty is present at the beginning of an interaction. As verbal communication between strangers increases, the level of uncertainty for each interactant in the relationship will decrease. As uncertainty is further reduced, the amount of verbal communication will increase.

2. As nonverbal affiliative expressiveness increases, uncertainty levels will decrease in an initial interaction situation. In addition, decreases in uncertainty level will cause increases in nonverbal affiliative expressiveness.

3. High levels of uncertainty cause increases in information seeking behavior. As uncertainty levels decline, information seeking behavior decreases.

4. High levels of uncertainty cause decreases in the intimacy level of communication. Low levels of uncertainty produce high levels of intimacy.

5. High levels of uncertainty produce high rates of reciprocity. Low levels of uncertainty produce low reciprocity rates.

6. Similarities between persons reduce uncertainty, while dissimilarities increase uncertainty.

7. Increases in uncertainty produce decreases in liking; decreases in uncertainty level produce increases in liking.

Uncertainty Reduction Theorems

Twenty-one theorems of URT were developed by Berger and Calabrese (1975). Taken together, Theorems 1 - 6 suggest that when the *amount of communication* between strangers in initial interaction increases, nonverbal expressions of interest (such as direct eye contact, head nods, pleasantness of voice), intimate communication content, liking, and similarity also increase. More communication creates less need for immediate and equal exchanges of information-seeking communication.

Figure 9.2
Uncertainty Reduction Theorems

1. Amount of verbal communication and nonverbal affiliative expressiveness are positively related.
2. Amount of communication and intimacy level of communication are positively related.
3. Amount of communication and information seeking behavior are inversely related.
4. Amount of communication and reciprocity rate are inversely related.
5. Amount of communication and liking are positively related.
6. Amount of communication and similarity are positively related.
7. Nonverbal affiliative expressiveness and intimacy level of communication content are positively related.
8. Nonverbal affiliative expressiveness and information seeking are inversely related.
9. Nonverbal affiliative expressiveness and reciprocity rate are inversely related.
10. Nonverbal affiliative expressiveness and liking are positively related.
11. Nonverbal affiliative expressiveness and similarity are positively related.
12. Intimacy level of communication content and information seeking are inversely related.
13. Intimacy level of communication content and reciprocity rate are inversely related.
14. Intimacy level of communication content and liking are positively related.
15. Intimacy level of communication content and similarity are positively related.
16. Information seeking and reciprocity rate are positively related.
17. Information seeking and liking are negatively related.
18. Information seeking and similarity are negatively related.
19. Reciprocity rate and liking are negatively related.
20. Reciprocity rate and similarity are negatively related.
21. Similarity and liking are positively related.

(from Berger, C.R., & Calabrese, R.J. (1975). Some explorations in initial interaction and beyond. Toward a developmental theory of interpersonal communication. *Human Communication Research, 1*, 99-112.)

Theorems 7 - 11 deal with nonverbal cues associated with affiliation or liking (factors of *nonverbal expressiveness*). These theorems suggest the greater the nonverbal expressiveness, the more intimate content, perceived similarity, and liking there will be. More nonverbal expressiveness reduces the need for information-seeking behavior and for equal, immediate exchanges of communication.

Theorems 12 - 15 are related to the intimacy level of communication content. As communication content becomes more intimate and personal, perceived similarity and liking between communicators increase. In addition, as self-disclosing messages become more intimate, people's tendency to seek inforation and need for immediate and equal exchanges of information decrease too.

Theorems 16 - 18 deal expressly with the concept of *information-seeking*. Theorem 17 suggests that strangers use less information-seeking communication as they begin to like each other more. As a relationship develops, there is less need to ask questions and "interrogate" one another. People are more willing to volunteer information about themselves.

Theorems 19 - 21 deal with *reciprocity, or rates of information exchange*. As two individuals perceive greater similarity and are more attracted to each other, they feel less need to exchange information with equal frequency. However, the theory also suggests that when uncertainty is high, communicators tend to reciprocate behavior; as one person increases information-seeking, the other person will also tend to seek more information.

Theorem 21 suggests that the greater the real and perceived similarity between communicators in a developing relationship, the more overall attraction or liking will exist. During the last twenty-five years, social psychological and communication researchers have conducted much research into the relationship between similarity and liking. For Uncertainty Reduction Theory, the key to this relationship is our need to reduce uncertainty. Berger and Calabrese (1975) suggest that the concept of uncertainty reduction accounts for many research findings concerning the similarity-attraction relationship.

In the almost fifteen years since the initial presentation of URT, many communication scholars have examined its assumptions through quantitative and empirical research. URT has been used to study the development and maintenance of romantic relationships (Parks & Adelman, 1983) and relationships between people of different cultures (Gudykunst & Nishida, 1984; Gudykunst, Nishida, Koike & Shiino, 1986; Gudykunst, Yang & Nishida, 1985). Lester (1986) studied uncertainty reduction in organizational communication. Berger and Calabrese (1975) suggest that, in our increasingly mobile society, we may all need to decrease uncertainty in new relationships several times during our lives. As we move from job to job, from city to city, and perhaps from one intimate relationship to another, we may spend a great deal of time developing new relationships by communicating to reduce uncertainty. Thus, these extensions of URT will be discussed in more detail below.

Moving Beyond Initial Interaction Stages

In an effort to explain how uncertainty reduction works *beyond* the initial stages of relational development, Berger (1979, 1986) has extended the boundaries of the original theory by including new concepts and refining the original ones. *Cognitive uncertainty* (the type of uncertainty presented in the original formulation of the theory) refers to a generalized state of uncertainty between individuals, while *linguistic* or *behavioral uncertainty* refers to the level of uncertainty felt in a *particular* conversation.

Three levels of knowledge are also described in the extended theory. *Descriptive knowledge* deals with statements people make to describe others' *current behavior.* A second level of knowledge, *predictive knowledge,* includes statements about others' *beliefs, attitudes, feelings,* and *future behavior.* Finally, an individual reaches the *explanatory* level of knowledge when he or she can explain *why* another person behaves or believes a certain way. Each level of knowledge includes the preceding level, and progression to each higher level becomes increasingly more difficult. As our desire to develop a significant and long-term relationship increases, so too does our need for higher levels of knowledge. The relative success of a long-term intimate relationship depends, in part, on one's ability to offer explanations of a partner's attitudes, beliefs, and behaviors. The three levels of knowledge can also be applied to the examination of *self.* Many people have high levels of *descriptive* and *predictive* knowledge about themselves. People generally know their own attitudes and can usually predict their own behavior. However, *explanatory* knowledge about oneself is often very difficult, perhaps even impossible, for any given person to acquire. Individuals frequently consult with experts such as psychologists or counselors to uncover explanatory knowledge about themselves.

Under several conditions, the desire to gain knowledge about others is quite strong. The first condition concerns *incentive.* We try to find out more about people who can provide us with rewards or satisfy our needs so that we may develop strategies to obtain the rewards. For example, we may develop relationships with fraternity or sorority members so that our new friends can help "get us in." When they can help us get what we want, these people possess *high incentive value* for us, so we monitor their behavior, as well as our own communication with them, more closely. For example, we may examine how they respond to praise. If we discover that they enjoy being complimented and are more gracious and giving after being praised, we may then compliment them frequently in order to develop the relationship more quickly.

A second motive which stimulates information-seeking is deviant or *unpredictable behavior* of others. When a person's communication behavior deviates from our expectations, we monitor their communication more closely to get additional information. We often respond less favorably to the unusual or unpredictable behavior of others than to behavior consistent with our expectations. One researcher found that as a stranger in an initial interaction gave more compliments, observers rated him as friendlier (Berger, 1979). However, they also judged him more dishonest and less sincere. Observers probably imputed *ulterior motives* to the stranger to explain the increase in compliments. Thus, when a person's communication follows conventional norms and rules, we may pay less attention to it. However, when a person's communication deviates from conventions, rules and norms, we pay closer attention to that behavior (increase our monitoring) to generate more reliable information about the person.

A third and final motive for acquiring information about others is the *likelihood of interacting with them in the future*. Generally, the expectation of or desire for future contact causes people to pay closer attention to their own and others' communication. Expecting future interaction can also strongly influence our evaluation of another's behavior. People who believe that they will be communicating with another person in the future may change their communication behavior to be viewed more favorably. People generally do not disclose intimate information to strangers. However, in two contexts this spontaneous and intimate self-disclosure to strangers does occur. The "stranger-on-the-plane" situation is one context in which we suspend normal communication rules because we never expect to meet the other person again. You may recall a long airplane ride during which your seatmate revealed intimate personal details after meeting you only a few hours earlier. An out-of-town pub or bar is another "special" context in which we may ignore the rules we typically follow for self-disclosure (Berger, 1979).

Strategies to Reduce Uncertainty

The development (extension) of Uncertainty Reduction Theory revealed three general strategies used to reduce uncertainty about others. *Passive strategies* involve watching someone without being observed. You may have engaged in a passive strategy to reduce uncertainty about someone you were attracted to. You may have unobtrusively observed this person talking with other students in class, in the cafeteria, or in the dormitory. Note that while you were gaining information, no *direct* communication occurred between you. We prefer to observe others in informal social situations where norms and rules are frequently relaxed and more revealing information may emerge (Berger, 1979). *Active strategies* of uncertainty reduction require more effort to discover information, but there is still no direct contact between the observer and the observed (target of observation). An active strategy may include finding out about another person by asking third parties for information. You may have discovered someone's "availability" for a relationship by asking friends whether the person was involved with someone. *Interactive strategies* include obtaining information *directly* through asking questions (interrogation) and offering personal information about yourself (self-disclosure). The self-disclosure strategy relies on the fact that self-disclosure by one person stimulates self-disclosure in another. If I reveal something important about myself to others, they feel "obliged" to reveal something equally important about themselves to me. A cocktail party is a good place to observe people using interactive strategies. When individuals give information about themselves, they may exaggerate or lie. Thus, it is important to be able to detect deception. One type of interactive strategy is *deception detection* strategies, including the careful scrutiny of nonverbal behavior (See Chapter 8). Much research has examined people's ability to detect deception in others (see esp. Knapp & Comadena, 1979).

A Test of Uncertainty Reduction Theory

Parks and Adelman (1983) tested Uncertainty Reduction Theory applied to *premarital romantic relationships*. Parks and Adelman suggest that all relationships are embedded within a larger social framework created by each partner's separate communication networks and relationships. This individual network may reduce uncertainty by providing "third party" information about one's romantic partner. For example, observing your partner interact with family may be quite telling in that they may communicate in ways you have never observed before. The mere act of meeting a partner's larger social network or family may reduce uncertainty. Indeed, failing to introduce a partner to one's friends and family may make the partner uncertain and provoke such questions as, "If I'm so important to you, how come I've never met your friends?" (Parks & Adelman, 1983, p. 58). Further, support from a partner's network or family may reduce uncertainty and help to make the relationship grow and stabilize. Using interviews and questionnaires, Parks and Adelman found that people who received more support for their romantic involvement from family and friends expressed less uncertainty about their relationships and were less likely to terminate them compared to people who received less support.

Predicted Outcome Value Theory

Predicted Outcome Value (POV) Theory, (a modification of Uncertainty Reduction Theory) emphasizes anticipated *rewards and costs* of relationships by stressing incentive value (Sunnafrank, 1986). Recall from the discussion above that incentive value consists of the perceived future rewards and costs likely to be experienced if the relationship develops. POV places less emphasis on the need for uncertainty reduction in initial interactions and greater emphasis on the need to ensure that future interactions with someone will lead to more positive experiences than negative ones. POV maintains that the need to maximize outcomes is central to the process of developing relationships. Beginning stages of any relationship are usually limited in the number of *actual* experiences and outcomes. Thus, *predicted* positive outcomes should influence a person's decision to seek, avoid or restrict further communication (Sunnafrank, 1986).

POV offers several key explanations for how people predict outcomes in developing relationships. Individuals who predict greater positive outcomes will be more attracted to relationships and will more often try to extend their relationships compared to people with lower predicted positive outcomes. On the other hand, individuals who predict greater negative outcomes will communicate specifically to block relational development. Further, individuals guide conversations toward topics that they expect will result in greater predicted positive outcomes (Sunnafrank, 1986, pp. 10-11). According to Predicted Outcome Value Theory, reducing uncertainty allows people to predict future outcomes better. They can thus control their communication to produce positive outcomes.

POV modifies all seven axioms of the original Uncertainty Reduction Theory by suggesting that *predicted outcome value* acts as a mediating variable and modifies the relationships between uncertainty reduction and communication factors such as amount of verbal communication, expressing affiliation nonverbally, seeking information, communicating intimate content, using reciprocal rates of communication, and feeling similarity and liking. Advocates of POV believe research shows these modifications strengthen Uncertainty Reduction Theory. Berger (1986) suggests that predicting an outcome value is itself one type of uncertainty-reducing activity. He views POV as an expansion of, not an alternative to, Uncertainty Reduction Theory. More research is needed to determine which theory best explains the role of communication in developing relationships. Additional research is also necessary to test whether these two theories accurately describe communication in the later stages of relationship development.

The Social Exchange Approach

Equity Theory and social exchange theories belong to the same "family." Social exchange theories have been of great interest to communication theorists, although these theories originally come from the disciplines of social psychology, sociology, and psychology (see Walster, Walster, & Berscheid, 1978). The *social exchange approach* to interpersonal communication suggests that people communicate to *maximize* positive outcomes, to *minimize* negative outcomes, and to achieve financial, physical and social rewards (Roloff, 1981). Like Predicted Outcome Value theorists, social exchange theorists believe individuals initiate, maintain, and terminate relationships on the basis of real and perceived rewards and costs associated with the relationship. For example, according to the social exchange approach, you date someone because you are receiving some *rewards* from the relationship: companionship, affection, love, and ego-gratification. *Costs* are associated with any relationship; they can include time, money, physical and emotional energy. If you believe the costs of maintaining a relationship greatly exceed the rewards you expect to receive from the relationship, you are likely to terminate the relationship.

Social exchange is "the voluntary transference of some object or activity from one person to another in return for other objects or activities" (Roloff, 1981, p. 21). Resources that people exchange through interpersonal communication include affection, prestige, services such as child rearing, goods or products such as jewelry, information such as advice, opinions, or instructions, and money (Foa & Foa, 1974). Interpersonal communication is a purposeful, goal-directed, and intentional activity which involves the exchange of symbols. Viewed from a social exchange framework, interpersonal communication can be thought of as the process by which individuals involved in a relationship provide each other with, and negotiate for, the exchange of resources (Roloff, 1981).

Equity Theory

Equity is sometimes discussed as *equality*. When people are engaged in an equitable relationship, then they perceive that their balance of rewards and costs is "fair" or "equal" compared to their partner's balance. Individuals evaluate the fairness of a relationship by calculating their own and their partner's *inputs* to and *outcomes* from the relationship. Inputs are the positive and negative contributions to the relationship, while outcomes are the consequences one receives from the relationship. If my ratio of rewards to costs is equal to my partner's, then equity exists. Many of us have witnessed inequitable relationships in which the number and value of one party's inputs greatly exceeded those of the relational partner. Partners may complain that they are responsible for giving all the affection in a relationship or that the "gifts" received from their partner are not equal in value to the gifts they give; "I bought a television for Mickey's last birthday, but Mickey only gave me a videotape for mine!"

Propositions About Equity. Although Equity Theory has generated a considerable amount of research, Walster, Walster and Berscheid (1978) suggest that Equity Theory can be summarized by four propositions. Proposition I states, "Individuals will try to maximize their outcomes (where outcomes equal rewards minus costs)" (Walster, Walster, & Berscheid, 1978, p. 6). This proposition suggests that people will behave in ways that enhance their own self-interest. The adage, "Every person has a price" is a maxim that could be derived from this proposition. The second proposition has two parts. In order to avoid constant conflict and to maximize positive collective group outcomes, compromise is necessary. This first part of the proposition emphasizes that groups develop sets of rules regarding what counts as a fair distribution of effort and resources in a relationship. The second half states that groups reward or punish members according to their fair or unfair treatment of others. Divorce laws constitute one attempt by society to ensure that the tangible aspects of a relationship (property, goods, money) are distributed somewhat equitably after a couple separates (Roloff, 1981).

Consequences of Inequity. Proposition III states, "When individuals find themselves participating in inequitable relationships, they become distressed. The more inequitable the relationship, the more distress individuals feel" (Walster, Walster, & Berscheid, 1978, p. 17). Both victims and beneficiaries in unfair relationships may feel distress if society tends to "blame the victim," although the victim of inequity may feel more distress than the victimizer. Some empirical research supports this assertion. In one experimental study, students who completed a "proofreading task" expected to receive two dollars for their efforts. Afterwards, all were told they had done a good job. However, some participants received one dollar (inequitably paid), some three dollars (overpaid), and some two dollars (equitably paid). When asked to describe their moods, equitably paid subjects were more content than the underpaid or overpaid participants (Walster, Walster, & Berscheid, 1978).

The final proposition in Equity Theory discusses how individuals respond to inequity. People in inequitable relationships try to restore equity to eliminate their distress. The more unfair the relationship, the more distressed one feels. People who are more distressed try harder than others to restore equity (Walster, Walster, & Berscheid, 1978). There are several explanations for why inequity may surface in a previously fair relationship. As we learn more about another, we discover new sources of inequity about which may have been unaware. Couples often experience greater conflict *after* marriage than before because they know more about each other and have more basis for disagreement (Roloff, 1981). A second reason individuals may suddenly feel a relationship is inequitable is that people grow and change during the stages of a relationship but may not communicate their changed needs to their partner. For example, suppose that as the relationship develops, Dale needs more demonstrations of affection. If Dale does not directly communicate this need to Jamie, and Jamie does not spontaneously demonstrate more affection, Dale may feel unfairly treated, as if Dale is giving more than Jamie. Important events in a relationship such as one partner's moving away to college or the birth of a baby may enhance feelings of inequity. The feelings may persist until the partners adjust their inputs. Finally, the partners may feel that the value of the rewards and costs and the "distribution" of profits in the relationship which they once considered equitable are in fact unfair. Roloff (1981) suggests that *societal influences* such as the women's movement and the media help convince some that equity in the distribution of relational rewards no longer exists.

Restoring Equity. Walster, Walster and Berscheid (1978) propose two ways to restore equity in a relationship: restoring *actual equity* or *psychological equity*. Restoring actual equity involves altering your own or your partner's gains in the relationship. *Behaviors* are altered in an attempt to create equity. For example, you may start to praise your partner less if you believe that he or she is praising you less, or you may more frequently seek out others who tend to praise you. When people engage in psychological equity restoration, they *distort reality* in an effort to convince themselves that an inequitable relationship is, in fact, equitable. Suppose Dana feels that Lyn is not showing enough affection. Dana may restore equity psychologically by saying, "I'm very lucky to have Lyn as my partner, so *whatever* amount of affection I receive, I'm fortunate to get!"

Equity and the Relational Development Process. When thinking of the development of intimate relationships involving friends, lovers, and spouses, you may feel that the application of Equity Theory is mercenary and unromantic. Many people feel that special types of interpersonal relationships are somehow above the economic metaphors of exchanging goods and services, costs and rewards, and the entire concept of social exchange in general. Recall that central to Equity Theory is the proposition that human beings think first and foremost of their own self-interest. This view contrasts sharply with more conventional beliefs about communication between spouses, lovers, friends, parents, and children. Conventional thought views communication in these contexts as the most profound demonstration of unconditional love, support, and giving. In these "special" interpersonal relationships, our own self-interests take a secondary role to the self-interests of our relational partners. In these relationships we become less concerned with getting and more concerned with giving. If we can suspend judgment for just a while, we may be able to discern more clearly whether Equity Theory accurately explains the development, escalation, maintenance, and possible de-escalation of intimate relationships.

Walster, Walster, and Berscheid (1978) suggest that relationships grow on the basis of equitable exchanges. Roloff (1981) contends that we become attracted to people who we believe can engage in equitable relationships with us. Intimate relationships usually involve deeper and more frequent *self-disclosures*. DeVito (1989) suggests that without self-disclosure of an honest and profound nature, a truly intimate relationship cannot exist. Thus, Equity Theory can be used to describe the nature of self-disclosure in an intimate relationship. If one partner engages in a great deal of self-disclosure, while the other does not, inequity may be said to exist. Those who self-disclose provide much input into a relationship through their self-revelations, with a great deal of potential cost. As many of us know, providing personal details about our lives to another, even to a special other, can be quite risky. Conversely, the person receiving self-disclosure receives much potential reward (in the form of information), but may sacrifice few costs. The inequity which exists in this type of relationship could signal distress for the participants. In order to alleviate this distress and restore equity, reciprocating self-disclosure with an approximately equal depth and amount of information must become more typical in the relationship. The more we reveal about ourselves to others, the more willing they should be to reveal important and intimate information about themselves. Indeed, some researchers (Davidson, Balswick, & Halverson, 1983) found that when married couples differed in self-disclosure, they had lower levels of marital adjustment compared to couples who reciprocated self-disclosure.

Characteristics of Intimate Relationships. Walster, Walster, and Berscheid (1978) acknowledge that Equity Theory is more difficult to calculate in intimate relationships than it is in less intimate or casual ones. Because intimate relationships tend to involve greater long-term commitments ("till death do us part" in marriage vows), equity may be especially difficult to calculate. Think about a long-term friendship of ten years or more. In relationships of this duration, calculating equity and inequity may be quite difficult. One might ask, "Do the seven dinners that Blair bought me eight years ago count today when we determine who should pick up tonight's dinner tab?" As a relationship endures over time, we dismiss the somewhat "one-for-one" exchanges in favor of a general sense of "averaging out" equity over the course of the relationship. Relationships of greater intimacy can tolerate long-term settlements of inequity because partners know they have the time for equity adjustments; casual relationships require more *immediate* equity adjustments. The value of the rewards exchanged by partners also differs with intimacy level. Generally, the more intimate the relationship, the more valuable the rewards exchanged (time, money, gifts, information, etc.).

The value of the costs is also more extreme in intimate relationships. A casual acquaintance may challenge our intelligence, honesty, or integrity without doing much damage to our self-concept. However, if our spouse or best friend were to make the same comments, we might feel psychologically devastated. People in casual relationships typically exchange more tangible and less symbolic resources: money, goods, services, and certain types of information. The exchange of affection (love) is more typical of intimate relationships. It is also true that the value of certain kinds of rewards (love, status, certain types of information) is less generally agreed upon than the value of other types of rewards. Values for these rewards tend to vary from person to person and from couple to couple. Intimate relationships also lend themselves more frequently to the *interchangeability of resources.* That is, if a casual friend lends you fifty dollars, you are generally obligated to repay that money by cash or check. However, if an intimate relational partner such as your girlfriend or boyfriend lends you fifty dollars, you can "repay" them in ways other than money. You could drive them to school for a month or do their laundry for two months.

Equity Concerns in Friendship Development. Research has supported the basic propositions of Equity Theory. Individuals involved in more equitable relationships are more satisfied with their interpersonal friendship and marital relationships. These findings appear consistent, even in inequitable relationships where one person seems to profit unfairly from the inequity. Roberto and Scott (1986) used Equity Theory to examine patterns of exchange between older adults and their friends. The researchers tested over one hundred senior citizens using interviews and a questionnaire to measure the perceptions of one's own and one's partner's inputs and outcomes in a relationship (The Walster Global Measure of Participants' Perceptions of Inputs, Outcomes, and Equity/Inequity; Walster, Walster, & Bersheid, 1978, pp. 234-236). Using formulas designed to translate equity into numbers, participants were classified as overbenefited, equitably benefited, and underbenefited in their interpersonal relationships. The researchers found that older individuals with equitable friendships reported less distress than those with inequitable interpersonal relationships.

Equity Concerns in Intimate Relationship Development. Intimate relationships promote more intense feelings of liking and loving than casual ones. Attraction research has explored factors that lead to the development of intimate relationships, and there are several issues involving interpersonal attraction which relate specifically to Equity Theory. Walster and Walster (1976) have defined interpersonal attraction as, "An individual's tendency or predisposition to evaluate another person or symbol of that person in a positive (or negative) way" (p. 280). How does Equity Theory relate to the concept of attraction, liking, and mate selection? Researchers have discovered that equity of self-disclosure promotes greater marital adjustment (Davidson, Balswick, & Halverson, 1983). Several proponents of Equity Theory suggest that equity considerations are important in dating and marriage relationships. Indeed, some equity theorists even offer a "Matching Hypothesis." This hypothesis states that the more equitable a romantic relationship is, the more likely the relationship will progress to permanence and/or marriage. How can we use Equity Theory to assess a potential partner? Walster, Walster, and Berscheid (1978) suggest that we judge potential mates on such traits as beauty or physical attractiveness, physical and mental health, and intelligence and education. Research indicates that, "Birds of a feather flock together"; that is, people with certain levels of these traits look for partners whose levels of the trait match their own. For example, if Lou is extremely attractive, Lou will seek out an extremely attractive relationship partner.

According to Equity Theory, individuals are attracted to potential mates who are their physical, intellectual, and educational equals. In a field experiment conducted by Kiesler and Baral (1970), some male participants were led to believe that they had done quite well on an "intelligence test." Others were told that they had done poorly. Each participant then interacted with a female associate (confederate) of the experimenters who was made up to appear either very attractive or very unattractive. The researchers found strong support for the "matching hypothesis." When the males' self-esteem was temporarily lowered, they behaved more romantically with the less attractive female. When their self-esteem was raised, they behaved more romantically with the more attractive female. The researchers suggest that the more desirable a man feels, the more physically attractive a woman he thinks he deserves. Thus, we are attracted to people we think can form equitable relationships with us. Using several of the propositions outlined in Equity Theory, Berscheid, Walster, and Bohrnstedt (1973) examined over fifty thousand responses to a survey published in *Psychology Today*. In general, they found that the more attractive a person was (compared to a partner), the richer, the more loving, and the more self-sacrificing the partner was. Equity can be achieved through an association with a dissimilar partner since people give greater amounts of one resource to compensate for the lack of another resource.

Evaluation of Equity Theory. Equity Theory does not view interpersonal communication in a very romantic way. It is, however, a clear, well-stated theory which has been studied extensively over the last twenty years. Equity Theory allows us to make predictions about interpersonal communication and relationship development in a wide range of contexts; the theory has a broad scope. The large number of studies produced by this theory have provided communication theorists and researchers with useful research techniques and hypotheses. Equity Theory thus has heuristic or research-generating value. Equity Theory findings also correspond well to "conventional wisdom" about relationships. Many of us can easily identify with the situations and communication patterns associated with the theory.

Attraction Theories and Relational Development

An interpersonal relationship will develop only if those involved like or are attracted to each other. The questions "Why do people like each other?" and "What attracts people to each other?" have stimulated almost a quarter century of research by theorists in communication and social psychology. Clearly, attraction is important to a variety of social outcomes and relationships of varying levels of intimacy. We choose to spend "the rest of our lives" with someone to whom we are attracted. We may hire someone or be hired because of attraction. We may temporarily feel "crushed" because someone we are attracted to does not share those feelings. We are often willing to tolerate uncomfortable situations and unpleasant behavior because we are attracted to a particular person. In extreme cases, people whose feelings of attraction are not returned respond with violence or threats.

Reinforcement Theory and Attraction

Donn Byrne, a pioneer in the study of interpersonal attraction, has devoted much of his career to studying why we like some people and dislike others. Byrne and other theorists sought to identify the many factors of interpersonal attraction and then to study each factor separately. They later attempted to combine the experimental findings to determine the relative contribution of each component to understanding the whole. This technique, *inductive* theory-building, involves collecting the many findings from specific and narrowly focused studies. Theorists then attempt to draw conclusions or to build a more general theory from the specific results.

Byrne felt that the principle of *reinforcement* explains most of interpersonal attraction. The reinforcement principle suggests that we like and are attracted to those people who reward us. Rewards can range from verbal compliments or praise to actual gifts. Similarly, we dislike and are repelled by individuals who punish us. Again, punishment can take many forms from unfavorable comments to uncomfortable or damaging experiences.

Similarity and Interpersonal Attraction

In studying reinforcement and attraction, Byrne (1971) focused on one primary component—similar *attitudes*. Byrne used Reinforcement Theory to explain the *attraction-similarity* research. If the behavior, attitudes, beliefs, values, abilities, and personality of another individual are similar to our own, they are positively rewarding to us. Research shows that people who believe others are similar to themselves are more attracted to them (Byrne, 1971; Sunnafrank, 1983, 1984, 1985; Sunnafrank & Miller, 1981). This factor, which is called "homophily" in communication and "similarity" in social psychology, is important when we evaluate those people with whom we intend to develop a relationship. Rogers and Bhowmik (1970) argued that *perceived similarity*, (the degree to which we *believe* another's characteristics are similar to ours) is related to attraction.

Several consistent findings have emerged in the research on similarity. We are more likely to be persuaded by communicators if we believe they are similar to us (Berscheid, 1966). Similar communicators communicate more with each other (Rogers & Bhowmik, 1970). Numerous studies report greater overall liking and attraction between similar than between dissimilar communicators. Similarity is made up of several factors or dimensions (Andersen & Todd-Mancillas, 1978). Berscheid and Walster (1978) suggest that similarity consists of six dimensions: attitude, personality, physical characteristics, social characteristics, intelligence, and education. McCroskey, Richmond, and Daly (1975) offer four dimensions of similarity: attitude similarity, value similarity (morality), background similarity, and appearance similarity. They developed a questionnaire to measure perceived similarity between communicators and tested it with high school, college, and adult participants. For all groups, attitude similarity was the most important factor in perceived similarity.

Communicators frequently make judgments about the attractiveness of others based on inferred, rather than actual, characteristics. Cappella (1984) suggests that, "We are as much studying who people think they are attracted to as who they are attracted to" (p. 241). Byrne's research and that of many interpersonal attraction researchers, including Berscheid, Walster, Sunnafrank and Miller, is conducted under the law-governed method of inquiry. The research methods used to test hypotheses and research questions about interpersonal attraction and attitude similarity are designed to establish *causes* of attraction.

In conducting much of his research on attraction and attitude similarity, Byrne employed the "bogus stranger" technique. In this method, participants completed an attitude questionnaire (scale). They were then given another scale supposedly completed by a stranger. Actually, the researcher chose the answers on "the stranger's" questionnaire. The researcher divided people into two groups to create two experimental conditions: the "similar" and "dissimilar" attitude conditions. In the "similar" condition, the stranger's scale almost duplicated the responses of the research participant. In the "dissimilar" condition, the questionnaire had almost opposite responses from those of the participant.

Researchers have also studied the effect of other kinds of similarity. Byrne, Griffitt, and Stefaniak (1967) have suggested that another's similarity to oneself, whether it be similar behavior, ability, or attitude, makes one more comfortable. Similarity provides reassurance and reinforcement that the person is functioning in a logical and meaningful way because the interaction seems more understandable and predictable.

Evaluating the Attraction-Reinforcement Research

Interpersonal attraction research was one of the first efforts to find that similar attitudes *cause* interpersonal attraction. It provided several useful research techniques (like "bogus stranger") which were later used in many experimental studies of interpersonal communication. Some critics (Eiser, 1980; Gergen, 1980) have challenged Byrne's experimental methods as too contrived and artificial to predict how people actually are attracted to each other. For example, we rarely read questionnaires completed by those we have just met and might be considering as friends. These critics feel that, because the studies were so artificial, the findings cannot be generalized to actual attraction situations and thus are not very useful. Other critics have described more fundamental limitations of the early work. Duck (1985) suggests that the studies investigating the relationship between attitude similarity and attraction did not describe *how* people recognize reinforcing attitudes in normal, everyday encounters with strangers. Early researchers did not study the *communication* of attitudes, beliefs, and values between individuals. Perhaps some people fail to communicate the right messages about their attitudes, inadequately self-disclose to others, or have difficulty with expressions of warmth, concern, and interest (Duck, 1985). Some people even consciously hide or disguise their real attitudes to be more attractive to others (Snyder, 1974, 1979). It may be very difficult for people to interpret messages about others' attitudes. Perhaps only very competent communicators can accurately discern others' "real" attitudes. Skill and knowledge of interpersonal communication are critical elements in the attitude similarity-attraction relationship. As Duck (1985) states, "relationship development requires different sorts of knowledge and communicative skill at different points" (p. 661). The early attraction-attitude similarity research failed to recognize the importance of these factors. Byrne's research also failed to acknowledge that an individual's attitudes may change as a relationship develops. This change in attitudes may affect a person's ability or desire to reward the partner.

The Interpersonal Goal-Oriented Theory of Attraction

Communication theorists have expanded our understanding of the similarity-attraction relationship. The early research failed to include the influence of *actual* conversation in the process of interpersonal attraction. The influence of outside factors such as status differences between people and environmental factors was not studied. Sunnafrank and his associates have studied the similarity-attraction relationship from a goal-oriented, communication-based perspective. They have examined the influence of "normal" communication and attitude information during the early acquaintance stages of relationships, since most first encounters between strangers include conversations. As Uncertainty Reduction Theory suggests, more personal information is exchanged as relationships become more intimate (Berger & Calabrese, 1975). Recall that Uncertainty Reduction Theory suggests that uncertainty makes individuals seek information to reduce feelings of discomfort. In Sunnafrank's (1986) Perceived Outcome Value (POV) Theory, people seek information about others in order to enhance the *quality* (or perceived outcome value) of their interactions. Thus, both Uncertainty Reduction Theory and Perceived Outcome Value Theory predict that people seek information *prior* to an initial encounter when they anticipate meeting someone new. People may believe that simply knowing the attitudes of a stranger will help them better predict and control the situation. Such information as age, sex, or social status can be obtained from mutual acquaintances or from the context in which the people meet. Attending the same house of worship, political rally, class, party, or professional meeting reveals certain shared characteristics.

Sunnafrank and Miller (1981) designed an experiment to discover how a "normal" first conversation between strangers affected the relationship between similar attitudes and attraction. Participants were told that they would be working on a project with a stranger who had attitudes either like or unlike their own. Half the participants then engaged in a five-minute interaction with their partner; the other half did not. The participants next completed a questionnaire that measured how much they were attracted to their partner. Results indicated that participants who did not have a chance to communicate preferred the "similar" stranger. Those who did communicate were more attracted to a stranger unlike themselves. Initial, non-threatening communication appears to make people more attracted to dissimilar others. To explain this finding, Sunnafrank and Miller suggest that when people engage in brief encounters with strangers, they feel better able to predict the stranger's behavior in future interactions. This feeling of stability and control, in turn, influences attraction. To underscore this point, the researchers reported that participants who met dissimilar strangers but had no opportunity to communicate with them were *least* attracted to the strangers. This study appears to support the assumptions of Uncertainty Reduction Theory, which suggests that individuals strive to predict and control their environments. Sunnafrank (1983) suggests that meeting these goals is the most important factor in determining attraction. Stable and predictable environments are reinforcing to individuals; unstable ones are not.

Sunnafrank extended this research by studying later stages of conversations about attitudes. He discovered that both first conversations and first conversations followed by discussions of attitudes made people more attracted to dissimilar, but not similar, strangers. If you already believed that a stranger shared your attitudes, confirmation would simply support your expectations. It would not necessarily increase your attraction to the stranger. However, if you believed that you would meet someone very different from you (an anti-nuclear energy person meeting a pro-nuclear energy person), a normal first conversation should reduce the threat associated with the different attitudes, and you should be more attracted to that person than before. Sunnafrank's goal-oriented theory of attraction seems to explain the later stages of the process of developing relationships. The similarity-attraction relationship discovered by earlier researchers best explains relations between individuals *before* communication takes place. When we communicate with others who are different from us at work, at school, or at parties, the communication may reduce our tendency to be attracted only to those we think are like ourselves. Sunnafrank's (1985) work also extended the previous findings to include interactions between *opposite-sex* partners. Since opposite-sex interaction constitutes a large percentage of first meetings, this extension is very important.

A Rules Theory of Interpersonal Communication and Relationship Development

The theories discussed so far used the law-governed perspective. As discussed in Chapter 3, some scholars think that communication is best understood from a rules perspective. These theorists feel that communication takes its significance from shared rules which guide the choices that people make when they encode and decode messages.

Relational Development From A Rules Perspective

Cushman and Florence (1974) argue that *developing, presenting, and validating our individual self-concepts* is the primary goal of interpersonal communication. When individuals communicate, they "create" identities for themselves and others. This identity creation enables us to discover what we can and cannot *do* and who we can and cannot *be* in the presence of others. When people "agree" on created identities, then the climate necessary to develop an interpersonal relationship is established. For example, if Sandy wants to be seen as intelligent and insightful and Jess accepts that image by responding favorably when Sandy acts intelligently and by complimenting the keen insights, Sandy and Jess "agree" on Sandy's identity. Of course, they probably never actually debate what kind of person Sandy is. They simply fall into a pattern which indicates both accept the self-definition. Jess' behavior is called *reciprocal self-concept support*. Different *types* of self-concept support lead to different interpersonal relationships: friends, lovers, intimates. Different *degrees* of self-concept support lead to different levels of an interpersonal relationship: acquaintance, friend, or best friend.

The Self-Concept and Interpersonal Attraction

Cushman, Valentinsen and Dietrich (1982) suggest that *perceived self-concept support* is linked to interpersonal attraction. In order to support another's self-concept, a person must be able to recognize the uniqueness and special configuration of another's self-concept and must know the communication rules to communicate support (Cushman & Cahn, 1985). A person must be able to identify cues presented by a receiver that indicate the receiver understood the message. This ability is called *perceived understanding* (Cahn 1983, 1986; Cahn & Shulman, 1984).

According to Cushman's rules-based theory, three propositions explain the relationship between self-concept and interpersonal attraction. First, individuals are attracted to those with the ability to convey support for their self-concept (perceived self-concept support). Second, *actual* similarity in self-concepts between individuals has no influence on attraction. Third, perceived self-concept support can be controlled by communication. The focus (who will be the recipient of the support) and the intensity (how strongly the support will be felt) can vary. Perceived understanding and support are essential to validate self-concepts. According to the theory, we are attracted to and form relationships with those who validate our self-concepts.

A Three-Stage Rule-Based Model of Relationship Development

Cushman and his associates use the practical *syllogism* (a method of reasoning which consists of two premises and a conclusion) to explain communication during relationship development. Individuals who wish to form a new relationship know that they must follow certain communication rules. People consciously, purposively, and intentionally communicate in ways which foster a new relationship. Three factors influence the formation of interpersonal relationships: honesty, trust, and self-concept support. These factors are necessary in the growth of intimate and friendly relationships.

Cushman and his associates have developed a three stage model of how friendships are formed. According to this model, people have a group of individuals whom they can expect to encounter called a *field of availables*. The field of availables is affected by such forces as birth and death rates, the age and sex distributions of a population, and by social, educational, religious, and economic structures. The socialization process also reduces one's field of availables. Cushman and Cahn (1985) stress that *communication rules* which govern interactions among our field of availables are fairly standardized for all individuals. Within the field of availables, there exist a number of individuals with desirable attributes and with whom we would consider developing a relationship. Cushman and his associates call these people the *field of approachables*.

Three communication rules limit the field of approachables. These rules form the basis of subsequent interactions which guide the development of the relationship (Cushman, Valentinsen, & Dietrich, 1982):

1. The more you think that the qualities you admire for yourself are actually found in someone else, the more likely you are to communicate with the other.
2. The more favorably you think that someone will respond to an offer of friendship or self-concept support, the more likely you are to communicate with the other.
3. The more self-concept support someone provides you, the more you will think that the person wants to be your friend.

Within the field of approachables, there exists a subset of individuals with whom we will begin to develop relationships and who will actually become our friends. These people are our *field of reciprocals*. Two communication rules limit the field of reciprocals (Cushman, Valentinsen, & Dietrich, 1982):

1. The more our interactions support our initial feelings that the other person possesses qualities we like and admire, the greater the chance that a relationship will develop.
2. The more we openly show respect for each other's self-concept, the greater the chance that our relationship will develop.

According to this rules theory, developing relationships, especially friendships, are characterized by honesty, trust between individuals, and support for each other's self-concept. This same three-stage model is also used to explain how more intimate relationships develop. In *mate formation*, the model emphasizes physical attraction, reciprocal affection, and perceptions of an ideal mate.

Cahn's Theory of Perceived Understanding

Cahn (1984) has advanced a rules-based theory of interpersonal communication with the core concept of *perceived understanding*. Sometimes called the "perception of being understood/ misunderstood," perceived understanding is, "the communicator's assessment of his success or failure when attempting to communicate with another person" (Cahn, 1981, p. 1). The perception of being understood/misunderstood is linked to an individual's interpretation of messages.

The Perceived Understanding Scale

Cahn and Shulman (1984) designed a questionnaire (scale) to measure perceived understanding. The questionnaire consists of two dimensions: some questions measure perception of being understood or *feeling understood*, and some measure perception of being misunderstood or *feeling misunderstood*. The first dimension contains the characteristics identified most often with the feeling of being understood: satisfaction, relaxation, pleasure, good, acceptance, comfortableness, happiness, and importance. The second dimension contains the characteristics identified most often with feelings of being misunderstood: dissatisfaction, annoyance, discomfort, insecurity, sadness, failure, incompleteness, and disinterest. In completing the questionnaire, individuals are first asked to identify in writing one person with whom they have recently talked. Then they are requested to use each adjective on the questionnaire to indicate how they felt during and immediately after trying to make themselves understood by the person they identified. Cahn and Shulman believe that it is possible to feel both somewhat understood and somewhat misunderstood at the same time. They feel that the questionnaire can be used to measure the intensity of the development of an interpersonal relationship and to identify communication behaviors which contribute to perceived understanding.

Perceived Understanding and Relationship Development

Theorists have suggested that individuals in the beginning stages of relationship development seek information to reduce uncertainty (Berger & Calabrese, 1975) or to enhance their perceived outcome value (Sunnafrank, 1986). Cahn (1983, 1986, 1987) believes that perceived understanding is also a factor in the relationship development process. People feel understood when, for example, what Kerry thinks of an object or concept (Kerry's *direct perspective*) and what Kerry imagines Sam thinks Kerry thinks about that object or concept (Kerry's *meta-metaperspective*) are congruent. The perception of feeling understood or misunderstood involves comparing one's meta-metaperspective with one's own direct perspective (Cahn, 1987). For example, suppose Kerry likes and engages in outward displays of affection such as hand-holding, touching arms and shoulders, and kissing; this is Kerry's direct perspective. Kerry also has a meta-metaperspective; Kerry believes Sam thinks that Kerry does *not* like outward and visible expressions of affection. Whether or not Kerry is correct about what Sam thinks, Kerry may feel misunderstood. Feelings of being understood or misunderstood serve as reasons for individuals to continue or abandon certain courses of action. If you feel someone understands you, you are more likely to continue to interact with that person. Feeling understood promotes closeness and feelings of emotional intimacy with others. These feelings surface because people believe they are following rules appropriate to the interaction. If people feel consistently misunderstood when they interact with someone, then they will probably communicate with that person less frequently. When feelings of misunderstanding surface, people believe that they behaved by "the wrong set of rules." Individuals who feel misunderstood frequently ask questions like, "What happened?" "What went wrong?" "Where did I fail?" and "What am I supposed to do now?" (Cahn, 1987, p. 12).

Consequences of Perceived Understanding

Perceived understanding seems to enhance one's satisfaction with a relationship. Individuals who felt their partners understood them were more attracted to and more trusting of others than individuals who felt misunderstood (Cahn & Frey, 1982). Feeling understood or misunderstood may play a more important part in the later stages of relationships as well (Cahn, 1983; Cahn & Hanford, 1984). Perceived understanding has been called an index of the intensity of relationship development. As an intensity variable, the more the relationship develops, the stronger the effect of perceived understanding. Cahn (1983, 1984, 1987) examined perceived understanding between teachers and students. The factor most associated with students' evaluation of teachers was perceived understanding. Three teacher communication behaviors were related to perceived understanding: classroom/platform behavior, student-centered behavior, and democratic/participatory teaching style. Cahn's theory extends communication theories about how relationships develop. Perceived understanding can be added to the list of factors that help connections grow.

A Systems Model of Relational Interaction

Millar and Rogers (1976, 1987) offer a systems-oriented view of interpersonal communication. Their relational approach suggests that communication scholars studying interpersonal dynamics should focus on *patterns of exchange* during interaction. They believe that individuals and messages cannot be studied separately or in isolation. Instead, patterns of messages and responses must be examined *over time*. The Millar and Rogers model is consistent with the principles of the systems approach; a relationship is viewed as a joint product of behavior and is more than the sum of the individual parts. The Millar and Rogers (1987) interpersonal dynamics model suggests that relationships emerge from patterns of interaction made up of "redundant, interlocked cycles of messages, continually negotiated and co-defined rather than unilaterally caused by personal qualities and/or social role prescriptions" (p. 118). According to this systems theory, interpersonal relationships are much less influenced by causes (law-governed) or social rules (rule-governed) than by patterns of message exchange.

The Dimensions of Interpersonal Relations

There are three types of message exchange patterns: *control, trust* and *intimacy*. Control is exhibited in messages such as, "'I'm in charge here'; 'You can't talk to me like that'; and 'You don't have the right to tell me what to do'" (Millar & Rogers, 1987, p. 120). The control dimension refers to which partner currently has the right to define and direct the actions of the pair (dyad). The partner who creates the most relational definitions or defines the system's actions is the partner who has the most control. According to Millar and Rogers, relational control can be measured by *redundancy* (how much change there is in partners' negotiation over rights), *dominance* (how much one partner dominates the interaction) and *power* (the potential to influence or restrict a partner's behaviors). Trust requires both members of a relationship to be trusting and trustworthy. By trusting, people admit that they are dependent on another and that they believe the partner will not exploit them or take advantage of their trust. Intimacy measures how often partners use the other to confirm their feelings of "separateness or connectedness" in the relationship (Millar & Rogers, 1987, p. 123). Very intimate relationships involve a great deal of mutual self-confirmation, behavior in which partners use each other primarily to fulfill their needs. Intimacy is communicated in such comments as, "'No one understands me the way you do'; and 'I couldn't live without him'" (Millar & Rogers, 1987, p. 124).

Coding Relational Messages

This approach to communication assumes that messages contain both *content* and *relational* dimensions. For example, the phrase, "Open the door" is understood by the content ("open the door") and the relational ("I command you to . . .") aspects. In their research, Rogers and Farace (1975) code messages by focusing on *relational control* rather than the content of messages. They code *message sequences* rather than individual message units. The purpose of the coding is to determine the relationship of one utterance to what precedes it. In message pairs, the second utterance defines the transaction because it indicates whether the receiver accepts the other's control, exerts control, or remains on an equal level (is not controlled or controlling). Each message is categorized according to a three-digit code. The first digit designates who is *the speaker*. The second digit designates the *grammatical form* of the message: (1) Assertion; (2) Question; (3) Talk-Over; (4) Noncomplete; (5) Other. The third digit is the most important. This digit designates the *response of the message* relative to the previous message. Rogers and Farace (1975) developed nine categories of responses:

1. Support: acceptance, approval, or agreement with the previous statement;
2. Nonsupport: disagreement, rejection, or a challenge to a previous utterance;
3. Extension: utterance which continues the flow of a previous utterance;
4. Answer: a direct answer to a question;
5. Instruction: a qualified or suggested order;
6. Order: a direct and unqualified instruction;
7. Disconfirmation: refusing to acknowledge the previous utterance;
8. Topic change: denotes a change of topic;
9. Initiation—termination: code for the beginning or ending of a discussion;
10. Other

Three levels of control can also be coded for the messages and their relationship to previous messages. An attempt to assert or gain control is considered a *one-up statement* (↑). A request, acceptance of the other's definition of the relationship, or an attempt to yield control is considered a *one-down statement* (↓). A nondemanding, leveling movement which neutralizes control is considered a *one-across statement* (→). For example, a question that supports a previous utterance would be coded as a one-down. Several researchers have used this coding scheme in studies during the past ten years.

The Millar and Rogers systems model has helped researchers understand patterns of control in interpersonal relationships. The dimensions of control, trust and intimacy have stimulated much research and theory building in interpersonal communication.

Summary

This chapter explored several theories of communication in interpersonal contexts. Theories were presented to explain and predict communication during the process of developing relationships. Some of the theories reviewed reflect the law-governed approach to understanding communication:

Uncertainty Reduction Theory, Perceived Outcome Value Theory, Equity Theory, Reinforcement Theory, Attraction Theory, and Interpersonal Goal-Oriented Theory of Attraction. Two action or rule-governed theories were also presented: Cushman, Valentinsen and Dietrich's Rules Theory of Interpersonal Communication and Cahn's Theory of Perceived Understanding. A systems model of interpersonal dynamics by Millar and Rogers was reviewed. Major assumptions, propositions and principles of each theory were discussed. Examples of communication research which tested the theories were provided.

Questions To Consider

1. Describe the beginnings of the study of interpersonal communication in the 1960s.
2. How do the laws, rules, and systems perspectives differ in their approaches to interpersonal communication?
3. What are the assumptions and predictions Uncertainty Reduction Theory makes about communication?
4. In what ways does Predicted Outcome Value Theory modify Uncertainty Reduction Theory?
5. How does Equity Theory explain the development of interpersonal relations?
6. According to Reinforcement Theory, why are people attracted to each other?
7. How is relationship development explained from a rules perspective?
8. What are the stages and main concerns of the rules-based model of relationship development?
9. How do relationships develop according to the Theory of Perceived Understanding?
10. How is interpersonal communication studied from a systems perspective?
11. Explain the difference between one-down, one-up, and one-across messages.

References

Altman, I., & Taylor, D.A. (1973). *Social penetration: The development of interpersonal relationships.* New York: Holt, Rinehart and Winston.

Andersen, P.A., & Todd-Mancillas, W. (1978). Scales for the measurement of homophily with public figures. *Southern Speech Communication Journal, 43,* 169-179.

Argyle, M., & Dean, J. (1965). Eye contact, distance and affiliation. *Sociometry, 28*, 289-304.

Barnlund, D.C. (1968). *Interpersonal communication: Survey and studies.* Boston, MA: Houghton Mifflin.

Bateson, G., Jackson, D.D., Haley, J., & Weakland, J.H. (1956). Toward a theory of schizophrenia. *Behavioral Science, 1*, 251-264.

Berger, C.R. (1986). Uncertainty outcome values in predicted relationships: Uncertainty reduction theory then and now. *Human Communication Research, 13*, 34-38.

Berger, C.R. (1979). Beyond initial interaction: Uncertainty, understanding, and the development of interpersonal relationships. In H. Giles & R.N. St. Clair (Eds.), *Language and social psychology* (pp. 122-144). Oxford: Basil Blackwell.

Berger, C.R., & Calabrese, R.J. (1975). Some explorations in initial interaction and beyond: Toward a developmental theory of interpersonal communication. *Human Communication Research, 1*, 99-112.

Berscheid, E. (1966). Opinion change and communicator-communicatee similarity and dissimilarity. *Journal of Personality and Social Psychology, 4*, 670-680.

Berscheid, E., & Walster, E.H. (1978). *Interpersonal attraction* (2nd ed.). Reading, MA: Addison-Wesley.

Berscheid, E., Walster, E., & Bohrnstedt, G. (1973). The body image report. *Psychology Today, 7*, 119-131.

Byrne, D. (1971). *The attraction paradigm.* New York: Academic Press.

Byrne, D., Griffitt, W., & Stefaniak, D. (1967). Attraction and similarity of personality characteristics. *Journal of Personality and Social Psychology, 5*, 82-90.

Cahn, D.D. (1987). *Letting go: A practical theory of relationship disengagement and reengagement.* Albany, NY: SUNY Press.

Cahn, D.D. (1986). Perceived understanding, superior-subordinate communication, and organizational effectiveness. *Central States Speech Journal, 37*, 19-26.

Cahn, D.D. (1984). Teacher-student relationships: Perceived understanding. *Communication Research Reports, 1*, 65-67.

Cahn, D.D. (1983). Relative importance of perceived understanding in initial interaction and development of interpersonal relationships. *Psychological Reports, 52*, 923-929.

Cahn, D.D. (1981, April). *Feeling understood as a research concept.* Paper presented at the meeting of the Central States Speech Association, Chicago, Illinois.

Cahn, D., & Frey, L. (1982, November). *Interpersonal attraction and trust: The effects of feeling understood/misunderstood on impression formation processes.* Paper presented at the meeting of the Speech Communication Association Convention, Louisville, Kentucky.

Cahn, D.D. & Hanford, J.T. (1984). Perspectives on human communication research: Behaviorism, phenomenology, and an integrated view. *Western Journal of Speech Communication, 48*, 277-292.

Cahn, D.D., & Shulman, G.M. (1984). The perceived understanding instrument. *Communication Research Reports, 1*, 122-125.

Cappella, J.N. (1984). The relevance of the microstructure of interaction to relationship change. *Journal of Social and Personal Relationships, 1*, 239-264.

Cushman, D.P., & Cahn, D.D. (1985). *Communication in interpersonal relationships.* Albany, NY: SUNY Press.

Cushman, D.P., & Florence, T. (1974). Development of interpersonal communication theory. *Today's Speech, 22,* 11-15.

Cushman, D., Valentinsen, B., & Dietrich, D. (1982). A rules theory of interpersonal relationships. In F.E.X. Dance (Ed.) *Human communication theory* (pp. 90-120) New York: Harper & Row.

Cushman, D., & Whiting, G. (1972). An approach to communication theory: Toward a consensus on rules. *Journal of Communication, 22,* 217-238.

Davidson, B., Balswick, J., & Halverson, C. (1983). Affective self-disclosure and marital adjustment: A test of equity theory. *Journal of Marriage and the Family, 1,* 93-102.

DeVito, J.A. (1989). *The interpersonal communication book* (5th ed.). New York: Harper & Row.

Duck, S.W. (1985). Social and personal relationships. In M.L. Knapp & G.R. Miller (Eds.), *Handbook of interpersonal communication* (pp. 655-686). Beverly Hills, CA: Sage.

Eiser, J.R. (1980). Prolegomena to a more applied social psychology. In R. Gilmour & S.W. Duck (Eds.), *The development of social psychology* (pp. 271-292). New York: Academic Press.

Foa, U.G., & Foa, E.B. (1974). *Societal structures of the mind.* Springfield, IL: Charles C. Thomas.

Gergen, K.J. (1980). Toward intellectual audacity in social psychology. In R. Gilmour & S.W. Duck (Eds.), *The development of social psychology* (pp. 239-270). New York: Academic Press.

Giffin, K., & Patton, B.R. (1971). *Fundamentals of interpersonal communication.* New York: Harper & Row.

Goffman, E. (1959). *The presentation of self in everyday life.* Garden City, NY: Doubleday/Anchor.

Gudykunst, W., & Nishida, T. (1984). Individual and cultural influence on uncertainty reduction. *Communication Monographs, 51,* 23-36.

Gudykunst, W., Nishida, T., Koike, H., & Shiino, N. (1986). The influence of language on uncertainty reduction: An exploratory study of Japanese-Japanese and Japanese-North American interactions. In M. McLaughlin (Ed.), *Communication Yearbook, 9* (pp. 555-575). Newbury Park, CA: Sage.

Gudykunst, W., Yang, S., & Nishida, T. (1985). A cross-cultural test of uncertainty reduction theory. *Human Communication Research, 11,* 407-454.

Hall, E.T. (1959). *The silent language.* Garden City, NY: Doubleday/Anchor.

Keltner, J.W. (1970). *Interpersonal speech-communication: Elements and structures.* Belmont, CA: Wadsworth.

Kiesler, S., & Baral, R. (1970). The search for a romantic partner: The effects of self-esteem and physical attractiveness on romantic behavior. In K. Gergen & D. Marlowe (Eds.), *Personality and Social Behavior* (pp. 155-165). Reading, MA: Addison-Wesley.

Knapp, M.L., & Comadena, M.E. (1979). Telling it like it isn't: A review of theory and research on deceptive communications. *Human Communication Research, 5,* 270-285.

Knapp, M.L., & Miller, G.R. (Eds.) (1985). *Handbook of interpersonal communication.* Beverly Hills, CA: Sage.

Lester, R.E. (1986). Organizational culture, uncertainty reduction and the socialization of new organizational members. In S. Thomas (Ed.), *Culture and communication: Methodology, behavior, artifacts and institutions* (pp.105-113). Norwood, NJ: Ablex.

McCroskey, J.C., Larson, C., & Knapp, M.L. (1971). *An introduction to interpersonal communication*. Englewood Cliffs, NJ: Prentice-Hall.

McCroskey, J.C., Richmond, V.P., & Daly, J.A. (1975). The development of a measure of perceived homophily in interpersonal communication. *Human Communication Research, 1,* 323-332.

Millar, F.E., & Rogers, L.E. (1987). Relational dimensions of interpersonal dynamics. In M.E. Roloff & G.R. Miller (Eds.), *Interpersonal processes: New directions in communication research* (pp. 117-139). Newbury Park, CA: Sage.

Millar, F.E., & Rogers, L.E. (1976). A relational approach to interpersonal communication. In G.R. Miller (Ed.), *Explorations in interpersonal communication* (pp. 87-103). Beverly Hills, CA: Sage.

Millar, F.E., Rogers, L.E., & Bavelas, J. (1984). Identifying patterns of verbal conflict in interpersonal dynamics. *Western Journal of Speech Communication, 48,* 231-246.

Miller, G.R., & Steinberg, M. (1975). *Between people: A new analysis of interpersonal communication*. Chicago, IL: Science Research.

Newcomb, T.M. (1963). Stabilities underlying changes in interpersonal attraction. *Journal of Abnormal and Social Psychology, 66,* 376-386.

Parks, M.R., & Adelman, M.B. (1983). Communication networks and the development of romantic relationships: An expansion of uncertainty reduction theory. *Human Communication Research, 10,* 55-79.

Pearce, W.B., & Cronen, V.E. (1980). *Communication, action, and meaning: The creation of social realities*. New York: Praeger.

Roberto, K.A., & Scott, J.P. (1986). Equity considerations in the friendships of older adults. *Journal of Gerontology, 41,* 241-247.

Rogers, E.M., & Bhowmik, D.K. (1970). Homophily-heterophily: Relational concepts for communication research. *Public Opinion Quarterly, 34,* 523-538.

Rogers, L.E., & Farace, R.V. (1975). Analysis of relational communication in dyads: New measurement procedures. *Human Communication Research, 1,* 222-239.

Rogers-Millar, L.E., & Millar, F.E. (1979). Domineeringness and dominance: A transactional view. *Human Communication Research, 5,* 238-246.

Roloff, M.E. (1981). *Interpersonal communication: The social exchange approach*. Beverly Hills, CA: Sage.

Snyder, M. (1979). Self-monitoring processes. In L.Berkowitz (Ed.), *Advances in experimental social psychology*, (Vol. 12, pp. 85-128). New York: Academic Press.

Snyder, M. (1974). Self-monitoring of expressive behavior. *Journal of Personality and Social Psychology, 30,* 526-537.

Sunnafrank, M. (1986). Predicted outcome value during initial interactions: A reformulation of uncertainty reduction theory. *Human Communication Research, 13,* 3-33.

Sunnafrank, M. (1985). Attitude similarity and interpersonal attraction during early communicative relationships: A research note on the generalizability of findings to opposite-sex relationships. *Western Journal of Speech Communication, 49,* 73-80.

Sunnafrank, M. (1984). A communication-based perspective on attitude similarity and interpersonal attraction in early acquaintance. *Communication Monographs, 51,* 372-380.

Sunnafrank, M. (1983). Attitude similarity and interpersonal attraction in communication processes: In pursuit of an ephemeral influence. *Communication Monographs, 50,* 273-284.

Sunnafrank, M.J., & Miller, G.R. (1981). The role of initial conversations in determining attraction to similar and dissimilar strangers. *Human Communication Research, 8,* 16-25.

Thibaut, J.W., & Coules, J. (1952). The role of communication in the reduction of interpersonal hostility. *Journal of Abnormal and Social Psychology, 47,* 770-777.

Walster, E., Berscheid, E., & Walster, G.W. (1973). New directions in equity research. *Journal of Personality and Social Psychology, 25,* 151-176.

Walster, E., & Walster, G.W. (1976). Interpersonal attraction. In B. Seidenberg & A. Snadowsky (Eds.), *Social psychology: An introduction* (pp. 279-308). New York: Free Press.

Walster, E., Walster, G.W., & Berscheid, E. (1978). *Equity: Theory and research.* Boston: Allyn & Bacon, Inc.

Chapter 10

Organizational and Group Contexts

Organizational and group communication are two of the most popular contexts for theory building by scholars of communication. Organizational communication involves exchanging messages to stimulate meaning within and between organizations and their environments. Organizational communication involves one-on-one communication (communication between superiors and subordinates), small group communication (meetings), public communication (public speeches by a chief executive officer), and mass communication (press releases, company newsletters, new product announcements using teleconferencing, perhaps even internal corporate television programs). Each of these forms of communication may occur between members of the same organization or may be used by organizations to coordinate behavior with each other or with their environment (customers, the government, or competitors). Small group communication involves exchanging messages to stimulate meaning between about 5-12 people who share a common goal and consider themselves members of a group (unit). Research about communication processes in small groups and organizations has been strongly influenced by the work of scholars in fields such as management, sociology, and social psychology. For example, many organizational communication textbooks discuss theories of organizations such as scientific management and human relations. You may be familiar with these two families of theories from courses in other academic departments. Because we wish to focus on communication theory building, this chapter will not attempt to survey theories developed

303

in other fields which have influenced communication research. Rather, we will limit ourselves to a brief introduction to organizational theory in order to focus on the body of theory and research developed by scholars in communication.

In this chapter we have chosen to discuss theories of organizational and small group communication together because they are closely related. While some theories of organizational communication discuss message processes at an organization-wide level, many deal with communication between group leaders and members or between a pair of individuals such as a superior and subordinate. Thus, an effective organizational communicator must also be an effective interpersonal and small group communicator. Since one level of the organizational systems hierarchy is the small group, and since many organizational communication textbooks discuss small group communication theories (particularly leadership theories), we have chosen to combine the two contexts.

Development of Organizational and Group Communication

Before the Industrial Revolution in England, most businesses were small, family-operated enterprises. The owner and the employees knew each other well. After the increased mechanization of the Industrial Revolution, manufacturing businesses grew much larger. With this expansion came the rise of a class of managers hired by the owner to make a business run smoothly. At the same time, theories were developed to explain how managers could more efficiently and effectively perform their jobs. Tompkins (1984) has identified the communication implications of these organizational and managerial theories.

The classical theory of organizations was developed based on the work of three important theorists. Max Weber (1909-1948) wrote about the benefits of bureaucracy. Weber believed that written messages in the organization's files created permanency for the organization (Tompkins, 1984). Henri Fayol (1916-1949) identified key principles of management such as division of work, centralization of power, and the scalar chain of command, "the chain of superiors and subordinates which stretches from the top to the bottom of the organization" (Tompkins, 1984, p. 664). Fayol developed the idea of the bridge or gangplank, a horizontal chain of communication between employees on the same hierarchical level but in different departments. This concept appears later in this chapter in the discussion of Farace, Monge, and Russell's (1977) systems Theory of Organizations. Fayol advocated oral, face-to-face communication contacts.

Frederick W. Taylor's (1911) *Scientific Management* Theory was meant to correct the unsystematic ways in which organizations of his time operated.

As was appropriate to the technology with which he was concerned, Taylor stressed efficiency and a scientific analysis of tasks to increase productivity. Time and motion studies, for example, would indicate the most efficient means of producing goods. Taylor advocated piecework, paying workers for the number of units they produced rather than for the length of time they worked. As Kreps (1986) notes, "According to classical theory, the organization is a machine, and organization members are mere cogs in the machine" (p. 79). However, Taylor's theory also led to recognition of the importance of upward and downward communication along the organizational hierarchy. Taylor advocated upward communication, not only as a method of receiving feedback for managers, but also as a means for managers to learn the rules-of-thumb that workers had developed for performing their jobs (Tompkins, 1984).

A change in perspectives of management was marked by the Hawthorne studies conducted from 1925 to 1932 at the Western Electric Hawthorne Plant in Cicero, Illinois (Roethlisberger & Dickson, 1939). Researchers trying to determine the optimum level of lighting found that productivity increased whether they increased or decreased the illumination in the plant. The researchers attributed their findings to what we now call the Hawthorne effect. The attention of the researchers, not the level of lighting, increased productivity. Through anonymous interviews, the researchers encouraged workers to ventilate their dissatisfactions; workers reported that these interviews helped them to regard their jobs and the organization more positively and to resolve their problems. In yet another experiment, the researchers found that workers set informal norms which in some cases blocked management attempts to speed up production. As a result of the Hawthorne studies, theorists began to consider the effect of communication and human relations upon productivity. Managers were taught to consider informal as well as formal organizational communication systems. The Hawthorne studies showed that workers' social needs and desire for informal communication were important. Managers were taught to listen to their employees and to stimulate upward communication. Chris Argyris (1957) and Rensis Likert (1971) further developed human relations theories of leadership and supervision. Argyris taught that the incongruence between workers' needs and the organization's demands led to alienated workers. Likert stressed open communication and participative decision making as means of increasing satisfaction and productivity.

Other theorists and practitioners have extended the work of these primary theorists. In Theory X and Theory Y, Douglas McGregor (1960) summarized the assumptions about people and work that undergirded scientific management and the human relations movement, respectively. Theory X managers assume that workers would prefer to avoid work if possible; they work only because they must to earn money. Thus, workers must be directed, controlled, and even threatened with punishment for the organization to achieve its objectives (Tompkins, 1984). Theory X identifies the assumptions typical of scientific management. Theory Y managers, like human relations theorists such as Likert and Argyris, believe that work is natural to human beings. Workers are self-directed and will be committed to organizational objectives if the organization can connect its goals with the workers' own needs for achievement and self-actualization. Workers desire to be creative and responsible in performing their jobs. McGregor draws on the work of Mary Parker Follett (1971). Follett stressed the role of communication in helping organization members adjust to other members and to the environment. She believed that the *manner* of communicating orders was extremely important. Chester Barnard (1938-1968), a successful businessman as well as theorist, also noted the central role of communication for the executive. More recently, Katz and Kahn (1966) have developed a systems approach to organizations. Reacting against the assumptions of both scientific management and human relations that there is one best way to manage all workers, Fielder (1967), Reddin (1970), and others have developed contingency theories of group leadership; these theories stress using different styles of leadership appropriate to the needs created by different organizational situations (contingencies). The remainder of this chapter will discuss examples of current theory building in organizational and group communication from the laws, rules, and systems perspectives.

Theories of Organizational Communication

The Theory of Independent-Mindedness

In Chapter 5, you read about the communication trait of argumentativeness, a person's tendency to present and defend his/her positions on controversial issues while refuting the positions of another (Infante & Rancer, 1982). Covering laws researchers have investigated argumentativeness in interpersonal communication inside organizations through a theory relating independent-mindedness to organizational communication. This theory was developed in response to several recent attempts to suggest how American workers might be more productive. The recent economic success of Japan has led to much interest in the culture of Japanese businesses. Quality circles, decision by consensus, workplace harmony, and "a caring, nurturing management style" (Gorden & Infante, 1987, p. 149) are some of the characteristics of Japanese management that have been studied for possible application by American managers. However, as Ouchi (1981) cautions in *Theory Z*, one of the most popular books about the advantages of Japanese management techniques, Japanese management models must be adapted to American society. Japan has a homogeneous and hierarchical culture, whereas American culture is more individualistic than that of any other country (Hofstede, 1980). Therefore, Japanese management techniques will not be as productive in America because the values of American workers differ markedly from those of Japanese workers. In order for management techniques to be effective, values held by the general society must also be affirmed in the workplace (Infante & Gorden, 1987). Based on this assumption that macro and microstructures will be most effective when their values are consistent, theorists have linked the American value termed "independent-mindedness" to organizational communication and job satisfaction. Independent-mindedness involves the tendency for Americans to have their own thoughts and opinions rather than passively accepting the opinions of others and to advocate those personal views.

There are eight premises linking independent mindedness to organizational communication:

1. Freedom and individuality are fundamental values in the United States.
2. Therefore, United States society predisposes people to express their individuality freely in daily life.
3. This expressiveness is revealed through a person's communicator style and willingness to argue opinions (See Chapter 5).
4. However, organizations depend on employees' complying with rules and authority.
5. In the United States, compliance is achieved by mutual negotiations characterized by giving good reasons and disputing points within a framework of good will (by argumentativeness).
6. On the other hand, verbal aggressiveness is a style of disputing which attacks another's self-concept and therefore interferes with cooperation in accomplishing tasks (Infante & Wigley, 1986).
7. Based on premises 1-5, workers in the United States ought to value communication characteristics that promote independent-mindedness, individuality, and independence in making decisions and carrying out tasks.
8. Because workers value these characteristics, workers will be more productive and satisfied and perceive their supervisors as more effective when these values operate in the workplace (Infante & Gorden, 1987).

Even though this theory emphasizes the individual, it is properly classified as a covering laws theory because it does not focus on individual freedom to *choose* values. Instead, it implies that those who live in a particular culture will be influenced to adopt the values of that culture. Being immersed in United States culture for a number of years thus *causes* us to value independent-mindedness. The theory does not investigate why or how individuals come to prefer these values to others; it assumes that the force of culture is so strong that individuals influenced by United States culture *will* value independence. If you were born and raised in the United States, you might be willing to grant this assumption. Certainly, as children, we did not deliberately decide to adopt or reject the values of our culture. Some adults do reject mainstream cultural values (for example, hippies in the 1960s who chose to live collectively in communes), but most people adopt the values of their culture without making a conscious decision to do so. The influence of society is so strong that it has shaped us to conform to values upheld by our culture. The Theory of Independent-Mindedness also has a hint of a systems perspective in that it treats individuals and organizations as part of a larger cultural system. The theory assumes that organizations must reflect the larger culture of their workers if they wish to manage effectively. So, while investigations of the Theory of Independent-Mindedness have focused on superior-subordinate communication and relationships (a form of interpersonal communication), the theory itself suggests applications for group and organization-wide communication. It thus deals with four levels of a system—cultural, organizational, dyadic (superior-subordinate), and individual—and implies a fifth level, small group communication.

Recently, researchers have begun to test the Theory of Independent-Mindedness through a series of studies relating communication behaviors which reflect independent-mindedness to organizational effectiveness, measured by productivity and job satisfaction. First, they investigated the relationship between verbal aggressiveness and argumentativeness and satisfaction with one's supervisor and the supervisor's upward influence (Jablin, 1980; Pelz, 1952). Upward influence is the supervisor's ability to influence those at higher levels of the organization. Researchers hypothesized that subordinates who perceived their supervisors as very argumentative but not verbally aggressive would be more satisfied with their jobs and more argumentative themselves (Infante & Gorden, 1985). Research on homophily and interpersonal similarity suggests that we like people we think are similar to us (see Chapter 9), so subordinates with very argumentative superiors should also be argumentative. If subordinates are satisfied with their jobs, they should also think themselves similar to their supervisors, since satisfaction with a superior was one way researchers measured job satisfaction in the study. Other components of job satisfaction were career satisfaction, number of promotions, salary, satisfaction with a superior's effectiveness with higher management, and satisfaction with employee rights. Two hundred sixteen members of a variety of midwestern organizations completed questionnaires measuring the variables listed above. The hypothesis was strongly supported. The most satisfied subordinates had very argumentative but not verbally aggressive supervisors. These subordinates felt their superiors were more effective in influencing upper management (upward influence) than did subordinates with other types of supervisors. One part of the hypothesis received little support: similarity between subordinates' and supervisors' argumentativeness was not strongly related to subordinate satisfaction. The authors concluded that, "candid dispute appears positively associated with a satisfying corporate culture" (Infante & Gorden, 1985, p. 124). Another investigation replicated this finding and indicated that subordinates were more satisfied with supervisors who encouraged them to argue work-related issues, even if the subordinates themselves did not like to argue (Gorden, Infante, & Graham, 1988).

Researchers also wondered how an organizational environment supporting employee rights and employee job satisfaction would affect supervisors' argumentativeness. They believed that subordinates who felt employee rights were respected by their organizations would have very argumentative but not verbally aggressive supervisors and would be more satisfied with their jobs than other employees. Using the same data described above, the investigators found that employees who believed the organization respected their rights did not have immediate supervisors who were verbally aggressive. However, they found no relationship between respect for employee rights and highly argumentative supervisors. Employees who perceived that their rights were protected reported higher salaries, more career satisfaction, and more satisfaction with their superiors and the superiors' upward influence (Gorden & Infante, 1987). These results indicate the key factor in a culture supporting employee rights may be the degree that subordinates like to argue and are encouraged to do so.

Finally, investigators using 131 superior-subordinate dyads from a variety of organizations investigated the communicator styles associated with argumentativeness and verbal aggressiveness and the relationship between communicator style (see Chapter 5). Norton's (1983) concept of communicator style indicates how things are said, not what is said. A speaker's communicator style indicates how receivers should interpret his or her words (Norton, 1978). The researchers expected that differences in communicator style would explain differences in supervisors' argumentativeness and influence with those at the top of the organizational hierarchy (upward influence). Using questionnaires, supervisors rated themselves on upward effectiveness and their subordinates on communicator style (Montgomery & Norton, 1981), argumentativeness (Infante & Rancer, 1982), and verbal aggressiveness (Infante & Wigley, 1986). Subordinates rated their superiors on upward effectiveness, communicator style, argumentativeness, and verbal aggressiveness. Supervisors who were verbally aggressive but not very argumentative were rated very inattentive and somewhat unfriendly and low on impression leaving, relaxed, and communicator image by their subordinates. Supervisors who had verbally aggressive subordinates found the subordinates dramatic, dominant, and open, but less friendly, less attentive, and less relaxed. Subordinates who were perceived to be more argumentative were thought to have strong communicator images and to be precise, attentive, animated, relaxed, impression leaving, dominant, and friendly. Next, the researchers related the superiors' upward effectiveness to superiors' argumentativeness, verbal aggressiveness, and communicator styles, as perceived by subordinates. The results confirmed the experimenters' expectations. Argumentativeness most strongly predicted upward effectiveness. Superiors with relaxed and impression leaving communicator styles who thought they had high upward influence were judged more effective with higher management by their subordinates (Infante & Gorden,1987).

This last experiment is especially important because it links communication to upward influence, a variable related to organizational effectiveness. Research shows that supervisors and subordinates find argumentativeness to be a positive trait in each other. Furthermore, argumentativeness and some communicator style variables are related to both superiors' and subordinates' ratings of the superiors' upward influence in the organization. There are several implications in these results. First, argumentativeness was viewed favorably in the series of studies presented. Second, argumentativeness is related to organizational effectiveness. Thus, the results of these studies supported the Theory of Independent-Mindedness. These studies indicate that organizations in the United States should foster independent-mindedness rather than Japanese collectivist values in order to be more effective businesses (Infante & Gorden, 1987). In fact, superiors should be trained to encourage subordinates to argue corporate issues (Infante, 1987a), since this encouragement is an important part of the organization's communication climate (Gorden, Infante, & Graham, 1988). Based on these findings, organization members should be trained in the following communication skills:

1. argumentation
2. interpersonal communication (to teach an affirming communicator style)
3. freedom of speech and communication research methods (to enable participants to understand the connection between communication climates and independent-mindedness)
4. public speaking and small group communication (Infante, 1987a)

If the Independent-Mindedness model became the foundation of communication education, organizational communication training would eventually make workers more satisfied and organizations more productive (Infante, 1987a).

The Theory of Independent-Mindedness provides an example of the benefits of covering laws research in organizations. It has four major strengths: (1) The theory is testable; a series of studies have shown that argumentativeness is a favorable trait and that it is related to satisfaction with supervisor and upward effectiveness. Empirical support for the theory has begun to accumulate; (2) The theory is consistent with other theories and research in the field. Although the theory challenges the conventional wisdom that organizations should demand unquestioned obedience to authority, it produces research consistent with theories of employee voice (Pacanowsky, 1982); (3) The theory is useful; it indicates how organizational training should be changed to increase members' productivity; and (4) researchers have tested the theory using actual superiors and subordinates in organizations rather than by asking inexperienced participants to predict what they *might* do. One of the problems with organizational communication research is that many early researchers drew conclusions from research involving inexperienced participants who role-played organizational situations.

Most of the weaknesses of the theory relate to its newness. Support for the theory was weaker than expected in one experiment (Gorden & Infante, 1987), but overall the research confirms the theory's predictions. Researchers involving more participants will continue to test the theory. Some might criticize the theory as an interpersonal communication theory masquerading as an organizational theory. So far only dyadic communication has been investigated. However, the suggestions about small group and public speaking training and the broad theoretical underpinnings of the theory suggest that the authors plan to extend it to additional levels of the organization.

Scholars in business might challenge some of the fundamental assumptions of the theory. The theory claims that independent-mindedness is closely associated with organizational effectiveness. Business and economic theorists believe that productivity has declined in the United States and increased in Japan because of several economic factors: The United States has maturing industries, whereas Japan is just now experiencing the growth curve of productivity that the United States experienced in the period after World War II. Plants and equipment in basic U.S. industries such as steel are much older than those in newer Japanese factories. The Japanese government and banks are closely associated with and support key Japanese businesses; business and government are relatively more independent in the United States. These business and economic reasons for changes in productivity might better explain the current situation than the Theory of Independent-Mindedness, and they are characteristic of a systems approach to organizations. A systems theory would focus on external environmental factors like the economy and government as well as internal variables such as management practices to account for differences in productivity. Nevertheless, much has recently been written about the failure of current American management practices and the loyalty of Japanese workers to their organizations (Ouchi, 1981). Gorden and Infante do relate interpersonal communication to culture, an element of the environment in which organizations operate.

Rules theorists might object that the research has ignored what individuals mean when they say they are satisfied with their supervisors and jobs. In most of the studies, participants completed questionnaires which yielded scores on different variables. Then the researchers related argumentativeness to satisfaction and supervisors' upward effectiveness using statistical methods. A rules researcher might prefer to interview workers and ask them *why* they were or were not satisfied with their supervisors. Asking them whether or not their supervisors encourage argumentativeness and whether that encouragement is an important part of their job satisfaction might demonstrate a more direct association than the type of research conducted by covering laws researchers.

Perhaps workers are satisfied with supervisors who allow independent decision-making as well as those who encourage arguing, and it is the independent decision-making and lack of close supervision, not the arguing, that makes them most satisfied with supervisors. Rules researchers would emphasize workers' self-knowledge about what management styles and supervisor characteristics are most effective and satisfying. On the other hand, laws researchers might respond that asking someone why he or she is satisfied with a supervisor might be like asking someone why he or she has fallen in love. If asked that question, you might list positive traits about your beloved, but you might not be able to give a "real" answer. We can give a response to the question, but we might admit to ourselves that we really do not know the "true" reason; we simply know how we feel. Similarly, the covering laws researcher would say asking people why they are satisfied with their supervisors will result in a response, but the answer might only focus on a recent incident or it might compare the current supervisor with an extremely difficult former supervisor. Neither of those responses would truly answer the question asked. If the question requires individuals to produce self-knowledge that they do not possess, their replies will not be valid. Their answers will not indicate the "true" reasons for differences in supervisor satisfaction, even though the answers are honest attempts to do so.

Additional criticisms are directed at some of the theoretical connections made in the Theory of Independent-Mindedness. The theory deals with rather abstract concepts like independent-mindedness and culture. However, independent-mindedness is studied by measuring only one variable, arguing in a particular style (being highly argumentative), rather than as a cluster of variables. Critics have charged that this rather simple way to study such an abstract concept oversimplifies the main concept of the theory. Tests of the model have been incomplete. Recall that the theory states that organizations which foster independent-mindedness will be more productive. Yet, to date researchers have never examined *actual* productivity variables such as hourly production rates. They have *assumed* that worker satisfaction leads to greater productivity, an assumption which the organizational literature does not always support. Further testing of the theory will be needed before scholars can be confident that fostering independent-mindedness and high argumentativeness will make business more productive.

Uncertainty Reduction Theory

Another study of organizational communication from the covering laws perspective relies on a theory presented in Chapter 9, Berger and Calabrese's (1975) Uncertainty Reduction Theory. Lester (1987) extended Uncertainty Reduction Theory by applying it to the process of socializing new organizational members. Like students taking a new course, new members of an organization try to predict how successful they are likely to be. In order to achieve success, new members must make choices their supervisors consider most appropriate from a range of behaviors available to organizational members. Lester believed that new members would have more confidence in predicting how they were likely to be evaluated (evaluative confidence) as they became more certain about what behaviors the organization viewed as effective (behavioral certainty).

Lester (1987) developed thirteen postulates relating uncertainty reduction to evaluative confidence measured as the new member perceives them. The first set of relationships relates to organizational variables and activities. Organization members will increase their evaluative confidence as they become more certain about appropriate behavior in the organization. When the available gains and losses (pay, promotion, job risks) for organization members differ widely throughout the organization, a newcomer's evaluative confidence will be low. When gains and losses are similar across the organization, evaluative confidence will rise. Receiving feedback (whether positive or negative) and participating in initiation rituals such as orientation programs will increase both behavioral certainty and evaluative confidence. Hearing a variety of different organizational stories repeated by different people will increase behavioral certainty because the stories will give the new member information about how the organization has evaluated members' behaviors in the past. Clear organizational identity and goals will also increase behavioral certainty. Communicating will increase both the member's behavioral certainty and the perceived level of influence within the organization. Increases in status relative to other organization members will also increase perceived influence. High degrees of perceived influence will increase evaluative confidence. In the event that employment (or activity) with an organization is not successful, organization members will look to alternative organizations as possibilities for employment or other types of involvement, such as membership. Individuals who have much relevant prior experience and who have many links to other, similar organizations will feel more independent from the organization. Feeling independent will increase members' evaluative confidence. While Lester (1987) has formed an impressive set of hypotheses by combining previous research findings, these hypotheses have yet to be investigated. Lester's Theory of Uncertainty Reduction in Organizations must be tested through empirical research.

Superior-Subordinate Communication Effectiveness

An extension of the Coordinated Management of Meaning (CMM) rules theory to organizations provides an excellent contrast to Gorden and Infante's Theory of Independent-Mindedness because Laird, Johnson, and Downs 1982) also attempted to investigate productivity and satisfaction with supervisor. You will notice the differences in methodology as you read more about the study below. You might want to review the section in Chapter 3 about the

Coordinated Management of Meaning to refresh your memory about the key points of that theory, although some will be repeated here.

Laird, Johnson and Downs (1982) attempted to discover what the Central Reservations Control (CRC) Department of a major airline considered to be productive behavior, an example of a definition (constitutive) rule. Then they investigated what behavior (regulative) rules governed how productive and unproductive people related to others at work. They wanted to find out what speech acts and other behaviors were obligatory and which ones were prohibited in order for a person to be considered productive. They also tried to determine how much each employee knew about the rules superiors and subordinates in the group followed. First, the researchers conducted interviews with 150 employees of CRC; they interviewed four reservations agents, four supervisors, and all three managers. They found that the department had one overall manager to oversee two functional managers. One manager supervised operations, and one services. The two functional managers each managed three or four supervisors. The list of interview questions (interview schedule or protocol) consisted of questions designed to lead respondents to give examples of productive and unproductive behavior in the organization. Also included were questions about knowledge of others' rules, such as, "What things does your manager consider most productive about an agent?" (Laird, Johnson, & Downs, 1982, p. 19). The data from the interviews revealed that all the employees agreed on six types of productive behavior: "(1) employees should follow a chain of command when making suggestions; (2) managers should provide clear and timely information; (3) superiors should reinforce employees when they do a good job; (4) superiors must be fair and consistent; (5) criticism should only be offered in private; (6) and superiors must delegate authority as well as responsibility" (Laird, Johnson, & Downs, 1982, p. 19). The employees disagreed about whether four types of behavior were productive: (1) whether managers should closely monitor agents' work by walking around the department; (2) whether subordinates should approach supervisors for help with personal matters; (3) whether subordinates should frequently visit a supervisor's office; and (4) whether performance and company rewards were strongly related.

Using the interview data, Laird, Johnson, and Downs (1982) constructed four scenarios of interaction between agents and supervisors. These scenarios represented episodes according to the Coordinated Management of Meaning Theory. In Episode One both supervisor and agent behaved productively according to the organizational rules discovered in the interviews. Episode Two portrayed ineffective behavior on the part of both supervisor and agent. Episodes Three and Four were designed to explore behaviors about which interviewees disagreed. In Episode Three the researchers expected all respondents to agree that the agent's behavior was effective but to disagree about the supervisor's behavior. In this episode, the supervisor closely monitors an agent's work, interrupting the agent's phone call to offer a correction and suggestion. The supervisor comments, "Well, I just like to watch all the agents doing their jobs, so that I can get an idea of everyone's performance. I'll be checking by again this afternoon" (Laird, Johnson, & Downs, 1982, p. 44). While some interviewees had indicated this type of monitoring was productive behavior, most agents interviewed felt it was ineffective. Episode Four explored a disagreement about agent effectiveness. The company allowed discussion of personal problems with supervisors, and managers and supervisors reported they actively encouraged this type of discussion. However, some agents had indicated they were afraid negative information revealed during counseling might be held against them in future performance reviews. For example, "One agent commented that she had once gone to her supervisor with a problem that she was having with her baby, only to be told a few months later in a performance appraisal meeting that she did not devote herself totally to the job because she was too concerned with personal family problems" (Laird, Johnson, & Downs, 1982, p. 25). In Episode Four, the agent enters the supervisor's office to ask for help and some time off without pay. The agent begins to cry about the breakup of a marriage and problems with children and the house. The supervisor expresses sympathy and willingness to consider the request if the agent will change schedules with another agent if necessary. The agent agrees and thanks the supervisor for helping. Follow-up interviews indicated that the original interviewees agreed the situations seemed realistic and judged productivity in the ways expected.

Employees completed questionnaires consisting of the four scenarios followed by questions which asked respondents to evaluate the superior and subordinate in each episode on qualities such as communication competence and productivity. Respondents were also asked whether or not they could have predicted the behavior of the second party given the action of the first person mentioned in the episode and whether alternate actions would have been appropriate. Six CRC departments were the focus of the analysis. The CRC manager had rated two as highly productive, two moderately productive, and two low in productivity. However, only a total of 3 questionnaires were received from members of the rather unproductive departments, so the researchers could only compare highly and moderately productive departments for this organization.

The results revealed several differences between managers' and agents' rules for productivity and evaluation. In Episode One, while both managers and agents agreed the agent's behavior was productive, agents expected the employee to be more highly rewarded than did managers. The authors attribute this difference to differences in definition and behavior rules about which actions deserve rewards. In the interviews one manager had commented that employees expected to be rewarded too often for merely performing their jobs. However, agents complained that they seldom received positive feedback. In Episode Three managers did tend to see the supervisor's close monitoring behavior as more productive than did agents, but this difference was not statistically significant. An interesting pattern emerged between departments for the fourth episode, the one concerning discussing personal problems with the supervisor. Members of one moderately productive department felt the employee's self-disclosure was more productive than members of the other moderate or the two highly productive departments. Although the differences were small, departments differed quite often about how much choice individuals had in obeying rules and their ability to predict outcomes. The authors believe these differences indicate members of less productive departments may be merely obeying implicit organizational rules about productivity rather than understanding them in a deeper fashion. Members with a greater degree of communication competence understand not only what the rules are but also the logic behind them. They know not only that a particular behavior is productive but also understand the broader rule that explains why the action is productive. Therefore, they are able to imagine other actions which also might satisfy the productivity rule even though those actions might not have been previously specified to them. Their deeper understanding of the rules makes them more competent communicators because they are able to imagine how the rules would operate in new situations. The connection between communication and productivity was confirmed by the fact that respondents agreed that, "How well I communicate significantly affects how productive I am in my job" (Laird, Johnson, & Downs, 1982, p. 25).

This study illustrates some of the strengths as well as problems of rules approaches to the study of communication. It is quite interesting because it explores meanings below the surface to discover organizational members' deeper understandings of what productivity means (definition rules) and what one should do to be productive or rewarded (behavior rules) by the organization. It is unfortunate that a low questionnaire return rate prevented the authors from comparing the rules and communicative competence of members of low and high productive departments. By understanding the reasons for lack of communicative competence, managers in the organization might clarify the definitions and rules for productivity so that both managers and agents would be more satisfied.

The theory, however, has several weaknesses. First, the rules experiment was more complicated and time-consuming than the covering laws research reported earlier. In the covering laws experiments on independent-mindedness, the researchers defined argumentativeness for respondents and asked them to identify such behavior, then related argumentativeness to satisfaction. It took a much more complicated process for the Coordinated Management of Meaning theorists to investigate individuals' understandings of the terms. The rules researchers share the same problem as the argumentativeness researchers. Neither can state with absolute certainty that their experiments have established the relationship of their variable (communicative competence or argumentativeness) with productivity. The rules experiment was more costly in terms of experimenter time and effort because it involved several stages of interviews, designing a comparatively long questionnaire and four scenarios, then analyzing the interviews and questionnaire data. The greater experimental costs of rules research have been responsible in part for the relative scarcity of these types of experiments. Second, the theory as presented would be difficult to disconfirm. What if the researchers had found that unproductive groups and very productive groups had the same behavior and definition rules for productivity? Would that result have "counted against" the Coordinated Management of Meaning Theory? Could the researchers have replied that the groups shared understanding but not the training or ability necessary to perform? If the researchers had suggested testing to see whether there were differences in communicative competence between the groups, what would have happened if no differences were found? What if the researchers suggested that the members of unproductive groups followed informal group rules for low productivity rather than formal organizational rules? It is difficult to think of a "test" by which the use of rules themselves could be disproved. (See Brenders, 1987, for a comprehensive, theoretical critique of CMM).

In contrast, if the experiments on independent-mindedness had indicated that subordinates with superiors who valued argumentativeness were *not* more satisfied than others, that finding would have provided strong evidence against the hypothesis that organizations must affirm values consistent with larger cultural values, at least with regard to independent-mindedness. The covering laws theory is more clearly able to be tested and thus more strongly supported when confirming evidence is found. For example, think about the finding that members of one moderately productive department felt the employee's self-disclosure in Episode 4 was more productive than members of the other moderate or the two highly productive departments. While this could indicate that members of one department had different productivity rules, it might also simply show that one supervisor was a more sympathetic and supportive counselor than the other three and that he or she acted consistently to "practice what he/she preached." The experimental result itself does not actually confirm the presence of different rules although different rules are one of the inferences that can be drawn from this finding. In general, the Laird, Johnson, and Downs (1982) experiment provides a good illustration of the earlier statement that rules theories are strong in explanation but weaker in prediction than covering laws theories. Comparing the Gorden and Infante and Laird, Johnson, and Downs research provides an excellent contrast of how theorists using different paradigms investigate similar topics of productivity and satisfaction in organizations through very different methods and by asking very different questions.

Two Systems Theories of Organizational Communication

In the next section two systems theories will be discussed to illustrate the point in Chapter 3 that systems theories do not contain the same level of philosophical assumptions about the nature of reality as do laws and rules theories. Instead, the developers of systems theories imply that systems are held together by law, rules, or both. We have chosen two theories to exemplify the difference in rule-governed and law-governed theories of organizations as systems.

Weick's Theory of Organizational Information

Karl Weick's (1969) book, the *Social Psychology of Organizing*, has been very influential in the field of organizational communication. Note that the title of Weick's book refers not to organizations but to organizing. Weick's model focuses on the idea that organizations come into being through continuous human activity. What is your college or university? You may identify its location or the buildings on campus, but they are not really the "heart" of the school. The school is made up of the people who come together to organize themselves into an educational institution. It is this organizing activity that Weick's theory attempts to explain. Weick considers communication the crucial means by which organizing occurs, and information is the key feature of the organizational environment. Weick borrows his concepts of information from information theory in which information is synonymous with "necessary information" or "what you need to know that you do not know yet" (see Chapter 4). Suppose you attempt to register for a closed class, and the registrar's office requires three items: (1) a clearance form stating you have paid your previous bills and owe no fines; (2) a computer registration card that indicates you have been admitted, have declared a major, and have met appropriate minimum grade point requirements; and (3) a permission card with the appropriate permit number to be admitted to a closed class. If you ask a friend what you need to get into the class and the friend replies, "A permit number," you have reduced 1/3 of the previous uncertainty in the system. However, if you stand in line with only the permit number, you will not be allowed to register since all three pieces of information are needed. Having some information helps you to reduce uncertainty. If you are attempting to repair a broken office copier which shows a red trouble light, and you know that the machine shows a yellow light when there is a paper jam, you do not have to consider problems with the paper feeding system. Having the information about the meaning of red and yellow lights allows you to reduce the possible causes of the trouble, so you have fewer alternatives to consider, fewer parts of the machine to check. In this sense, information helps to reduce the number of decisions you must make.

Weick uses the concept of uncertainty reduction from information theory to show that organization members perform communication activities to reduce uncertainty from their environment. Rules and communication-behavior cycles allow organizations to cope with the uncertainty (equivocality) in messages they receive from the environment. Information that is equivocal may be interpreted in several different ways. Suppose a professor assigns the class a term paper, then leaves town for the three weeks until the paper is due. The professor has given no further instructions, has no teaching assistant, and no one else on the staff knows anything about the assignment. For students who have taken classes from the professor before, that message is less equivocal than for students who have never written a paper for the professor. If the professor has graded previous term papers of yours, you have a much clearer idea of what to expect than if this is your first class with him or her. Weick's model predicts that students familiar with the professor's standards and expectations will approach the situation differently from students taking the professor's class for the first time. Students familiar with the professor will probably follow the procedures that have been successful for them in previous courses. New students will probably ask students familiar with the professor a series of questions designed to "pin down" just what the professor wants in a term paper. What does the professor consider a term paper? What sort of topic is appropriate? How long must the paper be? What type of research material is acceptable? Does the professor put more emphasis on outside reading or on original evaluation of the material? What footnote or reference form is required? These are just a few of the many questions you might have in mind. Organizations follow similar processes in interpreting environmental messages. "Organization members decipher information inputs, interpreting the level of ambiguity of messages, just as an individual decodes messages in creating meanings for them. Organization members create their appropriate responses to information inputs just as an individual encodes message responses" (Kreps, 1986, p. 118).

According to Weick's theory, if the information received is clear (has a low level of ambiguity or is unequivocal), organizations use *rules* to process and react to the information. They apply previously adopted rules to decide how ambiguous the message is, then search through the "standard responses" the organization has created in the past to deal with such situations. Students familiar with the professor in the example above used rules formed in the past in the professor's courses to write the paper for the new course. A form letter is another good example (Kreps, 1986, p. 119). If you are a customer service representative for a radio manufacturer and receive a letter complaining about a broken part in a new radio, you probably will have a form letter and a standard set of procedures to use. The letter probably assures the customer that the radio is still in warranty, so the part will be replaced without charge. It may provide a list of authorized service dealers or instructions for returning the radio to the manufacturer. It probably ends with an apology for the inconvenience and a statement that the organization values the customer's continued business.

If, however, you receive a request for a part for an antique radio that your company stopped producing in 1950 from a customer who is an antique dealer with a very valuable radio, you would not have a form letter to handle the inquiry. The information in the customer's letter is very equivocal or ambiguous compared with the "categories of customer inquiries" the organization has developed. In order to help the customer, you must perform a series of *communication-behavior cycles*. You might first ask your supervisor what part of the company handles repair parts. Then you would contact someone in that division to see if the part is still available. If it is not and you truly wish to help the customer, you might check to see if the supplier who manufactured the parts for your company in 1950 is still in business and call to see if the supplier makes an equivalent part. Then you might be sure to keep a copy of your records and the correspondence in case you get a similar inquiry in the future.

According to Weick (1969), organizations follow three major steps during the organizing process. The first step is *enactment*. During this phase, the organization members attend to information in the surrounding environment. As they interpret the incoming information, they re-create (enact) the environment in a sense. Does the information that interest rates are increasing rapidly indicate a favorable or unfavorable economic environment? That depends on whether you are a borrower or a lender. If you need to borrow money to buy a car, the environment is unfavorable for you. If you have just earned a big salary at a summer job and put the money in a money market account to pay next year's tuition, the news may make you smile. Similarly, during enactment organization members must decide what the information means for their organization and transmit that message. In transmitting the information as they have interpreted it, they re-create or reenact the environment.

In the enactment phase, rules and cycles are used to interpret and process the information. If you are a new student, your reaction to the term paper in the example above will depend upon the answers you received to the questions you asked. Those questions and answers constituted cycles of double interacts. A double interact is "a three-part exchange of conditionally related messages: act, response, and adjustment" (Kreps, 1986, p. 119). Thus your question, the answer, and your follow-up question or other response formed a double interact. You performed several cycles of double interacts until you felt you had sufficient information to complete the term paper (or until you had exhausted the patience of your classmates).

One of the key principles of Weick's theory is called the *principle of requisite variety*. Organizations attempt to interpret information to produce an optimal level of uncertainty (equivocality) for their members. In order to do so, organizations should use processes with the same level of equivocality as the messages themselves for optimum effectiveness. In other words, very complex or equivocal messages require equivocal organization processes (communication-behavior *cycles*) to enact them. On the other hand, simple, routine, unambiguous messages require only simple, uncomplicated processes (following organizational *rules*) for enactment. You can see that form letters save time for organizations. It would be unnecessary and wasteful to draft a separate letter every time the organization received a repair request if the organization deals with many requests of that type. Similarly, if the organization wishes to retain customer loyalty and provide service, it would be a mistake to respond to unusual inquiries with form letters. In response to an inquiry about the cost of a questionnaire, one of your authors received a form letter from an organization which publishes training materials. The letter consisted of a list of sentences with blanks beside them for the customer service representative to check. One appropriate sentence was checked, but nowhere was there the price and quantity information requested. This letter was an example of an organization's using rules to deal with relatively equivocal information when it should have used cycles. As Weick (1969) states, "It takes equivocality to remove equivocality. This means that processes must have the same degree of order or chaos as there is in the input of these processes" (p. 40). We will return to the principle of requisite variety, that the complexity of organizational processes should match the complexity of the environmental inputs, in our discussion of research investigating Weick's theory.

The second major organizational process is *selection*. During this phase, the organization makes decisions about the information it has processed using rules or cycles. Is it sufficiently clear to be useful, or does the equivocality need to be further reduced by using new rules and cycles? In the term paper example, when you feel you have a clear enough understanding of what the professor requires to select a topic and begin to search for information, you have entered the selection phase. At some point you might decide you need further information about footnotes and length and decide to repeat your cycles of questions and answers. Or you may decide you should ask a different classmate for the information to see whether the answers you are given by different people are consistent. If you have discovered that a classmate who is talkative, self-confident and willing to answer all your questions has a very low grade-point average, you might place less confidence in the information. You might decide the information is more equivocal than you at first thought, and you need to repeat more cycles to clarify or confirm the professor's expectations.

The final, *retention* phase corresponds to keeping a copy of the records and correspondence in the radio company example presented above. In this phase the organization decides whether or not to change its standard ways of responding to different inputs. The organization evaluates the rules and cycles used to see whether they should be dropped or retained for future use. Maybe the radio company will draft a separate form letter for obscure parts requests. Perhaps you will identify one particular classmate as a source of valid information about what professors expect on term papers and decide to interact with that person in the future should the need arise, or you may decide you like the professor's approach to term papers so well that you will adopt his or her requirements as your standard rules for approaching term papers. The repertoire of rules developed in the retention phase constitutes *organizational intelligence* (Kreps, 1986, p. 123). It is information stored in the organization's collective memory which may be used in the future to guide the group's actions more effectively.

Why is Weick's theory considered a rule-governed or human action theory of organizations? Of course, he uses the term *rules* to identify an important process in his model. In addition, Weick emphasizes the individual's or individual organization's *interpretation* as a key feature of the theory. The concepts that organizations must re-enact or recreate the environment during the enactment phase and that they actively choose to use rules, cycles, or both and select and retain them for future reference are evidence that Weick's theory is firmly grounded in assumptions about interpretation and choice-making. Note that, like the Coordinated Management of Meaning organizational communication theory just discussed, Weick's theory lists the types of behaviors available, rules and cycles, but does not specify the *content* of an individual organization's rule. Nevertheless, Weick's principle of requisite variety does have implications for organizational effectiveness.

For his Ph.D. dissertation, Gary Kreps (1980) tested Weick's principle of requisite variety. For one academic year, he investigated how the University of Southern California faculty senate used rules and cycles to process information. The faculty senate represents the faculty in university government. Tasks are accomplished by discussing and voting on motions, then presenting the motions to higher levels of the university government. The researcher considered two types of senate motions, those with high or low information equivocality. As the equivocality of motions increased, the researcher predicted that the number of communication-behavior cycles in the form of discussion by faculty senate members would also increase. In other words, motions with low equivocality would result in short discussions, while highly equivocal motions would provoke much discussion and debate; many cycles of communication interacts would result. Using written and audio transcripts, Kreps studied the 24 motions acted on during the 1977-78 academic year. He measured the equivocality of motions by surveying faculty senators, who rated each motion on three semantic-differential type scales: complicated-uncomplicated, unpredictable-predictable, and ambiguous-unambiguous (See Appendix for information about semantic differential scales). He then classified Senators' responses to each motion as acts, responses, or adjustments. Based on the questionnaire results, Kreps divided the 24 motions into two categories, high and low equivocality. Analysis indicated that there were statistically significant differences in the number of cycles used to respond to the two different categories of motions, indicating that the central assumption of Weick's model is accurate. Future researchers should investigate additional message variables proposed in the model.

Structural-Functional Systems

Farace, Monge, and Russell (1977) also adopt a systems perspective, but their theory suggests that organizational systems are governed by covering laws, not rules. Their theory provided an early, very influential synthesis of systems concepts for organizational communication. In fact, it has been called an "elegant integration" (Wilson, Goodall, & Waagen, 1986, p. 17). Farace, Monge, and Russell take a structural-functional approach to systems. They first identify key elements of the organizational structure. An organizational system consists of interdependent parts which use energy to process environmental inputs (information and materials), produce throughputs, and finally outputs or products. The analogy here refers to a manufacturing process which transforms raw material such as iron ore into a final product, steel bars, through several intermediate steps with intermediate products (throughputs). Like Weick, Farace, Monge, and Russell borrow from information theory in discussing communication in terms of uncertainty reduction. Two types of communication are important for organizations. *Absolute information* refers to the total amount of knowledge present in a system. In our office copier example, this would be the total number of parts that might break down to cause the red trouble light to appear. *Distributed information* is information which has circulated through the organization; it has been communicated. "Questions of absolute information deal with what is known; questions of distribution deal with who knows it" (Littlejohn, 1983, p. 257).

The theory describes four sublevels of the system hierarchy: individual, dyadic, group, and organizational. At every level, communication is structured in formal and informal networks. Inputs (such as messages) may be relatively complex or relatively simple and *flow* to individuals at a particular rate per unit of time (5 telephone calls per hour, for example). When the flow is too great to manage, a person experiences communication *overload*. If the rate is too slow, *underload* occurs. The concepts of rate, flow, complexity, overload and *underload* may also be used to describe other levels of the organizational hierarchy. It is possible for the entire organization to experience communication overload during a time of changing environmental conditions, such as the deregulation of the United States airline industry during the Carter administration. Information in organizations flows in patterns called *networks*. The communication structure or micronetwork is the network which links individuals in the group. Groups also are affected by power structures and leadership structures.

The network along which messages are transmitted between groups in the organization is the macronetwork. The macronetwork forms the organization's overall communication structure. The network consists of members and links (communication ties) between members. Links have five important characteristics: symmetry, strength, reciprocity, content, and mode or channel. *Symmetry* refers to the degree to which the link is initiated or used equally by both members. Do both give and take equally, or does one person always seek information and the other always provide it? If one person usually sends and the other receives, the link is an asymmetrical one. The strength of a link refers to use. A *strong link* is one that is frequently used, while a *weak link* is used only occasionally. Links are *reciprocal* (high in reciprocity) if both organization members report the link. If one person reports frequently using the link and the other says that no communication took place, the link is considered *unreciprocated* (low in reciprocity). *Content* of communication passing along the network might be work-related or social. *Mode* or *channel* refers to how the communication takes place: by telephone, in person, through group meetings, or in writing.

Organizational members may play different network roles. Members who have few or no links with others on the network are called *communication isolates*. *Bridges* and *liaisons* link two groups, but play different roles. A *liaison* links two groups but is not a member of either group. A *bridge* is a group member who links two groups and actually belongs to one of them. A *mediator*, a neutral third party like an ombudsman who helps settle a conflict, might perform a liaison role between two groups. A good example of an organizaional bridge was observed by a telephone company service representative. The group of service representatives were responsible for scheduling telephone installations and receiving customer complaints, while the repair department actually performed the work. There were communication problems between the two departments. The repair department felt service representatives frequently made unreasonable promises to customers, and the service representatives felt that the repair and installation employees often provided poor service and created unnecessary delays. Several steps were taken by management to improve communication between the two groups. First, all of the service representatives toured the repair department, which was located in another building in a different part of the city. Repair supervisors explained the duties of the department and the steps involved in completing orders written by the service representatives. Then, the managers appointed one service representative and one repair clerk to act as bridges between the groups. The service representative had previously worked in the repair department, so she understood their procedures and problems and had friends there. She also had had considerable experience as a service representative. When a customer had a difficult problem with a repair or installation order or needed a special request, the service representative who took the call asked the bridge representative to contact the repair department to solve the problem. While this procedure increased the number of links in the chain between the customer and the repairer or installer, it was effective because the quality of communication between the bridges was better than that between other members of each group. While one bridge was a service representative and the other was a repair clerk and each acted as a member of her own group, by talking to each other they helped improve the communication link between the two departments.

The second part of structural functionalism, as the name implies, consists of the functions which the parts of the system perform. Communication enables the organization: (1) to produce throughputs and outputs (*production*); (2) to change the system and generate new ideas for procedures and products (*innovation*); and (3) to maintain interpersonal relations among organizational members (*maintenance*). Even though the major purpose of an organization may be to produce automobiles, for instance, organization members must direct the work, coordinate the delivery of parts and distribution of finished automobiles, and control the entire production process on the assembly lines. *Production, innovation,* and *maintenance* are the three essential activities of communication systems.

No doubt you noticed many similarities between Weick's model of organizing and Farace, Monge, and Russell's structural functionalism. Both theories explain systems in terms of the vocabulary and properties of systems presented in Chapter 3. Both take a broader perspective than either the laws or rules theories presented at the beginning of this chapter. However, there are some differences. Weick's model emphasizes the organization's *understanding* of information, while structural functionalism analyzes key elements of the system's *structure* and identifies key activities. Weick's theory is more developed in that predictions such as the one tested by Kreps (1980) can be made from the model. Farace, Monge, and Russell (1977) are primarily concerned with identifying elements; extensions of the theory are needed to relate specific elements or properties to effective operation of the system. Even though we have identified Weick's theory as "systems plus rules," it is important to note that the principle of requisite variety is stated in the form of a covering law. Recall the statement quoted earlier, "It takes equivocality to remove equivocality" (Weick, 1969, p. 40). This principle is clearly presented in the form of a "law of nature" unresponsive to human choice or interpretation. The relationship between environmental equivocality and equivocal communication processes such as communication-behavior cycles is a necessary one produced by inherent characteristics of information and processing methods. Nevertheless, Weick's system theory places a strong emphasis on the role of rules and interpretations in enabling the system to function well in its information environment.

Both systems theories exhibit the typical strengths and weaknesses of this perspective. They focus our attention on the environment and multiple levels of the hierarchy, but away from individuals. In both systems theories, organization members are treated as interchangeable units who perform a particular function. For instance, a researcher investigating the role of bridges using structural-functionalism would be unlikely to deal with the personalities of the individuals performing that role. Another strength of both theories is the emphasis on interaction and *boundary-spanning*. In Weick's theory, it is clear that enactment takes place at the boundary between the organization and its environment. Most of the group roles and properties described by Farace, Monge, and Russell are designed to help groups coordinate their activities and communicate better. More and more theories in communication and other fields are incorporating interactions as important keys to explaining and predicting human behavior. This particular strength of systems theory is especially clear in the Fisher and Hawes Interaction System Model presented next.

Small Group Communication Theories

Fisher and Hawes' Interaction System Model

Fisher and Hawes' (1971) Interaction System Model was chosen to illustrate systems theories because it clearly relates patterns of interacts to small group communication. Fisher and Hawes argue that scholars studying small group communication should form theories based not on individual human behaviors but on interactions. Recall from the discussion of Weick's organizational communication theory that an *interact* is a behavior followed by a response from another individual. A *double interact* is a pattern of behavior-response-adjustment. By analyzing three levels of interaction patterns in small groups, Fisher and Hawes generated a theory explaining group behavior.

First, Fisher and Hawes categorize statements as belonging to one of six task categories. Each category represents the function a member's comment might perform with regard to a proposed decision. A member might: (1) interpret another's proposal; (2) substantiate another's claim; (3) clarify or (4) modify another's statement, or (5) agree or (6) disagree with a proposal. By counting how frequently different types of statements occur in different groups, the researcher can identify chains of interacts, patterns in which one type of statement consistently follows another type. Based on Fisher's (1980) work, Trenholm (1986) has synthesized a coding scheme for analyzing relational interacts. Relational messages are grouped into one of five categories— domineering, structuring, equivalence, deferring, and submitting—based on their relationship to the previous statement. These categories indicate attempts to communicate about the power balance in the relationship. For example, a domineering, or one-up statement, is a statement like an order or a challenge which indicates an attempt to control the other's behavior. An equivalence statement does not attempt to change the power balance of the interaction. Repetitions and agreements would be coded as equivalence statements by Fisher. Agreements and requests for information are considered one-down statements (deferring) because they indicate that the speaker is willing to give up conversational control to the other, at least temporarily. Unlike some small group coding schemes, in the Fisher and Hawes model a statement can be coded in both task and relationship categories at the same time.

Patterns of interacts called *interact phases* are identified in the second step of the Fisher and Hawes (1971) model. Fisher (1970) identifies four phases through which decisions emerge in task groups: orientation, conflict, emergence, and reinforcement. The *orientation phase* is characterized by tentative and ambiguously phrased statements. The discussion is filled with silences and pauses, and group members are polite, uncertain, and unwilling to commit to a decision. The *conflict phase* is more active than the orientation phase. Members introduce proposals more directly than before. They debate alternative proposals, form coalitions, and struggle for dominance and leadership. For example, if a group exhibited many agreement-disagreement interacts, these interact phases might indicate that the group was in the conflict phase. The *emergence phase* gets its name from the fact that the final solution tends to emerge during this part of the discussion. Conflict and arguments are reduced; coalitions formed earlier tend to dissolve. As in the orientation phase, there is much ambiguity, as members who previously had opposed solutions are able to express support for them in general terms. Consensus marks the *reinforcement phase*, in which the group supports and reinforces agreements reached in the emergence phase.

After all statements of a group transcript have been classified into interact categories, researchers identify phases by making a chart listing all possible interact categories on both the vertical and horizontal axes. Coders then fill in the matrix by placing a mark in the appropriate cell. For example, suppose the coders were to consider only the first three of the six task categories discussed above. They would then produce a 3 X 3 matrix like the one below:

	(1) Interpretation	(2) Substantiation	(3) Clarification
(1) Interpretation	1	1	
(2) Substantiation			
(3) Clarification			

If a coder found an interpretation following an interpretation, a tally would be placed in the upper left hand corner of the matrix. If a substantiation followed an interpretation, a tally would be placed in the cell to the immediate right of the previous cell, as the chart indicates. The coder would code each statement in the entire transcript, combining tallies to form a total number of interacts for each category. These interact patterns form the four phases mentioned above.

The third part of the model is the analysis of groups of phases, called cycles. Fisher (1980) found that decisions are modified by the group in a cyclical fashion. Several decisions are proposed and briefly discussed; later, some are reintroduced. The proposals seem to be produced in clusters when the group's energy for generating new solutions is high. Fisher's research indicates that these decision modification cycles tended to be one of two types. When conflict is high, group members appear to be debating and persuading each other to accept various proposals. The group reintroduces proposals in language equally as abstract as that in which they were first proposed while continuing to evaluate proposals in clusters. When conflict is relatively low, proposals are reintroduced in more specific form than the original presentation. Instead of saying, "Let's pass a law against drunk driving," discussants might reintroduce the proposal in more detail, for example, "Let's make driving while intoxicated punishable by a mandatory thirty-day suspension of a driver's license for a first offense." Instead of debating, the group follows a pattern similar to Dewey's (1910) reflective thinking model: state the problem, discuss criteria for a good solution, introduce an abstract solution, then present the solution in concrete form. The last two steps of decision modification are repeated in clusters for each decision considered.

The Fisher and Hawes (1971) Interaction System Model has made an important contribution to the field of communication because of its focus on interacts. True to its systems assumptions, the theory focuses on patterns of behavior and response. An additional strength is its emphasis on the interaction of message patterns. The model deals with three levels of message systems. Like other small group models, researchers have had difficulty in coding transcripts reliably; that is, coders often disagree about how to classify a particular act or interact. The coding is also time-consuming and tedious. The theory was developed by examining data, then describing the patterns that emerged. It remains to be extended to explain and predict effectiveness in small group decision-making.

An Input-Process-Output Problem-Solving Model

A recent experiment by Jarboe (1988) provides an excellent example of theory building from a covering laws perspective in small group communication. It also illustrates the difficulty of conducting research on small group behavior for some of the reasons mentioned for the Interaction System Model. After reviewing many studies of small group communication, Jarboe tested four competing models of small group problem-solving processes. She attempted to find the model that best explained why one group solved problems more effectively than another. Referring to the diagrams of these models presented in Figure 10.1 will be helpful as you read the description below.

The first is an *Input-Output Model*. Two major input variables are *discussion procedures* and *solution multiplicity*. Small group theorists use two major discussion procedures. One popular method is called reflective thinking, based on John Dewey's (1910) *How We Think*. This model is a very traditional one, but it is still used and taught in small group classes today. The reflective thinking procedure involves "careful exploration of symptoms, causes, and generation of criteria for an effective solution before a conclusion is reached" (Jarboe,

1988, p. 123). An alternative procedure, the nominal group technique, is also often taught to increase small group effectiveness. The nominal group technique is very different from reflective thinking. Each member of a nominal group first generates written ideas. These ideas are compiled into a list. Then, each member, one after the other, writes comments about the ideas, and the comments are circulated. Next, individuals rate or rank the ideas, then explain the reasons for their decisions. The last step produces a final ranking or rating. As you can see, the nominal group technique, as its name implies, produces a "group" in name only. There are very strict turn-taking, evaluation, and decision-making rules and procedures followed with the nominal group technique. In previous research, both reflective thinking and nominal group techniques have led to effective decision-making groups. Jarboe's second input variable, *solution multiplicity*, refers to the number of possible, effective solutions. A task with high solution multiplicity has a large number of "correct" solutions. A task with low solution multiplicity has few "correct" solutions, so the group has a limited range of alternatives (Shaw, 1963, 1981). The researcher chose a problem-solving task similar to those performed by organizational work-groups, since previous small group research had been criticized for presenting groups with unrealistic tasks (Hackman & Morris, 1975).

Jarboe found that the best measures of group effectiveness are two output variables: *productivity* and *satisfaction*. She studied three dimensions of each variable. Productivity was measured by number of ideas (or solutions) produced, number of *unique* ideas produced, and quality of ideas/solutions. Jarboe investigated how satisfied group members were with the problem-solving procedure used (reflective thinking or nominal group technique), with the group's product (the solution), and with the group. Jarboe combined the input and output variables to create the Input-Output Model I. She notes that both the nominal group technique (Delbecq, Van de Ven, & Gustafson, 1975; Van de Ven, 1973) and reflective thinking (Brilhart & Jochem, 1964; Maier & Thurber, 1969) produce high quality ideas, but she was the first researcher to compare the two procedures directly.

Jarboe then wanted to compare her Model I, which related input and output variables, with a model that included communication *processes*. After reviewing different coding schemes, she selected fifteen categories of messages produced by group members: solidarity, tension release, agreement, procedural suggestion, suggests solution, gives opinion, gives information, draws attention, asks for opinion, disagrees, tension increase, shows hostility, ego defensive, procedural remark, and other. Procedural remarks were comments about the group's process which did not include suggestions for change, for example, "Can't we speed up this discussion?" Jarboe (1986) had previously investigated the effects of discussion method and solution multiplicity on the fifteen types of statements through Model II, the *Input-Process Model*.

Jarboe (1988) also created Model III, the *Process-Output Model*, suggesting that the fifteen process variables would be directly related to satisfaction and productivity, the same output variables included in Model I. Jarboe (1988) created her final model by combining the other three. Previous research indicated that it is important to continue to study communication as a process variable (Cragan & Wright, 1980; Hirokawa, 1980; Poole & Folger, 1981). Jarboe also found that earlier research on input-process-output models was difficult to interpret (Katzell, Miller, Rotter, & Venet, 1970; Sorensen, 1973). As Hewes (1986) recommends, Jarboe used the Input-Output Model I to serve as a baseline to compare the communication Process-Output Model III to test whether communication or the input variables (discussion procedures and solution multiplicity) were more closely related to satisfaction and productivity. Thus, her first research question was: (1) Does communication or discussion procedures and solution multiplicity best explain differences in satisfaction and productivity between groups? Jarboe then investigated how communication affects satisfaction and productivity by comparing Model IV to the other models through her second research question, (2) Does adding communication to the Input-Output Model change the results or better explain the relationships between input and output variables? (See Figure 10.1).

Figure 10.1
Four Models of Small Group Communication
Model I: Input-Output Model

Discussion Procedures   Productivity

Number of Solutions ————————————————————→
(Solution Multiplicity)   Satisfaction

Model II: Input-Process Model

Discussion Procedures   Communication

Number of Solutions ————————————————————→
(Solution Multiplicity)   (Types of Statements)

Model III: Process-Output Model

Communication   Productivity

(Types of Statements) ————————————————————→ Satisfaction

Model IV: Input-Output-Process Model

Discussion Procedures   Productivity

Number of Solutions ————————————————————→
(Solution Multiplicity)   Types of Statements   Satisfaction

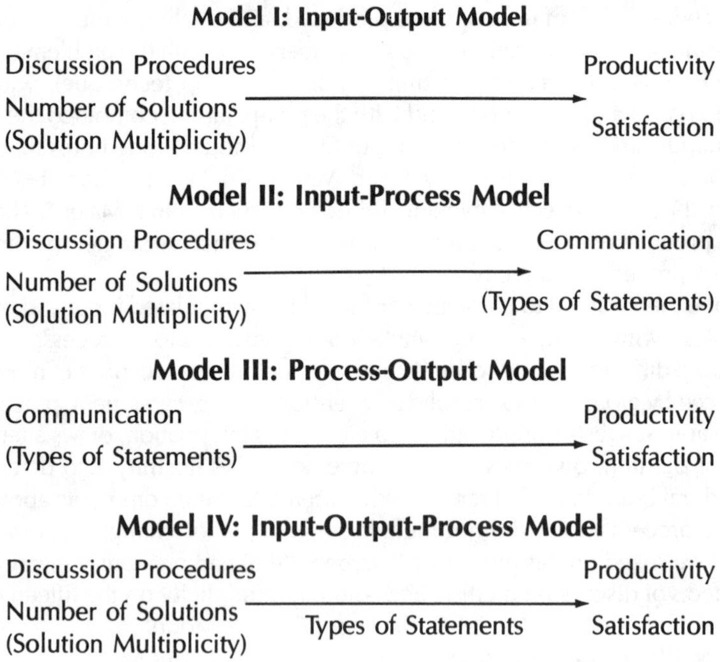

Jarboe (1988) investigated these research questions through an experiment involving 160 students in a group discussion class. The students were divided into ten four-person decision-making groups. After being trained in the problem-solving technique they were to use, students were asked to generate solutions to the following questions: "What can be done to prevent American teenagers from starting to smoke?" and "What can be done to prevent American teenagers from starting to drink?" The questions presented above formed the high solution multiplicity condition. Students in groups working in the low solution multiplicity condition had a greatly reduced number of possible solutions from which to choose. The group discussions, each lasting about thirty minutes, were videotaped. Then participants completed a satisfaction questionnaire designed to give information about their satisfaction with the group, the solution, and the problem-solving procedure. A team of coders counted the number of ideas and number of unique ideas produced, and a panel of expert judges (social scientists, teachers, and health care professionals) rated each solution for effectiveness, practicality, and social acceptability.

Overall, Model IV, the Input-Process-Output Model, best accounted for satisfaction with the group and with the solution. Model III, the Process-Output or Communication Model, best explained differences among group members in satisfaction with the procedure. Model I, the Input-Output Model, was least effective in predicting satisfaction, a fact which indicates that discussion procedures and solution multiplicity are not closely related to satisfaction. Therefore, Jarboe (1988) concludes, "Satisfaction . . . is understood better when communication is taken into consideration" (p. 140). Discussion procedures and solution multiplicity are related to differences in productivity, but Model IV, The Input-Process-Output Model, provided the best explanation of differences in all three productivity measures. Jarboe concludes that discussion procedures and solution multiplicity must be considered when explaining group productivity, just as communication cannot be ignored in explaining satisfaction. Model IV, the combined model, provided the best explanation for five of the six productivity and satisfaction outcome measures. Thus, the evidence seems to favor the Input-Process-Output Model as the best description of important variables in small group decision-making.

Jarboe's research has made a contribution to theory building in the area of small group decision-making. Her model integrates previous research and enables her to test competing theories of the variables that affect group productivity and satisfaction. Her model and experiment are especially interesting because they allow her to compare models that include communication with those that do not. Her conclusion that communication is essential to understanding satisfaction but that input variables are more closely associated with productivity is an important one that will need to be confirmed by further investigation.

As Jarboe (1988, p. 140) herself notes, while her model includes inputs, processes, and outputs, it is not a true systems model. Her process variables are really additional input variables, since both directly affect the output variables. In a true systems model, the effects of the input variables would be modified by communication (mediating variable) to produce satisfaction and productivity (the output variables). As indicated in the Fisher-Hawes (1971) model of small group communication presented above, true systems models consider sequential patterns of communication (rather than independent statements), and Jarboe's does not. For example, she does not code her transcripts for patterns such as "requests for opinions leading to ego defensiveness followed by tension increase" as a systems theorist would. Such interaction patterns might be very useful in explaining the communication process, perhaps more so than Jarboe's communication variables, which are measured only as percentages of the total number of statements. It is possible that two groups, each with many requests for opinions, might have exhibited those requests in very different communication contexts. Perhaps one group followed the "requests for opinions-ego defensiveness-tension increase" pattern suggested above, a pattern which indicates a high degree of interpersonal conflict, while the other's discussion followed a pattern of "requests for opinions-giving opinions-draws attention-clarifies." We might expect that these groups would have different levels of satisfaction and possibly productivity since the interaction patterns are so different. Jarboe's model does not yet take interaction sequences into account.

An additional weakness of Jarboe's research is the fact that her participants were undergraduate college students. Even though Jarboe's students were members of real class groups who received group rather than individual grades during the course, many social scientists would argue that the stakes and levels of experience in group problem solving are higher, group histories longer, and tasks more complicated and perhaps more involving in real work situations. If Jarboe's findings can be repeated with experienced business people who are members of actual work groups, her model will gain a strong measure of additional support. Perhaps then she can begin to derive hypotheses and make predictions to extend the model to produce a theory. At present her research is descriptive, indicating what variables are important and how they are related. Future research should work to strengthen the theoretical framework, suggesting and testing reasons to explain the pattern of relationships Jarboe found.

Bormann's Symbolic Convergence Theory

The final small group theory to be presented, Bormann's (1983) Symbolic Convergence Theory, is quite different from the two theories just discussed. While not a rules theorist, Bormann makes human action assumptions which are both typical of interpretive approaches and compatible with the focus on individual interpretation and choice-making that characterizes the rule-governed approach. Like other interpretive theorists, Bormann believes that stories and anecdotes shared by group and organization members reveal important rules and norms of the group. Stories which groups create about themselves and outsiders enable members to share a group identity and teach and reinforce norms about how "we" behave.

You will recall from the discussion in Chapter 4 that *fantasy theme analysis* is the method used by Bormann and those studying his theory to discover what meaning the stories have for the group. The symbolic communication of the group reveals the group's shared culture and values: its beliefs about who the group is and what its members are like. If you have ever discussed with a friend the different "personalities" of different colleges and universities, you have analyzed group identity and norms. Perhaps you have had friends who felt they could best explain what their school was like by telling you stories, creating a dramatic world of characters and plots related to important aspects of the college culture. Stories are involving for the speaker and audience and may excite and energize group members more than explanations. They may illustrate desirable behavior better than a set of rules and regulations. They also serve a persuasive function in motivating members to behave according to group norms. Bormann believes that, when several group members listen to a dramatic story, they share the group fantasy. By being caught up in the drama of the story, members identify with the heroes and against the group's enemies. Often group narratives in organizations concern the group's founder or a hero who exhibits the highest virtues of the organization.

Bormann analyzes group narratives by grouping them according to common fantasy themes. For example, your authors are familiar with a college which prides itself on its communication focus, especially on the ability of graduates to be effective public speakers. The kinds of stories told at the college upheld the importance of performance values and good delivery skills. Some stories dealt with famous personalities who had attended the school, worked hard, performed well on the senior speech exam, then achieved fame and fortune in the entertainment industry. Other stories concerned the school's founder and his personal theory of communication, which was taught to all freshmen and transfer students, regardless of major. Still other stories were tales of what it was like to be a student at the school's major competitor, which was located less than a mile away in the same city. Stories about the competitor emphasized the large class sizes and impersonal approach of faculty to contrast with the intimate, participative approach to education valued by students of the smaller college. These stories reflect two fantasy themes: the importance of performance skills and the value of a personal educational atmosphere. Narratives with the same fantasy theme may involve different characters and settings, but the "moral" or point of the story will be the same.

Narratives which attempt to answer a question or address a problem are called fantasy types. In the example above, fantasy types explained why students chose the smaller college and why the college had been so successful in producing famous actors and television personalities. Other colleges might have fantasy types designed to emphasize how difficult courses are or how difficult it is to be admitted. During freshman orientation in 1967, the president of Rice University in Houston, Texas, told students at the assembly to notice the people seated to their left and right. He concluded, "They won't be there when you graduate," indicating that only one-third of the freshmen present would eventually graduate from Rice. This story seems unusual now when colleges are working very hard to retain students enrolled as freshmen. However, in 1967 the president intended this story to motivate students by warning them how hard they would have to work and how special they would be if they graduated. They were already among the elite because they had been admitted; they would be even more elite if they worked hard enough to graduate. These examples indicate just a few of the types of fantasy themes found on college campuses.

Bormann believes that by sharing fantasies and fantasy types, group members come to share a *rhetorical vision*—a view of their identity in relation to each other and to non-group members. The vision forms a rhetorical community which cheers its heroes and boos its villains. Those who do not share the vision become outsiders. A fantasy theme which further illustrates this point is the "Quaker family" theme adopted by the Quaker Oats company. The company's symbol is a man in traditional dress associated with members of the Society of Friends. However, the Quaker Oats company has no association with the Quaker religious sect. The company adopted the Quaker symbol long ago as representative of sound, traditional, family values. That theme has remained strong at Quaker Oats up to the present. During orientation, employees are told that they are becoming part of the "Quaker family." At a small pet-food plant in Lawrence, Kansas, the plant manager knew each of the approximately 140 employees by name. In turn, they called him by his first name and frequently inquired about the welfare of his family, as he did theirs. Managerial and non-managerial employees mixed in outside groups such as the golf team for the plant. At lunch, managers were encouraged to sit with employees they supervised; a managers-only lunch table was strongly discouraged. Most of the employees were married with families. The "Quaker family" image was a fantasy theme which the company actively encouraged throughout its operations.

One of the strengths of Symbolic Convergence Theory is its focus on stories and other forms of symbolic behavior to explain group processes such as creating cohesiveness and developing norms and rules. Unlike the two theories presented earlier, fantasy theme analysis does not focus on categories of statements, but on the broader messages contained within the dramatic framework of the stories. One criticism of the theory is based on the breadth of its analysis. Some rhetorical critics charge that Bormann (1983) has not sufficiently explained how a fantasy theme is different from other rhetorical forms. Neither does Bormann's theory adequately explain how organizations choose among competing fantasy themes. Contemporary rhetorical critics analyze organizational stories and rituals to learn their meaning for the organization. It is not precisely clear how a fantasy theme differs from another type of organizational story that presents heroes and villains or how fantasy themes develop or are prevented from developing.

Summary

This chapter has traced the study of organizational communication from its roots in management theories developed after the Industrial Revolution gave rise to a class of professional business managers. Frederick W. Taylor's Scientific Management Theory summarized important key concepts from classical theory, such as upward and downward communication. The human relations movement emphasized the importance of horizontal and informal communication networks. Theorists such as Likert and Argyris emphasized the importance of integrating worker and organizational goals and of participative decision making. McGregor summarized the assumptions underlying scientific management and human relations theories in his Theory X and Theory Y. Other authors such as Follett and Barnard wrote explicitly about the importance of communication. Two of the most recent approaches to organizational communication theory are the systems perspective, first articulated in this context by Katz and Kahn, and the contingency leadership theories of authors such as Fiedler and Reddin.

Theories reflecting the laws, rules, and systems perspectives as they are applied to organizational and group communication were presented. In organizational communication, Infante and Gorden's Theory of Independent-Mindedness and Lester's work on Uncertainty Reduction Theory represented covering laws approaches to organizational communication. Laird, Johnson, and Downs used the Coordinated Management of Meaning, a rules theory, to study superiors' and subordinates' perceptions of organizational effectiveness and the firm's rules for achieving it. Two theories, Farace, Monge, and Russell's structural-functionalism and Weick's Organizational Information Theory, represented the systems perspective on organizational communication.

A similar pattern was followed for group communication. Fisher and Hawes' Interaction Systems Model of small group communication reflects theory building from the systems perspective. Jarboe conducted a test of four communication models from the covering laws perspective to see which was most accurate in predicting group satisfaction and productivity. Finally, Bormann's Symbolic Convergence Theory, a human action approach to group communication, was discussed.

Questions To Consider

1 What are the classical influences on contemporary group and organizational communication theory?

2 According to the Theory of Independent-Mindedness, what type of communication will make organizations more productive?

3 Why is the Theory of Independent-Mindedness considered a laws model? What criticisms would rules and systems theorists make?

4 How has Uncertainty Reduction Theory been applied to organizational communication?

5 How has the Coordinated Management of Meaning Theory been used to investigate organizational communication?

6 In what way is Weick's Theory of Organizational Information both a systems and a rules theory?

7 In what way is Structural-Functional Systems Theory a systems theory which also reflects the laws approach?

8 How does the Fisher-Hawes Interaction System Model analyze communication in small groups?

9 How is group communication studied according to the laws approach of the Input-Output Model of group communication?

10 Why is Bormann's Symbolic Convergence Theory of group communication considered a rules theory?

References

Argyris, C. (1957). *Personality and organization.* New York: Harper & Row.

Barnard, C. I. (1968). *The functions of the executive.* Cambridge, MA: Harvard University Press. (Original work published 1938).

Berger, C. R., & Calabrese, R. J. (1975). Some explorations in initial interaction and beyond: Toward a developmental theory of interpersonal communication. *Human Communication Research, 1,* 99-112.

Bormann, E. (1980) *Communication theory.* Reissued 1989. Salem, WI: Sheffield.

Brenders, D. A. (1987). Fallacies in the Coordinated Management of Meaning: A philosophy of language critique of the hierarchical organization of coherent conversation and related theory. *Quarterly Journal of Speech, 73,* 329-348.

Brilhart, J. K., & Jochem, L. M. (1964). Effects of different patterns on outcomes of problem solving discussion. *Journal of Applied Psychology, 48,* 175-179.

Cragan, J. F., & Wright, D. W. (1980). Small group communication research of the 1970s: A synthesis and critique. *Central States Speech Journal, 31,* 197-213.

Delbecq, A. L., Van de Ven, A. H., & Gustafson, D. H. (1975). *Group techniques for program planning: A guide to nominal group and Delphi processes.* Glenview, IL: Scott Foresman.

Dewey, J. (1910). *How we think*. Boston: D.C. Heath.

Farace, R. V., Monge, P. M., and Russell, H. (1977). *Communicating and organizing*. Reading, MA: Addison-Wesley.

Fayol, H. (1949). *General and industrial management*. London: Pitman. (Original work published 1916).

Fiedler, F. E. (1967). *A theory of leadership effectiveness*. New York: McGraw-Hill.

Fisher, B. A. (1970) Decision emergence: Phases in group decision-making. *Speech Monographs, 37,* 53-66.

Fisher, B. A., & Hawes, L. (1971) An interact system model: Generating a grounded theory of small groups. *Quarterly Journal of Speech, 57,* 444-453.

Follett, M. P. (1971). The giving of orders. In D. S. Pugh (Ed.), *Organization theory*. Baltimore: Penguin. (Original work published 1925).

Gorden, W. I., & Infante, D. A. (1987). Employee rights: Content, argumentativeness, verbal aggressiveness and career satisfaction. In C. A. B. Osigweh (Ed.), *Communicating employee responsibilities and rights: A modern management mandate* (pp. 149-163). Westport, CT: Quorum Books, Greenwood Press.

Gorden, W. I., Infante, D. A., & Graham, E.E. (1988) Corporate conditions conducive to critical involvement: A subordinate perspective. *The Employee Responsibilities and Rights Journal, 1,* 101-111.

Hackman, J. R., & Morris, C. G. (1975). Group tasks, group interaction process and group performance effectiveness: A review and proposed integration. In L. Berkowitz (Ed.), *Advances in experimental social psychology* (pp. 45-99). New York: Academic.

Hewes, D. E. (1986). A socio-egocentric model of group decision-making. In R. Y. Hirokawa & M. S. Poole (Eds.), *Communication and group decision-making* (pp. 265-291). Beverly Hills: Sage.

Hirokawa, R. Y. (1980). A comparative analysis of communication patterns within effective and ineffective decision-making groups. *Communication Monographs, 47,* 312-327.

Hofstede, G. (1980). *Culture's consequences: International differences in work-related values*. Beverly Hills, CA: Sage.

Infante, D. A. (1987a, May). *An independent-mindedness model of organizational productivity: The role of communication education*. Paper presented at the annual conference of the Eastern Communication Association, Syracuse, NY.

Infante, D. A. (1987b, August). *Argumentativeness in superior-subordinate communication: An essential condition for organizational productivity*. Paper presented at the Fifth Summer Conference on Argumentation. Alta, UT.

Infante, D. A., & Gorden, W. I. (1985). Superiors' argumentativeness and verbal aggressiveness as predictors of subordinates' satisfaction. *Human Communication Research, 12,* 117-125.

Infante, D. A., & Gorden, W. I. (1987). Superior and subordinate communication profiles: Implications for independent-mindedness and upward effectiveness. *Central States Speech Journal, 38,* 73-80.

Infante, D. A., & Rancer, A. S. (1982). A conceptualization and measure of argumentativeness. *Journal of Personality Assessment, 46,* 72-80.

Infante, D. A., & Wigley, C. J., III. (1986). Verbal aggressiveness: An interpersonal model and measure. *Communication Monographs, 53,* 61-69.

Jablin, F. M. (1980). Superiors' upward influence, satisfaction, and openness in superior-subordinate communication: A reexamination of the "Pelz Effect." *Human Communication Research, 6*, 210-220.

Jarboe, S. (1988). A comparison of input-output, process-output and input-process-output models of small group problem-solving effectiveness. *Communication Monographs, 55*, 121-142.

Jarboe, S. C. (1986). The effects of discussion procedure, task solution multiplicity, and topic on group communication, productivity, and satisfaction. (Doctoral dissertation, University of Wisconsin, 1986). *Dissertation Abstracts International, 47*, 1925A.

Katz, D., & Kahn, R. (1978). The social psychology of organizations (2nd ed.). New York: Wiley.

Katzell, R. A., Miller, C. E., Rotter, N. G., & Venet, T. G. (1970). Effects of leadership and other inputs on group processes and outputs. *Journal of Social Psychology, 80*, 157-169.

Kreps, G. L. (1980). A field experimental test and revaluation of Weick's model of organizing. In Nimmo, D. (Ed.), *Communication Yearbook 4* (pp. 389-398). New Brunswick, NJ: International Communication Association, Transaction Books.

Kreps, G. L. (1986). Organizational Communication: Theory and practice. New York: Longman.

Laird, A., Johnson, K., & Downs, C. (1982, May). *Communication and productivity: From structure to structuration.* Paper presented at the annual convention of the International Communication Association, Boston, MA.

Lester, R. E. (1987). Organizational culture, uncertainty reduction, and the socialization of new organizational members. In S. Thomas (Ed.), *Studies in communication: Culture and communication.* (Vol. 3, pp. 105-113). Norwood, NJ: Ablex.

Likert, R. (1971). The principle of supportive relationships. In D. S. Pugh (Ed.), *Organization theory.* Baltimore: Penguin.

Littlejohn, S. W. (1983). *Theories of human communication* (2nd ed.). Belmont, CA: Wadsworth.

Maier, N. R. F., & Thurber, J. A. (1969). Limitations of procedures for improving group problem solving. *Psychological Reports, 25*, 639-656.

McGregor, D. (1960). The human side of enterprise. New York: McGraw-Hill.

Montgomery, B. M., & Norton, R. W. (1981). Sex differences and similarities in communicator style. *Communication Monographs, 48*, 121-132.

Norton, R. W. (1978). Foundations of a communicator style construct. *Human Communication Research, 4*, 99-117.

Norton, R. W. (1983). *Communicator style: Theory, applications, and measures.* Beverly Hills, CA: Sage.

Ouchi, W. G. (1981). *Theory Z: How American business can meet the Japanese challenge.* New York: Avon.

Pacanowsky, M.E. (1982). Organizational identities vs. organizational products: Presentation of self among Valley View Police. *The Communicator, 12*, 20.

Pelz, D. (1952). Influence: A key to effective leadership in the first-line supervisor. *Personnel, 29*, 209-217.

Poole, M. S., & Folger, J. P. (1981). A method of establishing the representational validity of interaction coding systems: Do we see what they see? *Human Communication Research, 8*, 26-42.

Reddin, W. J. (1970). *Managerial effectiveness*. New York: McGraw-Hill.

Roethlisberger, F. J., & Dickson, W. J. (1939). *Management and the worker.* Cambridge, MA: Harvard University Press.

Shaw, M. E. (1981). *Group dynamics: The psychology of small group behavior* (3rd. ed.). New York: McGraw-Hill.

Shaw, M. E. (1963). *Scaling group tasks: A method for dimensional analysis.* [Tech. Rep. No. 1, ONR Contract NR 170-266, Nonr-580 (11)]. Gainesville, FL: University of Florida.

Sorensen, J. R. (1973). Group member traits, group process, and group performance. *Human Relations, 26,* 639-655.

Taylor, F. W. (1911). *Scientific management*. New York: Harper & Row.

Tompkins, P. K. (1984). The functions of human communication in organizations. In C. C. Arnold & J. W. Bowers (Eds.), *Handbook of rhetorical and communication theory* (pp. 659-719). Boston: Allyn & Bacon.

Trenholm, S. (1986) *Human communication theory.* Englewood Cliffs, NJ: Prentice-Hall.

Van de Ven, A. H. (1973). An applied experimental test of nominal, Delphi, and interacting decision-making processes. (Doctoral dissertation, University of Wisconsin, 1972). *Dissertation Abstracts International, 33,* 3094A.

Weber, M. (1948). *The theory of social and economic organization* (A. Henderson & T. Parsons, Trans.). New York: Oxford University Press. (Original work published 1909).

Weick, K. (1969). *The social psychology of organizing*. Reading, MA: Addison-Wesley.

Weick, K. (1973). Amendments to organizational theorizing. *Academy of Management Journal, 17,* 487-502.

Weick, K. (1976). Educational organizations as loosely coupled systems. *Administrative Science Quarterly, 21,* 1-19.

Weick, K. (1979). *The social psychology of organizing* (2nd ed.). Reading, MA: Addison-Wesley.

Wilson, G. L., Goodall, H. L., Jr., & Waagen, C. L. (1986). *Organizational Communication*. New York: Harper & Row.

Chapter 11

Mass Media Contexts

Mass Communication in Contemporary Society

Contemporary society not only influences mass media and communication but is itself influenced by mass or mediated communication (see Cathcart & Gumpert, 1986; Lowery & DeFleur, 1983). Rarely a day goes by without some mention of how the media and mass communication affect our lives. Newspaper and radio reports scream headlines such as, "Studies link teen suicides with TV news and movies," and, "Rock videos found to be less violent than prime-time TV." Through mass media, people learn almost immediately about major happenings across town or across the globe. As viewers, we are frequently eyewitnesses to global events both joyous and tragic. Most American homes have at least one television set and one radio. More often than not, new mediated technologies are also found in our homes: videotape recorders, cable and satellite television, and personal computers linked to large centralized databases via modem. These technologies are changing the very nature of "mass" communication.

One consequence of these innovations and of the changing nature of media use has been the development of new theories of mass communication. These theories try to explain how individuals respond to media, predict how rapidly a society will adopt these innovations, and attempt to determine what effect

341

mass communication has on individuals, society, other forms of human communication, and culture. DeFleur and Ball-Rokeach (1982) suggest three broad
questions have stimulated much of the research and theory building in mass
communication:

1. What is the impact of a society on its mass media?
2. How does mass communication take place?
3. What does exposure to mass communication do to people?
   (DeFleur & Ball-Rokeach, 1982, p. 13).

Until recently, few mass communication research efforts were designed to
explore the first question. Currently, mass communication research efforts
examine the role of society, culture, and the individual in the *production* of
mass communication content. The second question examines how mass communication differs from other forms of human communication. The distinction
between mass communication and interpersonal communication has stimulated a considerable amount of investigation by communication researchers.
Some theories have examined how mass communication and interpersonal
communication *jointly* influence an individual's decision-making processes.
Other theories attempt to offer a new synthesis of interpersonal and mass communication, which has been labelled mediated interpersonal communication.
The bulk of mass communication theory and research has addressed Question
3. Many theorists have investigated how mass media messages affect people's
perceptions and behaviors. Examples of those theories will be detailed in this
chapter. Some of the theories seek to understand audience involvement in mass
communication. Other theories seek to explain how mediated messages shape
our perceptions of reality. Yet another body of research examines how communication rules are used to guide audience members' collective interaction
with mass media.

The Influence of Mass Communication

Regardless of which questions the theories address, it appears clear that the
mass media exert a powerful influence on society, culture, and individual
behavior. Indeed, mass communication may have become one of the most
powerful influences in contemporary society. Loevinger (1979) offers what is
called the "Reflective-Projective" Theory of mass communication. This theory
asserts that the mass media act like "mirrors of society." These mirrors reflect
ambiguous images in which each individual sees or projects not only an
individual vision, but also a vision of society. The media not only reflect
society's attitudes and values but also project the many visions of the members
of a society. Audience members see in the media their own visions or images.
Loevinger compares this process to an ink-blot or Rorschach test. This test,
commonly used by psychologists, allows individuals to project their own ideas,

images, and visions to interpret ambiguous stimuli such as an ink-blot. Similarly, the mass media offer selected images which provide the basis for individual interpretation. These interpretations may vary due to the intellectual, emotional, and sensory character and responsiveness of the individual. As evidence of the impact of the media in contemporary society, Loevinger argues that nations or communities are not necessarily formed by maps or geographical boundaries. Rather, nations or communities are formed by common images and visions, along with common interests, ideas, and culture. The *mass media* reflect the social image of the masses.

Early Theory Building Efforts in Mass Communication

The Development of "Mass" Society

As society became increasingly larger and more "mass" in nature, there was a concomitant growth in mass communication. Theories were developed to explain the influence of these new forms of communication on society. During World War I, the new mass media were used to help mobilize the population (the mobilization function) and to create support for the various war efforts. The term "propaganda" first emerged during this time. Messages designed to stimulate and encourage support for the war effort were presented over the mass media. The newly developed media were used effectively to promote the beliefs of the warring nations. Mass communication became an important tool used by individuals engaged in large scale persuasive efforts. After World War I, American society witnessed an increasing growth of individuality; the society became less homogeneous. Individuals were no longer so closely dependent upon one another. The term "mass society" was created by sociologists to describe not merely a large number of people in a given culture, but the *relationship* between the individuals and the social order around them (DeFleur & Ball-Rokeach, 1982). India and China, for example, are cultures which have large numbers of people. The social order of those two cultures does not exhibit heterogeneity, independence, individuality, and autonomy, as American "mass" society does.

The "Magic Bullet" Theory

Sometimes referred to as the "Hypodermic Needle Theory" or the "Mechanistic Stimulus-Response Theory" of mass communication, the "Magic Bullet" Theory was one of the first theories developed to account for the presumed all-powerful effect of the media on audiences. The bullet theory and the many subtle variations of it were derived from the stimulus-response view taken by several early mass communication theorists and researchers (e.g., Lasswell, 1927). This view asserts that any powerful stimulus such as a mass media message can provoke a uniform reaction or response from a given organism, such as an audience. Recall that the mass media at this time were thought to exert powerful, direct influence over the audience. The "Magic Bullet" or "Hypodermic Needle" Theory suggested that the mass media could influence a very large group of people *directly* and *uniformly* by "shooting" or "injecting" them with appropriate messages designed to trigger a desired response. The popularity of these early stimulus-response theories of mass communication was consistent with that of the existing psychological and sociological theories of mass society. In addition, "evidence" of the power of the media existed in its ability to mobilize support for the country's war effort. The newly emerging mass media did have a profound effect on the audience, but several other intervening factors also exerted considerable influence on audiences during that time. After many years of additional research, mass communication theorists concluded that the early stimulus-response theories lacked full explanatory and predictive power. They developed alternative theories which address not only the power of the media to influence attitudes and behavior, but also the influence of different message sources and different audience reactions. Examples of these alternative theories will be presented later in this chapter.

The Two-Step Flow Theory of Mass Communication

One of the early theories of mass communication which recognized that many variables intervene to modify the effect of messages on audience response was the *Two-Step Flow Theory* of mass communication (Katz & Lazarsfeld, 1955). To test the hypothesized powerful and direct influence of the mass media on audience behavior, several researchers designed a study to examine how individuals from different social groups select and use mass communication messages to influence votes (see Lazarsfeld, Berelson, & Gaudet, 1944). The researchers expected to find empirical support for the direct influence of media messages on voting intentions. They were surprised to discover, however, that *informal, personal contacts* were mentioned far more frequently than exposure to radio or newspaper as potential sources of influence on voting behavior. When questioned further, several participants revealed that they had received their information about the campaign *first* from *others* (who had received information directly from the mass media).

Armed with this data, Katz and Lazarsfeld developed the *Two-Step Flow Theory* of mass communication. This theory asserts that information from the media moves in two distinct stages. First, individuals who pay close attention (are frequent "attenders") to the mass media and its messages receive the information. These individuals, called *opinion leaders*, are generally well informed people who pass their information along to others through informal, interpersonal communication. Opinion leaders pass on their own interpretations as well as the actual media content. The term "personal influence" was coined to refer to the process intervening between the media's direct message and the audience's ultimate reaction to that message. Over the last forty-five years a great deal of research has led to considerable knowledge about opinion leadership. Several characteristics of opinion leaders have been identified. Opinion leaders are quite influential in getting people to change their attitudes and behaviors and are quite similar to those they influence. Think of an individual whom you consult before making a major purchase. Perhaps you have a friend who knows a great deal about cars. You may hear a number of messages on television about the favorable qualities of the Ford Tempo and the Toyota Camry. The mass media have clearly provided you with information about each car, but do you rely solely on this information to decide which car to buy? If you are like most people, probably not. You may go to the library and check *Consumer Reports* to determine what it says about those two cars. Will this information be enough to persuade you to prefer one car to the other? Possibly, but chances are you will also seek out the advice of someone you consider an opinion leader on the topic of automobiles.

The Two-Step Flow Theory has improved our understanding of how the mass media influence decision-making. The theory refined our ability to *predict* the influence of media messages on audience behavior, and it helped *explain* why certain media campaigns may have failed to alter audience attitudes and behavior. Despite this contribution, the Two-Step Flow Theory has also received its share of criticism. First, some major news stories seem to be spread directly by the media with only modest intervention by personal contact. The stock market crash of October 19, 1987, may be one event which most people heard first from the media, then discussed interpersonally. Second, definitions of opinion leadership are often vague. Severin and Tankard (1988) suggest that some opinion leaders are self-nominated, but not reported to be opinion leaders by their supposed followers. Another difficulty is that opinion leaders have been found to be both active and passive. The Two-Step Flow Theory argues that opinion leaders are primarily active media seekers, while their followers are primarily passive information "sponges." This distinction between media behavior of leaders and followers does not necessarily hold true. Finally, while Katz and Lazarsfeld argue the need for a *two-step* model, the process of media dissemination and audience behavior can involve more steps. Thus, the Two-Step Flow Theory gave way to the *Multi-Step Flow Theory* of mass communication. This Multi-Step Flow Theory is often used to describe the *diffusion of innovations.*

Diffusion Theory

Research dealing with *diffusion* examines how new ideas are spread among groups of people. The Two-Step Flow Theory of mass communication was primarily concerned with the exchange of information between the media and others. Diffusion research goes one step further. Diffusion research centers around the conditions which increase or decrease the likelihood that a new idea, product, or practice will be adopted by members of a given culture. Diffusion research has focused on five elements: (1) the *characteristics of an innovation* which may influence its adoption; (2) the *decision-making process* that occurs when individuals consider adopting a new idea, product or practice; (3) the *characteristics of individuals* that make them likely to adopt an innovation; (4) the *consequences* for individuals and society of adopting an innovation; and (5) *communication channels* used in the adoption process (see Rogers, 1983).

It is in the area of communication channels that the Two-Step Flow Theory has been expanded. Communication channels include both the mass media and interpersonal contacts. The multi-step flow and diffusion theories expand the number and type of intermediaries between the media and the audience's decision-making. In multi-step diffusion research, opinion leaders are still found to exert influence on audience behavior via their personal contact, but additional intermediaries called change agents and gatekeepers are also included in the process of diffusion. *Change agents* are those professionals who encourage opinion leaders to adopt or reject an innovation. *Gatekeepers* are individuals who control the flow of information to a given group of people. While opinion leaders are usually quite similar to their followers, change agents are usually more educated and of higher status than either the opinion leaders or their followers. A change agent might be a representative from a national cable television company who tries to persuade local opinion leaders in a community (town selectmen and officials, for example) that cable television should be installed in their town. Another example of a change agent is a computer company representative who convinces local school officials to introduce a particular personal computer into the school system. This representative is probably more knowledgeable about the computer system than the opinion leaders (school officials). However, the task of influencing the town's electorate to budget money for these computers still rests with the local opinion leaders. Recall that opinion leaders are similar to those they represent. Previous research (see Chapter 9) suggests that similarity or homophily enhances attraction, liking, and influence. A gatekeeper might be the editor of a local news show or newspaper. This person decides what stories will be printed or broadcast. Gatekeepers represent yet another intermediate step in the flow of information between the media and audience. Thus, the process of information dissemination and influence is more complicated than the Two-Step Flow Theory suggests.

Contemporary Mass Communication Theory

The last two and a half decades have seen explosive growth in the theory building in interpersonal, persuasion, organizational, nonverbal, and intercultural communication contexts. Theory building efforts in mass communication have paralleled growth observed in the other contexts, beginning with early theory building efforts which relied heavily on psychological and sociological theories and ending with current efforts to build unified theories of mass communication (McQuail, 1987). The field of mass communication has produced theory which can "stand on its own" without relying on other fields such as psychology and sociology for theory building efforts. Several contemporary theories developed by communication scholars will be presented below. The first theory, the functional approach, has developed from the early research and continues to be refined today.

The Functional Approach to Mass Communication Theory

The mass media and mass communication serve many functions for our society. Clearly, one of the main attractions is escapism and entertainment value. We come home after a hard day at school or the office and turn on our favorite television comedy, game show, or dramatic program. Another major use of the media is to provide information. Driving to school or work, we turn on the radio and catch the latest news, weather, and sports scores. Or, we may listen to our favorite talk program to hear what others think about improving relations between the United States and the Soviet Union. Two scholars, Lasswell (1948) and Wright (1960), have studied the functions of mass communication. Lasswell articulated three functions of mass communication: *surveillance, correlation* and *cultural transmission*. A fourth function, the *entertainment* function, was added by Wright. Thirty years later, these four functions continue to form the basis of the functional approach to mass communication. Recently, McQuail (1987) added a fifth function called *mobilization*.

Five Functions of Mass Communication

The first function, *surveillance*, is considered the information and news-providing function of mass communication. When we turn on the radio to obtain the latest weather, traffic, or stock market reports, we are using the media primarily for its surveillance function. On Monday, October 19, 1987, the stock market dropped a record 508 points. Millions of Americans turned on their radio and television sets to obtain information about the stock market plunge. In every major office in the country that day, workers were "glued" to their radios to discover how much their companies' stocks had fallen. Individuals who did not own stock read in-depth reports in local newspapers concerning the potential influence of the stock market crash on the U.S. and global economies.

The second function, *correlation*, deals with how the mass media select, interpret, and criticize information about the environment. The editorials on radio and television and the persuasive campaigns waged using the media are primary examples of the correlation function. "USA for Africa," "Live Aid," "Farm Aid," and "Hands Across America" were campaigns whose origins and major fund-raising drives were stimulated by and developed in connection with the media. The outpouring of funds to help the starving people of Ethiopia was largely stimulated by the horrible images which came into our homes via television. Many political critics suggest that the media, and not the American people, select or choose who our politicians or political leaders will be. They point to the tremendous media coverage and scrutiny given to the fledgling campaign of Gary Hart as an example of the correlation function of the media. If the media had not so heavily exposed the private life of Senator Hart, perhaps his 1988 Presidential campaign would not have been derailed. Along with the criticism and selection of events, the correlation function of the media also *confers status* on selected individuals. The mass media choose to highlight a number of individuals who then become "legitimized" to audiences. When the media selects one person instead of another to highlight, pursue, and advocate, then this person emerges as an *opinion leader*. Previous research has discovered that opinion leaders influence our attitudes, beliefs and behaviors (see especially Katz & Lazarsfeld, 1955; Rogers & Shoemaker, 1971).

The third function, *cultural transmission*, refers to the media's ability to communicate norms, rules, and values of a society. These values may be transmitted from one generation to another, or from the society to its newcomers. Cultural transmission is a teaching function of the media, which brings many social role models into the home. Those role models frequently engage in behaviors which are considered appropriate in a given society (prosocial behaviors). Johnston and Ettema (1986) cite shows such as *Mister Rogers' Neighborhood, Sesame Street* and the *ABC After School Specials* as examples of children's programs which attempt to teach or to promote such prosocial behaviors as being polite, dealing with anger or fear, handling new situations, coping with death, persisting at tasks, caring, and cooperating. Prime-time television shows such as *Family Ties* and the *Bill Cosby Show* have been mentioned as programs which promote values such as respect for authority, family harmony, and the American work ethic. As the average American continues to watch more and more television, regional and subcultural differences appear to be decreasing. The media's powerful cultural transmission of "common" messages has caused us to speak, think and dress alike. These common or unifying messages may have further "homogenized" the American culture by dictating the "proper" way to act.

The fourth function of mass communication, *entertainment*, may be the most potent one. Entertainment is, "Any activity designed to delight and, to a smaller degree, enlighten through the exhibition of the fortunes or misfortunes of others,

[and] through the display of special skills by others and/or self" (Zillmann & Bryant, 1986, p. 303). Mass communication helps fill our leisure time by presenting us messages filled with comedy, drama, tragedy, play, and performance. The entertainment function of mass communication allows us to escape from our daily problems and concerns. The media introduce us to aspects of culture, art, music, and dance that may not have been readily available to us. When presenting sports events mass media can stimulate excitement in individuals. The media can also calm us with broadcasts of comedies or cultural events. They can comfort us or help us avoid discomfort (Zillmann, 1982; Zillmann & Bryant, 1985). The entertainment function of mass communication provides relief from boredom, stimulates our emotions, fills our leisure time, keeps us company, and exposes us to images, experiences, and events that we could not attend in person. Although the entertainment function of the media has been frequently criticized, current thinking by mass communication scholars allows for the functional consequences of media entertainment. Indeed, Zillmann and Bryant (1986) redefine the concept of escapism as "recreational success" (p. 321). There are, however, numerous critics who continue to assert that the media and its messages lower taste, and reduce fine art to pop art.

McQuail's (1987) fifth function of mass communication, *mobilization*, refers to the ability of the media to promote national interests and certain behaviors, especially during times of national crisis. While this mobilization function may be especially important in developing nations and societies, it can occur anywhere. We may have seen evidence of it in the United States during the days after the assassination of President John F. Kennedy, or in the wake of the explosion of the space shuttle Challenger, when the media's central function was not only to inform us, but to counsel, strengthen, and pull us together.

The Agenda-Setting Theory of Mass Communication

A number of scholars describe *agenda-setting* as a function of mass communication (e.g., McCombs & Shaw, 1972; Severin & Tankard, 1988). Others refer to agenda-setting as a theory (e.g., Wimmer & Dominick, 1987), while at least one mass communication scholar refers to it as a hypothesis (McQuail, 1987). Whether agenda-setting is considered a function, theory, or hypothesis, the concept has received considerable attention from mass communication theorists. As such, it will be detailed here. *Agenda-setting* describes a very powerful influence of the media, the ability to tell us what issues are important. Those issues or individuals that the media choose to publicize ultimately become the issues and individuals we think and talk about. According to the theory, those topics, issues and individuals we think are important become important *because of the media attention* they received. For example, if the media chooses to highlight a particular event such as the stock market plunge of late 1987, then the stock market becomes an important issue to us, regardless of the level of importance we placed on it before the media attention. Shortly after the media attention to the issue, books concerning the stock market started to sell well across the country. Suddenly, people were interested in knowing what "margin calls" were. Several entertainers immediately introduced jokes and stories about the "crash" into their routines. Agenda-setting has been the subject of attention by media analysts and critics for several years. As far back as 1922, the newspaper columnist Walter Lippman stated that the media helps put "pictures in our heads." (Wimmer & Dominick, 1987, p. 385). It was, however, a study by McCombs and Shaw (1972) which stimulated the flurry of empirical investigations into the agenda-setting function of the mass media.

Investigating the agenda-setting function of the mass media in the 1968 presidential campaign, McCombs and Shaw (1972) attempted to assess the relationship between what voters in one community *said* were important issues, and the *actual* content of media messages used during the campaign. Using interview techniques, the researchers concluded that the mass media exerted a major influence on what voters considered to be the major issues of the campaign. Wimmer and Dominick (1987) report that in recent years, agenda-setting is enjoying increased attention from mass communication theorists. In addition, the focus of this research is broadening from attention to political campaigns to issues including history, advertising, foreign, and medical news.

The many previous studies investigating the agenda-setting function of the media are producing a theory of agenda-setting (Williams, 1985). Indeed, Williams argues that the hypothetico-deductive method, a law-governed causal approach, is one method used to build an Agenda-Setting Theory of mass communication (see Chapter 3 and the Appendix for more about the hypothetico-deductive method). Conversely, McQuail argues that, despite recent research on agenda-setting, there is insufficient evidence to show a causal connection between the order of importance placed on issues by the media and the significance attached to those issues by the public. He argues that, at least for the time being, Agenda-Setting Theory remains, "Within the status of a plausible but unproven idea"(McQuail, 1987, p. 276).

A Theory of Mediated Interpersonal Communication

Few communication theorists today deny the impact of mass communication on interpersonal communication, or vice versa. The union of mass and interpersonal communication is not a new phenomena. Like Katz and Lazarsfeld (1955), other researchers have recognized the role the individual plays in the mass communication process. Cathcart and Gumpert (1983) suggest that the media play a significant role in the development of one's self-image. Self-image is considered largely media dependent. The Theory of Mediated Interpersonal Communication attempts to unite interpersonal and mass communication research in theory building. Cathcart and Gumpert argue that media is not synonymous with mass communication. Mass communication is the "relatively immediate communication over time and space to large, heterogeneous groups" (Cathcart & Gumpert, 1986, p. 90).

The critical focus of this theory consists of the social and personal uses that people have for mass communication. Cathcart and Gumpert argue that the term *media* should not be excluded from other forms of human communication such as intrapersonal, interpersonal, group, or public. When we talk with a friend on the telephone, we are using a medium to make possible our interaction. When we interact with others on a ham or CB radio, we are using a medium to facilitate interpersonal communication. When we use a modem and personal computer to log on to a computer service like CompuServe, are we not engaged in mediated small-group communication? Cathcart and Gumpert (1983) claim: (1) Some interpersonal communication situations require media; (2) Along with a complex of other variables, the media influence attitudes and behavior; (3) Media content both reflects interpersonal behaviors and contains projections of them; and (4) The development of an individual's self-concept is dependent on the media (p. 268).

The Media and Self-Image Creation

At the core of Cathcart and Gumpert's theory lie two premises. The first suggests that the media alter relationships between individuals. The second, and perhaps most important, is that a person's *self-image* is in large part media-dependent. Cathcart and Gumpert reason that, if an individual's self-image is formed through interpersonal interaction and interpersonal interaction is heavily media related, then communication theorists should devote more attention to the effect of the media on self-image. From childhood on, we hear or view media-projected images of what is acceptable," "standard," "normative," or "perfect." We then compare those images to our self-perceptions. More often than not, an individual's self-perception does not compare favorably with the media images. Advertisers have learned to associate products with media images of perfection. Individuals portrayed in the ads frequently exhibit the characteristics that we have been taught to value. As Cathcart and Gumpert (1986) suggest, "The more they project that image, the more we see ourselves in them. The more we see ourselves in them, the more we strive to produce a self-concept which confirms that same image" (p. 97). Self-concept is no longer primarily dependent upon face-to-face interaction, but relies heavily upon mediated communication. Photography, music videos, radio, motion pictures, and television play a significant part in the development and maintenance of an individual's self-image. Thus, Cathcart and Gumpert advocate that interpersonal communication scholars incorporate this concept of mediated image into their theory building efforts.

Mediated Interpersonal Communication

Cathcart and Gumpert offer the term "mediated interpersonal communication" to refer to any situation in which a mediated technology is used to
replace face-to-face interaction. Telephone conversations, the exchange of
audio and videotape cassettes, electronic mail, mediated teleconferences
between individuals or groups, interpersonal interactions via personal
computer and modem, t-shirts, and bumper stickers are "media" which are
used to facilitate interpersonal interaction. *Media-simulated interpersonal communication* refers to the feeling of audiences that they know a performer in
a very personal way, as they know their friends. Constant monitoring of a
performer's voice and gestures leads the audience to make personal judgments
about performers in much the same way they make judgments about their
friends. In fact, many people feel that they "know" their favorite media
personality better than they know their friends. After repeatedly watching David
Letterman, for example, we may begin to believe that we actually "know" him,
even though we experience only the illusion of an interpersonal relationship
with him. The skillful disc jockey or television talk host uses communication
behaviors which help build this relationship.

One form of mediated interpersonal communication which bridges mediated
and media-simulated interpersonal communication is *teleparticipatory media.*
The most familiar teleparticipatory medium is the two-way talk radio program
in which callers and host communicate with each other. Some people call
a favorite talk host daily or weekly, and even prefer this communication to
interaction with real friends (see Avery & Ellis, 1979). Group telephone
services such as Talk-About are like party-lines over which several people can
communicate simultaneously. For a charge, you can call one of these services
and communicate with those already on the line. Newspapers have reported
that some adolescents have used telephone party-line services so much that
their parents have received bills as high as a thousand dollars per month!
The popularity and abuse of these services have stimulated efforts to encourage
the FCC to regulate them. One study conducted by an undergraduate student
research team (Scholder, Lalumia, & Murphy, 1987) discovered that many
callers preferred this mediated interaction to face-to-face interpersonal contact.
Research by Avery and McCain (1982) has found that, for many individuals,
mediated teleparticipatory interaction supplements face-to-face interpersonal
communication.

Cathcart and Gumpert's theory indicates that it is dysfunctional to ignore
the pervasiveness of media when we develop theories of human communication. Theorists should incorporate the concept of media in their efforts to
build theories of intrapersonal, interpersonal, group and public
communication.

Uses and Gratifications Theory

One thoroughly researched, yet controversial, theory of mass communication is Uses and Gratifications Theory. Some contemporary communication theorists argue that the body of research labelled uses and gratifications "has made substantial contributions to our understanding of the mass communication process" (Swanson, 1987, p. 237). Recent critics have challenged the theory. Uses and Gratifications Theory attempts to explain why people use the mass media. The theory attempts to explain the *uses* and *functions* of the media for individuals, groups, and society in general.

Rubin (1985) states that Uses and Gratifications Theory is grounded in a "functional paradigm of social influence" (p. 202). Since the functional approach examines the relationships between the media, individuals, and society, it represents the *systems perspective*, one theory building paradigm detailed in Chapter 3. Rubin argues that mass communication represents one social system or subsystem of society. One tenet of the systems approach is that a change in one part of the system will, of necessity, cause a change in another part of the system. Many claim the home video cassette recorder (VCR) has altered television viewing patterns. For example, one consequence of videotaping television programs is that many people fast forward through the commercials. This phenomenon has caused advertisers and advertising agencies to re-examine the placement and the format of commercials shown during network programming. The five functions of mass communication described earlier represent the functions of the *content* of mass media. These content functions do not adequately describe the way an audience *uses* that content. The analysis of how an audience member uses the media is best explained by Uses and Gratifications Theory.

Assumptions of Uses and Gratifications Theory

At the core of Uses and Gratifications Theory lies the assumption that audience members actively seek out the mass media to satisfy individual needs. For example, Rubin (1979) uncovered six reasons why children and adolescents use television: for learning, for passing time, for companionship, to forget or escape, for excitement or arousal, and for relaxation. Television viewing for passing time and for arousal and relaxation emerged as the most important uses of television for Rubin's participants. Another assumption of Uses and Gratifications Theory is that audiences use the media to fulfill expectations. For example, you may watch a science fiction program such as *Star Trek: The Next Generation* to help you fantasize about the future and to escape the pressures of the day. A third assumption of this theory is that audiences actively select media and media content to satisfy their needs. Two types of television viewers have been identified. The first type consists of a time-consuming (habitual) information seeker who watches television for *ritualized* use. This person is a "more frequent, generalized user of TV, who has high regard for television" (Rubin, 1984, p. 68). This viewer uses television primarily as a diversion. The second type of viewer is a non-time-consuming (non-habitual) entertainment-information seeker who attends to television for *instrumental use*. This person exhibits a natural liking for a television program or programs. This individual uses media content primarily for information. This person is more selective and goal-oriented when watching television and does not necessarily feel that television is important. Rubin (1984) argues that *ritualized* television use represents a more *important* viewing experience for the audience member, while *instrumental* television use represents a more *involving* experience for the viewer.

Rubin (1979) designed a questionnaire called the *Television Viewing Motives Instrument* to discover reasons why people view television. Complete the survey in Figure 11.1 to get a sense of your primary motives for watching TV.

A fourth assumption of Uses and Gratifications Theory is that audience members are aware of and can state their own motives for using mass communication. Studies which investigate how individuals use the media for gratification primarily employ *self-report measures*, questionnaires which ask participants to tell their underlying motives for using the mass media. The *Television Viewing Motives Instrument* is one such questionnaire. A fifth and final assumption of this theory is that the underlying motives and gratifications of media use must be more fully understood before attempts are made to address the cultural significance of media content (Katz, Blumler, & Gurevitch, 1974; Rubin 1985, 1986). Before we attempt to assess the positive and negative outcomes to society from the media, we must learn more about the uses people have for the media and how media use gratifies individual needs.

Objectives of Uses and Gratifications Theory

Communication theorists had three objectives in developing uses and gratifications research. First, they hoped to explain *how* individuals use mass communication to gratify their needs. They attempted to answer the question: *What* do people do with the media (Rubin, 1985)? A second objective is to discover the *underlying motives* for individuals' media use. *Why* does one person rush home (or stay up late at night) to watch the local news on television while another person prefers reading the newspaper during breakfast or after dinner? Why do some people only watch HBO movies? These are some questions that uses and gratifications theorists attempt to answer in their research. A third objective of this line of theory building is to identify the positive and negative *consequences* of individual media use. It is with this third objective that the *systems* aspect of Uses and Gratifications Theory emerges. The systems approach to building communication theory attempts to identify relationships between the system and its subsystems. In Uses and Gratifications Theory, relationships between the individual and the mass media,

Figure 11.1

Television Viewing Motives Instrument

Instructions: Here are some reasons that other people gave us for watching TV. Please tell us how each reason is like your own reason for watching television. (Put one check in the correct column for each reason.)

I watch television . . .	A Lot	A Little	Not Much	Not At All
1. Because it relaxes me	____	____	____	____
2. So I won't be alone	____	____	____	____
3. So I can learn about things happening in the world	____	____	____	____
4. Because it's a habit	____	____	____	____
5. When I have nothing better to do	____	____	____	____
6. Because it helps me learn things about myself	____	____	____	____
7. Because it's thrilling	____	____	____	____
8. So I can forget about school and homework	____	____	____	____
9. Because it calms me down when I'm angry	____	____	____	____
10. When there's no one to talk to	____	____	____	____
11. So I can learn how to do things I haven't done before	____	____	____	____
12. Because I just like to watch	____	____	____	____
13. Because it passes the time away	____	____	____	____
14. So I could learn about what could happen to me	____	____	____	____
15. Because it excites me	____	____	____	____
16. So I can get away from the rest of the family	____	____	____	____
17. Because it's a pleasant rest	____	____	____	____
18. Because it makes me feel less lonely	____	____	____	____
19. Because it teaches me things I don't learn in school	____	____	____	____
20. Because I just enjoy watching	____	____	____	____
21. Because it gives me something to do	____	____	____	____
22. Because it shows how other people deal with the same problems I have	____	____	____	____
23. Because it stirs me up	____	____	____	____
24. So I can get away from what I'm doing	____	____	____	____

[From Rubin, A. (1979). Television use by children and adolescents. *Human Communication Research, 5,* 109-120.]

Figure 11.2

Scoring Instructions for Television Viewing Motives Instrument

Give a numerical value for each statement in each column. Use the following scale:

A Lot = 4
A Little = 3
Not Much = 2
Not At All = 1

Add your score for *each* of the following viewing motive factors:

Viewing Motive	Statement Numbers	Mean Score
Relaxation	1, 9, 17	2.41
Companionship	2, 10, 18	1.68
Habit	4, 12, 20	1.97
Pass Time	5, 13, 21	2.13
Learning About Things	3, 11, 19	1.84
Learning About Myself	6, 14, 22	1.84
Arousal	7, 15, 23	1.67
Forget/Escape	8, 16, 24	1.67

After you have added up the scores for each factor, divide that score by 3 to obtain a mean or average score for each television viewing motive factor. Compare your average score on each dimension with the norms obtained from a nonrandom sample of 464 adults (Rubin, 1983).

media content, the social system, alternative channels of communication (such as friends), and the consequences of media choice are examined.

The Historical Development of Uses and Gratifications Research

Efforts to discover media use patterns have existed for almost fifty years. As early as 1940, researchers began to explore radio listenership patterns via the uses and gratifications perspective (e.g., Lazarsfeld, 1940). Early uses and gratifications research investigated topics ranging from children's use of comics to how it feels to be without a newspaper during a newspaper strike. The early uses and gratifications studies were similar in that researchers used open-ended questions on surveys and in personal interviews to explore mass media use. Qualitative research techniques were used to collect and analyze data. Early researchers generally ignored the relationship between psychological needs and motives for media use (Rubin, 1985). In the 1960s and early 1970s researchers emphasized individual use of television instead of radio or print media. Greater interest in psychological factors involved in media use also emerged during this period. Finally, greater reliance on quantitative techniques of data gathering and analysis was evident (McQuail, 1984).

McQuail (1984) and Rubin (1986) suggest that current research efforts in Uses and Gratifications Theory can be classified under several broad headings. First, many studies have explored how *children* use the media. A uses and gratifications approach to understanding *political communication* has emerged. A third line of inquiry has explored characteristics of *audience experience, audience interpretations,* and *audience activity.* Some studies examine the information-seeking use of the media. Understanding *audience motives* of media use has stimulated considerable research. Another line of research examines the *social and psychological circumstances of media use.* These studies examine how factors such as family viewing, environment, personality, interpersonal interaction, and social activity influence media consumption. Finally, research efforts aimed at theory development and modeling the uses and gratifications process are currently under way (McQuail, 1984).

Current Examples of Uses and Gratifications Research

One tenet of Uses and Gratifications Theory is that audiences are active rather than passive in their media use. That is, individuals actively choose the communication media to which they attend. Levy and Windahl (1984) identified three types of audience activity. The first activity type, called *preactivity*, is practiced by individuals who deliberately seek certain media to gratify intellectual needs. For example, certain viewers deliberately select newscasts for such gratification. The second type of audience activity, called *duractivity*, deals with the degree of psychological attentiveness or involvement audience members exhibit during a TV viewing experience. This type of activity may best be understood from a *constructivist* orientation (see Personal Construct Theory, Chapter 3). The focus of this activity is on assessing how individuals interpret and decifer mediated messages. The comprehension, organization, and structuring of media messages leads to certain intellectual and emotional gratification for viewers. For example, trying to figure out the plot or ending of a dramatic program on television is one example of the duractivity use of the media. The third type of audience activity, *postactivity*, deals with audience behavior and message use after exposure to mediated messages. People involved in postactivity attend to a mediated message because they feel the information may have some personal or interpersonal value. Individuals who actively seek out television news as content for interpersonal communication such as "small talk" exhibit postactivity audience behavior.

In a study of Swedish television users, Levy and Windahl (1984) discovered that people who watch TV news vary in the degree to which they can be considered active users. The results of this study supported the assumption of an active audience. Participants were able to describe how particular media gratified certain needs. The researchers also found that the primary motivation for watching TV news was to gain information about the world, rather than for diversion.

Rubin (1983) designed a study to explore adult viewers' motivations, behaviors, attitudes, and patterns of interaction. The study also sought to explore whether TV user motivations could predict behavioral and attitudinal consequences of television use. Five primary television viewing motivations were examined: pass time/habit, information, entertainment, companionship, and escape. All factors, except information and pass time/habit, were related to consequences of television use. The strongest viewing motivation relationships were found between pass time/habit and both companionship and escape viewing. It appears, then, individuals use television as an escape mechanism and a companion. They do so to pass the time or as a habit. Two viewer types were also identified in this study. The first type uses TV to pass time and out of habit. The second type uses TV to seek information or as a learning tool. The viewer types are consistent with Rubin's (1984) *ritualized* and *instrumental* users of television discussed earlier.

Media Usage Lifestyle Types. One study addressed several social and psychological factors associated with patterns of audience media use. Donohew, Palmgreen, and Rayburn (1987) tested a random sample of subscribers to cable television. Through telephone and mailed questionnaires, they collected demographic (age, sex, income, education, marital status), lifestyle, and attitudinal data. Participants also provided information on their social, political, economic, cultural, and communication-related behaviors. The researchers also asked questions about need for arousal (stimulation), perceived gratifications sought from cable TV, satisfaction with cable TV offerings, number of hours of cable TV viewing per day, and number of newspapers and magazines subscribed to. Four lifestyle types emerged. Type I was labeled the *Disengaged Homemaker*. This individual was primarily female, middle-aged, lower in education and income. Members of this type were lowest in need for arousal (stimulation). They did not use the media for informational purposes, but for companionship and to pass the time. According to Rubin's (1983, 1984) classification, they appear to represent the *ritualized* media user. The second type of individual was labeled the *Outgoing Activist*. Demographically, this person was female (but less likely to be so than Type I), somewhat younger, well-educated, had a good income, and was less likely to be married. Outgoing activists were highest in need for stimulation among the four types. They enjoyed staying informed and were primarily print media users. They did not watch a great amount of television and were least gratified by cable TV. Donohew, Palmgreen and Rayburn speculate that Type II's active lifestyle leaves them little time for TV viewing. The third type of individual was labeled the *Restrained Activist*. These individuals were older and had the highest educational levels. More than half were female, and they were likely to be married and have relatively high incomes. They had low need for sensation but high need for intellectual stimulation. They exhibited strong informational needs and viewed themselves as opinion leaders. They were heavy users of both print media and television, especially for informational purposes. Their media use patterns follow those of Rubin's (1983, 1984) *instrumental* user. The final type of user identified was called the *Working Class Climber*. This person was primarily male, lower in education and income, and middle-aged. Most were married. Donohew, Palmgreen, and Rayburn (1987) suggest that this person "is most typified by the aspiring and somewhat chauvinistic male from blue collar or low level white collar occupations" (p. 270). Working Class Climbers were ambitious and self-confident. They did not engage in an activist lifestyle. They ranked low in need for intellectual stimulation. They were highest among the types on television exposure and satisfaction with cable TV. They were quite low on print media usage. According to Rubin's taxonomy, they would be classified more as ritualized than as instrumental media users. The results of this study helped clarify our understanding of the many lifestyle variables which influence mass media use. In addition, the study added support for Rubin's theory of ritualized and instrumental media use patterns.

Criticisms of Uses and Gratifications Theory

Since its inception, Uses and Gratifications Theory has enjoyed widespread popularity among mass communication theorists, researchers, and practitioners. The theory has also received its share of criticism. Blumler (1979) and Windahl (1981) provide powerful criticism when they suggest that uses and gratifications does not represent a single theory. These critics call uses and gratifications an umbrella concept in which several theories reside. McQuail (1984) argues that this lack of a unified theory has led to misuse of the empirical method of inquiry. Social and political objections have also been raised concerning Uses and Gratifications Theory. The theory's grounding in the functional paradigm has been challenged. McQuail argues that functionalism forces a researcher to use a conservative model of the social system. This conservative view increases the chances that the mass media will be used to manipulate people. It is argued that media manipulators will soon move from the knowledge of "why people like what they get" to the view "that people get what they like" (McQuail, 1984, p. 182). This will reduce the application of new knowledge about media dependence discovered through these many research efforts. Rubin (1985) suggests that uses and gratifications audience motive research has been too compartmentalized within particular cultures or demographic groups. This has thwarted synthesis and integration of research results, activities which are critical to theory building. He also argues that there are too many different meanings associated with the terms "audience motives," "uses," and "gratifications," which has slowed unified theoretical development in this area. Finally, Uses and Gratifications Theory and research has been criticized on methodological grounds. Self-report questionnaires have typically been used in uses and gratifications studies. As with other communication investigations, the *reliability* and *validity* of self-report data has been questioned. For example, some critics believe that individuals cannot respond accurately to questions about their own feelings and behavior. This criticism is tempered, however, by the use of instruments that have been judged as reliable and valid *a priori.* (See the Appendix for a discussion of reliability and validity.)

The Rules Approach in Mass Communication

Lull (1980a, 1980b, 1982) has used the rules approach to investigate media use and interpersonal communication activity in the home. Lull and others (e.g., Fry & McCain, 1980; Wolf, Meyer, & White, 1982) argue that the communication rules paradigm presents a fruitful way of resolving problems regarding theory building in mass communication.

Law-Governed Models and Media Activity

Lull suggests that the factors of human free will, choice, time, and numerous communication contexts make it difficult to measure and predict people's media activity. Traditional law-governed models have been useful to guide theory building efforts in understanding audience consumer habits and political activity, but the cause and effect models and quantitative measurement techniques of the law-governed approach are limited in their ability to explain and predict complex media-related interaction behavior such as family television viewing patterns. As in other contexts, the rules perspective has emerged as an attractive alternative paradigm to guide mass communication scholars in their theory building efforts. These scholars argue that communication rules exist not only in face-to-face interaction but between the parts of a mediated symbol system as well. Recall from our earlier discussion in Chapter 3 that communication rules can range from idiosyncratic rules developed by two people or a family unit to more generalized rules considered appropriate and normative by an entire culture or society.

Lull's Rules-Based Theory of Mass Media and Audience Behavior

The rules perspective views mass communication use as an interactive, choice-making activity. This paradigm represents an alternative to probabilistic, cause and effect, law-governed explanations of media-related communication activity. Lull (1982) suggests that the rules approach in communication can be profitably applied to studying issues such as television's effect on children, uses and gratifications, the agenda-setting function of the media, and the way people construct their leisure time. Rules of mass communication activity can be studied either on a *micro* or *macro* level. On a micro level, we would study how smaller audience units such as families use the media. In this context, the mass communication theorist would study audience members' relationships with one another as they watch television, listen to a radio broadcast, or attend to other forms of mass media. On a macro level, we can study behaviors of the entire society or culture associated with media use. For example, a researcher could examine a culture's media content. Radio and TV broadcasts could be studied to determine dominant themes of the culture's media messages.

Family TV Viewing Rules

Many of us may recall rules in our families regarding appropriate television viewing behavior. Examples include how much time you were allowed to watch TV each day, what types of programs you were allowed to watch, which member of the family got to choose the program the family would watch, and what behaviors you could (or could not) engage in during family viewing hours. One of your authors vividly remembers that loud talking to a sister was prohibited during family TV viewing hours. If you engaged in this "rule violation behavior," you risked being scolded by a parent! As with most communication rules, some rules of family media use were explicitly stated or "spelled out" for us. How many of you can recall examples of such rule-governed media behavior as "No TV after 10 PM!" or "No TV until all your homework is done!" Other rules were not explicitly stated but were still apparent to us. Some rules are "learned" through observing behavior of family members. One such communication rule related to TV viewing that many of us have learned through observation is, "When watching TV with members of the family, one does not change the channel without first asking permission."

Lull (1982) identified three classes of rule behavior and television viewing in the family. *Habitual rules* are rules which are typically non-negotiable, frequently instituted by those in positions of authority, and have negative consequences (punishments) if violated. Habitual rules frequently deal with the amount, time, or content of TV viewing allowed in a family.

Parametric rules are used to describe patterns of action considered appropriate within certain mutually understood boundaries or parameters. These parametric rules are frequently, but not always, verbally stated. As with habitual rules, parametric rules are typically dictated by an authority figure in the family. The major difference between habitual and parametric rules is that parametric rules are somewhat negotiable. In other words, parametric rules provide us with opportunities to choose from a range of acceptable behaviors. Lull cites the negotiation of TV program preferences or times for TV viewing as examples of parametric rules of TV-related family viewing behavior. For example, a family may favor informational programs designed to teach children academic or social skills. If a program of this nature was on television one evening, a child could negotiate so that the entire family would watch that program. "Extended talk only during commercial breaks" is another example of a parametric rule which influences family television viewing behaviors. Lull states that the major difference between habitual and parametric rules of TV viewing rests with the *degree* to which the rule is negotiable. With habitual rules, parents and older siblings impose *non-negotiable* rules. Parametric rules are more *negotiable*.

The third type of rules identified by Lull is termed *tactical rules*. These rules are used to achieve some personal or interpersonal objective. Tactical rules are created by individuals, groups, or the culture in general to solve problems or realize goals. Cushman and Pearce's (1977) notion of a rules-based *practical syllogism* can be used to provide an example of a tactical rule. What may seem like choice-making activity involving television may actually be the nurturing of relational harmony. For example, Terry desires to maintain marital harmony with a spouse, Pat. To do so, Terry determines that "giving in" on certain TV viewing is one means to achieve that goal. Thus, Terry changes the channel to Pat's favorite show (Lull, 1982, p. 9). In the form of the practical syllogism, if Terry wants to make Pat happy, Terry will choose to "give in" to let Pat watch a favorite show. Families also use television for other social purposes. Some family members turn on the television in order to withdraw from family conflict. Other families use television viewing as a reward or punishment. Families of this type tend to develop elaborate "social control rules" which parents use to control their children's viewing habits. Tactical rules such as these suggest that television use is a form of behavior regulation. Two examples of social-control rules described by Fry and McCain (1980) are: "When I want to reward my child for doing something good, I often let him/her watch extra television," and "When my child is bad, I often take his/her TV privileges away as punishment."

Relational Uses of Television: A Qualitative Study

Wolf, Meyer and White (1982) conducted a qualitative study to identify a couple's rule-governed media behavior. The researchers studied how one couple, Bob and Carolyn, used the media to construct and structure their own social reality. Over a two-year period the researchers observed, interviewed and recorded samples of the couple's conversations. The study revealed that this couple used media content for four social purposes: communication facilitation, affiliation/avoidance, social learning, and competence/dominance. Television content helped the couple create topics for talk or reminded them of feelings and experiences which they self-disclosed to each other and to friends. These uses are representative of the communication *facilitation* function of media content. Television content frequently establishes a common ground for people, reduces anxiety, clarifies values, and "sets the agenda" for talk. Couples also use media content for affiliation and/or avoidance.

Watching a heartrending drama frequently brings a couple closer together, as it stimulates the couple to disclose feelings, needs and desires. Television viewing could also be used for avoidance. A couple can "tune each other out" by turning on the television. A third use of television is for *social learning.* Some people watch game shows such as *Jeopardy!* as a way of learning about history, geography, literature and art. Fourth, media content can be used to display competence or dominance. Watching television commercials prompted Bob and Carolyn to challenge the sponsors' claims. In this way, displays of knowledge and competence emerged. Certain role-appropriate behaviors (such as "provider" or "protector") become clearer through television's mediated images. These images can help remind people of situations in which they should act in role-appropriate ways. For example, a television program may detail how loving, attentive, and supportive a husband is during his wife's pregnancy. Viewing this program may help reinforce role-appropriate behaviors in men whose wives are pregnant.

As students of communication, you can act as researchers to investigate rules of family media activity. You can attempt to locate patterns of rules-based media activity if you know what to *observe* and what questions to *ask.* Noting the frequency of recurring patterns of behavior is one way to identify communication rules. Who is the first one to turn on the television after dinner? Who controls the remote control channel changer? What types of verbal and nonverbal negotiation occur when the family decides to watch television? These are a few of the behaviors you can look for to determine rules of family viewing.

Benefits of the Rules Approach in Mass Communication

The communication rules approach has emerged as a profitable alternative paradigm to theory building in mass communication. Lull (1982) suggests that the rules approach acts as a bridge between "effects" theories of human interaction and critical researchers who analyze media content and its relationship to the economic and political structure. The rules perspective views audience members as active participants in the communication process. The rules paradigm can be used to bridge the gap between those who advocate direct media effects and the uses and gratifications theorists. Employing a multi-perspective orientation should increase the likelihood of building sound theories of mass communication.

Cultivation Theory

The Cultivation Theory of mass communication effects has largely been developed by Gerbner and his associates at the Annenberg School of Communication at the University of Pennsylvania. The theory has been developed and tested over the last twenty years by numerous empirical studies.

Cultivation Theory asserts that the media, especially television, exerts a tremendous influence by altering individuals' perceptions of reality. Cultivation Theory (Gerbner, Gross, Morgan & Signorielli, 1980, 1986) suggests that television is largely responsible for the development of perceptions of day-to-day norms and reality. The dramatizing and display of a culture's norms and values was once the job of formal religion. Today, television serves as the major medium from which a society acquires its norms and values. Television has become the major cultural transmitter for today's society (Gerbner & Gross, 1976a, b). Television has become the medium by which most people develop standardized roles and behaviors, so its major function is *enculturation*. "Living" in the world of television cultivates a particular view of reality. Some argue that television provides an experience that is more alive, more real, and more vivid than anything we can expect to experience in real life!

The Interaction of Media and Reality

One of the authors recently read an article in a local newspaper which illustrates our tendency to mistake a real event for a television enactment. The reporter had stopped his car at the intersection of a rural road and a larger highway. He noticed a car speeding on the highway at approximately 100 miles per hour! As the car reached the point where the reporter was stopped, it suddenly tried to make a left turn without slowing down. It clipped a light pole and flipped over on its back, wheels still spinning. No one else was in sight. The reporter described staring forward, not believing what he had just seen. He recalled his mind saying to him very clearly, "What you are seeing isn't real. You are just watching a movie." For almost ten seconds he just sat there, waiting to see what would happen next. Of course, nothing happened, and he realized that it was up to him to help. As he approached the car, he was scared to death, but in true movie style, for the wrong reason. On TV and in the movies, any overturned car soon catches fire and explodes. Fortunately, in "real life" cars rarely explode. In the movies and on TV, no "real man" minds approaching a dead or horribly mutilated body. The reporter was very afraid that he would encounter such a scene. This story reveals that television and the movies are making it difficult to distinguish between illusion and reality. We sometimes mistake a real event for a televised one, as in the example cited above. We probably make the opposite mistake more frequently. We frequently mistake television or movies for the real thing. This phenomenon provides the basis of the research into Cultivation Theory.

"Heavy" versus "Light" Television Viewers

Individuals frequently confuse media constructed reality with actual reality. Gerbner and Gross (1976b) reported that in the first five years of the broadcast life, *Dr. Marcus Welby* (a fictional doctor portrayed by Robert Young on television), the show received over a quarter of a million letters from viewers. Most of the letters contained requests for medical advice! Gerbner and his colleagues report that people who watch a great deal of television see the world as more dangerous and frightening than those who watch less television. They have identified two types of television viewers who differ in perceptions of reality. Heavy viewers are defined as those watching an average of four or more hours per day. Light viewers watch an average of two hours or less each day. Gerbner has reported that heavy viewers overestimate their chances of being involved in a violent crime. They also overestimate the number of law enforcement workers in society. Television overrepresents both the number of crime victims and law enforcement officials in society. One reason the influence of television in the cultivation process is so strong is that many of us do not have an opportunity to observe some aspects of reality as frequently as we observe mediated reality. We may have limited opportunities to observe the internal workings of a real police station, hospital operating room, or municipal courtroom. Thus, the media images become our images of reality. Have you noticed that the New Year's Eve parties we attend *never* seem quite as exciting as the New Year's Eve parties we see on television?

Cultivation studies have kept factors such as education and newspaper reading constant in determining the media's influence on perceptions of reality. Although education and newspaper reading did have some influence, the impact of heavy television viewing was still powerful. The only factor that seemed to have an independent effect on perceptions was age. Respondents under 30 consistently reported that their responses were more influenced by television than those over 30 (Gerbner & Gross, 1976b). Since people 30 and under have been "weaned" on television, the influence of media messages may be especially potent. As Gerbner and his colleagues report, the more time one spends "living" in the world of television, the more reality and the media's pictures of reality become congruent.

Refinement of Cultivation Theory

In response to challenges to the theory, Gerbner and his associates introduced the factors of mainstreaming and resonance to help add explanatory power to the cultivation effect (Gerbner, Gross, Morgan, & Signorielli, 1980). *Mainstreaming* suggests that differences in perceptions of reality due to demographic and social factors are diminished or negated by heavy TV viewing. Heavy television viewers who are highly educated with high incomes tend to respond more like heavy TV viewers with less education and lower incomes. As Gerbner and his colleagues suggest "Heavy viewers of all groups tend to share a relatively homogeneous outlook" (Gerbner, Gross, Morgan, & Signorielli, 1980, p. 15). *Resonance* implies that the influence of the media's messages on perceptions of reality is intensified when what people see on television is what they see in life. This double dose of the televised message tends to amplify the cultivation effect.

Criticisms and Modifications of Cultivation Theory

Despite the large data set supporting the theory, the cultivation effect has encountered several challenges. Hughes (1980) and Hirsch (1980) reanalyzed data from the National Opinion Research Center General Social Survey used in the original research and failed to support the core assumptions of Cultivation Theory. Critics of the theory argue that Cultivation Theory may be incorrect. Hughes (1980) reports that television may actually cultivate realistic and functional perceptions of the world. Recall some of the research identifying the prosocial functions of the media. It has been argued that major assumptions of Cultivation Theory may be correct, but the procedures used to study it may be incapable of uncovering the effect. Hughes (1980) suggests that the measures of heavy viewing only relate to total exposure to television, not specifically to what is watched. Certain personality characteristics which are related to the selection of television programs were not controlled for in the earlier studies. Hawkins and Pingree (1982) reviewed 48 research studies conducted on the cultivation effect. They concluded that there is modest evidence to support the influence of television viewing on perceptions of reality. They suggest that this influence is strongest for violent programs. More recently, Potter (1986) grouped subjects on several perceived reality dimensions. *Perceived reality* is the degree of reality that people "see" in mediated messages. This factor is more psychological in nature than variables used in previous tests of the theory. Potter (1986) concluded that the cultivation effect may be more complex than is currently stated; the amount of exposure to television may be less important than the attitudes and perceptions of individuals exposed. There is no doubt that the controversy surrounding the media's influence on our perceptions and behavior will continue to rage. We can expect more research from scholars of mass communication in this area. New findings will refine and advance our efforts to build mass communication theory.

Summary

The mass media exert a powerful influence on culture and on individual behavior. The media reflect a culture's attitudes and values and project many visions of a society to its members. Several early theories of mass communi-cation were outlined. The Magic Bullet Theory suggested that the mass media influences a large group of people directly and uniformly. The Two-Step Flow Theory argued that several variables intervene between media messages and audience reaction: informal, interpersonal contacts and the influence of opinion leaders. Diffusion Theory grew out of these early models. It identified conditions which influence the likelihood that a new idea, product, or practice will be adopted. Several contemporary theories of mass communication were presented. Mass communication serves five functions for a society: surveillance, correlation, cultural transmission, entertainment, and mobilization. The media also serve an agenda-setting function; they influence our attitudes by selectively focusing attention on certain issues. Gumpert and Cathcart's Theory of Mediated Interpersonal Communication examines the interaction of media and interpersonal communication. This theory recognizes the impact of mediated technology on interpersonal communication and the influence of face-to-face interaction on media. Uses and Gratifications Theory attempts to explain the underlying motives for individuals' use of mass communication. A core assumption of this theory is that an audience is an active group who seek out and use the media to satisfy certain needs. A rules-based theory of mass communication and audience behavior was presented. Lull's Rules Theory of Audience Behavior identifies three classes of rule-governed behavior and family television viewing. The media's influence on perceptions of reality is explained by Cultivation Theory. This theory suggests that television is largely responsible for the development of perceptions of day-to-day norms and reality. The theory argues that television has become the medium by which many people develop standardized roles and behaviors.

Questions To Consider

1. What questions have guided mass communication research and theory building?
2. What does the Reflective-Projective Theory say about the effects of the mass media?
3. What are five functions which mass media serve in society?
4. Explain the concept of media agenda-setting.
5. How do the Magic Bullet Theory and the Two-Step Flow Theory differ in explaining mass media effects?
6. What is the focus of Diffusion Theory? What does it predict about mass communication innovations?
7. How does the Theory of Mediated Interpersonal Communication attempt to combine interpersonal and mass media concerns?
8. How does the Uses and Gratifications Theory conceptualize mediated communication?
9. Discuss some examples of research conducted from a Uses and Gratifications framework.
10. What are the main assumptions of Lull's rules theory of mass media and audience behavior?
11. What does Cultivation Theory say about mass media effects?

References

Avery, R.K., & Ellis, D.G. (1979). Talk radio as an interpersonal phenomenon. In G. Gumpert & R. Cathcart (Eds.), *Inter/Media: Interpersonal communication in a media world* (pp. 108-115). New York: Oxford University Press.

Avery, R.K., & McCain, T.A. (1982). Interpersonal and mediated encounters: A reorientation to the mass communication process. In G. Gumpert & R. Cathcart (Eds.), *Inter/Media: Interpersonal communication in a media world* (2nd ed.), (pp. 29-40). New York: Oxford University Press.

Blumler, J.G. (1979). The role of theory in uses and gratifications studies. *Communication Research, 6*, 9-36.

Cathcart, R., & Gumpert, G. (1983). Mediated interpersonal communication: Toward a new typology. *Quarterly Journal of Speech, 69*, 267-277.

Cathcart, R., & Gumpert, G. (1986). I am a camera: The mediated self. *Communication Quarterly, 34*, 89-102.

Cushman, D., & Pearce, W.B. (1977). Generality and necessity in three types of communication theory. *Human Communication Research, 3*, 344-353.

DeFleur, M.L., & Ball-Rokeach, S. (1982). *Theories of mass communication* (4th ed.). New York: Longman.

Donohew, L., Palmgreen, P., & Rayburn, J.D. (1987). Social and psychological origins of media use: A lifestyle analysis. *Journal of Broadcasting & Electronic Media, 31*, 255-278.

Ettema, J.S., & Whitney, D.C. (Eds.) (1982). *Individuals in mass media organizations.* Beverly Hills, CA: Sage.

Fry, D., & McCain, T.A. (1980, August). *Controlling children's television viewing: Predictors of family television rules and their relationship to family communication patterns.* Paper presented at the Association for Education in Journalism and Mass Communication, Boston, MA.

Gerbner, G., & Gross, L. (1976a). Living with television: The violence profile. *Journal of Communication, 26*, 172-199.

Gerbner, G., & Gross, L. (1976b, April). The scary world of TV's heavy viewer. *Psychology Today*, pp. 41-45, 89.

Gerbner, G., Gross, L., Morgan, M., & Signorielli, N. (1980). The "mainstreaming" of America: Violence profile no. 11. *Journal of Communication, 30*, 10-29.

Gerbner, G., Gross, L., Morgan, M., & Signorielli, N. (1986). Living with television: The dynamics of the cultivation process. In J. Bryant & D. Zillmann (Eds.), *Perspectives on media effects* (pp. 17-40). Hillsdale, NJ: Lawrence Erlbaum.

Gumpert, G., & Cathcart, R. (Eds.) (1986). *Inter/Media: Interpersonal communication in a media world* (3rd ed.). New York: Oxford University Press.

Hawkins, R.P., & Pingree, S. (1982). Television's influence on social reality. In D. Pearl, L. Bouthilet, & J. Lazar (Eds.), *Television and behavior: Ten years of scientific progress and implications for the eighties: Vol. 2. Technical reviews* (pp. 224-247). Washington, DC: U.S. Government Printing Office.

Hirsch, P. (1980). The "scary world" of the non-viewer and other anomalies. *Communication Research, 7*, 403-456.

Hughes, M. (1980). The fruits of cultivation analysis: A reexamination of some effects of television watching. *Public Opinion Quarterly, 44*, 287-302.

Johnston, J., & Ettema, J.S. (1986). Using television to best advantage: Research for prosocial television. In J. Bryant & D. Zillmann (Eds.), *Perspectives on media effects* (pp. 143-164). Hillsdale, NJ: Lawrence Erlbaum.

Katz, E., Blumler, J.G., & Gurevitch, M. (1974). Utilization of mass communication by the individual. In J.G. Blumler & E. Katz (Eds.), *The uses of mass communications: Current perspectives on gratifications research* (pp. 19-32). Beverly Hills, CA: Sage.

Katz, E., & Lazarsfeld, P.F. (1955). *Personal influence: The part played by people in the flow of mass communication.* New York: Free Press.

Lasswell, H.D. (1948). The structure and function of communication in society. In L. Bryson (Ed.), *The communication of ideas* (pp. 37-51). New York: Harper.

Lasswell, H.D. (1927). *Propaganda technique in world wars.* New York: Knopf.

Lazarsfeld, P.F. (1940). *Radio and the printed page.* New York: Dvell, Sloan and Pearce.

Lazarsfeld, P.F., Berelson, B.R., & Gaudet, H. (1944). *The people's choice: How the voter makes up his mind in a presidential campaign.* New York: Columbia University Press.

Levy, M.R., & Windahl, S. (1984). Audience activity and gratifications: A conceptual clarification and exploration. *Communication Research, 11,* 51-78.

Loevinger, L. (1979). The ambiguous mirror: The reflective-projective theory of broadcasting and mass communication. In G. Gumpert & R. Cathcart (Eds.), *Inter/Media: Interpersonal communication in a media world* (pp. 234-260). New York: Oxford University Press.

Lowery, S., & DeFleur, M.L. (1983). *Milestones in mass communication research: Media effects.* New York: Longman.

Lull, J. (1978). Choosing television programs by family vote. *Communication Quarterly, 26,* 53-57.

Lull, J. (1980a). Family communication patterns and the social uses of television. *Communication Research, 7,* 319-334.

Lull, J. (1980b). The social uses of television. *Human Communication Research, 6,* 197-209.

Lull, J. (1982). A rules approach to the study of television and society. *Human Communication Research, 9,* 3-16.

McCombs, M.E., & Shaw, D.L. (1972). The agenda-setting function of mass media. *Public Opinion Quarterly, 36,* 176-187.

McQuail, D. (1984). With the benefit of hindsight: Reflections on uses and gratifications research. *Critical Studies in Mass Communication, 1,* 177-193.

McQuail, D. (1987). *Mass communication theory: An introduction.* Beverly Hills, CA: Sage.

Potter, W.J. (1986). Perceived reality and the cultivation hypothesis. *Journal of Broadcasting & Electronic Media, 30,* 159-174.

Rogers, E.M. (1983). *Diffusion of innovations* (3rd ed.). New York: Free Press.

Rogers, E., & Shoemaker, F. (1971). *Communication of innovations.* New York: Free Press.

Rubin, A.M. (1979). Television use by children and adolescents. *Human Communication Research, 5,* 109-120.

Rubin, A.M. (1983). Television uses and gratifications: The interactions of viewing patterns and motivations. *Journal of Broadcasting, 27,* 37-51.

Rubin, A.M. (1984). Ritualized and instrumental television viewing. *Journal of Communication, 34*, 67-77.

Rubin, A.M. (1985). Uses and gratifications: Quasi-functional analysis. In J.R. Dominick & J.E. Fletcher (Eds.), *Broadcasting research methods* (pp. 202-220). Boston, MA: Allyn and Bacon.

Rubin, A.M. (1986). Uses, gratifications, and media effects research. In J. Bryant & D. Zillmann (Eds.), *Perspectives on media effects* (pp. 281-301). Hillsdale, NJ: Lawrence Erlbaum.

Rubin, A.M., & Rubin, R.B. (1985). Interface of personal and mediated communication: A research agenda. *Critical Studies in Mass Communication, 2*, 36-53.

Scholder, S., Lalumia, T., & Murphy, M. (1987). *The creation of mediated "friendships": Meeting others via telephone.* Unpublished manuscript, Emerson College, Boston, MA.

Severin, W.J., & Tankard, J.W. (1988). *Communication theories* (2nd ed.). New York: Longman.

Swanson, D.L. (1987). Gratification seeking, media exposure, and audience interpretations: Some directions for research. *Journal of Broadcasting & Electronic Media, 31*, 237-254.

Williams, W.W. (1985). Agenda-setting research. In J.R. Dominick & J.E. Fletcher (Eds.), *Broadcasting research methods* (pp. 189-201). Boston: Allyn and Bacon.

Wimmer, R.D., & Dominick, J.R. (1987). *Mass media research* (2nd ed.). Belmont, CA: Wadsworth.

Windahl, S. (1981). Uses and gratifications at the crossroads. In G.C. Wilhoit & H. deBock (Eds.), *Mass communication review yearbook,* (Vol. 2, pp. 174-185). Beverly Hills, CA: Sage.

Wolf, M.A., Meyer, T.P., & White, C. (1982). A rules-based study of television's role in the construction of social reality. *Journal of Broadcasting, 26*, 813-829.

Wright, C.R. (1960). Functional analysis and mass communication. *Public Opinion Quarterly, 24*, 606-620.

Zillmann, D. (1982). Television viewing and arousal. In D. Pearl, L. Bouthilet, & J. Lazar (Eds.), *Television and behavior: Ten years of scientific progress and implications for the eighties: Vol. 2. Technical reviews* (pp. 53-67). Washington, DC: U.S. Government Printing Office.

Zillmann, D., & Bryant, J. (1985). Affect, mood, and emotion as determinants of selective exposure. In D. Zillmann & J. Bryant (Eds.), *Selective exposure to communication* (pp. 157-190). Hillsdale, NJ: Lawrence Erlbaum.

Zillmann, D., & Bryant, J. (Eds.) (1986). *Perspectives on media effects.* Hillsdale, NJ: Lawrence Erlbaum.

Chapter 12

Intercultural Contexts

Intercultural communication is one of the newer contexts for communication research. The growth of intercultural communication theories is in part due to changes taking place in the international environment. More United States firms are doing business in international markets, more firms are becoming multinational (having profit centers in more than one country), and more and more products of other countries are available in America. The 1987 United States stock market crash and its reverberations around the world indicated that we now have a global economy; economic events in one country have major repercussions on the economies of other nations. More and more people are traveling internationally on vacation as well as on business. Satellite communication has brought the world closer together; we can witness major events and disasters around the globe as they are happening. The suppression of the 1989 student demonstrations in Tienanmen Square, Beijing, China, emphasized that our world has become a "global village" in which we know people and events in other countries almost as well as residents of small villages know their neighbors (McLuhan, 1964).

Another social change which has affected intercultural communication is the growing attempt in the United States to celebrate cultural differences within our own society. The many ethnic festivals held in cities such as Chicago and Boston and widely attended by people from many different backgrounds are an attempt to create awareness of and sensitivity to the variety of cultures from which Americans have come. Although residents of the United States all have much in common as Americans, regional, socio-economic, religious, and ethnic differences are some of the factors which create many varieties of experiences, values, and ways of looking at the world. These variations create common communication patterns among people with similar backgrounds and influence communication between members of different regions and ethnic origins. Americans no longer view their country as a melting pot in which differences have been submerged but rather as a patchwork quilt made beautiful by a wide variety of different patterns (Kim, 1977b).

The Development of the Study of Intercultural Communication

The increasing importance of intercultural communication, mediated communication, and communication between members of subcultures has led to a burst of theory building in intercultural communication in the last twenty to thirty years. Theories of intercultural communication were first developed by anthropologists. Edward Hall, whose theories of proximity and social distance were presented in Chapter 8, is a cultural anthropologist who greatly influenced the field of communication. The creation of the Peace Corps by President John F. Kennedy in the early 1960s also led to an increased interest in and need for knowledge about how people of different cultures can communicate more effectively. Since the early work of Hall and the early studies of Peace Corps volunteers, theories of intercultural communication have broadened to include theories of language, mass media, and intercultural conflict (e.g., Asuncion-Lande & Womack, 1982). Theories have been used to train representatives of government, business, the military, and others who plan to live abroad. This chapter will first describe the different areas of theory building in intercultural communication and will then present key concepts from the field. Finally, examples of theory building from the laws, rules, and systems perspectives will be discussed.

Just as you learned in Chapter 1 that scholars disagree on what the best definition of communication is, there are many disagreements among scholars from different fields about the most appropriate definition of culture. For our purposes, culture is not a social system, "the behavior of people who share a common culture" (Gudykunst, 1987, p. 848), nor a society, people "who share a common culture and social system" (Gudykunst, 1987, p. 848), but "the traditions, customs, norms, beliefs, values, and thought-patterning which are passed down from generation to generation" (Prosser, 1978, p. 5).

Gudykunst (1987) divides the study of intercultural communication into nine different areas, some of which are described below. *Intercultural communication* refers to communication between individuals or groups from different cultures or from different subcultures (for example, Chicanos; see Asuncion-Lande, 1977) of the same sociocultural system. Intercultural communication research might describe how American and Japanese business negotiations are conducted or how Mexican Americans and Oriental Americans communicate with each other. *Cross-cultural communication* compares the intercultural communication behavior of different combinations of people, so Japanese and American negotiation tactics would be compared and contrasted in a cross-cultural communication study. *International communication* refers to the study of mass-media communication within different cultures. For instance, international communication research might describe the social role of television in India. *Comparative mass communication* theories compare media systems from different cultures, for example, India and England. *Communication and international relations* is an area of the field involving the study of communication between nations and their political leaders. The relationship between communication and political change is now studied not only by political scientists but also by scholars of communication.

Developmental communication spans the border between mass communication and interpersonal communication. It is communication related to social change, often in developing countries. Two kinds of processes, internal and external, lead to developmental communication (Fagen, 1966). In the external model, socioeconomic changes cause changes in media, lifestyle, and opportunities for members of a society. Then, people begin to perceive themselves and their place in the world differently. Finally, these different perceptions lead to behavior which affects the political system of the society. The internal model begins with the selection of political strategies which will change communication patterns. Next, the communication patterns lead to different self-perceptions and world-views, which finally lead to changes in the political system, although not necessarily the changes planned by those who set the process in motion. Developmental communication recognizes that communication can be used to facilitate social change; scholars in this area attempt to describe and analyze the variables and effects of the policies involved in using communication as an agent of social change.

Key Concepts in Intercultural Communication

Verbal Codes

Intercultural communication, the study of communication between individuals or groups of people from different cultures, involves several important areas of exploration. As a member of a particular culture, a person learns particular patterns of perceiving the world through learning symbol systems such as language and nonverbal behavior. While all members of a culture may share the same language, members of a nondominant culture may develop their own set of symbols. These symbols unify them against the dominant culture and reinforce their identity as members of the subculture. When the dominant culture adopts the symbols, they no longer serve the original purpose, so they are changed. An example of this phenomenon may be seen in the changing of teenage slang when it becomes adopted by adults.

The Sapir-Whorf or Whorfian Hypothesis

The importance of language in influencing a culture is an important point of the linguistic relativity theory of Edward Sapir (1958, 1964) and his student Benjamin Lee Whorf (1956). As you recall from Chapter 7, the Whorfian or Sapir-Whorf hypothesis indicates that language shapes culture and individual thought-patterns. For example, in English, you can say "brother" or "sister" when speaking of your sibling. You do not need to specify age unless you want to distinguish between two sisters or to emphasize the age relationship, as in "older sister." However, in Mandarin Chinese, there is no generic term for "brother," "sister," "uncle" or "aunt." Perhaps because of the greater importance of specific family relationships in Chinese culture, the only words available for relative specify quite precise relationships such as "big (first-born) older sister," "small (second-born but still older than the speaker) older sister," "younger brother," and "uncle on my mother's side." The Whorfian hypothesis indicates that language influences the way the speakers of that language perceive the world. Because Chinese must make more mental relationship distinctions to speak in Mandarin, they are likely to be more sensitive to differences in specific family relationships than are speakers of English.

However, because English has many more words for color than Mandarin Chinese, Chinese are likely to see fewer shades of color than English speakers. For example, think of all the words you can which are synonyms or varieties of "red": "pink," "pale pink," "salmon pink," "petal pink," "rouge," "cranberry," "rose," "maroon," and "russet" are just a few. Mandarin Chinese has only one word for "red," with additional designations for shades of "light" and "dark." A friend once bought a Chinese padded jacket in a store in Taipei, Taiwan. There were about fifteen jackets, all the appropriate size, hanging from a bar high over her head and the head of the salesclerk. With a hook, the clerk selected the first jacket and asked if it was the one our friend wanted. When she replied that she wanted a "light red" (actually pink or magenta) jacket, the clerk picked the next in line, which was a shade lighter than the first, but very different from the shade our friend had in mind. There was no way in Mandarin to specify the exact color, and the salesclerk did not speak English, so our friend finally had to point with her hand to the jacket she wanted. The salesclerk's language gave her a different set of categories from those of speakers of American English and influenced her perception. To the salesclerk all the jackets were approximately the same color; differences were slight and unimportant. On the other hand, our friend saw an entire range of shades of pink and red, all substantially different. The language each had learned influenced the mental category systems used to perceive the outside world.

Nonverbal Codes

The importance of the nonverbal code for influencing others' perceptions and for communicating meaning has been addressed in Chapter 8. Many of the ways in which people use nonverbal behavior to initiate interaction, clarify relationships, direct conversational turn-taking, guide emotional expression, and terminate conversations vary substantially from culture to culture. The examples below will briefly illustrate several important areas of nonverbal communication differences which vary with different cultures.

Ekman and Friesen's (1969) five types of bodily movement are emblems, illustrators, affect displays, adaptors, and regulators. (Refer to Chapter 8 for a more thorough treatment of them.) Emblems, movements which serve the same purpose as words, may easily be misunderstood (Ekman & Friesen, 1969). For example, when Americans want to motion to a friend to "come closer," they cup their hands with fingers pointed upwards and pull their fingers toward them in "a roughly clockwise motion" (Condon & Yousef, 1975, p. 133). Chinese living on Taiwan cup their hands with fingers pointing downward and pull their fingers toward them in "a roughly counter-clockwise motion" (Condon & Yousef, 1975, p. 133). In addition, Americans usually hold their hands between shoulder and waist level when summoning friends, while Chinese hold their hands with arms extended straight by their sides so that their hands are below waist level. An American might interpret this gesture as, "Stay back" (directed at someone following the person gesturing).

Illustrators, gestures which accompany words for emphasis, also vary from culture to culture. Jakobson (1972) discusses the difficulty that Russian and Bulgarian soldiers had in 1877-78 during a war with Turkey. To signal "no," Russians turned their heads from side to side, while for Bulgarians, that gesture indicated "yes." When these illustrators were used as emblems to substitute for spoken words, the Bulgarians were never sure whether a Russian soldier shaking his head at them meant "yes" or "no."

Affect displays, bodily movements which express emotion, are perhaps more similar between cultures than other types of movements (Condon & Yousef, 1975), but even affect displays may indicate different meanings. Smiling may indicate that a Chinese person is trying to cover up embarrassment. A friend once had a dispute with customs officials who smiled more and more as our friend became visibly angrier and angrier. The officials were not laughing at her but were attempting to maintain a pleasant interaction and to avoid open display of disagreement, a very uncomfortable situation for those raised in Taiwan. Morsbach (1982) notes that Japanese also use smiles and laughter to mask anger, sorrow or displeasure. This discussion of emblems, affect displays, and illustrators should help you understand how people from different cultures might misunderstand each other's nonverbal codes.

Another category of nonverbal behavior which often varies is eye contact. In America, people who avoid eye contact may be considered shy or even evasive and untrustworthy. Japanese, however, are taught as children to look at superiors at about their Adam's apple or where a knot on a necktie would be. Looking a Japanese person directly in the eye in order to be frank is likely to have the effect of making him or her very nervous, since a cultural taboo has been violated (Morsbach, 1982).

The nonverbal (non-word) elements of language including pitch, stress, and voice quality called *paralanguage* provide an additional source of intercultural differences. A tonal language is one that depends on a combination of pitch, stress, and sound patterns to indicate differences between words. For example, in Mandarin Chinese, *mai* with a rising tone (as if you were asking a question) means "to buy" whereas *mai* with a falling tone means "to sell." Tonal languages such as Mandarin, Taiwanese, and Cantonese, three Chinese dialects, are spoken with more vocal variety than a non-tonal language such as English. A native English speaker might infer that two speakers of these Chinese dialects were either very excited or very angry with each other because these are two of the relatively few situations in which pitch varies greatly in spoken English. In fact, the Chinese speakers might be conducting a calm conversation. It is easy to fall into the trap of interpreting sounds in another language to mean what they would mean if English were the language being spoken. Another example of differences in paralanguage involves the nonverbal (non-word) sounds of encouragement we use when talking on the telephone to indicate we are following the conversation. In American English, one often says, "Uh huh," or "Ummm." Mandarin speakers on Taiwan make a louder noise that sounds to American ears like a grunt. The sound is "Ugh!" spoken louder than "Uh huh" and with a falling tone. Hearing that sound, an American might think something terrible had happened to the person on the other end of the line!

The last illustrative category of nonverbal differences is perhaps the most famous because of the pioneering work of Edward Hall. Through books such as *The Silent Language* (1959), *The Hidden Dimension* (1966), and *Beyond Culture* (1976), Hall introduced many concepts which communication scholars have found useful in building intercultural communication theory. Recall the example of the South American and British diplomats talking in Chapter 8. The British diplomat is likely to think the South American pushy because the South American stands so close. On the other hand, the South American keeps trying to get closer because the British citizen is standing so far away that conversation is uncomfortable. Distances for the intimate, casual-personal, socio-consultative, and public zones are different for people from different cultures and comprise an important category of nonverbal influences on intercultural communication.

While many other examples of different nonverbal cultural codes could be provided, those presented above are sufficient to illustrate the numerous possibilities for misunderstanding if people from different cultures assume that they can interpret nonverbal behavior according to the rules of their own cultures. Since nonverbal differences may not be as readily apparent as differences in language, nonverbal communication mistakes are more likely to go unnoticed or to cause responses which puzzle people who have no idea that their nonverbal behavior might have been misinterpreted. The rules and roles discussed below provide an important context for nonverbal behaviors since the rules for using nonverbal behaviors may vary with the social role or family relationship of one's conversational partner.

Rules and Roles

In addition to sets of verbal and nonverbal symbols, a group member learns sets of appropriate behaviors called *roles* and rules for using them. The role of wife or husband is certainly very different now in the United States than it was thirty years ago when the majority of women cared for children in the home and the majority of men provided the sole economic support for their families. Cultures differ as to how closely a member is expected to fulfill his or her role expectations. Some cultures and roles allow more flexibility than others. Although the role of wife has changed in the United States, the role of mother has remained similar to that of thirty years ago, thus creating the phenomenon of "superwoman" or "supermom," the woman who tries to fulfill both the traditional role of mother and the new role of businesswoman or executive. When roles are changing or unclear, additional stress is created for the person trying to adopt the role.

In intercultural communication situations, individuals from other cultures may be viewed negatively because they do not know the appropriate role behaviors and therefore do not exhibit them. Chinese students in Taiwan were taught that one must never behave in a casual or flippant way toward a teacher. An American friend thought she understood these role distinctions between teacher and student very well; after all, she knew what it meant to be respectful in her own culture. However, she learned how much she did not know one day when she walked around the classroom collecting papers that were due. She caught one student by surprise. He had one hand on his homework paper and the other in his pocket. She started to take the paper from his hand rather than delay the beginning of class any longer. He almost ripped the pocket off his pants getting the other hand out so that he could hand the paper to her, his teacher, with two hands and a slight bow. To do otherwise would have been disrespectful to the teacher. The teacher had put him in an awkward position because she did not know the specific behaviors he had to enact in order to fulfill his role of "student submitting a paper to the teacher." This incident made her wonder how many older Chinese had thought her careless and flippant because she did not use proper nonverbal demonstrations of respect.

Low- and High-Context Cultures

Roles and rules for social behavior are more apparent in some cultures than in others. Edward Hall (1966) made an important contribution to intercultural communication when he distinguished between high- and low-context cultures on the basis of their communication patterns. In a *high-context culture*, most information in a message is encoded in the physical context or in the person's mental catalog of rules, roles, and values. In a *low-context culture*, most of the information in a message is contained in the explicit or verbal message. While there are both low- and high-context messages in all cultures, Hall believes that one form or the other tends to predominate. Thus, American culture is low-context; for instance, Americans express conflict or dissatisfaction openly. Oriental countries such as China and Japan tend to have high-context cultures, where much interpretation depends on intuitive or common-sense understanding of what is meant, rather than on the specific words that are spoken (Ting-Toomey, 1984). In Chinese and Japanese culture, for example, when one disagrees with what is said, one remains silent. It is not polite to disagree openly. Thus, in China, silence means disagreement, whereas in America, silence usually means agreement. Such a different interpretation for essentially the same behavior (silence) can certainly add complications to the process of intercultural negotiation (Womack, 1983).

Value Differences

Value differences are another source of ambiguity or difficulty in intercultural communication. Kluckhohn and Strodtbeck (1961) identified five different problems around which all societies appear to develop values that influence day-to-day interactions. (1) First is the problem of the proportion of good and evil in human beings. Is human nature primarily good, primarily evil, or a mixture of good and evil? (2) The second problem concerns the relationship of human beings to nature. Should humanity subdue nature, be subdued by it, or live in harmony with it? (3) Time is an important part of nonverbal behavior. Some cultures place a high value on tradition, while others associate change and the future with progress. Yet others live in the present, paying little attention to past or future. (4) The fourth problem concerns being, doing and becoming. Cultures which value "being" hold the spontaneous expression of an individual's personality to be the most important activity. Those which value "doing" invest worth in activities outside the individual. Current American society is an example of a "doing" culture; the first question you ask someone you have just met at a cocktail party is, "What do you do?" Yet a third type of culture values "being-in-becoming"; this type of culture emphasizes who a person is or has become through personal growth, not what activities a person is involved in. (5) The final question deals with the relationship of the individual to society. Individualistic cultures value individual autonomy. Cultures which focus on the family lineage and ancestors, or continuity of a group over time, are said to value lineality. Cultures which value collaterality also value the group more than the individual, but these cultures focus on the extended group, such as a tribe or racial or religious group.

Ethnocentrism

Stereotypes. Because people of a particular culture share values and verbal and nonverbal code systems, they have a tendency to be *ethnocentric*, to judge other groups according to the categories and values of their own culture rather than being open to cultural differences. Stereotypes are "beliefs about groups of individuals or objects" (Ruhly, 1976, p. 27) based on learned opinions rather than information about a specific individual. Stereotypes allow us to organize unknown information more quickly; by using stereotypes, we can respond to professors without first having to become familiar with each individual professor. By using stereotypes, we can behave on the basis of a minimal amount of information: in this case the person's role, that of professor. After we get to know each individual professor and his or her rules for attendance, for interacting with students, and for submitting assignments, we can differentiate our behavior. The danger of stereotypes is that we may never get beyond them to know the person as an individual. By treating members of a group according to ideas we believe are "typical" of that group, we may not notice how the person differs from other members of the group or be aware when our stereotypes are completely inaccurate.

Prejudice. If we are prejudiced, we prejudge individuals by stereotypes before getting to know them. Prejudice results in selective exposure, selective perception, and sensitized perception (Ruhly, 1976). *Selective exposure* means that we expose ourselves only to messages with which we agree. We tend to avoid messages which we believe will contradict our beliefs or which are being sent by someone against whom we are prejudiced and therefore believe is "not worth hearing." If you have strong feelings about a particular political candidate, you will avoid hearing the candidate's opponent (unless you attend the speech in order to heckle). The same phenomenon presents a special barrier to intercultural communication. Because we are likely to have more differences with those from other cultures or subcultures than with people from our own group, we are more likely to avoid exposing ourselves to the new and different messages that someone from another culture may send. By cutting ourselves off from this new information, we reinforce our prejudices and avoid learning that our stereotypes may be wrong.

Perceptual Barriers. Selective perception also affects communication with someone from a different culture. Because our culture gives us perceptual or mental categories and because our stereotypes and prejudices may "harden" those categories and make them resistant to new information, we perceive new information in terms of our old ways of seeing the world. We may ignore positive aspects of an intercultural encounter and pay ,attention only to information which confirms our stereotype or prejudice. We are especially likely to use the defense of selective perception if we are exposed against our will to a message we do not wish to hear.

Sensitized perception is the type of perception which results when a person is exposed frequently over time to messages perceived in a hostile setting. Messages which might have annoyed us at first come to make us angrier and angrier when they are repeated over time. Thus, racial epithets may be especially hurtful because of sensitized perception. Rich (1974) identifies five types of categories of negative statements which hamper intercultural communication between racial groups in the United States. She found that members of Chicano, African American, and Native American groups were particularly offended by these types of statements: (1) stereotypical statements about a racial group, (2) statements that reflect a lack of sympathy with the minority group's complaints about "the establishment," (3) condescending statements, (4) statements or terms such as "squaw" which demean women of color, and (5) statements that reflect an attempt by members of the majority group to cross ethnic barriers, such as, "My uncle by marriage is a Chicano."

Intercultural Training

Many theorists have studied intercultural communication to help people overcome the barriers to effective communication mentioned above. Two skills or attitudes are especially important in intercultural communication: empathy and the ability to step outside one's own culture to consider different explanations for a puzzling event (Ruhly, 1976). *Empathy* is the ability to share the other person's feelings, to feel as the other does. Once a person has developed these skills, two types of training may improve intercultural communication. The first type, *culture specific training*, is often given to people who will be living or working in a culture different from their own. The goal of culture specific training is to provide information about a particular other culture to give a sojourner some knowledge about common rules, roles, values, and interpretive patterns. This knowledge will make the sojourner more able to understand others' feelings and to develop a repertoire of possible explanations for events that includes explanations from the host culture (the culture in which the sojourner will be living).

On the other hand, *culture general training* includes sensitizing individuals to rules and norms of their own culture and indicating general categories of cross-cultural differences, such as differences in verbal and nonverbal codes. By making people more aware of the biases and limitations their own culture imposes upon them, culture general training makes them more receptive and sensitive to differences. Then people may become better intercultural communicators because they are more flexible in inferring motives or attributing meaning to another's behavior. They are more aware of the possibilities for different interpretations of communication.

Some Representative Intercultural Communication Theories

Even though the study of intercultural communication by communication theorists is relatively new, theories of intercultural communication have developed rapidly. It is especially interesting to note that some theories presented in earlier chapters have been adapted to help solve problems or explain events in the context of intercultural communication. The remainder of the chapter will present theories selected to illustrate the differences in theory building across the laws, rules, and systems perspectives.

A Covering Laws Approach to Intercultural Communication Theory

In Chapter 9, you read about Berger and Calabrese's (1975) Uncertainty Reduction Theory. Recall that Uncertainty Reduction Theory assumes that, during the initial phase of interaction, the primary goal of communication is to reduce uncertainty about one's conversational partner. Thus, communication behavior in the entry phase of interpersonal relationships is primarily an attempt to discover information about the other and to share relevant information about oneself in order to explain, predict, and control the relationship. Since people of different cultures are likely to have an even higher degree of uncertainty about each other than two strangers who share a similar culture, Uncertainty Reduction Theory seems especially appropriate to explain initial encounters in intercultural communication. Gudykunst and his colleagues have pursued a research program of testing and extending Uncertainty Reduction Theory in the context of intercultural communication.

Gudykunst and Nishida (1984) reasoned that Uncertainty Reduction Theory was general enough to explain communication both across cultures and between people of different cultures. Using an experimental design, the researchers tested the influence of culture, cultural similarity, attitude similarity, and self-monitoring on several aspects of uncertainty reduction between Americans and Japanese. All American and Japanese participants were asked to pretend that they had been "introduced" by a friend at a social gathering to a stranger of the same sex. A written description of the stranger was provided, (i.e., the "bogus stranger" technique described in Chapter 9 was used). Participants expected to interact with the stranger and were asked how they planned to behave during the meeting. This "stranger" was identified as either an American or a Japanese with attitudes similar to or different from those of the participant. Several axioms and theorems derived from Uncertainty Reduction Theory were fully or partially supported by the research. Overall, the study revealed cultural differences in the use of uncertainty reduction strategies. Japanese were less likely than Americans to self-disclose and ask questions (use interrogation) as uncertainty reduction strategies.

Another experiment extended the previous research by contrasting uncertainty reduction processes used for an acquaintance and those for a friend. This experiment was similar to the first except that all participants were Americans. Participants completed questionnaires responding about their relationships with culturally similar or dissimilar same sex friends or acquaintances. Results of the experiment generally confirmed Uncertainty Reduction Theory, except that some relationships were not so strong as expected. Some of the Uncertainty Reduction Theory axioms and theorems apply best to initial interactions; behavior changes once people begin to form relationships (Gudykunst, 1985).

Gudykunst, Yang, and Nishida (1985) extended previous investigations in two ways: (1) They studied members of three cultures, the United States, Japan, and Korea, and (2) they compared communication behavior of acquaintances, friends, and dating partners. The authors felt this was important because Uncertainty Reduction Theory was developed from research based on white participants in only one country, the United States. They wanted to know whether the theory would apply to different cultures and to more intimate types of relationships than conversations with strangers, so they tested the model in an experiment involving students from the three countries. Using questionnaires, participants described their communication with both an acquaintance and a friend of the same sex and with a dating partner of the opposite sex. Statistical analysis indicated that the Uncertainty Reduction Theory was confirmed by the data for acquaintance, friend, and dating partner relationships in all three cultures. Thus, the experiment provides support for extending the model beyond initial interactions to more intimate types of relationships. Extending theories in this way is one important method of building upon previous research. However, Gudykunst and his associates noted that Uncertainty Reduction Theory does not allow researchers to examine *changes* in communication as the relationship develops over time, nor does it take into account the broader social context, such as how involved the relational partners are in each other's communication networks. The authors felt the social context ought to be especially important in high-context cultures (Hall, 1966) such as Korea and Japan, where context is very important in predicting the other person's behavior. Individuals who share friends and acquaintances (are very involved in each other's social and communication networks) may be better able to predict each other's behavior based on information such as norms and values obtained from the network of friends rather than direct knowledge of the specific individual. This experiment confirmed Uncertainty Reduction Theory, extended it to new cultural and relational contexts, and suggested modifications, especially for high-context cultures.

Gudykunst, Nishida, Koike, and Shiino (1986) decided to explore in greater detail the role of language in uncertainty reduction. Using participants from a Japanese university, the researchers investigated whether the language in which a conversation took place influenced methods of reducing uncertainty. Like Gudykunst and Nishida (1984), the researchers asked participants to imagine that they were being introduced to a new student at their university ("bogus stranger" technique). The new student was either a Japanese or North American and the meeting would take place in either Japanese or English. As in the experiment by Gudykunst, Yang, and Nishida (1985), while the results tended to confirm the theory, they also indicated that Uncertainty Reduction Theory may need to be modified for high-context cultures in which knowing strangers' backgrounds and sharing communication networks, as well as directly communicating with the stranger, may be important additional ways of reducing uncertainty.

Based on the previous studies, Gudykunst, Nishida, Koike, and Shiino (1986) suggested five new hypotheses regarding uncertainty reduction in encounters between strangers from high- and low-context cultures. (1) Uncertainty differs in high- and low-context cultures. Uncertainty reduction in high-context cultures involves predicting whether strangers will follow group or cultural norms. In low-context cultures, uncertainty reduction involves predicting individual behavior. (2) Members of high-context cultures focus on predicting adherence to *norms* when speaking their *native* language; when speaking English, they try to predict *individual* behavior, just as a low-context native English speaker would. (3) Knowing someone's background or having mutual friends may reduce uncertainty for members of high-context cultures. Therefore, not having contact with strangers' communication networks before the initial interaction increases uncertainty for high-context cultures, but not for low-context cultures in which norms provide much less information. The same reasoning is used to explain the relationships noted in the two hypotheses which follow. (4) Being unable to empathize with strangers will increase uncertainty in high-context cultures, but not in low-context cultures. (5) Lack of knowledge about a stranger's background will increase uncertainty in high-context cultures, but not in low-context cultures.

Finally, Gudykunst, Chua, and Gray (1987) further explored the effect of cultural differences on Uncertainty Reduction Theory by studying people from a wide variety of cultural backgrounds. One key aspect was the degree of dissimilarity between the students' cultural backgrounds and the culture of the United States, in which they were living and studying. Respondents completed a questionnaire about their communication with either a friend or acquaintance from the United States All acquaintances or friends were the same sex as the student. The results revealed that cultural dissimilarities had less effect on communication as relationships developed. This finding confirmed earlier research by Gudykunst, Nishida, and Chua (1986), presented above.

The research program of Gudykunst and his colleagues applying Uncertainty Reduction Theory to intercultural communication offers an excellent example of theory building. First, the studies described above illustrate how scholars in one context may borrow or adapt a promising theory to study a different communication context. The research conducted by this team generally confirmed Uncertainty Reduction Theory but also suggested some changes for high-context cultures and for more intimate relationships. Thus, Gudykunst and his colleagues have extended Uncertainty Reduction Theory not only beyond the original context, but also beyond the relationship stage that the theory originally explained. The new hypotheses suggested by Gudykunst, Nishida, Koike, and Shiino (1986) will no doubt be tested in further experiments conducted by this team of communication scholars.

A Rules Approach to Intercultural Communication Theory

Using the Coordinated Management of Meaning Theory described in Chapter 3, Barnett Pearce and his students have explored differences in interpretive rules used by members of different cultures. Wolfson and Norden were interested in exploring "the meanings and implications of interpersonal conflict in Chinese and American cultures" (1982, p. 1). The researchers showed both Chinese and American students one of two segments from a film which presented the daily routine and relationships between teachers and students at an American high school. A segment showing a heated argument between a student and teacher was the "high-conflict" episode. The "low-conflict" episode presented a conversation between student and teacher about college plans. Participants in the experiment completed a questionnaire about the level of conflict in the film and agreed or disagreed with such statements as, "This is a tense conversation." Then they were asked to pretend that they were the high school student shown in the film. They wrote what they would say next, then completed a questionnaire about how much freedom they felt they had to choose a response. For example, contrasting statements such as, "The situation that I find myself in requires me to respond with this particular message," and "I would respond in this way in order to have the pattern of conversation go the way I want," were included on the questionnaire.

The questionnaire about freedom of response was included to measure the concept of logical force. You may recall from Chapter 3 that two kinds of rules, definition rules and behavior rules, are very important to the Coordinated Management of Meaning Theory. Definition rules tell people how words or phrases should be interpreted. Behavior rules tell actors what they should do in a given situation. For example, if a participant in this experiment had a behavior rule which said, "Students should be polite to teachers," the student might have indicated on the questionnaire above that the student would act in a particular way in order to "be polite." Logical force refers to the strength of the influence that meanings and rules have on behavior. So, for example, if the student's rule about being polite to teachers had relatively weak logical force, the student would have several options to choose from in selecting an appropriate behavior. If the rule had strong logical force, "Students must *always* be polite to teachers no matter what happens," the student would have relatively little freedom in deciding how to behave.

Statistical analysis revealed strong cultural differences between the American and Chinese students, both in perceptions of the conflict and in the logical force of their behavior rules. Chinese (who generally avoid overt expressions of conflict and show deference to authorities, especially teachers) perceived the conflict episodes as more harmonious, agreeable, and friendly than the Americans did. Logical force in the situation was also stronger for Chinese than for Americans. While Americans chose responses based on their anticipated effect on the teacher and conversation ("I would respond in this way in order to have the pattern of conversation go the way I want," for example), Chinese students felt less free to choose responses. A related finding was that the Chinese students felt they must act in a particular way regardless of the teacher's actions. Americans, more than Chinese, felt that they must manage the conversation to enhance their self-images.

In a related experiment, Wolfson and Pearce (1983) investigated differences between Chinese and American rules for self-disclosure. They hypothesized that members of Far East Asian cultures differ from Americans in what they consider confidential or public information. Barnlund (1975) found that Americans were more likely than Japanese to self-disclose in a variety of contexts. Alexander, Cronen, Kang, Tsou, and Banks (1980) discovered that Chinese rely more on (unspoken) demographic information to know others, whereas Americans rely more on verbal exchanges of personal information. (This observation is similar to the differences in uncertainty reduction theory in high- and low-context cultures noted by Gudykunst and his colleagues.) Wolfson and Pearce (1983) wanted to explore differences in Chinese and American perceptions of self-disclosure and in the influence of self-disclosure on subsequent communication. The researchers had participants read parts of a conversation written in English. The low-disclosure conversation concerned attitudes about music; the high-disclosure conversation involved a student's expressing doubts about his sexual adequacy as the result of an incident that occurred on spring break. As in the experiment described above, the student participants filled out questionnaires describing how they perceived the conversations, indicating what they would say in response to the self-disclosure, and revealing how free they felt to choose what to say next. The Chinese participants perceived both dialogues as less harmonious than did the Americans. The Chinese also felt more constrained by the logical force of their rules in the high-disclosure conversation than did Americans.

The two experiments described above again indicate differences between the rules and covering laws approaches to building communication theory.

Recall that the covering laws experiments by Gudykunst and his colleagues involved respondents' selecting strategies for interacting with a stranger, acquaintance, or friend. In the rules experiments, Wolfson and her colleagues asked participants to write the actual words they would say and to indicate how free they felt to choose their responses. This attempt to explore the logical force of the rule is unique to rules theory; it implies that, while choice may be limited, the respondents are consciously aware of their limitations. In the Uncertainty Reduction Theory experiments described above, respondents were not asked the reasons for their choices, because those choices were presumed to be tightly constrained by social laws (norms) governing the situation. While both the laws and rules researchers are studying patterns of behavior influenced by social rules or laws, the laws research treats the laws as "given" by a society, whereas the rules research is designed to explore the individual's perception of the rules.

A Systems Approach to Intercultural Communication Theory

An immediate contrast can be seen in the systems theory of intercultural communication by Young Kim. Kim's work has focused on the communication patterns of Korean immigrants to the United States. Through a series of studies, she has investigated different types of communication networks and their effects on acculturation. Because Kim was one of the initial researchers to explore the relationship between communication and acculturation, she first attempted to describe communication behaviors. The descriptive research presented in her early studies was necessary before theorists could begin to explain the communication behaviors that occur during acculturation.

Kim (1977a) hypothesized that immigrants who participated in networks of the host country would be more acculturated than immigrants who were involved only in immigrant communication networks. Kim developed a communication model to explain immigrant acculturation. A diagram representing her model is pictured in Figure 12.1. The model indicates that intercultural acculturation is quite dependent on perception; Kim considers acculturated immigrants to have relatively complex perceptions of the host society. Four factors are necessary to create complex perceptions: (1) potential for interacting with members of the host society and for consuming its media, (2) competence in the host language (English), (3) motivation or eagerness to learn about and participate in the host culture, and (4) the availability of mass media (access to host newspapers, radio, and television). These four factors affect the outcome variable—perceptual complexity—through the influence of two mediating or intervening variables. Mediating variables modify the effect of the four causal variables on perceptual complexity. In other words the model in Figure 12.1 might be stated as follows: interaction potential, English competence, acculturation motivation, and mass media availability create perceptual

Figure 12.1
Young Kim's Acculturation Model

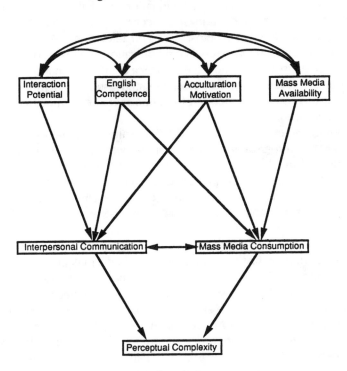

Reprinted with permission from Kim, Y. Y. (1977). Communication patterns of foreign immigrants in the process of acculturation. *Human Communication Research, 4,* p. 70.

complexity through the influence of interpersonal communication and mass media consumption.

Kim (1977a) tested the acculturation model by using a mail survey of 400 Korean households in Chicago. The survey included questions designed to reveal the number of American friends and organizations with which the immigrants were associated, how much difficulty the Koreans had in speaking and understanding English, how strongly they desired to make friends with Americans and to learn about current events in the United States, how many American people they had contact with daily, and to what types of electronic and print media they had access. Statistical analyses were used to compare the model with the questionnaire results. The first three causal variables shown in the model, (1) potential for interacting with members of the host society and for consuming its media, (2) competence in the host language (English), and (3) motivation or eagerness to learn about and participate in the host culture, were strongly related to perceptual complexity (acculturation). Only (4) the availability of mass media (access to host newspapers, radio, and television) was not related to acculturation, probably because the only differences among respondents involved access to print media. More than 95% of the respondents owned both radios and televisions. While both of the mediating variables, interpersonal communication and mass communication, were important in acculturation, the influence of interpersonal communication was stronger. Overall, the results of the study supported Kim's model. In particular this research supported the importance of communication in the acculturation process.

In a follow-up examination, Kim (1977b) explored the nature of the Korean immigrants' interpersonal communication with other Koreans and with Americans. Using the results of the survey reported above, Kim attempted to track the development of the immigrants' acculturation over time by comparing different groups of people who had been in the United States for varying periods of time. She analyzed four types of interpersonal relationships: casual acquaintances, casual friends, intimate friends, and membership in organizations. She found that the number of casual American acquaintances increased during the first nine years, then reached a plateau. In their first year in the United States, Koreans on average had eleven casual American acquaintances. By the time Koreans had lived in the United States from seven to nine years, they had an average of 124 casual American acquaintances. Patterns of friendship with Americans and with other Koreans differed. For both casual and intimate friends, the number of Korean friends was higher than American friends and increased for the first five to seven years. Friendships with Americans followed the same patterns, except immigrants had more Korean friends. After five to seven years, however, the number of American friends continued to increase, while the number of casual and intimate Korean friends declined. The immigrants participated in more Korean than American organizations. The pattern of participation followed that of friendship, with both American and Korean organization memberships increasing for the first several years. Then membership in American organizations continued to increase, while membership in Korean organizations decreased. This deeper exploration of interpersonal communication was important because it indicated that the Koreans maintained active membership both in the host society and in their own ethnic community. It was also interesting that ethnic friends are more important in shaping attitudes during an immigrant's first several years in the host society. As time passes, friends from the host culture became more influential.

The extensive information that she had gathered through her questionnaire led Young Kim (1978) to further analyze the immigrants' attitudes toward and perceptions of American society. After additional statistical analysis of the questionnaire results, Kim found that immigrants who had large numbers of interpersonal contacts in the ethnic community also tended to have large numbers of contacts with Americans. The immigrants' mass media behavior followed the same trend as the development of interpersonal relationships mentioned above. Consumption of both host and ethnic mass media increased during the first few years; thereafter, use of Korean media declined, while use of American media increased. The immigrants perceived cultural differences between Korea and the United States to be most important during the early part of their stay. Those who had lived longer in the United States were more likely to recognize cultural similarities. The immigrants' attitudes toward the United States followed a similar pattern: they became more positive as they spent more time in the new country. A final and very important conclusion of this study is that interpersonal communication contacts played a more important role in learning about the host society than did mass media. This finding was also mentioned in the first study presented (1977a).

In a later study, Kim (1987) explored the interpersonal networks of the immigrants in even more detail. This study was an attempt to build theory about the relationship between interpersonal communication and acculturation based on findings from the studies discussed above. Kim explored interpersonal network properties, some of which were discussed in Chapter 10. *Network heterogeneity* referred to the proportion of communication relationships held with Americans (the heterogeneous population for Koreans) compared to those held with Koreans (the homogeneous population). Another important network concept that Kim considered was the *strength of the tie* between two individuals, the degree of intimacy of their relationship. The more heterogeneous the immigrant's communication network and the stronger the ties with Americans, the more likely the immigrant was to communicate competently in the host culture. A person who has many direct contacts in a network is considered quite *central* on the network. Someone who is less central might have to send messages through other people to reach the ultimate receiver, just as in a university students do not usually voice their opinions directly to the residence hall manager or director but lodge complaints or make comments through their resident advisor. Kim recommended that future studies focus on *centrality*, since centrality might indicate how closely natives were integrated into the immigrant's support system. Kim also suggested two additional areas of exploration needed to develop the theory: (1) studying number and type of communication ties with other, non-Korean immigrants; and (2) observing changes in communication activities and their effect on immigrant perceptions over time. Overall, Kim concluded that participating in ethnic communication activities did not facilitate and might actually impede acculturation into the host culture.

Kim (1987) also modified the model she had first introduced in 1977(a). This second model is pictured in Figure 12.2. While it is quite similar to the first model, it differs in that it introduces the concept of host communication competence. Figure 12.3 pictures the elaboration of host communication competence which Kim introduced in the study. In the newer model, mass

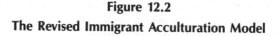

Figure 12.2
The Revised Immigrant Acculturation Model

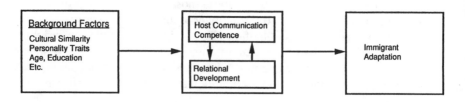

Reprinted with permission from Kim, Y. Y. (1987). Facilitating immigrant adaptation: The role of communication. In T. C. Albrecht and M. B. Adelman (Eds.), Communicating social support (p. 200). Newbury Park, CA: Sage.

media consumption has been dropped since it was found to be less important than interpersonal communication in influencing Korean immigrants' perceptions. Interpersonal communication has been analyzed to include communication competence in the host culture and relational development. Background factors (such as age and personality traits) have been added to the original model. The model in Figure 12.2 concerns more internal factors and is presented as a model entitled, "Background Factors Facilitating Adaptation" (1987, p. 200). Kim appears to use adaptation and acculturation synonymously; the models in Figures 12.1 and 12.2 illustrate the growth of theory both by intention (internal development and expansion) and extension (broadening the theory to include a larger domain; see Chapter 2). The addition of host communication competence is an example of extending the theory to cover a variable not present in the original model. Figure 12.3 presents even further evidence of intentional development of the theory. It pictures the components which make up communication competence in the host culture. Kim was able to add variables included in the affective, cognitive, and behavioral dimensions in part by reading others' research and thinking closely about the adaptation process and in part by analyzing the implications of her own research presented in the studies above. Finally, Kim's communication model of cross-cultural adaptation was complete (1988, p. 79). The finished model combines the internal, communication, and environmental factors present in earlier models; it is presented in Figure 12.4. Kim's model of immigrant acculturation provides a good example of systems theory because it includes variables from all levels of the cultural system: internal psychological and linguistic variables, communication network variables, and mass media

Questions To Consider

1. What factors have led to an interest in theory building in intercultural communication?
2. How can the Whorfian hypothesis help us understand intercultural communication?
3. In what ways do nonverbal communication behaviors differ between people of different cultures?
4. Explain the distinction between high- and low-context cultures.
5. How do value differences pose problems in intercultural communication?
6. What has been the nature of intercultural communication training?
7. How do stereotypes and prejudice affect intercultural communication?
8. How has Uncertainty Reduction Theory been applied to the study of intercultural communication? What changes in the theory have resulted?
9. How has the Coordinated Management of Meaning been used to study cultural differences?
10. How has a systems approach been used to study the importance of communication in acculturation?

References

Alexander, A., Cronen, V., Kang, K., Tsou, B., & Banks, J. (1980, November). *Patterns of topic sequencing and information gain: A comparative study of relationship development in Chinese and American cultures.* Paper presented at the annual meeting of the Speech Communication Association, New York.

Asuncion-Lande, N. (1977). Chicano studies: Current status and future directions. *Association for Communication Administration Bulletin, 22,* 36-40.

Asuncion-Lande, N., & Womack, D. F. (1982, August). *Communication and conflict management across cultures.* Paper presented at the meeting of the International Political Science Assn., Rio de Janeiro, Brazil.

Barnlund, D. (1975). *Public and private self in Japan and the United States.* Tokyo, Japan: The Simul Press.

Berger, C. R., & Calabrese, R. J. (1975). Some explorations in initial interaction and beyond: Toward a developmental theory of interpersonal communication. *Human Communication Research, 1,* 99-112.

Condon, J. C., & Yousef, F. S. (1975). *An introduction to intercultural communication.* New York: Bobbs-Merrill.

Ekman, P., & Friesen, W. (1969). The repertoire of nonverbal behavior: Categories, origins, usage, and coding. *Semiotica, 1,* 49-98.

Fagen, R. R. (1966). *Politics and communication.* Boston: Little, Brown.

Gudykunst, W. B. (1985). The influence of cultural similarity, type of relationship, and self-monitoring on uncertainty reduction processes. *Communication Monographs, 52*, 203-217.

Gudykunst, W. B. (1987). Cross-cultural comparisons. In C. R. Berger & S. H. Chaffee (Eds.), *Handbook of communication science* (pp. 847-889). Newbury Park, CA: Sage.

Gudykunst, W. B., Chua, E., & Gray, A. J. (1987). Cultural dissimilarities and uncertainty reduction processes. In M. L. McLaughlin (Ed.), *Communication Yearbook 10* (pp. 456-469). Newbury Park, CA: Sage.

Gudykunst, W. B., & Nishida, T. (1984). Individual and cultural influences on uncertainty reduction. *Communication Monographs, 51*, 23-36.

Gudykunst, W. B., Nishida, T., Koike, H., & Shiino, N. (1986). The influence of language on uncertainty reduction: An exploratory study of Japanese-Japanese and Japanese-North American interactions. In M. L. McLaughlin (Ed.), *Communication Yearbook 9* (pp. 555-575). Newbury Park, CA: Sage.

Gudykunst, W. B., Yang, S. M., & Nishida, T. (1985). A cross-cultural test of uncertainty reduction theory: Comparisons of acquaintances, friends, and dating relationships in Japan, Korea, and the United States. *Human Communication Research, 11*, 407-455.

Hall, E. T. (1959). *The silent language*. Garden City, NY: Doubleday.

Hall, E. T. (1966). *The hidden dimension*. New York: Random House.

Hall, E. T. (1976). *Beyond culture*. Garden City, NY: Doubleday.

Jakobson, R. (1972) Nonverbal signs for "yes" and "no." *Language and society, 1*, 91-96.

Kim, Y. Y. (1977a). Communication patterns of foreign immigrants in the process of acculturation. *Human Communication Research, 4*, 66-77.

Kim, Y. Y. (1977b). Inter-ethnic and intra-ethnic communication: A study of Korean immigrants in Chicago. In Jain, N. C. (Ed.), *International and Intercultural Communication Annual* (Vol. 4, pp. 53-68). Falls Church, VA: Speech Communication Association.

Kim, Y. Y. (1978). A communication approach to the acculturation process: A study of Korean immigrants in Chicago. *International Journal of Intercultural Relations, 2* (2), 197-224.

Kim, Y. Y. (1987). Facilitating immigrant adaptation: The role of communication. In T. L. Albrecht & M. B. Adelman (Eds.), *Communicating social support* (pp. 192-211). Newbury Park, CA: Sage.

Kluckhohn, F., & Strodtbeck, F. (1961). *Variations in value orientations*. New York: Row, Peterson.

McLuhan, M. (1964). *Understanding media*. London: Routledge & Kegan Paul.

Morsbach, H. (1982). Aspects of nonverbal communication in Japan. In L. A. Samovar & R. E. Porter (Eds.), *Intercultural communication: A reader* (3rd ed.) (pp. 300-315). Belmont, CA: Wadsworth.

Prosser, M.H. (1978). *The cultural dialogue: An introduction to intercultural communication*. Boston: Houghton Mifflin.

Rich, A.L. (1974). *Interracial communication*. New York: Harper and Row.

Ruhly, S. (1976). *Orientations to intercultural communication*. Chicago: SRA Modcom.

Sapir, E. (1958, 1964). In D. G. Mandelbaum (Ed.), *Selected writings of Edward Sapir in language, culture and personality*. Berkeley: University of California.

Ting-Toomey, S. (1984, May). *Intercultural understanding: An interpretive perspective.* Paper presented at the annual meeting of the Eastern Communication Association, Philadelphia.

Whorf, B.L. (1956). In J. Carroll (Ed.), *Language, thought and reality: Selected writings of Benjamin Lee Whorf.* Cambridge, MA: Technology Press, MIT.

Wolfson, K., & Norden, M. F. (1982, May). *Responses to filmed interpersonal conflict: A comparison between Chinese and American cultures.* Paper presented at the annual meeting of the International Communication Association, Boston.

Wolfson, K., & Pearce, W.B. (1983). A cross-cultural comparison of the implications of self-disclosure on conversational logics. *Communication Quarterly, 31,* 249-256.

Womack, D. (1983, May). *A model of negotiations in intercultural and organizational settings.* Paper presented at the annual meeting of the International Communication Association, Dallas.

Conclusion

After completing this book, you should have a greater appreciation of the process and extent of theory building in the communication field. As a student, you may be amazed at the numerous theories included in the text. However, your authors are aware of the many theories and theoretical approaches which had to be omitted in this limited space. In this last section, we want to make readers aware of other approaches that we could not include in detail and to set forth trends in communication theory building that we believe will continue for the next several years. In addition, we want to reiterate the understanding you should have gained from reading the book.

As we mentioned in Chapter 4, the field has experienced a trend toward theory building in specific contexts. You may remember that in Chapter 2 we contrasted a general communication theory, designed to explain all types of communication with one theoretical framework, with specific theories which describe and explain how communication functions in particular contexts. Recent communication theories have been context-bound, and we believe the trend will continue. While several contexts were explored in Part III of this book, others were not presented for reasons of space. Two of the newest fields, health communication and political communication, will continue to grow in theory building and research. More studies will be conducted in legal communication and in communication in conflict and negotiation. The fields of small group and interpersonal communication will remain strong, while rganizational communication and mass

ᵇriefly indicated in this text is the rich
ᵐ rhetorical/critical and interpretive
cholars in this area will continue
ory building. Consistent with the
ᵊ new communication theories
· including the rules approach.
ᵇuilding in specific contexts
ᵗems perspectives. In sum,
ᵧ communication scholars
ieve that this approach is
for answering the varied
iety of philosophical and
st productive environment

V
de
we
will
healtl
questic
method
for build.
Recently
Communic.
Even though
it reflects a tre
domain of evei
away from its i
conceptualizatio.
While oral comn
concerned with me
emphasis on study i
department titles. Ma.
Communication or Mɛ
many more will continue
of the field from artistic ᵖ
sense of performance as cr
Association sponsored jc
members of the field w
performers are condu
dramatic interpretati
emphasize research
stronger in the futi
performance con
communication
in the future as
is for commu
recommendati
communicatior

ᵗe name of the Speech
ᵗunication Association.
ow margin), we believe
mmunication view the
appears to be turning
nd toward a broader
ᵗitten, and mediated.
chief focus, scholars
ᶠorm they occur. The
ue to be reflected in
names from Speech
ication Studies, and
ᵗs a shift in emphasis
ᵗnance, often in the
ᵗch Communication
ᵗrly indicates, many
ᵗly as teachers and
heory of oral and
ᵗities increasingly
ᵗs trend will grow
ᵗsted solely in oral
ᵗritical theory and
ᵗly remain stable
v. The challenge
ᵗearch to make
many different
ᵧ, it is important

that we not neglect the communication skills which are so pervasive in everyday life.

No matter how inclusive the text or how astute the authors, no book can ever truly capture the state of communication theory building at a particular time. You have learned specifics of many different theories in studying this book. No matter what your field of future employment, communication will continue to be a vital part of your life. Learning to communicate effectively is a lifelong process, and communication is a skill that can affect your job performance and how fast and far you are promoted. Effective communication can also sustain and enrich your personal and family life. Your authors hope you have read about some theories which will help you to communicate more effectively in your social and work life. But we also hope you have learned something much more important. Ten years from now, many of the theories you have studied in your communication classes will have been revised, replaced, or faded from popularity. There will always be new theories and even new theoretical perspectives. The most important skill a course in communication theory building can provide is the ability to be a critic of theories. We hope that you are now able to recognize the perspectives and theoretical assumptions which lie beneath the surface of communication theories. We hope that you have learned to judge a theory's strengths and weaknesses and that you have developed your own criteria for a good theory. We hope that you have come to understand that theory and research are "two sides of the same coin." In a communication theory course, many students experience for the first time a feeling of discomfort and uneasiness; they feel they have been unable to grasp the "big picture." While such discomfort is not unusual for graduate students and professors, it can be quite disconcerting the first time you experience it. We hope you have come to realize that the "big picture" in a course in communication theory is not related to any one theory or group of theories but to the critical framework of theory building on which all theories depend. By presenting this framework, we hope the book has helped you to see as much of the "big picture" of communication as you are able at this point in your academic career. If you are at the end of your academic career, we hope the book has helped you to integrate all of the communication classes you have taken into a larger framework. We hope that the book has broadened your knowledge of the many different areas studied by communication scholars and has stimulated your interest, perhaps in an area of which you were previously unaware. Sometimes we encounter the misconception that "research" means sitting in the library. Certainly, academic research involves reading about what others have discovered, but it involves much more. Communication research is an exciting activity for each of us, and we hope through reading this book you have come to share some of that excitement.

Appendix

Communication Research Methods

We would now like to introduce you to the methods used in communication research. It is important to understand how scholars conduct research to obtain knowledge about communication. While we have already explored a good deal of information about human communication, we believe it will be more meaningful if you have a sense of *how* that information was discovered.

There are many methods to investigate the nature and origin of knowledge. In fact, one of the major areas of study in philosophy, epistemology, is devoted solely to that purpose. Although almost all of the knowledge in this book was learned through the practice of *behavioral science,* that is not to say that other methods of studying communication—such as the critical methods of the rhetorical critic—are unimportant. Presenting all possible methods of research is not our intent, but we would like to highlight the framework behind many of the theories we have discussed. Thus, this appendix will describe in some detail what is involved in doing behavioral science research.

The underlying foundation of this research is uncomplicated: *behavioral science research in communication involves controlled observation of humans in order to understand their communicative behavior.* The two key words in this definition are **controlled** and **observation.** Control is achieved by design. That is, procedures are followed so that a social scientist's confidence in what is observed about humans approaches the confidence that physical scientists have in fields such as biology. Thus, *research design* is a major type of method which we will examine. The second key word, observation, pertains to what is of interest in a study and how it is observed. Specifically, the concern is with *measurement*. Numerous ways of measuring various aspects of communication will be surveyed.

The Scientific Method

Before examining research design and measurement, we will discuss some basic ideas about scientific research. Let us consider a research problem to illustrate the ideas. Imagine you are interested in the impact MTV music videos have on viewers. At this point you do not know exactly what aspects of music videos you are interested in or what effects to look for. Raymond Cattell's (1966) outline of the scientific method offers guidelines for how your thinking on this problem could develop:

> **Induction** leads to **hypothesis**,
> which leads to **deduction**
> and finally to **experimentation**.
> Then, experiments lead to **new inductions**.

The induction phase involves understanding the research problem. In our example you could observe, read, talk, and/or think about music videos. Suppose you decide that your primary interest is to determine whether music videos have an impact on how the audience likes the song. Your thinking is that a music video provides the viewer with a fantasy and that fantasy will have a favorable effect on how the song is evaluated. When you begin speculating like this, you are entering the second phase—hypothesis. In the hypothesis phase, you make a prediction based on your thinking. Thus, you might hypothesize that a person's fantasy ability will influence (mediate) the effects of music videos. Specifically, when viewers are low in fantasy ability, music videos will make songs more likeable, but videos will have no effect when viewers are high in fantasy ability because they do not need others to provide fantasies for them. When you specify the outcomes which should occur if your thinking is correct, you are in the third phase—deduction. In our example your deduction is, "How much a song is liked, in terms of ratings on a scale, will be affected positively by music videos only when people are low in fantasy ability." Experiment is the fourth phase; an experimental design begins to emerge when the deduction phase is complete. The experiment must provide a test of the hypothesis. What design would allow us to see whether the deduced effects will occur? The design is straightforward. Select a group of viewers. Determine whether they are high or low in fantasy ability. Have half of the high fantasizers and half of the low fantasizers view a music video and then rate the song on a set of attitude scales. Have the other research participants (again, half high and half low fantasizers) listen to the song (no video) and then rate the song. This design can be depicted as a 2 x 2 design [two levels of fantasy ability (high and low) by two types of music stimuli (song alone and music video)]. This design is represented in Figure 1.

Figure 1

A Research Design

	Music Video	Audio Only
High Fantasy Ability		
Low Fantasy Ability		

Let us suppose you conducted this study. Would that be the end of it? According to the model, no. Even if you pursued this area no further, the investigative process has the potential to continue. What this means is the set of results of the experiment join the set of particulars which inspired the original hypothesis. This new information, along with the old, creates a new configuration which has the potential for stimulating new hypotheses to be tested. The process continues on and on (it is recursive). We never learn everything about an area of research.

Let's extend our example. If your hypothesis was supported, you might reflect on the results (the inductive phase). Perhaps it is not fantasy ability so much as another trait (the need for stimulation, for example) which best explains the effects of music videos. Or, the impact of music videos on how much people like the song may not be as important as how music videos influence political and social attitudes. Are the women in music videos treated as "sex objects" so music videos influence viewers to have sexist attitudes toward women? These are just two examples of new inductions with numerous implications for hypotheses, deductions, and experiments. Even if your original hypothesis was not supported, the feedback would be sufficient to energize the induction process. For instance, you might decide your hypothesis did not receive a good test because your measure of fantasy ability might have measured IQ rather than the ability to fantasize. Thus, a new study with a different measure of fantasy ability would be in order. If the process is recursive, then theories should not be accepted as fact. There is always the possibility that a new theory will provide better explanations than the original theory and also explain events not addressed by the existing theory.

Fundamental Concepts

Several concepts are fundamental to research design and measurement and to understanding research.

Variable

The most obvious attribute of a variable is that it varies. Aside from that, the notion of a variable is an important and not a simplistic concept in communication research. The words "concept," "construct," and "variable" are used interchangeably. They represent an abstraction or a way of referring to a class of things. For instance, fantasy ability refers to the ways in which people use their imagination. Whether one word or the other is used depends upon the level of discourse. When discussing something at the theoretical level, scientists usually use "concept" or "construct," as in "a person's fantasy ability is a *construct* which is necessary in order to explain the effects of MTV." On the other hand, when discussing the level of measurement and analysis, scientists commonly use "variable," as in "fantasy ability is a difficult *variable* to measure with a scale."

Continuous and dichotomous variables. Some variables can have only two values. Whether someone has seen the video for a song on MTV may be viewed as a dichotomous variable; there are only two values. You have or you have not seen the video. In communication research, the most common variable treated as a dichotomy is biological sex; you are either male or female. However, some variables are continuous in that there is a meaningful high and low value for the variable with increments between the extremes so that you could say a variable applies to a person to a certain degree. Fantasy ability is an example. We can conceive of what it is like to be very high or very low in the ability to fantasize; people can also be located at any one of numerous positions between the two extremes. Scientists may convert continuous variables—those with a range of values—into a dichotomy to make them more convenient to study and easier to observe through an experiment. They usually do this by splitting a group of scores at the middle score (the median). Thus, if we wanted to study how the fantasy ability of 200 students affected their liking of a song, we could (1) administer a measure of fantasy ability such as the Richness of Fantasy Scale (Hovland & Janis, 1959), which measures fantasy ability as a continuous variable, (2) find the median score for the group, then (3) classify all students who scored above the median as "highs" and all those who scored below the median as "lows." Although this procedure loses distinctions (Do people who are very high differ from those who are moderately high?, for example), it does provide a way to address the basic issue of whether fantasy ability matters in judging songs.

Independent and dependent variables. In experimental research, independent and dependent variables have a cause-effect relationship to each other. Independent variables (causes) are studied to determine their effects on dependent variables (results). Variables not of interest to the study (such as snacking while viewing the video, viewing alone, or viewing with friends) are kept constant. When variables are studied as independent variables, they are either manipulated or they are not. Manipulating a variable means the experimenter changes something to create at least two conditions for the variable: present and absent. The condition in which the variable is absent is called the control condition. The minimum conditions for manipulating exposure to MTV videos to determine effects on liking of the song would be to have one group of participants watch and listen to a video and a second group listen only to the soundtrack. This second group would serve as a control group because they are exposed to the control condition; they do not see the MTV video, our independent variable. A more complex design could involve more degrees of exposure. An experiment with four conditions for the variable would have groups exposed to the video three times, two times, or once, plus exposure to the soundtrack only. When variables are not manipulated, it is often because they cannot be manipulated feasibly or ethically. *Attribute variables* are characteristics of research participants; they are probably the most common non-manipulated variables. Usual attribute variables in communication research pertain to: physical characteristics such as biological sex; demographic characteristics such as age; and personality characteristics such as communication apprehension. Instead of sending people to Denmark to undergo sex change operations or conditioning them to have stage fright habitually when they previously had none, researchers select groups of people who reflect the attribute variable they wish to study. If we wish to contrast the levels of fantasy ability in males with those of females, we select a group of research participants that is evenly divided between men and women. For example, we might test our participants until we found two groups of 50 males and 50 females each. One male and female group would be high in fantasy ability and the other would be low in fantasy ability. However, when a variable is not manipulated we lose confidence that it is the cause of an effect. If a variable is not under the direct control of the experimenter, there is always the possibility that it is not the true cause of the effect but is only related to the actual cause. For example, male-female biological differences may have no effect on fantasy ability but how children are raised in our society might. So, if we found that females who viewed the video rated the songs much more favorably than their high fantasy ability male counterparts, we could not be sure whether the difference was due to biological sex or to cultural influences.

Dependent variables are the effects in the cause-effect model. A variable is dependent if you are interested in explaining it in terms of other variables which influence it (independent variables). In our example, liking for the song in a music video is the dependent variable because liking is assumed to be affected by the images in a video and the fantasy ability of the viewer (the independent variables). The idea of measurement is very important when considering dependent variables and nonmanipulated variables and will be covered in the final section of this chapter.

Definitions

Two types of definitions provide crucial foundations for scientific research: *constitutive* and *operational definitions*. A *constitutive definition* defines a concept by using other concepts. Thus, liking for a song could be defined as "a learned predisposition to evaluate a song in a consistently favorable or unfavorable manner." This incorporates several concepts: a learned predisposition, to evaluate, in a consistent . . . manner. Utilizing other concepts is an indication that the given concept can be made theoretically meaningful (Kerlinger, 1986, p. 28). *Operational definitions* define something in terms of the operations or procedures which were followed in order to experience the object of definition. This is very important in terms of *replication* in scientific research. That is, one scientist, working independently, should be able to duplicate the results of another researcher. Operational definitions provide a mechanism for this.

There are two types of operational definitions: *measured* and *experimental*. A measured operational definition presents essential information about how a variable was measured. For instance, an operational definition of how liking for a song was measured might be: "Liking for the song was measured by a set of six, seven-space semantic differential scales [to be explained later] representing the evaluative dimension of meaning: beautiful-ugly, nice-awful, pleasant-unpleasant, exciting-dull, interesting-boring, valuable-worthless. These scales were pretested with 50 students who were from the same population as the 200 students used in the actual experiment." (A description of the statistical procedures for assessing reliability and validity would follow.) If the operational definition is accurate, you could re-create the results by following the same procedures specified by the researchers. Sometimes, as in the case of published scales, a measured operational definition can be quite brief. For instance: "Fantasy ability was measured by the Richness of Fantasy Scale (Hovland & Janis, 1959)." If the procedures used in measurement have been published, you generally do not need to repeat them since the duplication is considered unnecessary. That is, the procedures used for published scales are considered common knowledge in the research community. (Of course, persons should read the published source if they are unfamiliar with the scale).

An experimental operational definition outlines the procedures followed in manipulating a variable. Thus, if other researchers want to study that independent variable, they would know how to replicate what the original researchers studied. Regarding the earlier example, a researcher might be interested in whether sexist music videos affect viewers' attitudes toward women. An experimental operational definition of sexist music videos might be: "Thirty individuals, who were similar to the people used in the actual experiment, were shown the 20 top music videos for 1989 and asked to rate each on a ten-point scale in terms of how much women were derogated in the video. The three rated highest and the three rated lowest were selected for the experiment. Participants in the experiment viewed either the three derogatory or the three nonderogatory videos (the independent variable) and then completed a scale for measuring attitudes toward women (the dependent variable)."

Hypothesis

Three kinds of hypotheses are important in scientific research. A *research hypothesis* is the prediction of the results of an experiment. That is, if the thinking which is the basis for a study is correct, then certain results ought to be obtained. If the hypothesized results are observed, this supports the thinking or theory. Theories are tested by testing hypotheses. For our MTV example, a research hypothesis might be: "Music videos will have a favorable effect on how much a song is liked when people are low in fantasy ability but will have no effect when people are high in fantasy ability." Research hypotheses are verbalizations of predicted outcomes; they need to be tested by being compared to something else. The most obvious test is a statistical one. The *statistical hypothesis* in our example is: "the mean (average) score for liking of the song by participants who are low in fantasy ability and who view the music video will be greater than the mean for participants who are low in fantasy ability and who hear only the soundtrack, while the means will not differ for participants who are high in fantasy ability." A problem is that the statistical hypothesis cannot be tested directly because of error. Because of measurement and sampling error, we cannot be certain that the means which we obtain for the four groups are exactly what we would have obtained if we had measured everyone in the population to which we wish to generalize our results. That is, we cannot be sure that testing 200 people in Boston or Cleveland will allow us to predict what would be true for the entire populations of those cities. If the results contained no error, we would simply look at the four means and see whether they corresponded to our predicted pattern.

Because of error, we need a standard for testing the statistical hypothesis. The standard is the *null hypothesis*: "There is no real difference between means." Probability theory and inferential statistics provide the full explanation, but we will simplify the concept to say that the logic of testing the null hypothesis is to determine whether it is likely that the difference among means is due to error. If you measure some variable (height, weight, or communication apprehension, for example) for four groups of people, the four means almost always will differ. However, the issue is whether the differences are real or whether the observed differences could be due to error. Error might be caused, for example, by using a faulty measuring stick to calculate height or by chance as in unwittingly forming groups consisting of only very confident or very apprehensive people. Using the methods of probability theory and inferential statistics, we can calculate the amount of error probably present in a given mean or average. Then we can examine the difference between two means. Taking into account the error in each mean, we can make a claim about how likely it is that the difference could be caused simply by error. Suppose we did this for two means and concluded that the probability of obtaining *by chance or error* a difference between means as large or larger than the difference we *measured* was .62. We would not be very confident that our difference was real. That is, 62 times out of 100 a difference was is, in reality, no difference at all. It would be too "chancy" to reject the null hypothesis. If something is different from something else, there should be a very low probability that the difference could be explained by error. The probability standard in the behavioral sciences for rejecting the null hypothesis is .05. That is, the chance has to be less than five times out of a hundred that a difference could have occurred due to error or chance. When the probability is low that a difference is simply due to chance fluctuations, the researcher concludes the difference observed probably is real—a non-chance occurrence.

The logic of hypothesis testing, then, is if the null hypothesis for a predicted difference is rejected, this supports the statistical hypothesis which in turn supports the research hypothesis. Further, if the null hypothesis is not rejected, the statistical hypothesis is not supported and this provides no support for the research hypothesis. This may seem a bit "round-about" to you, but the null-statistical-research sequence is particularly valuable because probability statistics allow us to state our results with a specific degree of confidence. For instance, you would regard the following situations differently: (1) calculations show the difference between groups A and B could occur by chance 20 times out of 100; (2) the probability is one out of 1000 that the difference between groups A and C is due to chance. In this example it is apparent that you would have more confidence that A is different from C than that A differs from B. If you were to bet on which difference is real based on probability theory, you should bet on the A-C difference.

Research Questions

At times it is not possible to state a hypothesis for a study because theory does not provide a basis for predicting what will happen. Also, there are times when one framework suggests a particular result while a second theory predicts another outcome. When this happens, a research question is stated instead of a hypothesis. Suppose we are interested in whether male or female viewers are influenced more to derogate women after watching sexist music videos. On the one hand, we might predict male viewers would derogate women more because sexist music videos reinforce the notion of male dominance and thus encourage males to "put down" women. On the other hand, if we were familiar with research which has found that women derogate other women more than women are derogated by men (e.g., Miller & McReynolds, 1973), we might predict that female viewers would derogate women more. Because of this uncertainty of outcome, the research would center upon the research question: Do male and female viewers differ in how they evaluate women after watching sexist music videos? This difference would have theoretical importance and answering the research question would provide a basis for the next study which would state a hypothesis. If a research question is presented for study instead of a hypothesis, the researcher should explain why it was not possible to offer a hypothesis. Unfortunately, this is not always done in research articles and consequently the theoretical significance of such studies is blurred.

Sampling

Seldom, if ever, is an entire population of interest studied. Instead, a part of the population is examined in hopes that what is found will be valid for the whole. For example, if we are interested in the communication characteristics of superiors in organizations which relate most to their subordinates' commitment to the organization, the population would be superior-subordinate pairs in corporate America. Because of the influence of culture, we would not try to generalize to all of the superior-subordinate pairs in the world. Sampling is necessary because it is seldom practical or even possible to study an entire population. At times, populations can be relatively small; e.g., P.O.W.s in the Vietnam war. However, sampling is usually necessary even with small populations because of the difficulty of avoiding exclusions.

Random Sampling. Random sampling involves selecting individuals from a population in such a manner that each member of the population has an equal chance of being selected. If this ideal of an "equal chance of being selected" is achieved, we would be rather confident that our sample is not biased, that the selection process has created a "population in miniature." Suppose we wanted to study the communication traits of state governors in the United States. The number in the population is 50. If we decided to take a random sample of 20 governors, each governor would have a 1 in 50 chance of being selected. Imagine we have the names of the 50 governors on folded slips of paper in a box. We draw the first name and put the slip of paper on a table. Then we draw a second name and put it with the first. We do this 20 times. Have we drawn a random sample according to the ideal? No, we have not. The first name drawn had a 1 in 50 chance of being drawn but the second had a 1 in 49 chance, the third a 1 in 48 chance, etc. This procedure is called sampling without replacement. *Sampling with replacement* means once a name is selected it is returned to the original pool so that the chance for successive draws remains constant. We seldom can determine if a random sample is representative of the population. A common way to assess the representativeness of a sample is to compare it to the population on a number of demographic variables such as age, education, income, etc. To find no differences regarding these variables is reassuring. However, that does not guarantee that the sample is typical of the population with reference to the variable of interest in a study. In our music video example, we could not be certain that our group is randomly distributed in their liking for a song on a music video.

Stratified Random Sampling. A stratified sample is one which is partitioned according to some meaningful criteria. Often the most recent census data are used to determine the proportions of each type selected. For instance, census data on religious affiliation could be used to determine the number of Catholics that should be included in a sample in order for the sample to represent the population. A sample of Governors could be stratified so that five are selected from each of the major geographic regions of the United Sates. A *stratified random sample* can be more representative, in practice, than a regular random sample. The reason is that unless the random sample is very large, the extreme cases tend to be underrepresented. For example, if there are 2000 rich people in a state with a population of 5 million people, a random sample of 200 could miss the rich because it takes a while for extremes to show up in a random sample. A sample of only 200 does not give the random process much time. Thus, if the characteristics of a population that matter for a particular study can be determined, a stratified random sample can produce a sample that we can be confident is truly representative.

Available Sampling. An available sample is not a random or a stratified sample. Instead the sample is selected because it is convenient. For instance, in studying the communication characteristics of superiors which predict their subordinates' organizational commitment, we might select 200 superior-subordinate pairs from a wide variety of companies in our geographic area. If we live in New York, the greater New York City area would be an *available or convenient sample.* However, our interest in studying this problem is not to specify the communication characteristics of New York managers which inspire corporate commitment in New York subordinates. Rather, we want to be able to say something that is valid with reference to all American managers. Thus, available samples are taken with the assumption that they are representative of the population. Researchers with available samples do not say their results apply only to this group of research participants, at this point in time, etc. Instead, results are discussed as if they pertain to the entire population. Over the years, this practice has stirred debate among behavioral scientists who are concerned that the widespread use of available samples may be producing knowledge which is not generalizable. The most frequently mentioned concern is the widespread use of college students as research participants. The issue raised is: if college students are not typical of the population, then the knowledge claimed in so many behavioral studies may say little about other people. The other school of thought on this issue maintains that available samples, as long as they are within normal ranges in terms of intellect, emotional health, etc., produce results in studies which are equivalent to what would be found in the population. While it is possible to take a variable such as education and create a scenario where it really matters in terms of how people respond in a study, in reality such variables seldom explain much variability in response. Thus, it is said, sampling "purists" have inflated the amount of error in a typical available sample. This position says, in essence, that "people are people" and going to the lengths necessary for a true random sample does not return results worth the time, effort, and expense.

Research Design

We will examine two types of research designs. *Experimental designs* involve *manipulation* of at least one variable. A manipulated or independent variable, as we explained earlier, is under the direct control of the experimenter. In our example, the number of times research participants are shown a music video in a communication laboratory would be the independent variable. A manipulated variable is viewed as the cause of the dependent variable. *Non-experimental designs* do not involve manipulation of variables. Instead, variables are measured, and the relationships between variables are studied. Because other causes generally cannot be ruled out, as in an experiment, claims about causality based on non-experimental designs do not inspire much confidence. This type of result is usually termed *correlational* data and is discussed in terms of one variable being related to or associated with another instead of one variable causing or being responsible for another. A non-experimental design for the effects of music videos would be to ask people whether or not they have watched a particular music video and to have them rate the song in terms of liking. This method will permit a conclusion as to whether liking for a song is related to seeing a video based on the song. However, we cannot conclude that the video caused more liking for the song. It might be that people who most like contemporary rock simply watch TV more. Thus, their liking a song might have nothing to do with watching music videos. Other variables such as watching the video with friends and being influenced by their opinions might also have affected the song ratings.

General Purpose of Research Design

The general purpose of research design is to *isolate* the variables of interest in a study. This means being able to distinguish one variable from another. At first, this does not appear to be a very complicated task. However, it is quite a feat, one that is responsible for much of what has been achieved by science. Research design is an important part of the scientific method. Many procedures have been developed for isolating variables so that they can be studied and understood. The scientific method in general, and research design in particular, provides a way of knowing, one that is regulated by *confidence*. Thus, when established procedures have been followed for isolating the effects of a variable, confidence is strong that the knowledge gained is valid. On the other hand, if the design of a study is faulty because a necessary procedure was not used, confidence is weak and there is serious doubt as to whether knowledge about the variable was gained.

How does research design permit confidence? This is primarily achieved by controlling any variables which can influence results. Research design, then, represents a set of procedures for isolating how variables relate to one another by accounting for and controlling variables which could influence results. As you might suspect, we can never have total confidence in the results of a study because it is always possible that the results were due to a variable which we did not anticipate because our theory was not sophisticated enough. Also, results could simply be due to chance. Random occurrences—such as people liking everything because they are in an unusually good mood—cannot be predicted. In our example of the effects of music videos, the research design attempted to isolate the variable exposure to music videos in terms of one effect, liking of the song. Let us suppose that in actually running the study, we conducted the two conditions (music video and audio-only) in an unairconditioned room during a hot and humid period of August. Further, suppose all of the sessions with the music videos were in the morning and all of the audio-only sessions were in the late afternoon. If our results showed that people in the music video condition liked the song more than those in the audio-only condition, could we have much confidence in the results? As you may have concluded, the answer is no. When people are distracted by an uncomfortable environment, they tend to make less favorable judgments. Thus, the results may not have been due to the music video at all. Rather, results could have varied according to comfort. Of course, the temperature may not have made any difference. The music video may have been totally responsible for the difference in liking of the song. However, we can never know for certain when the design of a study is faulty. *If a variable could have mattered and is not controlled, the study is invalid.* We may have gained some information about how to study the problem of interest, but no actual knowledge was gained regarding the original research question or hypothesis.

Achieving Control by Random Assignment

Research design attempts to rule out other possible causes of the relationship observed in a study. In experimental research, the most powerful procedure for accomplishing this is *random assignment of participants to the experimental conditions.* If some people happen to possess an expected quality which could affect the results, they will be equally distributed across the various experimental conditions when randomly assigned to experimental groups. Thus, variables that might matter in a study "cancel out" in terms of their impact and therefore do not affect the results. Here is how the principle operates. Suppose we select 50 people to view a music video and a second group of

50 to listen to the sound track only; we then measure liking of the song on a 10-point scale with 10 representing the most liking. Suppose the first group consists of 50 students enrolled in an Introduction to Mass Communication course. Unknown to us, they are very representative of the population of young adults to which we wish to generalize our results. Suppose the second group is a class of 50 students enrolled in an Organizational Communication Theory course. This group is typical of the population except they are more conservative and like the rock-and-roll of the 1950s and 1960s better than contemporary rock. In fact, on a 10-point scale, they tend to like today's songs about 3-points less than the population's rating. You can see the problem in using these two groups. Since the groups differ initially and in all likelihood we would not know this, the results of the experiment could show a difference between means. However, this result would be an illusion since the difference could have been due to their preference for rock-and-roll not because of music videos. For illustration, suppose all people in the music video condition rated the song 8 and all people in the audio-only condition rated it 5. Because of the possibility that some initial difference between the two groups of participants could be responsible for this rating difference, we can have little confidence that the 3-point difference says anything about the effects of music videos.

With random assignment of participants to experimental conditions, this would not be the case. If chance is allowed to operate, about 25 people with a conservative rock-and-roll predisposition would be assigned to the music video condition and about 25 to the audio-only. This would also be the case for the other 50 people. Thus, in each condition, 25 people will reduce a song's "normal" rating by 3 points. This could be termed "error", but *because it is equally present in both conditions*, it is canceled as a factor in the study. We will give two examples to show how this works. Suppose, in reality, music videos do not matter in terms of liking for the song. Using the data from the previous example, suppose we observe 25 scores of 8 and 25 ratings of 5 on the 10-point scale in the music video condition and also in the audio-only condition. Each group would have a mean (average) of 6.5, reflecting exactly the fact of no difference; i.e., the error canceled. However, let us suppose there actually is a 2-point difference in liking caused by music videos. If the 25 representative participants in the music video condition rate the song 8 and the 25 conservative people rate it 5, the mean would be 6.5. If the 25 representative people in the audio-only condition rate the song 6 (2 points lower than in the video condition because of the 2-point effect) and the 25 conservatives rate it 3 (also a 2-point effect), the mean would be 4.5. The difference between the 6.5 and 4.5 means is 2.0, which is exactly what we said the "real" difference is between the two conditions. In this second example, having 50 "biased" research participants had no effect on the outcome of the study because they were evenly distributed in the groups. The "3 points" of bias possessed by each of the 50 persons was canceled out because of random assignment. If we allow chance to operate, such differences in a sample will almost always balance out. Of course as mentioned earlier, there is always the very small possibility that chance will result in a biased distribution. That is why we said we can never have complete confidence in our results. We must always be aware that there is some level of probability that the results of a study could be due to error or chance.

Validity of Designs

When designing research, it is necessary to be aware of the various ways the *internal* and *external* validity of a study can be threatened (Campbell, 1957; Campbell & Stanley, 1963). *Internal validity* pertains to whether the actual procedures followed in a study rather than the variables of interest could be responsible for the results. External validity relates mainly to the generalizability of results: to whom do the results of a study apply?

Four major threats to *internal validity* are history, maturation, measurement and selection. *History* is concerned with the things which take place during the time of the study. If people are exposed to a music video once a day for five consecutive days and then liking for the song is measured, a concern would be whether anything happened during the exposure before the measurement of liking which could have influenced the results. For instance, if the recording artist for the song is accused of a serious crime during the exposure, liking for the song could be affected. Even if little time passes between exposure and measurement, an event could occur which will affect validity. For instance, suppose an audience is exposed to a music video and their liking is measured afterward. If the experimenter shows liking of the song by his or her nonverbal behavior (e.g., facial expression), the research participants' ratings might be influenced because the experimenter's response could serve as a "model" for how the participants should respond. *Maturation* refers to changes in the research participant which could affect results. This is a problem in studies which are conducted over a period of time. A study of the long-term effects of music videos, for instance, would be complicated by the possibility that the research participants' taste in music might have changed, perhaps in the direction of classical music. However, there are also changes that can take place during a relatively short laboratory session. For example, if we have people watch a fairly large number of new music videos and then ask which one they like best, results could be in error due to "confusion." The participants' cognitive systems could be overloaded with "too much of a good thing." *Measurement* is a threat to the validity of a study when the measurement procedure affects how the person reacts. This is especially troubling when a study measures something before an experimental treatment (a pretest) and again afterwards (a posttest) to see how much change was caused by the treatment. People realize they are expected to change when they are tested before an event and again after the event. Thus, they might change in order to be seen as "cooperative." A common misperception is that a pretest is necessary if you want to see whether a treatment affected someone. Since random assignment of participants to treatments equalizes the groups, the effects of a treatment can be seen by looking only at a posttest. Thus, a posttest-only design is superior to a pretest-posttest design because the former increases internal validity. *Selection* ruins the internal validity of a study because of a bias in assigning research participants. Suppose an independent variable of interest in studying music videos is how familiarity with the musical group enhances liking for the song. Perhaps the hypothesis is, "Liking for a song is enhanced more when the group is familiar because with a new group we give more attention to the group than to the song." To study this, we select music videos of new songs by five well-known groups and new songs by five unfamiliar groups. We would not use only one group for each condition because any difference could be due to something unique about the two groups (such as a difference in their clothing), therefore, our results would not be valid for all familiar and unfamiliar groups. Suppose when each participant arrives at our research laboratory, we greet him or her and then make a decision to have the person watch one of the five familiar-group videos or one of the five unfamiliar-group videos. This procedure would invalidate the study because a bias of which we may have been unaware might have led us to assign people to view particular videos to increase the chance that our hypothesis would be supported. For instance, we might assign older people to the unfamiliar-group videos because they are more established in their likes and therefore would be less likely to be attracted immediately to a new group and its song. The correct procedure, as described earlier, would be random assignment of participants to the groups (we could use a table of random numbers, or draw lots).

External validity is concerned with the generalizability of the results obtained in a study (Campbell & Stanley, 1963). Four factors which can influence this are pretesting, experimental arrangements, sampling, and multiple treatment effects. A *pretest* may increase or decrease how a research participant will react to an experimental treatment. As noted above, the pretest sensitizes the person to the idea of change as the focus of the study. The *experimental arrangements* can affect external validity because a response to an independent variable in the relatively "artificial" environment of a laboratory may be different from how people respond to the variable in more naturalistic settings. For instance, music videos might have little impact on liking for the song in a laboratory since people cannot relax as well as they do when watching music videos in the comfort of their living rooms. Thus, results of an experiment may be misleading. A solution which greatly increases the confidence we have about our conclusions is to gather more than one type of data. In addition to experimental data, evidence could be gathered from a survey or an interview. If several different types of data all point to the same conclusion, we can be more confident that the conclusion is valid. *Sampling* is a major threat to the external validity in most social science research because of the predominant tendency to use an available, convenient sample rather than a true random sample. Thus, if a convenient sample differs from the population we want to measure, the results will not be generalizable. For example, in studying how familiarity with a rock group affects liking for a song in a music video, suppose we select by chance a group of participants who are so knowledgeable about rock groups that they are equally aware of our "well-known groups" and our "new, unfamiliar groups." Our results would not be generalizable. We might find no difference in liking because, unknown to us, we actually compared reactions to other familiar groups. However, in the general population there may be an actual difference in liking for songs of familiar and unfamiliar groups. *Multiple treatment effects* result when research participants are exposed to more than one experimental treatment; how they respond in one treatment affects how they respond in another. In our example so far, each participant experienced one condition. Later we will see that under certain circumstances, a very valuable research design involves having a person exposed to more than one condition. However, learning becomes a problem. Having participated in one condition may influence someone's response to another condition. Suppose we are interested in how familiarity with a rock group in a video affects remembering the song. Research participants view a video of a familiar and an unfamiliar rock group (random order for each person). At the conclusion of each, the experimenter asks the participant to recite the lyrics. The problem here is that participants will do better for the second video. Because they know they will be expected to recite the lyrics, they will pay closer attention to them and probably practice subvocally during the second video.

Experimenter Effects

Even if all of the above seem like enough problems to have to contend with in conducting research, another major source of potential error is the *experimenter* (Brooks, 1970). In a valid experiment, participants' responses should be due to the independent variables, not to the person running the experiment. If a characteristic, trait or behavior of an experimenter is equally present in all of the conditions in an experiment and if it has an equal impact in all conditions, then there is no real problem in terms of the outcome of the study because this is comparable to adding or subtracting a constant from each participant's dependent variable score. A real problem occurs when something about the experimenter distorts how people respond in one condition, thus affecting the statistical comparison of that condition with all of the other conditions. There are several ways that this can occur. *Biological characteristics* of the experimenter such as sex, age, race, and physical attractiveness can affect participants' responses. For instance, male participants may be more cooperative when the experimenter is female. This could manifest itself by the participants' displaying a good deal of change. The experimenter's *personality traits* are one of the most potent sources of bias. Some of the more obvious ones are dominance, hostility, sociability, communication apprehension, and self-esteem. This becomes a serious problem if a trait is expressed more when the experimenter conducts one condition as compared to another. For example, if the experimenter is more sociable in an experimental treatment than in a control condition, results might be biased because the friendly behavior might motivate participants to give the experimenter what he or she seems to want. Thus, there might seem to be a difference between experimental and control conditions when in fact there is no difference caused by the independent variable. *Experimenter modeling* occurs when the experimenter shows the participant how to respond. For instance, when conducting a music video condition, the experimenter might seem to be reacting favorably to the song (e.g., tapping a finger to the music's beat), while in the audio-only condition the experimenter's behavior might be very neutral. The experimenter's behavior provides the participant with a model of how to react to the song and biases the experiment. A somewhat different problem is *experimenter expectancy*. This occurs when the experimenter communicates his or her research hypothesis to the research participants by reinforcing "correct" behavior. That is, behavior which supports the researcher's hypothesis *conditioned*. Subtle cues of approval (e.g., a nod and a slight smile) could be given when a participant begins to show liking for a song in the music video condition and cues of disapproval (e.g., a slight frown or a blank stare) when a person in the audio-only condition begins to reveal liking. The experimenter might be completely unaware of his or her expectancy behavior, making the problem particularly troublesome.

Controlling Experimenter Influence

There are several established procedures for neutralizing the impact of the person conducting a study (Brooks, 1970). *Using several experimenters* and rotating them throughout the various conditions serves to lessen the impact of a particular experimenter, he or she does not have contact with all of the participants. *Training the experimenters to standardize their behaviors* is a very important technique for solving this problem. Often a script for an experiment is written. Just as in a theatrical performance, the players practice their lines with the director, who in this case is the director of the research project. The idea is to standardize the experimental experience for all participants. *Blind contact with participants* means the experimenter does not know in which condition the person is participating. This procedure is easily employed in pharmaceutical studies, for example. The basic idea is the experimenter who has contact with the participants does not know which person is receiving the experimental drug treatment and which person receives a placebo. The same procedure could be used with a music video and an audio-only condition. The experimenter would greet participants when they arrive, give them a sealed envelope containing instructions unknown to the experimenter for either viewing a video or listening only to the sound, take them to a place for the stimulus to be presented, leave and have either a second experimenter or a computer present the video or audio-only condition. Later, the first experimenter could return to administer the liking scale and debrief participants about the purpose of the study. *Using written or recorded instructions* as much as possible is another way to reduce the impact of the experimenter by standardizing instructions. Often it is possible for the experimenter to say very little and to have minimal contact with participants. When this is achieved through the use of written or recorded instructions, confidence increases that the experimenter did not bias the study. Finally, *procedures can be developed for masking the research hypothesis.* Often this involves the use of deception; participants are led to believe the study is about one thing but it is actually about something else. There have been debates in the fields of psychology and communication on the ethics of misleading people in this manner. A reasonable position appears to be that deception should be used only when it is necessary and the participants must then be debriefed about the study's real purpose.

Experimental Research Designs

There are numerous ways to design an experiment (for example, see Edwards, 1972). We will describe three of the most common designs used in communication experiments. Other designs such as incomplete factorials, Latin Squares, and nested designs are rarely, if ever, used in communication research so they will not be covered. In the *completely randomized factorial design* all independent variables are manipulated and research participants are randomly assigned to the various conditions. A manipulated variable, you will recall, is created by and therefore under the direct control of the experimenter. The number of manipulated variables in communication studies typically varies from one to three for practical reasons. A study can become virtually unmanageable with a large number of manipulated independent variables. In our music video example, the following is a completely randomized factorial design for studying three manipulated variables. Each research participant would be randomly assigned (1) to view a music video or to listen to the audio portion only for a new song, (2) the musical group would be either a well-known group or a new one, (3) the participant would be exposed to the treatment on one, two, or three occasions (consecutive days). This design is illustrated in Figure 2.

Because each independent variable is present at every level of every other independent variable, there are a total of 12 conditions. Multiplying the number of levels of each variable produces this total (2x2x3). Adding just one more independent variable, with three levels, to the design (e.g., whether the group is all male, all female, or male and female) would increase the number of

Figure 2
Completely Randomized Factorial Design.

Familiarity of Group

	Well Known			New		
Days of Exposure:	1	2	3	1	2	3
Music Video Condition:	___	___	___	___	___	___
Music Audio Only Condition:	___	___	___	___	___	___

conditions to 36 (i.e., 2x2x3x3). If you can imagine using groups of about 20 people in each of the 36 conditions, you can appreciate the point made earlier that as the number of manipulated variables in a study increases, difficulty in conducting the study also increases. The experimenter would need a minimum of about 720 participants for 36 conditions.

A *randomized blocks design* (also termed a "mixed design") involves a combination of manipulated and nonmanipulated independent variables. This is a favorite design in communication experiments because of the interest in personality and gender differences. Personality traits and sex variables are studied as they are found in people. That is, the experimenter does not change or manipulate anything, and therefore personality and gender are nonmanipulated independent variables. The idea of "randomized blocks" means blocks of people are identified, e.g., people who are high or low in self-esteem. Then the individuals within each block are randomly assigned to the levels of the manipulated variables. An example would be: (1) people who are either high or low in fantasy ability, (2) would be shown a music video or listen to the audio-only, (3) on one, two, or three consecutive days. This design is presented in Figure 3. This design "looks like" the previous one. However, when a variable is not manipulated, what can be said about its influence is limited. That is, our confidence in discovering a cause of something is highest when we have manipulated the believed cause.

In the *repeated measures design* participants are exposed to all levels of one or more manipulated variables. The previous two designs were different because each participant experienced only one of the conditions. In the example for the first design (Figure 2) 12 different groups of participants would be needed. However, if participants are exposed to more than one level of an independent variable, the number of participants needed in a study can be substantially reduced. Thus, a repeated measures design can be very economical. Another benefit is that the participant serves as his or her own control group. It is nearly impossible to match people for a valid comparison in an experiment. As a result a "matched samples" design is seldom used

Figure 3

Randomized Blocks Design.

Music Condition

		Music Video			Audio Only		
Days of Exposure:		1	2	3	1	2	3
Fantasy Ability:	High	___	___	___	___	___	___
	Low	___	___	___	___	___	___

in research. Comparing a person to him or herself excels even a sample of matched identical twins. Here is an example to illustrate how this would work. Let us turn the example for the first design (See Figure 2) into a repeated measures design. Instead of twelve groups of research participants, we will only need two groups because we will have repeated measures over two independent variables: (1) familiarity with group and (2) one, two, or three exposures. Several new songs would be recorded by a well-known group and also by a new group. These would be systematically varied so that they appeared equally in the various conditions and so each participant would be exposed to two new songs. Participants would be told the study is investigating how we get to know a new song. The researchers would say: (1) that they were able to acquire the music videos for two new songs or that they were able to acquire audio recordings of two new songs and (2) that each participant would hear two songs on three consecutive days. One group would participate in the music video condition. They would watch a music video of a song by a well-known group and also one by a new group. They would rate each song on a set of scales. The order in which songs by the well-known and by the new group appeared would be varied for each participant. This procedure would be repeated on the second and third days. The second group of participants would be exposed to the audio-only. The same procedures would be followed here as with the previous participants. You can see how economical this design is. Instead of 12 groups of participants, we need only two—or about 40 people rather than 240. In light of this difference, you might wonder why repeated measures designs are not used for all experiments. The answer is that the repeated measures design is only appropriate when exposure to one condition does not influence how the person responds to another condition. Unfortunately, for many independent variables of interest in communication research, if a person is exposed to one level of an independent variable, the first exposure would have an effect on how he or she reacted to another level of the variable. For example, learning might take place between the first and second exposures as in the example above about recalling lyrics from the songs. However, there are instances, and our music video example may be one, where a repeated measures design is appropriate.

Nonexperimental Research Designs

The value of experimental research designs is fairly obvious. When a variable is manipulated and other variables controlled, resulting effects can be viewed as caused by the manipulated variable. Confidence in a supposed causal relationship is greatest when this degree of control is achieved by the researcher. That is why Kerlinger (1986) claimed the ideal of science is the controlled experiment. The researcher should deviate from this ideal only when it is necessary. Although the standards of experiments are highly desirable, the reality of communication research is that many of the areas of interest do not lend themselves readily to experimental research. Some variables are difficult or not feasible to manipulate. It is easier to study such variables naturally, as they already exist. However, when this is done, the researcher does not have control over the independent variables. These designs are not less valuable than experimental designs, but they are different in that statements about what causes what are not warranted. Thus, the researchers using nonexperimental designs are concerned about what is related to what, how things vary together. We will examine three nonexperimental designs. There is no manipulation of variables in these designs. However, the concern with controlling variables which can influence results is just as strong as it is with experiments. Nonexperimental research can and should be rigorous.

When diagrammed, an *investigational design* has the appearance of an experiment. However, the critical difference is that no variable is manipulated. This is illustrated by the design in Figure 4. The design involves males who are either high,moderate, or low in fantasy ability and who are either younger or older. They are shown a music video with a number of attractive female actors and then asked to complete a scale which measures liking of the video. The hypothesis could be that the video will be liked most by younger males who are lower in fantasy ability. The reasoning might be that music videos satisfy fantasy needs and young males who are low in fantasy ability and inexperienced might need the fantasies more than others and hence be more receptive to sources which provide satisfaction. Nothing is manipulated in this study. That is, need for fantasy is measured by a personality scale. Males are classified as high, moderate, or low according to norms for that scale. The

Figure 4

Investigational Design.

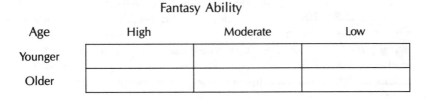

Fantasy Ability

Age	High	Moderate	Low
Younger			
Older			

second independent variable is created by the person's age. For instance, teenage males could be classified as "younger," while males beyond their teens could be termed "older." Because there is no manipulation, an important procedure of experiments for controlling other variables cannot be followed. Research participants cannot be randomly assigned to the various parts of the design. Rather, participants in effect assign themselves according to their level of need for fantasy and their age.

Field research is conducted in natural settings as contrasted to investigational designs which are conducted in a laboratory. Experiments can be conducted in the field, but communication researchers have seldom done so. Organizational communication research probably is the most common form of field research in the communication discipline. Researchers go to the participants in their natural setting (their workplace) instead of having the participant come to the researcher (the laboratory or college campus). As with the investigational design, no variable is manipulated. All of the variables of interest are measured, and the associations among the variables are studied. Hypotheses about predicted relationships are tested. In addition, a field study can be exploratory in that no hypothesis is tested. Instead, the purpose is to determine what should be studied in future investigations.

The basic design of *survey* research is to select a sample from a population in order to infer how frequently certain variables occur and how they are related in the population. Interviews and mail surveys are two major types of surveys. Each is capable of yielding a good deal of information. Personal interviews of participants are expensive in terms of time and effort. However, the span and depth of information gained can make the cost worthwhile. Mail surveys are easier to conduct. However, a major disadvantage is a typical low return rate, often below 50 percent. The results from a study with a low return rate can be very misleading because if everyone had returned the survey, the results could have been significantly different. The "missing data" could matter greatly, but there is no way to determine the difference other than the exhausting and sometimes impossible task of studying those who did not return the survey. An alternative to the mail survey of a random sample of people is to go in person to available groups such as students in classes, church and social groups, and people in professional meetings. A major advantage is that participation is usually near 100 percent. However, an important disadvantage is that the sample is not random; it is a convenient sample. The group could have peculiarities which could account for results; for instance, all members of the social group might have a high ability to fantasize. A good procedure to test for this possibility is to gather demographic data on the sample and compare it to the characteristics of the population of interest. If there are no differences, the researchers can have some confidence that the sample is not biased.

The music video topic could be investigated using survey methodology. A mail survey would involve selecting a random sample and sending participants a scale which contained a list of music videos. People could be asked how often they have seen each in the past week. Next, a scale could be used to measure liking of the song in each video. Demographic questions could be included. Also, a personality scale measuring the need for fantasy for example, could be a part of the questionnaire. You can see how this survey could address some of the same concerns as the experiments designed earlier in the chapter, such as whether frequency of exposure to a video enhances liking of the song. The major difference between this study and earlier experiments would be in terms of what is claimed. An experiment which manipulates exposure may be justified in contending that causal relationships are present; e.g., "more exposure *produces* greater liking." However, a survey which *measures* rather than *manipulates* exposure would be on firmer ground if it stated an *association*; e.g., "more exposure *is related to* greater liking." You might think the difference between these two claims is minute, hair-splitting, or "picky." However, A being the cause of B is different from A and B both being the effects of cause C. Without the control of an experiment, the second claim is a possibility, so it is not prudent to claim the first. For instance, in a survey of music videos, exposure might be related to liking for the song in a video; however, both of these effects could be produced by socioeconomic status. That is, teenagers from wealthier households might have had more exposure to the video tested because they have more leisure time to watch TV, and they might like the particular song more because it appeals to people who are wealthy but is repugnant to others. An experiment would control for this potentially biasing factor because random assignment of participants to the experimental conditions probably would equalize family income across the manipulated levels of exposure, hence canceling its influence.

Measurement

Most of the results of studies cited in this book were derived from questionnaires where people rated themselves, another person's behavior, messages, ideas, or aspects of a communication situation. Measurement ratings can be at any of four different levels: nominal, ordinal, interval, and ratio. The *nominal level of measurement* involves assigning an object of judgment to a category. A nominal level variable in communication is biological sex. A person is classified as either male or female. In terms of data, male could be coded "1" and female "2". However, the numbers are meaningless as data other than to identify a person's category. That is, a 2 is not greater than a 1. In the *ordinal level* of measurement, the levels of a variable are ordered and meaningful. This is commonly termed rank order data. If five speeches were rank ordered from 1 to 5 with 1 meaning "best," the speech ranked first would be better than the speech ranked second, and so forth. What you cannot tell from this rank order data is "how much better" each speech is than the next. It is not necessarily true that a speech rated 2 is twice as good as a speech rated 4.

There are many possible patterns. The best speech might be much better than the other four, which are clustered together. Or all five might be extremely close or clustered. These two very different patterns could not be distinguished by the ordinal data since the rank order would be exactly the same in both cases. *Interval data* are different in that the intervals between data points are equal, or at least approximately equal. Thus, if we had a 10-point interval scale for measuring speech quality, quality would increase an equal amount from 1 to 2, from 2 to 3, and so forth on the scale. A speech rated 8 would be considered 4 points higher in quality than a speech rated 4; we could state that there is a 4-point difference. If one speech was rated 8 and other speeches were rated 4 or lower, this scale would clearly reflect that one speech was far superior to the others. *Ratio data* are similar to interval data because the assumption of equal intervals between data points also applies. The major difference is that a meaningful zero point exists for a ratio measure but not for an interval measure. Weight is an example of a ratio scale. Zero is a clear starting point. Moreover, it registers on a scale. Speech quality is not a ratio scale. It is not clear what it means for a speech to have zero quality. In fact, there have been few, if any, ratio scales in communication research. Because ratio scales have a zero point, it is meaningful to multiply and divide scores. For instance, you can say one score is twice another. Thus, a 200-pound person is twice as heavy as a 100-pound person. Or, one person is half as heavy as another. We could not do that with the speeches rated 8 and 4 in the above example. Since we do not know where zero quality is for a speech (it is somewhere below 1), we cannot say that the speech rated 4 was only half as good as the speech rated 8. If there is a "true" zero that we are not aware of, and if, for example, it is considerably below 1, 4 might really be only three fourths as good as 8. Thus, if zero is unknown for a scale, it does not make sense to use multiplication or division in interpreting the data.

Measurement in communication research has utilized four primary methods: rating scales, behavioral observation, content analysis, and physiological measures. We will explain each briefly and develop an illustration based on our music video example.

Rating Scales

Most communication research data has come from rating scales. Three types have been employed almost exclusively: semantic differential, Likert scales, and simple linear scales. *Semantic differential scales* were developed by Osgood, Suci, and Tannenbaum (1957) in conjunction with their theory of meaning. They believed that the meaning of something can be located in "semantic space," which has three major dimensions: *evaluation, potency,* and *activity*. These dimensions are measured by scales composed of *bipolar terms* which allow an object of judgment to be placed somewhere on the continuum between the polar opposites. For instance good-bad is a pair of bipolar adjectives which measure the evaluative (or attitude) dimension of meaning. Typically, the continuum between the poles is represented by seven spaces. For each pair of bipolar adjectives, a check in the space next to the favorable end is given a score of "7"; the second space is given a score of "6," etc. A total score is then computed by summing across all pairs of the bipolar adjectives for a given object of judgment. Figure 5 contains an example of a semantic differential scale used to measure how much a song in a music video is liked. (A rating of liking is considered a measure of attitude toward the object of judgment.) Notice the instructions and also the scale format. The order of the bipolar adjectives, in terms of whether the favorable or unfavorable adjective appears on the left, is varied to discourage people from checking straight down a column without thinking of the given pair of adjectives as it applies to the concept being rated. Having to determine the location of the favorable and unfavorable ends of the continuum results in the person's considering the pair of bipolar adjectives at least briefly.

Figure 5
A Semantic Differential Scale.

Rate the song to which you just listened on the following set of six scales. For each pair of adjectives, a check in the space next to the word means "extremely"; the second space from the word means "moderately"; the third space means "slightly"; the middle space means "neutral." Remember, use only one check for each pair of words (six checks total on this page). Please make your checkmark on one of the blanks not the spaces.

I personally feel the song was:

Beautiful	____:	____:	____:	____:	____:	____:	____ ugly
awful	____:	____:	____:	____:	____:	____:	____ nice
unpleasant	____:	____:	____:	____:	____:	____:	____ pleasant
exciting	____:	____:	____:	____:	____:	____:	____ dull
interesting	____:	____:	____:	____:	____:	____:	____ boring
worthless	____:	____:	____:	____:	____:	____:	____ valuable

Likert scales (1932) are based on the idea of determining belief statements that are relevant to the object of judgment, assessing the extent to which the research participant accepts each statement, and then summing the person's acceptance across the total set of beliefs to derive a score for the person's attitude toward the object. Acceptance of a belief statement is usually measured by a five-point scale which spans from "strongly agree" to "strongly disagree." In order to discourage an automatic pattern of responses, word half of the statements positively and half negatively. This pattern is illustrated in Figure 6: an example of a Likert-type scale for measuring attitude toward a song in a music video. The mix of positively and negatively worded items also guards against "yeasaying" and "naysaying" response tendencies. That is, some people tend to agree with statements that are positive, while other people tend to disagree with anything worded negatively. Having a mix of items controls at least somewhat the degree that these tendencies influence scores. This scale is scored by giving a 5 to the "strongly agree" response to a positively worded statement, a 4 to "agree", a 3 to "undecided," etc. The scoring is reversed for the negatively worded items. That is, "strongly disagree" is given a 5, "disagree" a 4, etc. Scores on the statements are summed to arrive at the individual's total score.

Figure 6
A Likert Scale

Several statements about the song to which you listened are presented. Indicate the extent to which you agree or disagree with each statement by placing a number in the space to the left of the statement. Use the following scale:

5 = strongly agree
4 = agree
3 = undecided
2 = disagree
1 = strongly disagree

_____ 1. That was one of the best songs I have heard in some time.
_____ 2. I do not care if I ever hear that song again.
_____ 3. I would buy a recording of the song.
_____ 4. If that song comes on my car radio I would change the station.
_____ 5. I experienced very pleasant and favorable feelings while listening to the song.
_____ 6. The song fails to make a good impression.

Simple linear scales are usually five- or seven-point scales which rate something along a dimension specified by the endpoints. For instance, a scale item might ask you to rate the organization of a speech on a five-point scale which spans from "poor" to "excellent." Or an item could ask the degree of something (e.g., how much you liked something) on a seven-point scale using "not at all" to "greatly" as endpoints. One of the most used formats to measure personality and communication traits presents a statement and asks how often the statement is true for you; e.g., "I get a great deal of pleasure out of watching music videos." The rating scale usually consists of five points: "almost never true, occasionally true, sometimes true, often true, almost always true." Notice, the endpoints specify "almost" rather than never or always. People are reluctant to say never or always because confidence is seldom high for such absolute judgments. "Almost never" provides a margin for error in judgment and thus is preferred. Because of this tendency, a five-point scale that does not include "almost" with the endpoints becomes in effect a three-point scale since people tend not to use the endpoints in the rating.

Behavioral Observation

In addition to studying what people *verbally report* on questionnaires, communication researchers sometimes observe other behaviors of interest. The behavior might be studied "live" or videotape-recorded. The researcher usually does not rate or categorize the participant's behavior because the purpose of the study could cause the researcher to distort what is seen, e.g., to see support for a hypothesis when there is no support. Instead, researchers usually train research assistants who do not know the purpose of the study to observe the behavior of interest. Sometimes researchers ask participants to report whether they engaged in certain behavior. In our music video study, we could observe behavior instead of or in addition to gathering questionnaire data. For instance, participants could be videotaped while watching a music video. Then a research assistant could look for behavior which was specified before the experiment as relevant. Some of the behaviors might be: amount of time smiling during the video; how often the person beat time with hand, head, or foot; moving lips in synch with the lyrics, etc. A week later the participants might be asked whether they had purchased a recording of the song. *Reliability* of measurement is just as important with behavioral observations as it is with questionnaire data. Reliability of behavioral observations is assessed by having a second research assistant observe the behavior of the participant. The research assistants should not do this together because they could influence one another, thus giving the illusion of agreement and hence reliability. In fact, the only reliable behavior might be one assistant's ability to influence the other. The observations of both assistants are compared and a reliability coefficient is computed. If the coefficient is too low, the categories of behavior and instructions may have to be revised extensively, new assistants trained, and the process repeated. A weakness in behavioral data obtained as self-reports from research participants is that reliability and validity are seldom checked. In the example above, if we asked participants a week after viewing the video whether they had purchased a recording of the song, we probably would accept their answers as fact because it would be impractical to check to determine that they actually had such a recording.

Content Analysis

A limited amount of communication research has employed content analysis. In this very useful method of measurement, messages are examined for the occurrence of certain themes, types of language, organizational structures, language intensity, types of evidence, reasoning, etc. The procedures are similar to those used for behavioral observation: categories of things to look for in the message are formed ahead of time or after a preliminary reading of the messages if theory does not provide guidance for the categories; coders are trained to use the category system; if satisfactory reliability is not achieved, the category system and instructions are revised and the process is repeated. Content analysis can be used in a number of ways. For example, a single speech by a political leader could be analyzed for types of reasoning, for example, or a number of speeches by the person could be analyzed to look for trends. A number of individuals' messages on a topic could be analyzed; e.g., after viewing a music video, research participants could be asked to write an assessment of the video. Content analysis also can be used to analyze the interaction between people. For instance, the dialogue between husbands and wives in happy or troubled marriages could be analyzed to determine the occurrence of certain types of verbally aggressive messages, supportive messages, and instances of intense language.

Physiological Measures

A relatively small number of communication studies have used measures of involuntary responses such as heart rate and, to a lesser extent, blood pressure and skin conductivity. These measures have been used in studying communication apprehension—probably a good place to begin since an increase in heart rate, for instance, is often associated with presenting a speech. It probably would be beneficial if more research examined how changes in our central nervous system relate to and influence communication. As Bostrom (1980) pointed out, there are a large number of causes of physiological change: alcohol, tobacco, caffeine, tranquilizers, various other drugs, controlled substances such as marijuana, and physical states such as fatigue, pain, hunger, and stress. Given this range of factors, it may be somewhat uncommon to talk with someone who is in a completely unaltered physiological state. These factors tend to have two types of effects: stimulants or depressants. For example, stimulants can result in greater persuasion while depressants can reduce persuasion. Using physiological measures to study how altered physiological states function in other areas of communication besides communication apprehension and persuasion may yield some interesting knowledge. For instance, do stimulants or depressants influence how attracted we are to new acquaintances? Perhaps future research will take that direction.

Summary

A model of scientific research which involved induction, hypothesis, deduction, experiment, and feedback to the induction phase was discussed. Several concepts fundamental to behavioral research in communication were explained: variables (continuous-dichotomous, independent-dependent, manipulated-attribute), constitutive definitions, operational definitions (measured-experimental), hypotheses (research-statistical-null), research questions, sampling (random-stratified-available). Types of research designs were introduced in terms of whether manipulation of variables was involved. The purpose of research designs is to isolate the variables of interest in a study. Random assignment in experiments is a primary means for achieving control of extraneous variables which could influence results. Four threats to the internal validity of a study are history, maturation, measurement, and selection. External validity can be threatened by pretesting, experimental arrangements, sampling, and multiple treatment effects. Biological and personality characteristics of the experimenter, experimenter modeling, and expectancy can bias results. Experimenter bias can be controlled by using several experimenters, standardizing behavior, having blind contact with participants, using written or recorded instructions, and masking hypotheses. Three experimental research designs were explained: the completely randomized factorial design, the randomized blocks design, and the repeated measures design. Three types of nonexperimental research discussed were investigational, field, and survey. Four levels of measurement were specified: nominal, ordinal, interval, and ratio. Measurement in communication research has generally utilized four methods: rating scales, behavioral observation, content analysis, and physiological measures. Rating scales used most have been the semantic differential, Likert scales, and linear scales.

Questions To Consider

1. What steps are involved in the scientific method?
2. What concepts are particularly fundamental in communication research?
3. How do experimental and non-experimental designs differ?
4. Why is control so important in the design of research?
5. How is control achieved in research?
6. In what ways can the internal validity of a research design be threatened?
7. How can the external validity of a research design be threatened?
8. How can the experimenter be a source of error in a study? What can be done to control this problem?
9. What are the major experimental designs used in communication research?
10. What are the major non-experimental designs used in communication research?
11. What are the four levels at which measurement may take place?
12. What are the main methods of measurement which have been used in communication research?

References

Bostrom, R.N. (1980). Altered physiological states: The central nervous system and persuasive communications. In M.H. Roloff & G.R. Miller (Eds.), *Persuasion: New directions in theory and research* (pp. 171-196). Beverly Hills, CA: Sage.

Brooks W.D. (1970). Perspectives on communication research. In P. H. Emmert & W.D. Brooks (Eds.), *Methods of research in communication* (pp. 3-8). Boston: Houghton Mifflin.

Campbell, D.T. (1957). Factors relevant to the validity of experiments in social settings. *Psychological Bulletin, 54*, 297-312.

Campbell, D.T., & Stanley, J.C. (1963). Experimental and quasi-experimental designs for research on teaching. In N.L. Gage (Ed.), *Handbook of research on teaching* (pp. 171-246). Chicago: Rand McNally.

Cattell, R.B. (Ed.). (1966). *Handbook of multivariate experimental psychology.* Chicago: Rand McNally.

Edwards, A.L. (1972). *Experimental design in psychological research* (4th ed.). New York: Holt, Rinehart and Winston.

Hovland, C. I., & Janis, I.L. (Eds.). (1959). *Personality and persuasibility.* New Haven, CT: Yale University Press.

Kerlinger, F.N. (1986). *Foundations of behavioral research* (3rd. ed.). New York: Holt, Rinehart and Winston.

Likert, R. (1932). A technique for the measurement of attitudes. *Archives of Psychology,* No. 140.

Miller, G.R., & McReynolds, M. (1973). Male chauvinism and source competence. *Speech Monographs, 40*, 154-155.

Osgood, C.E., Suci, G.J., & Tannenbaum, P. H. (1957). *The measurement of meaning.* Urbana, IL: University of Illinois Press.

Glossary

Absolute information. Total amount of knowledge present in a system (e.g., the total number of parts that might break down to cause the red trouble light to appear on an office copier).

Adaptors. Bodily movements which serve a physical need, but have been employed to express one's personality and individuality; two forms are person adaptors and object adaptors. An example would be scratching one's nose during periods of anxiety or stress.

Affect displays. Bodily movements which express emotion. An example would be widening the eyes and raising the eye brows to indicate surprise.

Affective-cognitive consistency. Idea that cognitions about an object and feelings about an object tend toward a state of consistency.

Affective dimension of communication. The communication of emotion. Research indicates that emotions are more effectively conveyed through the nonverbal than the verbal code.

Agenda-setting. Function of mass media to influence the relative importance of our attitudes on issues. The perceived importance of issues is related to the attention given to those issues by the media.

Aggression. Applying physical and/or symbolic force to dominate and even destroy the locus of attack.

Animated style. Tendency to expend considerable energy when communicating. This is in contrast to a very controlled style of communicating.

Anomaly. Unexplained event or finding often resulting from research under an old paradigm during a period of scientific change.

Antecedent conditions. Events occurring earlier in time which are related to some later (subsequent) conditions or effects.

Anticipatory function of a theory. Aspect of a theory whereby humans anticipate events they may never have encountered. Also conceptualized as a "what if" analysis.

Argumentativeness. Personality trait in which individuals present and defend positions on controversial issues while attempting to refute the positions of other people.

Argumentative skill deficiency. Cause of verbal aggression due to inability to argue skillfully; attack and defend needs are not satisfied.

Assertiveness. Personality trait exhibiting dominant, ascendant, and forceful behavior. Involves four dimensions: directiveness, social, defense, independence.

Asymmetrical link. Communication link used unequally by two organization members; i.e., only one member initiates communication with the other while the other merely responds when contacted.

Atheoretical. Lacking a theoretical foundation.

Attentive style. Tendency to listen carefully to others.

Attitude. Learned predisposition to respond favorably or unfavorably toward an object.

Attitude similarity. One of the factors associated with interpersonal attraction; degree of perceived or actual similarity in attitudes between people.

Attribute variables. Characteristics of research participants which are studied as independent variables; e.g., age, sex, dogmatism.

Audience adaptation. Making a message compatible with receivers' attitudes and values and the nature of the situation.

Available sample. Group of research participants selected based on convenience and lack of evidence that the group is biased.

Because-motive. Term used by Alfred Schutz to label the reason for taking some action based on an event that happened in the past.

Behavior rules. In the Coordinated Management of Meaning theory, rules that individuals use to decide how to behave.

Behavioral observation. Method of measurement which involves observing behavior, classifying it according to a framework, and determining the reliability of the classification.

Biological time. Cycles or rhythms that our bodies follow: ultradian (hour and a half), circadian (daily).

Bit. Binary digit, such as 0 and 1; components of the binary number system representing a two-choice situation. A measure of the amount of information in a message.

Body orientation. Degree to which a person's shoulders and hips are turned toward another person.

Bogus stranger technique. Method used to manipulate degree of similarity to an unknown other in attraction research. Technique where "information" about the stranger is created by the researcher.

Boundary-spanning. Activity of going beyond the boundary of a system to link it with its environment.

Bridge. Group member who links two groups and actually belongs to one of them. (See liaison.)

Bureaucracy. Organization characterized by hierarchical chains of command and power, each with its own separate function. The organization is governed by rules accepted by the members in order for efficient mass administration.

Causation. Relationship in which previous (antecedent) events produce later (consequent) effects.

Centrality. Numerous direct contacts in a communication network.

Change agent. Individual who exerts influence on opinion leaders to adopt an innovation.

Channel. Means by which a message is conveyed from source to receiver, i.e., radio, television, telephone, face-to-face.

Chronemics. Study of how time is used in communication.

Classical model of communication. The oldest and most frequently employed theoretical perspective in communication theory and research. Based on the philosophical theory of logical positivism, this model suggests that theory is best developed by trying to discover law-like regularities in nature which operate according to cause-and-effect principles.

Classical theory of organizations. The earliest theory of organizations; classical theory emphasizes the study of structures and power relationships. The organization is compared to a machine, and workers are considered to be one of several means of production, like capital and raw materials.

Closed system. System that has little or no interaction with its environment. System that is not open to new information.

Clothing predispositions. Tendencies toward selecting particular clothing. Some research suggests that there are four dimensions: clothing consciousness, exhibitionism, practicality, designer.

Code. Set of rules or symbols used to translate a message from one form into another.

Code switching. Process of moving from one linguistic code or dialect to another.

Coercion. Social influence where the message receiver is not given a choice of how to respond to the message.

Cognitive complexity. As used by George Kelly, refers to a system of personal constructs which contains numerous interrelated abstract constructs.

Cognitive dissonance. Exists when two related beliefs are incompatible with one another or when one belief does not logically follow given the other. For example, knowledge that one smokes and knowledge that smoking is harmful may create dissonance.

Cognitive dissonance theory. Theory developed by Festinger (1957) which predicts that persuasion will be greatest when the magnitude of cognitive dissonance is highest.

Cognitive uncertainty. Generalized state of uncertainty intrapersonally or between individuals.

Collaterality. Cultural value which focuses on the extended group, such as a tribe or racial or religious group.

Communication. Humans manipulation of symbols to stimulate meaning in other humans.

Communication apprehension. Fear or anxiety associated with real or anticipated communication with others. Can take four forms: trait like, context-based, audience-based, situational.

Communication-behavior cycles. In Weick's theory, procedures of communication interacts (such as questions and answers) that an organization uses to process complex information received from the environment.

Communication competence. Involves appropriateness and effectiveness, can be viewed as traitlike, context or situation-bound.

Communication isolates. Organization members who have few communication links or contacts with others within the organization.

Communication plan. Set of verbal and nonverbal behaviors selected to accomplish a purpose.

Communication trait. Hypothetical construct invented to account for certain kinds of communicative behaviors. Argumentativeness, verbal aggressiveness, and communication apprehension are examples of communication traits.

Communicator style. How an individual manipulates the verbal and nonverbal message codes to signal meaning.

Comparative mass communication. Study of theories comparing media systems from different cultures, for example, India and Great Britain.

Completely randomized factorial design. An experimental research design in which all independent variables are manipulated and research participants are assigned randomly to treatment conditions.

Compliance. Social influence where perceived pressure, especially in terms of relationships with the source, rather than attitude toward a proposal, controls response to a message.

Compliments. Utterances in which a speaker bestows positively valued attributes upon a listener.

Concept. Abstraction referring to a class of things, a term used at the theoretical level.

Connotative meaning. Subjective associations, feelings or emotional attachments people associate with symbols.

Constructivism. Another name for the communication perspective based on George Kelly's Theory of Personal Constructs.

Content analysis. Method of measurement for studying the content of messages, which utilizes a category system and checks the reliability of categorizing message units.

Contentious style. Tendency to challenge others when disagreements occur.

Context. Specific situation in which communication occurs.

Contingency rules theory. Theory of persuasion which predicts persuasive strategy selection and response to the strategy from self-evaluative and adaptive contingency rules.

Contingency theories of group leadership. Leadership theories which stress that a particular leadership style will be variably effective according to the needs created by different organizational situations.

Continuous variable. When there are meaningful degrees of a variable between the highest and lowest values.

Coordinated Management of Meaning. Communication theory based on Searle's Speech Act theory. The theory assumes that individuals use definition and behavior rules to guide their conversations with others.

Constitutive definition. Definition of a concept which utilizes other concepts.

Construct. Abstraction referring to a class of things, a term used at the theoretical level.

Constructivistic model of credibility. Analysis of source credibility in terms of how people use their systems of personal constructs to create images of sources in persuasion situations.

Control. Interpersonal need to influence one's environment.

Control group. Group of participants in a study used for comparison purposes, who do not receive experimental treatment(s).

Convergence. Strategy where individuals alter their speech to adapt to each other. (see Speech Accommodation Theory).

Conversational analysis. Analysis of conversational form and content. Also referred to as discourse analysis.

Correlation. Process of mass communication through which the media select, interpret and criticize information about the environment.

Covering laws. Group of regular patterns observable in nature.

Covering laws perspective. Developed from logical positivism, a theoretical paradigm which asserts that the true nature of reality is contained in regular, observable natural patterns. Research conducted under this paradigm often uses variable analytic methods.

Cross-cultural communication. Communication of different combinations of people, i.e., a cross-cultural communication study might compare and contrast Japanese and American negotiation tactics.

Cross-situational consistency. Consistency of behavior across situations, involves validity of trait approaches to behavior.

Cultivation. Theory which asserts that the media (especially television) exert great influence in altering perceptions of reality.

Culture. Traditions and patterns of thought which are passed down through generations of people.

Culture-bound. Appropriate only for a particular culture or group of people; not true for all cultures.

Culture general training. Intercultural communication training designed to sensitize individuals to rules and norms of their own culture and to indicate general categories of differences across cultures, such as differences in values, perceptions, and verbal and nonverbal codes.

Culture specific training. Intercultural communication training designed to provide information about a particular culture to give the trainee some knowledge about the rules, roles, values, and interpretive patterns common in the other culture.

Cybernetic systems. Open systems which are self-regulating. A thermostat, which monitors the air temperature and adjusts a heater to cycle on and off to maintain a preset temperature, is an example of a cybernetic system.

Deception. Verbal and nonverbal behaviors which communicate that an individual is not telling the truth.

Decoding. The process of giving meaning to a message that has been received.

Definition rules. In the Coordinated Management of Meaning theory, rules that individuals use to interpret another's words and actions.

Denotative meaning. The objective, descriptive or agreed upon meaning of a word.

Dependent variables. Presumed effect in a cause-effect relationship, what is predicted from independent variables.

Descriptive models of communication. Specifies what is in the domain of interest and speculates on the structure of the domain.

Developmental communication. Communication related to social change, often in developing countries.

Dialectic. For Plato, a question-and-answer method philosophers use to arrive at truth; for Aristotle, a form of reasoning from principles agreed upon by most people.

Dichotomous variables. Variable with two discrete values.

Disclosiveness. Personality trait which reveals personal information to others according to five dimensions: intent, amount, positive/negative, depth, honesty.

Diffusion. How new ideas, information, and innovations spread out among a society or social system.

Discourse. Expression of thought through extended speech.

Disdain. Cause of verbal aggression which involves attacking another person verbally in order to communicate dislike.

Displacement. Moving mentally from the present to either a past or future time framework. In language study, the ability to communicate about things that cut across time, space, reality and fantasy.

Distributed information. Information which has been communicated throughout an organization.

Divergence. Accentuating vocal and linguistic differences to underscore social differences between speakers. See Speech Accommodation Theory.

Dogmatism. Degree of willingness to consider other persons' belief systems for controversial issues.

Dominance. Degree to which one partner is said to dominate a dyad's interaction.

Dominant style. Tendency to lead and take control in social situations.

Double interact. Pattern of behavior-response-adjustment, such as a question, answer, and follow-up question.

Downward communication. Communication from higher members of the organization (i.e., managers, vice-presidents) to members lower in the organizational hierarchy (subordinates).

Dramatic style. Tendency to tell stories, exaggerate, to "act" when talking with others.

Dramatism. Rhetorical theory of Kenneth Burke; dramatism emphasizes the drama as a metaphor for understanding human communication.

Duractivity. Degree of psychological involvement audience members exhibit during a television viewing experience.

Ectomorph. Body shape which is thin, lacks strength, hips and shoulders same width.

Ego-involvement. Characterized by a wide latitude of rejection, and narrow latitudes of acceptance and noncommitment.

Ego-involvement theory. Predicts persuasion is most likely when a message falls within the person's latitude of acceptance.

Elocutionists. 19th and 20th century rhetoricians who emphasized appropriateness and importance of delivery.

Emblems. Bodily movements which are functionally equivalent to words.

Emotional leakage. Unintentional nonverbal behavior which is a symptom of an internal state.

Empathy. Ability to share another person's feelings, to feel as the other does.

Enactment. In Weick's theory, the first phase of organizing. In this phase the organization uses rules and cycles to interpret information received from the environment.

Encoding. Process of taking an idea and getting it ready for transmission.

Endomorph. Body shape which looks heavy, soft, hips wider than shoulders, high body fat level.

Entertainment function of media. Use of the media to delight, stimulate, enchant, escape.

Enthymeme. Pattern of deductive reasoning like the syllogism, but with one or more premises suppressed.

Entropy. Chaos, randomness and disorder in a system. Entropy is the final state of a closed system.

Epistemology. Philosophical study of the ways of knowing.

Equifinality. Concept that there are many different ways by which a system may reach the same end state.

Equilibrium. Point of balance.

Equity theory. One of the social exchange theories of relational development. Suggests that relational satisfaction is greatest when there is an equal distribution of rewards and costs between partners in a relationship.

Ethnocentric. Judging other groups according to the categories and values of one's own culture rather than being open to cultural differences.

Evidence. Information or data used to support the truth or probability of a proposition, or a speaker's claims.

Evolution of ideas. Variety, selection and retention of ideas through communication.

Experimental research designs. Involves manipulation of at least one variable, control of variables that could influence results.

Experimenter effects. Error in a study caused by the experimenter's characteristics and/or behavior.

Experimenter expectancy. Experimenter reinforces behavior of the research participant which supports the research hypothesis.

Experimenter modeling. Experimenter shows the research participant the hypothesized behavior.

Exploitive orientation. Tendency to take, by cunning or force, what is valuable to other people.

Extension. Process in which a theory grows by adding knowledge and new concepts.

External validity. Concerned with the generalizability of a study, major threats are pretesting, experimental arrangements, sampling, multiple treatment effects.

Eye behavior. Nonverbal behavior which communicates attitude, interest, dominance-submission.

Factor model of credibility. Analysis of source credibility in terms of perceived attributes of a source.

Fantasy theme analysis. Method of rhetorical criticism used by Bormann to analyze the symbolic communication of a group in order to discover the group's shared culture and values.

Fantasy-type. In Symbolic Convergence Theory, a recurring story or script in a group's culture.

Fashion innovativeness. Extent to which the individual is current in dress, willing to adopt most recent fashion trends.

Fear appeal. Argument or persuasive appeal designed to scare or frighten receivers into compliance.

Feedback. Verbal and/or nonverbal reactions to a message which are received by the source.

Feeling misunderstood. Emotional state associated with feelings of dissatisfaction, annoyance, discomfort, failure.

Feeling type. Personality type which perceives time mainly in terms of the past.

Feeling understood. Emotional state associated with feelings of satisfaction, acceptance, pleasure, importance.

Field of approachables. Subset of field of availables. Those individuals who possess desirable attributes and with whom we would consider relational development.

Field of availables. All individuals with whom we can expect contact in order to develop a relationship.

Field of reciprocals. Subset of field of approachables. Those with whom we will begin the relational development process.

Field research design. Research conducted in a naturalistic setting.

Flow. Stream of communication messages.

Forewarnings. Messages which announce to receivers the nature of the topic and the direction of the argument in a message.

Formal communication systems. Communication links and networks determined and sanctioned by the organization. See also bridge and liaison.

Friendly style. Tendency to praise, encourage, and express liking for others.

Functional model of credibility. Analysis of source credibility in terms of the degree to which the source satisfies receiver's wishes.

Functions of communication. According to Cicero, to entertain, inform, and persuade; to stimulate was added later.

Gangplank. Horizontal chain of communication between employees on the same hierarchical level but in different departments (See also bridge).

Gatekeeper. Individual who controls the flow of information to a group of people.

General theories. Universal explanations which account for broad classes of events. Such theories are neither style-specific nor culture-bound.

Hawthorne effect. Conclusion from research conducted at the Western Electric Hawthorne plant that attention paid to workers causes workers to increase their performance; workers are also influenced by their peers.

Heuristic function of a theory. Role a theory plays in leading to new discoveries by stimulating future research.

Hierarchy. Ordering in which parts are related to each other in subordinate or superordinate fashion. For example, they may be more or less important, large, or complex. A system is composed of a hierarchy consisting of subsystems and suprasystems.

High-context culture. Culture in which most of the information in a message is encoded in the physical context or in the person's mental catalog of rules, roles, and values.

Hoarding orientation. Tendency to collect what is perceived as desirable and to keep such goods from other people.

Holistic. Like a holon, an entity that cannot be divided into parts without destroying its nature. Systems are holistic (sometimes spelled wholistic).

Homeostasis. Process of self-regulation by which a cybernetic system maintains an equilibrium.

Horizontal chain of communication. Communication between organizational members on the same hierarchical level, i.e., between two managers, or between two subordinates.

Hostility. Personality trait where symbols are used to express irritability, negativism, resentment, and suspicion.

Hypothesis. Tentative statement about the relationships between concepts of a theory; a statement of prediction about the relationships between variables. Three forms are research hypothesis, statistical hypothesis, null hypothesis.

Identity objective. Desired image which the individual wants to communicate.

Illustrators. Bodily movements used in conjunction with words to clarify meaning, especially with regard to shape, distance, spatial reasoning, and emphasis.

Impression leaving style. Tendency to try to create a lasting image in the minds of receivers.

Independent-mindedness. Characteristic values of individuality and constructive argument.

Independent variable. Variables which cause and/or predict dependent variables. Variables *from* which we predict.

Individualistic cultures. Cultures which value individual autonomy.

Informal communication systems. Communication links and networks (not determined by the organizational chart) which arise through natural human interaction. For example, two workers who might have no formal communication links may be connected in the informal communication system because they both play on the company golf team or eat lunch together.

Informal norms. Standards for behavior (i.e., production rates) which are shared, often implicitly, by work group members. These norms may contradict formal, management-directed norms.

Information. As used in information theory, the amount of uncertainty in a message.

Inoculation theory. Approach to preventing persuasion based on the biological analogy of preventing disease.

Innovation. Function of a communication system to change itself and to generate new ideas.

In-order-to-motive. Term used by Alfred Schutz to refer to the mental picture of a goal that someone wants to attain. We think about such goals as though they had already been completed in the future.

Inputs. Raw materials which an open system receives from its environment.

Instrumental objective. Pertains to the communicator's task goal.

Intension. Process in which a theory grows by developing a deeper understanding of the original concepts and variables.

Intentionality. Criteria for determining whether communication occurred.

Interact. Behavior followed by a response from another individual, such as a question followed by an answer.

Interact phases. Patterns of interacts identified in the second step of the Fisher and Hawes group communication model. Four interact phases are identified: orientation, conflict, emergence, and reinforcement.

Interaction involvement. Tendency to participate with another in conversation, composed of three dimensions: responsiveness, perceptiveness, attentiveness.

Interactionist. Approach to communication which emphasizes accounting for both traits and situational variables in explanations of communication.

Intercultural communication. Communication between individuals or groups from different cultures or from different subcultures (for example, ethnic groups) of the same sociocultural system.

Internal validity. Check to determine whether something other than independent variables in a study could be responsible for the results. Possible sources are history, maturation, measurement, selection.

Interpersonal attraction. Perceived liking for another individual based primarily on: similarity, proximity, attractiveness (physical, task and social), and reinforcement.

Interpersonal communication. Communication between two people.

Interpersonal objective. Concerned with forming and maintaining relationships with other people.

Interpretive perspective. Theoretical paradigm whose followers believe that the true nature of reality can best be discovered by understanding individuals' subjective interpretation of reality.

Interval measurement. Level of measurement where the points on the scale are assumed to increase or decrease by a constant degree.

Intimacy. Degree to which each partner in a relationship uses the other for self-confirmation.

Intuitive type. Personality type which perceives time mainly in terms of the future.

Investigational research design. A design where no independent variable is manipulated; conducted in a laboratory.

Kinesics. Study of how bodily movement communicates. Includes body movement, gestures, facial expressions and eye movements.

Language intensity. Quality of speaker's language about objects, concepts which indicates a difference in attitude from neutral.

Laws. Regularities involving behavior.

Learning. Approach to persuasion which emphasizes how feelings are conditioned to an object of persuasion.

Liaison. Person who links two groups but is not a member of either group (See bridge).

Likert scales. Rating scale which utilizes a five- or seven-point agree-disagree format to rate value statements about an object.

Lineality. Cultural value which focuses on the family lineage and ancestors, or on continuity of a group over time, rather than on the individual.

Linear process. Viewing communication in terms of one thing leading to another which in turn leads to something else.

Linear scale. Rating scale which specifies placing an object along a continuum, often dealing with degree or quantity.

Linguistic uncertainty. Level of uncertainty felt in a given interaction or communication encounter.

Linking function. Inherent function of communication which involves the person establishing relationships with the environment.

Logical force. In the Coordinated Management of Meaning theory, the strength of the influence that meanings and rules have on behavior.

Logically consistent. Theory that does not contain contradictory propositions. Opposite predictions should not be possible.

Logical positivism. Philosophical position that events can be explained by laws which have the formal structure of deductive reasoning, i.e., If some prior event occurs, then another, consequent event will follow. The prior event is said to be the cause of the later event.

Low-context culture. Culture in which most information in a message is contained in the explicit or verbal message.

Machiavellianism. Personality trait which involves manipulating other people as a basic strategy of social influence.

Macronetwork. Network along which messages are transmitted between groups in the organization.

Magic bullet theory. Theory which suggests that the mass media influence a large group directly and uniformly. Also referred to as the "hypodermic needle theory."

Mainstreaming. Argues that heavy television viewing diminishes differences in perceptions of reality caused by demographic and social factors.

Maintenance. Function of a communication system to maintain interpersonal relations among organizational members.

Manipulated variables. Variables whose levels are created by an experimenter.

Marketing orientation. Tendency to try to sell goods to other people.

Marketplace of ideas. A way of viewing a free society.

Mass communication. Communication to large audiences which is mediated by electronic or print media.

Matching hypothesis. States the more equitable a romantic relationship is, the more likely it will progress to permanence. See Equity Theory.

Mechanistic approach. Theoretical perspective which compares human behavior to that of machines. Actions are thought to occur because of prior events without the necessity of individual purposes or goals.

Mediated interpersonal communication. Any situation where mediated technology (e.g., telephone, computer) is used to advance face-to-face interaction.

Mediator. Neutral third party who helps settle a conflict.

Mentation function. Inherent function of communication which stimulates the development of higher mental processes.

Mesomorph. Body shape which is muscular, wide shoulders, low body fat level.

Message. Set of verbal and/or nonverbal symbols sent to a receiver.

Meta-metaperspective. What you think others think you think about an object, person or concept.

Micronetwork. Network which links individuals within a group.

Mindlessness. Tendency to avoid cognitive effort and behave automatically.

Mobilization. Function of mass media to promote rational interests and certain behaviors during national crises.

Need for social approval. Desire to receive positive feedback from others and to avoid negative feedback.

Networks. Patterns through which messages flow between individuals or groups in an organization.

Noble self. Tendency to be inflexible in expressing a position, to base behavior on a rigid conception of self.

Noise. Any physical or psychological stimulus which inhibits the receiver from accurate message reception. Any distortion in a communication channel.

Nominal group technique. Procedure for small group decision-making in which members form a group in name only without personal contact. Members of nominal groups individually generate written ideas which are compiled into a round-robin list and commented on using very strict turn-taking, evaluation, and decision-making rules and procedures.

Nominal measurement. Level of measurement which results in assigning an object to a category.

Non-experimental research designs. Involves no manipulation of variables.

Nonsummativity. Characteristic of a system which indicates that a system cannot be accounted for only by adding up the contributions of each individual part. The interactions of the parts also contribute to the system. Thus, changing one part causes changes in the entire system.

Nonverbal expressiveness. Nonverbal cues associated with affiliation or liking.

Nonverbal response matching. Matching another's nonverbal behavior in order to create perceived similarity which leads to trust.

Normal science. Period of time during which most scientists accept a particular theoretical paradigm to guide their research; i.e., not during a scientific revolution.

Null hypothesis. Statement that relations observed were due to chance.

Object adaptors. Involves using objects to express individuality.

Open style. Tendency to reveal feelings, thoughts, and personal information.

Open system. System that interacts with its environment, interchanging inputs and outputs.

Operational definition. Definition of a concept in terms of the operations utilized in order to experience the concept.

Opinion-leader. Person who influences the opinions, attitudes, beliefs and behaviors of others through informal communication.

Opinionated acceptance language. Language which expresses a favorable attitude toward people who agree with the speaker.

Opinionated language. Highly intense language which indicates a speaker's attitude toward topics and attitude toward others.

Opinionated rejection language. Language which expresses an unfavorable attitude toward people who disagree with the speaker.

Orators. Those who practice speechmaking.

Ordinal measurement. Level of measurement where objects are rank ordered according to some standard.

Organization. Hierarchically organized group of people so large that personal relationships with every member of the group are impossible. Organizations tend to outlive individual members and to be regulated by formal structures and rules.

Organizational communication. Communication between and among the individuals and groups which make up an organization.

Organizational intelligence. In Weick's theory, the repertoire of rules which the organization developed in the retention phase.

Outputs. Finished products which an open system sends to its environment.

Overload. Occurs when the flow of messages is too great for a person to manage.

Paradigm. "Grand model" or "world view" consisting of theoretical assumptions which a group of scientists use to guide their research.

Paradigm shift. Situation in which one theoretical paradigm replaces another in popularity among a group of scientists.

Paralanguage. Vocal (but nonverbal) dimension of speech; the manner in which something is said rather than what is said.

Parsimony. Simplicity of deductive structure. A parsimonious theory contains as few propositions as possible.

Pentad. In Kenneth Burke's dramatism, the five terms used to analyze rhetorical events: act, scene, agent, agency, and purpose.

Perceived Outcome Value Theory. Modification of uncertainty reduction theory which focuses on perceived future rewards and costs in the process of relationship development.

Perceived understanding. Ability to identify and isolate cues which indicate that a given message has been understood.

Personal construct. Bipolar set of terms which the individual applies to the environment to obtain meaning.

Personal construct theory. Theory invented by the psychologist George Kelly; also referred to in the communication field as Constructivism. Kelly believed that individuals develop mental perceptual categories called personal constructs in order to explain, predict and control their environments.

Personal knowledge. As used by Polanyi, this term refers to a scientist's feeling that a particular theory is "correct" and will prove profitable for future research.

Personal space. Zones of space which surround us: intimate, casual-personal, socio-consultative, public.

Persuasibility. The trait to be influenced easily regardless of the topic, source, or situation.

Persuasion. Attitude change toward a source's proposal resulting from a message designed to alter a receiver's beliefs about the proposal.

Persuasion situations. Defined by differences in intimacy, dominance, resistance, rights, personal benefits, consequences.

Physiological measures. Method of measurement which quantifies involuntary responses such as heart rate and blood pressure.

PONS Test. Profile of Nonverbal Sensitivity Test used to measure ability to decode nonverbal messages.

Postactivity. Audience behavior and message use after exposure to mediated messages.

Posture. Position of the body which communicates approach, withdrawal, expansion, contraction.

Power. Relationship between people including the ability to control the behavior(s) of others. The potential to influence or restrict a partner's behaviors.

Preactivity. Activity of individuals who seek certain media to gratify intellectual needs.

Precise style. Tendency to be extremely accurate and thorough in communication.

Predicted outcome value. Predicted positive and negative outcomes associated with relational development which influence decisions to seek, avoid or restrict contact with others.

Predispositions toward verbal behavior. Characteristic ways of using the voice, especially in terms of hesitating, forcefulness, length of utterance, verbosity, dominance.

Prejudice. Prejudging others using positive or negative attitudes based on stereotypes rather than information about a specific individual.

Pre-Socratic philosophers. Natural philosophers who lived from the beginning of the sixth to the middle of the fifth century B.C. They were the first to investigate questions such as, "How did the universe come into being?"

Preventatives. Devices used by speakers to gain permission to violate conversational rules.

Principle of requisite variety. In Weick's theory, the principle that organizations can most effectively process information by using processes with the same level of equivocality as the messages themselves. Very complex or equivocal messages require equivocal organization processes, communication-behavior cycles, while simple messages only require the application of rules.

Probabilistic. Occurring with a particular probability (usually less than 100%) rather than always. The statement, "There is a 60% chance of rain today," reflects a probabilistic relationship.

Probabilists. Communication theorists who advocate a probabilistic view of covering laws and causality; this view recognizes the presence of human choice.

Process. View that communication is unique, continual, and not repeatable.

Production. Function of a communication system to produce throughputs and outputs.

Productive character orientation. Involves respect for knowledge, and both work and play.

Proposition. Statement about the relationships between concepts of a theory.

Proxemics. How people use space to communicate.

Psychological equity restoration. Distortion of reality to make one believe that an inequitable relationship is, in fact, equitable.

Public communication. Involves a speaker addressing a large audience.

Pupil dilation. Indicates interest and perhaps cognitive effort.

Quality circles. Usually voluntary groups of workers who meet during work to suggest ways that organizational products can be improved.

Random assignment. Method of achieving control in an experiment by utilizing probability theory to cancel the effects of potentially biasing conditions.

Random sample. Selecting individuals from a population so that each member of the population has an equal chance of being selected to represent the population.

Randomized blocks design. Mixed research design involving a combination of manipulated and nonmanipulated independent variables.

Rapid fading. Fleeting, nonpermanent nature of verbal messages.

Rate. Speed with which communication messages flow.

Ratio measurement. Level of measurement which entails a natural zero point and a constant and equal difference between points on the scale.

Receiver. Destination of a message.

Receiver apprehension. Fear of misinterpreting and/or not being able to adjust psychologically to the messages sent by others.

Receptive orientation. Belief that benefits only come from other people.

Reciprocal self-concept support. Agreement on created identities thereby confirming each other's conception of self.

Reciprocated link. Communication link which both organization members report using.

Redundancy. Repetition; lack of information (as used in information theory).

Referent. Person, object, or event to which a word or symbol can refer.

Reflective-projective theory. Asserts that mass media not only reflect societal attitudes and values but project visions of what society is and/or should be.

Reflective thinking. Procedure for small group decision-making based on John Dewey's How We Think (1910). The reflective thinking procedure leads group members to identify a problem and its causes and to identify criteria for an effective solution before solutions are discussed and one eventually selected.

Regulating interaction. Involves greetings, turn-taking, leave-taking and is accomplished efficiently by the nonverbal code.

Regulators. Bodily movements used to guide how interaction takes place, especially in terms of greetings, turn-taking, and leave-taking.

Regulatory function. Inherent function of communication where the individual is influenced by people and thereby learns to influence.

Reinforcement principle. Suggests that we like, and are attracted to, those people who reward us.

Relaxed style. Tendency to show no signs of stress when communicating.

Reliability. Accuracy, stability or consistency of a scale, test or measure across time.

Repairs. Conversational devices used to smooth or reduce "troubles" that arise in conversation.

Repeated measures design. Research design where research participants are exposed to all levels of one or more manipulated variables.

Replicate. To repeat an experiment (often one performed by another scientist) hoping to find similar results. Replication is a way of confirming or supporting the conclusions of the original experiment.

Research hypothesis. Prediction of the results of a study based on a theoretical framework.

Research question. Question guiding investigation, usually used when a hypothesis is not warranted.

Resonance. Argues that media's influence on perceptions are intensified when media depicts "real life."

Retention. In Weick's theory, the third and final phase of organizing. In this phase the organization decides whether or not to change its standard ways of responding to different inputs. The organization evaluates rules and cycles used to see whether they should be dropped or retained for future use.

Rhetor. Communication scholars today use this Greek word to refer to someone who is both a rhetorician and orator.

Rhetoric. Use of symbols to prompt a particular response from other humans; persuasion.

Rhetorical communities. Groups of people who share a rhetorical vision and style.

Rhetorical reflector. Tendency to be too flexible in expressing a position by ignoring self and telling people only what they want to hear.

Rhetorical sensitivity. Tendency to be flexible in adapting to others in communication, to base behavior on a complex network of perceived selves.

Rhetorical vision. In Bormann's theory, group members' shared view of their identity in relation to each other and to nongroup members.

Rhetoricians. Those who study the principles of rhetoric.

Ritual. Type of sign which is partly natural and partly arbitrary.

Rules. Rules may refer either to socially agreed upon norms or to individual guidelines for behavior. In Weick's theory, standard procedures an organization has developed to process simple information received from the environment.

Rules approach to persuasion. Replaces the central concept of the laws approach, attitude, with the idea of contingency rules.

Rules perspective. Theoretical paradigm whose followers believe that the true nature of reality can best be discovered by understanding the subjective experience of people acting in the situation. Behavior is assumed to be governed by socially agreed upon norms or individual guidelines for behavior, both of which may be called rules.

Sampling. A method of studying part of a population in order to draw conclusions about the entire population.

Sapir-Whorf hypothesis. Theory which suggests that the language we speak influences or shapes our perceptions, thoughts and behavior. Also referred to as "linguistic relativity."

Scalar chain of command. Hierarchy of superiors and subordinates in an organization.

Scientific management. Organizational theory developed by Frederick W. Taylor stressing efficiency and a scientific analysis of tasks to increase productivity.

Scientific method. Consists of four interdependent phases: induction, hypothesis, deduction, experiment.

Scientific revolution. Scientific revolutions constitute major scientific change in which long-accepted theories are rejected in favor of theories that indicate new metaphors, new concepts, or other new ways of knowing. A scientific revolution often comes about when some problem in a field cannot be solved by current theories or paradigms.

Script. Sequence of events which a person expects in a situation.

Selection. In Weick's theory, the second phase of organizing. In this phase the organization makes decisions about the information processed using rules or cycles.

Selective exposure. Exposing oneself only to agreeable messages; avoiding situations, such as public speeches by a political opponent, requiring us to listen to those with whom we disagree.

Selective perception. Perceiving new information in terms of previous perceptual frameworks. During this process some information perceived is highlighted, and other information is ignored.

Self-adaptors. Involve touching or doing something to one's body to express individuality.

Self-concept. Image people have of their attributes which influences their communicative behavior.

Self-disclosure. Communication in which information about self normally hidden is revealed honestly and accurately to another.

Self-esteem. Evaluation of self in a favorable or unfavorable manner.

Self-monitoring of expressive behavior. Tendency to concentrate extensive attention on one's image and the impression made on others.

Self-report measures. Paper and pencil instruments (scales) in which individuals are asked to evaluate their behavior, attitudes and perceptions.

Semantic differential. Rating scale which uses a seven-point continuum bound by bipolar terms in order to locate an object in semantic space.

Sensation type. Personality type which perceives time mainly in terms of the present.

Sensitized perception. Type of perception which results when a person is exposed frequently over time to messages perceived in a hostile setting, for example, racial epithets.

Sign. Something that stands for or represents something else and bears a natural, nonarbitrary relationship to it. For example, dark clouds, thunder, and lightening are signs of rain.

Signal. Another category of sign. That which stands for something by virtue of a natural relationship of causality, contingency or resemblance. For example, a blinking yellow light signals drivers to slow down.

Situationist. Approach to understanding communication which emphasizes the impact of situational variables.

Small group. Group of fewer than 20 people who develop regular patterns of interaction and share a common purpose; members influence and are influenced by each other.

Small group communication. Communication between and among the members of a small group; communication involving several people.

Social exchange theories. Asserts that we develop relationships when we believe that our rewards will be greater than our costs.

Social learning. Cause of verbal aggression brought about by direct reinforcement of verbally aggressive behavior or by modeling the behavior after an esteemed person.

Social penetration theory. Theory which describes interpersonal relationships in terms of the breadth and depth of communication on various topics.

Sophists. Educators who traveled throughout the Greek city-states teaching rhetoric. They were considered knowledgeable or especially clever in effective speaking or arguing.

Source. Originator of a message.

Source credibility. Set of attitudes toward a source's expertise, trustworthiness, and dynamism which influence response to the source's message.

Speech act. Term used by Searle to refer to a statement designed to perform some specific function; e.g., to give a command or to ask a question.

Speech Accommodation Theory. Asserts that during communication, people try to adjust their style of speech to gain approval, increase communication efficiency, and maintain positive social identity.

Statistical hypothesis. Statement of a research hypothesis stated in mathematical terms.

Stereotypes. Beliefs about members of a group based on learned opinions rather than information about a specific individual.

Stratified random sample. Partitioning a population and then drawing a random sample at each level of stratification.

Strong link. Communication link that is frequently used.

Structural functionalism. Form of systems theory such as the communication systems theory developed by Farace, Monge, and Russell, which stresses the structure and functions of systems.

Subjective experience. Individual's unique experiences and perceptions of reality.

Subsequent conditions. Events occurring later in time which are related to some earlier (antecedent) conditions or effects.

Subsystems. Smaller units which are part of a system's hierarchy.

Suprasystems. Larger units which make up a system; suprasystems are composed of subsystems.

Surveillance. Information and news providing function of mass media.

Survey research. Interviews and mail surveys.

Syllogism. Method of reasoning which consists of a major and minor premise and a conclusion.

Symbol. Type of sign which is arbitrary, agreed upon, and is used to stimulate meaning. That which stands for or represents something else but bears no natural relationship to it.

Symbolic Convergence Theory. Bormann's theory which explains how people unite through sharing symbol systems, including group fantasies.

Symmetrical link. Communication link used equally by two organization members; i.e., each initiates communication with the other.

Symptom. Type of sign that bears a natural relation to an object.

System. Set of interdependent units which work together to adapt to a changing environment. An organization is one type of system.

System perspective. Theoretical paradigm whose followers believe that the true nature of reality is contained in systems, interdependent units which work together to adapt to a changing environment. This perspective is based on the General Systems Theory of biologist Ludwig von Bertalanffy.

Tactilics. Use of touch to communicate.

Tag questions. Phrase added to the end of an assertion or statement that asks for agreement with the speaker, i.e., "that's a beautiful dog, isn't it?"

Teleological. Property of open systems which indicates that they try to reach specific end states or goals.

Territoriality. Claiming that one has rights to a given area, responding to boundary violations.

Testable. Good theories must be capable of being disproved or falsified.

Theory. Group of related propositions designed to explain why events take place in a certain way.

Theory Z. Management theory developed by William Ouchi which stresses a modification of effective Japanese management techniques (i.e., quality circles) for use in American society.

Thinking type. Personality type which perceives time as flowing from the past through the present to the future.

Throughputs. Partially modified products which are passed from one subsystem of an open system to another during the process of being transformed into outputs.

Topoi. Common topics that a speaker can use to analyze the material of any subject.

Touch deprivation. Lack of stimulation to the skin can retard physical development, be psychologically upsetting.

Touch functions. Five functions of touch in communication are: functional-professional, social-polite, friendship-warmth, love-intimacy, sexual-arousal.

Trait approach. Approach to communication which maintains there are broad predispositions which account for behavior.

Transactional process. People exchanging messages and influencing one another.

Transference. Cause of verbal aggression which involves using verbal aggression against people who remind one of unresolved sources of conflict and pain.

Transition relevance places (TRPs). Those places in a conversation where a change of speaking turn is possible.

Trust. Faith in the behavior of another. Promotes confidence in risk-taking.

Turn-taking. Behavior which exhibits the exchange of source and receiver roles during conversation.

Two-step flow. Theory which asserts that information from media is processed first by opinion-leaders who then pass it along via interpersonal channels.

Uncertainty Reduction Theory. Theory which asserts that, during relational development, individuals seek to reduce uncertainty about each other.

Underload. Communication underload occurs when the flow of messages is too slow for a person; i.e., workers are able to manage more information than they receive.

Unreciprocated link. Communication link which only one organization member reports. If one person reports frequently using the link and the other says that no communication took place, the link is unreciprocated.

Unwillingness to communicate. Tendency to devalue and avoid communication, the more global of the apprehension traits.

Upward communication. Communication from lower members of the organizational hierarchy (subordinates) to members higher in the organization (i.e., managers, vice-presidents).

Uses and gratifications. Theory attempting to explain the underlying motives for people's use of the mass media.

Validity. Ability of a scale, test, instrument or measure to measure what it says it does.

Value-expectancy. Concept that the more an object is expected to have valued attributes, the more favorable the attitude toward the object will be.

Variable. Abstraction referring to a class of things, a term often used at the level of measurement.

Variable-analytic. Approach to studying persuasion which focuses on analyzing important variables rather than developing theories.

Verbal aggressiveness. Tendency to attack the self-concept of people in order to deliver psychological pain.

Verbal intensifiers. Adverbs which moderate, decrease intensity and reduce the strength of an utterance.

Verbal plan. What a speaker plans to say in a specific or general communication situation.

Verbal qualifiers. Expressions such as "possibly," and "perhaps," which modify and reduce the strength and impact of an utterance.

Vertical chain of communication. Communication between members of different levels of the organizational hierarchy; i.e., between managers and subordinates.

Vocalics. Study of how we use our voice to communicate.

Weak link. Communication link used only occasionally.

Writing apprehension. Fear of having one's writing behavior evaluated, expecting to fail in writing activities, avoiding situations where writing is a requirement.

Name Index

Subject Index